STATE ARCHIVES OF A

VOLUME XVI

FRONTISPIECE. *Head of a winged human-headed bull guarding the entrance to the palace of Esarhaddon in Calah (Nimrud).*
ANE 118893.

STATE ARCHIVES OF ASSYRIA

Published by the Neo-Assyrian Text Corpus Project
of the University of Helsinki
in co-operation with
Deutsche Orient-Gesellschaft

Editor in Chief
Simo Parpola

Managing Editor
Robert M. Whiting

Editorial Committee
Frederick Mario Fales, Simo Parpola, Nicholas Postgate
Julian Reade, Robert M. Whiting

VOLUME XVI

Mikko Luukko and Greta Van Buylaere

THE POLITICAL CORRESPONDENCE OF ESARHADDON

HELSINKI UNIVERSITY PRESS

Publication of this volume was made possible by a grant
from the University of Helsinki

Set in Times
Typography and layout by Teemu Lipasti
The Assyrian Royal Seal emblem drawn by Dominique Collon from original
Seventh Century B.C. impressions (BM 84672 and 84677) in the British Museum
Ventura Publisher format by Robert M. Whiting
Custom fonts designed and developed by Timo Kiippa and Robert M. Whiting
Electronic pasteup by Simo Parpola andKaisa Åkerman

Helsinki University Press
Vuorikatu 3 A 2, FIN-00100 Helsinki, Finland
Tel. 358-9-701 02363, Tfx. 358-9-701 02374

ISBN 951-570-001-9 (Whole Series, Paperback)
ISBN 951-570-002-7 (Whole Series, Hardbound)
ISBN 951-570-539-8 (Volume 16, Paperback)
ISBN 951-570-538-X (Volume 16, Hardbound)

THE POLITICAL CORRESPONDENCE OF ESARHADDON

by

MIKKO LUUKKO and GRETA VAN BUYLAERE

with Contributions by

SIMO PARPOLA

Illustrations
edited by

JULIAN READE

HELSINKI UNIVERSITY PRESS

2002

FOREWORD

The edition of the texts presented here and the introduction to the volume were done by Mikko Luukko and Greta Van Buylaere. The specific contributions of Simo Parpola are set forth in the Preface.

This volume brings to completion the publication of the Assyrian language correspondence of Esarhaddon found at Nineveh. The other parts of this correspondence are to be found in SAA 10 and SAA 13.

The Project expresses its thanks to the Trustees of the British Museum for permission to publish texts and illustrative material in their custody, and to the staff of the Department of the Ancient Near East of the British Museum for their wholehearted and enthusiastic cooperation. Professor R. Borger (Göttingen) kindly checked the museum and publication numbers of the tablets included in the edition. We also express our gratitude to the Musée du Louvre and the département des Antiquités orientales for permission to use AO 20155 for Fig. 1, and to the Vorderasiatisches Museum, Berlin, for permission to use VA 956 for Fig. 8.

We are grateful to the University of Helsinki for its long-standing support for the State Archives of Assyria Project.

Helsinki, December 2002 Robert M. Whiting

PREFACE

In early 2000, Professor Simo Parpola asked us if we were interested in editing the SAA volume on the political correspondence of Esarhaddon. His question first struck us with surprise, but after a moment of hesitation we answered: yes, of course! We were very delighted to have this unexpected opportunity to prepare a volume for the SAA series.

At that time we were provided with all the necessary computer files for the volume, including transliterations extracted from the database of the Neo-Assyrian Text Corpus Project. The original goal was to have the volume ready for publication by the end of 2001. It became clear early on, however, that this schedule could not be kept, as our work on the Assyrian-English-Assyrian dictionary of the Neo-Assyrian Text Corpus Project did not leave us much time to concentrate on the Esarhaddon letters. The volume was thus temporarily placed second in our order of priorities. Therefore we finished the first draft of the translations only around Easter 2001. Later, in February 2002, we went to the British Museum for a week to collate many of the texts. The introduction to the volume was written after the collation trip.

Our cordial thanks are due to Prof. Parpola under whose guidance we prepared the volume. We are extremely grateful that he gave us this chance. Moreover, he corrected numerous errors and improved many inconsistencies. He also established the final order of the letters, and generously added even more letters, all edited by him, to the volume, including letters that were originally assigned to the Assurbanipal volume of the series (nos. 14-20, 111-117, 158, 160, 162, 164-165 and 175-176). The translations of nos. 59-61 and 100 are also based on his work. We wish to thank Dr. Julian Reade for the magnificent illustrations he provided for this book. We also owe thanks to Mr. C. B. F. Walker, Deputy Keeper of the Department of the Ancient Near East, who permitted us to prepare copies and collations at the British Museum, to the helpful staff of the Students' Room, to Dr. Heather D. Baker, who corrected our English, and to Prof. Matthew W. Stolper (Chicago), on whose unpublished work our translation of no. 78 is largely based. We are grateful to the Trustees of the British Museum for permission to publish the ten previously unpublished texts and fragments included in this volume, and to Prof. W.G. Lambert (Birmingham) for communicating his preliminary translations of K 19787, K 19979, K 19986 and K 20565 to the SAA project many years ago.

Finally, we wish to extend our thanks to the Finnish Cultural Foundation and the Graduate School of the Institute of Asian and African Studies of the University of Helsinki for the financial support provided to Mikko during the years 2001-2002, without which this work could not have been completed.

Ostend, October 2002 Mikko Luukko Greta Van Buylaere

CONTENTS

INTRODUCTION

This volume completes the publication of the Assyrian letters attributable to the reign of Esarhaddon. SAA 10 (letters from scholars) and SAA 13 (letters from priests) form the other parts of the correspondence of this king in Neo-Assyrian.[1] Here, as in SAA 10 and SAA 13, Esarhaddon's own correspondence is seamlessly connected with letters addressed to Assurbanipal.[2] This fact reflects Assurbanipal's pre-eminent position after he was nominated crown prince of Assyria in 672, more than three years before his own reign started.[3] There are also political letters addressed to both Esarhaddon and Assurbanipal in Neo-Babylonian; these will soon be published in the SAA series, and thus will not be discussed here.

Esarhaddon's reign is one of the best-documented reigns of the Neo-Assyrian Empire. In addition to letters, other types of documents are abundantly preserved from his time: royal inscriptions,[4] chronicles,[5] treaties,[6] literary texts,[7] queries to the sun-god,[8] legal transactions,[9] administrative texts,[10] astrological reports,[11] prophecies,[12] and a land grant.[13]

Although the title "The Political Correspondence of Esarhaddon" accentuates the nature of the letters edited in this volume, the word "political" should not be understood in the narrow sense, but rather broadly. While this book contains many royal letters of a political nature, it also includes some unofficial letters (cf. Chapter 6), and letters of a more private nature (e.g., no. 28).

The real political letters of the volume relate to the domestic affairs of Assyria, as well as to Assyria's foreign policy. These domestic affairs include, among others, complaints to the king and the crown prince about mistreatment and injustice at the hands of some high officials;[14] people appealing for workers and seeking favour with the king and his high officials;[15] reports on work in progress and references to building activities,[16] reports of conspiracy, disloyalty and crimes,[17] infringement of the privileges of the city of Assur,[18] and so on.

Correspondingly, some letters shed light on the relations of Assyria with its neighbours to the east, south, west and north. Situations in far-away provinces and neighbouring states are clarified by means of intelligence reports, or, more telling in some instances, letters are based on quotations from first-hand intelligence activities.[19] References to actual battles, military activities or campaigns are scarce (see below, "Relations between Assyria and its Neighbours"). In the letters concerning foreign policy, both peaceful and hostile relations are attested.[20] A few letters relate to the transportation of goods from abroad, be it by means of trade, receiving tribute, taking booty or acquiring gifts.[21]

As is often the case with Neo-Assyrian royal letters, those edited in the present volume rarely give us explicit information on political issues or on the exact role of many individuals in important political affairs. Thus, important pieces of information are to be gathered from implicit hints, mostly found in seemingly meaningless details scattered here and there, and often in a broken context. Consequently, these snippets of knowledge have to be combined with the information obtained from other sources. In fact, many of the chief events of the reign of Esarhaddon, known primarily from his royal inscriptions, are not touched upon in these letters at all. For instance, we do not read anything about his successful and significant campaigns to Sidon in the west (676 B.C.) and Šubria in the north (673 B.C.). There is nothing about the Elamite raids to Babylonia in the first half of his reign. Neither Esarhaddon's military campaigns to Egypt nor his programmatic public works in Babylonia are mentioned, not even in passing.[22] Fortunately, many people who appear in these letters are also known from other documents, and this additional information can often be helpful in the interpretation of the texts.[23]

The Correspondents

A conspicuous feature of the letters edited in the present volume is that the titles or professions of many of the letters' senders are not exactly known. Excluding the letters from king Esarhaddon himself, only ten people are represented by more than two letters:

Nabû-ra'im-nišešu (a military official at Der)[24]	11
Assurbanipal, crown prince	7
Bel-iqiša (a high official)	7
Anonymous Informer	7
Ubru-Nabû, scribe of the New Palace of Calah	6
Šamaš-šumu-ukin, crown prince of Babylon	4
Itti-Šamaš-balaṭu (a royal agent in Phœnicia)	4
Šamaš-metu-uballiṭ, prince	3
Nabû-rehtu-uṣur (a servant of the queen mother?)	3
Another anonymous informer[25]	3

As to the other senders of this volume, no more than one or two letters can be assigned to any of them with certainty. Nevertheless, it is beyond dispute that the letters were sent by high-ranking members of the administrative and military personnel of the Neo-Assyrian Empire. However, when compared, for instance, with the correspondence of Sargon, the difference is great, as many of the senders there are identifiable as provincial governors. This is one of the reasons why the letters from the reigns of Sargon and Esarhaddon are so different in their nature and subject matter. Since there are no extant letters by provincial governors from the reign of Esarhaddon, it seems likely that their letters were already being written in Aramaic on papyrus or parchment.[26]

Datable Letters

None of the letters are explicitly dated. Their approximate dating to the reign of Esarhaddon is based on prosopographical evidence and on their contents, where they can be connected with events known from other sources. Therefore only a small group of letters can be dated to a specific year and very few of them more accurately to a specific month or day, and even then with certain reservations.[27] Fortunately, quite a number of letters can be roughly dated since they are linked with the crown princehood of Assurbanipal (and Šamaš-šumu-ukin), a well-documented period, or with a handful of known historical events which took place in Esarhaddon's reign (680-669) or shortly before it.

In chronological order, the most important events referred to or hinted at in the letters are as follows:

681-I	Esarhaddon's flight before his accession to power (no. 29)[28]
681-X-20	Sennacherib's death and the subsequent unrest in Assyria (no. 95)[29]
680-II	Esarhaddon's accession (no. 29)[30]
674	Conclusion of a peace treaty between Assyria and Elam (no. 1)
672-II-12	Esarhaddon's succession treaty (nos. 21, 59-61, 71, 126, 150)[31]
672-669	Time of two crown princes, Assurbanipal and Šamaš-šumu-ukin (passim)
670	Conspiracy against Esarhaddon (especially nos. 59-61)[32]

In the following table (Table I), approximate dates are proposed for the letters which can, one way or another, be linked with historical events known from Esarhaddon's reign. Naturally, the degree of certainty of these dates varies, from certain to very speculative. Column 1 gives the name of the sender, his profession and domicile (if known); column 2, the number of the letter in the volume; column 3, the proposed date; and column 4, the grounds for the dating or references to passages which elucidate the underlying reasoning.

TABLE I. *Approximately datable letters*

Sender, profession, domicile	**Letter**	**Proposed date**	**Grounds for dating**
ROYAL LETTERS			
Esarhaddon, king, Nineveh	no. 1	674 (or 673?)	After the peace treaty with Elam
Assurbanipal, crown prince, Nineveh	nos. 14-20	all 672-669, most 670	Crown princehood 672-669
Šamaš-šumu-ukin, crown prince, Babylonia	nos. 21-24	most likely in 670	See Parpola, Iraq 34 (1972) 27
Šamaš-metu-uballiṭ, prince, Nineveh	nos. 25-27	672-669	As son of Esarhaddon it is not likely that he had sent any letters before Assurbanipal and Šamaš-šumu-ukin were made crown princes
Šerua-eṭerat, princess, Nineveh	no. 28	most probably 672 or 671	To Libbali-šarrat, wife of Assurbanipal, perhaps not long after the latter married Libbali-šarrat
LETTERS FROM ASSYRIA			
Mardî, servant of the governor of Barhalza	no. 29	probably 680	References to Esarhaddon's flight (l. 6) and his accession (l. 13)
Ibašši-ilu, *pahhizu*	no. 30	perhaps 680	The author had probably appealed to Sennacherib earlier. The lawsuit and its consequences are unlikely to have taken many years
Kudurru, son of Šamaš-ibni of Bit-Dakkuri, in confinement in Nineveh	no. 31	674?	If the "previous expedition" referred to (obv. 6) is Esarhaddon's campaign in Babylonia in 675. Cf. Nissinen Prophecy, p. 133
Nabû-zer-ketti-lešir, overseer	nos. 32-33	early in Esarhaddon's reign (680-679?)	References (no. 32 r. 8, 33 r. 2) to Sennacherib's orders
Šumaya	nos. 34-35	early 672?	To the crown prince
unidentified	no. 36	672-669	The crown prince is mentioned
unidentified	nos. 37-38	672-669	Crown prince. See Nissinen Prophecy, p. 129f
Nabû-tukulti, Nabû-šumu-lešir, Mutakkil-Adad	no. 41	672-669	The crown prince is mentioned
Iqbi-Aššur, scribe of Kar- Shalmaneser	no. 44	early part of Esarhaddon's reign?	Iqbi-Aššur was active already in the late reign of Sennacherib

Sender, profession, domicile	Letter	Proposed date	Grounds for dating
Nabû-zeru-lešir, chief scribe	no. 50	before 672 (IV-8)	Cf. below, "Note on an Influential Family of Scholars"
Nabû-rehtu-uṣur	nos. 59-61	671/670	Conspiracy against Esarhaddon. See Nissinen Prophecy, p. 117ff.
Anonymous	nos. 62-68	672-669	No. 63 r. 4-5, 14, no. 66 r. 6 sons of the king; no. 65:2 Sasî, r.4 crown prince
Anonymous	nos. 69-70	672-669	To the crown prince
Mannu-ki-Libbali, scribe working under the palace scribe, Nineveh	no. 78	672-669	Kushite girls. Presumably after the occupation of Egypt (671)
Mannu-ki-Libbali and Kanunayu, deputy of the palace scribe	no. 79	672-669	No. 79 seems to be earlier than no. 78, since Mannu-ki-Libbali is still serving under the palace scribe in no. 79
Nabû-sagib, son of Parruṭu, goldsmith of the queen's household	no. 81	late in Esarhaddon's reign?	Related to no. 65?
unidentified, Assur	no. 95	680	Governor of Assur(?) acts after Sennacherib's death. Letter to Esarhaddon?
Mayors and elders of Assur	no. 96	late in Esarhaddon's reign	If to be taken literally, "your son's son" (r. 4) can only occur in the late reign of Esarhaddon; however, cf. LAS II A, p. 50
Ubru-Nabû, scribe of the new palace in Calah	no. 105	675?	A reference to Sippar shortly before or after the Elamite raid?
Bel-iqiša, high official	no. 116	672-669	Letter to the crown prince (r.4). This letter has a different greeting formula from the other letters authored by him alone
Babilayu	no. 118	672-669	Crown prince
Nanî	no. 124	672-669	To the crown prince
LETTERS FROM OTHER PARTS OF THE EMPIRE			
Itti-Šamaš-balaṭu	no. 126	672 or 671	No. 126:19-26 referring to and quoting from Esarhaddon's succession treaty
unidentifed, referring to Damascus	no. 133	672-669	Crown prince

Sender, profession, domicile	**Letter**	**Proposed date**	**Grounds for dating**
Nabû-ra'im-nišešu and Salamanu (high military official and his deputy)	nos. 136-145	675-679	See below, "The East and Southeast," and n. 42
unidentified (Nabû-ra'im-nišešu?)	nos. 146-147	673 (cf. SAA 2 p. XXXI) or 672-669	Humbariš of Esarhaddon's succession treaty
Aššur-ušallim	no. 148	672 (-669)	Blessing the crown princes. Cf. SAA 4 p. LXXV n. 247.
unidentified, Bit-Hamban	no. 149	672-669	Crown prince
unidentified	no. 150	672	Provided that *adê* refers to the succession treaty
unidentified	no. 155	672-669	Crown prince
		ADDITIONS TO SAA 10 AND 13	
unidentified scholar	no. 164	673?	Asakku. To be combined with the campaign against Šubria(?), see below.
Urdu-Nanaya	no. 165	671-669	Cf. SAA 10 p. XXVI
Mar-Issar, scholar, Esarhaddon's agent in Babylonia	no. 171	probably 671-669	Mar-Issar's letters (SAA 10 347-370) date to 671-669
Nabû-šumu-iddina, superintendent of the Nabû temple of Calah	nos. 175-177	probably either late reign of Esarhaddon or early reign of Assurbanipal	Cf., e.g., PNA 2/II p. 885 s.v. Nabû-šumu-iddina 15
		UNASSIGNED AND UNATTRIBUTED LETTERS	
Nabû-ahhe-šallim	no. 181	probably from the late reign of Esarhaddon	Balṭaya, cf. PNA 1/II p. 260f s.v. Balṭi-Aia 6-7
unidentified	no. 207	672-669	Crown prince. See Nissinen Prophecy p. 129f
unidentified	no. 217	672-669	If the Rear Palace in r.7 is correct, then probably 672-669

It is very likely that most of the letters which cannot be dated even approximately to any specific year in Esarhaddon's time were written in the years 672-669, considering the high density of datable letters during these years. It is not excluded that a few of them could also belong to the early years of Assurbanipal's reign.[33]

Relations between Assyria and its Neighbours

Compared with Esarhaddon's royal inscriptions and numerous queries (SAA 4) which record his worries and problems at the various frontiers of the Assyrian Empire, the letters of the present volume are surprisingly silent about military campaigns or diplomatic overtures. For instance, only a few military clashes are mentioned, and even then in a rather broken context (nos. 77, and 149; perhaps also 135, 231, and 243). Since SAA 4 already includes a recent discussion of some political and historical events during the reign of Esarhaddon,[34] only a short geographically orientated summary of those events to which the letters of this volume relate is given here, offering some glimpses of Assyrian foreign policy during the reign of Esarhaddon.

The East and Southeast

The evidence of the relations between Esarhaddon and the states east of Assyria is scattered. The first letter of the volume refers to the bilateral treaty between Esarhaddon and Urtaku, king of Elam, which was concluded in 674.[35] The letter emphasises the peaceful relations between Assyria and Elam. Furthermore, the letter gives an absorbing example of the reciprocal exchange of royal children. This practice of pledging princes and princesses as "hostages" was undoubtedly carried out in order to safeguard the mutual peace treaty.[36] Whether the exchange of children was also intended to result (in a later phase) in royal marriages between the rulers' children, in order to confirm more formally the good relations between the countries, is uncertain, but doubtful.[37]

Elsewhere, however, the Elamites occur in an unfavourable light. There is an often discussed passage in a letter from Šamaš-šumu-ukin to Esarhaddon (no. 21) which is interesting in this respect. The prince writes concerning Aššur-nadin-šumi, the eldest son of Sennacherib, who was enthroned as the king of Babylon in 700:[38] "Moreover, he (a denounced astrologer) has assembled the people who captured Aššur-nadin-šumi (and) delivered him to Elam. He has concluded a treaty with them, adjuring them by Jupiter (and) Sirius."

If this passage is to be understood literally, it is somewhat surprising to find that, approximately 25 years after the delivery of Aššur-nadin-šumi to Elam by some Babylonians,[39] these same Babylonians were still alive, despite all the vindicative measures taken by Sennacherib against Babylonia. We do not know what kind of feelings Esarhaddon, a brother of Aššur-nadin-šumi, harboured in the matter, but it is reasonable to suppose that if those men were still alive, Esarhaddon would have pursued them from the moment he learned their names. Hence it is very interesting that the names of the men are not actually stated in the letter. Does this mean that the Assyrians already knew who they were, or had these men succeeded in keeping their identity a secret for almost 25 years? In any case, the picture we get from the situation is not very clear.

It is difficult even to imagine Esarhaddon punishing the culprits, if one takes into consideration that one of his main concerns was to regain the trust of the Babylonians after his father's atrocious retribution against Babylonia. Picking up the old matter of Aššur-nadin-šumi again might have fuelled new discord between the Assyrians and Babylonians, and possibly between the Assyrians and Elamites also. But instead of new conflicts arising between the Assyrians and Elamites, we can cite the conclusion and maintenance of the aforementioned peace treaty between Esarhaddon and Urtaku, king of Elam.

On the whole, Assyrian-Elamite relations during the reign of Esarhaddon are far from clear.[40] Apart from the two letters already discussed, Elamites occur only in the reports of Nabû-ra'im-nišešu and Salamanu, two officials keeping an eye on the situation in the Babylonian-Elamite border zone.[41] Some of their letters seem to date from 675-674, but others could be later, as one of them certainly dates from (the beginning of) the reign of Assurbanipal.[42]

It seems plausible to identify the Humbariš who is mentioned in two fragmentary letters (nos. 146 and 147) with Humbariš of Nahšimarti, one of the Median 'city-rulers' with whom Esarhaddon concluded his succession treaty. The most conclusive evidence for identifying Humbariš of these letters with Humbariš of the succession treaty is the reference to "(military) help, aid" (*kitru*) in no. 147.[43] Another eastern partner of this treaty can be identified in no. 150, where the emissaries of Mazamua are mentioned in a context that clearly relates to the conclusion of the succession treaty.[44]

Despite this treaty, the tension between Assyria and the territories to the east does not seem to have eased off significantly after 672, since all potential deserters from Mannea, Media or Hubuškia were at that time to be sent immediately to the crown prince according to no. 148 (for this letter see also below, "North and Northwest").[45]

The main reason for the continuing tension between Assyria and the eastern countries was undoubtedly the pressure caused by the migrations of the Cimmerians and the Scythians. These migrations brought them from the north up to the eastern side of the Zagros mountains during the reign of Esarhaddon. The letters of the present volume are not very illustrative in this matter, but they provide us with some stray remarks: one small letter fragment (no. 149) informs us of fighting in Bit-Hamban, probably against the Cimmerians or the Scythians,[46] and mentions the crown prince. Also two letters (nos. 15 and 16) by crown prince Assurbanipal himself confirm the presence of the Cimmerians in the east.[47]

Moreover, no. 15 is of particular interest to the early history of Media, because it might confirm — the context is unfortunately broken — that the son of Cyaxares (= U(m)aksatar, l. 20) was Phraortes (perhaps something like *Paramurtu* in NA, if the name mentioned in no. 15:24 really refers to him). It should be noted that the U(m)aksatar mentioned here is not the later king of the Medes, son of Phraortes, but most likely the Median city-ruler of Nartu.[48]

The South and Southwest

As already noted, we do not have any letters telling us directly about the Assyrian campaigns to Egypt and Kush. Sources attesting to these events are to be found elsewhere, e.g. Esarhaddon's royal inscriptions and the Babylonian chronicles. Nor are trade or other possible connections between the Assyrians and Egyptians mentioned in the present letters.[49]

We do have, however, two interesting references related to the consequences of Esarhaddon's Egyptian policies. No. 78 refers to the settling of some Kushite girls in the royal palace, presumably after the conquest of Memphis.[50] In one private letter (no. 55), the writer petitions his master to settle a case on behalf of three mistreated people with Aramaic or West Semitic names whose belongings have been sold to Egyptians.

Assyrian-Babylonian relations only rarely crop up in the letters. The majority of Esarhaddon's Babylonian correspondence is either lost or written in Neo-Babylonian and therefore falls outside the scope of this volume. However, some information about the Babylonians is available.

For example, in Šamaš-šumu-ukin's well-known letter to Esarhaddon already discussed above (no. 21), three Babylonians denounce the allegedly treacherous actions of three scholars, a haruspex named Aplaya and two astrologers named Bel-eṭir and Šamaš-zeru-iqiša. On the surface this is simply evidence of the loyal behaviour of the Babylonians, as the stipulations of Esarhaddon's succession treaty, which certainly also applied to Babylonia, obliged all Assyrian subjects to inform the king of any suspicious actions they heard about or saw.[51] However, it cannot be excluded that these three Babylonians were in reality acting out of ultimately anti-Assyrian motives. Perhaps they intended to further their own personal interests at the cost of the denounced individuals, at least one of whom (Aplaya) may have been an Assyrian, or maybe they were simply pleased to be able to inform against (Assyrian) scholars?

The contrary case is attested in no. 65, where the king is informed that an Assyrian goldsmith of the queen's household had hired and settled in his house a Babylonian scholar to teach his son extispicy, exorcism and astrology. This letter is discussed in greater detail below.

A broken letter (no. 154) refers to people of Sarrabanu (south of Larak) who are said to hold houses in Babylon, Nippur and Uruk and in the Itu'u land, and are reported to have requested and obtained houses from a royal official. This letter may pertain to deportations that had taken place after raids to Babylonia under Tiglath-pileser III, Sargon II or Sennacherib, and it is not certain whether it dates from Esarhaddon's reign or from the time of one of his predecessors.[52]

If nos. 137 and 138 by Nabû-ra'im-nišešu's indeed originate in Esarhaddon's reign (see p. XXII, above), then a date earlier than 674 is out of the question.[53] It is easier to imagine that a messenger of Nippur had had dealings with the Assyrians and reported on the delegate of Araši after 675,[54] since several anti-Assyrian *šandabakku*s of Nippur were removed by Esarhaddon between 680 and 675.[55] In addition to these two letters, no. 31, a letter by Kudurru, the imprisoned son of the captured and executed Šamaš-ibni of Bit-Dakkuri, may also be connected with the consequences of events in Nippur and its surroundings in and after 675.[56]

No. 105 concludes with the intriguing remark, "With regard to Sippar, may the king, my lord, be vigilant, so we can relax" (r.16-18). Otherwise the letter, which was written in Calah, does not have anything to do with Sippar. Whether this throwaway remark can be connected with the Elamite raid in Sippar in 675 remains uncertain.

A Chaldean is reported to have appealed to the king in no. 17, a letter from the crown prince Assurbanipal to Esarhaddon. This letter may well be linked to no. 155, which also mentions the Chaldeans in connection with Kunaya and the crown prince.[57] It is unlikely, however, that the latter was authored by Assurbanipal, as some of the signs used in no. 155 do not agree with the orthographical conventions of Assurbanipal.[58] The sender was more likely Šamaš-šumu-ukin (cf. no. 21).

Nabû-ra'im-nišešu and Salamanu were apparently responsible for the territory around Der and they probably lodged in that city, as Nabû-ra'im-nišešu states in 140 r.14-16: "Let a messenger stay at our disposal in Der."[59] However, it should be noted that the letter itself was probably not written in Der but in Dunni-Šamaš, close to Der and Malaku.[60] In another letter (no. 136), Nabû-ra'im-nišešu informs the king that the governor of Der has sent deserters to him.

The West

The west, and particularly the eastern part of the Mediterranean coast, is fairly well represented in the correspondence. Interpreting the information offered by the letters is, however, often an intricate problem. Many of the incidents between Assyria and the Levantine coastal cities seem to relate to economic undertakings. It is needless to point out that many people wanted to participate in this lucrative trade, but it may come as a surprise to learn that Esarhaddon evidently gave a pretty free hand to many of the local kings, chieftains and traders, and tolerated some of their actions even when they conflicted with his own interests.[61] This is at least the impression one gets from two letters (nos. 127 and 128) by one Itti-Šamaš-balaṭu, whose exact status is not known, but who was probably a royal agent (*qēpu*) appointed to observe the situation in the northern part of the east Mediterranean coast.

These letters by Itti-Šamaš-balaṭu shed some light on Assyrian-Phœnician relations in the closing years of Esarhaddon's reign. For example, in no. 127 Ikkilû,[62] the king of Arwad, is reported to have hindered boats from approaching the Assyrian port, appropriating the whole trade for himself and favouring those traders who came to do business directly with him. And as if this were not incriminating enough, he is further said to have killed those traders who ventured to dock at the Assyrian harbour, and stolen their boats. Furthermore, one Ilu-ma'adi, a man from Ṣimirra, is reported as working as an agent for him in order to find out what was happening in Assyria. Such accusations can be considered extremely grave, especially if one compares them with the conditions stated in Esarhaddon's treaty with Baal, king of Tyre.[63] We may surmise that the king of Arwad had either contracted a similar treaty or was in some other way subjected to Assyrian rule, which dictated his rights.

Running business in the Phœnician coastal cities was certainly so profitable that the threats advanced by Ikkilû and the merchants against Itti-Šamaš-balaṭu are quite understandable. Those threats seem to have caused plenty of trouble to Itti-Šamaš-balaṭu, who represented the interests of the Assyrian king in northern Phœnicia. However, a rather puzzling aspect of the matter is the role of some Assyrians: "There are many in the entourage of the king, who have invested silver in this house — they and the merchants are systematically scaring me" (127 r.7-10).[64] Possibly SAA 4 89, a query by the crown prince Assurbanipal concerning a message to Ikkilû, resulted from Itti-Šamaš-balaṭu's complaints to Esarhaddon, who may himself at that time have been on his way to Egypt. Perhaps Ikkilû knew about it and wanted to profit from the occasion. In any case, Ikkilû must have enjoyed a considerable degree of freedom in his activities. He was not killed, replaced, or otherwise severely punished because of his schemes, but was able to keep his position as the king of Arwad even after Esarhaddon's reign, since he is attested as paying tribute to Assurbanipal.

Another letter (no. 129), probably also by Itti-Šamaš-balaṭu, records raids by Arabs, but its broken condition does not allow us to draw clear conclusions.

Some inland areas close to the eastern Mediterranean coast are also referred to. Arpad, for example, is mentioned twice. In no. 48 Tabnî petitions the palace scribe to treat better his friend Abnî, the sheep-tax master of Arpad, who is coming to Nineveh,[65] and no. 135 concerns some disorders around Arpad. Interesting is the reference in no. 63 r.9ff to one Halbišu, a Samarian, and Bar-uri from Sam'al, who had told the anonymous informer the latest news about Guzana. These men were possibly spying for Esarhaddon.[66] Damascus appears in two fragmentary letters (nos. 133 and 134). A merchant from Carchemish is killed by his own servants in no. 105. Augurs from Hamath occur in a broken context in no. 8. Iqbi-Aššur, the scribe of Kar-Shalmaneser (Til-Barsip), complains about his problems to the king (no. 44). The governor of Que is said to hate someone in Harran in a letter by an anonymous informer (no. 71). Šamaš-šumu-ukin presents to the king a horse from the governor of Raṣappa (no. 22).

The North and Northwest

If one were to judge solely from Esarhaddon's royal inscriptions and queries, there would seem to have been a great deal of turmoil and trouble in the north and northwest of Assyria under his reign. One of his main military campaigns was directed against Šubria in 673,[67] and his queries repeatedly record threats posed by the Cilicians and Scythians. On the other hand, judging solely by the evidence provided by the preserved correspondence of Esarhaddon, the north and northwest would appear to have been the quietest points of the compass during his reign.

One badly broken letter (no. 151) deals with Assyria's relations with Urarṭu, which may have been peaceful throughout the reign of Esarhaddon. For the present, the role which Urarṭu played at this time remains, however, uncertain.[68] The Cimmerians invasions of Urarṭu at the end of the eighth and the beginning of the seventh century had presumably weakened the country so decisively that the Assyrians did not perceive much of a threat from that direction.[69]

This may be one of the reasons why these letters inform us so poorly about Urarṭu, but it is not the whole truth. It seems that the Assyrians were still very alert with regard to Urarṭu and kept a close eye on it, although only one fragmentary intelligence report from the border of Urarṭu has survived to us (no. 18).[70] That report, by the crown prince Assurbanipal,[71] clearly documents Assurbanipal's involvement in political and military matters during his father's reign.[72] The bulk of the letter is destroyed, but it apparently consisted chiefly of a long quotation from a report by an Assyrian official responsible for the border district between Assyria and Urarṭu. This may be compared with no. 148, where the king is quoted as urging the guards of the fortresses on the border of Urarṭu to be attentive and quickly send to the crown prince any deserters who may cross over the border. It may be noted, however, that the letter does not mention any deserters from Urarṭu, even though the guards of the fortresses of Urarṭu are mentioned before all the other guards in the letter. This suggests that the Assyrian intelligence service was more concerned about nomadic warrior peoples, such as the Cimmerians and Scythians, who were present in Urarṭu at that time, than about the Urarṭians themselves. Esarhaddon fought with the Cimmerians early in his rule, and a reference to the Cimmerians in a fragmentary letter datable to the year 680 may indicate a threat in the north (see no. 95). At the end of Esarhaddon's reign the Cimmerians are attested around Mannea and Media in the east (see "The East and Southeast," above). That does not exclude their presence in the north as well.

Assyrian Domestic Affairs

One can easily imagine that the political climate in Assyria after Sennacherib's surprising and heinous murder was almost paranoid. One letter (no. 95) gives a glimpse of the restless situation at Assur after Sennacherib's death. However, labelling the general frame of mind following Sennacherib's murder as paranoid seems not only exaggerated but also too simplistic. As Sennacherib's successor, Esarhaddon took careful precautions to ensure the continuity of the Sargonid dynasty, and these arrangements cannot but be seen as wise acts when viewed against the background of the political events before Esarhaddon's time. His glorious grandfather had been killed ominously on the battlefield and his father had been murdered by his own son, a brother of Esarhaddon. Against this background, Esarhaddon's reign seems surprisingly stable, or, conversely, it is because of this background that we can easily understand the rationale of his domestic policy.

A number of letters sent to the crown prince Assurbanipal attest to his deep involvement in domestic politics after he was appointed as crown prince of Assyria.[73] He is not mentioned by name in any of these letters, but because many of them concern purely Assyrian matters, it seems certain that the crown prince referred to was Assurbanipal rather than Šamaš-šumu-ukin. In fragmentary letters, such as nos. 37 and 38, there is of course no way of proving for certain that they were sent to Assurbanipal. We assume, however, that not even a single letter in this volume was sent to Šamaš-šumu-ukin.

Military matters are not exceptional in the letters addressed to Assurbanipal. This is not surprising in view of the fact that Esarhaddon explicitly ordered intelligence reports from the eastern and northern borders of the Empire to be sent to Assurbanipal: "Should a deserter from Mannea, Media or Hubuškia fall in their (the frontier guards') hands, you are to put him immediately in the hands of your messenger and send him to the crown prince. And if he has something to say, you will tell it to the crown prince accurately" (no 148:19-r.7). Note also the fragmentary letter no. 149, in which a bodyguard of the crown prince is mentioned in a context referring to a battle.

The king himself was at that time presumably either in the battlefield, concentrating on the more problematic issue of the Egyptian frontier, or confined to bed, struggling against the fits of his illness, which had taken a turn for the worse.[74] Thus it is no surprise that Esarhaddon wanted to share the responsibilities of his reign with Assurbanipal. Although Šamaš-šumu-ukin had been nominated as crown prince of Babylon, Assurbanipal's activities were probably not restricted to the north and east; he may have been involved in Babylonian matters as well (cf. nos. 17 and 155). Assurbanipal's position as crown prince at the end of Esarhaddon's reign is on the whole well comparable to that of Sennacherib during the latter half of the reign of Sargon.[75]

Letters from Prince Šamaš-metu-uballiṭ and Princess Šeru'a-eṭerat

In addition to seven letters from Assurbanipal and four from Šamaš-šumu-ukin, all from the period of their joint crown princehood (672-669), the present volume contains four letters from two other children of Esarhaddon: three letters authored (or dictated) by a prince named Šamaš-metu-uballiṭ and one by the princess Šerua-eṭerat.[76] These letters are interesting rarities.

Šamaš-metu-uballiṭ's letters illustrate the necessity of getting the king's permission even for performing rather minor tasks: in no. 25 the king is expected to give the order to repair a chariot wheel which the prince had broken at the king's guard, in no. 26 the royal order is needed to engage a physician to take care of a sick court woman, and no. 27 may likewise relate to a healing ritual to be performed at court, again at the king's orders. These letters, the so-called Zakutu treaty (SAA 2 8) and some administrative documents in which Šamaš-metu-uballiṭ is mentioned[77] suggest that his role may principally, if not exclusively, have been confined to the affairs of the royal court.[78]

Šerua-eṭerat's letter to Assurbanipal's wife Libbali-šarrat (no. 28) vividly illustrates the undercurrent tensions between two high-ranking women at court.[79] Note that Šerua-eṭerat is annoyed that Libbali-šarrat might be publicly referred to as her "sister" (*ahātu*). This use of *ahātu* resembles the usage of the word *ahu* ("brother") in letters, where it mostly means "colleague, fellow." Presumably in this letter, too, the word carried the nuance "equal, equivalent, as good as." In any case, Šerua-eṭerat clearly did not want simply benevolently to instruct the newcomer to the royal family in the ways of the palace, but seems to have written the letter out of feelings of rivalry and jealousy. Was she afraid of losing influence and status among the Assyrian royal women? On the whole, it is quite remarkable that this kind of emotional letter was ever written by an Assyrian princess to the future queen of Assyria, and more so that the letter survives.

Petitions and Denunciations

It is perhaps no surprise to find complaints, petitions and denunciations among the letters sent to an Assyrian king. However, the great number of denunciations extant from the reign of Esarhaddon is rather extraordinary when compared with those sent to his predecessors. It probably results directly from several provisions in his succession treaty (SAA 2 6), concluded in 672, where he personally urges his subjects to send denunciations to him.[80] It seems that the king took pains to control the empire as tightly as possible, and that the purpose of these treaty provisions was to institute an efficient intelligence system which would nip in the bud potential rebellions, conspiracies and riots against the royal house. The dire fates of his father and grandfather clearly had made Esarhaddon strive to prevent history from repeating itself.

But did those controlling measures organised by Esarhaddon create greater justice and a feeling of safety in the empire? And was he perhaps more easily accessible to his subjects than the other Neo-Assyrian kings? This may indeed have been the case, at least for a while, if he followed the advice of the writer of no. 64 (cf. especially lines 10-r.5). However that may be, the more prosaic reality would probably soon have set limits to such a practice. In any case, the good intentions of the king definitely resulted in a high number of petitions, complaints and denunciations, sent both to the king and the crown prince and, more rarely, to the palace scribe.

The most typical reasons for petitions seem to have been unemployment, court intrigues, oppression by other, higher officials, unsettled legal cases, financial needs, and so on. Often the writers sought to improve their own personal status or position, trying especially to enter into royal favour, but in some petitions they also try to intercede on behalf of their friends, relatives or colleagues (no. 40: "brother"). It is impossible to determine in which petitions the writers are in really serious trouble and which of them simply record the ordinary worries of officials.

Of the eighteen denunciations included in the present volume, three (nos. 59-61, by an informer named Nabû-rehtu-uṣur) pertain to a conspiracy against Esarhaddon detected and crushed in 671/670. For these and some other letters in this volume which may be connected to the same conspiracy,[81] as well as on the persons involved in that conspiracy one way or another (in particular, Sasî), the reader is referred to the extensive discussion in Nissinen Prophecy (1998), pp. 109-153.

The Enigmatic Anonymous Informer

Seven letters presented in the volume (nos. 62-68) all originate from the same scribe, who writes to the king anonymously.[82] His letters are fairly exceptional because of their length and their appearance: the tablets are large, thick and heavy. The lengths of the letters vary as follows:

No. 62: 32 extant lines (originally 37?).[83]

No. 63: 72 lines (no lines missing).

No. 64: 24 lines (no lines missing). Out of all these letters, this one was originally the shortest. The brevity of the letter apparently caused the author to choose the horizontal format for it.

No. 65: 34 extant lines (originally at least 40).[84]

No. 66: 20 extant lines (originally at least 36).[85]

No. 67: 30 extant lines (originally about 44 or more).[86]

No. 68: 44 extant lines (originally 55 or more).[87]

Even in their present, partly fragmentary condition, the seven letters of this anonymous writer contain altogther as many as 256 lines. The original line total was presumably more than 308, i.e., 44 or more lines on the average per letter!

However, a more striking feature of the letters is that the anonymous author can indeed, with reason, be called "enigmatic." Use of the word "enigmatic" is well grounded here since the contents of the letters are not ordinary. They are denunciations informing the king of impending threats. The writer is clearly charged by the king himself with this task of ferreting out suspicious facts: "The king, my lord, wrote to his servant as follows: [...] Do not conceal from me anything that you see or hear" (no. 66:2-6).

With one exception (no. 65), this secretive author goes straight to the point in his letters, without presenting any blessings or introductory formulae which would even in their shortest form include the usual address, "To the king, my lord: your servant, PN." Though the letters are anonymous, it is possible to find out something about the writer by studying his letters. Actually, what do we know about this enigmatic man? What does he reveal about himself? Was he perhaps a royal agent or just an ordinary official?

The Contents of the Letters

The letters of the enigmatic informer deal with the following subjects:

(a) In no. 62 the writer reminds the king of the rites he should perform in a favourable month because of an event of which we do not know any details but which seems to have something to do with an individual called Nabû-kabti-ahhešu.[88] The writer also urges the king to ask one Hamnanu and an unnamed priest as to why and how Sasî had released them from a place that was probably mentioned in the broken part of the letter (or in another letter by the same author).[89] The formulation of the letter leads one to suspect that Sasî himself was not present to tell the king how he released these persons.

(b) In no. 63 several persons are said to have committed crimes in Guzana. It is not clear if the so-called "matter of Guzana" (obv. 6) is really discussed in the letter itself. It may be that "the matter of Guzana" refers to a possible stir in Guzana, which, in turn, may be connected with the conspiracy of 671/670 which had its roots in the nearby city of Harran. But that is uncertain, and our purpose here is not to give free rein to our imagination; this remarkable letter includes so many potential stumbling blocks that we have to refrain from discussing it to the extent it would deserve. A few interesting and problematical details in it can, however, be mentioned here in brief. For instance, the roles of Aššur-zeru-ibni (undoubtedly a high-ranking official either in Guzana or in the vicinity), Šamaš-emuranni (the governor), and Tarṣî (the scribe of Guzana) are somewhat difficult to fathom in the letter. Note that at the beginning of the letter, the wife of Tarṣî is mentioned among the alleged offenders but Tarṣî himself is not included, and it is only later in the letter that he is denounced (rev. 18ff). It is also not easy to assess whether Aššur-zeru-ibni's activities should be regarded merely as evil and deceitful — possibly so, at least if he had been implicated in Tarṣî's schemes. Other puzzling passages in the letter are obv. 21-26 and rev. 22-27, in which the author informs about the blasphemous and heretical behaviour of a chariot-driver named Qurdî and a priest (Adad- killanni), and about witchcraft by the wife of the priest and Zazâ, the wife of Tarṣî.

(c) In no. 64 the writer first advises the king as to how to proceed when people appeal for royal intervention. Secondly, he writes to the king about gold, but the partly broken lines at the end of the letter render the context irretrievably blurred.

(d) No. 65 is for the most part a denunciation of a goldsmith and his son (see the discussion below under "Goldsmith and his Son").

(e) The fragmentary state of no. 66 prevents us from drawing any far-reaching conclusions from it. As in almost every letter of the enigmatic informer, here, too, he quotes heavily from the king's sayings, giving the impression of an ongoing dialogue between him and Esarhaddon.

(f) No. 67 is fairly poor preserved but relates to stolen gold.

(g) In the fragmentarily preserved no. 68, the writer informs the king on some officials who are, one way or another, offending against the king's authority.

The Geographical Setting, Tone and Date of the Letters

As for geography, our informer refers only to a few places outside the royal court: Guzana in no. 63, the strategically important Harhar in a broken context (no. 64 r.11),[90] and Kar-Mullissi near Nineveh in no. 66 r.3. It is not clear whether the writer himself was visiting those places at the time he sent the letters to the king. He may have relied mostly on useful informants and agents (cf. no. 63 r.9-12). Thus it is possible that the author himself was usually based in Nineveh (cf. no. 63 r.15f) or in Calah, and that he belonged to the palace personnel (cf. no. 62 r.14f).

The author's incessant affirmations about his honesty and loyalty to the king are a recurrent topic in these letters. However, while fawning to the king, he at times uses a fairly demanding tone (no. 62:3-6), but after all his demands, he can suddenly become very humble again. His letters easily give the impression of one-sided denunciations, because we do not have any extant letters by the king to him. Nonetheless, there are two direct references to letters sent by the king to the enigmatic author, (91) and twice the author refers to his own earlier reports.[92]

All the letters of the enigmatic writer may date from the years 672-669. Taken literally, the reference to "the sons of the king" in no. 63 r.14 and no. 66 r.6 would permit a more general date, but in actual fact the phrase almost certainly refers to the two crown princes, Assurbanipal and Šamaš-šumu-ukin.[93] In any case, the reference to Esarhaddon's (succession) treaty in no. 63 r.4f clearly dates the letter to the period 672-669. Moreover, the writer explicitly mentions the crown prince's palace (in Guzana) in no. 63:32 and the crown prince himself in no. 65 r.4. Incidentally, the reference to the reign of Sennacherib in no. 63:12ff is interesting but quite puzzling. The purpose of the passage is to emphasise the earlier crimes of the denounced Kutî and Tutî. The modern reader cannot help wondering at the accuracy of the information the author seems to have about these old crimes, and at the possible source(s) of this information.

The Orthography and Paleography of the Anonymous Writer

The enigmatic writer is not identifiable by means of orthographic and epigraphic analysis. He remains anonymous for the time being. No known Neo-Assyrian letter-writer betrays conventions in writing that fully correspond to his.

Nonetheless, the many long letters extant from him reveal a well-established and distinctive orthography. He uses many signs in a consistent and functional manner, while at the same time allowing himself a certain freedom of alternation as well. A few observations on his writing conventions will suffice to illustrate the point. There follows a representative, though by no means an exhaustive summary of the most distinctive features of his orthography and paleography:

1. The subjunctive forms of verbs and pronouns and the ventive endings of third person masculine plural are written *plene* following the pattern *-Cu-u-ni* (not *-Cu-ni* or *-CVC-u/ú-ni*), with striking regularity.[94] There are few exceptions to this rule.[95]

2. The imperative and feminine plural endings are regularly written *-Ca-a-ni* in the ventive and subjunctive forms. *-Ca-a-ni* also occurs frequently in the plural forms of nouns, see 3. below. By contrast, words ending in *-anni* are regularly written *-an-ni*.[96]

3. The marking of vowel quantity is variable. The long vowel in the plural endings *-āni/-āti* and the abstract ending *-ūtu* is regularly indicated at the end of the word (e.g., *dul-la-a-ni*),[97] but left unindicated before pronominal suffixes (e.g., *dul-la-ni-šú*).[98]

4. Consonant doubling is regularly left unexpressed in perfect forms beginning with *i/a/uss*-and *a/i/utt*-(e.g., *i-sa-kan*, *a-ti-kip*), as well as in writings of the preposition /issi/ "with" (e.g., *i-si-šú*).[99] Note that the signs IS, IT, AS and AT are part and parcel of the writer's syllabary and could hence well have been used for writing these forms.[100] Otherwise, consonantal gemination can be either marked or left unmarked.[101]

5. The suffix *-tu* of feminine nouns is regularly written with the sign UD (= *tú*). Once *tú* occurs in final position in a verbal form, too: *i-mu-tú* (no. 63:18). Note the difference in spelling when the suffix is not in the final position: *a-bu-tu-u* (no. 62:4).

6. The signs ŠA and ŠÁ are both used for writing the relative pronoun/genetive particle *ša*, but otherwise there is a sharp difference in their use: ŠA occurs only independently, whereas ŠÁ can also occur in combination with other signs, as, e.g., in *šá-ni-ú*, *ú-ra-mu-šá-nu-u-ni*, *a-a-e-šá*.

7. The sign ŠU is used in initial and middle positions (e.g., *šu-te-tu-qe-e*, *ta-né-pi-šu-u-ni*),[102] and rarely for writing the third person singular possessive suffix.[103] The use of ŠÚ is restricted to the final position (e.g., *la-áš-šú*) and for the writing of the third person singular and plural pronominal suffixes.

8. "My lord" is regularly written EN-*iá*, only once EN-*ia* (63:9). Otherwise, the signs IA and IÁ occur in rather free variation.[104]

9. "King" is normally written with the sign LUGAL, but in four cases the sign MAN (actually the sacred number and logogram for "sun") is used.[105]

10. The word "if" is written *šúm-ma* (not *šum-ma* or *šum/šúm-mu*). The quotation particle of the first person is *nu-uk* (not *mu-uk* or *mu/nu-ku*).

11. In contrast to most writers of the reign of Esarhaddon, the enigmatic writer consistently uses LÚ* (the "short" form of LÚ) for writing the names of professions. He also regularly writes BA, ZU, SU and ŠA with tilted horizontal wedges (cf. the copies of nos. 63, 64, 66 and 68 in CT 53).

The vocabulary of the enigmatic writer includes rare and specialised words, several of them hapax legomena, e.g. *bunbullu*, *dannatānu*, *eqû*, *etāqu* Štn, *hiddu*, *ikīsu*, *luādu*, *maqaltānu*, *maṣātānu*. In the field of morphology, one may note the unusual syllabification *li-šá-al* (for /liš'al/), attested thrice in no. 62 r.3, 8 and 67 r.11. We know only two other examples from NA letters with the same spelling.[106]

The Scholarly Background of the Writer

The writing conventions of the author reflect his subtle insight into the grammar of Neo-Assyrian and reveal his scholarly background, which is confirmed by the allusion to (his) scholarly expertise in no. 62:6-13. On the other hand, e.g., the interpretation of the passage "two or three *reports* should be completed *by* my hand" in the same letter (rev. 9) remains uncertain, and it need not refer to the author's own scholarly activities.[107]

Even though the enigmatic anonymous writer of these denunciations remains unidentified, it cannot be excluded that he is somebody we already know by name from other Neo-Assyrian written sources. Though the evidence points to the writer having been a scholar, he could also have been a priest acquainted with exorcistic, extispical and astrological literature (no. 65). He certainly did not belong to the class of "magnates" (cf. no. 62 r.6f, "[...] who did not stand with us before the magnates," and no. 64 r.2f, "The magnates should be given clear instructions about it"), but he seems rather to have belonged to the inner circle of scholars or the upper echelons of the palace personnel, and clearly knew the king and both the crown princes well. The only detail known about the writer's family comes from a remark in no. 63 (obv. 10f) revealing that he had at least one son holding a high office, and that this son was personally allowed to bring horses to the king.

The writer repeatedly counsels and even reminds the king of his duties in a manner which was only permitted to the king's closest advisers, and it should be noted that only a very limited number of the most influential scholars could do that in the Neo-Assyrian Empire. It is not very likely that these letters were written at a time when Esarhaddon was seriously ill. Otherwise we would expect the letters to contain at least a few words of encouragement to the king — unless, of course, the author was unaware of his illness, a possibility which appears rather unlikely in view of the author's extensive knowledge of "what was going on." Other possible occasions for writing these letters could have been, for instance, Esarhaddon's absence from Nineveh, the writer's absence from Nineveh, Calah, or some other city having a royal palace, or perhaps both the writer and Esarhaddon were in fact in Nineveh, but in different palaces.

If the writer were an exorcist, haruspex, or astrologer/scribe, then his disapproval of the education given to a goldsmith's son in the relevant disciplines would become even more readily understandable (see below, "The Goldsmith and his Son"). However, as already noted, he did not necessarily have to be a representative of these disciplines, but could equally well have been a priest, a physician or a lamentation priest.

The Possible Identity of the Enigmatic Informer

We have taken considerable pains to identify the enigmatic anonymous writer among the influential and better-known scholars and priests known from SAA 10 and 13, comparing his roster of distinctive features against theirs with the help of the data found in LAS II Appendix M5-6. However, all our efforts have been frustrated; while there is no lack of candidates for the sort of *éminence grise* represented by our mysterious writer, none of the candidates considered could match all the distinctive features listed above. There is only one writer who may deserve to be seriously considered: Mar-Issar, Esarhaddon's special agent in Babylonia (see SAA 10 347-370 and no. 171 of the present volume).

His orthographical and paleographical conventions fulfil most of the criteria listed above (1-3, 5-8 and 10-11), and those criteria that are not fully met (4, 9) are partially fulfilled. Thus Mar-Issar, too, writes regularly *i-sa-* etc. in perfect forms, but unlike the anonymous informer, he writes *is-si* for "with" and uses the sign MAN almost exclusively for writing the word "king."

Like the anonymous informer, Mar-Issar probably also had a scribal background. He seems to have been appointed as Esarhaddon's special agent in Babylonia comparatively late, in Tammuz 671 (see SAA 10 347), and thus could have spent the early part of the period 672-669 in Assyria. This would account for the difference in format between his letters (which display a format resembling that of the Babylonian letters of the Sargonid period) and those of the enigmatic informer (which are externally quite different and much bigger). The slight differences in writing conventions would also be explicable if one assumes that the two dossiers of letters date from two different time periods.

However, it must be emphasised that the orthography of Mar-Issar also displays certain features which are not at all attested in (or are in conflict with) the orthography of the enigmatic informer (such as the use of the sign I as a glide in writing certain forms of finally weak verbs, or the use of the sign -*ṭí* for writing the assimilated perfect infix). Hence the possibility that the enigmatic informer is to be identified as Mar-Issar, fascinating as it seems, is far from having been established. More research is called for to settle the matter definitely.

The Other Anonymous Informer

The observations made above concerning the enigmatic anonymous writer largely apply also to the other anonymous informer, the author of nos. 69-71. This writer also seems to have been a scholar, but the c. 40 partly broken lines extant from his letters do not provide much ground for a comparable study. His letters, too, date from 672-669: nos. 69 and 70 are addressed to the crown prince, and Sasî is mentioned in nos. 69 and 71. The latter letter refers to Harran (obv. 6); even though the reference occurs in a quotation from another person's speech, its formulation makes it likely that the author himself had also visited the city. The orthography and other epistolary conventions of this informer clearly differ from those of the enigmatic one. His letters regularly open with an introductory blessing, are much shorter, and have the horizontal "report" format. In his orthography, he prefers *ú* to *u* in penultimate position.[108]

The Goldsmith and his Son

One of the most absorbing passages in the present correspondence occurs in no. 65, a letter by the enigmatic anonymous writer, where he gives vent to feelings of jealousy in protecting his own field of expertise against intrusive outsiders. He is very indignant at the teaching of specialised scholarly skills to the son of the goldsmith Parruṭu of the queen's household.

Our author's anger can be better understood when bearing in mind the importance of exorcism, extispicy and astrology at that time, and taking into consideration that their practice by people not authorised by the king was considered potentially harmful to the ruler himself and the whole monarchy.[109]

It is virtually certain that the unnamed son of the goldsmith is identical with Nabû-sagib, the author of no. 81, who in this letter actually identifies himself as "the son of the goldsmith Parruṭu of the queen's household."[110] The content of no. 65 may help explain why Nabû-sagib personally wrote a letter to the king. No. 81 relates to the delivery of jewellery, a matter that can easily be imagined to have been part and parcel of the work of royal goldsmiths. Of course, Nabû-sagib probably was a goldsmith, as his father, but he did not necessarily have to be a practitioner of the craft himself. Thus he might well have prepared the Pazuzu-heads mentioned in no. 65:4 himself, unless – more likely – there were several of those heads at the goldsmith's workshop.[111]

Anyway, Nabû-sagib could also be visualised as a type of courier, intermediary or apprentice, who was, among other things, running errands for the goldsmiths of the queen's household. Be that as it may, it is known that some people were specialised in two or more different occupations,[112] while others may even have held two or more offices at the same time.[113] The necessary prerequisites needed for many professions consisted of a wide variety of different skills. Scholars are good examples of this, since their education clearly was multi-faceted.[114] In the letter authored by Nabû-sagib, we witness him responding to an earlier missive of the king concerning the jewellery which the king had ordered Nabû-sagib to deliver to the palace, but which obviously had failed somehow to arrive, since Nabû-sagib explains: "I gave them (= the jewellery) to the gate-guard, Atanha-ilu, along with a letter, saying, 'Deliver them to the king, my lord!'" (r.4-6). This reference to another letter, probably also written by Nabû-sagib, which unfortunately has not survived, is interesting, since it suggests that there may have been still further letters written by him. The passage also illustrates the strict policy of admission to the royal palace: it shows that a person belonging to the household of the queen could not automatically enter the royal palace, even if delivering important and valuable items.

In the light of the previous discussion, it is not surprising that an exorcist called Nabû-sagib is actually attested. It seems quite possible that this exorcist is identical with Nabû-sagib the goldsmith's son.[115] At least the passage in no. 65 supports the assumption, clearly indicating that he received instruction in exorcism and that it was his plan (or his father's or someone else's plan) to become a scholar. The disapproving letter by the enigmatic anonymous writer may, of course, have led to actions intended to prevent the teaching of scholarly skills to the goldsmith's son, unless the king was already familiar with the matter, or unless some other significant factors favoured such an education. If the king did not know anything about the matter before reading or hearing the letter by the enigmatic anonymous writer, we might be informed of his reaction in another letter (no. 218). Unfortunately, in its present state, this letter cannot offer any further context whatsoever to elucidate the matter.

At this point it seems appropriate to ponder briefly whether a goldsmith's son could under any circumstances have become an exorcist. A categorical 'no' would in principle probably be the correct answer, the reason being that scholarly occupations, like many other ones, were strictly tied to family traditions.[116] Hence influential families of exorcists and other scholarly families would presumably have considered it an outrage if an outsider tried to "invade" their esoteric disciplines. Such a situation would not have been tolerated without protest. Actually, this is what happened in no. 65.

Nevertheless, the case might have been different if a protégé of the queen was in question, or even better, if the person concerned was a protégé of the queen mother. This possibility appears quite tempting to us, even though it has to be admitted that it involves some problems. We do not really know if the household of the queen was separate from the queen mother's household in the Neo-Assyrian period.[117] If there was only one entity, the household of the queen, then it might have been under the queen mother's control if she was alive.[118] If there were two separate entities (the queen's and the queen mother's households), they may have been so closely knit together that they partly shared the same palace(s), and so on.[119] A third possibility is that the household of the queen was a permanent institution even if there was, temporarily, no principal queen living.[120] In the first case, the living queen mother might still have been the most honoured person of the household, but not necessarily always the most influential person.

While a comprehensive study of the queen's household in the Neo-Assyrian period is beyond the scope of the present volume, we shall take a closer look at the queen's household referred to in the letters of goldsmith Parruṭu and his son Nabû-sagib, because it is essentially relevant to our enquiry. To establish the identity of the queen(s) under whom Parruṭu and his son served, we must, of course, first consider the dates of the relevant letters. As noted in Table I above, no. 65 can be certainly dated to 672-669. The dating of no. 81, by Nabû-sagib, is less clear, but it is also likely to come from the period 672-669.

During this period, Ešarra-hammat is known to have been an influential queen. Apparently she was the mother of Assurbanipal and Šamaš-šumu-ukin, and her importance, known from a handful of sources, would make her a good candidate here.[121] However, her early death (according to the Assyrian calendar in 673-XII-5/6, i.e. about February 7, 672 B.C.), rules her out.[122] Besides, it is not known if Ešarra-hammat ever played an active political role. In the present state of our knowledge it is impossible to decide if another wife of Esarhaddon was nominated queen after the death of Ešarra-hammat. Libbali-šarrat, the wife of Assurbanipal, was hardly called queen already in Esarhaddon's reign. So the most likely candidate for the queen of 672-669 is the queen mother Naqia.

Certainly, Naqia was influential enough to have a son of a goldsmith educated and become an exorcist, thus breaking the tradition of passing that esteemed profession from father to son. Moreover, Parruṭu himself was probably an exceedingly wealthy man. We do not see any obstacle in identifying him in one legal document (SAA 6 253, date lost), in which he sells a large estate to Issar-duri, the queen mother's scribe. This legal document does not expressly inform us of any tangible connections between Parruṭu and the scribe (the profession or position of the former is not mentioned in the document), but in general land sales were often carried out between parties who were familiar with each other. At the time when Parruṭu hired a Babylonian to teach his son, it is evident that the former was not intended to teach the mere rudiments of cuneiform writing to Nabû-sagib. Hence Nabû-sagib had presumably already acquired his basic education in the queen (mother)'s household, either from Issar-duri or some other scribe working for the queen's household, before the unnamed Babylonian scholar taught him specialised sciences.[123]

In our opinion it is not to be ruled out that Nabû-sagib enjoyed a special position in the queen (mother)'s household and thus might have gained a unique opportunity to learn the challenging and appreciated craft of the exorcist. More evidence is, of course, needed, but we are tempted to propose that the initiative to train a goldsmith's son to become a scholar, or more precisely an exorcist in this case, came from the queen mother Naqia in person; she herself is known to have had recourse to extispicy, astrology and oracles.[124]

Note on an Influential Family of Scholars

Apart from their scholarly activities, Esarhaddon's chief scribe Nabû-zeru-lešir and his son, Issar-šumu-ereš, who succeeded his father as chief scribe, also seem to have been involved in non-scholarly matters. There are some indications that the latter was a palace scribe before his promotion to the office of chief scribe. It is not known when exactly he was promoted to the rank of chief scribe after his father's death. In any case, the earliest extant letters written by Issar-šumu-ereš date to early 672.[125]

Nine letters of the present volume (nos. 48-50, 78-80, 87(?), 89 and 125) directly or indirectly pertain to Nabû-zeru-lešir, Issar-šumu-ereš, the chief scribe and the palace scribe.

Nabû-zeru-lešir is the author of a list (no. 50) which enumerates fourteen people permitted to enter the palace.[126] This list includes Nabû-zeru-lešir himself and his three sons, two daughters and daughter-in-law (names not mentioned). From other sources we know that his sons included Issar-šumu-ereš and the exorcist Šumaya.[127] The name of Nabû-zeru-lešir's third son is not known, but it is very likely that he was a scholar too. It seems that at the time this list was prepared only one of his sons was married, since only one daughter-in-law is mentioned.

Issar-šumu-ereš is most likely the author of a memorandum (no. 80) to the king. This memorandum shows that an essential part of the chief scribe's duty was the drawing up of financial records. Another typical task of the chief scribe is probably alluded to in no. 125 r.5-10, whose sender (name not preserved) urges the king to order "the chief scribe to write the name of the king on the stele, and at the same time to look up a favourable day for the (objects) to be placed in the door-jambs of the house."

Both the chief scribe and the palace scribe must have been extremely influential men at court, but this did not always result in riches and fortune, as the picturesque description of the chief scribe's house in no. 89 reveals: "The house of the chief scribe is a tiny house. Even a donkey would not enter there" (obv. 9-11).

The memorandum by Issar-šumu-ereš discussed above (no. 80) mentions a person called Kanunayu, who also occurs in no. 78 r.2 as "Kanunayu, the deputy (of the palace scribe)," whereas no. 79 is written by Kanunayu (title not given) and Mannu-ki-Libbali. Interestingly, at the end of this letter, which concerns building works, Kanunayu and Mannu-ki-Libbali ask the king to give an order to Issar-šumu-ereš, their own immediate superior. Is it possible that the palace scribe with whom Mannu-ki-libbali had problems (no. 78) was in fact Issar-šumu-ereš?

Scholarly Advice during Esarhaddon's Šubrian Campaign?

As already pointed out above, the present correspondence makes no reference to Esarhaddon's long campaign against Šubria. Not even the name of the country is mentioned in any of the letters. Nevertheless, one of the letters may be vaguely linked to the Šubrian campaign, and if so, then it would relate to an extraordinary incident which happened at a late stage in the campaign. Namely, Esarhaddon might have asked scholarly advice for the interpretation of Asakku's magical properties when the Šubrian ruler Ik-Teššup made his last attempt to save his life by creating a scapegoat statue called Asakku with a golden coat and presenting it to Esarhaddon. The enquiry about Asakku in no. 164:10-12 might refer to this scapegoat Asakku statue.[128] Of course, this suggestion is entirely hypothetical and impossible to verify because of the fragmentary state of no. 164. Another possibility is that the passage pertains to an astrological omen predicting an epidemic *asakku*-disease in the country.[129] In any case, the king's interest in hearing the scholarly analysis of Asakku's essence, power and sceptre, is unusual and favours the incident of the Šubrian campaign.

Bet bēli Reconsidered

The compound phrase *bēt bēli*, literally "the house of the lord," is attested in several letters of the present volume (see Glossary). In spite of the recent careful and extensive study of this term by Fales,[130] we believe that there is still room for a different and somewhat simpler interpretation, and would like to offer our alternative solution here.

It is easy to agree with Fales that all the Neo-Assyrian spellings of *bēt bēli* with the plural sign MEŠ are to be interpreted as singular,[131] MEŠ merely representing the lengthening of the genitive marker *-i* before a following possessive suffix.[132] However, our understanding of *bēt bēli* as such partly deviates from his views, because we think that *bēt bēli* can — possibly in all of its attestations — be interpreted literally as "the household of the lord,"[133] or rather, with the obligatory possessive suffix,[134] "the household of my/your/his/our/your/their lord."[135] We find this rendering preferable to "house of the lord," because a "household" can be understood as a larger entity than a "house," and possibly *bēt bēli* never meant a single physical house or building. Otherwise "the house of the lord" is, of course, an equally valid rendering.

In the basic meaning of the compound, the element "lord" can hardly refer to anybody other than the Assyrian king. Thus "the royal household, the ruling house," would also be acceptable translations.[136] The possibility that *bēt bēli* did not always refer to the Assyrian king remains, but we do not know any convincing examples of such a usage in Neo-Assyrian. It needs to be stressed that the literal translation of *bēt bēli* does not exclude different semantic nuances of the concept. It was probably understood concretely, but in a figurative use also abstractly. For instance, *bēt bēli* may often have been used in contexts where it was not desirable to repeat the word "king" all the time. Perhaps in some cases the phrase was simply used for stylistic reasons, to avoid tautology.

The fundamental purpose of using a concept like *bēt bēli* can be considered ideological or propagandistic: the phrase stresses the mutual bond between the royal household and its subjects. Interestingly, *bēt bēli* can be mentioned in the same breath with the royal palace and the land of Assyria.[137] In some cases, *bēt bēli* is also combined with forms of the verb *ra'āmu* "to love."[138] The use of *bēt bēli* in this kind of context strongly suggests that the concept had general currency as a means of expressing Assyrian patriotic or nationalistic feelings. Hence *bēt bēli*, as an ideological abstraction, may even be considered part of the Sargonid propaganda in its best form.[139] The passages with the verb "to love" emphasise the close relationship between the king and his subjects. Especially in contemporary Babylonian letters, the relationship of a royal servant (*ardu*) to the king is a recurring topic, see the references in note 138. In this respect it does not seem to make much difference whether the phrase is used by the king or one of his subjects. Only the viewpoint differs: the king emphasises the responsibilities of the subject vis-à-vis the ruling house and the privileges granted for a loyal servant siding with the king, while the subject confirms his allegiance to the king and his household.

The Neo-Assyrian Empire was truly multinational and it should be stressed that foreigners could "love" Assyria as well. Many non-native Assyrians were employed in high posts in the administration and army all over the empire. We do not see any reason why some Babylonians, for example, attested as high officials of the Assyrian king, would not address their overlord by using the phrase "my lord's household" to emphasise their allegiance and devotion to the Assyrian king.[140] Whether this "love" towards Assyria by non-native Assyrians was genuine, or merely pretended, is not our concern here.

At this point it is appropriate to compare the display of loyalty towards the ruling house with the display of disloyalty. Disloyalty is also attested in connection with *bēt bēli* and it manifests itself, among others, in crimes ("sins"), corruption, conspiracy and rebellion against the ruling house. All these things were constant worries and threats that could have corroded the Assyrian ruling house, either from inside or from outside. A telling example is a crime committed by some governors, or at least by the governor of Arrapha, against the king and the ruling house. The major-domo Ṣallaya and the scribe Asalluhi-ereš write in no. 42:

> The governors have squandered the household of our lord, (and) the king does not know. The governor of Arrapha has taken away the gift that the king gave to our lord. May it be known to the king, our lord, that our lord's household has been squandered.

It is a pity that the other "lord" of Ṣallaya and Asalluhi-ereš mentioned in the passage is not known. The context of the letter suggests that "the house of our lord" could here also be interpreted as referring to this other lord and not to the king. The major-domo (*rab bēti*) was a high official, usually associated with a palace, and served Assyrian and foreign kings, queens, crown princes, magnates or provincial governors. If the letter was sent from Arrapha and the other lord of Ṣallaya and Asalluhi-ereš was the governor of Arrapha, then the letter would be a denunciation of this immediate superior of theirs. However, this interpretation must for the time being remain uncertain.

In another letter referring to *bēt bēli*, royal magnates are similarly accused of having obstructed an explicit order of the king:

> As to what the king, our lord, wrote to us: 'I have ordered the magnates to do justice to you' — we have stood before them, but they have refused to render justice to the household of their lord. They have sold [all the servant]s of the crown prince for money and [finis]hed them up.[141]

It does not seem to matter whether the phrase *bēt bēli* occurs in letters sent from Assyrian cities, Babylonia, provinces annexed to Assyria or the countryside, since its meaning and connotations remain the same everywhere.[142] Moreover, the broad geographical distribution of the phrase confirms its currency and diffusion throughout the Neo-Assyrian Empire.

At present *bēt bēli* is attested in written documents attributable to the reigns of Sargon II, Esarhaddon, Assurbanipal and (once) Sin-šarru-iškun. An even earlier attestation may be available in CTN 2 186, a letter from Šarru-duri, the governor of Calah under Tiglath-pileser III and Sargon II, but the dating of this text is uncertain.[143] Therefore, the phrase may have originated as an ideologically loaded concept not earlier than the reign of Sargon.[144] The concept probably developed in time, and it may well have taken a while before all of its semantic nuances were fully established.

Surprisingly, perhaps, the phrase is not attested at all in Assyrian royal inscriptions. It seems to be confined to more informal types of text, such as letters. The only attestation of *bēt bēli* outside letters, a passage in the Succession Treaty of Esarhaddon (SAA 2 6:208), emphasises the adjured individual's personal relationship to the ruling house. The use of the phrase in the treaty indicates that by that time, at the latest, its ideological connotations were deeply rooted in Neo-Assyrian.

Seeing in *bēt bēli* an "informal" or "intimate" concept finds support in the possessive suffixes that were without exception attached to the phrase. Using the appropriate possessive suffixes clearly served to confirm the relationship of a person or persons to the ruling house, and their main purpose probably was to emphasise a person's allegiance to the latter: he/they was/were to protect and take care of "the household of his/their lord (= king)," for instance, by looking after its interests and by informing the palace of suspicious actions.

Rendering *bēt bēli* as "government," "government department" or "administrative department" seems a less fortunate solution. Much as our knowledge of the Neo-Assyrian Empire has increased during recent years, there is still very little positive evidence for the existence of an administrative body that could be called "government" in the modern sense. Thus it seems doubly difficult to posit the existence of specific "government departments" in Assyria. There were of course many governors and other high officials exercising their authority in the Assyrian homeland and the provinces, but ultimately decision-making always lay in the hands of the king. To use terms that would hint at the existence of a more diversified type of decision-making system in Assyria could be misleading. If the concept of "government" really existed in Assyria, then it would be safer to assume that the king himself took part in the governmental meetings than that the government gathered without the king. However, while there is some evidence for a group of magnates occasionally gathering to exercise justice with the Assyrian king and possibly secretly advising him on political matters, there are practically no direct references to the meetings of such an advisory body in the written record.[145] Probably a lot of interaction between the king and his trusted officials did precede the taking of many important decisions and the king may well have relied on his advisors — Assyrian royal correspondence shows that scholars, for instance, advised the king on an institutional basis[146] — but still it was always the king who made the final decisions. From this point of view, writing to the king in a fawning and flattering tone about one's "government (department)," divorced from the king, would not make much sense.

The political role of the king's magnates must have been considerable, but the way this role was organised is largely unclear. For example, the interaction between the king's magnates and the governors is not obvious. The (royal) magnates are often depicted acting collectively but it is never stated what that actually means, i.e., did they regularly gather to take counsel with the king? The fact that we do not have any letters by the magnates to Esarhaddon could imply that few such (cuneiform) letters were actually written.

On the Present Edition

Texts Included and Excluded

This volume contains all the remaining Neo-Assyrian letters datable to the reign of Esarhaddon that were not edited in SAA 10 (letters of scholars) and SAA 13 (letters of priests). In practice this means, for example, that the letters written by Assurbanipal to Esarhaddon, which were previously assigned to a separate Assurbanipal volume, as well as the letters written to Assurbanipal as crown prince, are included in the present volume. Seven of the letters included (nos. 52-58) are not addressed to the king or the crown prince but to various officials and private people.

The texts edited in this volume include ten previously unpublished letters or letter fragments (K 1273, K 15626, K 16521, K 16550, K 19787, K 19979, K 19986, K 20565, 83-1-18,147, 83-1-18,153, and 83-1-18,742 + Bu 91-5-9,149), which were identified as parts of the Esarhaddon correspondence by Parpola, and the editions are based on transliterations prepared by him. All of these texts were collated by us in February 2002, and virtually all of them were copied by Van Buylaere on 11-15/02/02 (see pp. 217-218). Only one fragment (83-1-18,147 = no. 191) was left uncopied because of its poor state of preservation.

The volume includes seven letters from a certain Bel-iqiša (nos. 111-117), who is mentioned in a letter of Ubru-Nabû (no. 110) and hence seems to belong to the reign of Esarhaddon. One additional letter of uncertain date (ABL 390) by Bel-iqiša has been excluded from the volume, however, because this writer is almost certainly to be identified with the homonymous governor of Gambulu under Esarhaddon and Assurbanipal, who revolted against the latter in 664 and died in obscure circumstances (see PNA 1/II p. 315f). It cannot be totally excluded that the author of ABL 390 and our Bel-iqiša were in fact one and the same person, or that ABL 390 was actually written to Esarhaddon, but the likelihood is that it was written to Assurbanipal after the revolt (cf. ABL 390 r.16-18 with ABL 896:10-12).

Furthermore, this volume includes several unassigned fragments which have a certain likelihood of belonging to the reign of Esarhaddon. Their fragmentary condition, scarcity of intact lines and lack of distinctive features, however, makes it impossible to date and attribute them to a specific Neo-Assyrian king with any degree of certainty. Some of them may predate Esarhaddon's reign, and if so, they most probably belong to the correspondence of Sargon II edited in SAA 1, 5 and 15. A few of these fragments may been written after Esarhaddon's reign, and thus date to the reign of Assurbanipal.

Two letters (nos. 98 and 99) edited in this volume may pre-date Esarhaddon's time. They have two things in common: (1) A scribe named Kabtî, who is the writer of no. 98 (there titled the "scribe of the palace superintendent") and is mentioned in no. 99 (there identified as "scribe of Aššur-da''in-aplu, son of Shalmaneser"), and (2) the "dissolved ordinances of the palace" (no. 98), which are reported as having been re-established in no. 99. It is obvious that the letters belong together, but their dating presents a problem. The son of Shalmaneser mentioned in no. 99 is most likely to be identified with Aššur-da''in-aplu, the rebellious son of Shalmaneser III (858-824), but the matter is complicated by two texts showing that a scribe called Kabtî also was active in Esarhaddon's time, in which case a(n otherwise unknown) son of Shalmaneser V (727-722) could also be in question (see Parpola, LAS II, p. 256:19, and cf. PNA 1/I and 2/I s.vv. Aššur-da''in-aplu and Kabtî). Since the letters would otherwise have had no place in any SAA volume, it seemed reasonable to include them in the present edition.

Sixteen further letters which were preliminarily assigned to the volume were subsequently excluded for various reasons:

ABL 1116, ABL 1167, CT 53 142, CT 53 619 and CT 53 968 belong to the Assurbanipal volume.

ABL 1272, CT 53 512, CT 53 683, CT 53 712 and K 16561 are letters to Sargon II.

CT 53 670 is fragment of an extispicy query to be added to SAA 4.

CT 53 399 is a literary text.

CT 53 412 and 548 are administrative texts to be added to SAA 11.

CT 53 531 is a legal fragment to be added to SAA 6.

The Order of the Texts

The letters are basically arranged according to the same principles as in previous volumes. All identifiable letters by the same sender have been grouped together into dossiers, and the dossiers have been ordered principally according to geographical criteria (the provenances of the letters), with letters from central Assyria (including the royal letters and other letters from the royal court and the capital) coming first and unassignable letters last. The only exception to this rule is constituted by Chapters 3 to 5 containing petitions, private letters, and denunciations, where the geographical criterion is not strictly applied.

Translations

Uncertain or conjectural translations are indicated by italics. Interpretative additions to the translation are enclosed within parentheses. All restorations are enclosed within square brackets. Untranslatable passages are indicated by dots.

Month names are rendered by their Hebrew equivalents, followed by a Roman numeral (in parentheses) indicating the place of the month within the lunar year. Personal, divine and geographical names are rendered by English or Biblical equivalents if a well-established equivalent exists (e.g., Esarhaddon, Nineveh); otherwise, they are given in transcription with length marks deleted. The normalisation of West-Semitic names follows PNA.

The rendering of professions is a compromise between the use of accurate but impractical Assyrian terms and inaccurate but practical modern or classical equivalents.

Critical Apparatus

The primary purpose of the critical apparatus is to support the readings and translations established in the edition, and it consists largely of references to collations of questionable passages, scribal mistakes corrected in the transliteration, alternative interpretations and other texts used for restorations. Collations given in copy at the end of the volume are referred to briefly as "see coll." Collations included in Waterman's RCAE and Ylvisaker's grammar (LSS 5/6) are referred to as "W" and "Y" respectively followed by page number (e.g, W 261 means a collation communicated in RCAE III p. 261).

The critical apparatus does contain some additional information relevant to the interpretation of the texts, but it is not a commentary. For the convenience of the reader, references to studies of individual letters and related letters in the Esarhaddon corpus are occasionally given, but with no claim to completeness. Comments are kept to a minimum, and are mainly devoted to problems in the text, The historical and technical information contained in the texts is generally not commented upon.

Glossary and Indices

The electronically generated glossary and indices, prepared by Parpola and checked by the editors, follow the pattern of the previous volumes. Note that in contrast to the basic dictionaries, verbal adjectives are for technical reasons mostly listed under the corresponding verbs, with appropriate cross-references.

The references to professions attached to the index of personal names have been provided by a computer programme written by Parpola. It is hoped that these will be helpful in the prosopographical analysis of the texts, but it should be noted that the program omits certain deficiently written professions and the references are accordingly not absolutely complete.

NOTES

[1] A minority of the letters in both SAA 10 and SAA 13 are Neo-Babylonian.

[2] Esarhaddon's letters and the letters from the early reign of Assurbanipal are in some instances almost inseparable from one another because they share the same archival context in Nineveh and the subject matters in their letters are rather similar. For the archival context and the types of texts from their reigns, see S. Parpola, CRRAI 30 (1986) 228ff.

[3] One conspicuous difference between this volume and SAA 10 and SAA 13 is that they also have letters from Assurbanipal's reign, whilst here all the Assurbanipal letters (possibly with two exceptions, see notes on nos. 129 and 143) are from the time of his crown princehood (672-669), i.e., from the late reign of his father, Esarhaddon.

[4] Borger Esarh. Since the publication of that volume, several additional articles have been published by Borger and others, see provisionally the list in Porter Images p. 177ff. A new volume on Esarhaddon's royal inscriptions is in preparation by E. Leichty, soon to be published in The Royal Inscriptions of Mesopotamia series.

[5] See Grayson Chronicles pp. 82ff and 125ff.

[6] SAA 2 4-7 and 14. It is not certain if SAA 2 13 dates to the reign of Esarhaddon, see SAA 2 p. XXXIV. Cf. also SAA 2 8 (and for this text ibid., p. XXXI) which was concluded after Esarhaddon's death in November 669.

[7] SAA 3 10 and 33. See SAA 3 p. XX, and H. Tadmor, B. Landsberger and S. Parpola, SAAB 3 (1989) 31f and 45ff. Possibly also SAA 3 9, see A. George, SAAB 1 (1987) 39.

[8] SAA 4 1-261. Of course, it is possible that some of the more fragmentary queries do not date to the reign of Esarhaddon.

[9] SAA 6 201-306. It is not impossible that a few of the texts in SAA 6 with numbers lower than 201 or higher than 306 originate from Esarhaddon's reign. In addition, there seems to be one document from his reign in SAA 14 (no. 474), see ibid., p. XXIII. For SAA 14 2 (671 or 666), see, e.g., the footnotes under SAA 6 287:7, SAA 14 2, Melville Naqia/Zakutu p. 63 n. 14, and also the references in PNA 1/I p. 233 s.v. Atar-ili 2. Moreover, SAA 14 3-7 are potentially from the reign of Esarhaddon but they are not accurately datable. Milki-nuri, eunuch of the queen, on whom this dossier contains information, is both known from the late reign of Esarhaddon and the early reign of Assurbanipal, see PNA 2/II p. 752 s.v. Milki-nuri.

[10] SAA 7 and SAA 11. Probably the majority of the texts in these two volumes date to the reign of Esarhaddon and the early years of Assurbanipal, cf. SAA 7 p. XIV.

[11] SAA 8. As is the case with many other Neo-Assyrian documents, the majority of the astrological reports dates to the (late) reign of Esarhaddon as well as to the early years of Assurbanipal. See ibid., pp. XX and XXII.

[12] SAA 9 1-7, possibly also 10. See SAA 9 p. LXVIIIff.

[13] For the time being only one land grant (SAA 12 24) can be dated to Esarhaddon's reign with certainty, see SAA 12 pp. XXIf and XXV. However, SAA 12 48 (land grant), 81 (schedule of offerings), and 89 (royal votive gift) may be attributed to his reign, cf. SAA 12 pp. XXV, XXXIII.

[14] Nos. 29, 32, 33, 41, 42, 45, 78, 82, and 112.

[15] Mostly in the previous and the following groups of letters.

[16] Cf. nos. 34, 79, 86, 111, 125, 183 and (in a fragmentary context) 184, 192, 197, 199, 204, 216, 217, 234, and 237.

[17] E.g., nos. 21, 43, 59, 60, 61, 63, 95, and 75.

[18] Nos. 96-97.

[19] Nos. 15-16, 18, 129, and 148.

[20] E.g., nos. 1, 15, 129, and 137.

[21] Nos. 131, 139, 140; perhaps also 141.

[22] An excellent source about these works is Porter Images.

[23] In some instances we have included cross-references to PNA, where the reader can find out more about the people attested in the present volume.

[24] The figure includes two letters of uncertain assignation (nos. 146 and 147). Six of these letters are signed by Nabû-ra'im-nišešu and Salamanu; nos. 139, 143, 144 are signed by Nabû-ra'im-nišešu alone; no. 141 lacks the beginning of the letter. At least no. 143 dates from the reign of Assurbanipal.

[25] Nos. 69-71. Furthermore, there are 3 fragmentary letters written by Nabû-šumu-iddina, superintendent of the Nabû temple of Calah, but these letters are less relevant here since they form the addenda to SAA 13.

[26] Cf. S. Parpola, "Assyrian Royal Inscriptions and Neo-Assyrian Letters," ARINH (1981), p. 122f., SAA 1 p. XVI and Melville Naqia/Zakutu, p. 67.

[27] More exact dates are mentioned in nos. 45, 52, 90, 100, 117, 125 and 197, but the correct year of these documents is not known.

[28] Cf. S. Parpola, CRRAI 26 (1980), p. 178 n. 39.

[29] Borger Esarh. p. 121: 681/0, Parpola, CRRAI 26 (1980) 171ff, Grayson Chronicles p. 81:34f.

[30] See, e.g., Borger Esarh. pp. 45:87, 121: 681/0, Grayson Chronicles p. 82:38, SAA 2 4 (accession treaty of Esarhaddon) and Leichty, CANE p. 951f.

[31] SAA 2 p. XXIX.

[32] For a thorough discussion of the conspiracy, see Nissinen Prophecy, pp. 108ff and 127ff.

[33] See the comments on nos. 129 and 143. For the dating of Esarhaddon letters, cf. the chronology of the letters in SAA 10 p. XXIXf and LAS IIA p. 48ff.

[34] SAA 4 p. LVIff.

[35] The treaty was broken by Urtaku ten years later. For the treaty and its background, see SAA 2 p. XVIIf and M. Waters, SAAS 12 p. 42ff.

[36] See Parpola, Iraq 34 (1972) 34 n. 66 and SAA 2 p. XVII.

[37] There is evidence that Esarhaddon gave, or at least was planning to give, two of his daughters in marriage to foreigners, see S. Dalley, SAAB 12 (1998) 84, and SAA 4 20-22. [Dalley stats that a daughter of Esarhaddon was married to Sheshonk, but the document on which this is based (SAA 6 142) is dated in 692, so it seems perhaps unlikely that the *hatna šarri* mentioned there was a son-in-law of Esarhaddon.] (HDB)

[38] See, e.g., Parpola, Iraq 34 (1972) 32f and J. Brinkman, JCS 25 (1975) 91f.

[39] Grayson Chronicles p. 78:42.

40 On the Assyrian-Elamite relations at the time of Esarhaddon, see M. Waters, SAAS 12 p. 37ff.

41 See nos. 136, 138, and 146-147.

42 See no. 143. On the whole, the evidence for dating Nabû-ra'im-nišešu's letters is rather elusive. For example, Šarru-iqbi, an Assyrian fortress on the Mannean border, mentioned in no. 142:8, is mentioned in a similar context also in the inscriptions of Assurbanipal, cf. Streck Asb p. 102 iii 71. On the other hand, one could hypothesise that no. 142 pertained to "Esarhaddon's Mannean War," cf. SAA 4 p. LIXf and no. 29. The reference (in no. 137) to the arrival of a messenger from the land Araši at Nippur in connection with a peace treaty could refer to 674, in which case the kings having made peace are Esarhaddon and Urtaku. One wonders if the unnamed Elamite(?) crown prince mentioned in no. 136:11-13 could be Urtaku (in 675)? A promising clue for dating Nabû-ra'im-nišešu's letters could be the person called Umban-kidinni. He has an Elamite name and occurs in four letters of Nabû-ra'im-nišešu. This Umban-kidinni must have been an influential man, but due to the frequency of his name, it is difficult to define his role in the NA correspondence more precisely, cf. Waters, SAAS 12 p. 115. The most well-known Umban-kidinni, however, was probably active around the mid-seventh century, see ibid., pp. 54, 114f.

43 In PNA 2/I p. 478 s.v. Humbareš, the city ruler mentioned in the succession treaty (= Humbareš 1.) is cautiously kept separate from the individual mentioned in nos. 146 and 147 (= Humbareš 2.), with the note "possibly identical with 2." However, it seems certain that one and the same person is in question in all instances, as *kitru* is attested in Esarhaddon's royal inscriptions in particular together with the Median 'city-rulers,' cf. M. Liverani, "The Medes at Esarhaddon's Court," JCS 47 (1995) 57-62, esp. 61f and SAA 2 p. XXXf.

44 See SAA 2 6:3 and p. XXX.

45 Cf. the discussion of the letter in SAA 4 p. LVIIIf.

46 For the presence of the Cimmerians and the Scythians in Mannea, see SAA 4 p. LXIf and ibid. nos. 35-40, also SAA 15 p. XXIX. The Cimmerians and Scythians are never explicitly mentioned acting together but are treated separately even in the same context, cf. SAA 4 p. LXIf. Although it is known that they were hostile towards each other, could it, however, imply that the Assyrians had some difficulty in distinguishing the Cimmerians from the Scythians and vice-versa, or that the Assyrians were rather inaccurate in some cases when speaking of them (cf. SAA 4 35-40, 65-67, 71)?

47 Compare the prophetic words about the Cimmerians by Mullissu to Assurbanipal, from the time he was crown prince, in SAA 9 7:14 and p. LXX (for further sources).

48 See SAA 4 pp. LXf and especially LXXV n. 255, cf. also the Table III in SAA 15 p. XXVII.

49 For the presence of Egyptians in Babylonia during the reigns of Esarhaddon and Assurbanipal, cf. Frame Babylonia p. 49 (especially n. 104 and the further sources mentioned there). For the economic connections between Assyrians and Egyptians, see M. Elat, "The Economic Relations of the Neo-Assyrian Empire with Egypt," JAOS 98 (1978) 20-34.

50 Inscriptions of Esarhaddon repeatedly refer to Kushite harem women deported to Assyria after the conquest of Memphis (671 B.C.), see Borger Esarh. pp. 99:43, 101:12, 114 §79:14 and §81:7.

51 Cf. Parpola, Iraq 34 (1972) 30f.

52 Assigning the letter to the reign of Tiglath-pileser III is in all probability excluded since the letter was found in Nineveh. Nevertheless, the city Sarrabanu is mostly known from his summary inscriptions, see Tadmor Tigl., Summ. 1:8, 2:13,. 7:15f, 9 r.11 and 11:13, and PNA 2/II p. 901 s.v. Nabû-ušabši 1. The contents of the letter may suggest that Šamaš-šumu-ukin – present in Babylonia as the crown prince of Babylon (c. 670) – was the sender of the letter, but we do not have any convincing arguments to support this.

53 Cf. n. 42 above.

54 To the southeast of Assyria, a region in the Zagros between Babylonia and Ellipi. In addition to the two attestations of this volume, the delegate of Araši is also mentioned in three letters sent to Sargon II: SAA 15 35:8, ABL 774 r.16-17 (NB), ABL 1275 e.19-r.1 (NB).

55 For the discussion of *šandabakkus* under Esarhaddon and further sources, see S. W. Cole, SAAS 4 p. 53f.

56 The letter was written at the time of Kudurru's confinement in Nineveh. See Nissinen Prophecy, p. 133ff. Kudurru was not executed in 675, contrary to, e.g., Cole, SAAS 4 p. 53, who probably follows Grayson's uncertain restoration, cf. Grayson Chronicles p. 126:19. For the connection of Nippur with Bit-Dakkuri, their resistance against the Assyrian rule, and Esarhaddon's Nippur policy, see Cole, SAAS 4 pp. 30ff, 72 n. 18, and 73ff.

57 Reading the fragmentary name in 155:6 as [K]unaya is virtually certain, as e.g. the readings Banaya, Buna'i, Dannaya, Ginnaya, Innaya and Nanaya are incompatible the copy.

58 Note, e.g., LÚ*.*kàl-d*[*a*]*-a-a* and *-ṭi-* in no. 17, as against LÚ.*kal-dà-a-a* and *-ṭí-* in no. 155.

59 Der was extremely important for the Assyrians in order to control the potentially common Elamite-Babylonian interests, see, e.g., J. Brinkman, "The Elamite-Babylonian Frontier in the Neo-Elamite Period, 750-625 B.C.," in *Fragmenta Historiae Elamicae. Mélanges offerts a M.-J. Stève* (Paris 1986), p. 202, and SAA 15 p. XXXIIff. For the letters from Der during the reign of Sargon, see SAA 15 112ff.

60 Cf. obv. 10. The town Malaku was significantly connected with the history of Der, for example, in Sargon's reign the Elamites had first laid siege to Malaku and plundered it, after which they were able to attack Der, see SAA 15 p. XXXV and no. 118.

61 For a summary of the economic conditions of the Levantine coastal towns and Assyrian control over them see, e.g., J. N. Postgate, "The Economic Structure of the Assyrian Empire," in M. T. Larsen (ed.), Power *and Propaganda* (Copenhagen 1979), pp. 198f, 206 and M. Elat, Festschrift Tadmor, pp. 21-35.

62 Also known as Iakin-Lû and Ikkalû, cf. PNA 2/I p. 488.

63 See SAA 2 p. XXIX and ibid. no. 5. Five years after the conclusion of the treaty (i.e., 671 B.C.), Baal was replaced and Tyre turned into an Assyrian province by Esarhaddon.

64 See also no. 128, which partly parallels no. 127.

65 Tabnî, the author of no. 48, might be identical with the haruspex Tabnî, the author of SAA 10 181 and 182 (however, cf. LAS II p. 373), and co-author of SAA 4 3, 18, 122, 139, 155, 185, SAA 10 177, cf. LAS IIA, p. 43.

66 The men in question, as other persons with Jewish names mentioned in the letter, were probably deportees from Samaria settled in Guzana during the reign of Sargon. The name Halbišu seems to have been Egyptian (see PNA 2/I p. 443 s.v. Hallabeše), but is also attested in Phœnician texts.

67 For this campaign see, e.g., E. Leichty, Festschrift Tadmor p. 52ff.

68 Was Urarṭu allied with the Cimmerians against Assyria at some point? That conclusion may be advanced on the basis of SAA 4 18. See ibid. p. LXI. On the other hand, contrary evidence may be adduced from the so-called letter to the god Aššur (or alternatively the letter to the gods by Esarhaddon), see E. Leichty, Festschrift Tadmor, pp. 55 and 57.

69 See, e.g., SAA 1 30-32; SAA 4 p. LIX, Kuhrt ANE p. 558, J. G. Macqueen, CANE p. 1102, and P. E. Zimansky, ibid., p. 1140.

70 Esarhaddon's suspicions regarding Urarṭu become clear from SAA 4 18-19.

71 The name of the sender is not preserved but can certainly be restored as Assurbanipal on the basis of the handwriting and orthographic analysis.

72 For Assurbanipal's active role in politics in the last years of Esarhaddon see, e.g., LAS II p. 235f and SAA 4 p. LIX.

73 Nos. 34, 35, 37, 38, 69, 70, 106, 107, 116, and 124.

74 For Esarhaddon's illness see LAS II p. 230ff.

75 See Starr, SAA 4 p. LIX, Kuhrt ANE p. 522f, and the letters from Sennacherib as crown prince, SAA 1 29-40 and SAA 5 281. The "Succession Palace" was the place from which the crown princes co-ruled with their fathers, see Parpola, CRRAI 30 (1986) 233.

76 According to Parpola, Festschrift Röllig p. 321 n. 18, Šerua-eṭerat is the writer of the letter.

77 SAA 7 131:6, 149 iii 3, 154 i 5, 157 i 2.

78 Šamaš-metu-uballiṭ was possibly the third eldest son of Esarhaddon, cf. SAA 2 8:4. For the children of Esarhaddon, see the list in LAS II pp. 117-9 and PNA 1/I p. 161ff s.v. Aššur-bani-apli.

79 Otherwise Šerua-eṭerat is almost exclusively attested together with the royal family: AfO 13 214:22, SAA 7 154 i 2, SAA 10 223 r.11, SAA 13 56 r.8, with one exception CT 53 966:9, a fragmentary letter in which she is mentioned together with Kandalanu and (the king of) Elam.

80 SAA 2 6: 73-82, 108-122, 130-161, 336-352, 499-507.

81 Such as nos. 31, 69, 71, and 207.

82 He certainly does not identify himself by name in four of the letters (nos. 62-65). The remaining three letters could theoretically have included his name, since they are all broken at the beginning.

83 Bottom edge with probably three lines and two lines on the reverse are missing.

84 Two or more lines are missing at the beginning of the obverse and the end of reverse, and two lines are missing from the upper edge.

85 Top, bottom and edges are gone, minimum number of missing lines is 16, provided that all edges were used for writing.

86 More than four lines are missing on the obverse, at least two lines on the reverse. Edges gone: approximately four or six missing lines. We do not know if there was writing on the left edge, but one can tentatively assume two written lines for it.

87 Top and bottom with their edges are broken away.

88 Interestingly, several different persons with the name Nabû-kabti-ahhešu are explicitly attested with a scholarly occupation: 1) the palace scribe of Sargon II (PNA 2/II p. 838 no. 1); 2) a scribe from Nineveh (after the reign of Assurbanipal, ibid. no. 4); 3) an exorcist of the Aššur temple in Assur (after the reign of Assurbanipal, ibid. no. 6); and 4) a scribe from Cutha, ancestor of several scribes (lifetime not exactly known, ibid. 7). We assume that also Nabû-kabti-ahhešu in no. 62 probably was either a scribe or an exorcist. Note that, so far, none of the persons known by the name Nabû-kabti-ahhešu can be shown to be anything other than scribes or exorcists by profession.

89 The enclitic *-ma* in *issu qannimma* suggests this interpretation.

90 On Harhar see SAA 15 p. XXVIff and SAA 4 p. LIX and ibid. nos. 51 and 77-78.

91 No. 65:11 and 66:3; possibly also 62 r.12.

92 No. 62:2-3 and 63:1.

93 See the discussion in SAA 6, pp. XXVII-XXXIV.

94 No. 62:7, r.6, 7, 13, 16; 63:10, 12, 18, 26, r.2, 12, 14, 16, 24, 31, s.3; 64:3, r.4; 65:9, 10; 67 r.8; 68:16, r.15 (in all, 24 examples).

95 *ta-*⌈*mar*⌉*-u-*[*ni*] 66:5, [*áš-pur*]*-ú-ni* 62:3, [*x x x*]*-bu-ni* 67:12. Note also *ú-lab-bi-i*[*š*]*-*⌈*ú*⌉*-*[*ka-ni*] 63:29 and *i-qa-bu-ni-ni* ibid. 33.

96 *i-šá-par-an-ni* 63 r.23, *áš-pur-an-ni* ibid. r.29, 64 r.6, *iš-pur-an-ni* 65 r.11, [*x x x x x x x x*]*-an-ni* 68 r.17, *li-ṭi-ba-a*[*n-ni*] 62 s.1, ᵐ10*—ki-la-an-ni* 63:3, [ᵐ10?]*—ki-la-an-ni* 68 r.11; *i-di-nak-kan-ni* 63:30, *a-da-ka-an-ni* 62:3, TA* *qa-an-ni-ma* ibid. r.5.

97 No. 62:8; cf. [*un-q*]*a-a-te* 63:19, *a-bat—šar-ra-a-*⌈*te*⌉ 64:1; SAG.DU*—pa-zu-za-a-ni* 65:4, *lum-*[*n*]*a-a-ni* 62:10, LÚ*.*mu-kil*—KUŠ.*a-pa-a-ni* 63:21, GIŠ.*ṣal-lu-ma-a-ni* 65:3; LÚ*.*ba-ru-u-te* ibid. r.9. The length of the vowel is left unindicated only in *ṭè-ma-ni* 62 r.9 and LÚ*.*a-ši-pu-te* 65 r.7.

98 No. 62:6; cf. *hi-ṭa-ni-šú-nu* 63:8.

99 The attestations are *i-sa-ṭa-ru* 63:14, *i-sa-kan* ibid. 23, *i-sa-al-šú-nu* ibid. e.33, *i-sa-ka*[*n* ibid. r.6, *i-s*[*a-ap-ra*] 66:3, *i-si-qi* 65 r.5; *a-sa-me* 63:27, *a-sa-a*[*l-ku-nu*] ibid. r.1, *a-sa-kan* 65:15; *i-si-ni* 62 r.6, *i-si-šú-nu* 63:7, *i-si-šú* 64:10; *ú-se-ši-ib*!*-šú* 65 r.6, *ú-sa-*[*x x x*] 67 r.2 (the sign *us-* is only once attested and then in a broken context: *ina* ŠÀ*-bi us-*[*s*]*ar*?*-x*[*x x*] 66:4); *i-ta-ma-lik* 63:25, *i-ta-an-na-ka-a* 67 r.12, *i-ti-ši* 67:2, *i-ti-din* 63 r.13, 21; *a-ti-kip* 63 r.32. Further, note the suppression of the gemination in the analogous preterite and present forms *la i-zi*!*-su-u-ni* 62 r.7, *la i-di-nu* 63:17, *i-di-nak-kan-ni* ibid. 30, *i-da-nu-u-ni* 65:10, and *li-di-nu-u-ni* 65:9; note also *i-ti-i-la* 64:10, *i-la-ku-u-ni* 64 r.4, and *li-li-ku-u-ni* ibid. 3.

100 Cf. *bi-is* (62:6, r.9, 64 r.3), *a-bi-it* 62:5, *ni-qi-it-te* ibid. r.1, *e-ki-it* 64:11, *ṣa-hi-it-tú* ibid. r.4, *ú-ka-ba-as* 63:22, *at-t*[*u-nu* 63 r.7, *ú-ba-at-ti-qu* 63:20, [ᵐ*ta*?]*-at-ti-i* 67:4 and *x*]*-si-at* 68 r. 18.

101 Cf., e.g., *q*]*i-ba-na-ši* vs. *ta-šá-al-an-na-*[*ši*, both in 63:35; *hi-ṭa-šú-nu* 63:12, *hi-ṭa-a-te* 62:11, vs. *hi-iṭ-ṭa-šú-nu* 63:10; *ub-ta-ti-qu* ... *ú-ba-at-ti-qu* 63:19f; *ú-lab-bi-i*[*š-k*]*a-ni* ... *i-di-nak-kan-ni* 63:29f.

102 No. 62:10 and 63:18.

103 [AR]AD.MEŠ*-šu* 63 r.7, LÚ*.*šak-ni-šu* 64:7, 8 *me-eh-ri-šu* 64 r.1

104 ᵐ*pal-ṭí—ia-u* no. 63:4, ᵐ*i-ri—ia-u* ibid. 4, 28, vs. ᵐ*pal-ṭí-iá-u* ibid. 27; TA* *pa-ni-iá* 66:6 vs. [prep. + I]GI*-ia* 62 r.10; *ina* ŠU.2*-iá* ibid. r.9 vs. *ina* ŠÀ*-bi uz-ni-ia* 63 s.2.

105 No. 63:12, 32, r.20; 65 r.14.

106 *li-šá-al* SAA 13 24:6, from Dadî, official of the Aššur temple, and *li-šá-a*[*l*!]-*šú-nu* SAA 13 31:12, from an official of the same temple named Iddin-Aššur (cf. PNA 2/I p. 504 s.v. Iddin-Aššur 6). The latter writer shares some orthographic features with our "enigmatic author," e.g. *-Cu-u-ni* endings for the subjunctive SAA 13 31:18, r.13, the alternation *ša/šá* in independent position, and the failure to mark gemination in perfect and preterite forms (*a-ti-din* SAA 13 31:8, *a-ta-ṣa* ibid. 9, *i-din* SAA 13 31 r.7). However, he cannot be identified with the latter, as he writes EN-*ia/be-lí-ia*, not EN-*iá*, for "my lord."

107 The interpretation "commands" for *ṭēmāni* is also possible, cf. the translation by Parpola in Nissinen Prophecy, p. 143.

108 Note *i-qab-bu-ú-ni* 69 r.4, *ú-bi-lu-ú-ni* 71 r.2, *áš-*]*mu-ú-ni* ibid. r.7; [*ir-t*]*u-ú-bu* 71 e.9; note also, in final position, [*am*]-*mì-ú* 70 r.2.

109 See Parpola, Iraq 34 (1972) 32 and Festschrift Röllig p. 321 n. 18.

110 The identity of the goldsmith's son in no. 65 was already inferred by Parpola, without stating the name of the person in question, see Festschrift Röllig p. 321 n. 18.

111 Evidence for goldsmiths or other metal workers producing Pazuzu-heads and figures is discussed in E. Klengel-Brandt, "Ein Pazuzu-Kopf mit Inschrift," Or. 37 (1968) 81-84. It is not excluded that magical treatments were performed by goldsmiths in some instances, as suggested by Klengel-Brandt (ibid. 83), even though this suggestion was to a great extent based on misreading the word *ṣarrāpu* "goldsmith" occurring in the inscription published as *zabbu*, a kind of ecstatic; for the corrected reading, see S. Parpola, "The Reading of the Neo-Assyrian Logogram LÚ.SIMUG.KUG.GI 'Goldsmith,'" SAAB 2 (1988) 79f.

112 For example, Nabû-ašared, a priest or official of the Aššur temple (PNA 2/II p. 806 s.v. Nabû-ašared 5), seems to have been quite versatile. He writes to the king, "I myself sketched the royal image which is in outline," and remarks on a royal image, "I myself do not agree with this and I will not fashion (it so) ... I myself should fashion the [bod]y, [but] they [don't a]gree" (SAA 13 34:14-15, r.7-8 and 15-17).

113 Some military personnel were able to carry several professional titles within the same year. Therefore it is sometimes difficult to decide whether different offices or only different descriptions of the same office were meant in reality, see SAA 14 p. XIIIff for Aššur-killanni and ibid. p. XV for Balasî. It seems possible that some occupations were only secondary "part time-jobs," like the function of a judge in court.

114 Therefore, it is not possible to say with certainty whether, e.g., the scholars who bore the title "chief scribe" indeed were first and foremost scribes. In general, Mesopotamian scholars can, despite the professional titles they bore, often be viewed as versatile, not confined to a certain field, but applying their theoretical and practical skills in a variety of ways.

115 In PNA 2/II p. 866, Nabû-sagibi, son of Parruṭu and goldsmith of the queen's household, and Nabû-sagibi, exorcist at the royal court (SAA 7 1 i 14), are (understandably!) treated separately as nos. 1 and 2.

116 See LAS II p. XVIIf.

117 So interpreted by Melville Naqia/Zakutu pp. 9, 19 and especially 105ff.

118 On the influence of the queen mother in the queen's household, the "harem," see, e.g., E. Leichty, CANE p. 949. Leichty's views about the harem are challenged by Melville in her Naqia/Zakutu, p. 2. How little we actually know about the queens and other royal women of the Neo-Assyrian Empire is aptly summarised in Kuhrt ANE, p. 526ff. However, some new evidence for the Neo-Assyrian queens is available, see, e.g., S. Dalley, "Yabâ, Atalya, and the Foreign Policy of Late Assyrian Kings," SAAB 12 pp. 83-98.

119 ND 2093:6-7 and SAA 13 108 may support this. "The queen mother's household" (*bēt ummi šarri*) is explicitly mentioned only twice, in SAA 6 255:2 (dated 678) and ND 2093:7 (629).

120 The career of Milki-nuri is interesting in this respect. So far he is explicitly attested as "eunuch of the queen" only in SAA 14 1-6. For the problem of dating some of the documents from his dossier (e.g., SAA 14 2-7), cf. n. 9 above. Otherwise Milki-nuri appears at the end of the reign of Esarhaddon (nos. 20 r.2, 60 r.12, 63 s.1) and at the beginning of the reign of Assurbanipal (SAA 14 1, dated 668), cf. L. Kataja, SAAB 1 p. 66.

121 That Ešarra-hammat was the mother of Assurbanipal and Šamaš-šumu-ukin seems certain, see Weissert, PNA 1/I p. 160f s.v. Aššūr-bāni-apli, and Radner, PNA 1/II p. 406f s.v. Ešarra-hammat.

122 For the Assyrian date of Ešarra-hammat's death see Grayson Chronicles pp. 85:22 and 127:23, and Borger Esarh. p. 124: 673/2 (cf. also ibid., p. 10 § 10). For the Julian date, see LAS II pp.190 and 382 (Appendix A).

123 That the queen mother had more than one scribe in her service becomes evident from SAA 6 253 in which her scribe Issar-duri acts as a purchaser and another scribe of hers is mentioned (name not preserved) as a witness (r.10). By name, also Asqudi (SAA 6 325:2, listed in Melville Naqia/Zakutu p. 108) is known to have been a scribe of the queen mother.

124 See Melville Naqia/Zakutu p. 27ff and SAA 9 1 v 13, 2 i 13; SAA 10 201, 313; SAA 13 76-77, 188.

125 See SAA 10 5 = LAS II 3 and SAA 10 6 = LAS II 1.

126 Nabû-zeru-lešir's letters all date either to 679 or 674, cf. PNA 2/II p. 911 s.v. Nabû-zeru-lešir 4.

127 SAA 6 314 r.13, SAA 10 257 r.7 and 291 r.1.

128 For the Asakku statue and the incident during Esarhaddon's Šubrian campaign, see E. Leichty, Festschrift Tadmor, p. 54f. On the other editions of the text, see ibid. p. 56, including, e.g., Borger Esarh. p. 105:18ff.

129 Cf., e.g., SAA 10 67.

130 Fales *bīt bēli* p. 231ff. Here we prefer the Assyrian form of the compound, *bēt bēli*, although the Babylonian form *bīt bēli* is justified as a variant form, since many of the attestations come from Neo-Babylonian letters.

131 Occasionally, this interpretation seems possible also when EN.MEŠ appears without É; cf. SAA 10 290:9 and the discussion in LAS II p. 215 (n. 352). However, a word of caution is appropriate here. While translating DUMU.MEŠ EN.MEŠ-*ia* in SAA 10 244:9 as "the sons of my lord" would superficially seem to make better sense than "the sons, my lords" of the edition, such a translation is excluded in SAA 10 187:17, where DUMU.ME EN.ME-*ka* can only mean "the sons, your lords," not "the sons of your lord."

132 See Fales *bīt bēli* p. 232, including references to previous literature on the matter.

133 The literal rendering is rejected by Fales *bīt bēli* p. 243: "I think that this usual rendering, in its complete "one-to-one" flatness, is not conducive for a deeper semantic and contextual perception such as will be sought here." In our opinion, using the "deeper semantic and contextual perception" in the case of *bēt bēli* may lead to far-fetched ideas which are based on passages whose interpretation seems questionable. Therefore, the tangled renderings of the concept may not correspond with the attested reality.

[134] The phrase never occurs without a possessive suffix. In É–EN.MEŠ ABL 402:12, the only attestation without a possessive suffix as cited by Fales (*bīt bēli* p. 232), the suffix is to be restored in the following break (É–EN.ME[Š-*šú*].

[135] "Her" not attested.

[136] The rendering "the ruling house" is not a new suggestion, cf., e.g., LAS II p. 107 ad ABL 620:3, Watanabe *adê* p. 183 ad 208 and Fales *bīt bēli* pp. 233, 245, 249.

[137] ABL 1342:13, 19-20. See the following note for bibliographical references.

[138] The references including attestations of *bēt bēli* with the verb *ra'āmu* and/or the land of Assyria are: ABL 277 r.8, ABL 288:9-11, ABL 290:14-r.12, ABL 402:10-14, ABL 521:18-22, ABL 561 r.1-6, ABL 964 r.9-11, ABL 1136 r.9-10, ABL 1311+ r.37, ABL 1342:13, 19-20, CT 54 62:20, 27, r.20 and no. 207:4-7 (except for the NA references ABL 561 and no. 207 all others are NB); in addition, cf. the passage from the succession treaty: "(...) one of you, who loves his lord and feels concern over the household of his lord," SAA 2 6 207-208. An illustrative example, for instance, is ABL 293+ (CT 54 484) 12ff, Fales *bīt bēli* p. 235. For some of these quotations, cf. de Vaan, "Idiom in Neubabylonischen (I). Erläuterungen zum Vokabular des Generals Bel-ibni," in M. Dietrich and O. Loretz (eds.), *dubsar anta-men*: *Studien zur Altorientalistik. Fs Römer* (AOAT 253, Münster 1998), p. 73ff. See also Fales *bīt bēli*, p. 237.

[139] Propaganda in the sense defined by B. N. Porter, "Assyrian Propaganda for the West: Esarhaddon's Stelae for Til Barsip and Sam'al," in G. Bunnens (ed.), *Essays on Syria in the Iron Age*. Ancient Near Eastern Studies Supplement 7 (Louvain 2000), p. 145ff.

[140] Examples are Bel-ibni, military commander of the Sealand (passim); Illil-bani, governor of Nippur and Aššur-belu-taqqin, prefect (in ABL 617+); probably Aqar-Bel-lumur, military official (CT 54 393); Rašil, high clergyman of Bel in Babylon (SAA 13 173); Inurta-ahu-iddina, scholar (SAA 10 373); Kudurru, governor of Uruk (ABL 277); presumably Nabû-ušabši, governor of Uruk (ABL 964); Nabû-taklak, official active in Bit-Dakkuri (ABL 897), and so on.

[141] No. 41:9-r.4. Cf. Fales *bīt bēli*, p. 241.

[142] Cf. ibid. p. 231.

[143] On the dating of Šarru-duri's governorship, see J. N. Postgate, *The Governor's Palace Archive* (CTN 2, London 1973), p. 11, and cf. Fales *bīt bēli*, p. 242f.

[144] Not any kind of proof, but perhaps indicative of the age of *bēt bēli* as a concept, is the fact that it is not attested in the so-called Nimrud Letters which to a great extent date from the reign of Tiglath-pileser III.

[145] See Parpola, "The Assyrian Cabinet," Festschrift von Soden (1995), pp. 379-401, esp. 83 with n. 15.

[146] For the evidence see LAS II p. 474ff.

Abbreviations and Symbols

Bibliographical Abbreviations

80-7-19 etc.	tablets in the collections of the British Museum
ABL	R.F. Harper, *Assyrian and Babylonian Letters* (London and Chicago 1892-1914)
AfO	Archiv für Orientforschung
AfO Bh	Archiv für Orientforschung, Beihefte
AJSL	American Journal of Semitic Languages and Literatures
AOAT	Alter Orient und Altes Testament
ARINH	F.M. Fales (ed.), *Assyrian Royal Inscriptions: New Horizons in Literary, Ideological and Historical Analysis* (Orientis Antiqui Collectio XVIII, Rome 1981)
AS	Assyriological Studies
BaM Bh	Baghdader Mitteilungen, Beihefte
BM	tablets in the collections of the British Museum
Borger Esarh.	R. Borger, *Die Inschriften Asarhaddons, Königs von Assyrien.* AfO Bh 9 (Graz 1956)
Bu	tablets in the collections of the British Museum
CAD	Chicago Assyrian Dictionary
CANE	J.M. Sasson (ed.), *Civilizations of the Ancient Near East* (New York 1995)
CRRAI	Rencontre assyriologique internationale, comptes rendus
CT	Cuneiform Texts from Babylonian Tablets in the British Museum
Deller Lautlehre	K. Deller, *Lautlehre des Neuassyrischen* (Vienna 1959).
de Vaan Bel-ibni	J.M.C.T. de Vaan, *Ich bin eine Schwertklinge des Königs* (AOAT 242, Neukirchen-Vluyn 1995).
DT	tablets in the collections of the British Museum
Fales Cento Lettere	F.M. Fales, *Cento lettere neo-assire* (Venice 1983)
Fales and Lanfranchi Lettere	F.M. Fales and G.B. Lanfranchi, *Lettere dalla corte assira* (Venice 1992)
Festschrift Röllig	B. Pongratz-Leisten, H. Kühne and P. Xella (eds.), *Ana šadî Labnāni lū allik. Festschrift für Wolfgang Röllig* (AOAT 247, Neukirchen-Vluyn 1997)

Festschrift Tadmor	M. Cogan and I. Eph'al (eds.), *Ah, Assyria ... Studies in Assyrian History and Ancient Near Eastern Historiography Presented to Hayim Tadmor*, Scripta Hierosolymitana 33 (Jerusalem 1991)
Festschrift von Soden	M. Dietrich and O. Loretz (eds.), *Vom Alten Orient zum Alten Testament, Festschrift für Wolfram Freiherrn von Soden* (AOAT 240, Neukirchen-Vluyn 1995)
Frahm Sanherib	E. Frahm, *Einleitung in die Sanherib-Inschriften*, AfO Bh 26 (Vienna 1997)
Frame Babylonia	G. Frame, *Babylonia 689-627 B.C. A Political History* (Istanbul 1992)
GPA	J.N Postgate, *The Governor's Palace Archive* (CTN 2, London 1973)
Grayson Chronicles	A.K. Grayson, *Assyrian and Babylonian Chronicles* (Texts from Cuneiform Sources 5, Glückstadt 1975)
Hämeen-Anttila Grammar	J. Hämeen-Anttila, *A Sketch of Neo-Assyrian Grammar* (SAAS 13, Helsinki 2000)
HANEM	History of the Ancient Near East, Monographs (Padua)
Ivantchik Cimmériens	A.I. Ivantchik, *Les Cimmériens au Proche-Orient* (OBO 127, Fribourg 1993)
JAOS	Journal of the American Oriental Society
JESHO	Journal of the Economic and Social History of the Orient
JSS	Journal of Semitic Studies
K	tablets in the collections of the British Museum
KAV	O. Schroeder, *Keilschrifttexte aus Assur verschiedenen Inhalts* (Leipzig 1920)
Ki	tablets in the collections of the British Museum
Kuhrt ANE	A. Kuhrt, *The Ancient Near East c. 3000-330 BC* (London 1997)
Lanfranchi Cimmeri	G.B. Lanfranchi, *I Cimmeri. Emergenza delle Elites militari iraniche nel Vicino Oriente (VIII-VII sec. a. C.)* (Padua 1990)
LAS	S. Parpola, *Letters from Assyrian Scholars to the Kings Esarhaddon and Assurbanipal* I, II (AOAT 5/1-2, Neukirchen-Vluyn 1970, 1983)
LAS II A	S. Parpola, *Letters ...*, Part II A: Introduction and Appendixes (Ph.D. diss., University of Helsinki, 1971)
Mattila Magnates	R. Mattila, *The King's Magnates* (SAAS 11, Helsinki 2000)
Melville Naqia/Zakutu	S.C. Melville, *The Role of Naqia/Zakutu in Sargonid Politics* (SAAS 9, Helsinki 1999)
NABU	Nouvelles Assyriologiques Brèves et Utilitaires
ND	field numbers of tablets excavated at Nimrud
NL	H.W.F. Saggs, *The Nimrud Letters* (Iraq 17 [1955], etc.)
Nissinen Prophecy	M. Nissinen, *References to Prophecy in Neo-Assyrian Sources* (SAAS 7, Helsiki 1998)
OA	Oriens Antiquus
OBO	Orbis Biblicus et Orientalis
OLZ	Orientalistische Literaturzeitung

Oppenheim Letters	A.L. Oppenheim, *Letters from Mesopotamia* (Chicago 1967)
Or.	Orientalia Nova Series
Payne Smith	J. Payne Smith, *A Compendious Syriac Dictionary* (Oxford 1903)
PKTA	E. Ebeling, *Parfümrezepte und kultische Texte aus Assur* (Rome 1952)
PNA	K. Radner and H. Baker (eds.), *The Prosopography of the Neo-Assyrian Empire* (Helsinki 1998-)
Porter Images	B.N. Porter, *Images, Power, and Politics: Figurative Aspects of Esarhaddon's Babylonian Policy* (Philadelphia 1993)
Postgate TCAE	J.N. Postgate, *Taxation and Conscription in the Assyrian Empire* (Studia Pohl, Series Maior 3, Rome 1974)
RA	Revue d'assyriologie
RCAE	L. Waterman, *Royal Correspondence of the Assyrian Empire*, I-IV (Ann Arbor 1930-1936)
RlA	Reallexikon der Assyriologie
Rm	tablets in the collections of the British Museum
SAA	State Archives of Assyria
SAAB	State Archives of Assyria Bulletin
SAAS	State Archives of Assyria Studies
Sm	tablets in the collections of the British Museum
StAT	Studien zu den Assur-Texten
Streck Asb	M. Streck, *Assurbanipal* I-III (Vorderasiatische Bibliothek 7, Leipzig 1916)
Tadmor Tigl	H. Tadmor, *The Inscriptions of Tiglath-pileser III, King of Assyria* (Jerusalem 1994)
TCL	Textes cunéiformes du Louvre
Th	tablets in the collections of the British Museum
Watanabe *adê*	K. Watanabe, *Die* adê-*Vereidigung anlässlich der Thronfolgeregelung Asarhaddons* (BaM Bh 3, Berlin 1987)
WO	Die Welt des Orients
WZKM	Wiener Zeitschrift für die Kunde des Morgenlandes

W and Y in the critical apparatus (followed by page number) refer to collations in RCAE and S. Ylvisaker, *Zur babylonischen und assyrischen Grammatik* (Leipziger Semitische Studien 5/6, Leipzig 1912) respectively.

Other Abbreviations and Symbols

Asb.	Assurbanipal
Esarh.	Esarhaddon
Sar.	Sargon
Tgl	Tiglath-pileser
MB	Middle Babylonian
NA	Neo-Assyrian
NB	Neo-Babylonian
OB	Old Babylonian

SB	Standard Babylonian
Syr.	Syriac
e.	edge
obv.	obverse
pl.	plate
r., rev.	reverse
col.	column
coll.	collated, collation
mng.	meaning
ms.	manuscript
unpub.	unpublished
var.	variant
!	collation
!!	emendation
?	uncertain reading
:	cuneiform division mark
*	graphic variants (see LAS I p. XX)
0	uninscribed space or nonexistent sign
x	broken or undeciphered sign
( )	supplied word or sign
(( ))	sign erroneously added by scribe
[[ ]]	erasure
+	joined to
(+)	indirect join

TRANSLITERATIONS AND TRANSLATIONS

Royal Letters

1. Letters from the King and the Crown Prince

FIG. 1. *Esarhaddon with his mother Naqia.*
AO 20155.

1. Letter to Urtaku, King of Elam

K 1542

1 DUB-*pi* ^{m}*aš-šur*—PAB—AŠ MAN KUR—*aš-šu*[*r*.KI]
2 *a-na* ^{m}*ur-ta-ku* LUGAL KUR.NIM.KI Š[EŠ-*ia*]
3 *šul-mu a-a-*[*ši*]
4 *šul-mu a-na* DUMU.MEŠ-*ka* DUMU.MÍ.MEŠ-*ka*
5 *šul-mu a-na* KUR-*ia* LÚ.GAL.MEŠ-*ia*
6 *lu šul-mu a-na* ^{m}*ur-ta-ku* LUGAL KUR.NIM.KI ŠEŠ-*ia*
7 *lu šul-mu a-na* DUMU.MEŠ-*ia* DUMU.MÍ.MEŠ-*ia*
8 *lu šul-mu a-na* LÚ.GAL.MEŠ-*ka ù* KUR-*ka*

---

9 *an-nu-rig ša* ^{d}*aš-šur* ^{d}30 ^{d}UTU ^{d}EN ^{d}AG
10 ^{d}15 *ša* NINA.KI ^{d}15 *ša* URU.*arba-ìl*
11 ^{d}[*m*]*a*!-[*a*]*n*!-*zi-ni-ri iq-bu-u-ni*
12 *ú-*[*sa-l*]*i-mu uk-ti-i-nu*
13 L[Ú!.EN—D]ÙG!.GA!-*ti-ni a-na ap-pi*! *ú-se-ṣi*!-*u*
14 ⸢*ú*⸣-[*ma-a an*]-*nu-rig ša šá-ka-an šu-me*
15 [*x x x x x*]*x x*[*x x*]*x x*[*x x x x x*]
rest broken away

Rev. beginning broken away

1′	[*x x x*]	[*x*]-*me*	1-[*me* 0?]	[*x x*]	[*x x x*]
2′	[*x x x*]	[*x*]-*me* 50	1-*m*[*e* 50?]	⸢5⸣ 5	[*x x x*]
3′	[*x x x*]	[*x-me*] 50	1-*me* 50	5 5	5 [*x x*]

rest uninscribed

ABL 918

1 A tablet from Esarhaddon, king of Assyria, to Urtaku, king of Elam, [my] br[other]. I a[m] well, your sons and daughters are well, my country and magnates are well. May Urtaku, king of Elam, my brother, be well, may my sons and daughters be well, may your magnates and your country be well!

---

9 Aššur, Sîn, Šamaš, Bel, Nabû, Ištar of Nineveh, Ištar of Arbela and Manziniri have now [fulf]illed and confirmed what they promised, (and) have developed our f[rie]ndship to (its) peak.

14 N[ow t]hen, [...] of establishing fame

15 [......]

(Break)

r.1 [...] [*1*]00 1[*00* x x x x]

2 [...] [*1*]50 1[*50*] 5 5 [x x]

3 [...] [*1*]50 150 5 5 5 [x]

(Rest destroyed)

2. King's Word to the Queen Mother

K 486

1 *a-bat* LUGAL *a-na*
2 MÍ.AMA—MAN
3 DI-*mu a-a-ši*
4 *lu* DI-*mu a-na*
5 MÍ.AMA—MAN
6 *ina* UGU ARAD *ša* ^{m}*a-mu-še*
7 *ša taš-pur-in-ni*
8 *ki ša* MÍ.AMA—MAN
9 *taq-bu-u-ni*

ABL 303

1 The king's word to the mother of the king: I am well. Good health to the mother of the king!

6 Concerning the servant of Amos, about whom you wrote to me — just as the king's mother commanded, in the same way I have

1 1-12 → Parpola and Watanabe, SAA 2 p. XVII. 11 See coll., cf. W 261. 13 See coll. Cf. ABL 878 r.9, 886:16 (both NB letters); Oppenheim, JAOS 61 (1941) 262.
2 Previous editions: Fales and Lanfranchi Lettere (1992) 130f; Melville, SAAS 9 (1999) 76f. 8-r.2 LAS II 186

10 *a-na-ku ina pi-te-ma*
r.1 *aq-ṭi-bi*
2 SIG$_5$ *a—dan-niš*
3 *ki ša taq-bi-ni*
4 *a-na mì-i-ni*
5 ^{m}*ha-mu-na-a-a*
6 *il-la-ak*
rest uninscribed

commanded. It is fine indeed, as you said.

r.4 Why does Hamunayu go?

3. King's Word to Issar-na'di

Sm 1942

1 *a-bat* LUGAL
2 *a-na* ^{md}15—I
3 DI-*mu ia-a-ši*
4 ŠÀ-*ba-ka lu* DÙG.GA-*ka*
5 *ina* UGU ^{md}*aš-šur*—AD—AŠ
6 [*ša taš*]-*pur-an-ni*
7 [*x x x l*]*a ṭa-bu-u-ni*
8 [*x x x i*]*q-ṭi-bi*
9 [*x x x x x x x x*]
r.1 [*še*]-*bi-la*
2 *ù de-e-qe*
3 *ša taš-pur-an-ni*
rest uninscribed

ABL 417

1 The king's word to Issar-na'di: I am well. You can be glad.

5 As to Aššur-abu-iddina, [whom you w]rote to me about,

7 [...] which is [no]t good

8 [...] has said [...]

r.1 [s]end me [...]! But it is good that you wrote to me.

4. King's Word to Ištar-[...]

K 13154

1 [*a-bat*] LUGAL *a-na* ^{md}15—[*x x x x*]
2 [DI]-*mu ia-a-ši* ŠÀ-*ba*-[*ka lu ṭa-ab-ka*]
3 [*ina* UG]U ERIM.MEŠ *ha-an-nu-ti* [*x x x x*]
4 [*ša ta*]*š-pur-a-ni um*$^{?}$*-ma en-n*[*a*$^{?}$ *x x x x*]
5 [*x x*] *ram*$^{?}$ *x*[*x x x*] *a* [*x x x x*]
6 [*x x x*] ⌜*x*$^{?}$⌝ [*x x x x x x x x x*]
rest broken away
Rev. for the figure on Reverse, cf. Bezold, Catalogue

ABL 300

1 The king's [word] to Ištar-[...]: I am [we]ll. [You can be gl]ad.

3 [As t]o these men [... about whom you] wrote: "No[w ......]"

(Rest destroyed or too broken for translation)

5. Settling Accounts and Preparing for Royal Visit to Harran

83-1-18,257 + Bu 91-5-9,137 (CT 53 967)

1 [*a-bat* LUGAL *a-na* ^{m}*x-l*]*i*$^{?}$*-i*
2 [DI-*mu a-a-ši* Š]À$^{?}$-⌜*ka*$^{?}$⌝
3 [*lu* DÙG-*ka an-nu-ri*]*g* [^{m}PAB-*bu-u*]
4 [*ina* UGU-*hi-k*]*a il-l*[*a-ka*]
5 [*ár-hiš* KA]SKAL *ina* GÌR.2.MEŠ-*šú* [0]
6 [*šu-kun*] *ku-zip-pi-ia ku-zip-pi*

CT 53 930+

1 [The king's word to ...*l*]*î*: [I am well], you [can be gl]ad.

3 [Ahabû] is [no]w co[ming to y]ou. [Make] everything ready for him [quickly]! [...] my garments (and) the garments [of] my

r.5, p. 181.

4 1 Restoring the name of the addressee as Issar-[na'di] (cf. no. 3) is unlikely, as obv. 4 indicates that he was a Babylonian.

7 [*ša* 2?] DUMU.MEŠ-*ia* SÍG.MEŠ
8 [*x x x*] ŠE.GIŠ.Ì.MEŠ GEŠTIN *mit-hu*[*r*?*-r*]*u*?
9 [ANŠE.*ku-d*]*in*.MEŠ ANŠE.*gam-mal*.MEŠ
10 [*di-na-áš-šú*] 20 MA.NA KUG.UD [[*x*]]
11 [TA IGI] ⌈m⌉*si-i*—AD [[*su*?]]*-ur-ha*
12 ŠE.ZÍZ.MEŠ ŠE.PAD.MEŠ ŠE.GIG.MEŠ
13 GIŠ.KIN.GEŠTIN.MEŠ *ki-i* KI.LAM
14 *mu-nu a-na* LÚ.TUR-*šú*
15 *di-ni e-gír-tú iṣ-ṣa* [[*ṣa*]]
16 *mu-ru-uq* : UDU.NITÁ.MEŠ *a-šur* :
17 GIŠ!!.ERIN.BAD.MEŠ *kur-ru* [[*x x*]]*x*
18 *ad-ri ša* LÚ.NU.GIŠ.SAR.MEŠ
19 *a-mur ina* ŠÀ-*bi* GIŠ.LI.U$_5$.UM
20 *šu-ṭur ina* ŠU.2 mIM.4-*i*
21 *še-bi-la* mPAB-*bu-u*
22 LÚ.ENGAR.MEŠ LÚ.SIPA.MEŠ
23 ⌈LÚ*⌉.NU.GIŠ.SAR.MEŠ
e.24 *is-si-šú lu-bi-la-ni*
25 NÍG.ŠID.MEŠ-*šú-nu lu-up-pi-šu*
26 ŠE.PAD.MEŠ *ša ina pu-u-hi*
r.1 *ta-di-na-ni pu-ru-us*
2 *šup-ra a-na-ku ina* ŠU.2 LÚ*.EN—*pi-qit-tú-ia*
3 *lu-ba-ʾi-a* TA IGI UN.MEŠ-*ia*
4 *i-sa-ap*?-[*pi*]*-qa* ⌈*at*!⌉*-ta qa-la-ka*
5 *a-na mi-nim-ma*!! m*la*—⌈*qe*⌉*-pu*
6 *e-pu-uš mu-uk* LÚ *kab-su*
7 *rad-di-u šu-ú* TÙR.MEŠ
8 *an-šu ma-ki-u tu-x*[*x*]
9 *at-ta ina* ⌈ŠÀ *da*?⌉*-te-ka tas-sa-*[*ka*]*n*? *ṣa-ad*
10 *man-nu-ma* ⌈*lu*? *la*?⌉ *i-*⌈*sa*?⌉*-ma-*[*x*]*-a*
11 *lu*! ⌈*la*⌉ *ip-par-ri-hi t*[*i*?*-x*]*-ka*
12 ⌈*la e-mar*⌉ *ina* URU.ŠE.MEŠ-*ti lu*
13 [*x x x* L]Ú.ENGAR.[M]EŠ *a-mur*
14 [*x x x x*]*x* [*x*] *ša* KUR *pát-hat-ú-ni*
15 [*x x x* LÚ.SIP]A.MEŠ ŠÀ-*bu ša-áš-kin*
16 [*x x dul-l*]*a-ku-nu ep-šá a-na-ku*
17 [*x x x x x* L]UGAL *a-mah-har*
18 [*x x x*] *ni su tú ma ù*? URU.KASKAL
19 [*al-la-k*]*a* DINGIR.MEŠ-*ia a-pal-làh re-eš* É-*ia*
20 [*a-na-áš*]*-ši ina* UGU-*hi* MÍ.MEŠ *am-ma-te*
21 [*ša x x*]*x-ni* [*á*]*š-pu-rak-kan-ni-ni*
22 [*x x x x*] *ʾa* ⌈*x*⌉ *ta-ta-ma-a-ra*
23 [*x x x x x x*]*-ra ina* É [0]
24 [*x x x x x x*]*-bi ma-a*
25e [*x x x x x x x*] *al-ka-ni*

[*two*] sons, [and give him] wool, [x] sesame, a corres[ponding] (amount of) wine, [mul]es and camels! ... [from] Sî-abu 20 minas of silver!

12 Count out emmer, barley, wheat (and) grapes according to the market price and give them to his manservant! Get the (relevant) document and destroy it!

16 Review the rams, deposit *šupuhru*-cedar! Inspect the threshing floors of the gardeners, write (a report) on a writing-board and send it to me via *Amurrî*!

21 Let Ahabû bring the farmers, shepherds, (and) gardeners with him, (and) let their accounts be made! Determine the barley given as a loan, write to me, (and) I will call my official to account.

r.3 It will be sufficient *for* my people, and you will keep silent. (But) why on earth did La-qepu do (it)? I said he is an old ram, a follower!

7 *Stalls*, weak and poor [...]

9 You have *put* in your ...

10 May nobody be unreliable and make difficulties! One should not see your [...]! Let [...] in the villages! Inspect the farmers!

14 [*Until* the ...] of the country *has been pierced*, encourage the [sheph]erds, (and) [...] do your (pl.) [wor]k!

16 I will receive the royal [...].

18 [...] ... [I shall com]e [to] ... and Harran, venerate my gods, and honour my house.

20 As to those women [about whom] I [...] wrote to you, did you see [......]?

23 [......] in the house

24 [......] said:

25 "[......] come!"

5 Join by S. Parpola, 20.4.83. Note that the obverse of copy CT 53 930 is now reverse, and vice versa. 6f The reference to the king's sons dates this letter to the reign of Esarhaddon; cf. SAA 10 13 r.3-8 and also note SAA 10 338:9-14. 14 Or: "to his apprentice". 17 GIŠ badly written (like ŠE or NUMUN). See coll. r.6 The translation of UDU.*kab-su* is based on Syr. *kabšo* "a wether sheep, old ram" (Payne Smith 204b). See also no. 22:8 and no. 236:4. r.8 See coll. r.9 Perhaps *ṭātu* "gift, bribe". Hardly *dātu* "you have put after/behind you." r.11 Or *parāku* N "to oppose; to be obstructed"? r.21 Or: "[whom ...] I sent to you".

FIG. 2. *Inventorying booty (cf. no. 5).*
ANE 124596.

6. Reading Letters to the King

K 7522

beginning broken away
1′ ⌜*ša*⌝ [*taš-pur-an-ni ma-a e-gír-tú*]
2′ *ša ina* UGU-*hi-ka* [*áš-pur-u-ni*]
3′ *la ta-as-si ma-*[*a la tap-ti*]
4′ *a-ke-e ana-ku an-ni-*[*tú la e-pu-uš*]
5′ *ki-ma e-gír-tú š*[*a ta-šap-par-an-ni*]
6′ *ina* UGU EN—*ṭe-e-*[*mì-ia ta-tal-ka*]
e.7′ [*qa*]*r-bat-te-šú e-gí*[*r-tú i-pa-ti*]
8′ [*ṭe*]*-en-šú* [*ú-šá-áš-man-ni*]
9′ [*a-k*]*e-e e-gír-tú* [*lu-ú as-si*]
10′ [*pa*]*-ni-ia ina* UGU-*hi-ia-m*[*a e-gír-tú*]
r.1 *a-mar la a-pa-ti la a-s*[*a-as-si*]
2 *ù* LÚ.A—KIN [*šá*?] *a-na* [*x x x*]
3 *lu-ú* LÚ.*šá*—EN.NUN *lu-u* [LÚ.*x x*]
4 *lu-ú* LÚ.*kal-lap*—[*ši-pir-ti x x x*]
5 *lu-ú-bi-lu* [*x x x x x x x*]
rest broken away

CT 53 391

(Beginning destroyed)

1 As [to what you wrote to me]: "You did not read [nor open the letter] which [I sent] to you."

3 How [would] I [not do] thi[s]? When a letter whi[ch you send to me comes] to [my re]porter, [*he pe*]*rsonally* [*opens*] the let[ter] and [makes me hear] its [infor]mation.

9 [W]hy [should I read] a letter? I take care of myself. (When) I see [a letter], I do not open it nor r[ead it].

r.2 Besides, the messenger [*who brings a letter*] to [*his lord*], whether a guard, [a ...], or a mounted [messenger ...] — let them bring [......]

(Rest destroyed)

7. Sealed Order

K 15635

beginning broken away
1′ *a-sap-*[*x x x x x x*]
2′ *a-du-na-k*[*a-ni x x x*]
3′ *ki-i un-q*[*u tal-lik-a-ni*]
4′ *qar-ba-ti-ia* [*x x x*]
5′ *a-sap-ra* [*x x x x*]
e.6′ *ba-la-at x*[*x x x x*]
7′ *ta-x*[*x x x x x*]
r.1 *ša* IGI *x*[*x x x x x*]
2 *la du-*[*x x x x x x*]
3 *qa-*[*x x x x x x x*]
rest broken away

CT 53 693

(Beginning destroyed)

1 I wro[te ......]

2 until n[ow ...]

3 When the seal[ed order came to me], I *personally* sent [......]

6 *without* [......]

7 you [......]

r.1 who is in the presence [......]

2 no [......]

(Rest destroyed)

8. Augurs from Hamath

K 10849

1 [*š*]*a* LÚ*.*da-gíl*—M[UŠEN.MEŠ *x x*]
2 [LÚ*].*ha-mat-a-a* NIN [*x x x*]
3 [*ina*] SAG LUGAL-*te up-*[*x x x*]
4 MU.AN.NA *ša da x*[*x x x x*]

ABL 1346

1 [*O*]*f* the augu[rs ...]

2 [the] (*king*) of Hamath, *the sister* [...]

3 [At] the beginning of the reign [...],

6 7 *qarbātēšu* also in SAA 1 89:12, and SAA 5 27:11; cf *qarbātija*, no. 8 r.6 and no. 7:4. 8f See coll. 10 Lit., "my face is on me." Cf. no. 78:15 and no. 34 r.15f.
7 6 Or: "the life (*ba-la-aṭ*) of".
8 The order of the sides is correctly determined in ABL (original collated): the obverse is flatter and the left side

5 *at-ta-ṣa-áš-šú ki-i* [*an-ni-i*]
6 [*q*]*ar-ba-ti-ia ina* IGI [*x x x x*]
7 [*nu*]*-uk* LÚ**.da-gíl*—MUŠEN.[MEŠ *x x*]
8 [*li*]*l*$^{?}$*-mu-du id-da-*[*x x x*]
9 [*x x x x*]*x*[*x*]*x*[*x x x x x x*]
rest broken away
Rev. beginning broken away
1′ *ik-te-r*[*u*$^{?}$ *x x x x x*]
2′ *ù at-t*[*a x x x x x x*]
3′ *ki-i ke-nu-ti* [*x x x x*]
4′ *ina* UGU*-hi-ia še-*[*bi-la x x*]
5′ [*x x*] *šú ma ma k*[*i x x x x*]
6′ [*x x x*]*x*[*x*] *x*[*x x x x x*]
7′ [*x x x x x x x x x*]
8′ [*x x x x x x x x x*]
9e [*x ina*] IGI LÚ**.ha-mat-*[*a-a x x x*]
s.1 [*x x x x x-š*]*i* ^{m}*ur-x*[*x x x x*]

4 the year *which* [...]
5 I brought him here, and [*p*]*ersonally* [*spoke*] as [follows] in the presence of [...]: "[*Let*] the augur[s *le*]*arn* [...]." *Therea*[*fter* ...]
(Break)
r.1 they *deposite*[*d* ......]
2 and yo[u ......]
3 loyally [...]
4 s[end ...] to me! [...]
(Break)
9 [*bef*]*ore* the (*king*) of Hamath [...]
(Rest destroyed or too broken for translation)

9. Fragment Referring to Bel and Offenders

K 7411

beginning broken away
1′ [*x x x x x*] ⸢*x*⸣ [*x x x x x*]
2′ [*x x x x x*]*-nu i-x*[*x x x x x*]
3′ [*x x x x ma*]*-a* 1*-en* [*x x x x*]
4′ [*x x x x š*]*úm-ma ú-*[*x x x*]
5′ [*x x x x*]*-ka ša ina* UGU*-hi-*⸢*ka*⸣
6′ [*x x x x x*]*x-a-su la ik-ri-ka-a*
7′ [*x x x x x m*]*a-a la* ^{d}EN *šú-u*
e.8′ [*x x x x*]*-i-ni*
9′ [*x x x x*] *lu ke-na-a-ka*
r.1 [*x x x x*]*x* ŠEŠ.MEŠ*-ka*
2 [*x x x x*] *an-na-ka la ú-du-u*
3 [*x x x* DU]MU ^{md}ŠÚ*-a ta-sa-nap-par-u-ni*
4 [*x x x x-t*]*e ú-ma-a at-ta*
5 [*x x x x*]*-bu-tu uh-tal-lil*
6 [*x x x x*]*-ra-ar ù* [*x x x*]
7 [*x x x x* E]N—*hi-i*[*ṭ-ṭi x x x*]
8 [*x x x x x*]*x hi* [*x x x x x*]
rest broken away

CT 53 351

(Beginning destroyed)
3 [... sayi]ng: "One [...]
4 [...] If [...]
5 your [...], which [...] upon you
6 Did he not gather [...]?
7 [... say]ing: "It is not Bel
8 [......]
9 [...] Be loyal!
r.1 [...] your brothers
2 [...] here do not know
3 [that] you keep sending [*letters to* the so]n of Marduka
4 [...] Now you
5 [...] *I have sounded*
6 [......]. And [...]
7 [... the o]ffen[der(s) ...]
(Rest destroyed)

10. They are Plotting to Kill You

Ki 1904-10-9,121 (BM 99092)

beginning broken away
1′ [*x x x*] ⸢*x*⸣ [*x x*].MEŠ*-ni is* [*x x*] ⸢*ni*⸣
2′ [*x x x*]*x-ia id-du-ub-bu ina ke-ti-ia*
3′ [*aq*]*-ṭi-bi at-ta-a-ma tah-ti-ik-im*
4′ *ša ina* UGU *du-a-ki-i-ka id-bu-bu-ni*

CT 53 977

(Beginning destroyed)
1 [...]s [...] have been plotting [*against*] *me*. [I t]old (this) truthfully, and you understood that they have (also) been plotting to

is readable in the same direction as the reverse. Cf. notes on no. 48 s.1 and no. 65. r.1 Cf. *ik-ter-ru* in no. 63:19. r.6 Cf. no. 7:4, SAA 1 54 r.11.
9 r.5 Or: "he".

5′ a-na-ku mì-i-nu la-áš-pu-⸢rak⸣-ka
6′ at-ta tu-ud-da [x x x x x x]
7′ it-ti-it-zi ù x[x x x x x]
8′ [ina I]GI-ia i-ba-áš-ši a-ta-a k[a-x x x]
9′ [T]A IGI-i[a x]x-me-du tú da x[x x x]
10′ [x x x x x]x ⸢x x⸣ ʾa [x x x]
11′ [x x x x x x x] a-na mi-[i-ni x x]
12′ [x x x x x]x-šú la a-na ka-[x x]
13′ [x x x x x x x x]x x[x x x x]
rest broken away
Rev. beginning broken away
1′ [x x x x x x x x x x] az [x]
2′ [x x x x x x x x x x] i [x]
3′ [x x x x x x x x x x] i [x]
rest broken away

kill you. What (else) should I write to you?

6 You know (that) [...] has stood [...] (and that) [...] is [in] my [pre]sence. Why [...] ... [...]?

(Remainder too broken for translation)

11. Fragment Referring to Thrones

K 7560

beginning broken away
1′ [x x]-⸢tal⸣-k[a x x x x x]
2′ [as]-⸢se⸣-me ⸢ma$^{?}$-a x x niš⸣
3′ [x]-a is-sa-⸢nap⸣-[pu-r]u
4′ [x]-ú tu-ur-a [x x.M]EŠ-ka
5′ [x x.M]EŠ-ka taš-[x x]-an-ni
6′ [x x x] la tu-šá-aṣ-bat-šá-⸢nu⸣-ni
7′ [x x x x x x x] i-qab-bi
8′ [x x x x x x]⸢x x⸣-ta
9′ [x x x x x]x nu-šá-aṣ-bat-ka
10′ [x x x ^{m}š]um-ma—MAN LÚ*.A—SIG$^{!}$
11′ [x x x x x x] qa-ni [x x]
12′ [x x x x x x x] ⸢x⸣ [x x]
Edge destroyed
r.1 [x x x x x x x x x x x]
2 [x x x x x x x x GIŠ].GU.ZA
3 [x x x x x x x x x x]x-ka
4 [x x x x x x x x l]a$^{?}$ a-bu-uk
5 [x x x x x x x]x e-ru-ub
6 [x x x x G]IŠ.GU.ZA i-ba-áš-ši
7 [x x x x x]x is-sa-na-al-lu-ka
8 [x x x x x]x i-qab-bu-ni-ka
9 [x x x x T]A GU.ZA ša LÚ.2-e
10 [x x x x] ⸢i⸣-ba-áš-ši-ma
11 [x x x x x l]e-e-mu-ru
12 [x x x x x x] le-e-pu-uš
13 [x x x x x x]⸢x x⸣[x x]-⸢ru⸣
rest broken away

CT 53 397

(Beginning destroyed)

1 [...] cam[e ...]

2 [I have he]ard *that* [...]

3 are continually se[n]ding [...]

4 Again, [(the fact) that] you *s*[*ent*] me your [...]s and your [...]s *but* do not provide them [with ...]

7 [......] says

8 [......]

9 We shall provide you [with ...]

10 [... Š]umma-šarru, a chariot fighter

11 [......] *outside* [...]

(Break)

r.2 [......] *throne*

3 [...] your [...]

4 [......] I did [*no*]*t drive away*

5 [......] enter

6 [...] the *throne* exists

7 [...] they are lying to you

8 [...] they tell you [...]

9 [... *wi*]*th* the throne of the deputy (governor)

10 [(...)] there is also [*another throne*]

11 [... M]ay he inspect and do [...]

(Rest destroyed)

11 2, 10 See coll. r.2, 6, 9, 10 Or: "chair."

12. ———-

K 15614

beginning broken away
1′ [*x x*]-*ku-nu* ⌜*x*⌝ [*x*] ⌜*x*⌝ IGI-*ia-ni*
2′ [*x x-t*]*a at-tu-nu*
3′ [*x x x x*]*x la tal-li-ka*
4′ [*x x x x š*]*a* AD-*u-a*
5′ [*x x x x x x*]*x-u-ni*
6′ [*x x x x x x x x*]*x*
rest broken away
Rev. completely broken away

CT 53 683

(Beginning destroyed)
1 your [......] ...
2 [...] you (pl.)
3 [...] you (pl.) did not go
4 [...... o]f my father
(Rest destroyed)

13. ———-

K 15685

beginning broken away
1′ *rih-ṣi* [*x x x x x*]
2′ *áš-pu-r*[*a-x x x x*]
3′ *i-bal-l*[*a*?-*x x x x*]
4′ *tu-bal-*[*x x x x x*]
5′ [*tu*]-*pa-a*[*s-x x x x*]
6′ [*x x*]*x* 1? *x*[*x x x x x*]
rest broken away
Rev. completely broken away

CT 53 715

(Beginning destroyed)
1 devastation [.....]
2 [about which] I wrote [......]
3 *liv*[*es ......*]
4 you *revi*[*ve ......*]
5 [you] *brin*[*g good news .....*]
(Rest destroyed)

14. ———-

K 1587

1 [*a*]-*na* LUGAL *be-lí-ia*
2 [ARA]D-*ka* ^{m}*aš-šur*—DÙ—A
3 *lu* DI-*mu a-na* LUGAL
4 *be-lí-ia*
5 *aš-šur* ^{d}EN ^{d}PA *a-na* LUGAL
6 *be-lí-ia lik-ru-bu*
7 [*x x x ina* U]GU LUGAL *be-lí-ia*
8 [*x x x x x*] *a—dan-niš*
rest broken away
Rev. entirely broken away

ABL 1001

1 To the king, my lord: your [serva]nt Assurbanipal. Good health to the king, my lord! May Aššur, Bel and Nabû bless the king, my lord.
7 [... t]o the king, my lord
8 [......] very
(Rest destroyed)

15. Report on the Cimmerians of Iyazê

K 4279 (CT 53 226) (+) K 5425a (ABL 1026)

1 [*a-na* LUGAL] *be-lí-ia* ARAD-*ka* ^{m}*aš-šur*—DÙ—A
2 [*lu* DI-*mu*] *a-na* MAN *be-lí-ia aš-šur* ^{d}EN ^{d}PA
3 [*a-na*] LUGAL *be-lí-ia lik-ru-bu ina* UGU ^{m}*ra-hi-iṣ*—U.U
4 [*ša*] LUGAL *be-lí-ia iq-bu-ni ma-a le-ru-ub*
5 [*ina pa-n*]*i-ka šá-al-šu qí-bi-a a-sa-al-šú*
6 [*ki*]-⌈*i*!⌉ *an-ni-i iq-ṭi-bi ma-a ša* MAN *iš-pur-ni-ni*
7 [*m*]*a*!-*a a-mur pa-ni šá* ^{m}*ia-ze-e a-ki*! *ma-a ina* UGU
8 ⌈LÚ*⌉.*gi-mir-ra-a-a am-mu-te qí-ba-áš-šú a-ki*
9 [*r*]*a-mì-ni-ka a-ta-lak ma-a pa-ni-šú a-ta-mar*
10 [*m*]*a-a pa-lìh a—dan-niš ma-a aq-ṭi-ba-šú ina* UGU LÚ*.*gi*!-[*m*]*i*[*r-ra-a-a*]
11 ⌈*ma*⌉ *a-ta-a* LÚ*.*gi-mir-a-a ta-ši*! *ma-a k*[*i*!]-⌈*i*!⌉ *a*[*n*!-*ni-i*]
12 *iq-ṭi-bi ma-a* LÚ*.KÚR *i—ba-ti* [x x x x x (x)]
13 *ina* UGU-*hi šu-u ma-a šu-tú x*[x x x x x x x x x]
14 1! *ma*!-*hu*!-*uṣ*! *ma-a a-*⌈*x*⌉ [x x x x x x x x x x]
15 *ma-a* ^{m}*a-a-ze-e iq*!-[x x x x x x x x x x]
16 ⌈*e*⌉-*ta-*⌈*kal*⌉ *m*[*a-a* x x x x x x x x x x]
short break; continued in CT 53 226
17′ *ma-a* [x x x x x x x x x x x]
18′ DI-*m*[*u* x x]*x*[x x x x x x x x x]
19′ *ma-a ha-di-u a—dan-*⌈*niš*⌉ [x x x x x x x]
20′ DUMU ^{m}*ú-ak-sa-t*[*a-ar* x x x x x x]
21′ *ma-a ina* UGU GÌR.2 *it-*[*ta-lak* x x x x x]
22′ ŠÀ-*bi ú-sa-ag-ri-r*[*i* x x x x x]
23′ *ša* MU.AN.NA *šá* MU.A[N.NA x x x x x]
24′ *ma-a a-na* ^{m}*pa-ra-m*[*u*? x x x x x x x]
25′ *ma-a ina* UGU GÌR.2 *i*[*t-ta-lak* x x x x x]
26′ *šú-nu ma-a* LÚ*.EN—[URU.MEŠ x x x x x x]
27′ TA* *a-he-iš qa-r*[*a-bu* x x x x x x x]
28′ *ša ip-hur-*[*u-ni* x x x x x x x]
r.1 2 URU.MEŠ *ú-*⌈*tú*⌉-[x x x x x x x x]
2 MU-*šú šá* 2-*tú* URU.*ku-*⌈*da*⌉-*na* MU *šá x*[x x x x x x]
3 *ša* ^{m}*a-a-ze-e* TA* *ú-x*[x x x x x]
4 *il-la-*[x]
rest uninscribed

ABL 1026+

1 [To the king], my lord: your servant Assurbanipal. [Good health] to the king, my lord! May Aššur, Bel and Nabû bless the king, my lord.

3 Concerning Rahiṣ-Dadi [about whom] the king, my lord, said: "Let him enter [into] your [presen]ce, interrogate him, and report to me" — I have interrogated him, and he told me as follows:

6 "The king having sent me, (saying) 'See how the *face* of Iyazê is, and give him a piece of your mind about those Cimmerians,' I went to see his *face*: he was very frightened. I said to him about the Cimmerians: 'Why have you removed the Cimmerians?,' and he said as follows:

12 "'The enemy *at the side* [......]
13 "On account of that he [.....]
14 "one was wounded [.....].'
15 "Iyazê [.....]
16 "has eaten [.....]
(Break)
18 "[*all is*] well [.....]
19 "they are very glad [.....]
20 "the son of Cyaxares [.....]
21 "*has g*[*ained*] *footing* [.....]
22 "has frightened my heart [.....]
23 "year by ye[ar .....]
24 "to *Phrao*[*rtes* .....]
25 "*has g*[*ained*] *footing* [.....]
26 "are [...]. The [city] lord[s .....]
27 "[are] fight[ing] with each other [.....]
28 "who have assembl[ed .....]
r.1 "They have [*taken*] two towns [.....].
2 "The name of the second one is Kudana; [*I don't know*] the name of [the first one. The ...] of Iyazê goe[s] with [.....]."

15 Previous editions: Lanfranchi Cimmeri (1990) 84f; Ivantchik Cimmériens (1993) 185-188. Indirect join and collations by S. Parpola, 28.7.78. 2 MAN *be* written over erased *be-lí*. 4 *be-lí-ia* erroneously written for *be-lí*. 7, 10f See coll. 15 1 *ma* written over an erasure. 21, 25 See the comment in SAA 9 3 i 13.

16. Cimmerians in Mindâ

83-1-18,283

illegible traces of two lines
1′ *[x x]-ra iq-ṭi-bi [ma-a]*
2′ *[it-t]a!-lak* MAN *liš!-⸢al!⸣-[šú]*
3′ *ina!* ŠÀ! DINGIR.MEŠ *an-nu-te ⸢ni?⸣-[x]*
4′ *ina ṭi-bu-te ša* MAN *bal!-ṭu*
5′ *ú-ma-a an-nu-ri*
6′ LÚ.*gi-mir-ra-a-a*
e.7′ *gab-bi-šu-nu it-ta-ṣa*
r.1 *[i-n]a* URU.*mì-in-da-a* [0]
2 *iz-za-zu ket-tú ud-di-ni*
3 ⸢TA*?⸣ MAN! ⸢*x x*⸣-*ú-ni*
4 *[x x]x[x]x[x x] ṭè? [x x]x*
rest broken away

ABL 1161

(Beginning destroyed)

1 [...]ra said: "He [has go]ne (away)." Let the king ask [him].

3 Thanks to these gods, [they are] *ca[lm]*, and they are alive *due to* the *kindness* of the king.

5 Now then he has brought all the Cimmerians, and they are staying in Mindâ. True, they have [not] yet ...

(Rest destroyed)

17. Report on Kunaya and Kudurru

Bu 91-5-9,3

1 *a-na* LUGAL *be-lí-ia*
2 ARAD-*ka* m*aš-šur*—DÙ—A
3 *lu* DI *a-na* LUGAL *be-lí-ia*
4 *aš-šur* dEN dPA *a-na* MAN EN-*ia*
5 *lik-ru-bu*
6 *ina* UGU m*ku!-na!-a-a*
7 m*ku-dúr-ru šá* MAN EN *iq-bu-u-ni*
8 *ma-a šu!-pur liš!-u-lu!*
9 *a-na* m*sa-si-i*
10 *ma-a šu-tú [ṭè]-en!-šú-[nu]*
11 *ú-da k[i-i] an-ni-i*
12 *is-sap!-[ra ma-a]*
13 *[x x x x x x x]*
rest broken away
Rev. beginning broken away
1′ *[x x x x x x]-te*
2′ *m[a-a* m*x x x x]-a*
3′ LÚ*!.*kàl!-d[a]-a-a*
4′ *a-mat* LUGAL *ina* UGU-*šú-nu*
5′ *iz-za-kar ma-a : iq-ṭi-bi-u*
6′ *ma-a* MÍ!.*[ár]-me-ti*
7′ 1-*et ma-a* TÚG.*hu-la-nu*
8′ *ina* GÚ-*šá ta-kar-ra-ár*
9′ *ma-a* TA* ARAD.MEŠ *ša* MAN
10′ *ta-za-az ma a-na-ku*
11′ TA* m*ab!-di—mil-ki ni-sa-al-lam*
12′ *an-ni-ti? tú šá ha x[x]*
13e *ma-a e-gír-tú šá ṭè-[me]*
14e *le-mu-ru*

ABL 1257

1 To the king, my lord: your servant Assurbanipal. Good health to the king, my lord! May Aššur, Bel and Nabû bless the king, my lord.

6 Concerning Kunaya (and) Kudurru about whom the king, my lord, said: "Send word that Sasî be interrogated, he knows about them" – he has writt[en] a[s] follows:

(Break)

2 "[PN], a Chaldean, has appealed to the king on account of them.

5 "They say that an *[Ar]amean* woman is putting a cloak on her neck and is staying with the king's servants, saying 'I and Abdimilki are making peace.'

12 "*This is* ... They should read the letter with the repo[rt]."

16 Previous editions: Lanfranchi Cimmeri (1990) 86; Ivantchik Cimmériens (1993) 196f. Collated by S. Parpola, 16.11.66. 2ff See coll. 3 Or: "By these gods." At the end of the line both ⸢*né*⸣-[*e-hu*] and ⸢*sa!*⸣-[*al-mu*] are possible. 4 Thus according to collation without question marks; W 311 (there obv. 6). r.2 *udīna/i* is also written *ud-di-ni* in SAA 10 349:9. r.3 See coll.

18. Report on the Border of Urarṭu

K 13046

1 [*a-na* LUGAL *be-lí-ia*]
2 [ARAD-*ka* ^{m}*aš-šur*—DÙ—A]
3 [*lu* DI-*mu a-na* LUGAL *be-lí-ia*]
4 *aš-šur* ⸢^{d}EN ^{d}PA *a*⸣-*n*[*a* LUGAL *be-lí-ia*]
5 *lik-ru-*[*bu*]
6 ^{m}*dà-ri*—MAN LÚ.[*x x x*]
7 *ša ina* UGU *ta-h*[*u-me*]
8 *ša* KUR.URI ⸢*pa*⸣-[*qid-u-ni*]
9 *ma-a* L[Ú.*x x x x x*]
rest broken away

CT 53 469

1 [To the king, my lord: your servant Assurbanipal. Good health to the king, my lord]! May Aššur, Bel and Nabû bless [the king, my lord].

6 Dari-šarru, the [...] app[ointed] over the bor[der] of Urarṭu says: "The [......]"

(Rest destroyed)

19. ———

83-1-18,22

1 *ana* MAN EN-*iá*
2 ARAD-*ka* ^{m}*aš-šur*—DÙ—A
3 *lu* ⸢DI-*mu*⸣ *ana* MAN U-*iá*
4 ^{d}PA *u* ^{d}[AMAR.U]TU *ana* MAN U-*iá*
5 *li*[*k-ru-b*]*u*
6 ⸢*us x*⸣ [*x x š*]*a*
7 [*x x x ina*] IGI-*iá*
8 [*x x li*]*p*-⸢*ru*⸣-*us*
e.9 ⸢*x x x*⸣ *a-na*-⸢*hu*⸣
Rev. uninscribed

CT 53 147

1 To the king, my lord: your servant Assurbanipal. Good health to the king, my lord! May Nabû and [Mard]uk b[les]s the king, my lord.

6 [...... o]f

7 [... *is* in] my presence.

8 [... may] decide

9 ...

20. Milki-nuri Curses the Crown Prince

K 1110

1 *a-na* MAN EN-⸢*ia*⸣ [ARAD-*ka* ^{m}*aš-šur*—DÙ—A]
2 *lu-u* DI-*mu a-na* [MAN EN-*ia*]
3 ^{d}PA *u* ^{d}AMAR.UTU *a-n*[*a* MAN EN-*ia*]
4 *lik*-⸢*ru*⸣-*bu*
5 ⸢*x* LÚ.*ki*⸣-*na*-⸢*al*⸣-*ti*
6 *ša* ^{m}EN—*šal-lim* LÚ.GAL—KAR
7 ⸢*ur-ta-am*⸣-*m*[*e i*]*d*—*da-tú*
rest broken away
Rev. beginning broken away
1′ *x*[*x x x*] ⸢*x x*⸣
2′ *aq-ṭi-bi a-na* ^{m}*mil-ki*—ZALÁG
3′ *a-ki ša* LUGAL *be-lí iq-ban-ni*
4′ *ina* UGU GÌR.2 *it-ta-gal*
5′ *it-at-na-ag-ra-ra*

CT 53 26

1 To the king, my lord: [your servant Assurbanipal]. Good health to [the king, my lord]! May Bel and Nabû bless [the king, my lord].

5 I rejected the [...] assembly of Bel-šallim, the chief of trade. Thereafter [...]

(Break)

r.2 I spoke to Milki-nuri as the king, my lord, had told me; he *looked* at the feet, and was trembling with fear.

17 6-11 Cf. SAA 11 156:14-19, "Kudurru and Kunaya ... are at the disposal of Sasî."
18 6ff → no. 148.
20 r.4 Cf. no. 15:21′, 25′. *it-ta-gal* is hardly a mistake for *it-ta-lak*, as the meaning "gain footing" (see SAA 9 3 i 13) does not fit the context here. r.5ff Cf. the different interpretations of the passage by von Soden, ZA 70 (1980)

6′ *aq-ṭi-ba-áš-šú nu-uk*
7′ *sa-gu ina* MURUB$_4$ *ul-li*
8′ ÚŠ.MEŠ-*ka mì-h*[*iṣ*?]
9e *iq-ṭi-bi m*[*a-a*]
10e *lu la* LUGAL-*t*[*u*?]
11e *a-na* A—MAN [*x x x x*]
s.1 [*x x x x x x* M]U.AN?.NA.MEŠ *ša* TI-*ku-ni*
traces of one line

6 I said to him: "Remove the *sash* from (your) waist and *stri*[*ke*] blood!"

9 He said: "*May not the king*[*ship be granted*] to the crown prince [...... the y]ears that I live."

147 (reading *it-ta*!-*na-aq-ra-ra*), and Deller, Or. 58 (1989) 259. s.1 AN? badly written with an extra vertical wedge.

2. Letters from Other Members of the Royal Family

FIG. 3. *Seal of Aššur-nadin-šumi.*
ANE 77612.

21. Treacherous Astrologers

BM 135586

1 *a-na* LUGAL *be-lí-i*[*a*]
2 ARAD-*ka* ^{md}GIŠ.NU$_{11}$—MU—GI.N[A]
3 *lu-u* DI-*mu a-na* LUGAL *be-lí-ia*
4 ^{d}AG *ù* ^{d}AMAR.UTU *a-na* LUGAL *be-lí-iá*
5 *lik-ru-bu* ^{m}*šá-ri-du* ^{md}PA—PAB.MEŠ—APIN-*eš*
6 DUMU KÁ.DINGIR.RA.KI
7 ^{m}EN—SUM-*na* DUMU BÁR.SIPA.KI
8 *e-gír-tú is-sa-ap-ru-u-ni*
9 *ma a-de-e* LUGAL *ina* UGU-*hi-ka*
10 *is-se-e-ni is-sa-kan*
11 *ma-a mi-i-ni ša ta-šá-ma-a-ni*
12 *a-na* EN-*ku-nu ta-qab-bi-a*
13 *ma-a ú-ma-a* ^{m}EN—KAR-*ir* ^{md}UTU—NUMUN—BA-*šá*
14 *ṭè-e-mu ša* LUGAL *iš-ka-nu-šá-nu-u-ni*
15 *ur-tam-mi-ú ša ra-ma-ni-šú-nu e-pu-uš*
16 ^{m}DUMU.UŠ-*a-a ša* LUGAL *iš-pur-šu-u-ni*
17 *ma a-lik* BARAG.MEŠ *ina* KÁ.DINGIR.RA.KI *kur-ru*
18 *is-si-šú-nu pi-i is-sa-kan*
19 MUL.MEŠ *e-mur-ru* UDU.*pu-ha-da-a-ni*

Iraq 34 21

1 To the king, m[y] lord: your servant Šamaš-šumu-ukin. Good health to the king, my lord! May Nabû and Marduk bless the king, my lord.

5 Šaridu (and) Nabû-ahhe-ereš, citizens of Babylon, (and) Bel-iddina, a citizen of Borsippa, have sent me the (following) letter:

9 "The king concluded a treaty with us concerning you: 'Tell your lord whatever you hear!' Now, Bel-eṭir (and) Šamaš-zeru-iqiša have neglected the order the king gave them (and) are acting on their own. Aplaya, whom the king sent (with the command): 'Go (and) set up sanctuaries in Babylon!', has made common cause with them. They are observing the stars (and) dissecting lambs, but he

21 Previous edition: Parpola, *Iraq* 34 (1972) 21-34.

FIG. 4. *Slaughtering lambs.*
ORIGINAL DRAWINGS IV, 25.

20 *i-nak-ki-su ina* UGU LUGAL BE-*i-ni*
21 DUMU—LUGAL KÁ.DINGIR.RA.KI *la i-qab-bi*
22 *ma-a* ^{m}DUMU.UŠ-*a-a ú-de-e-šú* LÚ.HAL
23 ^{m}EN—KAR-*ir* ^{md}UTU—NUMUN—BA-*šá*
r.1 LÚ*.A.BA UD-*mu*—AN—EN.LÍL *šú-nu*
2 *mu-šu kal-la*—UD-*mu* AN-*e i-da-gul*
3 ⸢*ù*⸣ UN.MEŠ *šá a-na* ^{m}*aš-šur*—*na-din*—MU
4 *iṣ-bat-*⸢*ú*⸣*-ni a-na* KUR.NIM.MA.KI *id-di-nu-u-ni*
5 *up-ta-hir-šú-nu a-de-e is-si-šú-nu*
6 *is-sa-kan ina* MUL.SAG.ME.GAR MUL.GAG.SI.SÁ
7 *ut-ta-me-šú-nu ú-ma-a ni-is-se-me*
8 *a-na* DUMU—LUGAL KÁ.DINGIR.RA.KI *ni-iq-ṭi-bi*
9 ^{m}ARAD—^{d}PA *e-gír-tú a-na* ^{m}EN—KAR-*ir*
10 *a-na* ^{md}⸢UTU⸣—NUMUN—BA-*šá is-sa-ap-ra*
11 *ma-a* LÚ*.IGI.DUB *ša*!! *il-lik-an-ni*
12 *ma-a šá la*!! LUGAL *it-tal-ka*
13 *ma-a ina* UGU-*hi pi-i-ia qa-li-la-šu*
14 ^{m}*su-la-a-a* ŠEŠ-*ú-ni*
15 *ina* UGU *a-bat* LUGAL *ina* KUR—*ma-šar-ti*
16 URU.*ni-nu-u ṣa-bit*
rest uninscribed

does not report anything concerning the king, our lord, or the crown prince of Babylon. Aplaya alone is a haruspex; Bel-eṭir (and) Šamaš-zeru-iqiša are astrologers, they watch the sky day and night. Moreover, he has assembled the people who captured Aššur-nadin-šumi (and) delivered him to Elam, and has concluded a treaty with them, adjuring them by Jupiter (and) Sirius. We have now heard (about it) and informed the crown prince of Babylon."

r.9 Urdu-Nabû has written to Bel-eṭir and Šamaš-zeru-iqiša as follows:

11 "The treasurer who came, has come without (the consent of) the king. Scold him on my behalf! Sulaya, our brother, is kept in the Review Palace of Nineveh by royal command."

22. Audience Gifts for the King

K 637

1 *a-na* LUGAL *be-lí-ia*
2 ARAD-*ka* ^{md}GIŠ.NU—MU—GI.NA
3 *lu-u* DI-*mu a-na* LUGAL EN-*ia*
4 ^{d}PA ^{d}AMAR.UTU *a-na* LUGAL
5 *be-lí-ia lik-ru-bu*
6 1-*en* ANŠE.KUR.RA
7 *ša* KUR.*ra-ṣa-pa-a-a*
8 1-*en* UDU.*kab-su*
9 *ša* ^{md}PA—DÙ—PAB.MEŠ
Rev. uninscribed

ABL 534

1 To the king, my lord: your servant Šamaš-šumu-ukin. Good health to the king, my lord! May Nabû (and) Marduk bless the king, my lord.

6 One horse from the (governor) of Raṣappa, one wether sheep from Nabû-bani-ahhe.

23. ———

K 5579

1 [*a-n*]*a* LUGAL *be-li-*[*ia*]
2 [ARAD]-*ka* ^{md}GIŠ.NU—MU—[GI.NA]
3 [*lu*] DI-*mu a-na* LUGAL *b*[*e-lí-ia*]
4 ^{d}AG *u* ^{d}AMAR.UTU *a-*[*na* LUGAL *be-lí-ia*]
5 *lik-ru-bu* DINGIR.MEŠ *x*[*x x x x*]
6 *hi-is-su-tú ša* [*x x x x x*]
7 *a-na* SIG$_{5}$ *ša a-*[*x x x x*]
8 *li-ih-su-su* [*x x*]

ABL 536

1 [T]o the king, [my] lord: your [servant] Šamaš-šumu-[ukin]. Good health to the king, [my lord]! May Nabû and Marduk bless the [king, my lord]! May the gr[eat] gods remember [the king, my lord], ve[ry] favourably [indeed...].

22 Previous edition: Parpola, *Iraq* 34 (1972), p. 21, n. 2. 7 KUR.*ra-ṣa-pa-a-a* also in SAA 5 254:8. Here the governor of Raṣappa. 8 See note on no. 5 r.6.

r.1 *hi-is-su-tú* [*x x x x*]
2 ŠÀ-*bi pa*-[*x x x x*]
two uninscribed lines
3 [*x*] 30 *x*[*x x x x x*]
4 [*x*] ŠÀ-*bi* [*x x x x*]
5 [*lid*]-*di-nu* [*x x x x*]

r.1 A reminder [......]
2 *my heart* [......]
3 [...] 30 [......]
4 [...] *there* [......]
5 [let] them give [......]

24. ———

K 5500

1 *a-na* [LUGAL *b*]*e-lí-ia*
2 ARAD-*k*[*a* ^{md}GIŠ].NU$_{11}$—MU—GI.NA
3 *lu* DI-[*mu a-na* LUGAL] EN-*iá*
4 [^{d}PA ^{d}AMAR].UTU
5 [*a-na* LUGAL EN-*iá lik*]-*ru-bu*
6 [*x x x x x x x*]*x-ki-ri*
rest broken away
Rev. broken away (and at least partly uninscribed)

ABL 535

1 To the [king], my [l]ord: yo[ur] servant [Ša]maš-šumu-ukin. Good hea[lth to the king], my lord! [May Nabû and Mar]duk [b]less [the king, my lord].

(Rest destroyed)

25. A Broken Chariot Weel

K 475

1 [*a-na* LUGA]L EN-*iá*
2 ARAD-*ka* ^{md}GIŠ.NU$_{11}$—UG$_{5}$.GA—TI.LA
3 *lu* DI-*mu a-na* LUGAL
4 *be-lí-iá* ^{d}PA *u* ^{d}AMAR.UTU
5 *a-na* LUGAL EN-*iá lik-ru-bu*
6 *it—ti-ma-li ina bé-et*
7 *i—da-at* LUGAL *al-la-kan-ni*
8 *ina qab-si* NINA.KI *e-tar-ba*
9 *ina* EN.NUN LUGAL SIG$_{4}$.MEŠ *šak-na*
10 [UMBI]N$^{?}$ *ša* GIŠ.GIGIR *is-se*$^{!}$-*niš*
11 [*it-t*]*a*-⌈*ha*⌉-*aṣ i*[*t*$^{!}$-*t*]*ak-sap*
12 [*ú*]-*ma-a* LUGAL *be-lí-ia*
r.1 *ṭè-e-mu*
2 [*l*]*iš-kun dul-lu*
3 [*ina*] UGU$^{!}$ *le-pu-šú*
rest uninscribed

ABL 766

1 [To the kin]g, my lord: your servant Šamaš-metu-uballiṭ. Good health to the king, my lord! May Nabû and Marduk bless the king, my lord.

6 Yesterday, when I was coming after the king, I entered the centre of Nineveh. There were bricks at the king's guard. [*The whe*]*el* of the chariot hit them (and) broke instantly.

12 [N]ow, let the king, my lord, give an order, so that they may do the work on it.

26. Doctor for a Sick Maid

82-5-22,174

1 *a-na* LUGAL EN-*ia*
2 ARAD-*ka* ^{md}GIŠ.NU$_{11}$—UG$_{5}$.GA—TI.LA
3 *lu-u* DI-*mu a-na* LUGAL EN-*ia*
4 ^{d}PA *ù* ^{d}AMAR.UTU

ABL 341

1 To the king, my lord: your servant Šamaš-metu-uballiṭ. Good health to the king, my lord! May Nabû and Marduk bless the

23 r.5 See coll.
24 3 See coll.
25 Previous edition: Fales and Lanfranchi Lettere (1992) 132f. 10 Possibly not enough room for UMBIN; see coll. r.3 W 231.

5 *a-na* LUGAL EN-*iá*
6 *a—dan-niš a—dan-niš*
7 *lik-ru-bu*
8 *ú-ma-a* GEMÉ *ša* LUGAL
9 MÍ.^{d}BA.Ú—*ga-me-lat*
10 *mar-ṣa-at a—dan-niš la ku-sa-pi ta-kal*
11 *ú-ma-a* LUGAL *be-lí*
12 *ṭè-mi liš-kun*
13 LÚ.A.ZU 1-*en*
r.1 *lil-li-ka*
2 *le-mur-ši*
rest uninscribed

king, my lord, very greatly.

[8] Now, Babu-gamilat, a female servant of the king, is seriously ill. She does not (even) eat bread. Now, may the king, my lord, give orders that a physician come and see her.

27. Report on Two Women

80-7-19,43

1 [*a-na* LUGAL EN-*ia*]
2 [ARAD-*ka* ^{md}GIŠ.NU$_{11}$—UG$_{5}$.GA—TI.LA]
3 [*lu-u* DI]-*mu a-na* LUGAL EN-*ia*
4 [^{d}]PA *ù* ^{d}AMAR.UTU *a-na* LUGAL EN-*iá*
5 [*a—dan-niš a*]—*dan-niš lik-ru-bu*
6 [*ina* UGU *x x ša*] LUGAL *iš-pur-an-ni*
7 *at*$^{!}$-*ta-lak*$^{!}$ *as-sa-ʾa-al-šú*
8 *ma-a* MÍ.*sa-an-gíl*$^{!}$—*ra-mat* MÍ-*šú*
9 [*ša*] $^{m⌈}$*a-bi*$^{!⌉}$—*i*$^{!}$-*li* LÚ.*ša*—GÌR.2
10 [MÍ.*x x x x x*]*x* MÍ-*šú ša* ^{md}PA—KAR-*ir*

ABL 1199

[1] [To the king, my lord: your servant Šamaš-metu-uballiṭ. Good hea]lth to the king, my lord! May Nabû and Marduk bless the king, my lord, [very] greatly.

[6] [Concerning ... about whom] the king wrote to me, I went (and) asked him. He said: "Saggil-ramat, the wife [of] Abi-ili, the *ša šēpi* guard, (and) [PNf], the wife of Nabû-eṭir [...]

26 Previous edition: Fales and Lanfranchi Lettere (1992) 130f. [8-10] → LAS II 151 r.8; n. 98.
27 Assignation to Šamaš-metu-uballiṭ based on affinities with no. 26. Coll. S. Parpola, 14.11.66. [r.1] Possibly

FIG. 5. *Chariot wheel (cf. no. 25).*
ANE 124945.

FIG. 6. *Libbali-šarrat, wife of Assurbanipal. Drawing by A. Billerbeck (1867) from a relief in Assurbanipal's North Palace, Nineveh, published in* F. DELITZSCH, *Babel und Bibel* (Leipzig 1903), Abb. 28.

11 [*x x x x x x*]-*ka-ši i-na*
12 [*x x x x x x*] ⌜*lu*⌝-*ú-bal-liṭ*
13 [*x x x x x x x x x x x*]
Rev. beginning broken away
1′ [*x x x x x*]-*hi-ti né-ep-pa-áš*
2′ *ša* ⌜*x x x ú*⌝-*ma-a* ^{md}U.GUR—DÙ-*uš*
3′ *li*$^{!}$-*iz-zi-iz a-di* MÍ *tal-la-kan-ni*
4′ *am-mu-ú-ti il-la-ku-ú ú-la-a*
5′ *pa-ri-is-tu* LUGAL *liš-pu-ra*
6′ *šum-ma* LUGAL *i*$^{!}$-⌜*qab*⌝$^{!}$-[*b*]*i*$^{!}$ ⌜*ša*⌝$^{!}$ UD-29$^{!}$-KAM
7′ *mu-sa-ah*$^{!}$-[*x x x x x*] *lit-bu-ku*
8′ [*x*]*x an* [*x x x x x*] SIPA
9′ [*x x x x x x x x*]-*áš*
s.1 [*x x x*] *ma t*[*a*] *di x*[*x x x*]
2 [*x x x*]*x pa* [*x x x x x*]
3 [*x x x*] *a* [*x x x x x x*]

[11] [......] *her in*

[12] [...] should heal (them)

(Break)

[r.1] We shall perform [......], *for* [...].

[2] Now, let Nergal-epuš stay until the woman comes. Should the aforementioned go? If not, the king should send definite (orders).

[6] If the king commands, let the [...] be poured out on the 29th.

[8] [......] the shepherd

(Rest too broken for translation)

28. Dressing Down the Wife of the Crown Prince

K 1619b

1 *a-bat* DUMU.MÍ—LUGAL *a-na*
2 MÍ.URU.ŠÀ—URU—*šar-rat*
3 *a-ta-a ṭup-pi-ki la ta-šaṭ-ṭi-ri*
4 IM.GÍD-*ki la ta-qab-bi-i*
5 *ú-la-a i-qab-bi-ú*
6 *ma-a an-ni-tu-u* NIN-*sa*
r.1 *ša* MÍ.^{d}EDIN—*e-ṭè-rat*
2 DUMU.MÍ GAL-*tú ša* É—UŠ.MEŠ-*te*
3 *ša* ^{m}*aš-šur*—NIR.GÁL—DINGIR.MEŠ—GIN-*in-ni*
4 MAN GAL MAN *dan-nu* MAN ŠÚ MAN KUR—*aš-šur*
5 *ù at-ti ma-rat kal-lat* GAŠAN—É *ša* ^{m}*aš-šur*—DÙ—A
6 DUMU—MAN GAL *ša* É—UŠ.MEŠ-*te*
7 *ša* ^{m}*aš-šur*—PAB—AŠ MAN KUR—*aš*

ABL 308

[1] Word of the king's daughter to Libbali-šarrat.

[3] Why don't you write your tablet and do your homework? (For) if you don't, they will say: "Is this the sister of Šerua-eṭerat, the eldest daughter of the Succession Palace of Aššur-etel-ilani-mukinni, the great king, mighty king, king of the world, king of Assyria?"

[r.5] Yet you are (only) a daughter-in-law – the lady of the house of Assurbanipal, the great crown prince designate of Esarhaddon, king of Assyria.

restore [*nahnā*]*hiti*, "nostril."

28 Previous editions and translations: Oppenheim Letters (1967) 158, no. 97; Fales and Lanfranchi Lettere (1992) 72ff.; Kuhrt Ancient Near East (1995) 529. [r.3] Aššur-etel-ilani-mukinni (abbreviation for Aššur-etel-ilani-mukin-apli) was an alternate name of Esarhaddon. See PNA 1/I p. 184.

Letters from Assyria

3. Petitions to the King and the Crown Prince

FIG. 7. *Doing the king's work (reign of Sennacherib).*
ANE 124823.

29. Debts of the Governor of Barhalza

K 1287

1 [*a-na* LUGAL] *be-lí-iá* ARAD-*ka* ^{m}*mar-di-i*
2 [^{d}NIN.URTA] ^{d}ZA.BA$_4$.BA$_4$ ^{d}U.GUR ^{d}DI.KUD
3 [^{d}AG$^{?}$ *a-na* LUG]AL *dan-nu u ki-i-nu be-lí-iá lik-ru-bu*

4 [TA* *re-e-š*]*i* LÚ*.ARAD-*šú a-na-ku* ŠEŠ-*u-a a-na* ^{m}EN—NUMUN—DÙ *uš-mat-tan-ni*
5 [GÌR.2 DUMU—LUGAL] *a-ṣa-bat ina e-kel-ti bu-bu-ti la—pa-ni us-se-zib*
6 [TA* DUMU—LUGAL *be*]*-lí-iá a-na* ŠÀ URU.*i-si-ti ah-tal-qa re-e-mu a-na* LUGAL *iṣ-ṣa-bat*
7 [*x x x* LÚ*].A—KIN DUMU—LUGAL *is-si-ia is-sap-ra*
8 [*ma-a hi-bi-la-te*]*-šú ša* LÚ.EN.NAM *šá* KUR.*bar-hal-za ih-bil-šú-ni tu-sa-har ta-dan-áš-šú*

9 [^{d}E]N ^{d}PA *u* ^{d}UTU *ka-a-a$^{!}$-man ina* UGU LUGAL EN-*ia ú-ṣal-li*
10 [*m*]*u-uk* DUMU—LUGAL *be-lí* GIŠ.GU.ZA LUGAL-*ú-tú šá* É—AD-*šú li-iṣ-bat*
11 *a-na-ku* ARAD-*su* UR.KU-*šú u pa-lih-šú i-na* GIŠ.MI-*šú la-mur nu-ú-ru*

12 ^{d}EN ^{d}PA *u* ^{d}UTU *ṣu-le-e-ka ki-i iš-mu-ú-ni*
13 LUGAL-*ti šá da-ra-a-ta* BALA-*e* GÍD.DA.MEŠ *a-na* LUGAL *be-lí-iá it-tan-nu*
14 *ù ki-ma ṣe-e-ta* ^{d}UTU-*ši* KUR.KUR *gab-bi ina ṣe-e-ti-ka nam-ru*
15 *ù a-na-ku ina* ŠÀ *e-ṭu-ti kar$^{!}$-rak me-me-ni a-di pa-an* LUGAL *la$^{!}$-a ú-qar-rab-an-ni*
16 *ha-ba-la-ta-ia ša a-na* DUMU—LUGAL EN-*iá ah-hur-u-ni* LUGAL *be-lí is-si-ia iš-pur-u-ni*

ABL 916

1 [To the king], my lord: your servant Mardî. May [Ninurta], Zababa, Nergal, Madanu [*and Nabû*] bless the strong and righteous [kin]g, my lord.

4 [From the beginn]ing I have been his servant. My brother tried to make Bel-zeru-ibni kill me, (but) I grasped [the feet of the crown prince], saved myself from it in darkness and hunger, and fled to *the tower* [with the crown prince], my [l]ord. Compassion took hold of the king; [*at my return*], the crown prince sent a messenger with me, [saying], "You are to give him back [the things] that the governor of Barhalza owes him."

9 I constantly prayed to [B]el, Nabû and Šamaš for the king, my lord, saying, "May the crown prince, my lord, seize the royal throne of his father's house! I am his servant and his dog, who fears him; may I see light under his protection!"

12 Bel, Nabû and Šamaš heard (this) prayer for you, and they gave the king, my lord, an everlasting kingship (and) a long reign. And like sunshine, all the countries are illuminated by your light. But I have been left in darkness; no one brings me before the king. My outstanding debts, because of which I appealed to the crown prince, my lord, and (because of which) the king, my lord, sent

29 Previous (unpublished) edition: Deller Lautlehre (1959) 89ff. → SAA 10 109. Horizontal tablet (obv. and rev. 1 written on the edges). 1 Surely the same Mardî, servant of the governor of Barhalza, who sells slaves and an orchard in SAA 6 90 (see PNA 2/II s.v. Mardî). In the present letter the crown prince = the king. This implies that it (like SAA 10 109) originates from the very beginning of Esarhaddon's reign, cf. especially the lines 7, 9f, 12 and 16. 2 There is not enough space for restoring [*lū šulmu ana šarri bēlīja* at the beginning of the line. 4 For the restoration cf. SAA 10 294:14. The name Bel-zeru-ibni is erroneously rendered as Bel-zeru-epuš in PNA 1/II p. 340. 6 For this line cf. SAA 10 109:11. *ana isīti halāqu* seems to be an idiom (or a code or periphrasis) in which the word *tower* may refer either to the northern, mountainous region, or a specific fort somewhere. In itself, URU.*i-si-ti* (and URU.*a-ši-ti* in SAA 10 109) could be taken as a syllabic spelling for the city Issete (normally written URU.I-*tú/te*). However, this is unlikely since Issete was not situated in the area where Esarhaddon escaped his assassination. The restoration [TA* DUMU—LUGAL] imposes itself from the context. 9 Y 83, W 260. 15 *kar$^{!}$-rak* coll. K. Deller 1966 ("perfectly clear *kar*"); cf. SAA 10 182 r.13 and 242:9, SAA 1 179 r.4, CT 53 169:10. *la$^{!}$* coll. W 260. 17 See coll.

17 *ma-a hi-bil-a-te-šú sa-ha-ra di-na*

r.1 *ú-ma-a* ^{m}*se-e'—ra-pa-a'* LÚ.EN.NAM *la i-ma-gúr la id-dan ma-a* LUGAL *mu-hur*$^{!}$
2 [*x x x x x x x x x x x x x*]*x-an-ni* KUR.*bar-hal-za-a-a i-zi-ru-u-ni*
3 [*x x x x x x x x x x x ma*]-⌈*a*⌉ A$^{!}$.ŠÀ GIŠ.SAR.MEŠ *la tu-sa-har la ta-dan-áš-šú*

4 [*x x x x x x x x x x x x x x x x x x x x*] *šá-me-e ep-šú*
5 [*x x x x x x x x x x x x x x x x x x x x*]*x ir-bu-u'*
6 [*x x x x x x x x x x x x x x x x x x x x*]*x la i-di-na*
7 [*x x x x x x x x x x x x x x x x x x x* ^{m}*lu*]*—šá-kín* LUGAL *liš-al-šú*
8 [*x x x x x x x x x x x x x x x x x x x x x x x x x x-i*]*a*
9 [*x x x x x x x x x x x x x x x x x x x x x x x x x x x*]*x*
10 [*x x x x x x x x x x x x x x x x x x x x x x x x x x-á*]*š*
11 [*x x x x x x x x x x x x x x x x x x x x x x x x x*]*-sa-ak*
12 [*x x x x x x x x x x x x x x x x x x x x x x x x x*]*x-bu*
13 [*x x x x x x x x x x x x x x x x x x x x x x x x x*]*-ni*
14 [*x x x x x x x x x x x x x x x x x x x x x x x x x*] *id-din-ak-kan-ni*
15 [*x x x x x x x x x x x x x x x x x x x x x* LUGAL *be-lí lu*] *ú-da*

(his messenger) with me, saying, "Give his outstanding debts back to him!" —

r.1 now Se'-rapa', the governor, refuses to give them (back), saying, "Appeal to the king!"

2 [......] the Barhalzeans hate me

3 [......] "Do you not give the field and orchards back to him!"

4 [......] have been done [*without*] listening to [...]

5 [......] ...

6 [......] he has not given

7 [...... Lu]-šakin. May the king ask him!

(Break)

14 [...... which] he gave to you

15 [...... The king, my lord, should] know [*this*].

30. May the King Save Me

K 505

1 *a-na* LUGAL *be-lí-ia*
2 ARAD-*ka* ^{m}Ì.GÁL—DINGIR
3 LÚ.*pa-hi-zu*
4 DUG_4.DUG_4.ME *ša a-hur-u-ni*
5 *a-na* AD-*ka aq-bu-u-ni*
6 ŠEŠ-*u-a ina* UGU-*hi*
7 *de-e-ke*
8 DUMU-*a-a ina pi-i-šú*
9 *ṭa-bi-ih*
r.1 BÀD$^{!}$ [*ma*]*-ki-i* LUGAL
2 LUGAL$^{!}$ *liš-al*
3 *a-na-ku ša du-a-ki*
4 *hal-qa-ku ad-du*$^{!}$*-al*
5 *ina* ŠÀ-*bi* LUGAL *at-*[*te*]*-'i-la*
6 LUGAL *lu-še-zib-an-ni*
rest uninscribed

ABL 166

1 To the king, my lord: your servant Ibašši-ilu, the ...

4 My brother has died on account of the lawsuit for which I appealed to your father, and my son is being slaughtered because of it.

r.1 The king is the bulwark of the [w]eak one. Let the king ask: I am about to be killed, lost, roaming about.

5 I have *found rest* in the reign of the king. May the king save me!

and cf. W 260. r.1 Reading *mu-hur*$^{!}$ as suggested by Deller Lautlehre p. 90. See coll. r.3 See coll. W 260. r.4 Or: "done [in] heaven." Syllabically written *šá-me-e* "sky, heaven" is extremely rare but possible, cf. SAA 8 57 r.3 by Nabû-ahhe-eriba. He also often wrote *ša-mu-ú* in his glosses, see SAA 8 glossary.

30 4-9 → Parpola, JSS 21 (1976) 173. r.1, 4 See coll. r.4 This is probably an ellipsis for the idiom *akī kalbi asabbu' adualla*, cf., for instance, SAA 13 190 r.20f, 15 288:5f.

31. May the King Let me See Light

Bu 91-5-9,110

1 *a-na* LUGAL EN-*ia* ARAD-*ka* ^{m}NÍG.GUB
2 DUMU ^{md}UTU—*ib-ni me-e-te*
3 *ša* LUGAL *ú-bal-liṭ-ú-ni*
4 *lu-u* DI-*mu a-na* LUGAL EN-*ia*
5 ^{d}*aš-šur* ^{d}UTU $^{d+}$EN *u* ^{d}PA *a-na* LUGAL
6 EN-*ia lik-ru-bu* KASKAL.2 *pa-ni-ú*
7 LUGAL *be-lí re-e-ši it-ti-ši*
8 [TA* Š]À (*i*)-*ri-kal-la us-se-la-an-ni*
9 [*mì-nu x x x*]*x a-di-ni ina a-bat* LUGAL
10 [*x x x x x na*]-⸢*ṣu*$^{!}$⸣-*niš-šú*
rest broken away
Rev. beginning broken away
1′ LUGAL *nu-ú-ru*$^{!}$ *lu-*⸢*kal-lim*$^{!}$⸣-*an-ni*
2′ *dà-lí-lí ša* LUGAL EN-*ia*
3′ *la-ad-lul ki-i kal-bi*
4′ *ina si-in-qi ina bu-bu-ti*
5′ *ša* NINDA.HI.A *lu la a-mu-ʾa-at*
rest uninscribed

ABL 756

1 To the king, my lord: your servant Kudurru, son of Šamaš-ibni, a dead man whom the king revived. Good health to the king, my lord! May Aššur, Šamaš, Bel and Nabû bless the king, my lord.

6 In the previous expedition the king, my lord, summoned me and raised me [from] the netherworld.

9 [*What*] have I given [...]? At the king's order they have [bro]ught [...] to me.

(Break)

r.1 May the king let me s[e]e light, and I will glorify the king, my lord! May I not die of distress and lack of food like a dog!

32. Justice Turned Upside Down

Bu 89-4-26,4

1 *a-na* LUGAL *be-li-ia*
2 ARAD-*ka* ^{m}⸢^{d}PA$^{!!}$⸣—NUMU[N$^{!}$—GI]N$^{!}$—⸢GIŠ⸣
3 LÚ.[*šá*—UGU—*hu-luh-hi*]
4 ⸢*lu*⸣-*u* DI-⸢*mu*⸣ *a-na* ⸢LUGAL EN⸣-*iá*
5 *aš-šur* $^{d+}$EN *u* ^{d}[UTU$^{?}$] *u* ^{d}⸢PA$^{?}$⸣
6 [*x x x x x x x x x*]
7 [*x x x x x x x x*]-*ti*
8 [*x x x x x x x x x*]
9 [*x x x x x x x x x*]
10 [*x x x x x x x x x*]
11 [*x x x x x x x x*] *aš-šur*
12 [*x x x x x x x x*]-*ši*
13 *a-na* [*x x x x x x*]-*din*
14 [*x x x x x x x*] MA.NA
15 [*x x x x x x x*]-*di*
16 [*x x x du*]*l*$^{?}$-*li-ia*
17 [*x x x x x x x x x*]
18 [*x x x x x x x x x*]
19 [*x x x x x x x x*]-*ši*
20 [*x x x x x x x x x*]
21 [*x x x x x x x x x*]
22 [*x x x x x x x x x*]
e.23 [*x*] *iš l*[*a x x x x x x*]
24 [*x*] *e* [*x x x x x x x*]
r.1 [^{m}]^{d}AMAR.UTU—MAN—PAB [*x x x x*]
2 [*li*]*p-qi-id is-si-i*[*a x x x*]

ABL 1250

1 To the king, my lord: your servant Nabû-ze[r-ket]ti-lešir, the [*overseer of white frit*]. Good health to the king, my lord! [May] Aššur, Bel and [*Šamaš*] and *Nabû* [bless the king, my lord].

(Break)

11 [......](-)Aššur
12 [......]
13 [ga]ve [...] to [...]
14 [......] mina(s)
16 [... for] my [*wo*]*rk*
(Break)

r.1 May [the king, my lord], appoint Marduk-šarru-uṣur [...], (and) may he do [......]

31 1 For Kudurru see Nissinen, SAAS 7 (1998) 133ff. 10 Cf. e.g. *na-ṣu-niš-šú* SAA 1 32:10; *-ni-šú* SAA 1 236 r.8, 245 r.2. r.1 See coll.
32 2 See coll. 16 *du*]*l*- very doubtful; see coll. r.3 See coll. r.5f Oppenheim, JAOS 61 (1941) 259. r.7 →

3 ⌜*le*$^{!?}$⌝*-pu-uš ú-ma-a x*[*x x x x*]
4 *de-e-ni la-a e-pa-áš* [0]
5 *da-ba-bu ša* LUGAL *la iš-me*
6 *e-ni ša* LÚ.NAM.MEŠ *i-da-gal*

7 *a-ni-na* LUGAL *be-li de-e-nu*
8 *ša* AD-*ka e-pu-šú-u-ni*
9 *ṭè-e-mu iš-ku-nu-u-ni*
10 *ú-ma-a an-nu-(rig) ú-sa-bal-ki-tú*
11 *ù a-na-ku* TA* ŠÀ É—AD-*ia gab-bu*
12 *ki-i kal-bi a-sa-ab-bu-u*ʾ
13 *ra*$^{!}$*-mì-ni-ia la-ah-ri-id*
14 *ma-ṣar-tu ša* LUGAL EN-*ia la-ṣur*
15 BÀD *ma-ki-i* LUGAL LUGAL *be-li*
16 *ki-i ša i-la-u-ni le-pu-uš*
17 *man-nu at-ta* LÚ.A.BA
18 *ša ta-sa-su-u-ni*
19 TA* IGI LUGAL EN-*ka la tu-pa-*⌜*zar*⌝
20 *ṭa-ab-ti ina* IGI LUGAL *qi-bi*
21 EN ^{d}AG *ṭa-ab-ta-ka*
22 *ina* IGI LUGAL *liq-bi-ú*

with m[e]. Now the [...] is not doing justice (to [me]) (and) does not obey the orders of the king, (but) is seeking favour in the eyes of the governors.

7 Hear me, O king, my lord! They have right now turned upside down the justice which your father did (and) the order that he gave. And I (alone) out of the entire house of my father am bounding about like a dog.

13 Let me keep vigil and watch for the king, my lord, on my own. The king is the bulwark of the weak one. Let the king, my lord, do as he pleases.

17 Whoever you are, O scribe, who are reading (this letter), do not hide it from the king, your lord! Speak for me before the king, so Bel (and) Nabû may speak for you before the king.

33. Partial Duplicate of No. 32

82-5-22,150

1 [*a-na* LUGAL] *be-li-ia*
2 [ARAD-*ka* ^{md}]PA—NUMUN—GIN—SI.SÁ
3 [LÚ.*šá*—UG]U$^{!}$*—hu-luh*$^{!}$*-hi*
4 [*lu-u* DI-*m*]*u a-na* LUGAL EN-*ia*
5 [*aš-šur* ^{d}30 ^{d}]*šá-maš* ^{d}EN ^{d}AG
6 [^{d}15 *š*]*a* URU.NINA.KI
7 [^{d}15 *š*]*a* URU.*arba-ìl*
8 [*a-na* LUGAL E]N-*ia li-ik-ru-bu*
9 [SUHUŠ GIŠ.GU].ZA LUGAL-*ti-ka*
10 [*a-na* UD-*me*] *ṣa-a-ti*
11 [*x x x x*]*x lu-ki-in-nu*
rest broken away
Rev. beginning broken away
1′ [*x x x x x*] *a-ta-a*
2′ [*ṭè-e-mu ša* AD-*k*]*a*$^{?}$ *iš-ku-nu-u-*[*ni*]
3′ [*de-e-nu ša e-pu-u*]*š-u-ni*
4′ [*ú-ma-a ú-sa-ba*]*l*$^{!}$*-ki-tú*
5′ [*a-na-ku* TA ŠÀ É—A]D$^{!}$*-ia gab-bu*
6′ [*ki-i kal-bi a-sa-a*]*b-bu-u*ʾ
7′ [*ina ra-mì-ni*]*-ia*$^{!}$ ⌜*la*$^{!}$⌝*-ah-ri-id*
8′ [EN.NUN *ša*] LUGAL EN-*ia la-aṣ-ṣur*
9′ [*x x* L]Ú *ša a-na* LUGAL EN-*šú*
10′ [*i-d*]*u-lu-u-ni*
11′ [*la i-mu-a*]*t* LUGAL *be-li*
12′ [*ki-i ša*] *i-la-*ʾ*u-u-ni*
13e [*le-p*]*u-uš*

ABL 1107

1 [To the king], my lord: [your servant] Nabû-zer-ketti-lešir, the [*oversee*]*r of white frit*. [Good hea]lth to the king, my lord! May [Aššur, Sîn], Šamaš, Bel, Nabû, [Ištar o]f Nineveh (and) [Ištar o]f Arbela bless [the king], my [lo]rd.

9 May they consolidate [the foundations of] your royal [thr]one [until] far-off [days ...]!

(Break)

r.1 [Now], why [have they turne]d upside down [the order that *yo*]*ur* [*father*] gave (and) [the justice which he d]id? [I (alone) out of my whole pate]rnal [house am boundi]ng about [like a dog].

7 Let me keep vigil and [watch for] the king, my lord, [on] my [own].

9 [... May] the man who [se]rves the king, his lord, [not die]! The king, my lord, [may] (however) do [as] he pleases.

Nissinen, SAAS 7 (1998) 110 n.428. r.17-22 → Oppenheim, AS 16 (1965) 256.
33 3 See coll. r.1-8 Paralleled by no. 32 r.8-16. r.7, 11 See coll.

34. Let me Finish my Father's Work in Calah

K 521

1 [a-na] DUMU—LUGAL EN-ia ARAD-ka ^{m}šu-ma$^{!}$-⌈a⌉-[a]
2 [lu-u] šul-mu a-na DUMU—LUGAL EN-i[a]
3 [^{d}]PA u ^{d}AMAR.UTU a-na DUMU—LUGAL EN-ia lik-r[u-bu]

4 dul-lu ša URU.tar-bi-ṣi ša e-pu-šu-[u-ni]
5 LUGAL AD-ka e-ta-mar at-ta-ah-[rid]
6 e-ta-pa-áš mu-uk šu-mì ina pa-an EN-[ia]
7 lu-u de-e-iq ú-ma-a LÚ*.A.BA
8 ša AD-ú-a a-na ma-né-e ša dul-li
9 TA* ŠU.2 LÚ.šak-ru-te ip-qí-du-u-ni
10 ù LÚ.A—SIG$_{5}$ ša AD-ia ša ina dul-li
11 pa-qu-du-u-ni qa-an-ni iš-mu-u-ni
12 ma-a LÚ.A.BA pa-qí-id dul-lu it-ta-ṣu
13 ur-ta-am-me-u ih-tal-q[u] ⌈É$^{?}$⌉ KUG.UD
14 ša re-eh-te dul-li [LUGAL b]e-lí
15 la id-di-na ú-ma-a šum$^{!}$-⌈ma$^{!}$ pa-an DUMU⌉—LUGAL
16 ma-hi-ir NÍG.ŠID$^{!}$-ia liš-ku-nu DUMU—LUGAL be-lí-iá
17 dul-lu lip-qid ù a-na-ku dul-lu
18 ša ina URU.kal-ha ša ina UGU AD-ia
19 le-e-pu-uš a-na DUMU—LUGAL la-ad-din
20 me-me-e-ni la-áš-šú la-a i-šá-man-ni
21 il-la-ka a-na la LÚ ina pa-an DUMU—LUGAL
22 a-tu-ar a-mu-at šum-ma DUMU—LUGAL be-lí
23 pa-ni-šú ina UGU-hi-ia us-sa-hi-ra
24 dul-la-ni ša DUMU—LUGAL ep-pa-áš
e.25 a-na DUMU—LUGAL EN-ia ad-dan
26 ki-ma a-na-ku la-a e-pu-uš
27 man-nu-um-ma le-e-pu-uš
r.1 a-na DUMU—LUGAL li$^{!}$-id-din$^{!}$
2 LÚ*.IGI—ma-né-e LÚ*.⌈šak$^{!}$-ru$^{!}$⌉-te
3 le-e-pu-šú DUMU—LUGAL be-lí lu-u da-ra
4 a-na-ku ina ŠÀ a-hi-ia GÌR$^{!}$.2-ia
5 a-na DUMU—LUGAL EN-ia la-ap-làh

6 DUMU—LUGAL be-lí liš-al TA* AD—AD-ia
7 ^{m}aš-šur—EN—GIN LÚ*.SAG la-a iz-zi-zi
8 id—da-te ki-i AD—AD-ka ina GIŠ.GU$^{!}$.ZA$^{!}$
9 ú-si-ib-u-ni a-na LÚ*.A.BA-[ú]-te
10 la iš-kun-šu-u ú-ma-a DUMU—LUGAL be-lí
11 lu la ú-ra-man-ni šu-mu ša AD—AD-šú
12 ma-za-as-su ša AD-ia TA* É-ka

ABL 885

[1] [To] the crown prince, my lord: your servant Šumay[a. Good] health to the crown prince, m[y] lord! May Nabû and Marduk ble[ss] the crown prince, my lord.

[4] The king, your father, saw the work that I did in Tarbiṣu. I did it caref[ully], thinking: "May my name be good before [my] lord."

[7] Now, the scribe whom my father appointed to count the work done by the *drunks*, and the *nobles* of my father who were assigned to the work — the moment they heard that a scribe had been appointed, they quit the work and ran away. [The king], my [l]ord, did not give me [*a hou*]*se* (nor) silver for the rest of [the] work.

[15] Now, if it is acceptable to the crown prince, let them settle my accounts, let the crown prince hand over the work, and let me do the work in Calah assigned to my father and deliver it to the crown prince.

[20] Nobody listens to me. (Should) it come to pass that I become a nobody before the crown prince, I will die. If only the crown prince, my lord, would turn his attention to me, I'd perform the works of the crown prince and deliver them to the crown prince, my lord. If I did not do it, who would do and deliver (them) to the crown prince? Would the accountant (and) the *drunks* do it?

[r.3] May the crown prince, my lord, live forever, (and) may I revere the crown prince, my lord, with my arms and feet!

[6] The crown prince, my lord, may enquire: Was my grandfather not assisted by the eunuch Aššur-belu-ka''in, (and) afterwards, when your grandfather ascended the throne, did he not appoint him to the position of a scribe? Now, may the crown prince, my lord, not forsake me! May the name of his grandfather and the position of my father not be

34 [1] See coll. [11ff] See LAS II 239:5. [13, 15] See coll. [17ff, 24f] Cf. LAS II 252:10. [23] Lit. "turns his face towards me." [e.26] See LAS II 156:11. [r.1f] See coll. [r.4] See coll. [r.4f] Cf. SAA 10 198 r.5 and LAS II 124 r.4. [r.6f] Or: "serve." [r.6-10] Contrary to the interpretation given in PNA 1/I p. 172 sub Aššur-belu-ka''in 5, we consider it more plausible that these negated rhetorical questions imply that Šumaya's grandfather was assisted by the eunuch Aššur-belu-ka''in and appointed as a (chief?) scribe by Sennacherib. Cf., e.g., *anāku lā ūdâ* "Do I not know?" in ABL 523:8, 1002 r.5. [r.8] See coll. [r.15f] Probably an elliptical variant of the phrase in obv. 23. [r.18] See coll. and W

13 *lu la i-hal-liq* AD-*u-a* AD—AD-*ia*
14 *ina* É-*ka it-ti-ti-is-su* LUGAL AD-*ka*
15 DUMU EN—*dul-li i-ra-am pa-ni-šú*
16 *ina* UGU DUMU EN—*dul-li ia-u mi-i-nu*
17 *hi-iṭ-ṭa-a-a* UR.KU *ša* DUMU—LUGAL
18 *a-na-ku*$^{!}$ *ina as-ku-pe-te ša* É-*ka*
19 [*a-du-a*]*l* DUMU—LUGAL *be-lí lu la ú-ra-man-ni*

20 [*a-na-ku*] *ú-da* DUMU—LUGAL *be-lí*

21 [*x x*] *ri*$^{?}$ *ni*$^{?}$ *u ni a-di an*-[*x x*]
22 [*x x*]*x* TA* *im* DUMU—LUGAL *ú-šab*

23 [*x x*] *ni šú* [*x x*] *mu*$^{?}$ *li*$^{?}$ [*x*] *me u* [*x*]
24 [*x x x x*] *li-is*-[*x x x*]

25e [DUMU—LUGAL] ⌜*be*$^{!}$-*li*⌝$^{!}$ *ú-da* [0]
26e [*x x*] EN—É *me*$^{!}$-*e-te*$^{!}$
s.1 É *i—da-tu-uš-šú i-hal-liq* DUMU—LUGAL *la-a ú-r*[*am-man-ni*]

lost from your house!

13 My father (and) my grandfather stayed in your house. The king, your father, loves the son of one who worked for him, feels concern for the son of one who worked for him. What is my fault? I am a dog of the crown prince, [running abo]ut at the threshold of your house. May the crown prince, my lord, not forsake me!

20 [I] know (that) the crown prince, my lord,

21 [...] ... *until* [...]

22 [...] ... the crown prince will ascend (the throne)

23 [...] *him* [...] ... [...] ... [...]

24 [...] *let* [...]

25 [The crown prince], my lord, knows (that) [*once* ...] the master of the house is dead, the house (too) will perish after him. May the crown prince not fo[rsake me]!

35. Paying back Father's Debts

83-1-18,111

1 *a-na* DUMU—LUGAL EN-*ia*
2 ARAD-*ka* ^{m}*šu-ma-a-a*
3 *lu-u šul-mu a-na* DUMU—LUGAL EN-*ia*
4 ^{d}AG *u* ^{d}AMAR.UTU *a-na* DUMU—LUGAL EN-*ia*
5 *lik-ru-bu* 1-*lim* ŠE.PAD.MEŠ *ša* LUGAL
6 *ina pa-an* AD-*ia ú-ma-a a-na-ku*
7 4-*me* ŠE.PAD.MEŠ TA* ŠÀ-*bi at-ti-din*
8 6-*me* ŠE.PAD.MEŠ *ina pa-ni-ia re-e-ha-at*
rest broken away
Rev. beginning broken away
1′ *nu*-[*x x x*]-*an*$^{?}$ *a-na* DUMU—LUGAL
2′ EN-*ia at-ta-har* DUMU—LUGAL *be-lí*
3′ *lu la ú-ra-man-ni*
4′ *me-me-e-ni le-e-pu-uš*
5′ [*ki*]-*i ša* UD-*mu an-ni-ú*
6′ [LÚ].MAH.MEŠ-*ni ša* KUR.KUR *gab-bu*
7′ [*ina pa*]-*an* AD-*ka e-ti-qu-u-ni*
8′ [*ki*]-⌜*i*⌝ *an-ni-im-ma ina pa-an* DUMU—MAN
9e E[N$^{!}$-*i*]*a*$^{!}$ 1-*lim* MU.AN.NA.MEŠ
10e [0 *le*]-*e-ti-qu*

ABL 948

1 To the crown prince, my lord: your servant Šumaya. Good health to the crown prince, my lord! May Nabû and Marduk bless the crown prince, my lord.

5 1,000 (homers) of barley from the king were at my father's disposal. Now I have given 400 (homers) of barley from it, 600 (homers) of barley remain at my disposal.

(Break)

r.1 [......] I have appealed to the crown prince, my lord. May the crown prince, my lord, not leave me in the lurch, (but) do something.

5 Just as today the emissaries of all the countries pass [bef]ore your father, so [may] they pass before the crown prince, [m]y lo[rd], for a thousand years.

254. r.25 See coll.
35 r.5-10 → Postgate, TCAE (1974) 126. r.9 See coll.

36. May the King Have Mercy on his Dog

K 1201

beginning broken away

1′ [*x x x x x x x x x x x x x*]*x sal*? ⌜*x*⌝
2′ *x*[*x x*]*x x*[*x x*]*x ka nu* [*x x*]*x* ⌜*x*⌝ *tu*? *ub*?
3′ *hi-ṭu dan-nu ina* É—EN.MEŠ-*ia ah-ti-ṭi*
4′ *ša du-a-ki a-na-ku la-a šá bal-lu-ṭi a-na-ku*
5′ LUGAL *be-lí re-e-mu a-na kal-bi-šú is-sa-kan*
6′ *i—ku-me a-na-ku mi-i-nu a-na* LUGAL EN-*ia*
7′ *ú-šal-lim* ŠÀ-*bi* Á.2.MEŠ-*ia* GÌR.2.MEŠ-*ia*
8′ *ina* KI.TA GIŠ.*mu-gir ša* LUGAL EN-*ia šá-kín*
9′ *ka-a-a-ma-nu* IGI.2.MEŠ-*ia* TA* LUGAL EN-*ia*
10′ *šak-na ù ka-a-a-ma-nu* DUMU—LUGAL *be-lí*
11′ ŠÀ-*bu i-šá-kan-an-ni a-du* DUMU—LUGAL *an-na-kan-ni*
12′ *a-na* DI-*me a-na* URU.NINA *la-a il-lak-u-ni*
13′ *a-na-ku a-ke-e le-e-pu-uš*
14′ *a-na* MAN [EN]-*ia ki-il-lu la-a áš-kun*
15′ LUGAL *be-lí re-e-mu ina* UGU UN.MEŠ-*šú*
e.16′ *li-i*[*š-kun*]
r.1 *a-du* DUMU—LUGAL *an-na-*[*kan-ni x x x*]
2 *li-iṣ-bat* DINGIR.MEŠ-*k*[*a lik-ru-bu-šú*]
3 *né-mal-šu a-na*! LUGAL EN-*ia lu-*[*kal-li-mu*]
4 LUGAL *re-e-mu ina* UGU *kal-bi-šú li-i*[*š-kun*]
5 LÚ*.ARAD *ra-ʾi-mu ša* EN.MEŠ-*šú a-na-ku*
6 LÚ*.ARAD *ša* ŠÀ-*bu-šú a-na* EN.MEŠ-*šú ga-mur-u-ni*
7 *a-na-ku la-a a-ki an-ni-e a-na* LUGAL EN-*ia aq-bi*
8 *mu-ku ki-na-ta-te-ia gab-bu li-iz-zi-ru-u-ni*
9 *mi-i-nu ep-pa-šu-u-ni mu-ku at-ta* LUGAL *be-lí*
10 *ú-de-*[*e-ka*] *is-si-ia*
11 *bi-*[*x x x x x*]*-a-te ša* LUGAL EN-*ia*
12 *x*[*x x x x x x*] LUGAL *be-lí lu-u dà-ri*
13 [LUGAL *be-lí re-e*]*-mu ina* UGU ARAD-*šú*
14 [*li-iš-kun ú-ma-a š*]*úm-ma ma-hir*
15 [*ina* IGI LUGAL EN-*ia a-na* U]RU.ŠÀ—URU
16 [*x x x x x x x*] LÚ* TÚG.*zi-zi-ik-tú*
17 [*x x x x x x x x*]*-ru-u-ni-ni*
18 [*x x x x x x x x*]*x* IGI ^{d}30
19 [*x x x x x x x x x x*]-⌜*e*⌝*-mu*
20 [*x x x x x x x x x x x x*]

rest broken away

ABL 620

(Beginning destroyed)

3 I committed a serious crime against the house of my lords. I (deserved) to be killed, not to be kept alive. Yet the king, my lord, had mercy on his dog. What I have rendered to the king, my lord, instead? My heart, my arms (and) my feet are placed beneath the chariot of the king, my lord. My eyes are constantly fixed upon the king, my lord, and the crown prince, my lord, constantly encourages me.

11 As long as the crown prince is here and not going for the audience to Nineveh, how should I act? I have not set up a wail to the king, my [lord], (but) the king, my lord, should h[ave] mercy on his people.

r.1 As long as the crown prince is he[re], let him seize [...]. [May] yo[ur] gods [bless him] and may they let the king, my lord, see him prosper!

4 May the king h[ave] mercy on his dog. I am a servant who loves his lords; I am a servant whose heart is entirely devoted to his lords. Have I not said to the king, my lord, as follows: "Even if all my colleagues curse me, what can they do to me? You are the king, my lord. Only [you] (are) with me."

11 The [...]s of the king, my lord, [......]. May the king, my lord, live forever! [May the king, my lord have mer]cy on this servant!

14 [Now, i]f it is acceptable [to the king, my lord, ...] to the Inner City.

16 [......] a man — the hem

17 [......]

18 [......] before Sîn

19 [... *mer*]*cy*

(Rest destroyed)

36 Deller, AOAT 1 (1969) 58 assigns this letter to Adad-šumu-uṣur. However, this is contradicted by the spellings *šúm-ma* and *mu-ku*, which are not attested in the letters of Adad-šumu-uṣur (cf. LAS II, Appendix M6). 2 See coll. 3ff Cf. LAS II 121:21. 3-11, r.5-7 → Fales, HANEM 4 (2000) 238a. r.3 See coll. r.8f → AOAT (1969) 58.

37. ———

K 7416

beginning broken away
1′ [*x x x x* DUMU—MA]N ˹EN˺-[*ia*]
2′ [*x x x x*] *a—dan-niš a—dan-niš*
3′ [*lik-ru-bu*] *mì-i-nu*
4′ [*ša ši-ti*]-*ni*
5′ [*x x x*]-*ka pa-ni-ka*
6′ [SIG$_5$].MEŠ *la-mur*
7′ [*la*]-*as-hu-ra*
8′ [*ina* U]GU *dul-li-ia*
9′ [*la-a*]*l-li-ka*
rest broken away
Rev. beginning broken away
1′ [*x x x x x x*]-*ia*
2′ [*x x x x x x*]-*ni*
3′ [*x x* DUMU—MAN] EN-*ia*
4′ [*x x x x x*]-*ti*
5′ [*x x x x*] DUMU—MAN EN-*ia*
6′ [*x x x x*]-*ni*
7′ [*x x x x*] *e-ta-mar*
8′ [*x x x ki*]-*i ha-nim-ma*
9′ [*x x x x x*] ˹*x x*˺ [*x*]
rest broken away

CT 53 353

(Beginning destroyed)

1 [May DNN *bless* the crow]n [prince, my] lord, [...] very greatly.

3 [May they ...] you what[ever it be].

5 May I see your [beautiful] face, and [may] I (then) [c]ome [b]ack [to] my work.

(Break)

r.1 [...] my [...]
2 [......]
3 [... *of* the crown prince], my lord
4 [......]
5 [... *of*] the crown prince, my lord
6 [......]
7 [...] he saw
8 [... i]n like manner
(Rest destroyed)

38. Fragment of a Letter to the Crown Prince

K 14601

Obv. completely broken away, except for ends of two lines seen reverse
1′ [*a-na* DUMU—LUGAL *be-lí-i*]*a*
2′ [*a—dan-niš a—dan-niš lik-ru-b*]*u*
Rev. beginning broken away
1′ [*x x x x*]*x x*[*x x x*]
2′ [ŠÀ-*bu š*]*a* DUMU—M[AN]
3′ [*be-lí-i*]*a lu* DÙG.GA
rest uninscribed

CT 53 538

(Beginning destroyed)

1 [May DNN bles]s [the crown prince, m]y [lord, very greatly].

(Break)

r.1 [......]

2 The cr[own] prince, [m]y [lord], can be [hap]py.

39. Appeal on Behalf of a Woman

Sm 1072

1 *a*-[*na* LUGAL *be-lí-ia*]
2 A[RAD-*ka* ^{m}*x x x x*]
3 *lu* D[I-*mu a-na* LUGAL *be-lí-ia*]
4 ^{d}PA [^{d}AMAR.UTU *a-na* LUGAL *be-lí-i*]*a*
5 *lik*-[*ru-bu*]
6 *ina* UGU [*x x x x x x*]
7 *šá* ^{m}[*x x x ina* UGU-*šá*?]
8 LUGAL [*i-hu-ru-u-ni*]
9 *ma-a* [LUGAL *be-l*]*í*

ABL 1061

1 T[o the king, my lord: your] se[rvant PN]. Good he[alth to the king, my lord]! May Nabû (and) [Marduk] bl[ess the king, my lord]!

6 As to [......] concerning whom (f.) [PN appealed to] the king, [saying]: "[The king,

10 *ú-d[a ki-i x x x]-ni*
11 *ma-a ina [x x x x x]x-šá*
12 *a-mu-at [ma-a* LUGAL *de]-⸢e⸣-ni*
13 *le-pu-uš an-nu-rig*
14 *a-na* LUGAL *be-lí-ia*
15 *as-sap-ra un-qu*
16e *liš-[pu]-ru*
r.1 *li-di-nu-ni-šú*
2 *mi-i-mi-ni is-si-šú*
3 *li-ip-qid-du*
4 *di-in-šú le-pu-šu*
rest uninscribed

m]y [lord], kno[ws that ......]. I am dying be[cause of] her [...]. Let [the king] do me [jus]tice!"

[13] Now, I am writing to the king, my lord. Let them se[n]d a sealed order and give it to him, and let them appoint somebody with him to do him justice.

40. Complaints by Blacksmiths

K 971

1 2-*me* GÍR.AN.BAR
2 1-*me pur-ṭí-e* AN.BAR
3 25 GAG AN.BAR *ša ki-pa-ni*
4 2-*me pa-ki* AN.BAR
5 *né-ta-pa-áš ni-ti-din*
6 2-*me-ma pa-ki* AN.BAR
7 [[*pa-ki* AN.BAR]] *la-mu-qa-ni*
8 *la né-pa-áš*
9 ŠEŠ-*u-ni ina* É LÚ*.NINDA
10 *i-mu-at ša dul-lu*
11 *an-ni-e gab-bi*
12 *bu-le-e me-me-ni*
13 *la i-di-na-⸢na⸣-[še]*
14 *ina* ŠÀ-*bi a-[x x]*
15 *la ni-ha-[ṣi-in x x]*
16 *⸢i⸣-[x x x x x]*
e.17 KUR? *x[x x x x x x]*
r.1 TA* ŠÀ-*b[i x x x x]*
2 *gab-bu la [x x x]*
3 17 LÚ*.SIMUG—AN.BAR *x[x x]*
4 *ša me-me-ni* A.ŠÀ-*šú x[x x]*
5 *la-a-šú ina ša* A.ŠÀ-*in-ni*
6 *la-áš-šú-ni* ŠE.NUMUN.MEŠ
7 *me-me-ni la i-di-na-na-še*
8 *dul-la-ni ša* É.GAL.MEŠ
9 *ina* UGU-*hi-ni i-da-nu*
10 LUGAL *liš-ʾa-al lu-ṣi-ṣi*
11 *ina* ŠÀ-*bi ni-ip-ta-ṣa*
12 *a-na* LÚ*.GAL—*ki-ṣir-a-ni*
13 LUGAL *liš-ʾa-al*
14 *ma-a* LÚ*.ERIM.MEŠ *a-le-e*
15 TA* *pa-an il-ki* LÚ*.ERIM.MEŠ
16 *[i]na* É.GAL.MEŠ *i-tal-ku*
17e *i-tar-bu*

CT 53 13

[1] We have made and delivered 200 swords of iron, 100 *purṭû*-weapons of iron, 25 nails of iron for ...s, (and) 200 *pakku*s of iron, but we cannot make another 200 *pakku*s of iron.

[9] A brother of ours is dying in the house of the baker. For all this work, nobody has given u[s] any firewood. Therefore we cannot *ta[ke care of* ...]

(Break)

[r.1] Out of all the [...s], no [......].

[3] [*We are*] 17 blacksmiths, (but) none (of us) has a field [...]. Because we have no field, nobody has given us seed corn.

[8] The works of the palaces have become a burden on us. May the king enquire and thoroughly investigate (this matter): we *have withdrawn* because of it.

[12] Let the king ask the cohort commanders: "Where are the men?" The men have gone away and entered the palaces because of the *ilku*-duty.

40 [2] *purṭû*s of copper are attested in TCL 3:393 (cf. also line 382). [4, 6, 7] *pakku*s of iron also attested in ND 2374:7 (Iraq 23 pl. 12). [r.1] Or: "from ther[e]." [r.8f] Cf. SAA 1 147:14f, 224:4; SAA 5 56 r.7f. [r.15] Cf. SAA 5 52:18. Alternatively, TA* *pa-an il-ki* can be translated as "because of (the hard) labour duty," cf. SAA 10 143 r.3.

41. Magnates Obstructing Justice

82-5-22,100

1 [*a*]-*na* LUGAL BE-*ni*
2 ARAD.MEŠ-*ni-ka*
3 ^{md}PA—*tukul-ti*
4 ^{md}PA—MU—GIŠ
5 ^{m}*mu-tak-kil*—^{d}IM
6 *lu-u* DI-*mu a-na* LUGAL BE-*ni*
7 *aš-šur* ^{d}*šá-maš a-na* LUGAL
8 BE-*ni lik-ru-bu*
9 *ša* LUGAL BE-*ni iš-pur-an-na-ši-ni*
10 *ma-a a-na* LÚ*.GAL.MEŠ
11 *ṭè-e-mu as-sa-kan*
12 *ma-a de-en-ku*$^{!}$*-nu*
13 *ep-pu-šú ni-ti-it-zi*$^{!}$
14 [*ina*] *pa-ni-šú-nu la*$^{!}$ *i*$^{!}$*-ma*$^{!}$*-gúr*$^{!}$
15 *de-e-nu ša* É—EN.ME-*šú-nu*
e.16 [*la*] *e-pu-šú*
r.1 [ARAD.ME]Š *ša*$^{!}$ DUMU$^{!}$—LUGAL$^{!}$
2 [DÙ]-*šú*$^{!}$*-nu ina kas*$^{!}$*-pi*$^{!}$
3 [*it-t*]*a-an-nu*
4 [*ug-da*]*m-mì-ru*
5 [LUGAL] BE-*ni*
6 [*x x x*]*x i-ba-šú-ni*
7 [*x x x*]*x ni-ip-ta-làh*
8 [*x x x*]*x* LUGAL *i-šam-me*
9 [*x x x*]*x tak*$^{!}$ ⸢*ka*$^{?}$⸣ *šú*$^{?}$
10 [*x x x*]*-ni*$^{!}$*-e ina kas*$^{!}$*-pi*$^{!}$
11 [*x x x*]*-bu-u-ni*
12 [*x x x*]*x de-ni-ni*
13 [*x x x*] *ina* UGU
14 [*x x x*]*x a-ṣu-du*
15 [*x i-b*]*a-áš-šú-u-ni*
16 [*x x x x x x*]*x-áš*
17e [*x x x x x x*]*x-tú*
18e [*x x*] *e-pa-áš*

ABL 1101

1 To the king, our lord: your servants Nabû-tukulti, Nabû-šumu-lešir (and) Mutakkil-Adad. Good health to the king, our lord! May Aššur (and) Šamaš bless the king, our lord.

9 As to what the king, our lord, wrote to us: "I have ordered the magnates to do justice to you" — we have stood before them, but they have refused to render justice to the household of their lord. They have [s]old [all the servant]s of the crown prince for money and [finis]hed them up.

r.5 [The king], our lord,
6 [...] there are
7 [...] we got scared
8 [...] the king will hear
9 [...] ...
10 [......] for money
11 [...] ...
12 [...] our lawsuit
13 [...] *concerning*
14 [...] the *aṣūdu*-dish
15 [...] there is
(Break)
18 performs [...]

42. Governor Appropriates a Royal Gift

Bu 91-5-9,157

1 *a-na* LUGAL *bé-li-ni*
2 ARAD.MEŠ-*ka*
3 ^{m}*ṣal-la-a-a* LÚ.GAL—É
4 ^{md}ASAL.LÚ.HI—KAM-*eš*
5 LÚ.A.BA
6 *lu-u šul-mu a-na* LUGAL EN-*ni*
7 ^{d}PA ^{d}AMAR.UTU *a-na* LUGAL EN-*ni*
8 *lik-ru-bu* É—EN.MEŠ-*ni*
9 LÚ.NAM.MEŠ ⸢*ub*$^{!}$⸣*-ta-di-du*$^{!}$
10 LUGAL *la ú-da*

ABL 415

1 To the king, our lord: your servants Ṣallaya, major domo, (and) Asalluhi-ereš, scribe. Good health to the king, our lord! May Nabû (and) Marduk bless the king, our lord.

8 The governors have squandered the household of our lord, (and) the king does not know. The governor of Arrapha has taken

41 9-r.3 Fales, HANEM 4 (2000) 241a-b. 12ff, r.1f See coll. r.15 See coll.
42 Previous edition: K. Deller "Neuassyrisch *qanû, qinītu* und *tidintu*," in Charpin and Joannès (eds.), *Marchands, diplomates et empereurs*, (Paris 1991), 352. 8-s.1 Fales, HANEM 4 (2000) 241b. 9 See coll. r.1f → LAS

11 LÚ.EN.NAM *ša* URU.*arrap-ha*
12 *ti-din-tu ša* LUGAL
13 *a-na bé-li-ni*
e.14 *id-di-nu-u-ni*
15 *ip-tu-ag-ga*
r.1 *a-na* LUGAL *bé-li-ni*
2 *lu ud-da-áš-šú ki-i*
3 É—EN.MEŠ-*ni ba-du-du-ni*
4 LUGAL *ú-da ki-i* EN-*ni*
5 TA* EN—*de-ni-šu*
6 *la i-da-bu-bu-u-ni*
7 *ù a-ni-nu* É *ni-da-bu-bu-ni*
8 *i-ha-as-su-na-ši*
9 LUGAL *ina pa-an* 1-*en*
10 LÚ.GUB.BA—*pa-ni-šu*
11 *li-ip-qi-da-na-ši*
12 *ša ṭè-mì-ni ina* IGI LUGAL
13 *i-qab-bu-ú-ni*
14e *ù* LÚ.*qur-bu-tú*
15e *ina* UGU É ARAD-*šú*
16e *lip-qid*
s.1 *de-na-ni ša* É *le-pu-uš*

away the gift which the king gave to our lord. May it be known to the king, our lord, that the household of our lord has been squandered.

r.4 The king knows that our lord does not argue with his adversary; and when we litigate, they mistreat us. May the king entrust us to someone of his entourage, who will tell our story before the king. Moreover, may he appoint a royal bodyguard over the house of his servant, so that he may settle the lawsuits concerning the house.

43. My Associate is a Criminal

K 893

1 [*a-na* LUGAL *be-li-ia*]
2 [ARAD]-*ka* ^{md}[*x x x x*]
3 LÚ*.A.BA *ša ina* IGI [*x x x*]
4 *ki-ṣir ša x*[*x x x*]
5 ^{d}PA ^{d}AMAR.UTU *a-n*[*a* LUGAL]
6 *be-li-ia lik-ru-bu*
7 LUGAL *be-li a-ki tak-mis*
8 *ip-taq-da-na-a-ši*
9 *ú-ma-a* ^{md}PA—MU—AŠ
10 *ša i-si-ia pa-ri-ṣu šu-ú*
11 ARAD.MEŠ *ša* LUGAL *ša* A.ŠÀ
12 *ša bir-te* URU *uh-ta-li-qi*
13 ÉŠ-*iš*-QAR.MEŠ *ša* LUGAL KÚ
14 UGU *ša a-qa-bu-u-ni*
15 *nu-uk a-ta-a*
r.1 ⸢ARAD?⸣.M[EŠ *ša* LUGAL *tu-hal-la-qa*]
2 ÉŠ.QAR.MEŠ [*ša* LUGAL KÚ]
3 *ma-a ta-ra-am bat-x*[*x x x*]
4 *ma-a ta-ra-am* [*x x x*]
5 *a-na* LÚ.GAR-*nu*.MEŠ *a-na* ⸢LÚ.(GAL)—*ki*⸣-*ṣir*.MEŠ
6 LUGAL *be-li liš-al-šú-nu*
7 *ina* UGU DUG$_4$.DUG$_4$ *an-ni-i*
8 LUGAL *be-li i-se-e-šú*
9 *lu-ki-na-a-ni hi-bil-a-te-šú-nu*
10 *ša* LÚ.DUB.[SAR].MEŠ
11 *ina* GIŠ.*le-ʾi* [*a-si-di*]*r*
12 *ša* GIŠ.*l*[*e-ʾu x x x x x*]

ABL 557

1 [To the king, my lord]: your [servant PN], the scribe who is in the service of [...], the cohort of [...]. May Nabû (and) Marduk bless the [king], my lord.

7 The king, my lord, appointed us as ... Now Nabû-šumu-iddina, my associate, is a criminal. He has wrecked the servants of the king outside and inside the city, (and) is utilizing the assigned quotas of the king.

14 In response to what I said — "Why [are you wrecking the servants of the king and using the king's] assigned quotas?" — he answered: "[I ...] the corn heap [of ...] (and) the corn heap [of ...]".

r.5 May the king, my lord, question the prefects and cohort commanders, and establish that I am right in this dispute with him. [I have liste]d the debts of the scr[ibe]s on a writing-board.

12 Of the writi[ng board ...]

II 4:10.

43 Previous edition: Postgate, TCAE (1974) 281f. r.5 GAL omitted by scribe. See coll. r.13 According to

13 KUG.UD *ša* ARA[D.MEŠ *ša* LUGAL *x x x*]
14 [*x x x*]*x x*[*x x x x x x*]
rest broken away
s.1 *ina* UGU ZI.MEŠ-*ia i-da-bu-bu* [*x x*]

13 the silver of the serv[ants of the king ...]
(Break)

s.1 He is plotting against my life [...]

44. May my Lord Appoint me

82-5-22,158

1 *a-na* LUGAL EN-*ia*
2 ARAD-*ka* ^{m}*iq-bi—aš-šur* LÚ.A.BA
3 *ša* URU.KAR—^{md}DI-*ma-nu*—MAŠ
4 *lu šul-mu a-na* LUGAL EN-*ia*
5 [*x x x*] *a-na* LUGAL EN-*ia*
6 [*lik-ru-bu*] $^{d+}$EN *u* $^{d+}$AG
7 [*x x x x* AN]-*e a—dan-niš*
8 [*x x x x x x*].MEŠ *ki*?
rest broken away
Rev. beginning broken away
1′ [*x x x x x x*] ˹*x x*˺
2′ [*x x x x*] ˹*x x*˺-*te-te*?
3′ [*ina*] *šul*!-˹*ma*˺!-*na-te i-du-ku-u-ni*
4′ [*be*]-*lí lip-qí-dan-ni ina* IGI LUGAL
5′ *is-si-šu-nu lu-ki-ii-ni*
6′ [T]A? *il-ki-ia*! *šat-*˹*b*˺*u*!-*a-ku-u*
7′ LUGAL *be-lí lu ú-di*

ABL 1234

1 To the king, my lord: your servant Iqbi-Aššur, the scribe of Kar-Shalmaneser. Good health to the king, my lord! [May DNN bless] the king, my lord. [May] Bel and Nabû, [*and the gods of* heav]en greatly [... the king, my lord]!
(Break)

r.3 are killing me [by] (giving out) bribes.
4 May my [lor]d appoint me, so I can settle (this lawsuit) with them in the presence of the king. Have I been removed [fro]m my duty? The king, my lord, should know (this).

45. Complaints from Naṣibina

Ki 1904-10-9,8

beginning broken away
1′ LÚ.A.BA [*x x x*] *a-na x*[*x x*]
2′ *ur-ta-am-me dul-li* LUGAL [*la e-pu-uš*]
3′ *ma-a a-ta-a* AD-*u-a x*[*x x x*]
4′ *ia-a-ši ku-um-mu-šu ip-*[*taq-du-ni*]
5′ *a-ti-it-zi* AD-*ka a*[*s*?-*x x x*]
6′ *ina* URU.*na-ṣi-bi-na ina* UR[U.*x x x*]
7′ *ina* URU.*ha-me-de-e* ˹*ú*˺-[*x x x x*]
8′ *dul-lu a-na* LUGAL *e-*[*ta-pa-áš*]
9′ LÚ.*hu-ub-tú a-na* LUGAL [*a-ti-din*]
10′ MU.IM.MA *ina* ITI.AB [*ki-i*?]
11′ *ina pa-an* LUGAL EN-*ia* [*a-na-ku-ni*?]
12′ *ṭè-mu ša* É.GAL *x*[*x x x x*]
13′ KUG.UD TA* IGI LÚ!.D[AM!.QAR.MEŠ]
14′ *a-ta-as-ha a-na* LUGAL? [*a-ti-din x x*]
15′ *ša* LUGAL EN-[*ia x x*]
16′ *ú-di-na l*[*a x x x x x*]
e.17′ *a-na* KUR.*bar-hal-za* [*x x x x x*]

ABL 1371

(Beginning destroyed)
1 The scribe [...] left [his *post* and did not do] the king's work, saying: "Why [...] my father?"
4 They ap[pointed] me in his stead, (and) I stood by and [*serv*ed] your father. I [...ed] in Naṣibina, [GN] (and) Hamedê; I [did] work for the king (and) [gave] booty to the king.
10 Last year in Kanun (X), [*when I was*] in the presence of the king, my lord, [...] *report* of the Palace [...]. I exacted silver from the me[rchants] and [gave] it to the king.
15 The [...] of the king, [my] lord, [...] had no[t] yet [...], [...] to Barhalza, (when) the scribe returned to my service [...]. He had

Postgate, a line with fragmentary signs follows. Between that line and s.1 two to five lines are broken,
44 2-3 According to S. Dalley, Abr-Nahrain 34 (1996/7) 68, the name Kar-Shalmaneser was not used for Til-Barsib after Shalmaneser III, except for the post-canonical-eponym Nabû-nadin-ahi of Kar-Shalmaneser. Nevertheless, in addition to this letter, the name Kar-Shalmaneser is also attested, at least, in RIMA 3 A.0.103.1 ii 9, A.0.104.2010:19; NL 40 r.4, SAA 11 r. ii 21, 178:14. Undoubtedly the same Iqbi-Aššur also in TB 14:3. Consequently, PNA 2/I p. 560 Iqbi-Aššur nos. 2-3 are to be combined. 8 See coll. r.2f See coll. r.6 See coll.

r.1 LÚ.A.BA *ina pa-na-tu-u-a* [*x x*]
2 *i-su-hu-ra i-x*[*x x x x*]
3 *bir-ti* LUGAL.MEŠ *i-ti-*[*ti-zi*]
4 DI-*mu ša* LUGAL *la iš-a*[*l x x x*]

5 *la iq-bi-ia ú-ma-a* LÚ.[*x x x*]
6 *ina pa-an* LUGAL *e-ta-rab i-*[*x x*]
7 *ba-la-at* LUGAL *up-ta-*[*ti-iu-u*]
8 *la im-mal-ku* É LUGAL [*x x x*]
9 MÍ.TUR-*a* UN.MEŠ-*a i-t*[*a-x x*]
10 *šu*$^{?}$*-tú*$^{?}$*-ú* KUR *ša* LUGAL *li-*[*x x x x*]

11 *ia-a-ši* LÚ.DAM.QAR.MEŠ-*ni x*[*x x*]
12 *ina* UGU *mì-i-ni a-ka-ni i-x*[*x x*]
13 *ina* UGU *ša ina pa-an* LUGAL EN-*ia a-*[*x x*]
14 LUGAL EN LUGAL.MEŠ-*ni be-lí liš-*⸢*al*$^{?}$⸣
15 *ša la x*[*x x*]*x ina ba-la-at* [LUGAL *x*]

16 [*x x x x x x x*] *ina du-x*[*x x x x*]
17 [*x x x x x x x x x*]*x*[*x x x x*]
18 [*x x x x x x x x x x x x x x*]

scribe returned to my service [...]. He had st[ood] in the middle of kings, [but] did not inqui[re about] the king's health and did not tell it to me.

[r.5] Now the [*scribe*] has entered the king's presence. [*They have*] dism[issed ...] without the king's permission, heedlessly [...ed] the king's house, and [*mistreated*] a girl servant of mine and my people.

[10] *Is it* a country of the king? May [...]!

[11] Why do the merchants [...] me here [...]?

[13] May the king, lord of the kings, my lord, enquire about what I [spoke] in the presence of the king, my lord. Without [...], without [...]

[16] [......] *in* [...]

[17] [......]

[18] [......]

46. Asking for Mercy

K 5539

beginning broken away
1′ [*re*$^{?}$*-e*]-⸢*mu*⸣ *liš-ka-*⸢*nu*⸣-[*šú*$^{?}$*-nu*]
2′ [*šum-ma* L]UGAL *be-li i-qa*[*b-bi*]
3′ [*x x x a-n*]*a* LÚ.EN—[*x*]
4′ [*x x x x x*] LÚ.GAL—⸢*da*⸣-[*ni-bat*]
rest broken away
Rev. beginning broken away
1′ ⸢*ú*$^{?}$⸣-[*x x x x x x x*]
2′ *li-*[*x x x x x x x*]
3′ *ṭè-*[*e-mu x x x x x*]
4′ ^{m}*iz-*[*x x x x x x x*]
5′ ⸢*an*⸣-*x*[*x x x x x x x*]
6′ *ù* [*x x x x x x x*]
7′ *ša x*[*x x x x x x x*]
rest broken away

CT 53 275

(Beginning destroyed)

[1] May they have [mer]cy [on them].

[2] [If the k]ing, my lord, ord[ers],

[3] [...] the [...]

[4] [...] the chief vic[tualler]

(Reverse too broken for translation)

47. Slander

83-1-18,742 + Bu 91-5-9,149

beginning broken away
1′ [*x x x x x x*]*x* É.GAL [*x x x x*]
2′ [*x x x x*]*x-ha-aṣ* [*x x*] *at-ta-ṣa* [*x x x x*]
Edge uninscribed
r.1 [*x x x x*]*x* ^{m}*hu*—BÀD *a-na* ERIM—É.GAL [*x x*

83-1-18,742+

(Beginning destroyed)

[1] [......] the palace [...]

[2] [......] I brought [...]

[r.1] [...] Ahu-duri *to* the palace personnel

45 Previous edition (transliteration only): Deller, JESHO 30 (1987) 14f. [7] See coll. [13] Coll. T. Kwasman *apud* Deller, ibid. [r.8] Or: "the royal house." [r.10, 14] See coll.

47 Previously unpublished; copy p. 218. Join by S. Parpola, 14.4.76. [r.1] The compound *ṣāb ekalli* is not attested

x x]
2 [*x x x p*]*a-an* LUGAL [E]N-*ia kar-ṣi-ia x*[*x x x x*]
3 [*x x x x*]-*ku* LUGAL ⌈LÚ*⌉.MUŠEN.DÙ *lu* [*x x x x*]
4 [*x x x x*]*x* LÚ.GAL.MEŠ LÚ.MUŠEN.DÙ [*x x x x*]
5 [*x x x*] ⌈LÚ*?⌉.*x*[*x*] LUGAL *ina* NAG [*x x x x*]
6 [*x x x x x*]-⌈*i-na*⌉ *a*-⌈*bu*⌉-*tú* [*x x x x*]
7 [*x x x x x x x x*] *na-ṣ*[*a x x x x*]
rest broken away

[...]
2 [...] slander[ed] me [be]fore the king, my [lord].
3 [...] May the king [...] the fowler,
4 [... let] the magnates [...] the fowler [...]
5 [...] the king's [...] to drink [...]
6 [......] *word* [...]
7 [......] *bringi*[*ng* ...]

elsewhere in the SAA corpus.

4. Petitions to Officials and Private Letters

FIG. 8. *Assyrian officials from Nineveh (reign of Sennacherib).*
VA 956.

48. Petition on Behalf of a Tax Master

K 175

1 *a-na* LÚ.A.BA—KUR EN-*iá*
2 ARAD-*ka* ^{m}*tab-ni-i*
3 *lu* DI-*mu a-na* EN-*iá*
4 *a—dan-niš* ^{d}AG *u* ^{d}MES
5 *a-na* EN-*iá lik-ru-bu*
6 TA* ŠÀ-*bi-ka* DÙG.GA
7 *a-na* URU.NINA.KI
8 *e-ru-ub pa-ni ša* ^{d}AG
9 *pa-ni ša* LUGAL
10 *ina* DI-*me a-mur*
11 *an-nu-ri* ^{m}*ab-ni-i*
e.12 GAL—MÁŠ
13 *ša* KUR URU.*ar-pad-dà*
r.1 *ina pa-an* EN-*iá* DU-*ka*
2 EN—*ṭa-ab-ti-ia*
3 *ša a—dan-niš šu-u*
4 *ù pa-lìh* TA* *pa-an*
5 EN-*iá ina* UGU UDU.MEŠ
6 *be-lí li-ir-hi-ṣa-áš-šú*
7 *ù bir-ti* IGI.2.MEŠ-*šú*
8 *ma-di-di a-na mì-i-ni*
9 *be-lí i-ha-si-šú*
10 LÚ *la a-še-er*
11 TA* EN.NAM *be-lí*
12e *lid-bu-ub* GAL—NÍG.ŠID$^{!}$.MEŠ
13e *lil-li-k*[*a* 0]
14e KASKAL *ina* GÌR.2.M[EŠ-*šú*]
s.1 *liš-kun*

ABL 221

[1] To the palace scribe, my lord: your servant Tabnî. The best of health to my lord! May Nabû and Marduk bless my lord! Enter Nineveh in good spirits and see the face of Nabû (and) the face of the king in peace!

[11] Now Abnî, the sheep-tax master of Arpad, is coming to the presence of my lord. He is a great friend of mine, and one who reveres my lord. My lord should trust him regarding the sheep. But give him clear instructions!

[r.8] Why does my lord mistreat him? The man has not been properly treated. May my lord speak with the governor, and may the chief of accounts come (and) help him out.

49. Petition on Behalf of Servants not Allowed to Enter the Palace

K 1274

1 *a-na* LÚ.A.BA—É.GAL EN-*ia*
2 GEMÉ-*ka* MÍ.*sa-ra-a-a*
3 ^{d}EN ^{d}GAŠAN-*ti-*[*ia*] ^{d}*be-let*—KÁ.DINGIR.RA.KI
4 ^{d}AG ^{d}*taš-me-tum* ^{d}15 *ša* NINA.KI
5 ^{d}15 *ša* URU.*arba-ìl a-na* EN-*ia*
6 *lik-ru-bu* UD.MEŠ GÍD.DA.MEŠ *ṭu-ub* ŠÀ-*bi*
7 *ṭu-ub* UZU.MEŠ *a-na* EN-*ia lid-di-nu*

ABL 220

[1] To the palace scribe, my lord: your maid Sarai. May Bel, Belti[a], the Lady of Babylon, Nabû, Tašmetu, Ištar of Nineveh (and) Ištar of Arbela bless my lord! May they give long days, happiness and physical well-being to my lord.

48 Previous editions: Kienast WO 19 (1988) 11f; Fales and Lanfranchi Lettere (1992) 66-69. → Postgate, TCAE (1974) 169 (obv.11-r.1); Deller, OA 25 (1986) 24f (obv.11-s.1); Neumann, AOAT 247 (1997) 287 (r.14-s.1). r.2f → LAS II 125:7. s.1 Text on the side here exceptionally runs in the same direction as the obverse. Cf. note on no. 65.

FIG. 9. *Sheep (reign of Sennacherib).*
ORIGINAL DRAWINGS IV, 15.

8 ARAD.MEŠ-*ni ša be-lí-ia*
9 *ša* LÚ.EN.NAM *ša* É—*na-a-a-la-ni*
r.1 *iš-šu-ú* 7 ZI$^{!}$.MEŠ *šu-nu*
2 *a-na* ^{md}AMAR.UTU—SU *it-ti-din-šu-nu*
3 *an-nu-rig* UN.MEŠ *an-na-ka šu-nu*
4 *it-tal-ku-nu ina* UGU-*hi-ia*
5 *ma-a ina pa-ni* LÚ.A.BA—É.GAL *qi-bi-i*$^{?}$
6 *ma-a a-du-u* É ^{md}AMAR.UTU—SU
7 *la ú-še-ra-ba-na-ši-na*
8 LÚ.SAG (*ša*) *be-lí ik-nu-ku-u-ni*
9 *an-nu-rig is-si-šu-nu*

[8] There are seven persons, servants of my lord, whom the governor of Bet-nayalani took and gave to Marduk-eriba.

[r.3] Now the(se) people are here. They have come to me, saying: "Speak in the presence of the palace scribe as long as Marduk-eriba does not allow us to enter."

[8] The eunuch (whom) my lord 'sealed' is with them at the moment.

50. List of People Entering the Palace

K 858

1 *kap*$^{!}$-*pu* ^{md}PA—NUMUN—GIŠ
2 *a-na* LÚ.GAL—É.GAL

---

3 :. ^{md}PA—*šar-hu—ú-ba-šá*
4 :. ^{m}NUMUN—15 GAL—*pil-ka-ni*
5 :. ^{m}*ár-ba-a-a* DUMU—É.GAL
6 :. ^{m}*mu-ṣur-a-a* DUMU—É.GAL
7 :. MÍ-*šú ša* LÚ.GAL—KUR
8 : 3 DUMU ^{md}PA—NUMUN—GIŠ
9 : MÍ-*šú ša* ^{md}PA—*šar-hu*—TÉŠ
10 : 2 DUMU.MÍ ^{md}PA—NUMUN—GIŠ

ABL 512

[1] A *list* of Nabû-zeru-lešir to the palace manager.

---

[3] : Nabû-šarhu-ubaša;
[4] : Zer-Issar, chief of public works;
[5] : Arbayu, courtier;
[6] : Muṣurayu, courtier;
[7] : the wife of the palace manager;
[8] : three sons of Nabû-zeru-lešir;
[9] : the wife of Nabû-šarhu-ubaša;
[10] : two daughters of Nabû-zeru-lešir;

49 [9] For *naiālu*, cf. Postgate, TCAE (1974) 367. [r.1] Y 78, W 90
50 [1] → Parpola, OLZ 74 (1979) 32.

11 : MÍ.É.GI$_4$.A-*su*
12 : UD-8-KÁM *ša* ITI.ŠU
13 ^{md}PA—NUMUN—GIŠ
14 *a-na* DUMU—É.GAL
r.1 PAB 14 LÚ.*e-rib-u-te*
rest uninscribed

11 : his daughter-in-law;
12 : 8th of Tammuz (IV).
13 Nabû-zeru-lešir, for courtier(s).
r.1 Total: 14 enterers.

51. List of Staff-bearers Coming in

K 11930

beginning broken away
1′ [*x x x x*]-⸢*ia-a*⸣ [0] ^{m}AD—ZALÁG
2′ [*x x š*]*a* É-*ma šú*$^{?}$-*nu*
3′ [*š*]*a be-lí ina* UGU-*hi*
4′ TA* GAL—*mu-gi id-bu-bu-ni*
5′ ^{m}PAB—*ia-u*
6′ ^{m}*bir*—DINGIR
7′ [^{m}]⸢*sam-si*⸣—*na-tan*
rest broken away
Rev. beginning broken away
1′ *š*[*a*] ⸢*ú-ma-a*⸣
2′ *e-r*[*a*]*b-u-ni*
3′ [P]AB 11 ERIM.MEŠ TU.MEŠ
4′ [*x*] ⸢LÚ*⸣.PA.MEŠ
5′ [*x x*] ⸢^{m}⸣^{d}*a-a—ba-ba*
rest uninscribed

CT 53 428

(Beginning destroyed)

1 [...]iâ, Abi-nuri [...]. *They are from the same household* about which my lord spoke with the *rab mūgi*.

5 Ahi-Iau, Bir-il, Samsi-natan

(Break)

r.1 wh[o] are com[i]ng in today. [T]otal, 11 men coming in.

4 [x] staff-bearers [*in charge of*] Aya-yababa.

52. Food for Schoolboys

K 1273

1 [^{d}]EN *ù* ^{d}GAŠAN-*ia* ^{d}AG ^{d}*taš-me-tum*
2 [^{d}]⸢MAŠ⸣ *ù* ^{d}*gu-la* ^{d}U.GUR ^{d}*la*-⸢*aṣ*⸣ [0]
3 DINGIR.MEŠ *an-nu-te* GAL.MEŠ *a-na* ^{md}AG—[*x x x*]
4 *lik-ru-bu-ka li-ṣur-ú-ka l*[*u-šal-li-mu-ka*]
5 *ṭu-ub lib*^{ib}-*bi ṭu-ub* UZU.MEŠ [*lid-di-nu-ni-ka*]
6 *ma-ṣar šul-me ba-la-ṭi is-si-k*[*a lip-qi-du*]
7 *am—mar ša a-na* DINGIR.MEŠ *an-nu-te t*[*a-hur-u-ni*]
8 *a—dan-niš a—dan-niš ha-an-ṭiš liš*-[*ru-ku-ka*]
9 *a-li-ma mi-i-nu ša x*[*x x x*]
e.10 *ina* IGI EN.MEŠ-*šú a-bat-su* [*x x x*]
r.1 *an-nu-rig a-na be-li*$_{8}$-*ia* [*as-sap-ra*]

K 1273

1 May Bel and Beltia, Nabû (and) Tašmetu, Ninurta and Gula, Nergal (and) Laṣ, these great gods, bless you, O Nabû-[...]! May they guard you, k[eep you in good health, and give you] happiness (and) physical well-being! [May they appoint] a guardian of health and vigour (to be) with yo[u]. Whatever you have [prayed] to these gods for, may they very, very quickly bes[tow it upon you].

9 *What else*? The word of [*my lord* is *respected*] before his lords.

r.1 [I am] now [writing] to my lord, (as)

51 1 Or: "Abu-nuri," cf. PNA 1/I p. 19. 6 Bir-il: cf. PNA 1/II p. 346. r.5 For Aya-yababa, prefect of staff-bearers, see SAA 7 30 r. iii 7 and PNA 1/I p. 90.

52 Previously unpublished; copy p. 217. Almost complete roundish horizontal tablet. The surface is dotted with tiny round holes and throughout more eroded than indicated on the copy. 4f For restored *lu-šal-li-mu-ka*, cf. SAA 10 130:10. 9, r.6 *alīma mīnu* (lit., "where is what?") also in no. 105 r.21. The expression seems to be used in the present letter in the same way as the more common epistolary idiom *mīnu ahhur* "what else?," for which see, e.g., SAA 13 40 r.4 and 41:13. r.3 *kispu* usually "funerary offering"; but is it here merely a question of "bread/food"?

2 QÀL.MEŠ-*šú-nu ina* URU.*kal-ha* TA* ŠÀ UD-1-KÁM-⸢*ma*⸣ [0]
3 *ša la ki-is-pi ina* É—*ṭup-pi la il-lu-*[*ku*]
4 *tab-ku ša* ITI.SIG$_4$ *be-li*$_8$ ARAD.MEŠ-*šú lu-bal-l*[*iṭ*]
5 *a-di* É ŠE.PAD.MEŠ GIBIL-*tu ta-ma-qu-ta-an-*[*ni*]
6 *a-li-ma mi-i-nu a-na* ^{d}AG *at-ta-har*
7 *ina* IGI *be-li*$_8$-*ia ip-taq-da-an-ni*
8 ^{d}AG *ab-bu-ti ina* IGI *be-li*$_8$-*iá i-ṣa-bat*

from the first day on their little ones in Calah cannot go to school without funerary offering(s). May my lord keep his servants al[ive] (with) the stored grain of Sivan (III), until a new barley ration falls to my share.

6 *What else*? I prayed to Nabû, and he appointed me to my lord's service. Nabû will intercede for me before my lord.

53. Adopting a Daughter

K 880b

1 [*x x x x x x*]
2 É—AD-*i*[*a x x x*]
3 *ta-*⸢*ta*⸣*-ha-za*
4 MÍ.DINGIR-*ú-sa* 2 DUMU.MEŠ-*šá*
5 MÍ.UGU-*hi*—DINGIR—*šá-ap-ka-ku*
6 DUMU.MÍ-*sa*
7 PAB 5 ZI.MEŠ
8 GIŠ.NÁ *a-di* GIŠ.DA
9 3 TÚG.*dáp-pa-sat*
10 TÚG.*qar-ra-ru*
11 GIŠ.GU.ZA.MEŠ GIŠ.⸢BANŠUR⸣
12 AD-*ia iq-ṭi-bi*
13 *ma-a* DUMU.MÍ-*sa*
r.1 *a-na* DUMU-⸢*ut-te*⸣
2 1-*te* HAR KUG.U[D]
3 1-*te da-áš-*⸢*šú*⸣ KUG.UD
4 PAB 32 GÍN KU[G].UD KI.LAL *šá-an-ši*
5 *pi-it-te* TA* ŠÀ-*bi-šá-ni*
6 *ta-ti-din*
7 *dul-lu ša ina* IGI EN-*ia*
8 *mah-hur-u-ni šu-u-tu*
9 *a-na-ku* NINDA.MEŠ *ina* ⸢*a*⸣*-kal-li-*⸢*i*⸣*a*
10 *la-áš-šú* EN *ú-da*
11 *mi-nu ša* EN *e-pa-áš-u-ni*
12 *le-pu-uš*

CT 53 9

1 You *took over* [*the property* of] m[y] father's house [...]: the woman Ilussa and her two sons, the woman Muhhi-ili-šapkaku and her daughter, a total of 5 persons; a bed including a wooden board, 3 blankets, a *bedspread*, chairs, (and) a table.

12 My father ordered: "Her daughter is to be adopted." She has given (her) in accordance with *her preference* one silve[r] bracelet (and) one silver *daššu*-implement. In all, 32 shekels of si[l]ver *on the golden weight*.

r.7 It is a deed that is *adverse* to my lord. I myself have no bread to eat; my lord knows that. May my lord do what he sees fit.

54. Silver for the Merchants

K 992

1 *ina* UGU LÚ.DAM.QAR$^!$.[MEŠ]
2 *ša be-lí iq-bu-u*$^!$*-n*[*i*$^!$]
3 *ma-a kas-pi-šú-nu la* ⸢*ú*⸣*-š*[*e*]*-*(*bi*)*-la*
4 *ma-a* KUG.UD ⸢*la*⸣*-áš-šú as-se-me*
5 14 MA.NA KUG.UD *be-lí lu-še-bi-la*

SAAB 4 5

1 Concerning the merchan[ts] about whom my lord said: "I have not sent their money, (for) there is no silver" — I have heard (it). My lord should send 14 minas of silver.

53 r.5 This adverbial idiom is not known from elsewhere. r.8 *mah-hur-u-ni* "adverse": cf. SAA 10 294 r.32. Theoretically, it is also possible (though less likely) to read *mah-hír-u-ni*, "acceptable."

54 Previous editions: Waterman, AJSL 29 (1912/3) 16 (copy only); Jas, SAAB 4/1 (1990) 3-5 (transliteration, translation, notes and copy). The exclamation marks in the present transliteration refer to Waterman's copy, which seems to have been made when the tablet was in a better state of preservation. 3 Less likely *la* ⸢*ú*⸣*-š*[*e*]*-la*, "I shall

6 *is—su-ri be-lí i-qa-bi*
7 *ma-a a-ke-e tak-ṣip*
8 4 LÚ.DAM.QAR.MEŠ 1/2 MA.NA-*a-a*
9 4 MÍ.ME-*šú-nu* 1/2 MA.NA-*a-*⸢*a*⸣
10 1 MÍ.*mu-ṣap-pi-tú* 1/2 MA.NA [0]
11 *re-e*[*h*]-⸢*tú*⸣ [*a*]-*sa*!-[*dir*]
12 *ina* [*x x x x x x x*]
13 *x*[*x x x x x x x x*]
rest broken away
Rev. beginning broken away
blank space of about 5 lines
1′ *ù* [*x x x x x x x*]
2′ *a-na* [*x x x x x x x*]
3′ *pa-an* KÁ.GAL [*x x*]
4′ *al-ka*
rest uninscribed

6 Perhaps my lord will say: "How did you figure it out?" Four merchants: half a mina each. Their four wives: half a mina each. One female dyer: half a mina. The re[st I shall i]tem[ise] (and) [...] in [a ...]
(Break followed by a blank space)

r.1 And [...] come to [...] in front of the city gate!

55. Petition on Behalf of Weavers

Sm 2077

1 [*x x x*] *ina bir-ti* KUR.MEŠ-*ni*
2 [*x x*] ⸢LÚ*⸣.UŠ.BAR—*ṣip-rat* ^{m}*ha-a-a*
3 [*x x x*] *ku* [T]A? ŠE.*tab-ki-šú-nu*
4 [*it-tal-ku-u-ni*? *m*]*a-a* ^{m}*se-e*ʾ*—ra-hi-i*
5 [*x x x x x*] LÚ*.*mu-ṣur-a-a*
6 [*x x x x*]-⸢*ri*?⸣-*šú-nu a-na* LÚ*.*mu-ṣur-a-a*
e.7 [*it-t*]*i-din*
r.1 [*ú-ma-a*] *an-nu-rig*
2 [*x x*] SIG_5 *na-ṣu-u-ni*
3 [*ina* IGI E]N-*ia i-za-zu*
4 [*be-lí*] *de-en-šú-nu le-pu-uš*
rest uninscribed

CT 53 134

1 [PN, a ...] between the mountains, [PN], a *scarf* weaver, (and) Haya, [a ... *have come to me wi*]*th* their stored grain, [clai]ming that Se'-rahî, [... *of*] the Egyptians, has [*so*]*ld* their [...] to the Egyptians.

r.1 [Now] then they are bringing good [...] and are standing in the [presence] of my [lo]rd. Let [my lord] settle their case!

56. Petition Concerning a Will

K 1585

1 ⸢*a*⸣-*na* MÍ.GAŠAN—⸢GIŠ EN⸣-*iá*
2 ARAD-*ki* ^{md}PA—PAB—AŠ

3 AD-*u-a* ⸢*gu*? *x*⸣
4 LÚ*.A—*šip-ri* ⸢*x x*⸣ [*x*]-*a*
5 *pa-(na)-at* ^{md}⸢PA?—NUMUN—AŠ *x*⸣
6 LÚ*.A.⸢BA?⸣ *ša* ^{m}[*x x x x*]

7 *ma-a* 15 MA.N[A *x x x*]
8 *a-na* ^{md}PA—*ba*[*l*?-*liṭ*? *x x*]
9 17 ZI.MEŠ [*x x x x x*]
10 4 UDU *x*[*x x x x x*]
11 *a-nu-*[*ut x x x x x x*]

CT 53 53

1 To (the lady) Balti-lešir, my lord: your (f.) servant Nabû-ahu-iddina.
3 My father [*has died*].
4 A messenger [of PN ...]
5 before *Nabû*-zeru-iddina [...]
6 the *scribe* of [PN],
7 saying: "[...] 15 min[as of ...]
8 to Nabû-*ba*[*lliṭ*]
9 17 people [...],
10 4 sheep [...],
11 utens[ils ...]

not set aside." Waterman reads *la it-tal-ka*, which is impossible. 7 *tak-ṣip*: Cf. SAA 7 79 r.11. Hardly *tak-sìp* as suggested by Deller in Jas' article. 11 *-sa-* shown in Waterman's copy. See coll.
55 6 Or: "given."
56 5 See coll. r.7 Cf. no. 85 r.4.

rest broken away
Rev. beginning broken away
1′ ^{m}⸢$^{d?}$⸣[*x x x x x x x x*]
2′ ^{md}[*x x x x x x x x x*]
3′ *i-x*[*x x x x x x x x x*]
4′ *ma-a ni-*[*x x x x x x x*]
5′ TA* LÚ*.GAL—[*x x x x x*]
6′ *ni-din bu-*[*x x x x*]

7′ *i—da-te a-s*[*a-ṭar*]
8′ *ina* IGI EN-*iá a-sa-*[*pa-ra*]
9′ *re-ši* ^{md}⸢PA⸣—[*x x x*]
10′ *li-ši-ú* ⸢AD-*u-a*⸣ [*iq-ṭi-bi*]

11′ *ma-a* UN.MEŠ ARAD.MEŠ
12′ *ša* É-*ia šu-nu*
13′ *an-na-ku za*$^{?}$ 1 *da x*[*x*]
14 [*x*]*x* [*x x x*]*x na* [*x*]

s.1 [*x x x x x*]*x-mu-na kar-ru i-na-šu-ni*
2 [*x x x x x*]*x-da li-ši*

(Break)
r.1 P[N, ...]
2 P[N, ...]
3 [...]:
4 "We [...]
5 with the chief [...]
6 we shall give [...]."
7 I have accordingly wr[itten it down and]
8 s[ent] it to my lord.
9 Let them summon Nabû-[... (and PN)].
10 My father [said]:
11 "The(se) people are servants of my household."
13 I ... [...]
14 [.....]
s.1 [...] are deposited in [...]muna; they are bringing it.
2 Let [*my lord*] take [...].

57. ———

K 13126

1 [IM ^{md}P]A—DINGIR-*a-a*
2 [*a-na* ^{m}*pu*]-*ṭi-ši-ri*
3 [*lu* D]I-*mu a-na* ŠEŠ-*ia*
4 [^{d}PA] ⸢*ù*⸣ ^{d}MES *a-na* PAB-*iá*
blank space of one line
5 [*lik-ru-b*]*u* 40$^{?}$ GIŠ.[*x x*]
rest broken away
Rev. completely broken away

CT 53 113

1 [A tablet of Na]bû-ila'i [to Pu]ṭiširi. [Good he]alth to my brother! [May Nabû a]nd Marduk [bles]s my brother.

4 *40 wooden* [...]
(Rest destroyed)

58. ———

81-2-4,425

1 *a-na* EN-*i-ni*
2 [^{m}*x*]-*i-pi-di*
3 [*x* DU]MU.MEŠ-*šú*
4 [*x x x*]*x-a-a*
5 [*x x* DU]MU.MEŠ-*šú*
6 [*x x x*] ⸢*x*⸣ [*x*]
rest broken away
Rev. completely broken away

CT 53 894

1 To our lord:
2 [...]ipidi
3 [...] his [s]ons
4 [...]aya
5 [...] his [so]ns
(Rest destroyed)

5. Denunciations

FIG. 10. *Attending to the royal parasol (reign of Sennacherib); cf. no. 63.*
ANE 124912.

59. The Conspiracy of Sasî

82-5-22,108 (+) K 13737 (CT 53 118)

1 *a-na* LUGAL [EN-*i*]*a*
2 ARAD-*ka* ^{md}PA—*re-eh-tú*—PAB ^{d}EN ^{d}GA[ŠAN ^{d}PA ^{d}*taš-me*]-*tum*
3 ^{d}15 *šá* URU.NINA ^{d}15 *šá* URU.*arba-ìl* UD.MEŠ GÍD.[MEŠ MU.AN.NA.MEŠ *da-r*]*a-ti*
4 *li-di-nu-nik-ka šá ina* ŠÀ *ṭa-ab-ti šá* AD!-[*ka ina* ŠÀ *a-de-e šá* AD]-*ka*
5 *ù ina* ŠÀ *a-de-e-ka ih-ṭu-u-ni* ^{d}NIN!.GAL [*x x x x* UN.M]EŠ-*šú-nu*
6 MU-*šú-nu* NUMUN-*šú-nu* TA* ŠÀ É.GAL-*ka hal-li-qí*! *a-na* [*x x x x x lu*]
7 *tak-ru-ur* UN.MEŠ *ša* TA ^{m}*sa-si-i ú-du-u-*[*ni ár-hiš li-mu-tu x x x*]
8 *a-ni-nu* LUGAL *be-li da-ba-bu šá* ^{d}NIN.GAL *ú-*[*da x x x x x x x*]
9 *li-mu-tu* ZI.MEŠ-*ka* ZI.MEŠ *šá qin-ni-ka* [*še-zib x x x x x x x*]
10 AD-*u*!-*ka*! AMA-*ka lu šu-nu li-im-tu-*[*hu x x x x x x x x*]
11 ZI.MEŠ-*ka la tu-hal-la-qa* LUGAL-*u-tu* TA ŠU.2-*k*[*a la tu-še-li*]
12 *a-ni-nu* LUGAL *be-*⸢*li*⸣ [*ina* Š]À *da-ba-bi* ^{d}NIN.[GAL *an-ni-e*]
13 *la ta-ši-*[*aṭ x x x*]-⸢*ú*⸣-*nim-ma* [*x x x x x x x x*]
14 *e-gír-tu* [*x x x x x*]*x x*[*x x x x x x x x x x*]
15 *ina* [*x x x x x x x x x x x x x x x x x x x x*]
uncertain number of lines broken away; K 13737:
1′ [*x*] *x*[*x x x x x x x x x x x x x x x x x x x x*]
2′ *ma-a a-*[*x x x x x x x x x x x x x x x x x x x*]
3′ *la ú-*⸢*ba-la*⸣ [*x x x x x x x x x x x x x x x x*]
4′ *ina* IGI-*šú iz-za-zu is-*[*x x x x x x x x x x x x x x x*]
5′ *pi-i-šú-nu šá-ki-in* [*x x x x x x x x x x x x x*]
6′ *ka-a-a-ma-nu ina* UGU ^{m}*sa-s*[*i-i x x x x x x x x x x*]
7′ *ma-a ina* IGI LUGAL *dam-mì-iq ma-*[*a x x x x x x x x x*]
8′ *le-pu-šú* TA* ^{md}PA—EN—[*x x x x x x x x x x x x*]
9′ TA ^{m}SUHUŠ—^{d}PA L[Ú.*x x x x x x x x x x x x x*]
10′ ⸢TA LÚ⸣.GAL.MEŠ *š*[*a x x x x x x x x x x x x x x*]
11′ [*x x x*]*x*[*x x x x x x x x x x x x x x x x x*]
rest of K 13737 broken away

ABL 1217+

1 To the king, m[y lord]: your servant Nabû-rehtu-uṣur. May Bel and Be[let, Nabû and Tašme]tu, Ištar of Nineveh (and) Ištar of Arbela give you long days and ever[lasting years]!

4 Nikkal [*has revealed*] those who sinned against [your] father's goodness, and your [father's] and your own treaty. Destroy their [peopl]e, name and seed from your palace! [May] she cast [......]! [May] the accomplices of Sasî [*die quickly*]!

8 Hear me, O king my lord! I k[now] the words of Nikkal. Let [the people] die! [Rescue] your life and the life of your family! Let [the goddesses ...] be your father and your mother, and let them li[ft up ......]! Do not destroy your life, [do not let] the kingship [slip] from your hands!

12 Hear me, O king my lord! Do not disre[gard these] words of Ni[kkal! Let ......] and [......]

14 a letter [......]

15 in [......]

(Break)

3 is not bringing [......]

4 are staying in his presence [......]

5 are making common cause [with ......]

6 [They are] constantly [......] to Sas[î ......]:

7 "Present (yourself) in good light with the king! Let [...] do [......] with Nabû-belu-[......]

8 with Ubru-Nabû [......]

9 with the magnates o[f/who ......]

59 Previous edition: Parpola *apud* Nissinen, SAAS 7 (1998) 109-111. r.4f LAS II p. 239 n. 412. r.13 *prefect*:

Rev. beginning broken away

1′ *is—su-ri i-*⸢*ba-áš*⸣*-*[*ši x x x x x x x x x x x x x x*]

2′ *liš-ú-lu ma-a* GEMÉ *šá* ^{m}EN—PAB—PAB *ina*$^{!}$ *q*[*a-n*]*i šá* ⸢URU⸣.K[ASKAL].2 *ina* U[GU *x x x x*]

3′ *ma-a* TA* ŠÀ ITI.SIG$_4$ *sa-ar-ha-at ma-a da-ba-bu* SIG$_5$ *ina* UGU-*hi*

4′ *ta-da-bu-bu ma-a a-bat* ^{d}PA.TÚG *ši-i ma-a* LUGAL-*u-tu a-na* ^{m}*sa-si-i*

5′ *ma-a* MU NUMUN *šá* ^{md}30—PAB.MEŠ—SU *ú-hal-la-qa* LÚ.GAL—*mu-gi-ka*$^{?}$

6′ *ina šap-la* KÁ.GAL *šá* É ^{d}PA É ^{m}EN—PAB—PAB *liš-al* LÚ.*še-e-pi*$^{!}$ [*šá*]

7′ GEMÉ *ina* É ^{m}*sa-si-i ú-bi-lu-ni lu-bi-lu-ni-ši dul-lu* LUGAL$^{?}$ [*x x x*]

8′ *ina* UGU-*hi-šá le-pu-šú* ^{m}EN—PAB—PAB TA* URU.KASKAL *lu-bi-lu-ni* ^{d}PA.TÚG [*x x x*]

9′ MU NUMUN *šá* ^{m}*sa-si-i šá* ^{m}EN—PAB—PAB *šá* UN.MEŠ *šá is-si-šú-nu ú-du-*[*u-ni*]

10′ *li-ih-li-iq* MU NUMUN *šá* LUGAL EN-*ia* ^{d}EN ^{d}PA *a-na* ⸢*ṣa*$^{!}$*-at*⸣ [UD.ME *lu-ki*]*n-nu*

11′ TA* ^{m}*ar-da-a lid-bu-bu ma-a* UD-27-KÁM *ina nu-bat-ti ma-a a-na* [^{m}*sa*]*-si-i*

12′ LÚ.*šá*—UGU—URU ^{m}15—SUM—A LÚ.A.BA *ma-a si-mu-nu ha-*[*an-ni-u bé-et*]

13′ *il-li-ku-u-ni* TA* ^{m}*a-ú-ia-a-ni* LÚ.*šak-ni* [*x x x x x x*]

14′ *ma-a* ^{m}15—SUM—A LÚ.A.BA *ma-a* ^{md}PA—KAR-*ir an-*⸢*ni*$^{!}$⸣*-*[*tú x x x x x x*]

15′ *ma-a* UD-28-KÁM *ma-a* ^{m}*sa-si-i mì-i-nu ina* UGU-*hi* ⸢*x x x*⸣ [*x x x x x x*]

16′ *ma*$^{?}$ *a*$^{!}$*-na*$^{!?}$ 2-*e* UD.ME ^{m}*sa-si-i is-si-ka* TA LÚ.[*x x x x x x x x*]

17′ *id-bu-bu ma-a a-*[*ta*]*-a mì-i-nu šá ta-m*[*u-ru-ni x x x x x x x*]

18′ LÚ.GAL—*mu-gi x*[*x x x x x x x x x*] ERIM.MEŠ [*x x x x x x x*]

19e ^{m}15—[SUM—A 0] LÚ$^{?}$.A$^{!}$.B[A *x x x x x*]

s.1 [*x x x x x x* UN.MEŠ *š*]*a*$^{!}$ *is-si-šú-nu* TA* ^{m}*sa-si-i ú-du-u-ni* [*li-mu-tú*]

2 [*x x x x x x* DUMU].MEŠ-*ka* ŠEŠ—AD.MEŠ-*ka* EN.NUN-*ka li-ṣu-ru*

3 [*x x x-k*]*a lu-pa-ah-*⸢*hi*⸣*-ir* [*x x x x at-ta*] *tu-qu-nu ina* É.GAL-*ka ši-bi*

4 [*x x*] *a-du* ⸢É⸣ [*la i-ha-ru-pu-ni* UN.MEŠ *li-mu*]*-tú* ZI.MEŠ-*ka še-zib*

(Break; continued in ABL 1217, rev.)

r.1 "Perhaps ther[e is ......]; let them ask [...].

2 "A slave-girl of Bel-ahu-uṣur [...] upon [...] in a suburb of Harran; since Sivan (III) she is *enraptured* and speaks nice words about him: 'It is the word of Nusku: The kingship is for Sasî. I will destroy the name and seed of Sennacherib!'"

6 Let your squadron commander question the household of Bel-ahu-uṣur under the gate of the Nabû temple; let the *ša-šēpi* guards who brought the slavegirl into the house of Sasî bring her here, and let the *king* [...] perform a(n extispicy) ritual on her (account). Let them bring Bel-ahu-uṣur from Harran and [...] Nusku. May the name and seed of Sasî, Bel-ahu-uṣur and their accomplices perish, and may Bel and Nabû establish the name and seed of the king, my lord, until far-off [days]!

11 Let them speak with Ardâ as follows: "On the 27th, at night, [*when*] the scribe Issar-nadin-apli at this particular moment went to [Sa]sî the city overseer, [*did* ......] with the *prefect* Awyanu? [*Did*] the scribe Issar-nadin-apli [...] this [*with* Nabû-eṭir? What [did] Sasî [......] concerning it on the 28th? Did Sasî speak with you and the [...] on the following day? Why have you [not reported] what you sa[w and heard]?"

18 [Let] the squadron commander [...] men/troops [... *arrest*] the scrib[e] Issar-[nadin-apli ......].

s.1 [The people w]ho conspire with them and with Sasî [should die]!

2 [......] Let your [son]s and uncles guard you.

3 Let [me] gather [yo]ur [...... As for you], stay in safety in your palace. [... Let the people di]e before [they get ahead (of you)]! Rescue your life!

reading LÚ.SAG "eunuch" also possible. See Nissinen, SAAS 7 p. 111 n. 432. s.2 "uncles," proving that Sennacherib had younger brothers, who were still alive more than ten years after his murder, cf. Frahm Sanherib p. 1.

60. More on the Conspiracy of Sasî

K 1034 + K 7395 (ABL 1031) + K 9204 + K 10541 + K 11021 (+) K 9821 (CT 53 107)

1 *a-na* LUG[AL] EN-*ia*
2 ARAD-*ka* ^{md}PA—*re*-⸢*eh*⸣-[*tú*—PAB ^{d}EN ^{d}]GAŠAN ^{d}⸢PA⸣ ^{d}*taš-me-tum*
3 ^{d}15 *šá* NI[NA.KI ^{d}15 *šá* URU.*arba-ìl* DINGIR.MEŠ]-*ka* (*šá*)
4 MU-⸢*ka*⸣ [*a-na* LUGAL-*ti iz-kur-u-ni šu-nu lu-bal-li-ṭ*]*u-u-ka*
5 *šá* [*ina* Š]À [*ṭa-ab-ti šá* AD-*ka ina* ŠÀ *a-de-e šá* A]D-*k*[*a u ina* Š]À *a-de-ka*
6 ⸢*i*⸣-*ha-ṭu-u-n*[*i šá ina* UGU ZI.MEŠ-*k*]*a* ⸢*i*⸣-[*da-ba-bu-u*]-*ni*
7 *šu-nu ina* ŠU.⸢2⸣-[*ka i-šá-ka-an-šú-nu*] MU-*šú-nu* [TA* KUR—*aš*]-*šur*.KI
8 TA* ŠÀ ⸢É⸣.[GAL-*ka tu-hal-la-qa*] *da-ba-bu an-ni-*⸢*ú*⸣
9 *šá* ^{d}NIN.LÍL [*šu-u* LUGAL *be-lí*] *ina* ŠÀ-*bi lu la i-*[*ši-aṭ*]
10 *ina* UD-6-KÁM *šá* I[TI.APIN$^{?}$ *di-ig-lu*] ⸢*a*⸣-[*d*]*a-gal ma-a x*[*x x x*]
11 *ma-a ina* ŠÀ-*b*[*i x x x-bi-da* EN—*a-de-e šá* LUGAL EN-*ia a-na-ku*]
12 *la mu-qa-a-a la ú-*[*pa-az-za-ar di-ib-bi šá x x x x x*]
13 *ki-i šá a-mur-u-ni ina* Š[À *x x x x x x x x x x x x x*]
14 *ak-ta-ra-ar a-na* M[UL$^{?}$].*taš-k*[*a-ti x x x x x x x x x x*]
15 LUGAL *be-li ú-da a-ki* ⸢É⸣ [*x x x x x x x x x x x x*]
16 *ki-i an-ni-i ina* ŠÀ *e-gír-t*[*i-šú šá-ṭi-ir ma-a x x x x*]
17 *lu iṣ-ṣi-a* ⸢*ma-a x x x*⸣ [*x x x x x x x x x x x*]
18 ⸢*x x x*⸣ [*x x x x x x x x x x x x x x x x x x*]

two or three lines broken away; continued by CT 53 107:

1′ [*x x x m*]*a-a* DUMU—L[UGAL$^{?}$ *x x x x x x x x x x x*]
2′ [*x x x-ṣ*]*i a-na* DUMU—LU[GAL$^{?}$ *x x x x x x x x x x*]
3′ *ma-*⸢*a* TA⸣ *a-he-iš ú-sa-ma-*[*hu-ni x x x x x x x x x*]
4′ *i-qab-bi ma-a an-nu-ti is-*[*x x x x x x x x x x x*]
5′ *ù ma-a* É.GAL *gab-bu* ⸢TA⸣ [*x x x x x x x x x x x*]
6′ *me-me-ni ma-a* DUMU.MÍ ^{m}*ba-am-ba-*⸢*a*⸣ [*x x x x x x x x x x x*]
7′ *ù* ⸢ERIM.MEŠ $^{md!}$⸣IM—⸢MU⸣—PAB ^{m}*ar-*[*da-a x x x x x x x x x*]
8′ *iq-ṭi-bu-u-ni ma-a* ⸢*bar-tu*⸣ *e-pu-*[*šu x x x x x x x x*]

CT 53 17+

1 To the ki[ng], my lord: your servant Nabû-re[htu-uṣur. May Bel and] Belet, Nabû and Tašmetu, Ištar of Ni[neveh (and) Ištar of Arbela, your] gods (who) [called] you by name [to kingship, keep] you a[live]!

5 Those who sin against [your father's goodness, yo]ur fat[her's and] your own treaty, and who [plot against yo]ur [life, shall be placed] in [your] hands, [and you shall delete] their name [from As]syria and from [your pa]lace.

8 This is the word of Mullissu; [the king, my lord], should not be ne[glectful] about it.

10 On the 6th of [*Marchesvan* (VIII)] I had a vi[sion]: "[...] in the midst [...]."

11 [I am bound by the treaty of the king my lord]; I cannot c[onceal the words of ...].

13 Just as I saw, [...] in [......]

14 I have put at (the culmination of) the *Tripl*[*et*] *s*[*tar* ......]

15 The king my lord knows that [......]

16 [It is written] as follows in the lette[r: "......]

17 "should have ... [......]

(Short break)

1 "[......] the *crown pr*[*ince* ......]

2 "[......] to the *crown prin*[*ce* ......]

3 "are in league with one another [......]

4 he says: "These [......]"

5 and: "The whole palace [is] with [......]

6 "anything; the daughter of Bambâ [......]

7 and the men of Adad-šumu-uṣur and Ar[dâ ......]

8 have said to me: "They are making a rebellion [......]

60 Previous edition: Parpola *apud* Nissinen, SAAS 7 (1998) 111-114. Joins by S. Parpola, 25.10.66.

9′ *ma-a šu-ú ina* UGU ŠÀ-˹*bi*˺ *ir-ti-hi-i*[*ṣ x x x x x x x*]
10′ *a-sa-kan ma-a šá* ^{d}EN! ^{d}PA ^{d}15 *šá* U[RU.*x x x x x x x x*]
11′ *ur-ta-am-me ma-a šá ra-mì-ni-šú* [*x x x x x x x x x*]
12′ ^{d}15 *šá* NINA.KI *ma-a a*-˹*x*˺-*x*[*x x x x x x x x x x x*]
13′ *e-tap-šú ma-a ú-sa-hi-x*[*x x x x x x x x x x x x*]
14′ [*ma*]-˹*a* TA*˺ ŠÀ É.[GAL *x x x x x x x x x x x*]
two lines and edge broken away
r.1 [*x x x x x x x x x x x x x x x x x x x x*]
2 [*x x x x x x x x x x x x x x x x x x x x*]
3 [*x x x x x x x x x x x x x x x x x x x x*]
4 *lu-ba-x*[*x x x x x x x x x x x x x x x x x*]
5 *ki-i an-ni-i q*[*a-b*]*i ma-a ina* ˹URU.KASKAL˺ [*x x x x x x x*]
6 *ma-a ina* UGU-*hi-ia a-ke-e ṭè-e-mu iš-kun* [*x x x*]
7 *ma-a iá-bu-tú šá* AD!-˹*ia*˺ *a*—˹*dan*˺-*niš ta-ta-aṣ*-[*ra*?]
8 *ma-a* É.GAL *a-na* ˹*x x x*˺ *x*[*x x t*]*a-sa-kan ma-a šá x*[*x x x*]
9 ˹*ma*˺-[*a* ER]IM.MEŠ-˹*ia*˺ *x*[*x x x x x*]*x*[*x x x x*]*x a-na g*[*i*?-*x x x*]
10 ˹*x* ^{m}*sa*?˺-*si*-˹*i*˺ [*x x x x x x x x x x x x x x x x*]
11 *ta-ku*-˹*la*˺ [*x x x x x x x x x x x x x x x x*]
12 *ma-a šu-nu* [*x x x x x x x x x x x x x x x x*]
13 TA* ^{m}*s*[*a-si-i x x x x x x x x x x x x x x*]
14 *lu-k*[*i-x x x x x x x x x x x x x x x x x*]
a few lines broken away; CT 53 17+:
1′ *ši* [*x x x x x x x x x x x x x x x x x x x*]
2′ *ma-a* [*x x x x x x x x x x x x x x x x x x*]
3′ *ma*-˹*a*˺ [*x x x x x x x x x x x x x x x x x x*]
4′ ˹*šá*˺ [*x x x x x x x x x x x x x x x x x x x*]
5′ *x*[*x x x x x x x x x x x x x x x x x x x x*]
6′ [*x x x x x x x x x x x x x x x x x x x x*]
7′ Z[I.MEŠ *x x x x x x x x x x x x x x x x x x*]
8′ ZI.ME[Š *x x x x x x x x x x x x x x x x x x*]
9′ [*ina* I]GI LÚ.GAL—˹SAG˺ [*x x x x x x x x x x x x x x x x*]
10′ ZI.MEŠ-*ka še-zib ár*-[*hiš x x x x x x x x x x x*]
11′ *ši-i* ^{m}*sa-si-i a*-˹*na*˺ *x*[*x x x x x x x x x x x x*]
12′ [^{m}*mi*]*l-ki*—ZALÁG ^{m}ARAD—15 *is-s*[*i-šú x x x*] ˹*ú*?˺-[*x x x x*]
13′ [0] *šá-ʾa-al-šú-nu* UN.MEŠ *a*[*m—mar x x*].*x-ti is-si-šú-nu* ˹*ú-du*˺-[*u-ni*]
14′ [*l*]*i-iq-bu-nik-ka* ˹UN?˺.[MEŠ *an-nu-t*]*i li-mu-tú la ta-pa-làh*
15′ ^{d}EN ^{d}PA ^{d}NIN.LÍL [*is-si-ka*] *iz-za-zu ár-hiš* UN.MEŠ
16′ *li-mu-tú* ZI.MEŠ-*k*[*a še-zib*] ˹*e*˺-*gír-tú an-ni-tú lu ši-ip-tú*
17′ *ina* UGU-*hi*-˹*ka*˺ *i*-˹*ma*˺-[*x ár-hi*]*š* UN.MEŠ *li-mu-tú*

9 "He has become confident in (his) heart [and is saying]: 'I have set [......].' He has rejected what Bel, Nabû, Ištar of [Nineveh and Ištar of Arbela have ...ed], and [......] of his own."

12 Ištar of Nineveh says: "[......]

13 "have done ...[......]

14 "from [your] pal[ace ......]

(Break)

r.4 may ...[......].

5 it r[ead]s as follows: "In Harran [......]

6 "What orders has he given [*to you*] about me? [......]

7 "You have guar[ded] the *word* of my father greatly, [and]

8 "you have turned the palace into a [...].

9 "My men [......]

(10) "*Sasî* [......]

11 "[I] trust [in ......]

12 "They [......]

13 "with *S*[*asî* ......]

14 let him *e*[*stablish* ......]

(Small break)

7 the l[ife of ......]

8 the lif[e of ......]

9 [in the pres]ence of the chief eunuch [......]

10 Rescue your life! [Let the people die] qu[ickly! ......]

11 Sasî to [......]

12 [Mi]lki-nuri and Urad-Issar [......] with [*him*].

13 Interrogate them! Let them tell you the [...] people who conspire with them, and let [these] people die! Have no fear; Bel, Nabû and Mullissu are standing [with you]. Let the people die quickly, and [rescue] your life!

16 May this letter be a spell, it will [...] upon you! Let the people die [quick]ly before

18′ *a-du la i-ha-*⸢*ru*⸣*-[pu-u-ni] a-ni-nu* LUGAL *be-li*
19e ZI.MEŠ-*ka ba-l[i-iṭ* ERIM$^{?}$.MEŠ *š]a* ^{m}*sa-si-i*
20e *šu-ub-tú ú-[se-ši-bu x x x] is-si-ni*
21e *i-da-bu-u[b ma-a a-du la i-h]a-ru-pu-u-ni*
22e *ma-a a-ni-[nu x x x x]x-šú*

s.1 *a-ni-nu* LUGAL *[be-li]* ⸢^{d}EN$^{!}$⸣ *a-n[a x x x x]* KUG.GI NA$_4$.MEŠ *šá* ⸢*ka*⸣*-a-*⸢*a*⸣*-[m]a-nu* 1 LÚ* *x[x x]x*
2 *lu-bi-*⸢*lu*⸣ *[at-ta tu]-qu-nu a-*⸢*na*⸣ *[*^{d}EN *sa-ri-ir* ZI].MEŠ-*ka lu-ur-rik ra-[man]-ka ú-*⸢*ṣur*⸣ KI.MIN KI.MIN
3 ZI.MEŠ-⸢*ka*⸣ [ZI.MEŠ *šá*] ⸢*qin*$^{!}$⸣*-ni-ka [še-zib x x* LÚ*].SAG.MEŠ ZI.MEŠ-*ka še-zib* [K]I.MIN KI.MIN
4 ŠÀ-⸢*ba*⸣*-k[a ṣa-ab-t]a* ⸢*x*⸣ *hu un x[x x x is-si-ka l]i-zi-zu* ŠÀ$^{!}$*-ba-šú-nu ga-mur-*⸢*ak*$^{!}$⸣*-ka*

they get ahe[ad] (of you).

18 Hear me, O king, my lord! Save your life! [The *men* o]f Sasî have [set] an ambush, [saying: "The moment the king] will speak with us, w[e shall kill] him [before he g]ets ahead (of us)."

s.1 Hear me, O king [my lord]! Bel [......]. Let the [...] bring gold and precious stones ...... [As for you, ke]ep in safety, [pray to Bel], and let him prolong your life. Take care of yourself, ditto ditto (= let the people die quickly)!

3 [Rescue] your life and [the life of] your family! Rescue your life [from the *hands* of the e]unuchs! Ditto ditto.

4 [Brace] yourself! [Le]t the [...] stand [with you]; they are loyal to you.

61. Partial Duplicate of No. 60

83-1-18,508

1 *[a-na* LUGAL EN-*ia]*
2 [ARAD-*ka* ^{md}PA—*re-eh-tú*—PAB ^{d}EN ^{d}GAŠAN ^{d}PA ^{d}*taš-me-tum]*
3 [^{d}15 *šá* UR]U.NINA ^{d}15 *šá* [URU.*arba-ìl* DINGIR.MEŠ-*ka ša* MU-*ka*]
4 *[a-na* LUGAL]-*ti iz-kur-u-ni šu-n[u lu-bal-li-ṭu-u-ka šá ina* ŠÀ]
5 *[ṭa-ab-ti] šá* AD-*ka ina* ŠÀ *a-de-e š[á* AD-*ka u ina* ŠÀ *a-de-e-ka]*
6 *[i-ha-ṭu-u-ni] šá ina* UGU ZI.MEŠ-*ka* ⸢*i*⸣*-[da-ba-bu-ni]*
7 *[šu-nu ina* ŠU.2-*k]a i-šá-ka-nu-šu-nu* ⸢MU⸣*-[šú-nu* TA* KUR—*aš-šur*.KI]
8 [TA* ŠÀ É.GA]L-*ka tu-hal-la-qa da-ba-bu [an-ni-ú]*
9 *[šá* ^{d}NIN.LÍ]L *šu-ú* LUGAL *be-li ina* ŠÀ-*bi lu l[a i-ši-aṭ]*
10 *[ina* UD-*x*-KÁM *š]a* ITI.APIN *di-ig-lu a-da-gal ma-a [x x x]*
11 *[ma-a ina* ŠÀ-*bi x x x x t]a*$^{?}$*-bi-da* EN—*a-de-e šá* LU[GAL EN-*ia a-na-ku]*
12 *[la mu-qa-a-a la ú-pa-az-z]a-ar di-ib-[bi šá x x x x]*
rest broken away
Rev. beginning broken away
1′ *[x]x x[x x x x x x x x x x x x x x x x x]*
2′ *ša ina* É.GAL-*ka* ⸢*ep-šu*⸣*-u-n[i x x x x x x x x]*
3′ *la iš-me la ú-da a-n[a x x x x x x x x x]*

CT 53 938

1 [To the king, my lord: your servant Nabû-rehtu-uṣur. May Bel and Belet, Nabû and Tašmetu, Ištar of] Nineveh and Ištar of [Arbela, your gods who] called [you by name to kings]hip, [keep you alive]!

4 [Those who sin against] your father's [goodness, your father's and your own] treaty, and who [plot] against your life, shall be placed [in yo]ur [hands], and you will delete [their] name [from Assyria and from] your [pala]ce!

8 [This] is the word [of Mullis]su; the king, my lord, should n[ot] be ne[glectful] about it.

10 [On the *6th* o]f Marchesvan (VIII) I had a vi[sion]: "[...] *spend the night* [...]"

11 [I am] bound by the treaty of the ki[ng, my lord; I cannot conce]al the word[s of ...]

(Break)

r.2 which have been done in your palace [......]

3 he has not heard, and does not know

61 Previous edition: Parpola *apud* Nissinen, SAAS 7 (1998) 114f.

FIG. 11. *Royal eunuchs (reign of Assurbanipal).*
ORIGINAL DRAWINGS VI, 50.

4′ PI.2-*ka lu la ta-sa-hu-r*[*a x x x x x x x x*]
5′ *hal-lu-qi a-na* [*x*]*x da x*[*x x x x x x x x x*]
6′ ⌜*ù*⌝ ᵐ*ba-am-ba-a a-*[*x x x x x x x x x x*]
7′ [*x*]*x* [*x*] ⌜*šú*⌝*-nu la ta-*[*x x x x x x x x x x*]
two lines broken away
s.1 [*x x x x x x x x x x*]*-tú ú-qa-*[*x x x x*]
2 [*x x x x x x x x x x*] ⌜*x x*⌝ [*x x x x x*]
two lines broken away

[......]
4 do not turn away your attention [......]
5 destroy ... [......]
6 and Bambâ [......]
7 do not [......] their [......]
(Rest destroyed)

62. The Case of Nabû-kabti-ahhešu and Sasî

K 4786 ABL 1308

1 [*ina* UGU *a-bi-ti šá*] ᵐᵈPA—IDIM—PAB.MEŠ-*šú*
2 [*šá ina pa-ni-ti*] *a-na* LUGAL EN-*iá*
3 [*ú-šá-áš-mu*]*-ú-ni a-ta-a* LUGAL *be-lí a-da-ka-an-ni*
4 [*l*]*a iš-al la ú-ṣi-ṣi a-bu-tu-u qàl-li-su*
5 *ši-i* LUGAL *be-lí a-na a-bi-it an-ni-te*

1 [Concerning the case of] Nabû-kabti-ahhešu [which I previously communica]ted to the king, my lord, why has the king, my lord, until now [nei]ther asked nor enquired (about it)? Is it an insignificant matter?

62 → Nissinen, SAAS 7 (1998) 143 (obv. 1-11, r.3-10). For r.4-8, cf. also Deller, Or. 30 (1961) 348 and Or. 34 (1965) 268 (obv. 27-30). According to Deller, this is the first part of a two-tablet letter, the second part being represented by no. 63 ("ABL 633 [i.e. CT 53 46] ... ist "Blatt 2" des Briefes ABL 1308," Or. 34 268). He does not state the reason(s) for this suggestion, but probably the argument is largely based on the considerable affinities of the two letters. However, it should be noted that contrary to the only clear example of a Neo-Assyrian "two-page" letter (SAA 10 197-198, see LAS II p. 111), whose two "pages" are of identical size and format, no. 62 is considerably smaller than no. 63: the former measures 87 mm, the latter 105 mm in width. Furthermore, while r.2f of the present letter does imply that the writer intended to continue his subject matter in another letter, it also makes it clear that this second letter was to follow only after the king had reacted positively to the present one. Hence, the theory of a "two-page" letter does not seem to be warranted in the case of no. 62 and no. 63, but it is by no means excluded that the two letters indeed belong together and were written in close succession. [SP] We have not been able to trace the tablet 83-1-18,456 which according to Deller (Or. 34 268) also belongs to ABL 1308 (without making a direct join). 1 The name Nabû-kabti-ahhešu is incorrectly read as Nabû-bel-ahhešu in PNA 2/I p. 448b sub Hamnānu. 3 On the restoration cf. SAA 5 52 r.1f, SAA 8 84 r.5 etc. 4 For the rendering of *qàl-li-su*, see LAS II 151 r.11. 6,

LUGAL *be-lí*
6 ⸢*lu*!⸣ *la i-ši-ia-ṭa bi-is* LUGAL *be-lí dul-la-ni-šú*
7 *le-pu-uš an-nu-rig* ITI.ZÍZ ITI.ŠE *e-tar-bu-u-ni*
8 ITI.MEŠ DÙG.GA.MEŠ *šu-nu a-na dul-la-a-ni e-pa-ši*

9 *ṭa-a-ba*! *ṭup-šar-ru-tú an-ni-tú a-na mi-i-ni*
10 ⸢*ú*⸣*-man-na a-na šu-te-tu-qe-e šá lum-*[*n*]*a-a-ni*
11 [*šá x*]*x-a-te šá hi-ṭa-a-te šá la ṭa-ba-te ep-šat*
12 [*x x x x x*] *šá* ^{d}É.A *i-ba-áš-ši*
13 [*x x x x x x*] *šá* ^{d}É.A *i-ba-áš-ši-i* LUGAL *be-lí*
14 [*x x x x x x x x x*] *ina* UGU *i-x*[*x x x*]
15 [*x x x x x x x x x x x*]*x*[*x x x x*]
Rev. beginning broken away
1′ [*x x x x x x*]*-li*? *šá ni-qi-it-te šu-*[*u*]
2′ [*x x*] *šá-*⸢*ni*⸣*-iu*!*-um-ma pa-ni-iu-u*[*m-ma* 0]
3′ [LUGAL *b*]*e-lí li-šá-al da-ba-bu šá-ni-iu-um-*[*ma*]
4′ [*i—d*]*a-te a-na* LUGAL EN*-iá a-qa-bi an-nu-ri*[*g*]
5′ ^{m}*ha-am-na-a-nu* LÚ*.SANGA *šá* ^{m}*sa-si-i* TA* *qa-an-ni-ma*
6′ *ú-ra-mu-šá-nu-u-ni i-si-ni ina* IGI LÚ*.GAL.MEŠ
7′ *la i-zi*!*-su-u-ni an-nu-te-am-ma* LUGAL *be-lí*
8′ *li-šá-al ma-a a-ke-e ra-mu-u-a-ku-nu*
9′ 2 3 *ṭè-ma-ni ina* ŠU.2*-iá liš-li-mu bi-is*
10′ [*x* I]GI*-ia i-har-ri-di* TA* *re-hu-u-te a-da-bu-bu*
11′ [*x x x x*]*-ma*? *lu e-mu-qi-ia* TA* *ma-a*ʾ*-du-te*
12′ [*x x x x* LUGAL] *be-lí a-na* ARAD*-šú iš-pu-ra*

13′ [*x x x x x i*]*r-tu-du-u-ni*
14e [*x x x x x x x* Š]À*-bi* É.GAL
15e [*x x x x x x x x le-r*]*u-ub lu-ṣi*
16e [*x x x x x x x x x a*]*-na*!*-ku-u-ni*
s.1 [*x x x x x x x x x* Š]À*-bi li-ṭi-ba-a*[*n-ni*]

5 O king, my lord! May the king, my lord, not disregard this matter! May the king, my lord, perform his rites at once!

7 Now then, the months of Shebat (XI) and Adar (XII) have arrived. They are favourable months, it is auspicious to perform the rites (now).

9 What do I count this scribal lore for? Is it made for the averting of misfortunes, [of ...]s, of sins, and of evil things?

12 [...] is of Ea.

13 Is [...] of Ea? The king, my lord,

14 [......] *upon* [...]

(Break)

r.1 [......] is of *revenge*.

3 The second [*matter*] is (the same as) the previous matter. May [the king], my lord, ask (about it); I shall then tell the other matter to the king, my lord.

4 Now then, Hamnanu (and) the priest whom Sasî released from ..., who did not stand with us before the magnates — may the king, my lord, ask these (people) how they were released.

9 Two or three *reports* should be completed *by* my hand; he will ... watch over my [...], (while) I speak with the rest.

11 May [...] also be my forces! Out of many (people),

12 [*why*] did [the king], my lord, write to his servant?

13 [...] they have [*p*]*ersecuted* me

14 [...... in] the palace

15 [...... ma]y *I* [g]o in and out

16 [...... that] I am [...]

s.1 [......] May my [h]eart become happy!

63. Crimes in Guzana

K 1366 (ABL 633) + K 11448

CT 53 46

1 [*ina* UG]U 6 LÚ*.ERIM.MEŠ 1 MÍ *ša a-na* LUGAL [EN*-iá áš-pur-an-ni*]
2 [^{m}]*ku-ti-i* LÚ*.A.BA ^{m}*tu-ti-i* LÚ*.[*x x x x*]
3 ^{m}10*—ki-la-an-ni* LÚ*.SANGA ^{m}*qur-di-i* LÚ*.*m*[*u-kil—*KUŠ.*a-pa-a-ni*]

1 [Concer]ning the six men (and) one woman about whom [I wrote] to the king, [my lord] — Kutî the scribe, Tutî [the scribe], Adad-killanni the priest, Qurdî the ch[ariot

9 See coll. r.7 See coll. r.11 Or: "let my troops (consist) of many (men)!" r.13 See coll. [*i*]*r-tu-du-u-ni* taken as a variant of /irtaddūni/ (pf. 3m pl. of *radādu* "to persecute"). Cf. *iddubbu* (passim) beside *iddabbu*, (pf. 3m pl. of *dabābu*). r.16 See coll. s.1 Cf., e.g., SAA 10 227:16, r.6, KAV 214:13, NL 54 r.7.

63 Same scribe as in no. 62. Previous editions: Fales, AfO 27 (1980) 27, 142-146; Cento Lettere (1983) 118-125

FIG. 12. *Priest.*
ANE 124948.

4 [^{m}]*ni-ri—ia-u* LÚ*.GAL—NÍG.ŠID.MEŠ ^{m}*pal-ṭí—ia-u* ⌜LÚ*⌝.[2]-*u*
5 MÍ.*za-za-a* MÍ-*šú ša* ^{m}*tar-ṣi-i* ARAD.MEŠ *ša* LÚ*.EN.NAM
6 *ina* UGU *a-bi-te ša* URU.*gu-za-na šúm-ma i-ba-áš-ši an-nu-te*
7 *ú-du-u šúm-ma la-áš-šú šu-nu-ma ú-du-u i-si-šú-nu*
8 LUGAL *be-lí lid-bu-bu hi-ṭa-ni-šú-nu šá-ni-iu-u-te*
9 *a-na* LUGAL EN-*ia la-qa-bi ša* ^{m}*ku-ti-i ša* ^{m}*tu-ti-i*
10 1-*en hi-iṭ-ṭa-šú-nu ša* DUMU-*a-a iq-ba-áš-šá-nu-u-ni ma-a*
11 ANŠE.KUR.RA.MEŠ *bi-la-a-ni ina ir-ti* LUGAL *lu-bíl*
12 *la i-ma-ga-ru-u-ni šá-ni-ú hi-ṭa-šú-nu* AD-*šú ša* MAN
13 EN-*iá* KUG.UD ÉŠ.QAR *ša* LÚ*.SIPA.MEŠ *ina* ŠÀ-*bi ni-ib-zi aš-šur-a-a*
14 *ina* ŠÀ-*bi ni-ib-zi ár-ma-a-a i-sa-ṭa-ru ina* ŠÀ-*bi* UZU.GÚ
15 *šá* ^{md}PA—ŠU.2—*ṣa-bat* LÚ*.IGI.DUB *ša* LÚ*.GAL—URU.MEŠ-*te ša* LÚ*.A.BA
16 *ni-bu ša* KUG.UD *ina* ŠÀ-*bi* UZU.GÚ-*šú-nu ina* ŠÀ-*bi un-qi*
17 *ik-ta-an-ku ma-a šum-ma* MU.AN.NA *an-ni-tú la i-di-nu*
18 *ma-a i-mu-tú ki-i ṭa-aʾ-tú ta-né-pi-šu-u-ni*
19 [*un-q*]*a-a-te* TA* UZU.GÚ-*šú-nu ub-ta-ti-qu ik-ter-ru*
20 [*x x*]-*nu-um-ma la ina ha-du-te-e šu-u ú-ba-at-ti-qu*
21 [^{m}*qur-d*]*i-i* LÚ*.*mu-kil*—KUŠ.*a-pa-a-ni* ANŠE.KUR.RA.MEŠ *na-kam-te*
22 [0$^{?}$ É].GAL *ú-ka-ba-as ina* UGU *bu-un-bu-ul-li*
23 [*ša* ^{d}15$^{?}$] Á.2-*šú i-sa-kan ma-a mah-ṣi-ni né-mur*
24 [*ma-a* GÍ]R.TUR AN.BAR *bi-la-a-ni la-ab-tu-qu ina qi-in-ni-te*
25 [*ša* LÚ*.E]N.NAM *la-áš-kun la mu-qa-a-a la-qa-bi*
26 [*mi-nu*] *ša man-ni iq-bu-u-ni* LÚ*.SANGA *uq-ṭa-ri-da-áš-šú*
27 [*ana-k*]*u a-sa-me* ^{md}UTU—IGI.LAL-*ni* LÚ*.EN.NAM TA* ^{m}*pal-ṭí—iá-u*
28 [TA*] ^{m}*ni-ri—ia-u i-ta-ma-lik ma-a a-a-e-šá ni-ṣi-bat*
29 *ma-a šu-nu a-na* LÚ*.EN.NAM *ma-a ša* SÍG.SA$_5$ *ú-lab-bi-i*[*š*]-⌜*ú*⌝-[*ka-ni*]
30 [*ša* H]AR KUG.GI GÍR KUG.GI *i-di-nak-kan-ni ma-a* [*x x x*]
31 [*x x*]*x* LÚ*.EN.NAM *ma-a ṣi-a* LÚ*.AB.BA.MEŠ URU [*x x x*]
e.32 [*ina*] IGI É.GAL *ša* DUMU—MAN *pa-hi-ra-a-*

driver], Niri-Ia'u the chief of accounts, Palṭi-Ia'u the [depu]ty, (and) Zazâ, the wife of Tarṣî, (all) servants of the governor — as to the matter of Guzana, they know if there is (such a thing), and if there isn't, they know it, too.

7 The king, my lord, should speak with them, but (first) let me tell the king, my lord, about their other crimes.

10 The first crime of Kutî and Tutî: When my son commanded them, "Bring me the horses, so that I can bring (them) to the king!," they refused.

12 Their other crime: (In the reign of) the father of the king, my lord, they wrote the silver quota of the shepherds on an Assyrian document (and) on an Aramaic document and sealed the amount of silver with the neck seals of the treasurer Nabû-qati-ṣabat, the village manager, (and) the scribe, with their neck seals (and) with the (royal) stamp seal, saying: "If they don't pay this year, they will die!" (But) when a bribe was made, they cut off the [stam]p seals (and) their neck-seals, (and) threw them away. Did they not cut (them) off arbitrarily?

21 [Qurd]î, the chariot driver of the treasury horses, is treading on (the authority of) the [Pa]lace. He has laid his hands on the *cone* [of Ištar], saying: "Strike (f. sg.) me! Let's see (what happens)! Bring me an iron knife, (so) I can cut it off and stick it in the [gov]ernor's ass!" I am unable to tell [what else] he has said about everybody.

26 The priest (Adad-killanni) has *encouraged* him; [I] am powerless.

27 Šamaš-emuranni, the governor, took counsel with Palṭi-Ia'u (the deputy) [and] Niri-Ia'u (the chief of accounts), saying: "Who(se feet) should we grasp?" They told the governor: "The one who dressed [you] in purple garments (and) gave you the golden [br]acelet (and) the golden dagger [......]." The governor said: "Go out and gather the elders of the city [*of Guzana* in] front of the

and 148-152; → Postgate, TCAE (1974) 287-289 (obv. 6-20); Radner, SAAS 6 (1997) 29ff (obv. 12-20). Join by K. Deller, 24.8.64. 20 [*man*]-*nu-um-ma*: cf. Fales, AfO 27 (1980) 143 and 145. 22 *bunbullu* also in SAA 3 7:3, cf.

ni la HAR.MEŠ l[a x x]
33 ⸢i⸣-qa-bu-ni-ni ma-a i-sa-al-šú-nu ma-a a-na a-⸢e⸣-[šá 0]
34 [pa-n]i-ku-nu ma-a e-ta-pal ^{m}10—sa-ka-a LÚ*.EN—GIŠ.GI[GIR 0]
35 [ma-a q]i-ba-na-ši a-na mi-i-ni ta-šá-al-an-na-[ši]
r.1 [ma]-a DUMU.MEŠ-ni šá-ʾa-la ma-a a-na ka-šá-nu-⸢u⸣-ma a-sa-a[l-ku-nu]
2 ma-a qi-ba-a-ni ma-a e-tap-lu-u-ni ki-i a-[ha-iš]
3 ma-a hi-ir-ṣu ša DUMU.MEŠ-ni ša DUMU.MÍ.MEŠ-ni ma-a [x x x x]
4 ^{m}aš-šur—NUMUN—ib-i-ni né-ta-kal ma-a EN—⸢a⸣-[de-e ša LUGAL]
5 a-né-e-nu ma-a ina UGU ^{m}aš-šur—PAB—AŠ pa-ni-ni š[a]k-n[u ma-a LÚ*.EN.NAM GIŠ.PA?]
6 TA* ŠU.2-šú ik-ta-ra-ra Á.2-š[ú] i[na x x]-šú i-sa-ka[n ma-a?]
7 [AR]AD.MEŠ-šu ma-a at-t[u-nu mi]-⸢i⸣-nu ta-dáb-[b]u-ba
8 [m]a-a É—AD-k[u-nu x x x]x-[k]a-ni ma-a a-na-ku
9 [UR]U-ku-nu [x x x x] $^{[m]}$hal-bi-šú URU.sa-mir-i-na-a-a
10 [x x]x ⸢x LUGAL EN-iá⸣ ^{m}bar—ur-ri LÚ*.SAG ma-qa-al-ta-a-nu
11 [ša ^{d}]bi-iʾ-li—ra-kab-bi ša URU.sa-ma-al-la
12 a-b[u]-tú an-ni-tú iq-ṭí-bu-u-ni ^{m}ta-ra-ṣi-i
13 LÚ*.A.BA ša URU.gu-za-na DUMU-šú É ^{m}aš-šur—NUMUN—DÙ i-ti-din
14 ^{m}aš-šur—NUMUN—DÙ ki-i TA* DUMU.M[EŠ—LU]GAL šu-tu-u-ni DUMU-šú ša ^{m}tar-ṣi-i
15 LÚ*.GAL—NÍG.ŠID.MEŠ šu-u ki-i 10 UD.MEŠ an-na-te ša ^{m}aš-šur—NUMUN—DÙ
16 ina URU.ni-nu-u-a i-du-lu-u-ni DUMU ^{m}tar-ṣi-i GAL—ka-ṣir
17 šu-u HAR KUG.GI GÍR KUG.GI TÚG.šá—ṣi-il-li
18 SAG ^{m}aš-šur—NUMUN—DÙ ú-ka-la ^{m}tar-ṣi-i an-ni-ú
19 LUGAL be-lí da-an-na-ta-a-nu ma-ṣa-ta-a-nu šu-u
20 ARAD.MEŠ ša MÍ—É.GAL ša DUMU—MAN ša É LÚ*.GAL.MEŠ
21 LÚ*.za-ku-ú up-te-ii-ṣi a-na É ^{m}aš-šur—NUMUN—DÙ i-ti-din
22 ù DUMU—šip-ri.MEŠ ša LUGAL be-lí [[x]] a-na URU.gu-za-na
23 i-šá-par-an-ni ^{m}ta-ra-ṣi-i MÍ-šú qu-la-a-li
24 ša i-šá-ka-nu-u-ni man-nu i-šam-me MÍ.za-za-a MÍ-šú ša ^{m}LAL-i
25 DUMU.MEŠ-šá la ša bal-lu-ṭi šu-nu LUGAL be-lí LÚ*.SANGA

crown prince's palace! [...] no bracelets, n[o ...]."

33 I am being told that he asked them (= the elders): "To whom are you [devoted]?" Adda-sakâ, a chari[ot] owner, answered: "Tell us, why do you ask u[s]? Ask our sons!"

He said: "It is you I have aske[d], so tell me!" They answered of one [accord]: "We have eaten the *slice* of our sons and daughters, and [that of] Aššur-zeru-ibni too, but we keep the t[reaty of the king], we are devoted to Esarhaddon."

r.5 [The governor] threw [the sceptre] from his hands, place[d] h[is] arms [on] his [chest], and said: "[You are] his [servant]s! [W]hat are you saying? You [...] yo[ur dynastic house! I [......] your [cit]y."

9 Halbišu the Samarian, [*a servant of*] the king, my lord, (and) Bar-uri, the eunuch (and) *maqaltānu*-official [of] Ba'al-rakkab of Sam'al, told me this matter:

12 Tarṣî, the scribe of Guzana, has given his son to the household of Aššur-zeru-ibni. When Aššur-zeru-ibni is with the son[s of the ki]ng, the son of Tarṣî is the chief of accounts. During these ten days when Aššur-zeru-ibni is lingering in Nineveh, the son of Tarṣî is the chief tailor, taking care of the golden bracelet, the golden dagger and the parasol of Aššur-zeru-ibni.

18 This Tarṣî, O king, my lord, is a powerful (and) influential man. He has *taken away* the servants of the queen, of the crown prince, of the household of the magnates (and) the exempts, (and) given them to the household of Aššur-zeru-ibni.

22 Moreover, the messengers whom the king, my lord, sends to Guzana — who hears (all) the slighting remarks that Tarṣî and his wife make (about them)? Zazâ, the wife of Tarṣî, and her sons should not be kept alive. O king, my lord! The priest is a brother-in-

the footnote in SAA 3 7:8. The translation "cone" is suggested by Neo-Aramaic *banbūl gelīdi* "icicle" (information courtesy Zack Cherry). 35 See coll. r.6 See coll. r.24-27 Reiner Astral Magic, 98. r.26f I.e., they are witches.

26 LÚ*.i-ki-i-su ša ^{m}tar-ṣi-i šu-u MÍ.MEŠ-šú-nu
27 ^{d}30 TA* AN-e ú-še-ra-da-a-ni LUGAL be-lí ina UGU
28 ina ŠÀ-bi e-gír-a-te-ia gab-bu ša ina UGU LUGAL EN-iá
29 áš-pur-an-ni 1-te ši-i a-bu-tú ina ŠÀ-bi
30 al-tu-u-da ina UGU da-ba-bi ša ⌈x x⌉
31e a-qa-bu-u-ni ku-um ^{m}aš-šur—NUMUN—[DÙ x x x]
32e ^{md}AMAR.UTU—HAL-ni a-ti-kip a-[x x x x x]
33e LUGAL be-lí ^{d}UTU ARAD ša LU[GAL EN-iá a-na-ku]
34e ⌈x⌉-ba la e-mar [x x x]
s.1 [ù ša] ^{m}mil-ki—ZALÁG LUGAL be-lí da-ba-ab-šú la har-ṣa 1-en [UD-mu ša ina IGI LUGAL e-ra-bu-u]-ni a-n[a 0]
2 [LUGAL] EN-iá a-qa-bi da-ba-ab-šú ina ŠÀ-bi uz-ni-ia šu-u ⌈a⌉-[na-ku pa-ni ša LUGAL EN-i]a la-a-mur [0]
3 [x x x].x šúm-ma LUGAL be-lí i-qa-bi ma-a ša taš-mu-u-ni [a-ta-a la taš-p]u-ra [x x x]

law of Tarṣî. Their wives bring down the moon from the sky!

27 O king, my lord, concerning (this), in all the letters which I have sent to the king, my lord, there is just this one matter. I have *been shamed*. On account of the words that I have spoken [...], instead of Aššur-zeru-[ibni ...], I have butted Marduk-išmanni [...].

33 The king, my lord, is the sun! [I am] a servant of the ki[ng, my lord], (but) I do not see [...].

s.1 [And] the words spoken [by] Milki-nuri, O king, my lord, are not accurate. I will tell [the king], my lord, the very first [day when I enter before the king]. His words are within my ears. Let me see [the face of the king, m]y [lord, ...]. Should the king, my lord, say: "[Why did you not wri]te what you heard?" — [...].

64. How to Deal with Appeals for Royal Intervention

K 5432a + K 11465 (CT 53 426)

1 ina UGU LÚ*.ERIM.MEŠ ša a-bat—šar-ra-a-⌈te⌉ [i-zak-ka-ru-u-ni]
2 LUGAL be-lí lu la ú-⌈ku⌉-uš ⌈LÚ*⌉.[ERIM.MEŠ]
3 li-li-ku-u-ni li-iq-⌈bi⌉-ú ⌈ina de-e⌉-n[i-šú-nu LUGAL]
4 le-ru-ub a-bu-tú š[a ina] IGI LUGAL mah-ra-tu-[u-ni]
5 ina ŠU.2-šú li-ṣi-bat ša [in]a IGI LUGAL EN-iá la mah-r[a-tu-u-ni]
6 LUGAL be-l[í lu-ra]-⌈am⌉-mi [š]úm-ma ARAD ša LUGAL šu-u ina [UGU]
7 LÚ*.šak-ni-šu ina UGU ⌈LÚ*.NAM⌉-šú iq-ṭí-bi bir-ti IGI.2
8 ša LÚ*.šak-ni-šu ina UGU-h[i-š]ú lu-[ma-di-d]u šúm-ma ur-du
9 ⌈ša⌉ aš-šur-a-a bir-te IGI.2-šú ⌈ša⌉ EN-šú lu-ma-di-du
10 [m]a-a ina ŠÀ-bi LUGAL i-ti-i-la [ma]-a me-me-ni i-si-šú
e.11 [lu] la i-da-bu-ub ma-a ina ŠÀ-[b]i e-ki-it! la ta-ra-di
12 [l]u la-a ú-kaš LUGAL be-lí E[RI]M.MEŠ-šú ú-ga-mar i—[su-ri]
r.1 [i]-lak a-na me-eh-ri-šu i-⌈qa-bi⌉ ma-a ina

CT 53 78+

1 Concerning the men who [appeal] for royal intervention, the king, my lord, should not tarry. Let th[e men] come and speak up, and may [the king] familiarise himself with [their] cases. May the king seize upon the matter whi[ch] is accept[able t]o him. What is not acce[ptable t]o the king, my lord, the king, [my] lord, [may] drop.

6 If one is a servant of the king and tells ab[out] his prefect or about his governor, his prefect should be given clear instructions about him; (and) if one is a servant of an Assyrian, his lord should be told in no uncertain terms: "He rests in the king's protection — nobody may litigate against him! You must not lead him to ..., he must not be detained!"

12 (Should) the king, my lord, *finish off* his m[e]n, one might [g]o to his comrade and say:

64 Previous editions: Postgate, RA 74 (1980) 180ff; Fales, AfO 27 (1980) 148; Fales and Lanfranchi Lettere (1992) 74ff. → Nissinen, SAA 7 (1998) 131 (obv. 2-6, r.1-5). Join S. Parpola 26.7.76. Coll. C.B.F. Walker, 1976. Same scribe as in no. 62. Horizontal tablet. 1 Or: "who [are invoking] the king's word (in order to get a royal intervention)." 10 Cf. no. 30 r.5. r.2 Or: "It was not said (*la qa-bi*) before the king." Cf. no. 63:9. r.5 See

FIG. 13. *Amulet stone with the head of Pazuzu (cf. no. 65).* ANE 91899.

IGI LUGAL-*ma*
2 *la-qa-bi ú-la* LUGAL *be-lí bir-te* IGI.2.MEŠ *ša* LÚ*.GAL.MEŠ
3 *ina* UGU-*hi lu-ma-di-du bi-is i-šam-me-ú* UN.MEŠ
4 *ma-a*ʾ-⌈*du-te i-la-ku*⌉-*u-ni ṣa-hi-it-tú ša* LUGAL [EN-*iá*]
5 *ina da-ba-bi ma-a*ʾ-*di ta-na-mar*! *ina* UGU KUG.GI *ša* [*a-na*]
6 ⌈LUGAL⌉ E[N]-*iá áš-pur-an-ni nu-uk šum-ma ṭè-e-mu ša* [*x x x*]
7 *an-ni-e ina* IGI LUGAL EN-*iá e-ta-rab nu-uk* ⌈LUGAL⌉ [*be-lí*]
8 *a-na* ARAD-*šú liš-pu-ra a-ta-a* LUG[AL *x x x x x*]
9 [*šúm*]-*ma* LUGAL *be-lí ina* UGU *da-ba-bi a*[*n-ni-e x x*]
10 ⌈*x*⌉-*te-e-ni a-na* LÚ*.*sar-tin-n*[*i x x x x x x*]
11e [*š*]*a*? URU.*har-ha-ra* LUGAL *be-lí* [*x x x x x x*]
12e IGI.2-[*š*]*ú-nu lu ina* UGU-*hi-šú* [*x x x x x x x*]

"I too want to speak before the king." *No*, O king, my lord! The magnates should be given clear instructions about it. They will hear it *at once* and many people will come. The desire of the king, [my lord], will be achieved through much talk.

r.5 As to the gold about which I wrote [to] the king, my lord: "If the report of this [...] comes to the king, my lord, the king, [my lord], should write to his servant" — why [*has*] the kin[g, my lord, *not written to me*]?"

9 [I]f the king, my lord, [...] about t[his] matter

10 [...] to the *sartinn*[*u* ......]

11 [*o*]*f* Harhar, the king, my lord [......]

12 [T]hey should keep their eyes on him [...]

Postgate, RA 74 (1980) 180 and Deller, Or. 56 (1987) 179.

65. Divination Taught to a Goldsmith's Son

83-1-18,121

1 *aš-šur* ^{d}UTU ^{d}EN ^{d}PA *a-na* LUGAL
2 EN-*iá lik-ru-ub* ^{m}*pa-ru*$^{!}$*-ṭu*
3 LÚ*.SIMUG.KUG.GI *ša* É$^{!}$ MÍ—É.GAL
4 *ki-i* LUGAL DUMU—LUGAL DUMU—KÁ.DINGIR.KI
5 *ina* ŠÀ-*bi* KUG.UD *i-si-qi ina* É *ra-mi-ni-šú*
6 *ú-se-ši-ib*$^{!}$*-šú* IM.GÍD.DA
7 *ina* ŠÀ-*bi* LÚ*.*a-ši-pu-te a-na* DUMU-*šú*
8 *iq-ṭí-bi* UZU.MEŠ *i-ba-áš-ši*
9 *ša* LÚ*.*ba-ru-u-te uk-tal-li-mu-šú*
10 *li-iq-te ša*$^{!}$ 1$^{!}$ UD—*a-na*—^{d}EN.LÍL
11 *i-ba-áš-ši lu e-ta-mar*
12 *i-na pa-ni ša* LUGAL EN-*iá*
13 *ina* UGU *da-ba-bi an-ni-e*
14 LUGAL *be-lí a-na* ARAD-*šú liš-pu-[r]a*
15 [*x x x x x x*] *šá x*[*x x x*]
rest broken away

Rev. beginning broken away
1′ ⸢*x x*⸣ [*x x x x x x x x*]
2′ ^{m}*sa-si-i x*[*x x x x x x x*]
3′ GIŠ.*ṣal*$^{!}$*-lu-ma-a-ni* NA$_{4}$.*ki-šá-*⸢*du*⸣
4′ SAG.DU—*pa-zu-za-a-ni ina* SAG-*šú*
5′ *i-ba-áš-ši ú-šar-qu-up*
6′ ⸢LÚ*$^{!}$⸣ *lu-sa-ni-qi lu-še-ṣi-a*

ABL 1245

1 May Aššur, Šamaš, Bel (and) Nabû bless the king, my lord.

2 Parruṭu, a goldsmith of the household of the queen, has, like the king and the crown prince, bought a Babylonian, and settled him in his own house. He has taught exorcistic literature to his son; extispicy omens have been explained to him, (and) he has even studied gleanings from Enuma Anu Enlil, and this right before the king, my lord!

13 Let the king, my lord, write to his servant on account of this matter.

15 [......] *that* [...]

(Break)

r.2 Sasî [......]

3 They are even *planting* amulets of black wood, a neck-stone (and) Pazuzu-heads on his head. Should I interrogate and bring out the man?

65 Same scribe as in no. 62. Collated by S. Parpola, 26.3.68. The order of the obverse and the reverse is possibly (though unlikely) to be inverted, since the left side (which is normally inscribed in the same direction as the reverse) is here inscribed in the same direction as the obverse. Cf. note on no. 48. 2f See coll. 2-8 → Nissinen, SAAS 7 (1998) 142. 4-12 → Parpola (1997) 321. 10 See coll. r.4 For an illustration and description of such a Pazuzu-head see Klengel-Brandt, "Ein Pazuzu-Kopf mit Inschrift," Or. 37 (1968) 81-84 and Tab. VII. r.5 *ú-šar-qu-up* is most

FIG. 14. *An amulet jewelstone.*
ANE 135114.

7′ LUGAL *be-lí ṭè-e-mu liš-kun*
8′ *ki-ma hi-id-du e-ti-qi-ši*
9′ *li-di-nu-u-ni šá da-a-ni*
10′ *ša la man-ni hi-id-du i-da-nu-u-ni*

11′ *ša* LUGAL *be-lí a-na* ARAD-*šú iš-pur-an-ni*
12′ *ma-a man-nu la-ma-a-nu ma-a'-du*
13′ *ú-kal-lam-ka le-ma-gúr a-na* MAN
14′ EN-*iá la áš-par šá-ti-ši*

15′ *pu-u-lu ina* UGU *lub-bi a-sa-kan*
16e *nu-uk a-ke-e lu-*⌈*sah*$^{!}$*-hi*⌉$^{!}$*-ri*$^{!}$
17e ARAD-*ka šup-ru*
s.1 LUGAL *be-lí li-ih-kim ina* UD-4-KAM U[D *x x x*]
2 LUGAL *be-lí ki ma-ṣi ah-ru* IGI.2.MEŠ [*x x x x*]

7 Let the king, my lord, give orders: if he daubs her with hiddu, they should give it to me. The hiddu must be given to me, (whether) by force, (or) without anybody('s permission)!

11 As to what the king, my lord, wrote to his servant: "Who displays much malice towards you (and) is disagreeable?" — would I not write to the king, my lord! ...

14 I put the foundation stone in a bag, (thinking): "How will *he* return it?" Send your servant.

s.1 May the king, my lord, understand! On the 4th day, [......].

2 O king, my lord! How long still [will *my*] eyes [...]?

66. Fragment Mentioning Kar-Mullissi

Ki 1904-10-9,84 (BM 99055)

beginning broken away
1′ [*a-n*]*a* ⌈LUGAL EN-*iá*⌉ [*x x x x x x*]
2′ [*x*] *lu la maš-la-ku* ⌈*šú ma x x x*⌉ [LUGAL *be-lí*]
3′ [*a*]*-na* ARAD-*šú ki-i an-ni-e i-s*[*a-ap-ra*]
4′ *ma-a* LÚ*.ERIM.MEŠ *ina* ŠÀ-*bi us-*[*s*]*ar*$^{?}$*-x*[*x x*]
5′ *ma-a mar ta-*⌈*mar*⌉*-u-*[*ni*] ⌈*x*⌉ [*x x x*]
6′ TA* *pa-ni-iá* ⌈*la*⌉ [*tu-pa-za*]*r* ⌈TA*⌉ [*x x x*]
7′ *up-ta-z*[*i*$^{?}$*-x x x x*]*x a* [*x x x*]
8′ [*ina* U]GU$^{?}$ [*x x š*]*a*$^{?}$ LUGAL *be-*[*lí x x x*]
9′ [*x x x x x x x*]*x* É *a x*[*x x x x*]
10′ [*x x x x x x x*] 3-*su* [*x x x x*]
11′ [*x x x x x* LUG]AL$^{?}$*-ni a-*[*x x x x*]
12′ [*x x x x* LUGAL] *be-lí x*[*x x x*]
rest broken away
Rev. beginning broken away
1′ [*x x x x x x x*] É.GAL *x*[*x x x x*]
2′ [*x x x x x*]-⌈*a*⌉*-te šá i-*[*x x x x*]
3′ [*x x a-n*]*a* ⌈URU⌉.*kar*—^{d}NIN.L[ÍL *x x x*]
4′ [*ir*$^{?}$]*-ta-kas šúm-ma iq-ṭí-bi-*[*ú x x x*]
5′ [*šúm-m*]*a la iq-bi-ú mi-i-nu* [*x x x x*]
6′ [*x x x x*].MEŠ *šá* LUGAL EN-*iá* DUMU.MEŠ-*iá* [*x x x x*]
7′ [*x x x x x x* ^{md}*x*]—MAN—PAB *i*[*š-x x x x*]
8′ [*x x x x x x x x k*]*a* [*x x x x x*]
rest broken away

CT 53 976

(Beginning destroyed)

1 [t]o the king, my lord [......]

2 [...] I am not like that [... The king, my lord], wr[ote t]o his servant as follows: "He has [...] troops there; [do] no[t concea]l from me anything that you s[e]e (or) h[ear]" — have I conce[aled ...] fr[om ......]?

8 [*As t*]*o* [*the ... about wh*]*ich* the king, [my] lor[d, wrote to me]: "[......] *house* [...]

10 [......] one third [...]

11 [... *ki*]*ngs* [...]

12 [... the king], my lord, [...]

(Break)

r.1 [......] the palace [...]

2 [(...) the ...]s which [...]

3 [... has] bound [... i]n Kar-Mullis[si]; whether [they] say [... o]r do not say, what [...]?

6 [... the son]s of the king, my lord, [*are*] my sons [...]

7 [...; ...]-šarru-uṣur [...]

8 [... *yo*]*ur* [......]

(Rest destroyed)

likely to be taken as pl. 3rd m. of *zqp* Š with a dissimilated first radical and an apocopated pl. ending (< *ušazqupu*); cf. *ir-qa-pu-u-ni* for *izqapūni*, StAT 2 173:8. r.8, 10 Or does *hiddu* act as a subject in these clauses? r.11-14 Cf. Nissinen, SAAS 7 (1998) 142. r.14 *áš-par* is a syncopated variant of *ašappār*(*a*) "shall I send?" (with interrogative intonation); cf. *as-par* = *assapār*(*a*) "I have sent," SAA 13 20 r.13 and 22 r.5. *šá-ti-ši* at the end of the line remains obscure. r.15 For *lub-bi*, cf. SAA 10 315 r.15. r.16 Or: "How will I return it?" See coll. r.17 "your servant": i.e., "me." s.2 *kī maṣi*: see Parker, SAAB 11 (1997) 37-54.

66 Same scribe as in no. 62. 2 Or: *lū lā mašlāku* "may I not be like that." 4 Or: "the troops [...] there."

67. Stolen Gold

K 4299

beginning broken away

1′ *ša* 6 MA.NA [TA* IGI ^{m}DINGIR-*ma*—ZU]
2′ *i-ti-ši ú-ma-a* [*šúm-ma* LUGAL *be-lí*]
3′ [*i-qa-b*]*i an-na-ka* [*x x x x x*]

4′ [^{m}*ta*$^{?}$]-*at-ti-i* DUMU [^{m}*x x x x x*]
5′ [TA* ^{m}]TE-*a-a* ^{m}*mu-x*[*x x x x x*]
6′ [*ih-ti*]-*ṭu* LUGAL *be-lí a-*[*na x x li-šá-al*]
7′ [*ma-a*] KUG.GI *ša* ^{m}DINGIR-*ma*—[ZU *x x x x*]
8′ [*i*]-*ta-nu-ni-ka-nu-u* ⌜LÚ*⌝.[*x x x x x*]
9′ *ša* ^{m}DINGIR-*ma*—ZU LÚ*.G[AL—*ki-ṣir x x x*]

10′ TA* IGI ARAD.MEŠ-*ia t*[*a x x x x x*]
11′ [LUGA]L$^{?}$ *be-lí i-ba-ta-q*[*u-ni x x x x x*]
12′ [*x x x*]-*bu-ni* KUG.GI LUGA[L *x x x x x*]
13′ [*x x ma*]-*a*ʾ-*du šu*$^{?}$-[*x x x x x x*]

rest broken away

Rev. beginning broken away

1′ [*x x x x*] LUGAL *be-lí* [*x x x x x x*]
2′ [*a-na* LUGAL] EN-*iá ú-sa-*[*x x x x x*]
3′ [*x x x x*] *šá* LUGAL *be-lí* [*x x x x x*]
4′ [*x*] ⌜*x*⌝-*ta-ra-a*$^{?}$-*te x*[*x x x x x x*]
5′ MÍ.É.GAL-*tú ina* ŠÀ-*bi* [*x x x x x x*]
6′ LÚ*.EN—*pi-qi-te-ma* [*x x x x x x*]

7′ *i-na-áš-ši* ŠU LUGAL [*x x x x x x*]
8′ *ú-ma-a šu-tu-u-ni* [*x x is—su-ri* LUGAL *be-lí*]
9′ *a-na* ARAD-*šú la i-qi-*[*ap x x x x x*]
10′ *aš-šur-a-a ša* LUGAL *be-lí* [*x x x x x x*]
11′ *li-šá-al ma-a* GIŠ.*x*[*x x x x x*]
12′ *i-ta-an-na-ka-a* [*x x x x x x*]
13′ *i-ba-áš-ši ina pa-ni* [*x x x x x x*]
14′ *a-qa-bi na-mir ša* [*x x x x x x*]
15′ *šúm-ma a-na-ku a—ma*[*r x x x x x x*]
16′ LUGAL EN-*iá ú-p*[*a-x x x x x x*]
17′ *ma* ⌜*x x x*⌝ *x*[*x x x x x x x*]

rest broken away

ABL 1291

(Beginning destroyed)

1 He took 6 minas worth [*of gold from Ilumma-le'i*]. Now, [if the king, my lord, command]s, [*I shall investigate* (the matter)] here.

4 [*T*]attî, son of [PN, *weigh*]*ed* [*the gold* with] Sukkaya (and) Mu[...].

6 The king, my lord, [should ask ... as follows]: "Did they [g]ive the gold of Ilumma-[le'i] to you (pl.)?"

9 The [...] of the [cohort] com[mander] Ilumma-le'i [...]

10 from my servants [......]

11 [the kin]g, my lord, parce[ls out ...]

12 [...] *the roya*[*l*] *gold* [...]

13 [... m]uch [...]

(Break)

r.1 [...] the king, my lord, [......]

2 *I have in*[*formed* the king], my lord, [...]

3 [...] *whom* the king, my lord, [.....]

4 [...]s [......]

5 the lady Ekallitu *in* [......]

6 an official carries [......]

7 The hand of the king [......]

8 (that) he now is [...]. [Perhaps the king, my lord], does not beli[eve] his servant!

10 May an Assyrian whom the king, my lord, [*trusts*], ask [...]: "Did [...] give you [...]?"

13 [...] is in charge of [...]

14 I will speak up. It is clear *that* [...]

15 Verily I do not co[nceal] any[thing that I ... from] the king, my lord, [...]

(Rest destroyed)

67 Same scribe as in no. 62. 6 For the restoration cf. *ih-ṭi-ṭu* in SAA 1 52 r.3. 9 Restored from SAA 14 2 r.6 (666 BC). r.5 It is tempting to suggest to read this PNf as Šadditu (= Esarhaddon's sister). We do not know any other case in which É.GAL would stand for *šaddû*, but because KUR can mean both *ekallu* "palace" and *šaddû* "mountain", therefore, interchangeably, we would not exclude the same interpretations for É.GAL. r.16 See coll.

68. Disloyal Officials

K 5424a

beginning broken away

1′ [*x x x x x x x*] *man ni*$^{?}$ [*x x x*]
2′ [*x x x x x x*] *áš* ⸢*x*⸣ [*x x x*]
3′ [*x x x x x x*]*x* LÚ.*si*-[*x x x*]
4′ [*x x x x x x* L]Ú.*x*[*x x x*]
5′ [*x x x x x x x x*]*x* [*x x x x*]

about 9$^{?}$ lines broken away; traces of one line

15′ *ša la* LUGAL EN-*iá ú-x*[*x x x x x*]
16′ *iq-bu-u-ni ma-a man-nu šu-n*[*u x x x x*]
17′ *ša* LÚ*.EN.NAM LÚ*.⸢3⸣.U_5.ME[Š LÚ*.*x x x*]
18′ LÚ*.*rak-su*.MEŠ LÚ*.A—SIG LÚ*.[*x x x*]
19′ LÚ*.GIŠ.GIGIR *ša* LÚ*.NAM URU.MEŠ [*x x x*]
20′ *ina* UGU-*hi* ^{m}*na-si—bar* LÚ*.[GAL—URU.MEŠ]
21′ ⸢*x x x*⸣ [*x x*] ⸢*x x x x*⸣ [*x x x x x*]

rest broken away

Rev. beginning broken away

1′ ⸢*x*⸣ *x*[*x x x x x x x x x x x*]
2′ NUMUN *x*[*x x x x x x x x x x*]
3′ SUM$^{?}$ [*x x x x x x x x x x x*]
4′ *x*[*x x x x x x*]*x x*[*x x x x*]
5′ LÚ*.ERIM.M[EŠ *x x x*]*x* LÚ*.*x*[*x x x x*]
6′ ^{m}⸢*su*$^{?}$⸣-*mu-ti*-⸢*i*$^{?}$⸣ ⸢LÚ*⸣.A.BA [*x x x x*]
7′ ^{m}⸢*na*⸣-*si—bar* LÚ*.GAL—URU.MEŠ *x*[*x x x x*]
8′ [*šu*]-*nu ú-du-u a-na* LUGAL [*x x x x*]
9′ [*ina* UG]U$^{?}$ ^{m}NUMUN—GIN *ki-i iq*-[*x x x x x*]
10′ [*a-n*]*a* LÚ*.3.U_5-*u-tú* LÚ*.*mu-kil*—K[UŠ.PA.MEŠ-*u-tú*]
11′ [^{m}10$^{?}$]—*ki-la-an-ni šu-u iq-ṭí-bi* [*x x x*]
12′ [*x x x x*]-*ni-ti ina šá-pa-lu*-[*uš-šú*]
13′ [*x x x x x*]*x* ⸢*šu*⸣-*u* LUGAL *be-lí* [*x x x*]
14′ [*x x x x x*] ⸢*ú*⸣-*se-li ug-da-x*[*x x x*]
15′ [*x x x ša* LUGAL *be*]-*lí iq-bu-u-n*[*i x x x*]
16′ [*x x x x x x x x*]*x la x*[*x x*]
17′ [*x x x x x x x x*]-*an-ni* [*x x*]
18′ [*x x x x x x x x*]-*si-at* [*x x*]
19′ [*x x x x x x x x*] LÚ*.ERIM.M[EŠ *x*]
20′ [*x x x x x x x x x-t*]*a*$^{?}$-[*x x*]

rest broken away

s.1 [*x x x x x*]*x aš-šur-a-a* LUGAL *be-lí* [*x x x x x*]
2 [*x x x x*] ⸢LÚ*⸣.LUL.ME *ú-šá-da-b*[*a-bu-u-ni x x*]
3 [*x x x x x*] *šá-ni-e* [*x x x x x*]

CT 53 80

(Beginning destroyed)

15 [*who* ...] without the king, my lord's permission, [*about whom the king, my lord*], said: "Who are the[y?" – *they are* ...s] of the governor, 'third men,' [...s], recruits, a chariot fighter, [...], the *horse trainer* of the governor. The towns [...]

20 *upon* Nasi'-bar, [the village manager ......]

(Break)

r.5 the me[n of ...], the [...s],

6 *Su*mutî, the scribe [...],

6 Nasi'-bar, the village manager [...]

7 [Th]ey know [*and will say it*] to the king, [my lord].

9 [As t]o Zeru-ken, when he [...]

10 [t]o *become* a 'third man' (or) a chariot-d[river],

11 [*Adad*]-killanni *himself* said: "[...]

11 [... *form*]*erly* under [*him*]

13 *He is* [...]." The king, my lord [...]

14 [...] *promoted* [...]

15 [... the king, my lor]d, said [...]

16 [......] *not* [...]

(Break)

s.1 [...] Assyrian(s). O king, my lord, [...]

2 [... who] incit[es] *criminals* [...]

3 [...] *another* [...]

68 Same scribe as in no. 62. → no. 63. 19 See coll. 20 Alternatively, "Concerning Nasi'-bar" or "against Nasi'-bar." r.9 See coll. r.11 [Adad]-killanni is possibly the same person as in no. 63:3, cf. PNA 1/I p. 28a. r.12 Possible restorations are *ina pa*]-*ni-ti*, *an*]-*ni-ti* or *šá*]-*ni-ti*. s.2 ME written like LAL. See note on no. 106:10.

69. Sin-balassu-iqbi Sends Gold to Sasî

K 724

1 ^{d}PA ^{d}AMAR.UTU *a-na* DUMU—MAN EN-*ia*
2 *lik-ru-bu*
3 ^{md}PA—PAB LÚ.*šá—hu-ṭa-ri*
4 *iq-ṭi-bi-ia ma-a* 1 MA.NA
5 KUG.GI ^{md}30—TI-*su—iq-bi*
6 DUMU ^{md}NIN.GAL—SUM-*na*
7 *ina* ŠU.2 LÚ.*mu-kil*—KUŠ.PA.MEŠ
e.8 *a-na* ^{m}*sa-s*[*i*]-*i*
r.1 LÚ*.*ha-za-nu* [*ša*?] ⸢DUMU?—MAN?⸣
2 *ú-še-bi-la*
3 *ma-a mì-i-nu ša* LUGAL *be-lí*
4 *i-qab-bu-ú-ni*
rest uninscribed

ABL 445

^{1} May Nabû (and) Marduk bless the crown prince, my lord.

^{3} Nabû-naṣir, the staff-bearer, has told me: ^{4} "Sîn-balassu-iqbi, son of Nikkal-iddina, has sent 1 mina of gold with a chariot driver to Sasî, the superintendent [of] *the crown prince*, saying, 'What is it that the king, my lord, commands?'"

70. May the Horse not Die!

K 1372

1 [^{d}PA *u* ^{d}AMAR.UTU *a-na* DUMU]—⸢LUGAL EN-*iá*⸣ *lik-ru-bu*
2 [*ina* U]GU ANŠE.KUR.RA *am-mì-i ú-ma-a*
3 [^{m}ARAD?]—⸢^{d}⸣15 *iq-ṭi-bi-a ma-a ki-i*
4 [*ša*] *ṭè-e-mu šak-na-ka-ni*
5 [*e-p*]*u-uš a-ni-na* DUMU—LUGAL *be-l*[*í*]
6 [ARA]D-*ka* ⸢*a*⸣-*na-ku a-na* DUMU—[LUGAL]
e.7 [*li*]*l?-li-ki* ⸢*x x*⸣ [*x* ANŠE.KUR.RA?]
r.1 [*l*]*a i-mu-u-at* ⸢LÚ⸣.[*x x x*]
2 [*am*]-*mì-ú ma-a a-ta-*⸢*a*⸣ [0]
3 [ANŠE.K]UR.RA.MEŠ *ša šap-a-lu-*[*a*?]
rest broken away

CT 53 178

^{1} May [Nabû and Marduk] bless the crown [prince], my lord.

^{2} [Concer]ning that horse, [Urdu]-Issar is now telling me: "[D]o [as] you were ordered to do!"

^{5} Hear me, O crown prince, [my] lord! I am your [servan]t. May it [*ha*]*ppen* to the [crown] prince that [...], may [*the horse* n]ot die!

$^{r.1}$ [Th]at [...] (official) is saying: "Why [the ho]rses that are under [*me* ......]?

(Rest destroyed)

71. Fragment Mentioning Sasî

K 1357

beginning broken away
1′ *x*[*x x x x x x x x x*]
2′ ⸢*i*⸣-*tan-*⸢*na*⸣ *x*[*x x*] *x*[*x x*]
3′ LÚ*.EN.NAM *ša* KUR.*qu-*⸢*e*⸣
4′ *i-zi-ir-ra-an-ni*
5′ *ma-a* LUGAL *a-na* ^{m}*sa-si-i*
6′ *liš-al ki-i ša* LUGAL *a-na* URU.KASKAL.K[I]

CT 53 44

(Beginning destroyed)

^{2} ["]He gave [......].

^{3} "The governor of Que hates me. May the king ask Sasî, just as the king wrote to us in

69 For the context of this letter see Nissinen, SAAS 7 (1998) 141f. Collated by S. Parpola, 1966. Roundish horizontal tablet. $^{r.1}$ Signs at the end of the line obliterated; reading ⸢DUMU—MAN⸣ (Harper) not excluded but uncertain. See coll. → Frame Babylonia (1992) 99 n.174. $^{r.2}$ *ú-še-bi-la* sic.
70 Same scribe as in no. 69. ^{5} For *a-ni-na*, see SAA 9 3 ii 13. ^{7} Thus if referring to the horse; otherwise, "may he not die."
71 Same scribe as in no. 69. Judging from the curvature, the first preserved line is written on "half-edge." ^{2}

7′ *[i]š-pur-an-na-ši-i-ni*
8′ *[ma]-a* LUGAL *ina* UGU-*hi-ia*
9′ *[ir-t]u-ú-bu*
e.10′ *[ma-a]* ⸢*a—dan*⸣*-niš* ⸢*ap*⸣*-ta-làh*
11′ *[x x]x-hi x[x x x]x ti* ⸢*x x*⸣
r.2 ⸢*ú*⸣*-bi-lu-ú-*⸢*ni i*⸣*-qab-bi [m]a-*⸢*a*⸣ LÚ.ARAD *ša* LUGAL *a-na-ku*
3 *[ma-a* A]D-*šú ina* ŠÀ-*bi a-de-e*
4 *[ú-s]e-ri-ba-an-*⸢*ni*⸣
5 *[ma-a mì]-i-nu ša ina* KUR.*gi-[mir*?*]*
6 *[a-šam]-mu-ú-ni ta-š[am-me]*
7 *[x x x]* ⸢*x x na*?⸣ *[x x x]*
rest broken away

Harran. The king [ra]ged at me and I got very scared."

11 [...... who] brought [...], says: "I am a servant of the king; his [fat]her [made] me enter the treaty. You will h[ear w]hatever [I he]ar in *Go[mer]*

(Rest destroyed)

72. I have Something to Tell the King

K 1128

beginning broken away
1′ *ba-la-ṭi* UD.ME[Š]
2′ *ar-ku-ú-te*
3′ ^{d}*aš-šur* ^{d}30 ^{d}UTU
4′ ^{d}IM *u* ^{d}AMAR.UTU
5′ *a-na* LUGAL EN-*iá*
6′ *li-iš-ru-ku*
7′ *ši-pir ep-še-te-ka*
8′ *da-an-qa-a-te*
9′ *[ina]* UGU-*hi* DINGIR.MEŠ
r.1 *[ka]-*⸢*la*⸣*-me*
2 *[lu-ṭ]i-ib-bu*
3 *[da-ba]-bu*
4 *[šu-ú ú]-ma-a i-ba-áš-ši*
5 *[a-na* LUGAL E]N-*iá*
6 *[la-aq]-bi*
rest uninscribed

ABL 603

(Beginning destroyed)

1 May Aššur, Sîn, Šamaš, Adad and Marduk grant [...] life (and) long days to the king, my lord, (and) [may] they [ma]ke the outcome of your good deeds pleasing [to a]ll the gods.

r.3 There is [a certain matt]er that [I would like to te]ll [the king], my [lo]rd.

73. May They Inform the King

Sm 421

beginning broken away
1′ ⸢*ú*⸣*-[di-ni šu]-nu*
2′ *la an-na-kan-ni*
3′ *e-gír-ti ina pa-ni-šú-nu*
4′ *is-si-si-ú*
5′ *ki-i an-ni-u*
r.1 *iq-ṭí-bi-ú*
2 *ma-a man-nu ša ina pa-ni-šú*
3 *in-na-mar-u-ni*
4 *ina* IGI LUGAL *li-iq-bi-u*
5 *[šip]-ṭa le-mì-du-šú*
6 *[x x x]-*⸢*a*⸣*-ni-ni*

ABL 1050

(Beginning destroyed)

1 [Even] b[efore th]ey were here, the letter was read in their presence and they were told to inform the king about anyone who is seen in his company, so he may be [pun]ished."

(Rest destroyed or too broken for translation)

See coll. 3-r.6 → Nissinen, SAAS 7 (1998) 141. r.3 See coll. r.3-4 For "entering the treaty," cf. SAA 10 6 and 7.
72 r.1 See coll.
73 r.8f Contra ABL copy, the left edge was not inscribed; these lines are to be interpreted as continuations of lines on the reverse.

7 [*x x x x* A]M.MEŠ
8 [*x x x x x x*]-*ru*$^{?}$
9 [*x x x x x x*]-⸢*x*⸣-*te-ra*
rest broken away

74. Fragment Referring to Trespassing

K 5487

beginning broken away
1′ [*e*]-*ta-mar š*[*a x x x x x*]
2′ *i-pa-ṭa-ra ma-a* ^{m}[*x x x x x x*]
3′ [LUG]AL *be-lí liš-al-šú m*[*a-a x x x x x*]
4′ [*x x i*]*h-ṭu-ni ma-*⸢*a*⸣ [*x x x x x*]
5′ [*x x x*]-*iṣ*$^{?}$ *a-kan-ni* [*x x x x*]
6′ [*x x x x*] ⸢*x*⸣ *x*[*x x x x x x*]
rest broken away
Rev. beginning broken away
1′ [*x x*]-*šú-nu* [*x x x x x x x x x x*]
2′ [*x x*] *la x*[*x x x x x x x x x x x*]
3′ [*x x*] *ša t*[*a*$^{?}$-*x x x x x x x x x x*]
4′ [*x x*] 2-*me* [*x x x x x x x x x x*]
5′ [*x x x*]*x šá*$^{?}$ [*x x x x x x x x x x x*]
rest broken away

CT 53 253

(Beginning destroyed)
1 "[He] saw [......]
2 "He is releasing [.....]
3 [The ki]ng, my lord, should ask [......]
4 "[... who t]respassed [......]
5 [...] now [......]
(Break)
r.1 [...] them [......]
4 [...] 200 [......]
(Rest destroyed)

75. A Crime Committed

83-1-18,838

beginning broken away
1′ [*x x x x x x x x*] *x*[*x x*]
2′ [*x x x x x x x*] *i-ba-áš-*⸢*ši-i*⸣
3′ [*x x x x x x x*] ITI.MEŠ
4′ [*x x x x x x x*]-*ma-ti ú-ši-ib*
5′ [*x x x x x x-a*]*m-ma hi-iṭ-ṭu ih-ṭi*
6′ [*x x x x x x*] ⸢*i*⸣-*ha-aṭ-ṭi*
7′ [*x x x x x x*] *ša e-pu-uš-u-ni*
8′ [*x x x x x x*]-⸢*t*⸣*u ša* MAN EN-*iá*
9′ [*x x x x x*]-*rad* LUGAL *a-na* ARAD-*šú*
10′ [*x x x x x l*]*u-sa-hi-ru*
11′ [*x x x x x x x x m*]*i-i-nu*
12′ [*x x x x x x x x x x x*]*x*
rest broken away
Rev. beginning broken away
1′ [*x x x x x x x x x x*]*x*
2′ [*x x x x x x x x x x*]-*šú*
3′ [*x x x x x x x x x x*]-*bi-ia*
4′ [*x x x x x x x x x x*]-*ti*
5′ [*x x x x x x x x x x x*]*x* UD-*me*
6′ [*x x x x x x x x x x*]
7′ [*x x x x x x x x x x*]-*u-ni-šú*
8′ [*x x x x x x x x x x*]-*bat*
9′ [*x x x x x x x x x x*]
10′ [*x x x x x x x x x x*] *šu-u*
11′ [*x x x x x x x x x x*]-⸢*ia*⸣
rest broken away

CT 53 954

(Beginning destroyed)
2 [......] is there [...]? [...] months
4 [... *W*]*hen did he* sit [...]?
5 [......] ... he committed a crime
6 [...... h]e commits (a crime)
7 [......] *which he has done*
8 [... the ...] of the king, my lord,
9 [...... *go*]*es down*. The king [has ...] *to* his servant [...]
10 [......] they [s]hould return
11 [...... w]hat [......]

(Reverse too broken for translation)

76. Fragment Mentioning a Nephew of Hanbî

83-1-18,153

Obv. completely broken away
Edge one line broken away
2′ [*x x x x x*].*x-te šu-nu*
3′ [*x x x x*].*x* ITI *e-tap-šu*
r.1 [*x x x*].*x-te ina* ŠÀ-*bi* URU
2 [*ú-se*]-*li-ia-a u* LÚ*.URU.MEŠ-*n*[*i*]
3 [*ih*]-*ta-sa-ʾu-šu* LUGAL *ir-tu-ʾa-*⌈*ba*⌉
4 [m.dMA]Š—PAB—PAB LÚ*.GAL—KA.KÉŠ
5 [m*x x x*].*x* DUMU—ŠEŠ-*šú ša* m*ha-an-bi-i*
6 [*x x x*].*x x*[*x x x x*].*x-nu*
rest broken away

83-1-18,153

(Beginning destroyed)

2 [...] they are [...]

3 They did [... *month after*] month.

r.1 [*He* m]oved the [...]s up to the town, but the townsmen [mo]lested him, and the king got angry.

4 [Inur]ta-ahu-uṣur, the chief tailor, and [PN], the nephew of Hanbî

(Rest destroyed)

76 Fragment from base. Previously unpublished; copy p. 218. r.1 Or: "I moved" r.3 Cf. *i*[*h*]-*ta-sa-ʾu*, SAA 1 179:16. r.5 For Hanbî, see PNA 2/I sub Hambî p. 447 and cf. no. 95 r.12.

6. Letters from Nineveh and the Royal Court

FIG. 15. *Embroidered garment (reign of Ashurnasirpal); cf. no. 84.*
LAYARD, *Monuments of Nineveh* I, Pl. 6.

77. Instructions for Battle

83-1-18,861

Obv. completely broken away
e.1′ [*x x x x x x x*] *x*[*x x x x*]
r.1 [*x x x x x x*]*x i-ša*[*p-par-u-ni*]
2 [LUGAL *be-li*] *ina* UGU-*hi lu ra-hi-*[*iṣ*]
3 [*ṭè-mu a-na*] LÚ.GAL.MEŠ-*ka šu-*⸢*kun*⸣
4 [*x x x-šú*]*-nu šá-zi-iz* LUGAL *be-lí*
5 [*a-na q*]*a-ra-bi lu la i-qar-ri-ib*
6 [*ki-i š*]*a* LUGAL.MEŠ-*ni* AD.MEŠ-*ka e-pa-áš-u-ni*
7 [*at-t*]*a ina* UGU *mu-le-e i-t*[*i-iz*]
8 [LÚ.G]AL.MEŠ-*ka qa-r*[*a-bu lu-pi-šu*]
9 [LUGAL] *be-li* [*x x x x x x*]
10 [*x š*]*a* ⸢ARAD⸣-[*šú x x x x x*]
rest broken away

CT 53 958

(Beginning destroyed)

r.1 [*Until* ...] se[nds ..., the king, my lord], may rely on it.

3 Give [orders to] your magnates and station their [...]! The king, my lord, should not advance [to the b]attle. [Just a]s your royal fathers have done, st[ay] on the hill, and [let] your [ma]gnates [do] the bat[tle].

9 [The king], my lord [......]

10 [... o]f [his] servant [......]

(Rest destroyed)

78. The Matter of the 'Third Man' of the Palace Scribe

K 662

1 *a-na* LUGAL EN-*ia* ARAD-*ka* [^{m}*man-nu—k*]*i*—URU.ŠÀ—URU
2 *lu* DI-*mu a-na* LUGAL EN-*ia*
3 ^{d}EN ^{d}PA *a-na* LUGAL EN-*ia lik-ru-bu*
4 *ina* UGU LÚ*.3.U$_5$ LÚ**.mu-kil*—KUŠ.PA.MEŠ *ša* LÚ*.A.BA—KUR
5 *ša* LUGAL *be-lí a-na* ARAD-*šú iš-pu-ra-an-ni*
6 *ma-a ina ket-te qi-bi-a a-ke-*(*e*) *a-na-ku*
7 TA* LUGAL EN-*ia la ket-tu ad-da-bu-ub*
8 *ina* ŠÀ MUN *an-ni-te ša* LUGAL *be-lí a-na* ARAD-*šú e-pu-šú-u-ni*
9 *a-na-ku ina ku-me mi-i-nu a-na* EN-*ia ú-sa-hi-ir*
10 MUN-*ú ša* LÚ*.A.BA—É.GAL *ina* UGU-*hi-ia te-te-qe*
11 IGI.2.MEŠ-*šú a-da-gal a-bu-tú ša a-mur-u-ni*
12 *áš-mu-u-ni a-na* LUGAL EN-*ia la-aq-bi*
13 TA* UD.MEŠ *am-ma-te a-ki ina* IGI-*šú a-za-zu-ni*
14 LUGAL *be-lí ú-da a-ki i-da-gal-an-ni-ni*
15 *ù pa-ni-šú ina* UGU-*hi-ia-a-ni* TA* *mar*

ABL 211

1 To the king, my lord: your servant [Mannu-k]i-Libbali. Good health to the king, my lord! May Bel (and) Nabû bless the king, my lord.

4 As to the matter of the 'third man' and the chariot driver of the palace scribe, about whom the king, my lord, wrote to his servant, saying: "Tell me the truth!" — how could I speak dishonestly to the king, my lord? What have I been able to give to my lord in exchange for this favour that the king, my lord, has shown his servant? Would the patronage of the palace scribe have had such an influence over me that I would still be obliged to him? (No), I shall tell to the king, my lord, the thing that I have seen and heard.

13 The king, my lord, knows from those times when I was (still) in his service how he used to regard me and what trust he used to

77 r.2 For the restoration, cf. SAA 15 90 r.22f.
78 The translation of this letter is essentially based on an unpublished translation by M. Stolper prepared in 1989. 10 Lit., "reach across to me." 13f, 16 "He" = the palace scribe. 15 "the fact that": lit., "ever since." 15-18 Cf.

LUGAL *be-lí*
16 *ina* [É-*šú*] *ip-qid-an-ni-ni ina* IGI-*šú la mah-ri*
17 [*ù ina*] UGU *la pa-qa-di-ia a-na* LUGAL EN-*ia*
18 [*i-da-bu-ub*] *a-ki* EN—*da-me i-da-gal-an-ni*
19 [*x x x*]-*šú it-ta-lak us-sa-ta-ʾi-da-ni*
20 [*a-na x x*]*x*.MEŠ *ù* LÚ*.ARAD.MEŠ-*šú ša* LÚ*.A.BA—KUR
21 [LUGAL] *be-lí liš-ʾa-al*
e.22 [*i—da*]-*a-te ú-ma-a a-ki* GEMÉ.MEŠ
23 [KUR.*ku*]-*sa-a-a-te nu-šá-aṣ-bat-u-ni*
24 [*ina* UG]U É *ša* LUGAL *ša* 2-*šú* 3-*šú*
r.1 *a-na* LUGAL EN-*ia áš-pur-an-ni*
2 ^{m}ITI.AB-*a-a* LÚ*.2-*ú ina* IGI-*šú*
3 *us-sa-an-zi-ir-an-ni ša a—dan-niš*
4 *a-ki* EN—*da-me-šú id-da-gal-an-ni*
5 *ina* UGU *an-ni-te* LUGAL *be-lí lu-ki-in-ma*
6 [*šú*]*m-ma a-bu-tú an-ni-tú ú-du-ni*
7 *áš-mu-u-ni ina* ŠÀ-*bi qur-ba-ku-u-ni*
8 *a-na* LUGAL EN-*ia la aq-bu-u-ni*
9 *ina* UGU *ša ina qab-si* URU.*kàl-ha áš-mu-u-ni*
10 MÍ-*šú ša* LÚ*.3-*šú ina* UGU-*hi-ia ta-da-bu-bu-u-ni*
11 *la a-ma-gúr-u-ni is-si-šá la a-da-bu-u-ni*

place in me. (But) ever since the king, my lord, appointed me to his household, it has been intolerable to him. [In fact, he told] the king, my lord, not to appoint me. He regards me as a mortal enemy. He has gone [...] (and) he has been spreading tales about me – [the king], my lord, should ask the [...]s and the servants of the palace scribe.

[22] Hence, now that we have settled the Kushite girls in the royal palace – a matter about which I wrote several times to the king, my lord – Kanunayu, the deputy, has made me out to be even more hateful to him, and he (now) regards me as very much of a mortal enemy indeed.

[r.5] It is in this light that the king, my lord, should determine what the truth is.

[6] I swear that I did not know (and) did not learn about this matter, that I am not implicated in it, that I have told the king, my lord, (the truth about) what I heard in the inner precinct of Calah, what the wife of the 'third

FIG. 16. *Kushite noblemen led away as prisoners of war (reign of Assurbanipal).*
ANE 124928 (detail).

12 *mu-uk* LUGAL *lu-ki-na-an-ni-ni*
13 ^{d}EN *u* ^{d}AG *uz-nu ra-pa-áš-tu*
14 *a-na* LUGAL EN-*ia it-ta-nu*
15 *a—ki-ma ina* ŠÀ *a-bi-te an-ni-te*
16 *qur-ba-ku* LUGAL *be-lí*
17 *a-na ši-ip-ṭi liš-kun-an-ni*
rest uninscribed

man' speaks against me, and (why) I refused to litigate with her, saying, "Let the king determine my veracity."

13 Bel and Nabû have given vast insight to the king, my lord. If I am implicated in this matter, let the king, my lord, punish me.

79. Work on the Inner City, Nineveh and Dur-Šarrukin

K 671

1 *a-na* LUGAL *be-li-ni*
2 ARAD.MEŠ-*ka* ^{m}ITI.AB-*a-a* ^{m}*man-nu—ki—*ŠÀ—URU
3 *lu* DI-*mu a-na* LUGAL *be-li-ni*
4 *ina* UGU *dul-la-ni ša* LUGAL *be-l*[*i-ni*]
5 *a-na* ARAD.MEŠ-*šú iš-pur-an-ni ma-*⸢*a*⸣ [0] *šu-u*
6 *ú-de-šu te-ep-pa-šá dul-lu š*[*a* 0]
7 *lu-u* URU.ŠÀ—URU URU.NINA URU.[B]ÀD—^{m}MAN—GIN
8 *am—mar dul-lu-ni ša* É—EN.[MEŠ-*ni* 0]
9 *ki-ma a-ni-nu la né-pu-uš* [*man-nu-ma ep-pa-áš*]
10 *ina* UGU LÚ*.ENGAR! LÚ*.SIPA LÚ*.[*x x x x*]
11 ⸢*a*⸣-[*na*] LUGAL *be-lí-ni x*[*x x x x x*]
12 *ša* SIG$_{4}$ *ša* GI.*ap-p*[*a-ri x x x x*]
13 *am-mu-te* ^{m}*ar-zi-i* [*x x x x x*]
14 *re-eh-tú* ^{m}*a-ri-ri a-*[*x x x x x*]
15 ARAD.MEŠ-*ni ša* LUGAL *ina* É [*x x x x x*]
16 [*x*]*x-ku a-na* LÚ*.EN.NAM [*x x x x x*]
17 [*ina* UG]U-*hi šu-*⸢*ú*⸣ *x*[*x x x x x x*]
18 [*x x x*] *x*[*x x x x x x x x x x*]
rest broken away
Rev. beginning broken away
1′ *a-na* IGI *x*[*x x x x x x x x x x*]
2′ ^{md}PA—*rém-a-ni i-*[*x x x x x x*]
3′ ^{md}PA—MU—AŠ *la* [*x x x x x x*]
4′ ^{m}⸢*ša—*$^{d?}$⸣[*x*]*x—a-né-nu* [*x x x x x x*]
5′ *a-n*[*a* LUGAL] *be-lí-ni x*[*x x x x x x*]
6′ *ina* UGU *re-hu-u-te a-na* ^{m}15—MU—APIN-*eš*
7′ LUGAL *be-lí ṭè-e-mu liš-kun*
rest uninscribed

ABL 845

1 To the king, our lord: your servants Kanunayu (and) Mannu-ki-Libbali. Good health to the king, our lord!

4 As to the works about which the king, [our] lor[d], wrote to his servants: "You are to do that alone" — be it work in the Inner City, Nineveh, [D]ur-Šarrukin (or) whatever work there is on the household of [our] lord, if we didn't do it, [who would]?

10 As to the farmer, the shepherd (and) the [...]

11 t[o] the king, our lord, [...]

12 of bricks (and) of re[ed ...]

13 those [...] Arzî [...]

14 the rest Ariri [...]

15 The servants of the king *in the house* [......] to the governor [......]

17 *That is why* [......]

(Break)

r.1 *to* [......]

2 Nabû-remanni [......]

3 Nabû-šumu-iddina [*does*] not [......]

4 Ša-[...]-anenu [......]

5 t[o the king], our lord, [......]

6 Let the king, my lord, give an order to Issar-šumu-ereš about the remaining ones.

80. Reimbursements

K 762

1 *e-gír-tú ša taš-li-ma-a-ti*
2 *ša* LUGAL *be-li ú-šal-lim-u-ni*
3 *ša* ^{m}ITI!.AB-*a-a-u ú-še-ṣa-an-ni*
4 *at-ta-na-šú us-sa-hi-ir us-se-ri-ba*

ABL 446

1 The document of the reimbursements (to be) paid by the king, my lord, which Kanunayu took out — I gave it to him, but he has

Deller, Or. 31 (1961) 235.
79 4-9 Fales, HANEM 4 (2000) 240a. 9 LAS II 156:11. 10 Y 83, W 246. r.6f LAS II, p. 464.

5 *lu-še-ṣu-u-ni lid-di-nu-ni*
6 *ina pu-u-ti taš-li-ma-a-ti lu-šal-lim*
Rev. uninscribed

brought it in again.

[5] May it be brought out and given to me, so that I can pay the reimbursement according to it.

81. Jewellery for the King

83-1-18,115

1 *a-na* LUGAL *be-lí-ia*
2 ARAD-*ka* ^{md}PA—*sa-gi-ib*
3 A ^{m}*pa-*⸢*ru*$^{!}$⸣*-ṭi* LÚ$^{!!}$.SIMUG.KUG.GI
4 *šá* É MÍ—É.GAL
5 *lu-u* DI-*mu a-na* LUGAL
6 [*be-lí*]*-iá* ^{d}AG *u* ^{d}AMAR.UTU
7 [*a-na* LU]GAL EN-*ia lik-ru-bu*
8 [*x x* MU].AN.NA TA* É
9 [*x x x x x i*]*š*$^{?}$*-al*$^{?}$*-u-ni*
10 [*x x x x x š*]*a* ITI.[*x*]*x*
rest broken away
Rev. beginning broken away
1′ [*x x x x x x x x*] ⸢KUG$^{?}$⸣.UD
2′ [N]A$_4$.BABBAR.DIL 3 ŠU.SI *ru-up-šá-šá*
3′ DAG.GAZ *šá* NA$_4$.IGI.ZAG.GA
4′ *a-na* ^{m}*a-tan-ah*—DINGIR
5′ LÚ.Ì.DU$_8$ *a-ti-din*
6′ *e-gír-tu is-se-niš*
7′ *mu-uk a-na* LUGAL *be-lí-iá*
8′ [*d*]*i*$^{!}$*-ni šum-ma it-ti-din*
9′ *šum-ma la id-din*
10′ LUGAL EN *liš-al*

ABL 847

[1] To the king, my lord: your servant Nabû-sagib, the son of Parruṭu, a goldsmith of the household of the queen. Good health to the king, my [lord]! May Nabû and Marduk bless [the ki]ng, my lord.

[8] It is [x y]ears (now) [since *the king, my lord, in*]*quired* [...]

[10] [...... o]f the month [...]

(Break)

[r.2] of agate, its width 3 inches, (and) a piece of *egizaggû*-stone. I gave them to the gate guard, Atanha-ilu, along with a letter, saying, "Deliver them to the king, my lord!"

[8] May the king, my lord, enquire whether or not he has delivered them.

82. Marduk-šarru-uṣur in Trouble

81-2-4,52

1 *a-na* LUGAL *be-lí-ia*
2 ARAD-*ka* ^{md}AMAR.UTU—MAN—PAB
3 *lu* DI-*mu a-na* LUGAL *be-lí-ia*
4 ^{d}AG *ù* ^{d}AMAR.UTU
5 *a-na* LUGAL *be-lí-ia lik-ru-bu*
6 LÚ.ARAD *ša mar-ṣa-šu-un-ni*
7 EN.MEŠ-*šú i-mah-har*
8 *a-na-ku mar-ṣa* LUGAL *be-lí a-ta*$^{!}$*-har*
9 LUGAL *be-lí lip-qi*$^{!}$*-dan-ni*
10 NÍG.ŠID-*ia* TA* LÚ.A.BA.MEŠ *lu-pi-šú*
11 LÚ.A.BA.MEŠ TA* ŠU.2 LUGAL
12 *uh-ta-li-qu-u-ni*
13 *an-nu-rig* TA* É LUGAL *be-lí*

ABL 347

[1] To the king, my lord: your servant Marduk-šarru-uṣur. Good health to the king, my lord! May Nabû and Marduk bless the king, my lord.

[6] A servant who is in trouble petitions his masters. I am (now) in trouble and petitioning the king, my lord. Let the king, my lord, appoint me, and let my accounts be made with the scribes. The scribes have *wrenched* me away from the king.

[13] Now, ever since the king, my lord, ap-

80 Horizontal tablet. This memorandum can be attributed with considerable certainty to the chief scribe Issar-šumu-ereš. Grounds are the use of *ša* as the determinative pronoun, the rare spelling *be-li* (l. 2) and his characteristic way of using the fuller writings of precative forms, as well as many other forms, cf. Parpola (1971) 32f. [3] See coll. For Kanunayu see PNA 2/I p. 602 (16).

81 [3] See coll. [9f] See coll. [r.2] Cf. SAA 13 28:4 *ina ša* BABBAR.DIL "in the *agate* standard." [r.8] See coll.

82 [6-8] Fales, HANEM 4 (2000) 245 n. 62. [8] *mar-ṣa*: a scribal error? One expects rather *mar-ṣa-ak* or *mar-ṣa-ku*.

14 *ip-qi-da-ni-ni*
15 TA* É-*ia* É.GAL *a-pa-làh*
16e *a-na la*! *e-pi-še*
17e *ina* IGI LUGAL E[N]-*i*[*a la a-tu-ur*]
r.1 LUGAL *be-lí* ⸢*ú*⸣-[*di x*]
2 *an-nu-rig* ⸢*la x x x*⸣ [*x*]
3 LUGAL *be-lí a-ki ša i-la-u-ni*
4 *le-pu-uš*
5 31 GÚ.UN *ṭi-bu* GADA
6 80 GÚ.UN SÍG.SA$_5$ KUR
7 7 GÚ.UN (SÍG).MI KUR
8 30 GÚ.UN NA$_4$.*ga-bu-u*
9 10 GÚ.UN NA$_4$.*ni-ti-ru*
blank space of one line
10 PAB 1-*me*-58 GÚ.UN
11 LUGAL *be-lí liš-al*
12 1 MA.NA 1/2 MA.NA
13 TA* ŠÀ-*bi me-me-ni*
14 *la i-di-na*

pointed me, I have been revering the palace together with my household. [I did not become] a do-nothing before the king, m[y] lo[rd].

r.1 The king, my lord, *kn*[*ows that*] now [...] *not* [...].

3 May the king, my lord, act as he deems best.

5 31 talents of twine of linen; 80 talents of red wool, *of the country*; 7 talents of black (wool), *of the country*, 30 talents of alum, 10 talents of natron. In all, 158 talents.

11 Let the king, my lord, ask (about the matter): nobody gave me a mina (or even) half a mina from it.

83. Wool for Weavers

K 1217

1 *a-na* LUGAL EN-*ia*
2 ARAD-*ka* ^{md}ŠÚ—MAN—PAB
3 *lu-u* DI-*mu a-na* LUGAL EN-*ia*
4 ^{d}AG ^{d}AMAR.UTU *a-na* LUGAL EN-*ia*
5 *lik-ru-bu* ^{md}PA—PAB.MEŠ—AŠ
6 LÚ.*qur*-ZAG *ša* LUGAL *be-lí*
7 [*ina*] UGU LÚ.UŠ.BAR.MEŠ
8 [*š*]*a*? LÚ.GAL.MEŠ *iš-pur-u-ni*
rest broken away
Rev. beginning broken away
1′ [*x x x*]*x*[*x* SÍG.SA$_5$] KAR
2′ 20 [GÚ.U]N *li-di-nu-u-ni*
3′ *le-*[*pu-šu*] *ku-zip-pi*
4′ [*x x*] ⸢*x*⸣ *bat ša e*!-*mì*!-*du-ni-ni*
5′ SÍ[G.SA$_5$?] *li-di-nu-ni*
6′ *la-ad-din le-pu-šu*

ABL 714

1 To the king, my lord: your servant Marduk-šarru-uṣur. Good health to the king, my lord! May Nabû (and) Marduk bless the king, my lord.

5 Nabû-ahhe-iddina, the royal bodyguard whom the king, my lord, sent concerning the weavers [*of*] the magnates

(Break)

r.1 [......] let them give me 20 [tale]nts of [red wool] *of the port* so they (can) m[ake it].

3 (As to) the [...] garment(s) [...] which they imposed on me, let them give me [red] wo[ol]; I will deliver it, and they will make it.

84. Providing Weavers with Red Wool

Bu 91-5-9,12

1 *a-na* LUGAL EN-*ia*
2 ARAD-*ka* ^{md}PA—MAN—PA[B!]
3 *lu-u* DI-*mu a-na* LUGAL EN-[*ia*]
4 ^{d}AG ^{d}AMAR.UTU

ABL 413

1 To the king, my lord: your servant Nabû-šarru-uṣu[r]. Good health to the king, [my] lord! May Nabû and Marduk bless the king,

ta!: see coll. 9, 16 See coll. r.1 Or perhaps: -[*da x*]. r.5-10 These huge amounts of twine of linen, wool and minerals must have been used for processing garments. In general, see SAA 7 pp. XXVI-XXIX and the pertinent texts (SAA 7 93-116), particularly SAA 7 110-111 and 115-116. These lines are written in a type of shorthand without using any prepositions or *ša*, which makes their exact interpretation difficult. Nevertheless, at least in theory, it might also be possible to translate: "31 talents for twine of linen, 80 talents of/for red wool of/for/from the country" and so on. r.6 SA$_5$ KUR passim in SAA 7, e.g. SAA 7 96:5 etc.

83 r.1 refers to a textile or wool quality.

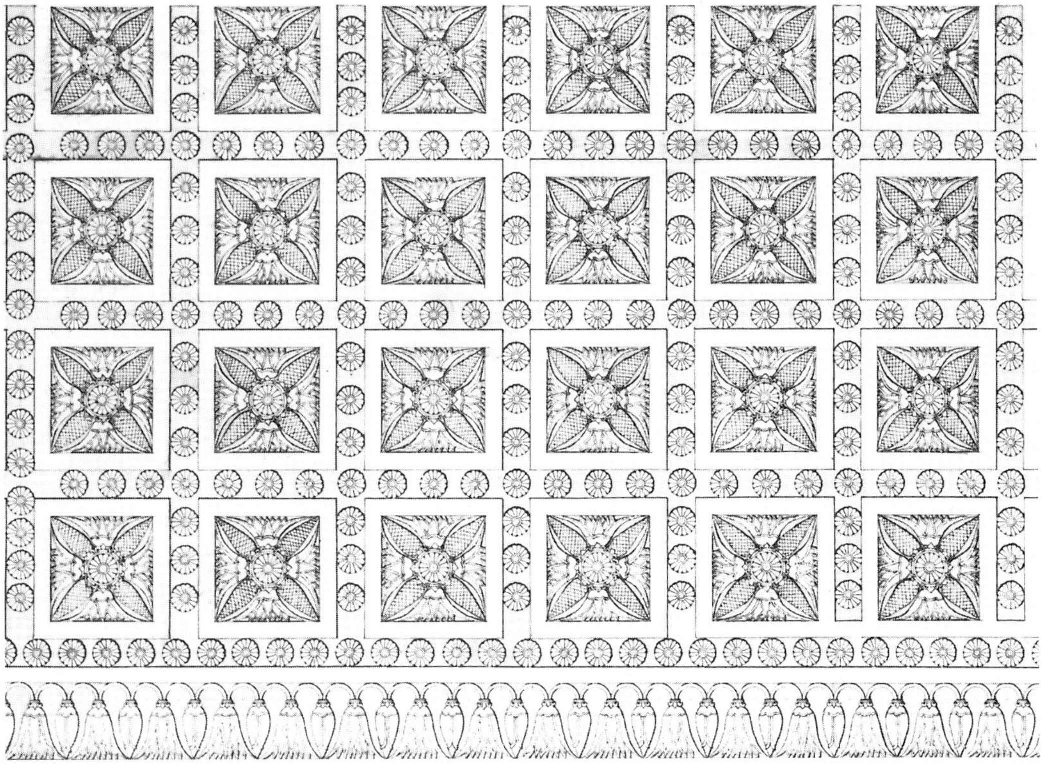

FIG. 17. *Stone threshold imitating a carpet.*
ORIGINAL DRAWINGS V, 60.

5 *a-na* LUGAL EN-*ia lik-ru-bu*
6 *ina* UGU *ša* LUGAL *be-lí*
7 *a-na* ARAD-*šú iš-pur-an-ni*
8 *ma-a ina* UGU TÚG.BAR.DIB.MEŠ
9 *a-na* ^{m}*ba-la-si-i*
10 *šá-ʾa-al* TA* *a-a-ka*
11 *id-da-nu-ni šup-ra*
12 *a-na* ^{m}*ba-la-si-i*
13 *as-sa-ʾa-al*
r.1 *ma-a* SÍG.SA$_5$
2 TA* ŠÀ É.GAL *ni-dan*
3 *ma-a šú-nu a-na ṭè-mì-šú-nu*
4 *ep-pu-šú*
5 *ù a-na* ^{m}A-*ia*
6 *as-sa-ʾa-al ma-a* SÍG.SA$_5$
7 *id-da-nu-na-ši*
8 *ma-a* LÚ*.UŠ.BAR.MEŠ
9 *ša* ^{d}15 *ša* URU.*arba-ìl*
10 *il-la-ku-u-ni*
11 *ina* URU.*kur-ba*$^{!}$*-ìl ep-pu-šú*
12 *ù bir*$^{!}$*-me ina* IGI *ir*$^{!}$*-te*
13 [*ša*] ^{d}IM *nu-x*[*x x*]
14e [*x x x x*]*x*[*x x x*]
s.1 *ša* LUGAL *ib-ta-aṭ-l*[*u*]

my lord.

6 As to what the king, my lord, wrote to his servant: "Ask Balasî about the robes and write me from where they will be delivered!"

— I have asked Balasî (and he answered): "We will supply red wool from the palace and they will do as ordered." Moreover, I have asked Aplaya (and he said): "They will give us red wool. The weavers of Ištar of Arbela will come (and) make (fabrics) in Kurbail."

r.12 Furthermore, we shall [...] the multi-coloured textiles (placed) before the breast [of] Adad.

s.1 They have stopped the [...] of the king.

84 2 See coll. r.5 → MacGinnis SAAB II/2 (1988) 67-72. Aplaia, the *šangû* of Kurbail, is also attested in SAA 13 186. r.11 Y 80, W 154. r.12 See coll. *ir*! W 154. r.13 See coll.

85. Itemising Textiles

83-1-18,118

1 *a-na* LUGAL EN-*ia*
2 ARAD-*ka* ^{md}AG—MAN—PAB
3 *lu-u* DI-*mu a-na* MAN EN-*ia*
4 ^{d}AG *ù* ^{d}AMAR.UTU
5 *a-na* LUGAL EN-*ia lik-*[*ru-bu*]
6 *ina* UGU *ša* LUGAL [*be-lí*]
7 [*x x*]*x x*[*x x x x x*]
8 [*x x x x x x x x*]
Rev. beginning broken away
1′ *ša* L[UGAL *x x x x x x x*]
2′ *ma-a šum-ma hu-*[*x x x x*]
3′ *ma-a al-*[*la-ka x x x*]
4′ *ma-a id—da-a-te a-sa-*[*dir x x*]

ABL 770

1 To the king, my lord: your servant Nabû-šarru-uṣur. Good health to the king, my lord! May Nabû and Marduk bl[ess] the king, my lord.

6 As to what the king, [my lord, *wrote me*]
(Break)
r.1 which the k[ing ......]
2 "if [...],
3 "I shall g[o and ...];
4 "thereafter I shall *item*[*ise them*]."

86. Working for the Royal Household

81-2-4,75

1 [*a*]*-na* LUGAL *be-lí-ia*
2 [ARAD]-*ka* ^{md}AG—MU—*iš-kun*
3 [*lu-u*] DI-*mu a-na* LUGAL *be-lí-ia*
4 [^{d}AG] ^{d}AMAR.UTU *a-na* LUGAL *be-lí-iá lik-ru-bu*
5 [^{d}EN] ^{d}AG ^{d}U.GUR *ma-ṣar* DI-*mu* TI.LA
6 [TA* L]UGAL *be-lí-iá lip-qí-du*
7 [*ina* UG]U! *ša* LUGAL *be-lí*
8 [*a-na*] ARAD-*šú ma-a-la ši-né-e-šu*
9 [*b*]*ir*!*-ti*! IGI.2.MEŠ *ša* ARAD-*i-šu*
10 *ú-ma-di-du-u-ni*
11 *ma-a dul-lu ša* É—EN.MEŠ-*ka*
12 *ina* ŠU.2-*i-ka ú-ba-*ʾ*a*
13 LÚ.EN—*pi-qit-ta-a-te*.MEŠ
14 [*ša* É]—EN.MEŠ-*ia i-ba-áš-ši*
15 [*x x x x x*] *id-da-nu-u-ni*
16 [*x x x x x x*]*x id-da-nu-u-ni*
17 [*x x x x x x x x x x*]-*u-ni*
rest broken away
Rev. beginning broken away
1′ [*x*] ^{d}MES *u* [*x x x x x*]
2′ [*u*]*b-bal-áš-ša-nu-*[*u-ni x x*]
3′ *dul-*[*lu ša*] É—EN.MEŠ-*šú-nu*
4′ [*x*]*x*[*x x x x x x*]-*u-ni*
5′ [*x x x x x i*]*-ba-áš-ši*
6′ [*x x x x x x ba*]*l-u-ṭi*
7′ [*x x x x x x* LU]GAL *be-lí*
8′ [*x x x x x x*]-*nu-šú-nu*
9′ [*x x x x x x*]-*ú-ni*
10′ [*x x x x* L]Ú.GAL—URU.MEŠ-*te*
11′ [*x x x x*].MEŠ *ša u-ṣu-u-ni*
12′ [*x x x x*] ⌜*e*⌝*-ra-šu-u-ni*

ABL 778

1 [T]o the king, my lord: your [servant] Nabû-šumu-iškun. [Good] health to the king, my lord! May [Nabû] (and) Marduk bless the king, my lord. May [Bel], Nabû (and) Nergal appoint a guardian of health (and) life [with the k]ing, my lord.

7 [As t]o what the king, my lord, impressed upon his servant once or twice, saying: "I shall hold you responsible for the work of your lord's household" — certain officials of my lord's [household] are giving me [...], are giving me [......].
(Break)

r.1 [...] Marduk and [......]
2 [who b]ring(s) *to* them [...]
3 The wo[rk of] their lord's household
4 [......]
5 [...... there] is
7 [...... the ki]ng, my lord,
10 [... the v]illage managers
11 [the ...]s who come out
12 (and) cultivate [...]

85 r.4 Or *a-sa-*[*par*] "I sent (word)," cf. ABL 879:7, GPA 186 r.24f. See coll.
86 7-17, r.3, r.15-20 Fales, HANEM 4 (2000) 241a. 9f Y 83, W 234. r.15 See coll.

13′ [*x x x*]-*nu e-pa-áš-u-ni*
14′ [*x x x*] *an-na-ka*
15′ [*re-e*]*h-te dul-li ša* É—EN.MEŠ-*iá*
16′ *e-pa-áš ma-ṣar-tu*
17′ *ša* É—EN.MEŠ-*iá a-na-ṣar*
18′ LUGAL *be-lí ú-da a-ki-i*
19′ *i—har-pu-u-te an-ni-e*
20′ *dul-lu gab-bu i-né-pa-áš-u-ni*

13 (and) do [...]

14 [...] here

15 I will do the [res]t of the work of my lord's household (and) keep watch over my lord's household.

18 The king, my lord, knows that all the work will be done in this spring.

87. Eunuchs for Officials

83-1-18,90

1 *a-na* LUGAL EN-*ia*
2 ARAD-*ka* ^{md}PA—MU—GAR-*u*[*n*]
3 *lu-u* DI-*mu a-na* LUGAL EN-*i*[*a*]
4 ^{d}PA ^{d}AMAR.UTU *a-na* LUGAL EN-[*ia*]
5 *lik-ru-bu* ^{d}EN ^{d}PA *ù* ^{d}[U.GUR]
6 *ma-ṣar* DI-*mu ù* T[I.LA]
7 TA* LUGAL EN-*ia lip-qi-d*[*u*]
8 *ina* UGU LÚ.SAG.MEŠ
9 *ša a-na* LÚ.*pi-qi-ta-*[*te*]
10 *ša a-na* LUGAL E[N-*ia*]
11 *a-hu-ru-*⌈*ú*⌉-[*ni*]
12 LÚ.A—KIN *ša* LU[GAL *x x*]
13 LÚ.A.BA—KUR *a-*[*sa-ʾa-al*]
14 *ṭè-e-mu* [*is-sa-kan*]
15 *ma-a* 3 [*x x x x x*]
16 *a-na* ^{md}P[A—*x x x x*]
17 *mi-mi-*[*i-ni x x x x*]
18 *ina* UD.MEŠ [*x x x x x x x*]
19 *im-*[*x x x x x x x x x*]
r.1 *tu-šam-*[*x x x x*]
2 LUGAL *be-lí* [*x x x x*]
3 *ina* ŠÀ-*bi x*[*x x x x*]
4 *li-*[*x x x*]
5 *bi-is dul-*[*lu x x x*]
6 *ú-ma-a* LUG[AL *be-lí*]
7 *a-ki-i ša* [*i-la-u-ni*]
8 *le-pu-*[*uš*]
rest uninscribed

ABL 779

1 To the king, my lord: your servant Nabû-šumu-išku[n]. Good health to the king, m[y] lord! May Nabû (and) Marduk bless the king, [my] lord. May Bel, Nabû and [Nergal] appoin[t] a guardian of health and l[ife] with the king, my lord.

8 As to the eunuchs for the official[s] about whom I appealed to the king, [my] lo[rd], the k[ing's] messenger [...]. I [asked] the palace scribe, (who) [gave] (the following) order: "Three [......]

16 *to* Nabû-[...]

17 any[body/thing ......]

18 *in the* days [......]

r.1 you [......]

2 Let the king, my lord [......] there, so [they can ...] the wo[rk].

6 Now let the ki[ng, my lord], d[o] as it [pleases him].

88. Donkey Trade at Nineveh

83-1-18,62

1 *a-na* LU[GAL *be-l*]*í-ia*
2 ARAD-*ka* $^{m⌈d⌉}$[PA—NUM]UN—PAB
3 LÚ*.A.BA *ša* LÚ*.*šá*—IGI—É.GAL
4 *lu-u* DI-*mu a-na* LUGAL EN-*ia*
5 ^{d}60 *u* ^{d}ŠÚ *a-na* LUGAL EN-*iá*
6 *lik-ru-bu*
7 LÚ*.SIPA.ME MÍ.ANŠE.ME

CT 53 151

1 To the ki[ng], my [lor]d: your servant Nabû-[ze]ru-uṣur, the scribe of the palace supervisor. Good health to the king, my lord! May Nabû and Marduk bless the king, my lord.

7 The herders of donkey mares used to

88 5 d60 is to be read Nabû according to LAS II 172 r.20. 16 Cf. SAA 5 104:12f, r.3f, 10f. 17f Or: "If (he

8 *ina* IGI É.GAL *ina* IGI *né-ri-bi*
9 *i-za-zu-u-ni* ANŠE.*ha-lup*.MEŠ SUM-*u-ni*
10 *ú-ma-a la i-ma-gu-ru la i-za-zu*
11 *ma-a* LÚ*.EN.NAM *ina* IGI URU.NINA
12 [*i*]*q-ṭi-ba-na-ši ma-a ina* ŠÀ É.GAL
13 *a-ta-mar-ku-nu gul-gu-lat-ku-nu*
14 *ú-mar-ra-qa ma-a* LÚ*.*qur*-ZAG
15 [*ina*] UGU-*hi-ni lil-li-ka* [0]
16 [*l*]*u-u-bi-la-na-ši*
17 [*m*]*a-a šum-ma la-aš-šú*
18 [*l*]*a ni-lak* ANŠE.ME *pa-ni-u-*[*te*]
19 [*š*]*a ina pa-ni-šú-nu* [*x x x*]
e.20 ⌜*x*⌝ *mu ub-ta-*[*x x x x*]
21 [*x x x*] ⌜*ik*⌝ [*x x x x x x*]
Rev. beginning broken away
1′ [*x x x x x x x x*]*x* HAR
2′ [*x x x x x x x x*]*x*
3′ [*x x x x x x x x*] *zu*
4′ [*x x x x x x x x*]*x*
5′ [*x x x x x x x x*]*x-šú-nu*
6′ [*x x x x x x x*]*x ta-za-za*
7′ [*x x x x x x*] *la e-mu-qa-a-a*
8′ [*x x la*] ⌜*a*⌝*-za-za*
rest uninscribed

stand in front of the palace, at the entrance, selling *covered* donkeys.

10 Now they refuse to stand (there), saying: “The governor told us in front of Nineveh, ‘Should I (henceforth) see you in the palace, I shall crush your skulls.’ A bodyguard should come to us and take us (there). Otherwise we shall not go (there).”

18 The earli[er] donkeys which were in their charge [...]
(Break)

r.5 [......] them
6 [...] “You shall stand [...]”
7 [...] I cannot stand [...]

89. The House of the Chief Scribe

K 978

1 [*a-na* LUGAL *be-lí-ia*]
2 [ARAD-*ka* ^{m}*x x x x*]
3 [*lu-u*] DI-*mu a-na* LUG[AL *be-lí-ia*]
4 [*ina* UGU] É ^{m}*aš-šur*—PAB-*i*[*r*]
5 [*ina* UGU] É LÚ*.GAL—A.BA
6 [*ša*] LUGAL *be-lí*
7 *ṭè-e-mu iš-kun-ni-ni*
8 *ma-a a-mur*
9 É LÚ*.GAL—A.BA É *qa-lál*
10 [AN]ŠE.NITÁ-*ma ina* ŠÀ-*bi-šú*
11 *la e-rab*
12 É ^{m}*aš-šur*—PAB-*ir*
13 DUMU—ŠU.SI.MEŠ SIG$_5$
14 *bat-qu ma-aʾ-da*
15 *ina* ŠÀ-*bi*
16 LÚ*.SAG *ša šap-r*[*u*?]-⌜*ni*⌝
Edge uninscribed
r.1 É ^{m}*aš-šur*—⌜PAB-*ir*⌝
2 *a-nu-*⌜*tu*⌝ *am—mar ina* [ŠÀ-*bi*]
3 *ik-ti-ri-i*⌜*k*⌝
4 *ina* É—ŠU.2.MEŠ-[*i*]*a*
5 *ina* É—*ma-a-a-*[*li-i*]*a*
6 [*i*]*k-ta-*[*ra-ra*]
7 [*li*]*q-bu-ni-šú x*[*x x x*]
8 [*gab*]-⌜*bi*⌝*-šú* [*x x x x*]

CT 53 14

1 [To the king, my lord: your servant PN. Good] health to the kin[g, my lord]!

4 [Concerning] the house of Aššur-naṣi[r and] the house of the chief scribe [about which] the king, my lord, ordered me: “Inspect them!”

9 The house of the chief scribe is a tiny house. Even a [do]nkey would not enter there. (Whereas) the house of Aššur-naṣir, *a nobleman*, is good (but) much repair (must be done) there.

16 The eunuch who was *se*[*n*]*t* (to) the house of Aššur-naṣir has collected all the equipment [there and] pi[led] them [up] in [m]y storehouses and in [m]y bedro[om].

r.7 [Let] him be told: “[...]
8 the [who]le [...]

does) not (come), we do not come.”

89 9ff Cf. Radner, SAAS 6 (1997) 84. 13 DUMU—ŠU.SI.MEŠ: possibly a rebus spelling for *mār banê*, cf. PNA 1/I (1998) p. 203b Aššur-naṣir 6. 16 *r*[*u*?] very doubtful; see coll.

9 [*x x x x x*]*x me*? [*x*]
10 [*x x x x x l*]*u-še-ṣu-ni*
traces of one line; rest broken away

9 [......]
10 [... let] them be brought out
(Rest destroyed)

90. Outriders for Brick Masons

83-1-18,64

beginning broken away
1′ [*x x ša* LUGAL *be-lí iš-pu*]*r-an-ni*
2′ [*ma-a x x x x x*].MEŠ-*ni*
3′ [*x x a-n*]*a*?-⸢*ku*⸣ *as-sa*⸣*-nam-me*
4′ 1-*en* LÚ*.SAG.MEŠ *lu-ṣi-a*
5′ *ṭè-e-mu liš-kun-šú-nu*
6′ *ù ina* UGU LÚ.*ú-ra-si*
7′ LÚ.*kal-lap qur-bu*
8′ LÚ.*kal-lap ma-a*ʾ-*d*[*a*]
9′ LÚ.*kal-lap* URU.*ub*-[*x*]
10′ LÚ.*kal-lap ša* É.[GAL]
11′ LÚ.*zu-k*[*u x*]
12′ *šum-ma ma-hi-ir ina* IGI [LUGAL EN-*iá*]
e.13′ *ú*-⸢*x*⸣ [*x x x x x x x x*]
14′ ⸢LÚ⸣.[*x x x x x x x x x*]
r.1 *x*[*x x x*] *x*[*x x x x x x*]
2 *li*-⸢*il-li*⸣*-ku-u-n*[*i x x x*]
3 *ku-um ina tak-ri-ma*-⸢*a*⸣-[*ti*]
4 *ina* ITI.DU$_6$ *a-na* LUGAL EN-[*ia*]
5 *iq-ab-bu-ni ma-a* LÚ.*kal*-[*lap*.MEŠ]
6 *la e-rab*-⸢*ú*⸣*-ni*
7 *a-na* ^{m}*aš-šur*—PAB-*ir a*-[*na*] ^{m}*da-ni-i*
8 LUGAL *li-iq-bi* L[Ú.*qu*]*r*-ZAG.MEŠ
9 *ša* MU.IM.MA *ina* UG[U-*hi-š*]*ú-nu*
10 *il-lik-u-ni ina* IGI L[UGAL] EN-*iá*
11 [*l*]*u-šá-zi-zu* LUGAL *ṭè-e-mu*
12 [*liš-k*]*un-šú-nu lil-li-ku*
13 [*x x li-b*]*u-ku-u-niš-šú-nu*
rest broken away

CT 53 150

(Beginning destroyed)

1 [... about whom the king, my lord, wro]te to me: "[......] – I *hear and obey*.

4 Let one of the eunuchs come out and give them orders. And regarding the *brick masons*, there are many outriders available: the outriders from Ub[...], the outriders of the Pa[lace], (and) the exempt [...]. If it is acceptable to the [king, my lord]

(Break)

r.2 let them come [...],

3 *lest* they will tell the king, [my] lord, in *the autumn*, in Tishri (VII): "The outr[iders] have not come in."

7 May the king command Aššur-naṣir and Danî that they station in the k[ing] my lord's presence the bodyguards who went to them last year. May the king [giv]e them orders to go (and) [fet]ch them [...].

91. Candidates for Courtiers

Bu 89-4-26,71

beginning broken away
1′ [*x x x*]*x x*[*x x x x x x x x*]
2′ [*l*]*a*! *a*!-*mur*! [*ina*] ⸢UGU⸣! [*x x x x*]
3′ *ina* [*x x*]-*ú-te ta*-[*x x x x*]
4′ *ša* [*x x*] *a-na mu-rab*-[*ba-nu-te x x*]
5′ *a-n*[*a ma*]-*za-az*—*pa-nu-te x*[*x x x x*]
6′ *a-na ta-da-ni ù ma-a ša* [^{m}*x x x x*]
7′ LÚ*.*ša*—IGI—*né-re-bi* ^{m}*man*-[*nu*—*ki*—*x x*]
8′ LÚ*.*ša*—IGI—É—ŠU.2 *ša* [*x x x x*]
9′ *in-nu-di-šu* SIG$_5$ *x*[*x x x x x*]

ABL 875

(Beginning destroyed)

2 I have [n]ot seen [...]. *As to* [......]

3 [...] ... [...]

4 who (*are*) to be given [...] to tut[orship ...] (or) t[o c]ourtiership [...].

6 Furthermore, he says: "[PN], the entrance supervisor (and) Man[nu-ki-...], the supervisor of the storehouse, *who* [...]

9 to *him alone* good [...]

90 3 Lit., "I keep listening."
91 Coll. S. Parpola, 16.11.66. 5 Cf. ABL 1222:7 (De Vaan Bel-ibni [1995] 304f).

10′ *i-ba!-qi-du-⸢šú?-nu?⸣-[ni x x x x]*
r.1 *ù* ^{md}PA—*šal!-lim!*—[*x* LÚ*.*x x x*]
2 *ša* IGI É *dan-na-*[*te x x x*]
3 Á.2-*šú ina* [*x x x x*]
4 ^{m}*ba-la-su* LÚ*.[*x x x x*]
5 ^{m}EN—MAN—PAB [LÚ*.*x x x*]
6 ^{md}PA—*rém-a-ni* [LÚ*.*x x x*]
7 ^{m}*a-du-nu—mil-*[*ku-ti* LÚ*.*x x x*]
8 ^{m}IGI—^{d}PA—*la-*[*mur* LÚ*.*x x x*]
9 PAB 5 *an-nu-te* [*x x x x*]
10 [*x x*]*x* [*x x x x x x x*]
rest broken away
s.1 LUGAL *ú-da ši-*[*x x x x*]
2 ARAD *ša* TA* EN.MEŠ-*šú la* [*ke-nu-ni x x x*]

10 are appointing [...]
r.1 But Nabû-šallim-[..., the ...] in charge of the main buildings, [*has laid*] his arm in [...].
4 Balassu, the [...], Bel-šarru-uṣur, [the ...], Nabû-remanni, [the ...], Adunu-Mil[kuti, the ...] (and) Pan-Nabû-la[mur, the ...]; all these five (men) [......]
(Break)
s.1 The king knows [that ...]
2 A servant who is not [loyal] to his lords [...].

92. Drink on the Accounts!

Bu 89-4-26,31

1 [*a-na* LUGAL *be-lí-ia*]
2 [ARAD-*ka* ^{m}*x x x*]
3 [*lu-u* DI-*mu a-na* LUGAL *be-lí-ia*]
4 ⸢^{d}EN⸣ ^{d}⸢AG!⸣ [*a-na* LUGAL]
5 *be-lí-ia lik-ru-bu*
6 *ina* UGU *ša* LUGAL *be-*[*lí*]
7 *iq-bu-u-ni ma-a* NIM.[MEŠ]
8 *ša a-ṣu-di hu-ur-*[*ṣa*]
9 *lu-ut-ka ha-ra-me-ma*
10 *ina* UGU NÍG.ŠID *ši-t*[*i-a*]
11 *šúm-mu ma-hi-ir ina* IGI [LUGAL]
12 *be-lí-ia* LÚ*.SUKKAL [*x*]
13 ⸢*ù*⸣ LÚ*.GAL—[*x x*]
14 [*x x x*] LÚ*.*qe-*[*e-pu*]
e.15 [*x x x x*]*x šu* [*x x*]
16 [*x x x x*]*x x*[*x x x*]
Rev. beginning broken away
1′ *nu* [*x x x x x x x*]
2′ *x*[*x x x x x x x x*]
3′ [*x x x x x x x x*]
4′ [*x x x x x x x x*]
5′ *x*[*x x x x x x x x*]
rest broken away

ABL 874

1 [To the king, my lord: your servant PN. Good health to the king, my lord]! May Bel (and) Nabû bless [the king], my lord.

6 As to what the king, [my] lor[d] told me: "Chec[k] and test the upper part of the *aṣūdu*-bowl and thereafter dri[nk] on the accounts!"

11 If it is acceptable to the [king], my lord, [let] the [...] vizier and the chief [......] the (royal) del[egate ...]
(Rest destroyed or too broken for translation)

93. May the Chief Baker Release Us

K 1556

beginning broken away
1′ *ki-*[*x*] ⸢*x x x*⸣ [*x x*]
2′ *ina* UGU ŠE *la-áš-a*[*l?*]
3′ ⸢*x*⸣*-ru-*⸢*qu?*⸣
4′ *a-*[*du?*] *e-ta-ka-ni? x*[*x x*]
5′ *né-*⸢*e*⸣*-*[*li*]

ABL 1451

(Beginning destroyed)

2 I will as[k] about the corn, [...]
4 *As* [*long as*] *we are on the alert*, [...]. We will climb up (and) [k]eep watc[h].

92 4 See coll.
93 Collated by S. Parpola, 31.10.66. 4 Cf. SAA 10 241 r.14 and 182 r.19. 5ff Cf. r.3ff. r.9f Arbela probably

6′ *ma-ṣar-[tu]*
7′ *ni-n[a-ṣ]a-a[r]*
8′ *a-na* LÚ.GAL—NINDA ^{d}[*x x*]
9′ *ṭè-e-[mu]*
10′ *liš-ku-[nu]*
11′ *lu-ra-ma-an-na-[ši]*
12′ *meš-lu te* [*x x*]
r.1 *ina* UGU *ziq-qur-r[a-te]*
2 *meš-lu te ni*$^{!}$ [*x x*]
3 *ina* ÙR ˹*x*˺ *x*[*x x x*]
4 *né-*˹*e*$^{?!}$˺*-l[i]*
5 *ma-ṣar-tu ni-iṣ-[ṣ]ur*$^{!}$
6 *ù* LÚ$^{!}$.˹*qur*$^{?!}$˺-[*bu-te*]
7 *a-na* URU.ŠÀ—[URU]
8 URU.*kal-[ha]*
9 URU.*arba-ìl*
10 ((URU.*arba-ìl*))
11 URU.BÀD—^{m}LUGAL—GI.NA
12 *liš-pu-ru*
13 [*x x*]*x* LÚ.GAL$^{?}$—˹*x*˺
rest broken away

⁸ Let the chief baker [*of DN*] be ord[ered] to release u[s] so we [*can put*] (one) half of [...] on the top of the ziggur[ats] and the other half of [...] on the roof [of ...]; we will climb up and keep watch.

r.6 Furthermore, let them send *bod[yguards]* to the Inner [City], Cal[ah], Arbela, (and) Dur-Šarrukin;

13 [...] the chief [...]
(Rest destroyed)

94. An Appeal to the Queen Mother

K 1527

beginning broken away
1′ [*x x*] ˹*ri*˺ [*x x x*]
2′ [*a*]*m-mu-ú-[ti]*
3′ [*š*]*a-ka-na-ku-u-ni*
4′ [*š*]*a ina ti-ma-a-l[i]*
5′ [AM]A—LU[GAL *t*]*a[š-pur]-an-ni*
6′ [*m*]*a-a it-*˹*tah*˺*-ru-u-[ni]*
7′ [*m*]*a-a* ˹*la*$^{?}$ *ig*$^{?}$˺*-ru-r[u]*
8′ [*x x*] ˹*x x x*˺ *na* UD ˹*x*˺
Edge broken away
r.1 [*x x x*]*x a x*[*x x*]
2 [*x*] *u*$^{?}$ ˹*x*˺ [*x x*] *ur* [*x*]
3 *hi*$^{?}$ [*x x x x x x*]
rest broken away

CT 53 182

(Beginning destroyed)

¹ [... about whom] I was given [t]hos[e orders] (and) [about wh]om the qu[een moth]er w[rote] to me yesterd[ay]: "They have appealed to [me]; they were not frightened [...]"

(Rest destroyed or too broken for translation)

erroneously repeated.
94 ³ Cf. SAA 5 27:9f, SAA 10 279:7, 287:3f.

7. Letters from Other Cities of Assyria

FIG. 18. *Entrance to the Inner City.*
W. ANDRAE, *Das wiedererstandene Assur* (Leipzig 1938), Abb. 3.

95. The Governor Acts after the King's Death

81-2-4,65

1 [MÍ]-*šú ša* LÚ.GAR.KUR LUGAL *it-tah-raš*$^{!}$-*ši*$^{!}$
2 *ina* É.GAL *ú-se-ri-ib-ši* UD-*mu ša ni-iš-mu-ni*
3 *ma-a* LUGAL *mé-e-ti* URU.ŠÀ—URU-*a-a*
4 *i-ba-ki-ú* LÚ.GAR.KUR TA* ŠÀ É.GAL
5 MÍ-*šú ú-se-ṣi-a* UDU.MÍ.ÁŠ.GÀR *taq-ṭu-lu*
6 LÚ.SAG-*šú a-na* LÚ.*ha-za-nu-ti*
7 *ú-se-še-eb* LÚ.SAG.MEŠ-*šú*
8 *ku-si*$^{!}$-*a*$^{!}$-*ti la-bu-šú* HAR.MEŠ KUG.GI
9 *šá-ak-nu ina pa-an* LÚ.*ha-za-ni i-za-zu*
10 ^{m}*qi-sa-a-a* LÚ.NAR TA* DUMU.MÍ.MEŠ-*šú*
11 *ina pa-ni-šú-nu* ⸢*i-za*⸣-*mu-ru ina* UGU *šá ni-iq-bu-ni*
12 *ma-a* [*x x x x x x*] *ki*

13 LÚ.GAR.KUR [*x x x x*] ⸢TA*⸣ ŠÀ ŠEŠ.MEŠ-*ni*
14 *ina* ⸢*bir-tú*⸣-[*x x x x x*] *ik-tar-ru*
15 2 LÚ.*x*[*x x x x a-na* ^{m}*aš-šur*]—NUMUN—DÙ

16 *it-tal-*[*ku x x x x x x x* LÚ.GAR].KUR
17 URU.ŠÀ—URU-[*a-a*$^{?}$ *x x x x x*]*x-u-ni*

18 KUR.*gi-m*[*ir-ra-a-a x x x x x x x x*]*x* [*x*]*x*
about 8 lines broken away

Rev. about 10 lines broken away
1′ *e-gír*$^{!}$-*a-ti* [*x x x x x x x*]
2′ *ú-ba-lu-ni-ni* ^{m}*d*[*a-na-a-a*]
3′ TA* *an-na-ka i-šá-ṭar x*[*x x x i-s*]*a*$^{!}$-*si*
4′ *ina* UGU-*hi* ^{m}*da-na-a-a ni-t*[*a-lak ina* UG]U *áš-li*
5′ KÁ.GAL *ip-te-ti* ^{m}*da-n*[*a-a*]-*a ú-se-ṣi*
6′ *a-ni-nu ina ir-ti* LÚ.ÚŠ$^{!}$
7′ *a-na ba-ke-e ni-tu-ṣi*
8′ LÚ.GAR.KUR TA* LÚ.ERIM.MEŠ-*šú*
9′ TÚG.GÚ.È.MEŠ *hal-lu-pu*
10′ ⸢GÍR⸣.AN.BAR.MEŠ *kar-ru né-ta-mar*
11′ *ni-ip-ta-làh a-na* LÚ.SUKKAL
12′ *a-na* ^{m}*ha-am-bi-i ni-iq-ṭí-bi*
13′ *nu-uk a-ta-a a-ni-nu ni-bak-ki*

ABL 473

[1] The king received the [wife] of the governor and brought her into the Palace. On the day we heard that the king was dead and the people of the Inner City were weeping, the governor brought his wife out of the palace. She burnt a female goat-kid, (while) he installed a eunuch of his as the mayor. His (other) eunuchs stand in the presence of the mayor, dressed in festive robes and wearing golden rings, while the singer, Qisaya, and his daughters keep singing (hymns) before them.

[11] Regarding what we said, he (told us): "[...]."

[13] The governor [and ...] threw [...] from our brothers in the middle of [...]

[15] Two [...s] went [to Aššur]-zeru-ibni [......].

[16] [The gove]rnor [*and the people of*] the Inner City [...].

[18] The Cimm[erians ......]

(Break)

[r.1] [...] used to bring letters [......]. D[annaya] from here used to write and read them [...].

[4] We went *straight* to Dannaya. He opened the gate and let Dan[nay]a go out.

[6] (As) we left for the (king's) corpse to weep (over it), we saw the governor with his troops dressed in armour and wearing iron swords. We got scared (and) said to the vizier and to Hambî: "Why are we weeping? The

95 Previous edition: Lanfranchi Cimmeri (1990) 43-47; Thompson (1937) 35ff. Discussion: Frahm Sanherib (1997) 184. Collated by S. Parpola, 1964. The order of obv. and rev. is determined by the direction of writing on the left side and is correctly indicated in Harper's copy. [8] See coll. [r.1] See coll. [r.2] According to collation, nothing missing after ^{m}*d*[*a-na-a-a*]; the signs -*s*]*a-si* in Harper's copy belong to the next line. [r.4] According to collation, there is room for the suggested restoration before *áš-li*. For *ina muhhi ašli* "straight," see LAS II 29 r.10. [r.6] See coll. and W 173. [r.11f] Hambî is attested in a legal document from Assur dated 707 (see PNA 2/I 447). [r.15]

FIG. 19. *Female singer (reign of Assurbanipal).*
ANE 124920.

14′ LÚ.GAR.KUR TA* LÚ*.ERIM.MEŠ-*šú* GÍR.MEŠ AN.BAR *kar-ru*
15′ *ina re-šú-un-ni i-za-zu*
16′ *ina* É.GAL *ina* É—*re-du-ti*
17e *ina* UGU *áš-li it-ta-lak*
18e *ma-a* GIŠ.IG *pi-ta-a-ni*
19e *ina* UGU LÚ.GAR.KUR *ni-ṣa-bat*
s.1 [*x x x x x a-na*] DUMU.MEŠ ᵐ*za-za-ki i-du-ak*

governor and his men are wearing iron swords and *taking care* of us."

16 He went *straight* to the Palace (and) to the Succession Palace, saying: "Open the door for me!" We will *seize upon* the governor.

s.1 [...] is killing the sons of Zazaki.

96. Privileges in Assur at Stake

K 543

1 *a-na* LUGAL EN-[*ni*]
2 [ARA]D.MEŠ-(*ka*) LÚ.*ha-*[*za-na-te*]
3 [LÚ.*pa*]*r-šú-mu-te š*[*a* URU.ŠÀ—URU]
4 [*lu-u*] DI-*mu a-na* [LUGAL EN-*ni*]
5 [DINGIR.MEŠ *ša*] É.ŠÁR.[RA]
6 [*a-na*] LUGAL EN-[*ni*]
7 [*a—dan-niš*] *lik-*[*ru-bu*]
8 [AD]-*ka* A[D—AD-*ka*]
9 [A]D *ša* A[D—AD-*ka*]
10 URU.ŠÀ—URU *ú-*[*za-ki-ú*]
11 *at-ta ú-tú-*[*x x x x*]
12 *ú-tú-ru-te t*[*a-sa-kan*]
13 *ú-ma-a ša* É ⌈LÚ⌉.[GAR.KUR]
14 LÚ.*qe-ba-a-ni*
15 *ina* UGU URU.ŠÀ—URU
16 *ip-ta-aq-du*
17 ŠE.*nu-sa-hi i-*⌈*na*⌉*-su*!*-*[*hu*]
18 ŠE.*ši-ib-še i-šab-bu-šú*!
r.1 *at-ta* NUMUN.MEŠ GIN
2 *ša* ᵐᵈ30—PAB.MEŠ—SU
3 *at-ta* DUMU-*ka*
4 DUMU—DUMU-*ka le-bu*
5 *a-na le-e-bi*
6 *aš-šur* ᵈUTU *ik-tar-bu-ka*
7 LUGAL-*u-tú ina* UGU-*hi-ni* [0]
8 *tu-pa-áš ina ti-ir-ṣ*[*i-ka*]
9 ŠE.*nu-sa-hi-ni i-*[*na-su-hu*]
10 ŠE.*ši-ib-še-ni i-*[*šab-bu-šú*]
11 *ina* UGU É.MEŠ [*ša* LUGAL EN-*ni*]
12 *iš-pur-an-*[*na-ši-ni*]
13 *ma-a mì-i-*[*nu* 0?]
14 *šu-tú-u-ni ni*?*-*[*sa-ʾa-al*]
15 *dan-na-a-te* [*x x x x*]
16 *ina* É LÚ.GAR.KUR [*x x x*]
17 *i-sa-ka-*[*nu x x x x*]
18 *i-qab-bi* [*x x x x x*]
19e LÚ.A—*šip-*[*ri ša* LUGAL EN-*ni*]
20e *lil-l*[*i-ka x x x*]
21e *lip-*[*qid x x x x*]
22e *ina x*[*x x x x x*]

ABL 442

1 To the king, [our] lord: (your) servants, the ma[yors] and [el]ders o[f the Inner City. Good] health to [the king, our lord]! May [the gods of] Ešar[ra greatly] b[less] the king, [our] lord.

8 Your [father, your] gran[dfather], (and) [the fath]er of [your] gran[dfather] e[xempted] the city of Assur. (And) you have [established] additional [*privileges for us*].

13 Now the men of the house of the [governor] have appointed officials over the Inner City. [They] are exac[ting] corn taxes (and) collecting straw taxes.

r.1 You are the true seed of Sennacherib. Aššur and Šamaš have blessed you, your son, your son's son, generation to generation. You exercise kingship over us. (Yet) in [your] reign, [they are exacting] our corn taxes (and) [collecting] our straw taxes!

11 As to the houses [about which the king, our lord], wrote to [us]: "Wha[t] is the matter (with these)?" — we [have asked] (about them).

15 *The (legal) documents* [...]

16 in the house of the governor [...]

17 [they] have placed and [...]

18 he will say [......]

19 May a messen[ger of the king, our lord], co[me ...] and appo[int ...].

22 in [......]

Literally: "standing at our head." r.19 Unclear whether still part of the direct speech or a statement by the writers of the letter. s.1 Zazaku was the eponym of the year 692.

96 → Postgate, TCAE (1974) 276f (obv.1-r.10); LAS II n. 412 (r.1f). 9, 12 See coll. 17 Y 80; cf. Borger Ash. ⌈185⌉ 2 III 8: liberation of corn taxes. 18 See coll. r.9f Postgate (TCAE 277) restores *i-*[*ši*] at the ends of these

97. The Mayor is a Criminal

83-1-18,20

1 [*a-na* LUGAL] *be-lí-ni*
2 [AR]AD.MEŠ-*ka* LÚ.*ha-za-na-ti*
3 LÚ.A.BA—URU LÚ.SAG.DU.MEŠ
4 *ša* URU.ŠÀ—URU URU.ŠÀ—URU!-*a-a*
5 TUR GAL *lu šul-mu*
6 *a-na* LUGAL *be-lí-ni*
7 DINGIR.MEŠ *ša* É.ŠÁR.RA
8 *a-na* LUGAL *be-lí-ni lik-ru-bu*
9 mdI5—I LÚ.*ha-za-nu*
10 URU.[ŠÀ—URU] *ih-ti-pi*
11 [*x x x i*]*r-ti-aq*
12 [*x x x x*]*x ba-tu-ba-ti*!-*ni*!
13 [*x x x*] *ina* UGU *ša pi-ni*
14 [*ina* UGU-*š*]*ú ni-ip-tu-ni*
15 [*x x-p*]*a*?-*ar si*? *mat*? *ti ni*
16 [*x x x*]*x ú-ma-a*
17 [*x x*] GÚ.UN KUG.UD
18 [*x x*] KUG.GI
19 [*x x*] MA.NA KUG.UD
20 [*x x*] *duh-ši-e*
r.1 [*in-ta*]-*at-ha*
2 [*x x*]*x* ⸢*x*⸣-*na-ni*!
3 [*x x*] ⸢*e*!⸣-*pa*-⸢*as*!⸣
4 [*a-ta-a*] *a-na* LÚ.*ha-za-nu*-⸢*ti*!⸣
5 [*li*]-*ip-qi-du-ni-šú*
6 [*par-r*]*i*!-*ṣu šu-ú*
7 [LÚ].⸢*da*!⸣-*a-a*-⸢*lu*!⸣
8 *la*? ⸢*x i*? *ni*! *ru*?⸣
9 *en*? [*x x*] *na ra am*? *ti*
10 *a-na* LUGAL EN-*ni ni-iq-te-bi*
11 *šum-mu a-na* LÚ.*ha-za-na-ti*
12 *i-pa-qi-du-ni-ši*
13 LÚ.ARAD.MEŠ-*ka* ÚŠ
14 2 *e-gír-a-ti*
15 *a-na* LUGAL EN-*ni ni-sap-ra*
16 *gab-ru-ú la né-mur*
17 Á.2-*ni a-na mi-tu-ti*
18 *ni-ti-din*? LUGAL LÚ.ARAD.MEŠ-*šú*
19 *lu la ú*!-*ra-ma*

ABL 1238

1 [To the king], our lord: your [ser]vants, the mayors, the city scribe, the principals of the Inner City and the citizens of the Inner City, young and old. Good health to the king, our lord! May the gods of Ešarra bless the king, our lord.

9 Issar-na'di, the mayor, has destroyed the [Inner Ci]ty.

11 [...] has become empty

12 [...] around us

13 [...] Because we opened our mouths [against hi]m, [he ...s] our [... and ...]

16 [...] Now he has picked up [x] talent(s) of silver, [...] gold, [x] mina(s) of silver, [x] coloured leather, (and) is *making* [...].

r.4 [Why should] he be appointed to the mayorship? He is a [crimi]nal.

7 The scout [...]

(Break)

10 We have told the king, our lord. If he is appointed to the mayorship, your servants will die.

14 We have sent two letters to the king, our lord, but we have not seen a reply. We have (already) surrendered to death. May the king not forsake his servants!

98. Dissolved Ordinances

81-2-4,113

1 *a-na* LUGAL *be-li-ia*
2 ARAD-*ka* m*kab-ti-i* LÚ.DUB.SAR
3 *ša* LUGAL *be-lí*
4 *ina* É LÚ.*ša*—IGI—É.GAL *ip-qi-da-ni*

ABL 733

1 To the king, my lord: your servant Kabtî, the scribe whom the king, my lord, installed in the house of the palace superintendent.

lines: "Re[move] (our taxes)!" r.13f Oppenheim, JAOS 61 (1941) 264 fn. 64 "to give (exact, reliable) information" (cf. no. 196:10ff).

97 According to PNA: Assurbanipal and later. 4 See coll. and W 326. 12 See coll.; Deller, Or. 35 (1966) 312: *ba-tu-ba-at*!-*te*!. 20 [KUŠ].*du*$_8$-*ši-e*: cf. Radner, SAAS 6 (1997) 301. r.2, 4 See coll. r.17f Oppenheim, JAOS

5 *lu šul-mu a-na* LUGAL *be-lí-ia*
6 ^{d}*aš-šur* LUGAL DINGIR.MEŠ *a-šib* É.ŠÁR.[RA]
7 *a-na* LUGAL EN-*ia lik-ru-ub*
8 UD.MEŠ GÍD.DA.MEŠ MU.AN.NA.MEŠ *ma-a'-du-[te]*
9 *še-bé-e lit-tu-tu a-na* LUGAL
10 [*be-lí-i*]*a li-id-*[*din*]
11 [*x x x*] ⸢ŠÀ⸣ [*x x x x*]
rest broken away
Rev. beginning broken away
1′ [*x x*]*x x*[*x x x x x x x*]
2′ *me*? *i*[*l*? *x x x x x x x*]
3′ *a-na* LUGAL EN-*ia mì-i-nu* [*la-aq-bi*]
4′ *ri-ik-sa-a-ni ša* É.GAL
5′ *pa-ṭu-ru ra-am-mu-u*
6′ *me-me-ni la-a i-šam-man-ni*
7′ TA* *bé-et* LUGAL *be-lí*
8′ *ip-qi-da-an-ni-ni*
9′ *ma-ṣar-tu*! *ša* LUGAL EN-*ia*
10′ *a-na-ṣar* ^{d}AG *u* ^{d}AMAR.UTU
11′ *a-na* LUGAL EN-*ia lik-ru-bu*

Good health to the king, my lord! May Aššur, the king of the gods, who dwells in Ešar[ra], bless the king, my lord. May he gi[ve] the king, [m]y [lord], long days, [nu]merous years and the satisfaction of extreme old age.

(Break)

r.3 What [can I say] to the king, my lord? The ordinances of the palace are dissolved and neglected. No one listens to me.

7 Ever since the king, my lord, appointed me, I have been keeping the watch of the king, my lord. May Nabû and Marduk bless the king, my lord.

99. Information on Accomplices of Aššur-da''in-aplu

Bu 89-4-26,16

beginning broken away
1′ *šúm-ma x*[*x x x x x*]*x* ⸢*x*⸣
2′ *a-se-me ri-i*[*k-s*]*a-t*[*i*]
3′ *am—mar ša pa-aṭ-ru-u-ni*
4′ *i-sa-hu-ru i-ku-u-nu*
5′ ^{d}PA *u* ^{d}*taš-me-tum* DINGIR.MEŠ *ša* É
6′ *ha-an-ni-i a-na* LUGAL *a-na* NUMUN-*šú*
7′ *a-na* NUMUN NUMUN-*šú lik-ru-bu*
8′ ^{m}*kab-ti-i* LÚ.A.BA
9′ ARAD *ša* ^{m}*aš-šur—da-in—*DUMU.UŠ DUMU ^{m}DI-*ma-nu—*MAŠ
10′ *ša e-gír-tú ar-me-tú id-din-an-ni*
e.11′ *a-na* LUGAL EN-*ia*
12′ *ad-din-u-ni*
13′ *i-qab-bi-'a-a*
r.1 *ma-a ina* UGU EN—*hi-iṭ-ṭi*
2 *ša a-na* LUGAL EN-*ia*
3 *aq-bu-u-ni*
4 *ma-a* DUMU-*šu ina* ŠÀ É.GAL *e-rab ú-ṣa*
5 *a-na ia-*⸢*a-ši*⸣ *i-qab-bi-'a-a*
6 *ma-a šum-m*[*a di*]*-ib-bi an-nu-ti*
7 *is-sa-*[*x x-a*]*n-ni*
8 *ma-a ana-k*[*u la-aq-ba*]*-ak-ka*
9 *ma-a* 8 L[Ú.*x x x*]*x*.MEŠ
10 *ma-a ša x*[*x x x a-na*] LUGAL EN-*ia*
11 *id-din-*[*u-ni x x x x x*]
12 [*ma*]*-a šul-ma-*[*nu x x x x u*]*b*
rest broken away

ABL 872

(Beginning destroyed)

1 If [......]

2 I have heard that all the ordinances which were dissolved have become stable again. May Nabû and Tašmetu, the gods of this house, bless the king, his offspring and his offspring's offspring.

8 The scribe Kabtî, a servant of Aššur-da''in-aplu son of Shalmaneser (III), who gave me the Aramaic letter which I gave to the king, my lord, is saying to me: "Regarding the offender about whom I spoke to the king, my lord, his son enters and leaves the Palace. He is telling me: 'If he [...s] these [wo]rds to me, I [will tell them] to you.'

r.9 "8 [..]s who gave [... to] the king, my lord, [......]

12 "a brib[e ......]

(Rest destroyed)

61 (1941) 268, translates this idiom as "to give oneself up." r.18f → Deller, Or. 30 (1961) 347. r.19 See coll.
98 r.4f Deller, Or. 30 (1961) 352. r.9 See coll. and W 226.
99 8f The reference to Aššur-da''in-aplu son of Shalmaneser (III) would seem to date this letter to the reign of

100. An Earthquake Hits Assur

Th 1932-12-10,301 (BM 123358)

1 *a-na* LUGAL *be-lí-ia*
2 ARAD-*ka* ^{md}PA—MU—GIN LÚ*.A.BA
3 *lu-u* DI-*mu a-na* LUGAL *be-lí-ia*
4 ^{d}PA *u* ^{d}AMAR.UTU *a-na* LUGAL *be-lí-iá*
5 *lik-ru-bu*
6 UD-21-KÁM *ša* ITI.KIN
7 *ri-i-bu ir-tu-bu*
8 EDIN URU *gab-bi-šu*
9 *i-ta-am-ri-ṭi*
10 BÀD *ša* EDIN URU *gab-bu*
11 *i-te-ṭi-ra*
12 30 1/2 KÙŠ TA* ŠÀ-*bi*
13 *i-ta*-am-la-ah*
14 *ina qab-si* URU *i-tu-qu-ut*
15 É—DINGIR *gab-bu i-ta-[am-r]iṭ*$^{!}$
16 *up-ta-ta-ṣi-[d]i*
17 DINGIR.MEŠ-*ni ša* LUGAL
18 *gab-bu* DI-*mu*
19 *ši-ib-šú-tú ša ap-te*$^{!}$
20 ⸢*ša*⸣ É—DINGIR
r.1 [*x x*]*x* ⸢$^{d?}$⸣PA ^{d}⸢IM$^{?}$⸣
2 [*x x x x x x x x*]
3 *šu* ⸢*x x x x*⸣ *har* [*x x*]
4 *x*[*x x x*]*x x*[*x x x x*]
5 *ša* É.*si-qur*$^{!}$*-ra*$^{!}$*-*[*te*]
6 *ša* É—1-*te ša* ⸢É$^{!}$ *x*⸣
7 *i-tu-uq-tu* 1-*e*[*n*] ⸢*x*⸣
8 TA* ŠÀ-*bi* É ⸢*x*⸣ *an-ni-te*
9 *i-tu-qu-ut*
10 *na-mi-ri ša* KÁ.GAL *qab-si-te*
11 *ša* KÁ.GAL ⸢*ša*$^{!}$⸣ *qa-ni*
12 *i-tu-qu-tu*
13 É—[1-*te*] ⸢1$^{?}$-*et*$^{?}$ *ša*$^{?}$⸣ *qa-ni* 0$^{!}$
14 É—*ma-ṣar-te ša* URU
15 É—1-*te* 1$^{!}$-*et* TA* ŠÀ-*bi*
16 *ta-tu-qu-ut*
17 LÚ*.SAG *ša* L[UGAL]
18 *lil-l*[*i-ka l*]*e-mu-ur*

Iraq 4 189

1 To the king, my lord: your servant Nabû-šumu-ka''in, the scribe. Good health to the king, my lord! May Nabû and Marduk bless my lord.

6 There was an earthquake on the 21st of Elul (VI). The outer town in its entirety was damaged (lit. "scratched") but the whole wall of the outer city was saved; (only a stretch of) 30.5 cubits was torn out of it and fell into the centre of the city.

15 The House of God in its entirety was dam[ag]ed and cracked, but all the gods of the king are well.

19 The architrave of the window-opening of the House of God (and) [the ... *of*] Nabû (and) Adad [......]

(Break)

r.5 of the ziggurat[s ... and] of the ... house of ... fell down; one [...] collapsed from this house.

10 The watchtowers of the middlemost gate and the outer gate have collapsed; (and) one [...] house outside the city garrison and one inside it have collapsed.

17 A royal eunuch should come and have a look.

101. Repairing Earthquake Damages

K 1948

beginning broken away
4′ ⸢LÚ*⸣.GA[L—*x x x x x x*]
5′ EN [*x x x x x x x*]
rest broken away

CT 53 216

(Beginning destroyed)

4 the chi[ef ......]

5 *together with* [......]

(Break)

Šamši-Adad V (823-811), see Introduction, p. XLV. In view of the reference to "the ordinances which were dissolved" (obv. 2), the scribe mentioned here may well be identical with the writer of no. 98. Cf. PNA 2/I 593. r.8f See coll.

100 Copy and previous edition: Thompson, Iraq 4 (1937) 186-189. Coll. S. Parpola 30.11.66. 13 *i-ta*-am-la-ah*: Normally *ta** was reserved for *issi/u* = TA*. 19 Normally, the word *šibšutu* is written as GIŠ.ŠÚ.A; cf. no. 101 r.6.

FIG. 20. *The temple of Aššur and the ziggurats.*
W. ANDRAE, *Das wiedererstandene Assur* (Leipzig 1938), Abb. 14.

Rev. beginning broken away
1′ ⌜*a-na* LÚ*.GAL⌝—[*x x x x*]
2′ *liš-al* LUGAL [*x x x x*]
3′ *a-ki* BÀD *x*[*x x x x*]
4′ *i-me-ri-du-n*[*i*? *x x x*]
5′ *a-na ma-qa-t*[*e x x x x*]
6′ GIŠ.ŠÚ.MEŠ *ú-*[*x x x x*]
7′ *a-ki ša* LUG[AL *be-lí i-qab-bu-ni*]
8′ *le-pu-u*[*š x x x*]
s.1 [ŠÀ-*bu ša* LUGAL EN-*ia a—d*]*an-niš lu* DÙG.GA

r.1 May [the king, my lord], ask the chief [...]. The king [...].
3 When the city wall [...]
4 was damaged [...]
5 to fal[l ...]
6 the door-beams [...]
7 I will do as the kin[g, my lord, commands].
s.1 [The king, my lord], can be glad [in]deed.

102. ———

K 16532

1 [*a-na* LUGAL *be-lí-ni*]
2 A[RAD.MEŠ-*ka* m*x x x*]
3 m[*x x x x x*]
4 *lu* [DI-*mu a-na* LUGAL EN-*ni*]
5 d*aš-š*[*ur x x x*]
6 *a-n*[*a* LUGAL EN-*ni*]
rest broken away
Rev. beginning broken away
1′ *ina* IG[I *x x x x x x x*]
2′ *ša* LU[GAL? *x x x x x*]
rest uninscribed

CT 53 794

1 [To the king, our lord: your] se[rvants PPN]. Good [health to the king, our lord]! [May] Ašš[ur and DN bless the king, our lord].
(Break)
r.1 befor[e ......]
2 of the ki[ng ......]

101 r.4 Cf. no. 100:9. r.6 GIŠ.ŠÚ.MEŠ: normally, the word *šibšutu* is written as GIŠ.ŠÚ.A; cf. no. 100:19.

103. ———

K 4710

beginning broken away
1′ *[x x]x[x x x x x]*
2′ *[x x]x[x x x x x]*
3′ ŠÀ$^{?}$ *[x x x x x]*
4′ *[x x x]* ⸢TA*⸣ URU.*x[x x]*
5′ *a-na* URU.Š[À$^{?}$—URU]
e.6′ *it-tal-ka [x x x]*
r.1 *a-na* ŠEŠ-*i[a x x]*
2 *i-ta-la[k x x x]*
3 *is-su-[hur$^{?}$ x x x]*
4 *ih-[x x x x x]*
5 ⸢*ra*⸣-*[x x x x x]*
rest broken away

ABL 1299

(Beginning destroyed)

4 [... fr]om the city [GN] he came to the *In[ner City ...]*.

r.1 He wen[t] to m[y] brother [...].

3 *He retu[rned ...]*

(Remainder destroyed)

104. On the River Tartaru

Bu 91-5-9,111

beginning broken away
1′ *[x x x x x]* ⸢*a-na*⸣ *[x x x]*
2′ *[x x x ina]* UGU ÍD.*tar-ta-ri*
3′ *[x x x]x-tu i-ma-la šú-u [x]*
4′ *[x x x i]l-li-ku-ni* [0]
5′ *[x x x] an-ni-tú a-na e-pa-še*
6′ *[x x x x x]x* ^{m}*aš-šur*—LUGAL—MU [0]
rest broken away
Rev. completely broken away

CT 53 961

(Beginning destroyed)

1 [......] to [...]

2 [...] on the river Tartaru

3 [...] is filling up [...]

4 [... *who* w]ent

5 [...] to do this

6 [......] Aššur-šarru-iddina

(Rest destroyed)

105. Killed in the Enemy Country

K 11

1 *a-na* LUGAL *be-lí-ia*
2 ARAD-*ka* ^{m}SUHUŠ—^{d}PA
3 *lu-u* DI-*mu a-na* MAN EN-*ia*
4 ^{d}EN ^{d}PA ^{d}15 *ša* URU.NINA
5 ^{d}15 *ša* É—*ki-di-mu-ri*
6 *a-na* MAN EN-*ia a—dan-niš a—dan-niš*
7 *lik-ru-bu ṭu-ub* ŠÀ-*bi*
8 *ṭu-ub* UZU.MEŠ *a-na* MAN EN-*ia*
9 *lid-di-nu* DI-*mu a-na* EN.NUN.MEŠ
10 *ša* LUGAL EN-*ia* ^{m}*šúm-mu*—DINGIR
11 DUMU ^{md}*a-ra-miš*—MAN—DINGIR.MEŠ
12 LÚ.*mu-šar-kis a-bat* LUGAL
13 *ina* IGI-*ia i-za-kar*
14 *ma-a* AD-*ú-a ina* KUR—*na-ki-ri*
15 *me-e-ti ma-a* 50 LÚ.ERIM.MEŠ

ABL 186

1 To the king, my lord: your servant Ubru-Nabû. Good health to the king, my lord! May Bel, Nabû, Ištar of Nineveh (and) Ištar of the Kidmuru temple very greatly bless the king, my lord. May they give happiness (and) physical well-being to the king, my lord. The garrisons of the king, my lord, are well.

10 Šumma-ilu, the son of Aramiš-šar-ilani, the recruitment officer, has appealed in my presence for royal intervention, saying:

14 "My father died in enemy country. The fifty men who were under his command, took

105 Previous editions and translations: Oppenheim Letters (1967) 177f, no. 125; Fales Cento Lettere (1983) 56-60, 83f. → Postgate, TCAE (1974) 136 (obv. 10-18); Elat, JESHO 30 (1987) 249f (obv. 10-r.11)

16 *ša* ŠU.2-*šú* 12 ANŠE.KUR.RA.MEŠ
17 *ina* ŠU.2-*šú-nu i-ṣab-tu-u-ni*
18 *it-tal-ku-ú-ni*
19 *ina bat-ti-bat-ti ša* URU.NINA
e.20 *kam-mu-su*
21 *ma a-na-ku aq-ṭi-ba-šú-nu*
22 *ma-a* AD-*ú-a*
23 *lu me-e-ti*
r.1 EN.NUN *ša* LUGAL *a-ta-a*
2 *tu-ra-am-me-a tal-lik-a-ni*
3 *ú-ma-a an-nu-rig*
4 *ina pa-an* LUGAL EN-*ia us-se-bi-la-áš-šú*
5 LUGAL *be-lí liš-al-šu*
6 *ki-i ša a-bu-tu-u-ni*
7 *a-na* MAN EN-*ia liq-bi*
8 LÚ.DAM.QAR *šu-u* URU.*gar-ga-mis-a-a*
9 ARAD.MEŠ-*šú i-du-ku-uš*
10 1-*en ina* ŠÀ-*bi-šu-nu*
11 *la ú-še-zib nu-ṣa-bi-it*
12 *ki-din-nu ša* ^{d}NIN.LÍL
13 *ša* ^{d}GAŠAN—*ki-di-mu-ri*
14 *ša* AMA.MEŠ *ša i-ra-ma-ka-a-ni*
15 *a-na* MAN EN-*ia us-se-bi-la*
16 *ina* UGU UD.KIB.NUN.KI LUGAL *be-lí*
17 *li-ih-hi-ri-id*
18 *ni-ip-šah*
19e DI-*mu* LUGAL EN-*ia*
20e *la-áš-me*
21e *a-li-ma mi-i-ni*

twelve horses in their hands and came (back); they are (now) staying in the surroundings of Nineveh. I said to them: 'My father may be dead, but why did you leave the royal guard and come (back)?'"

r.3 Now then I am sending him to the presence of the king, my lord. May the king, my lord, question him, and may he tell the king, my lord, how the matter is.

8 That merchant from Carchemish was killed by his servants, (but) not even one of them escaped, we have arrested (them all). I am sending to the king, my lord, the protection of Mullissu (and) of the Lady of Kidmuri, the mothers who love you.

16 With regard to Sippar, may the king, my lord, be vigilant, so we can relax.

19 Let me hear the health of the king, my lord, wherever what (= anything).

FIG. 21. *Guard horses (reign of Sennacherib).*
ORIGINAL DRAWINGS VI, 22.

106. Leftovers of Nabû for the Crown Prince

K 589

1 *a-na* DUMU—LUGAL EN-*ia*
2 ARAD-*ka* ^{m}SUHUŠ—^{d}PA
3 *lu-u* DI-*mu a-na* DUMU—MAN
4 *be-lí-ia a—dan-niš*
5 ^{d}EN ^{d}PA
6 ^{d}NIN.LÍL ^{d}GAŠAN—*ki-di-mu-ri*
7 ^{d}15 *ša* URU.*arba-ìl*
8 *ṭu-ub* ŠÀ-*bi*
9 *ṭu-ub* UZU.MEŠ
10 *šeb*$^{!}$-*e* TIN
11 *a-na* DUMU—MAN *be-lí-ia*
12 *lid-din-nu*
r.1 *re-ha-a-te*
2 *ša* ^{d}PA
3 *a-na* DUMU—LUGAL EN-*ia*
4 *ú-se-bi-la*
5 DI-*mu a-na* EN.NUN.MEŠ
6 *gab-bu lib-bu*
7 *ša* DUMU—LUGAL EN-*ia*
8 *lu* DÙG.GA-*šú*
rest uninscribed

ABL 187

1 To the crown prince, my lord: your servant Ubru-Nabû. The best of health to the crown prince, my lord! May Bel, Nabû, Mullissu, the Lady of Kidmuri (and) Ištar of Arbela give happiness, physical well-being, (and) *enjoyment* of life to the crown prince, my lord.

r.1 I have brought the leftovers of Nabû to the crown prince, my lord. All the guards are well. The crown prince, my lord, can be very glad.

107. ———

K 1048

1 *a-na* DUMU—LUGAL EN-[*ia*]
2 ARAD-*ka* ^{m}SUHUŠ—^{d}PA
3 LÚ*.A.BA *ša* É—GIBIL
4 *lu-u* DI-*mu a-na* DUMU—LUGAL
5 EN-*ia* ^{d}AG ^{d}AMAR.UTU
6 *a-na* DUMU—LUGAL EN-*ia*
7 *lik-ru-bu*
8 TA* ^{m}*aš-šur—še-zib-an-ni*
9 EN.NAM ⌈*ša*? DUMU?⌉—MAN [*x x*]*x*
rest broken away
Rev. broken away

ABL 189

1 To the crown prince, [my] lord: your servant Ubru-Nabû, the scribe of the new palace. Good health to the crown prince, my lord! May Nabû and Marduk bless the crown prince, my lord.

8 *From* Aššur-šezibanni, the governor *whom the crown prince* [...]

(Rest destroyed)

108. The Guard is Well

K 1000

1 *a-na* LUGAL EN-*iá*
2 ARAD-*ka* ^{m}SUHUŠ—^{d}PA
3 *lu-u* DI-*mu a-na* LUGAL EN-*iá*
4 ŠÀ-*bi* LUGAL EN-*iá lu* DÙG.GA
5 *ina* UGU-*hi* EN.NUN

ABL 188

1 To the king, my lord: your servant Ubru-Nabû. Good health to the king, my lord! The king, my lord, can be glad!

5 As to the guard which the king, my lord,

106 6 Cf. Nissinen, SAAS 7 (1998) 36f. 10 In this context the clearly written LAL must be considered a graphical variant of the ME sign; for a similar variant see CT 53 80 s.2 (L]Ú*.LUL.ME). Hence the most likely interpretation is either *me*$^{!}$-*e* TIN "water of life" or *šib*$^{!}$-*e* TIN "enjoyment of life."

6 *ša* LUGAL *be-lí*
7 *ip-qi-da-ni-ni*
8 DI-*mu a—dan-niš*
Rev. uninscribed

appointed to me, it is doing very well.

109. ———

K 1583

1 *a-na* LUGAL EN-*iá*
2 ARAD-*ka* ^{m}SUHUŠ—^{d}PA
3 *lu* DI-*mu a-na* LUGAL EN-*iá*
4 ^{d}PA ^{d}AMAR.UTU *a-na* LUGAL
rest broken away
Rev. entirely broken away

ABL 728

1 To the king, my lord: your servant Ubru-Nabû. Good health to the king, my lord! May Nabû and Marduk [bless] the king [my lord ...]

(Rest destroyed)

110. ———

Bu 91-5-9,46

1 [*a-na* LUGAL EN]-⸢*ia*⸣
2 [ARAD-*ka* ^{m}]SUHUŠ—^{d}PA
3 [*lu* DI-*mu a*]-*na* LUGAL EN-*iá*
4 [^{d}PA *u* ^{d}AMAR.UT]U *a-na* LUGAL EN-*i*[*a*]
5 [*lik*]-*ru-bu*
6 [*a-ki* ^{m}E]N—BA-*šá a-na* UR[U.*x x*]
7 [*x x*]*x* ⸢*x x*⸣ [*x x x x*]
rest broken away
Rev. beginning broken away
1′ [*x x x x x*] *bar*?
2′ [*x x x*] DINGIR.MEŠ LUGAL
3′ [*x x x*] *an* [*x*]
4′ [*x x š*]*a ina pi-i*-[*šú*?]
5′ [*x x x*] ⸢*a*⸣-*na* LUGAL E[N-*iá*]
6′ [*us-se-b*]*i-la* [0]
7′ [*x x x x x x*]

CT 53 960

1 [To the king, m]y [lord: your servant] Ubru-Nabû. [Good health t]o the king, my lord! [May Nabû and Mardu]k [bl]ess the king, m[y] lord.

6 [When B]el-iqiša [went] to the cit[y of ...]

(Break)

r.2 [...] gods *of* the king
3 [...] ... [...]
4 [... *whi*]*ch* in [his] mouth [...]
5 [...] to the king, [my] lo[rd],
6 [I have se]nt

111. The Queen's Palace in Kilizi

Sm 1034

1 *a-na* LUGAL *be-lí-ia*
2 ARAD-*ka* ^{m}EN—BA-*šá*
3 *lu* DI-*mu a-na* LUGAL EN-*iá*
4 ^{d}AG *ù* ^{d}AMAR.UTU
5 *a-na* LUGAL EN-*ia a—dan-niš*
6 *a—dan-niš lik-ru-bu*
7 *ina* UGU-*hi* É MÍ—É.GAL
8 *ša ina* URU.*kàl-zi*
9 *ša* LUGAL *be-lí ip-qi-da-ni-ni*

ABL 389

1 To the king, my lord: your servant Bel-iqiša. Good health to the king, my lord! May Nabû and Marduk very greatly bless the king, my lord.

7 Concerning the palace of the queen in Kilizi which the king, my lord, entrusted to

110 6 PNA 1/II p. 316 dates Bel-iqiša 9-10 to the reign of Assurbanipal and only 5 (p. 315, this letter) to the reign of Esarhaddon. All the Bel-iqiša attestations of this volume are now tentatively assumed to refer to only one person. Cf. also Texts Included and Excluded, p. XLIV.
111 Previous edition: Fales Cento Lettere (1983) 164ff, 185ff.

10 É *up-ta-ṭi-ir*
11 É *uš-še pa-te*
12 *uš-še a-na ka-ra-ri*
r.1 SIG$_4$.MEŠ *kar-mat*
2 *šum-ma* LUGAL *be-lí i-qab-bi*
3 *a-na* LÚ*.GAL—TIN.MEŠ
4 *ṭè-e-mu liš-ku-nu*
5 *lil-li-ka uš-še*
6 *li-ik-ru-ra*
rest uninscribed

me, I have demolished the house, the space for the foundations is open, and bricks have been stocked up for laying the foundations.

[r.2] If the king, my lord, commands, the chief of the master builders may be ordered to come and lay the foundations.

112. Fodder for Horses

K 117

1 *a-na* LUGAL *be-lí-ia*
2 ARAD-*ka* ^{m}EN—BA-*šá*
3 ^{d}AG ^{d}AMAR.UTU *a-na* LUGAL EN-*ia*
4 *lik-ru-bu šá-daq-diš ina* URU.⸢*tar*?⸣-*ni-nu*
5 2 *ú-rat ša* ANŠE.KUR.RA.MEŠ
6 LUGAL EN TA* KI.[TA *x x*]*x-a*
7 LÚ*.SAG.MEŠ *ša* [*x x x x*]
8 *a-na* ARAD-*šú it-ti-*⸢*din*!⸣
9 *ina* UGU LÚ*.IGI.DUB [*x x x*]
10 *ek-ka-la* TA* ^{md}PA—[*x x*]
11 LÚ*.A.BA ⸢*ša*!⸣ LÚ*!.[GA]L!—⸢É⸣
12 *ad-da-bu-*[*ub*]
13 *mu-uk ki-*[*su-tú pa*]*-ni-tú*
14 *a-na* ANŠE.KUR.RA.MEŠ *di-in*
15 *qu-la-le-e-a*
16 *is-sa-kan*
r.1 *ù i-qab-bi-a*
2 *ma-a a-na-ku* TA* É-*an-ni*
3 *a-pa-ra-as-ka*
4 *u* TA* É LUGAL EN *ina* É—EN.MEŠ-*ia*
5 *ip-qid-da-ni-ni*
6 *ina* UGU *me-me-ni ina* É—EN.MEŠ-*ia*
7 *la šal-ṭa-ak*
8 *ù* TA* LÚ*.A.BA *ša* ŠU.2-*ia*
9 *ad-du-bu-bu ina* UGU *d*[*u-a*]*-k*[*i-ia*]
10 *i-da-bu-ub*
11 É—EN.MEŠ-*ia gab-bi*
12 *ik-te-rik šap-lu-uš*
13 *is-sa-kan šul-ma-na-te*
14 *ú-za-zi i-du-kan-ni*
15 *ak* (*an*)*-ni-im-ma šul-ma-na-te*
16e *i-ti-din* LÚ*.A.BA
17e *ša ina pa-na-tu-u-a*
18e *it-ta-as-ha*
s.1 LUGAL *be-lí lu ú-da*

ABL 84

[1] To the king, my lord: your servant Bel-iqiša. May Nabû and Marduk bless the king, my lord.

[4] Last year in Tarninu the king, my lord, gave to his servant two teams of horses from the posse[ssion of ...] the eunuchs of [the *treasurer*]. They used to eat [...] at the expense of the treasurer.

[10] I have tried to speak with Nabû-[...], the scribe of the major domo, saying, "Give the [pr]evious (amount of) fo[dder] to the horses," but he has slighted me and is telling me: "I will cut you off from the inner quarters!"

[r.4] Ever since the king, my lord, appointed me in my lord's household, I have no authority over anybody in my lord's household.

[8] I have also spoken with my own scribe, but (the other) one is plotting to kil[l me]. He has wrapped up the whole house of my lord and subjected it to himself, and has been distributing gifts to have me killed. In the same way he has given out gifts and pulled out the scribe in my service.

[s.1] The king, my lord, should know (this).

112 [4] The suggestion of Fales, HANEM 4 (2000) 240 n. 68, to read *ina* URU.[*gu-za*]*-nu* is out of the question. See coll. [11] See coll. [15-s.1] Fales, HANEM 4 (2000) 240a-b. [r.6] Or: "anything."

113. Report on Guzana

83-1-18,157

1 *a-na* LUGAL EN-*ia*
2 ARAD-*ka* ^{m}EN—BA-*šá*
3 *lu-u* DI-*mu a-na* LUGAL EN-*ia*
4 [^{d}]AG ^{d}AMAR.UTU *a-na* LUGAL EN-*ia*
5 [*a—dan-niš*] *a—dan-niš lik-ru-bu*
6 [*x x x x*] URU.*gu-za-na*
7 [*x x x x*]*x ina* É—EN.MEŠ-*ia*
8 [*x x x x x*]-*ri-i*
9 [*x x x x x-d*]*a-an*
10 [*x x x x x x*]*x*
11 [*x x x x x x x*]-*ni*
12 [*x x x x x x x*]*x*
13 [*x x x x x x x*]*x*
rest broken away
Rev. entirely broken away

ABL 700

1 To the king, my lord: your servant Bel-iqiša. Good health to the king, my lord! May Nabû and Marduk [very] greatly bless the king, my lord.

6 [...] Guzana

7 [...] in my lord's household

8 [... *re*]*gular* [*sheep offering*]

9 [... *gi*]*ves*

(Rest destroyed)

114. Report on Shepherds

K 13139

1 *a-na* LUGAL [EN-*ia*]
2 ARAD-*ka* ^{md}[EN—BA-*šá*]
3 *lu* DI-*mu a-na* [LUGAL EN-*ia*]
4 ^{d}AG *ù* ^{d}AMAR.UTU [*a-na* LUGAL EN-*ia*]
5 *a—dan-niš a—dan*-[*niš lik-ru-bu*]
6 LÚ.SIPA.MEŠ *ša* [*x x x x*]
7 *ša* LUGAL ⌜EN⌝ [*x x x x*]
8 ^{md}PA—*še-zib* [*x x x x x*]
rest broken away
Rev. beginning broken away
1′ *ši*-[*x x x x x x*]
2′ *e*-[*x x x x x x*]
3′ LUGAL [*x x x x x x*]
4′ *a-na* [*x x x x x x*]
5′ *ma-a* [*x x x x x x*]
6′ *e-pu*-[*uš an-nu-rig a-na* LUGAL]
7′ EN-*ia at-ta-har* : LUGAL EN [*x x x*]
8′ *a-ta-a* : ^{md}PA—*še-zib* É—EN.MEŠ-*š*[*ú*? *x x*]
9e *ina ši-ia-a-ri* LUGAL *i-šam*-[*me*]
10e *ina* UGU *ša la a-kul-u-ni* [*x x*]
11e LUGAL *ina* UGU-*hi id*-[*du-kan-ni*]

ABL 1354

1 To the king, [my lord]: your servant [Bel-iqiša]. Good health to [the king, my lord! May] Nabû and Marduk very great[ly bless the king, my lord].

6 The shepherds of [...]about whom the king, my lord, [*wrote to me*] —

8 Nabû-šezib [...]

(Break)

r.3 The king [... said]to [......]:

5 "Do [......]!"

6 [Now then] I am appealing [to the king], my lord: [may] the king, my lord, [...]!

8 Why [does] Nabû-šezib [... h]is lord's household?

9 Tomorrow the king will hear (about it), and the king will k[ill me] on account of the fact that I have not consumed [...].

113 8 Possibly restore UDU.*da*]-*ri-i*.

115. These Men are Drunkards

K 613

1 *a-na* LUGAL *be-lí-ia*
2 ARAD-*ka* ^{m}EN—BA-*šá*
3 ^{d}PA ^{d}AMAR.UTU *a-na* MAN EN-*iá*
4 *lik-ru-bu*
5 ARAD.MEŠ *ša* É—EN.MEŠ-*ia*
6 *ša* LUGAL *be-lí* UD-*mu*
7 *an-ni-ú ú-par-ri-su-u-ni*
8 ^{m}*tab*-URU-*a-a* DUMU ^{m}EN—KASKAL—PAB—PAB
9 *ša a-na* LÚ*.GAL—*ki-ṣir-u-tú*
10 LUGAL *be-lí ú-še-lu-u-ni*
11 ^{md}PA—*sa-kib ša* TA* LÚ*.3.U_5.MEŠ
12 *ka-a.*(*a*)-*ma-nu-te*
13 LUGAL *be-lí ú-še-lu-u-ni*
r.1 ^{m}IGI.LAL—^{d}ŠÚ
2 *ša* TA* LÚ*.*qur*-ZAG.MEŠ
3 LUGAL BE *ú-še-lu-u-ni*
4 3 *an-nu-te* ERIM.MEŠ
5 *šá-ak-ra-nu-tú šú-nu*
6 *ki-ma i-šak-ki-ru*
7 LÚ GÍR AN.BAR
8 TA* *pa-an mì-hi-ri-šu*
9 *la ú-sa-ah-*(*ha*)-*ra*
10 *a-bu-tú ša ú-du-ú-ni*
11 *a-na* LUGAL *be-lí-ia*
12 *as-sa-pa-ra*
13e LUGAL *be-lí*
14e *ki-i ša i-la-u-ni*
s.1 *le-pu-uš*

ABL 85

[1] To the king, my lord: your servant Bel-iqiša. May Nabû and Marduk bless the king, my lord.

[5] The servants of my lord's household who(se status) the king, my lord, has *determined* (as of) today:

[8] Tabalayu son of Bel-Harran-ahu-uṣur, whom the king, my lord, promoted to the rank of cohort commander; Nabû-sagib, whom the king, my lord, promoted to the rank of permanent 'third man'; (and) Atamar-Marduk, whom the king, my lord, promoted to the rank of bodyguard –

[4] these three men are drunkards. When they are drunk, none of them can turn his iron sword away from his colleague.

[10] I have written to the king, my lord, (about) a matter that I know. The king, my lord, may do as he deems best.

116. Dispute Over a Bath

K 13177

1 [*a-na* DUMU—LUGAL EN-*ia*]
2 [ARAD-*ka* ^{md}EN]—BA-*šá*
3 [*x x x x x x*] ⸢^{d}⸣BE
4 [*x x x x x x*]*x*
5 [*a-na* DUMU—LUGAL E]N-*ia*
6 [*lik-ru-b*]*u*
7 [*x x x x*]-*ni*
8 [*x x x x*] ŠÀ-*bi-ni*
9 [*x*] ⸢É⸣ [0] DI-*mu*
10 [*x*] É—*ra-ma-ki* ⸢KALAG$^{?}$⸣
Edge uninscribed
r.1 [*šá*] ⸢*i*⸣-*ba-qu-*[*ru-ni*]
2 [N]A_4.ŠU.GUR.MEŠ
3 [*šá ina*] UGU-*hi*
4 [*a-na* DUM]U—LUGAL *liš-pu-ru*
5 [*l*]*e-mu-ru*

CT 53 505

[1] [To the crown prince, my lord: your servant Bel]-iqiša. [May DNN], Enlil, [and DNN bles]s [the crown prince], my [lo]rd.

[7] [......],
[8] [the ... that is] there
[9] [*and*] the house [are] well.

[10] (As to) the *large* bathroom
[r.1] [which] they are claim[ing],
[2] may the seal(ed document)s (available) on it be sent [to the] crown [pri]nce, and may he have a look at them.

115 Previous editions: Fales and Lanfranchi Lettere (1992) 72f; Fales, HANEM 4 (2000) 240b (translation of obv. 5-s.1). [7] Or: "decided, separated."
116 [10] Cf. LAS II 310:6. See coll.

117. No Shelter for the King's Wine

K 660

1 [a-na] LUGAL [EN-i-ni]
2 [ARAD.MEŠ]-ni-ka ^{m}[x x x]
3 ^{m}EN—BA-[šá]
4 ^{m}KÁ.DINGIR-a-a
5 lu-u DI-mu a-na L[UGAL]
6 EN-i-ni ^{d}aš-šur ^{d}[UTU]
7 ^{d}EN ^{d}AG UD.MEŠ
8 ar-ku-te MU.AN.NA.MEŠ
9 da-ra-a-te a-na LUGAL
10 EN-i-ni lid-di-nu
11 LUGAL EN-i-ni
12 ú-da ki-i
13 na-mur-tú ša ITI.AB
14 kar-ma-tu-ú-ni
15 ù ṣi-il-la-a-te
r.1 la-áš-šú É [GIŠ].GEŠTIN.MEŠ
2 ša LUGAL ni-šak-kan-u-ni
3 LUGAL EN-i-ni li-iq!-bi
4 É.MEŠ lu-kal-li-mu-na-ši
5 re-⸢e!-šu!⸣ ni-iš-ši
6 GIŠ.GEŠTIN ša LUGAL
7 ma-aʾ-da a-a-ka
8 ni-iš-kun

ABL 86

1 [To] the king, [our] lord: your [servant]s [PN], Bel-iqi[ša] and Babilayu. Good health to the k[ing], our lord! May Aššur, [Šamaš], Bel (and) Nabû give long days and everlasting years to the king, our lord.

11 The king, our lord, knows that the audience gift of Kanun (X) has been stocked up but there are no shelters where we could deposit the king's wine. May the king, our lord, command that (storage) rooms be shown to us, so that we may proceed.

r.6 There is much wine of the king — where should we put it?

118. Assyria is Well

K 4760

1 [a-n]a LUGAL EN-[ia]
2 [ARAD-k]a ^{m}KÁ.DINGIR.RA.KI-⸢a⸣-[a]
3 [DI-mu] a-na KUR—aš-š[ur.KI]
4 [DI-m]u a-na DINGIR.⸢MEŠ GAL⸣.MEŠ a-ši-b[u-ti KUR—aš-šur.KI]
5 [ša a-na LUGAL] EN-iá ú-ba-l[a-ṭu-u-ni]
6 [DI-mu a-na DUMU]—MAN DI-mu a-a-š[i]
7 [a-na x x] ša LUGAL EN-iá a—dan-[niš lu DI-mu]
8 [a-na LÚ.GAL].⸢MEŠ⸣-te u LÚ.TUR.MEŠ-te
9 [x x x x]x ⸢ra x x⸣.MEŠ ša LUGAL
10 [EN-iá a—dan]-⸢niš a⸣—[dan]-⸢niš⸣ l[u] ⸢DI⸣-mu
11 [x x x x x x x x x x]-ru-bi
12 [x x x x x x x x x x]-bi
13 [x x x x x x x x] ⸢e-te⸣-li-ú
14 [x x x x x x x x]-li-⸢e?⸣
15 [x x x x x x x x] qa? [x]
rest broken away

CT 53 73

1 [T]o the king, [my] lord: yo[ur servant] Babilayu.

3 Assy[ria] is [well]. The great gods who dw[ell in Assyria] (and) keep [the king], my lord, ali[ve, are we]ll. [The crown pr]ince [is well]. I am well. The bes[t of health to the ...] of the king, my lord! [May the magn]ates and manservants, [and the ... hor]ses of the king, [my lord], be [ve]ry well in[de]ed!

(Break)

13 [......] they have gone up

117 Previous editions: Postgate, TCAE (1974) 249; Fales Cento Lettere (1983) 166ff, 187f. r.3 See coll. and W 44. r.5 In W 44, šu is correctly drawn but transliterated as šú (and probably thus erroneously repeated by Postgate and Fales).

Rev. beginning broken away
1′ [*x x x x*] *a x*[*x x x x x*]
2′ [*x x x*.M]EŠ-*šú a-na* [*x x x x x*]
rest uninscribed

(Rest destroyed or too broken for translation)

119. Fragment Referring to Riding

K 4522

1 [*a-na* LUGAL] *be-lí-ia*
2 [ARAD-*ka* ^{m}]PA—KALAG-*in-an-ni*
3 [^{d}PA] *u* ^{d}AMAR.UTU *a-na* LUGAL EN-*ia*
4 [*lik-ru*]-*bu* TA* UGU ^{m}KÁ.DINGIR.R[A-*a*]-*a*
5 [LÚ.ARAD$^{?}$].MEŠ-*šú ša* LUGAL *be-lí*-[[*ia*]]
6 [*ṭè-mu iš*]-*ku-na-an-ni* [*x x*]
7 [*x x x*]-⌜*šú*⌝-*nu e-t*[*a-x x*]
rest broken away
Rev. beginning broken away
1′ [ŠÀ-*bu ša*] LUGAL *be-lí-iá a—dan-niš* [*lu*]
2′ [DÙG.GA *b*]*ir-ti* IGI.2 *ša* ^{md}[*x x x*]
3′ [*ina* UGU]-*hi-šú-nu un-ta-ad*-[*di-di*]
4′ [*a-na du*]*l-li-šú-nu ka-a-a-ma*-[*nu x x x*]
5′ [*x x*] *i-kar-ru-ru* [*x x x*]
6′ [ANŠE.K]UR.RA *i-ra-ak-ku-b*[*u x x*]

ABL 927

1 [To the king], my lord: [your servant] Nabû-da''inanni. [May Nabû] and Marduk [bl]ess the king, my lord.

4 As to Babilayu (and) his [*servant*]s about whom the king, my lord, [g]ave me [orders ......]

(Break)

r.1 The king, my lord, [may be glad] indeed.

2 I have given cl[ear] instructions to P[N ab]out them,

4 [and they are] constant[ly ...] their [wor]k.

5 [...] they are laying [...]

6 [they] are riding a [hor]se [...]

120. Soldiers for the Chief Cook

K 584

1 *a-na* LUGAL EN-*ia*
2 ARAD-*ka* ^{m}*ki-na-a*
3 *lu-u šul-mu a-na* LUGAL EN-*ia*
4 ^{d}AG *ù* ^{d}AMAR.UTU
5 *a-na* LUGAL EN-*ia lik-ru-bu*
6 LÚ.*zak-ku-ú*
7 *ša na-ṣa-ni-ni*
8 *an-nu-rig*
9 *ina qa*-[*ni* URU.*ar*]*ba-ìl*
10 *k*[*a*$^{?}$-*mu*$^{?}$]-*sa*
11 [*ú-ma-a*$^{?}$ LÚ].GAL—MU
12 [*iq-ṭi-bi-a*]
r.1 [*ma*]-*a* TA* ŠÀ É.GAL$^{!}$
2 *iq-ṭi-bu-u-ni*
3 *ma-a a-na* ^{m}*ki-na-a*
4 *ṭè-e-mu šu-kun*
5 *ma-a šu-u ina pa-ni-ia*
6 *i-sa-dir*
7 *i—da$^{!}$-tu-uk-ka*
8 *il-la-ka*
9 *ú-ma-a mì-i-nu*
10 *ša* LUGAL *be-lí*
11 *i-qab-bu-u-ni*

ABL 143

1 To the king, my lord: your servant Kinâ. Good health to the king, my lord! May Nabû and Marduk bless the king, my lord.

6 The exempt(s) who were brought to me [are] at the moment [*stay*]*ing* out[side Ar]bela.

11 [*Now*] the chief cook [*is telling me*]: "They have told me from the Palace: 'Order Kinâ to line up in my (= king's) presence (and) follow you.'"

r.9 Now what does the king, my lord, command?

119 7 See coll. r.4 Or: "he is."
120 r.7 See coll.

121. Approaching the King

K 651

1 *a-na* LUGAL *ki-na-a-te* EN-*iá*
2 ARAD-*ka* ^{m}EN—PAB-*ir*
3 *lu* DI-*mu a-na* LUGAL EN-*iá*
4 ^{d}PA *u* ^{d}MES *a-na* LUGAL EN-*iá*
5 *lik-ru-bu*
6 *ki-i* LUGAL EN *ina* URU.*arba-ìl*
7 *ina* UGU-*hi šá-ad-da-tu-u-nu*
8 *kam-mu-su-u-ni*
9 LUGAL *a-na* LÚ*.ARAD-*šú ir-tu-*[*a-ba*]
10 *ma-a qí-ri-ib ina* IGI Á.2-⸢*e*⸣-[*a*]
11 ⸢*ana*⸣-*ku a-ba-ak-ka la aq-ri-i*[*b*]
12 *up-ta-ši-iq a-na*! LUGAL EN-*iá*
13 *aq-ṭi-bi mu-uk ta-ri-iṣ*
14 *ù ina* IGI LÚ*.[ARA]D ⸢*ša*⸣ LUGAL
15 *ma* (blank) [*x x x x*]
16 *ša* LUGAL *a-na* [*x x x x*]-*iá*
rest broken away
Rev. beginning broken away
1′ [*x x x x x*]-*nu a-*[*x x*]
2′ ⸢*x x x*⸣ *kas* LÚ* *qi mu* BÀD ⸢*x*⸣
3′ *iq-ṭi-bu-u-ni*
4′ LUGAL EN *is-sa-al-šú-nu*
5′ *a-na* LUGAL EN-*ia aq-ṭi-bi*
6′ *mu-uk ki-i* ⸢*x*⸣ BURU$_5$!
7′ ^{m}ZALÁG-*i ih-tu-bur*
8′ *la ṭa-ab-tu* ⸢*e*⸣-*t*[*a-pa-áš*]
9′ *ù šu-u* ⸢*la*?⸣ [*x x x*]
10′ *is-sa-kan-an-n*[*a-ši*]
11′ *ša*!!-*nu-te*!-*šú a-na* LU[GAL EN-*ia*]
12′ *aq-ṭi-*[*bi* 0]
13′ *mu-uk* LUGAL EN *r*[*e-e-mu*?]
14′ *ina* UGU-*hi* LÚ*.ARAD.M[EŠ-*šú liš-kun*?]
15′ *am—mar ina pa-ni-*[*šú x x*]
16′ *ni-qar-rib-u-ni* UD-[*x*-KÁM]
17′ *a-na ṭu*?-*bi ina* IGI LU[GAL]
18′ *ni-iq-ri-ib* [0]
19e TA* *pa-an la-qa-ni* [0]
20e *lu la ni-qar-ri-ib*

ABL 333

1 To the king of justice, my lord: your servant Bel-naṣir. Good health to the king, my lord! May Nabû and Marduk bless the king, my lord.

6 When the king, my lord, was seated on the *šaddattunu* in Arbela, the king an[grily] told his servant: "Arrive before my arms!"

11 Weeping, I didn't arrive; I *explained* and told the king, my lord, that it was right (to do so). And in the presence of the king's [serva]nt, *they said*: "[...]."

16 That the king [...] to my [...]

(Break)

r.2 ....

3 They told it to me, (and) the king, my lord, questioned them.

5 I said to the king, my lord: "Nurî made noise like [a *swarm* of] locusts (and) did an evil thing. And he set u[s] a [...]."

11 A second time I said to the king, my lord: "[May] the king, my lord, [*have mercy*] on [his] servants, all those who used to arrive in [his] presence!"

16 On the [xth] day we will arrive in the ki[ng's] presence *with good intentions*. May we not arrive because of ...!

122. Who Angers the Gods?

K 7309

beginning broken away
1′ *š*[*ul-mu a-na x x x x*]
2′ *šul-m*[*u a-na x x x x*]
3′ *šul-mu a-*[*na x x x x*]
4′ *ša šul-m*[*u x x x x*]

ABL 1333

(Beginning destroyed)

1 [*Assyria* is] w[ell], [*the temples are*] wel[l], [...] i[s] well.

4 (The servant) who hears [that *his lord*] is

121 Coll. K. Deller 1966. 6f CAD Š/I 41b; cf. SAA 10 77:9. 12f Thus following CAD P s.v. *puššuqu*. r.11 *ša*!!: tablet *da*, scribal error. r.17 *ṭu*?: tablet *šu ma*; see coll. According to Deller, the sign after *ma* could also be read ⸢*nu*⸣.

122 1ff Cf. the introductory formulae of the letters of Sennacherib, (SAA 1 29-38), Ṭab-ṣil-Ešarra (SAA 1

5′ *i-šá-am-mu-*[*u-ni x x x*]
6′ *šu-lam-šú ina x*[*x x x x x*]
7′ *man-nu* DINGIR.MEŠ [*x x x x*]
8′ *ša* TA* [*x x x x*]
9′ *ina* KUR—*na-ki-ri* [*x x x*]
10′ *hi-ṭu ša* DINGIR.[MEŠ *x x x*]
11′ *man-nu* DINGIR.MEŠ [*x x x x*]
12′ *ša a-na-ku x*[*x x x x*]
13′ ⸢*x x x*⸣ [*x x x x x x*]
Rev. beginning broken away
1′ [*x x x*] KUR [*x x x x x*]
2′ [*x x x*]*x šú*? [*x x x x x*]
3′ [*x x a*]*k* [*x x x x x*]
4′ [*x x m*]*i*? *x*[*x x x x x*]
5′ [*x x x*]*x-ti šá* [*x x x x*]
6′ [*x x x*]*x-šú-nu* [*x x x x*]
7′ *in*[*a šá—še-r*]*a-a-t*[*i x x x*]
8′ *a-*⸢*du*?⸣ ^{d}15 *šá pa-*[*x x x*]
9′ EME.MEŠ-*šú-nu x*[*x x x x*]
10′ PI.2.MEŠ-*šú-nu* [*x x x x*]
11′ *ina šá—še-ra-ti* [*x x x x*]
12′ *ina pa-an* [*x x x*]
13′ DUMU.MEŠ U[RU?.*x x x x*]
14′ *ina* ŠÀ-*bi* [*x x x x x*]
15′ *al-ti*?-[*bi*? *x x x x x*]
16′ [*x*]*x x*[*x x x x x x x x*]
rest broken away

well, [...] his own health in [...].
7 Who [*angers*] the gods?
8 He who [*defects*] from [*his own country*] to the enemy country, [*commits*] a crime which the go[ds ...].
11 Who [...s] the gods?
12 What I [...]
(Break)

r.6 [...] their/them [......]
7 i[n the m]orning [......]
8 *as soon as* Ištar of [...]
9 their tongues [......]
10 their ears [......]
11 in the morning [...]
12 before [...]
13 the 'sons' of *A*[*rbela* ......]
14 there [......]
15 *I cir*[*cled* ......]
(Rest destroyed)

123. People for the Rab Mugi

K 9811

beginning broken away
1′ [*x x x x x x*]*x*[*x x x x x*]
2′ [*x x x x x*]*-a-ú*? *ša ku-x*[*x x*]*-šú*
3′ [*x x x x*] TÚG.*ša*—GIŠ.MI
4′ [*x x ina* ŠÀ]*-bi ep-pa-áš*
5′ [*x x x x*]*-ni* LÚ.NAR.GAL
6′ [*x x x x* D]UMU—URU.*arba-ìl*
7′ [*x x x x x*]*x* DUMU—URU.*arba-ìl*
8′ [*x x x* LÚ.A.B]A LÚ.*ar-ma-a-ú*
9′ [*x x x x x*] IGI LÚ.GAL—*mu-gi*
10′ [*x x x x x x*]*x* NIN-*šu*
11′ [*x x x x x x*] *šá* URU.*kam-mu-hi*
12′ [*x x x x x x x x x x*]*-me*
rest broken away
Rev. beginning broken away
1′ [*x x x x x*]*x* ⸢*x*⸣ *šu* [*x x x x*]
2′ [*x x x x*] AD *um-taš-šir*
3′ [*x x x x*]*x tu-mu-ṣu*
4′ [*x x x x*] *ib-bi-is-si*
5′ [*x x x x*]*-ni* ARAD.MEŠ *ša* MAN

ABL 1343

(Beginning destroyed)
2 [PN], a [...] maker —
3 [...] a parasol
4 he will make [the]re —
5 [PN], chief singer
6 [PN], from Arbela
7 [PN], from Arbela
8 [PN], an Aramean [scrib]e
9 [total x people] at the disposal of the *rab-mūgi*
10 [......] his sister
11 [PN, ...] of Commagene
(Break)
r.2 [...] has released
3 [...] ...
4 [...] *bundles*
5 [...], servants of the king [who] have

100-101), Aššur-bani (SAA 1 111-116) and Babilayu (no. 118 in this volume). r.7 See coll. r.7, 11 Cf. SAA 10 19:7, 59:9, 72:19, 79 s.1. r.9f Possibly referring to physical punishments to be ritually inflicted in Arbela because of the crimes alluded to on the obverse. r.13 See coll.

123 2f See coll. r.2 Or: "I have." The verb *muššuru* is a Babylonianism. r.5 Cf. the sold servants of the crown

6′ [*ša ina kas-p*]*i ta-ad-nu-u-ni*
7′ [*šum-ma* LUGA]L *be-lí i-qab-bi*
8′ [*lu-še-bi-l*]*a-šú-nu*
9′ [*x x x x*]*-ka ú-du-u-ni*
10′ [*x x x x x*]*x*.MEŠ *ni li*$^{?}$
11′ [*x x x x*] ⸢*i*⸣*-na* Š[À*-bi x x*]
rest broken away

been sold [for mon]ey.

7 [If the kin]g, my lord, commands, [I will sen]d them over.

9 [... whom] your [...] know(s)

(Rest destroyed or too broken for translation)

124. Shepherd Acting as an Informer

83-1-18,155

1 *a-na* DUMU—LUGAL EN*-ia*
2 ARAD*-ka* ^{m}*na-ni-i*
3 *lu-u* DI*-mu a-na* DUMU—LUGAL EN*-ia*
4 ^{d}AG *u* ^{d}AMAR.UTU
5 *a-na* DUMU—MAN EN-[*ia lik-r*]*u-bu*
6 *ki-i* LUGAL [*x x*] ⸢*ra*$^{?}$⸣ [*x x*]
7 [*x x*] *d*[*a x x x x x x x x*]
rest broken away
Rev. beginning broken away
1′ *il-lik-u-ni* TA* *x*[*x*]
2′ *šu-nu*
3′ *an-nu-rig* 1 LÚ*.SIPA
4′ *ina* IGI*-ia ina* URU.*kàl-ha*
5′ *i-ta-al-ka*
6′ [*b*]*a-te-qu-tú ú-tu-pi-*⸢*eš*⸣

ABL 950

1 To the crown prince, my lord: your servant Nanî. Good health to the crown prince, my lord! May Nabû and Marduk bless the crown prince, [my] lord.

6 When the king [......]

(Break)

r.1 [Ever since] they went, they have been with [...].

3 Now then one shepherd has come to me to Calah. He has acted [as an in]former.

125. Inscribing a Foundation Stone

K 1103

beginning broken away
1′ [*x x x x x lik-ru-b*]*u*
2′ [*x x x x x x x x*]*-ti*
3′ [*ša x x* URU].*a-di-a*
4′ [*x*] ⸢*x*⸣ [*x*]*x ug-dam-me-ru*
5′ *ša uš-še ka-ra-ri*
6′ *pu-u-lu pa-ni-u šá nu-pa-ṭi-ru-ni*
7′ *ga-ṣa-a-nu šu-u*
8′ *an-nu-rig* NA$_4$.*pu-u-lu šá-ni-u*
9′ *qu-ru-ub šum-ma* MAN *i-qab-bi*
10′ *šu-mu šá* MAN *ina* UGU*-hi liš-ṭu-ru*
11′ *ni-ir-ṣi-ip ú-la-a*
12′ MAN *i-qab-bi ma-a la-bi-ru*
13′ *ri-iṣ-pa mi-nu šá ina* IGI LUGAL
14′ *ma-hir-u-ni a-na* ARAD*-šú*
15′ *liš-pu-ra*
Edge uninscribed
r.1 *ina* UGU GIŠ.MEŠ
2 *šá ina bir-te pu-u-li*
3 *ni-ka-ba-su-u-ni*
4 MAN *liq-bi* TA* *bé-et i-da-nu-ni*

CT 53 25

(Beginning destroyed)

1 [May DNN bles]s [the king, my lord].

2 [Concerning the ... *in*] Adia, they have finished [...], (but) for laying the foundations, the earlier foundation stone which we loosened was (too) calcareous.

8 Now, there is another foundation stone at hand. If the king so orders, let the name of the king be written on that and we shall build it in. Alternatively, the king may command: "Build in the old one!" May the king write to his servant what the king finds acceptable.

r.1 As to the wood which we are to trample between the foundation stone, let the king command whence it will be given. Let the

prince in no. 41 r.1-3.
124 6 See coll. r.6 See coll.

5 *a-na* LÚ.GAL—A.BA
6 MAN *ṭè-e-mu liš-kun*
7 *na-ru-u šu-mu šá* MAN *ina* ŠÀ *liš-ṭur*
8 *ù šá ina si-ip-pa-ni šá* É
9 *i-šá-kan-u-ni is-se-niš-ma*
10 UD-*mu* DÙG.GA *le-mur*
11 [*x x*]*x-su šá* MAN *hu-ṭa-ru nu-bil*
12 [*ina* ŠÀ] *ni-ik-ru-ur*
13 [*x x* UD-*x*]*x*-KÁM *le-pu-šú*
14 [*x x x*] ITI.GUD
15 [*x x x x*]*x tal-lak*
traces at the ends of three lines; rest broken away

king order the chief scribe to write the name of the king on the stele, and at the same time to look up a favourable day for the (objects) to be placed in the doorjambs of the house.

11 We will bring the [...] of the king and a staff and lay (them) [there]. The [...] should be performed [on the x]th [day].

14 [...] Iyyar (II)

15 [...] *you* will go

(Rest destroyed)

125 r.10 Cf. SAA 10 14:12, 183:3. r.15 Or: "she will go."

Letters from Other Parts of the Empire

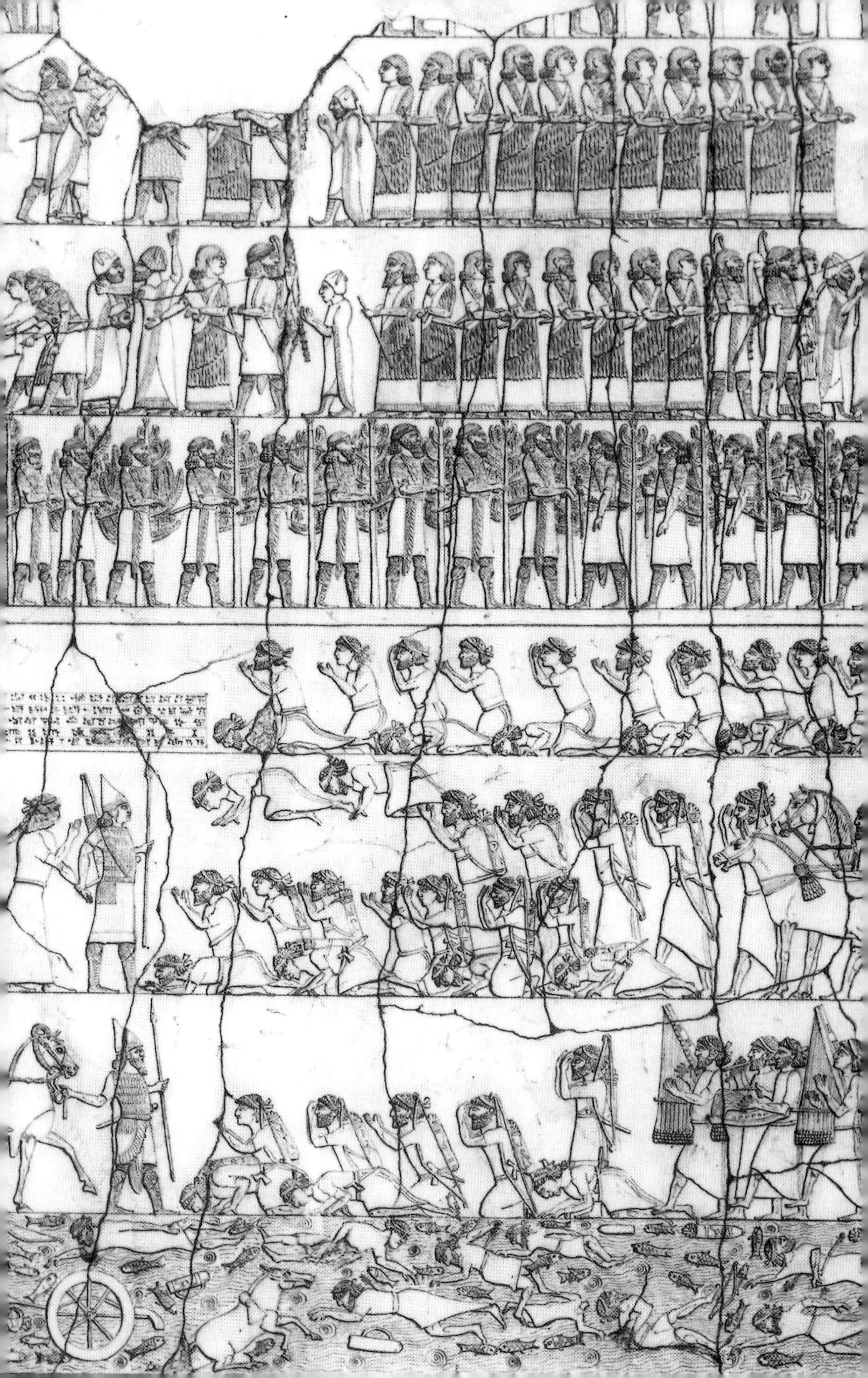

8. Letters from Phoenicia and Transpotamia

FIG. 22. *Enemies at the feet (reign of Assurbanipal).*
ORIGINAL DRAWINGS II, 5.

126. The Whole Country Blesses the King

83-1-18,55 (ABL 1110) + Bu 91-5-9,86

1 *a-na* LUGAL EN-*ia ke-e-nu šá-al-mu*
2 *ù ra-a-mu ša* DINGIR.MEŠ-*šú* ARAD-*ka* ^{m}KI—^{d}UTU—TIN
3 *lu-u šul-mu a-na* LUGAL *be-lí-ia*
4 ^{d}*aš-šur* ^{d}UTU ^{d}EN ^{d}PA ^{d}U.GUR
5 ^{d}15 *ša* NINA.KI ^{d}15 *ša* É—*kad-mu-ru*
6 ^{d}15 *ša arba-ìl*.KI UD-*mu* GÍD.DA.MEŠ
7 MU.AN.NA.MEŠ *da-ra-a-ti ṭu-ub* ŠÀ-*bi*
8 *ṭu-ub* UZU *hu-du-ú* ŠÀ-*bi a—dan-niš a—dan-niš*
9 *a-na* LUGAL *be-lí-ia lid-di-nu*
10 *a-ki-i ša* LUGAL *be-lí* TA* DINGIR *u* LÚ-*ti ke-nu-u-nu*
11 *ù ṣi-it—pi-i ša* LUGAL EN-*ia* ((*ša*)) *i-n*[*a*] UGU-*hi*
12 DINGIR *u* LÚ-*ti i-na* UGU-*hi ṣal-mat*—SAG.DU *ṭa-bu-u-ni*
13 *a-ki ha-nim-ma* DINGIR.MEŠ *ša* LUGAL EN-*ia dan-nu-ti*
14 *ša* TA* ŠÀ-*bi ṣe-he-ru a-du-ú ru-ú-bu*
15 *a-na* LUGAL *be-lí-ia ú-ra-bu-ú-ni*
16 *šu-nu-ma ep-pu-šú ú-gam-mu-ru a-na* LUGAL EN-*ia id-du-*⸢*nu*⸣
17 *ù ma-ri na-ga-ru-ti-ni* [*ša*] LUGAL *be-lí-ia*
18 *i-na sa-pal* GÌR.2 *ša* LUGAL EN-[*ia ú-šak-nu*]-*šú*
19 *a-ki-i ša i-na* ŠÀ-*bi a-de-*⸢*e*⸣ [*qa-bu-u-ni*]
20 *ma-a ša a-na* 15 *il-la-k*[*u-ú-ni* GÍR.MEŠ *le-ku-la-šú*]
21 *ma-a ša a-na* 150 *il-la-*[*ku-ú-ni* GÍR.MEŠ *le-kul-šú*]
22 *ma-a ina kaq-qar ṣ*[*u-ma-mit lap-lap-tú*]
23 *na-da-te-ku-ni lu t*[*a-hi-bi*]
24 DINGIR.[ME]Š *ša* LUGAL [*lu-ú ú-du-u*]
25 [*šum-ma*] ⸢*a*⸣*-ki-i ša* ⸢*i*⸣*-n*[*a* ŠÀ-*bi a-de-e qa-bu-u-ni*]
26 [*la e-pu-šu*]-*ni šum-ma* [*x x x x x x x*]
27 [*x x x*]*x x*[*x x x x x x x x*]
rest broken away
Rev. beginning broken away
1′ [*x x*]*x x*[*x x x x x x x x x x*]
2′ *pa-ni am-mu-t*[*i ša* LUGAL *be-lí-ia*]
3′ *dam-qu-ti* [*x x x x x x x x x*]
4′ *ù ki bi x*[*x x x x x x x x x*]

CT 53 148

1 To the king, my lord, the righteous, sincere, and beloved of his gods: your servant Itti-Šamaš-balaṭu. Good health to the king, my lord! May Aššur, Šamaš, Bel, Nabû, Nergal, Ištar of Nineveh, Ištar of the Kidmuri temple, (and) Ištar of Arbela very generously give to the king, my lord, long days, everlasting years, happiness, physical well-being (and) joy.

10 Just as the king, my lord, is truthful to god and man, and the command of the king, my lord, is good to god and man (and) 'the black-headed people,' in the same manner the powerful gods of the king, my lord, who raised the king, my lord, from childhood till maturity, will fully carry out (these blessings) and render them to the king, my lord. And [they will brin]g all the enemies [of] the king, my lord, [to submission] before the feet of the king, [my] lord.

19 As [it is said] in the treaty: "[May iron swords consume him] who go[es] to the south [and may iron swords consume him] who g[oes] to the north. May your waterskins b[reak] in a place of [severe] t[hirst]" —

24 [by] the gods of the king, [I have don]e just as [it is said] in [the treaty]

(Break)

r.1 [......]

2 that beautiful face [of the king, my lord]

4 and ... [......]

126 Join by S. Parpola, 29.10.66. 17 The dialectal *ma-ri na-ga-ru-ti-ni* stands for (*am*)*mar nak*(*a*)*rūtīni* of the standard language, see Parpola, OLZ 74 (1979) 27. 20f, 22f These two separate quotations from Esarhaddon's Succession Treaty are to be found in SAA 2 6:635f and 653f. 26 Apparently *šumma* here marks the continuation of

5′ *ik-ra-bu-*[*šú-nu x x x x x x*]
6′ *ú-ma-lu-šú-*[*nu x x x x x x x*]
7′ *lu-u me-tu x*[*x x x x x x x x x*]
8′ *be-lí a-na* [*x x x x x x x x x*]
9′ *a-ga-ni* [*x x x x x x x x x*]

10′ LUGAL *be-lí* [*x x x x x x x x x*]
11′ *ša* TA* *i-*[*x x x x x x x x x*]
12′ *ù pa-ni* [*x x x x x x x x x*]*x*

13′ *a-me-lu-ti* [*x x x x x x x* E]N.MEŠ-*šú*
14′ *ú-šal-lam* [*x x x x x x x x x*]*x*
15′ *šú-nu ṭa-a*[*b-tú x x x x x x*]*x-mu-šú*

16′ *ù ina dul-*[*li x x x x x x x x x*]*-*⸢*i*⸣
17′ *a-na—ma-ti* [*x x x x x x x x*.M]EŠ-*šú*
18′ *e-pu-su-nu* [*x x x x x*] ⸢*ú*⸣*-da-mì-qa*
19′ *ù* ŠÀ-*bi ša x*[*x x x x*] *ub-tal-liṭ*

20′ *ma-a-ti gab-bi-šú a-na* LUGAL EN-*ia i-kar-ru-bu*
21′ *a-a-i dul-lu ša* LUGAL *be-lí e-pu-su-su-nu*
22′ *ù ba-di-qu-nu ma-ri dul-lu*$^{!!}$*-nu*
23′ *ša* LUGAL *be-lí ep-pa-su-nu*
24′ *gab-bi-šú da-mu-qi*

5 [*who*] blessed [him ......]
6 (and) filled him [......]
7 be it a dead one [......]
8 my lord to [......]
9 *now* [......]
10 the king, my lord [......]
11 who *with* [......]
12 and *the face* [......]
13 mankind [......] repays his [lo]rds [......]
15 [let] them [repa]y the fav[our ...] to him!
16 And in wor[k ......],
17 *whenever* [...] he performed [...] to its [...]s,
18 [...] he made well [...]
19 and revived the heart of [...].
20 The whole country blesses the king, my lord.
21 What work has the king, my lord, done, that would have been repaired? All the work the king, my lord, performs, is well made!

127. Ikkilû of Arwad Steals the King's Boats

K 1281

1 [*a-na* LUGAL] KUR.KUR EN-*ia*
2 ARAD-[*ka*] ^{m}KI—^{d}UTU—TI.LA
3 [*lu-u š*]*ul-mu a-na* EN LUGAL.MEŠ EN-*ia*
4 [*aš-šur* ^{d}30] ^{d}UTU ^{d}EN ^{d}PA ^{d}U.GUR
5 [^{d}15 *š*]*a* NINA.KI ^{d}15 É—*kid-mur-ra*
6 [^{d}15] *ša arba-ìl*.KI UD-*mu* GÍD.DA.MEŠ
7 [M]U.AN.NA.MEŠ *da-ra-a-te*
8 *ṭu-ub* ŠÀ-*bi ṭu-ub* UZU *hu-du-ú* ŠÀ-*bi*
9 *a-na* LUGAL EN-*ia lid-di-nu*

10 TA* *bé-et* ^{d}UTU *i-nap-pa-ha-an-nu*
11 *a-du-ú i-rab-bu-ú-nu*
12 *ina sa-pal* GÌR.2 *ša* LUGAL EN-*ia ú-sak-niš*

13 KUR *bé-et* LUGAL *be-lí iš-ku-ni-ni*
14 *a-ge-e ša e*[*p*]*-sa*$^{!}$*-tu-ni* LUGAL EN *ú-du*
15 ^{m}*ik-ki-lu-ú la ú-ra-am-mu* GIŠ.MÁ.MEŠ
16 *ina ka-a-ru ša* LUGAL EN-*ia la e-la-a-ni u*
17 *ka-a-ru gab-bi a-na pa-ni-šú us-sah-hir*
18 *ša a-na pa-ni-šú il-la-kan-ni*

ABL 992

1 [To the king] of the lands, my lord: [your] servant Itti-Šamaš-balaṭu. [Good h]ealth to the lord of the kings, my lord! May [Aššur, Sîn], Šamaš, Bel, Nabû, Nergal, [Ištar o]f Nineveh, Ištar of the Kidmuri temple (and) [Ištar] of Arbela give long days, everlasting [y]ears, happiness, physical well-being (and) joy to the king, my lord.

10 From where the sun rises to where it sets, he (= Šamaš) has brought (all lands) to submission before the feet of the king, my lord.

13 The king, my lord, knows the nature of the land where the king, my lord, placed me. Ikkilû does not let the boats come up to the port of the king, my lord, but has turned the whole trade for himself. He provides for

the oath. r.9 *a-ga-ni*: probably for *akanni*, cf. lines 17 and r.22. r.22 *ba-di-qu-nu*: cf. Syr. *bdq* "to repair, restore." *lu*$^{!!}$: tablet KU (scribal error).

127 → Kienast WO 19 (1988) 12f (obv. 14-21); Neumann, AOAT 247 (1997) 287 n.37 (obv. 18-21); Parpola *Iraq* 34 (1972) 27 (r.5-6); Elat JESHO 30 (1987) 238 (r.6-13); Deller WZKM 57 (1961) 41 n.31 (r.11-13). 14 *a-ge-e* for

19 KASKAL.2 *i-na* GÌR.2-*šú i-šak-kan*
20 *ša a-na ka-a-ru ša* KUR—*aš-šur*.KI *il-la-ni*
21 *i-du-ak* GIŠ.MÁ-*šú ú-pa-ṣi*
22 *ma-a* TA* ŠÀ-*bi* É.GAL *is-sa-par-u-ni*
23 [0] *ma-a ša*! *ṭa-ba-kan-ni e-pu-*⸢*uš-ma*⸣

e.24 [0] {m!}DINGIR!—*ma-a-di i-qab-bu-niš-š*[*u*]
25 1! URU.*ṣi-mir-a-a šu-ú*
26 *šu-ú a-na* KUR—*aš-šur*.KI *il-lak*
27 *il-la-ka mi-i-ni*
r.1 ⸢*šá*!⸣ *a-ba-tu-ni mi-i-ni ša ṭè-mu-ni*
2 *i-har-ra-ṣi il-la-ka i-qab-ba-šú*
3 *is—su-ru* LUGAL *be-lí i-qab-bi*
4 *ma-a a-ta-a la ta-aṣ-bat-si*
5 *i-na pa-ni-šú šu-ú pal-ha-ak ša la*! LUGAL
6 EN-*ia la a-ṣab-bat-si* LUGAL EN *lu ú-du*
7 *ma-du-ti ina* LÚ.*man-za-za—pa-ni ša* LUGAL EN-*ia*
8 *ša* KUG.UD *a-na* É *an-ni-i id-di-nu-u-nu*
9 *šu-nu* TA* LÚ.DAM.QAR.MEŠ
10 *i-na bat-ta-ta-a-a ú-pal-làh-u-ni*
11 *a-na-ku a-na* UGU LUGAL EN-*ia tak-ku-lak*
12 1 GÍN 1/2 GÍN *a-na me-me-e-ni la ad-dan*
13 *a-na* LUGAL EN-*ia ad-dan*
14 LUGAL *be-lí lu-ú ú-du*
15 *kal-bi me-e-ti a-na-*⸢*ku*!⸣
16 *i-na li-mu mu-ta-ni* LUGAL EN *ub-tal-*[*liṭ-a*]-*ni*
17 LUGAL DINGIR-*a-a ù* LUGAL ⸢*du*!-*ma*!-*qi*!⸣
18 [*še*]-*zib-an-ni ù lu la a-mu-*[*a*]*t*
19 [*sa-a-ri ina*] ŠÀ-*bi* É.GAL *ša* LUGAL EN-*ia lu ú-da*
20 [*x x* ŠÀ] ⸢É⸣.GAL *ša* LUGAL EN-*ia lu-za-in*
21 [DINGIR.MEŠ *ša*] AN-*e ù ša*? KI.TIM
22 [*a-na* LUGAL] EN-*ia lik-ru-bu*
23 [*x x x*] ⸢ŠÀ?-*bi ha ʾa*? *ti ù*?⸣
rest broken away

anyone who comes to him, but kills anyone who docks at the Assyrian harbour, and steals his boat. He claims: "They have written to me from the palace: 'Do only what is good for you!'".

24 There is a man called Ilu-ma'adi, from Ṣimirra. He goes back and forth to Assyria, finds out in detail whatever matter (and) news there is, and goes and tells it to him.

r.3 Perhaps the king, my lord, will say: "Why haven't you arrested him?" He is in his presence. I am afraid, I cannot seize him without the king, my lord's permission. The king, my lord, should know that there are many in the entourage of the king, my lord, who have invested silver in this house — they and the merchants are systematically scaring me. I (however) put my trust in the king, my lord. I don't give one shekel (or even) half a shekel to anybody but the king, my lord. The king, my lord, should know (this).

15 I am (but) a dead dog; the king, my lord, has revived me (from) a thousand pestilences. The king is my god and the king is my decor. [Res]cue me, do not let me die! May I know [the *brooms* in] the palace of the king! May I decorate [the interior of] the palace of the king, my lord! May [the gods of] heaven and earth bless [the king], my lord!

(Rest destroyed or too broken for translation)

128. The Merchants are Systematically Scaring Me

K 1016

1 *a-na* LUGAL KUR.KUR EN-*ia*
2 ⸢ARAD⸣-*ka* {m}KI—{d}UTU—*ba-la-ṭu*
3 *lu-ú* DI-*mu a-na* LUGAL EN-*iá*
4 {d}*aš-šur* {d}UTU {d}EN {d}PA {d}U.GUR
5 {d}15 *ša* ⸢NINA⸣.KI {d}15 *ša* URU.*arba-*⸢*ìl*⸣
6 UD-*mu* GÍ[D.D]A.MEŠ MU.AN.NA.MEŠ
7 *da-r*[*a*]-*a-ta ṭu-ub* ŠÀ-*bi*
8 *ṭu-ub* ⸢UZU⸣ *hu-du-ú* ŠÀ-*bi*
9 *a-na* ⸢LUGAL EN-*ia lid*⸣-*di-n*[*u*]
10 ⸢TA* *bé-et* {d}UTU *i-nap-pa-ha-an-nu*⸣
11 [*a-du*]-⸢*ú*⸣ *i-rab-bu-un-nu*
12 [*ina sa*]-*pal* [GÌR.2] *ša* LUGAL EN-*iá*
13 [*ú-šak-ni*]-*iš*

CT 53 16

1 To the king of the lands, my lord: your servant Itti-Šamaš-balaṭu. Good health to the king, my lord! May Aššur, Šamaš, Bel, Nabû, Nergal, Ištar of Nineveh (and) Ištar of Arbela give lo[n]g days, everlasting years, happiness, physical well-being (and) joy to the king, my lord.

9 From where the sun rises [to whe]re it sets, [he (= Šamaš) has brought] (all lands) [to submission be]fore [the feet] of the king, my lord.

akê.

14 [*x x x x*].*x* KUR *an-ni-ti*
rest broken away
Rev. beginning broken away
1′ [*ṭ*]*u*[*p*?]-*pu x*[*x x ma-du-ti*]
2′ *ina* ŠÀ-*bi* LÚ.*man-za-za—pa-ni ša* MAN EN-*iá*
3′ *ša* KUG.UD TA* LÚ.DAM.QAR.MEŠ
4′ *a-na* É *an-ni-e i-di-nu-u-nu*
5′ *ù sa-la-mu dan-nu a-na* U[GU?]
6′ *ru-*⸢*qi qa*⸣*-ru-*⸢*x x x x*⸣*-bu*
7′ *ina* ⸢*bat-ta*⸣*-ta-*⸢*a-a ú*⸣*-p*[*a-l*]*a-*⸢*hu*?⸣*-nu*
8′ ⸢*ṭa*⸣-[*ab-t*]*a-ni-ma an-na-ka*
9′ [*l*]*a-áš-šú a-na-ku a-na* UGU-*hi*
10′ LUGAL EN-*ia ta-ku-la-ak*
11′ 1 GÍN 1/2 GÍN *a-na mì-mì-i-ni*
12′ *la a-dan-nu a-na* LUGAL EN-*iá*
13′ *ad-dan-nu* LUGAL EN *ina* ŠU.2-*šú-nu*
14e *la-a ú-ra-ma-an-ni*
15e *kal-bi me-e-ti a-na-ku*
16e *sa-a-ri ina* ŠÀ-*bi* É.GAL
17e ⸢*ša* LUGAL⸣ EN-*iá lu-ka-*⸢*i*⸣
s.1 [*x* Š]À ⸢É⸣.[G]AL *ša* LUGAL EN-*iá*
2 [*lu-za-i*]*n* DINGIR.ME[Š] AN-*e u* KI.TIM
3 [0] *a-na* MAN E[N]-⸢*iá*⸣ *lik-ru-bu*

13 [...] this land
(Break)

r.1 [t]a[b]let [... There are many] in the entourage of the king, my lord, who have invested silver together with the merchants in this house and [*there is*] a strong alliance over the distance [...].

7 They are systematically scaring me. There is no fr[ien]d of mine here. I put my trust in the king, my lord. I do not give one shekel (or even) half a shekel to anybody but the king, my lord.

13 May the king, my lord, not leave me in their hands. I am (but) a dead dog. May I *wield* the brooms in the palace of the king, my lord! [May I decorate the inte]rior of the palace of the king, my lord! May the gods of heaven and earth bless the king, my lord!

129. Raids by Arabs

K 5580

beginning broken away
1′ ⸢EN-*iá ta*?⸣*-x*[*x x x x x x x x x*]
2′ LÚ.KÚR *ša* LUGAL EN-[*iá x x x x x x*]
3′ *šu-mu dam-qa a-na* L[UGAL EN-*iá i-šak-ku-nu*]

4′ DINGIR.MEŠ *ša* LUGAL EN-*iá x*[*x x x x x*]
5′ *ú-gam-mu-ru a-na* LU[GAL EN-*iá id-du-nu*]
6′ *ši-pir-ti* É LUGAL *be-lí* [*iš-pur-an-ni*]
7′ *pa-zu-u hi-ṭu ina* ŠÀ-*b*[*i x x x x x*]
8′ *gab-bi* DINGIR.MEŠ *ša* L[UGAL? *x x x x x*]
9′ *a-na* LUGAL EN-*iá it-*[*x x x x x x*]

10′ [m]*ú-mi-te-e a-na* [*x x x x x x*]
11′ *ni-sa-par ši-mu-nu š*[*a* DINGIR.MEŠ *ša* LUGAL]
12′ EN-*iá šu-mu dam-qa* ⸢*a*⸣-[*na x x x x x*]
13′ *iš-kun-u-nu a-na* ⸢*a*⸣-[*a-ši*? *x x x x x*]
14′ *ina* ŠÀ-*bi x*[*x x x x x x x x x*]
e.15′ *an-ni-*[*x x x x x x x x x x x*]

CT 53 289

(Beginning destroyed)

1 my lord [......]

2 [May they ...] the enemy of the king, [my] lord, (and) [establish] a good name to the k[ing, my lord].

4 The gods of the king, my lord, will finish off [... and deliver them] to the ki[ng, my lord]!

6 When king, my lord, [sent] a message [to me],

7 ... a crime in [......]

8 All the gods of *the k*[*ing* ......]

9 *de*[*livered* ...] to the king, my lord.

10 We have sent Umitê to [......].

11 The moment th[at *the gods* of the king], my lord, established a good name to [..., ...] to me

14 there [......]

15 thi[s ......]

128 r.5-9 Cf. Elat JESHO 30 (1987) 238 n.17. r.17 *lu-ka-i*: taken as a scribal error or dialectal variant for *lu-ka-i-*(*il*), from *kullu* "to hold, employ, wield."

129 Although Ammi-ladin (r.13) and Ammi-leti (r.8) are attested in the reign of Assurbanipal, the idiolect and writing conventions of the letter strongly support attribution to Itti-Šamaš-balaṭu, and thus possibly dating to the late reign of Esarhaddon. Alternatively Itti-Šamaš-balaṭu could have served Assurbanipal after Esarhaddon's death, but probably then in a somewhat more southern location than in Esarhaddon's reign (cf. Introduction, p. XXIVf). 10 Umitê (= /Uwitê/) possibly stands for Iauta', king of the Arabs/Qedarites (cf. PNA 2/I p. 497f s.v. Iauta', and note especially the name form Uaite' = /Uwaite'/ discussed ibid. under c), since otherwise Umitê would be a *hapax legomenon* personal name. This suggestion is in keeping with Itti-Šamaš-balaṭu's spelling conventions, which (like

16′ *as-pur-⸢an⸣-[ni x x x x x x x x x]*
17′ *⸢mi⸣-i-ni [x x x x x x x x x x]*
18′ *[x] nap-šá-te [x x x x x x x x x x]*
r.1 *i-pa-qid ina* UGU *x[x x x x x x x x x]*
2 *as-sap-ra* LUGAL *b[e-lí x x x x x x x]*
3 *gab-bi ú-di di-du-[x x x x x x x x]*
4 *a-na-ku* LUGAL *be-lí ki-i š[a? i-la-ʾu-nu]*

5 *le-pu-šú ina* UGU *ar-b[a-a-a ša a-na]*
6 LUGAL EN-*ia ni-is-pur-an-ni [x x x x x]*
7 TA* *pa-ni mi-ih-iṣ ša m[i?-x x x x x]*

8 ^{m}*am—li-ta na-pi-šá-a-a [*^{m}*x x x x]*
9 *maš-ʾa-a-a is-su-hu-ru-nu [x x x x x]*
10 *ina pa-ni-ni* 1-*me* 30 LÚ.*[x x x x x]*
11 TA* ^{m}*am-ra-aʾ* LUGAL *ša [x x x x x]*
12 *mi-ih-zi-a-ni d[i?-x x x x x x]*
13 *ša* ^{m}*am-mu-u—la-[din x x x x x]*
rest broken away
s.1 DINGIR.MEŠ *ša* LUGAL EN-*iá [lik-x x x x x x]*

16 I wrote [......]
17 what [......]
18 [...] life [......]
r.1 appoints [......]
2 I have sent [......]. The king, [my] l[ord]
3 knows everything [...].
4 I am [......]. May the king, my lord, do as [he deems best].
5 As to the Ar[abs about whom] we wrote to the king, my lord, [...], because of the raid that [......], Ammi-leti of Napisu [and PN] the Mas'ean have returned [...].
10 Before us, 130 [...]-men [...] *from* Amrâ, the king of [...].
12 *raids* [......]
13 *of* Ammu-la[din ......]
14 May the gods of the king, my lord, [......]!

130. Fragment Referring to an Insurgent

Sm 169

beginning broken away
1′ *[x x x x x x x x x x]-nu*
2′ *[x x x x x x x x x]-bi?-ia* [0]
3′ *[x x x x x x x* ^{m}*]a-du-ni—[ba-al]*
4′ *[x x x x x x x x x]x pa-ni-[šú]*
5′ *[x x x x x x x x x] iš-ku-n[u]*
6′ *[x x x x x x* EN—*si]-i-hi šú-⸢ú⸣*
7′ *[x x x x x x* ^{m}*ru]-ki-ib-t[ú]*
8′ *[x x x x x x x š]a* KUR—*aš-šur*.[KI]
9′ *[x x x x x x x x] ket-tú* [0]
rest broken away
Rev. as far as preserved, uninscribed

CT 53 813

(Beginning destroyed)
3 [......] Aduni-[*Ba'al*]
4 [...... his] face
5 [......] set
6 [......] he is an [insur]gent
7 [... *Šarru-lu-dari son of* Ru]kibtu
8 [...... o]f Assyria
9 [......] *truly*
(Rest destroyed)

his name and idiolect) contain Neo-Babylonian features and suggest that he originated in Babylonia. 11 *ši-mu-nu* is taken to be an 'unorthographic' (Babylonian) spelling for *simunu* "time," see Parpola, Festschrift Röllig (1997), 318 n. 10. r.7, 12 *mi-ih-iṣ* (or *mi-ih-iz*) and *mi-ih-zi-a-ni* probably for *mihṣu* "attack," even though the sign ZI was not used in NA for writing *ṣi*. Other non-Assyrian features of the letter include *pazû*, *aspur*, *nispur*, *damqa*, *mīni*, *iškunūnu*; also *šipirtu* and *gabbi ūdi*. r.8 Ammi-leti: this attestation is to be added to PNA 1/I p. 105 Ammi-leti (2). r.11 Or: "with." r.13 For Ammu-ladin, see PNA 1/I pp. 104f.

130 To judge from its phraseology and subject matter, this fragment may actually be part of an extispicy query. 3 Possibly referring to Aduni-Baʾal, son of Yakinlû, king of Arwad (cf. no. 127), see PNA 1/I p. 54. 7 On Rukibtu, king of Ashkelon appointed by Tiglath-Pileser III, see PNA 3/1 p.1053f. His son Šarru-lu-dari, appointed king of Ashkelon by Sennacherib, is referred to in the fragmentary query SAA 4 83.

131. Sending Caravans to the King

K 1083

1 [*a*]-*na* LUGAL EN-*ia*
2 [ARAD]-*ka* ^{m}10—KALAG-*an*
3 [*lu* DI]-*mu a-na* LUGAL EN-*ia*
4 [*aš-šur* ^{d}UTU] *a-na* LUGAL EN-*ia lik-ru-bu*
5 [*x x x x*] ⸢*x*⸣ ŠÀ-*bi x*[*x x*]
rest broken away

Rev. beginning broken away
1′ [*x*] ⸢*x*⸣ [*x x x*]*x* ⸢^{d}AMAR$^{?}$⸣.UTU *a-x*[*x x*]

2′ [*ú*]-*ma-a an-nu-rig* 2 KASKAL.MEŠ-⸢*tú*⸣ *ma-ki*-[*u-te*!]
3′ [*x*] KASKAL.MEŠ *a-šá-re-du-te a-na* LUGAL EN-*ia*
4′ [*ú*]-*se-bi-la ki-i ša ina* IGI LUGAL
5e [*ma-h*]*i*!-*ru-u-ni le-pu-šú*
6e [*x x*]-*tú ú-ma-a šúm-ma ma-hi-ir*
7e *ina* IGI MAN EN-*ia*
Side broken away

ABL 981

1 [T]o the king, my lord: your [servant] Adad-dan. [Good hea]lth to the king, my lord! May [Aššur (and) Šamaš] bless the king, my lord.

5 [... *hap*]*piness* [...]

(Break)

r.1 [......] *Marduk* [...]

---

2 [Ri]ght now [I] am sending 2 *infer*[*ior*] caravans and [x] *well equipped* caravans to the king, my lord. Let the king do as it [ple]ases him.

6 [...] Now, if it is acceptable to the king, my lord, [...]

(Rest destroyed)

132. The King's Gods are Ready for Battle

82-5-22,146

1 [*a-na* LUGAL EN-*ia* ARAD]-*ka* ^{m}10—KALAG-*an*
2 [*lu* DI-*mu a-n*]*a* LUGAL EN-*ia*
3 [^{d}*aš-šur*] ^{d}*šá-maš* ^{d}30 ^{d}NIN.GAL
4 *a-na* LUGAL EN-*ia lik-ru-bu* [DINGIR.MEŠ *ša* A]N-*e*
5 *ka-li-šú-nu* MURUB$_4$ *ra-a*[*k-su-t*]*e*.MEŠ
6 *ina pa-na-at* LUGAL EN-*ia* [*lil-li-k*]*u*
7 LÚ.KÚR.MEŠ-*te ša* LUGAL EN-*ia* [*ár-h*]*iš*?
8 *ina* KI.TA GÌR.2.MEŠ *ša* LUGAL E[N]-*i*[*a lu-š*]*a*[*k*!-*ni-šú*!]
9 *ṣu-um-mu-rat ša* LUGAL EN-[*ia lu-šak-š*]*i-d*[*u*]
10 *kal-bu qa-ni kal-ba*-⸢*a*⸣-[*ni a-na*]-*ku*!
11 LUGAL *be-lí na-ma-a-ru* [*x x x x x*]
rest broken away

Rev. beginning broken away
1′ [*x x x x x x x x*]*x-u-ni x*[*x x*]
2′ [*x x x x x x x x*]*x ina pi*-⸢*i*⸣$^{?}$ [*x*]
3′ [*x x x x x x x x x*] MÍ.KUR *ta*
4′ [*x x x x x x x la*]-*a ap-ṭu-ra*
rest uninscribed

ABL 1228

1 [To the king, my lord]: your [servant] Adad-dan. [Good health t]o the king, my lord! May [Aššur], Šamaš, Sîn and Nikkal bless the king, my lord.

5 All the [gods of hea]ven are ready (for battle). [May they march] in the presence of the king, my lord, and [bring] the enemies of the king, my lord, [quick]ly to submission before the feet of the king, m[y] lo[rd! May they let] the wishes of the king, [my] lord, [be fulfilled].

10 I am (only) a dog among (other) dogs. The king, my lord, [...] brightness [...]

(Break)

r.2 [......] *in the mouth*

3 [......] ...

4 [...] I di[d not] release [...].

131 r.2f → von Soden, Or. 26 (1957) 137f; cf. SAA 15 30:17ff: *la a-ša-ri-du-um-ma ... la ma-ki-iu-ú*.
132 4f See coll. 5 On *qablē rakāsu* see LAS II 171:23 and cf. SAA 9 1 ii 26′; 5:4. Lit., "All the gods of heaven have girded their loins." 8 Cf. no. 127:12. 9 Cf. SAA 10 123:7ff. r.2 Or: "by the command."

133. Fragment Referring to Damascus

81-2-4,388

beginning broken away

1′ [*x x x x x š*]*a* DUMU—LUGAL
2′ [*x x x x*] ⌜*ša*⌝ LÚ.*sar-ten-ni*
3′ [*x x x x* L]Ú.GAL.MEŠ
4′ [*x x x x*.ME]Š *aš-šur-a-a*
5′ [*x x x x*] *a-na* URU.*di-maš-qi*
6′ [*x x x x x*]*x-ti ša* URU.*di-maš-qi*
7′ [*x x x x x*]*x id-da-nu-u-ni*
8′ [*x x x x x*]*x* KÁ.GAL.MEŠ
9′ [*x x x x x x x-ma*]*h-har*
10′ [*x x x x x x x x*]*x-u-ni*
11′ [*x x x x x x x x x x*]*x*
rest broken away
Rev. entirely broken away

ABL 1421

(Beginning destroyed)

---

1 [...... o]f the crown prince
2 [...... o]f the chief judge
3 [...... the m]agnates
4 [......] Assyrian [...]s
5 [......] to Damascus
6 [...... the ...]s of Damascus
7 [...... which] they give
8 [......] the (city) gates
9 [...... will re]ceive
(Rest destroyed)

134. Fragment Referring to Damascus

83-1-18,272

1 *a-na* LUGAL EN-*ia* ARAD-*ka* [^{m}*x x x x*]
2 *lu-u šul-mu a-na* LUGAL EN-[*ia*]
3 ^{d}PA *u* ^{d}AMAR.UTU *a-na* LUG[AL] ⌜EN⌝-[*ia*]
4 *a—dan-niš a—dan-niš lik-ru-bu*
5 *ina* UGU LÚ*.GAL—URU.MEŠ *ša* É—⌜*un*⌝-*qi-a-a*
6 *ša ina* URU.*di-maš-qa ša ina* IGI LUGAL E[N-*ia*]
7 ⌜*aq*⌝-*bu-u-ni* ⌜*ma-a*⌝ *ša q*[*ur-x x*]
rest broken away
Rev. beginning broken away
1′ [*x x x*]-⌜*a-a* LÚ*⌝.[*x x x x x*]
2′ [*x*] ⌜*x x*⌝ GAL *ša ni-z*[*a-x x x*]
3′ ⌜*x*⌝ [*x*] ⌜*a*? *ina*⌝ [ŠÀ]-*bi-šú-nu na-ṣa*
4′ [L]UGAL ⌜*be-lí*⌝ *ki-i*
5′ [*š*]*a* ⌜*i-la-u-ni*⌝ *le-pu-uš*
rest uninscribed

CT 53 936

1 To the king, my lord: your servant [PN]. Good health to the king, [my] lord! May Nabû and Marduk very greatly bless the kin[g, my] lord.

5 Concerning the village manager of the *Bit-Unqian* in Damascus about whom I spoke in the presence of the king, [my] lo[rd], he says: "*(One) who is pre*[*sent*]

(Break)

r.1 [...]â, the [...] (official)
2 [...] which we [...]
3 [...] of them is bringing [...]

4 [The k]ing, my lord, should do as he deems best.

134 5 Besides this occurrence, *bēt unqi* is only attested in SAA 13 127:13, where it clearly means "sealed building." Here, however, a gentilic derived from the toponym Unqi (see Hawkins, RlA 4 160ff) seems to be in question.

135. Fragment of a Military Report

81-2-4,492

1 *a-na* [LUGAL *be-lí-ia*]
2 ARAD-*k*[*a* ^{m}*x x x x x*]
3 LÚ*.A.BA [*x x x x x*]
4 *ša ina* ŠÀ [*x x x x x*]
5 DI-*mu a-*[*na* LUGAL *be-lí-ia*]
6 ^{d}AG [*u* ^{d}AMAR.UTU]
7 *a-na* LUGAL [*be-lí-ia lik-ru-bu*]
8 ^{m}*ar-ba-a-a* [*x x x x x*]
9 ^{m}*qi-il-ti-*[*i x x x x*]
10 ^{m}PAB—*šá-an-ši* [*x x x x*]
11 ^{m}SU—^{d}15$^{!}$ [*x x x x x*]
12 4 *ah-ma-x*[*x x x x x*]
13 *ki-i ár-hiš* [*x x x x*]
14 *ša* LUGAL *b*[*e-lí x x x*]
15 [*l*]*a*$^{?}$*-a il-l*[*i*$^{?}$*-x x x*]
rest broken away
Rev. beginning broken away
1′ [*x x x x*]*x x*[*x x x x*]
2′ [^{m}*x x x* L]Ú.*kit*$^{?}$-[*x x x x*]
3′ ^{m}⸢*ṣil*⸣—LUGAL ⸢LÚ*⸣.[*x x x*]
4′ *pi-i-šú* : *i*[*s-si-šú-nu*$^{?}$]
5′ *i-sa-kan* : *x*[*x x x x*]
6′ *ša* LUGAL : [*x x x x*]
7′ *ú-hal-l*[*u-qu x x x*]
8′ 2 LÚ*.*qur-b*[*u-te x x x*]
9′ TA* IGI-*šú l*[*u x x x*]
10′ *ina* ŠÀ LÚ*.KÚR [*x x x x*]
11′ LÚ*.ARAD.MEŠ [*ša* LUGAL]
12′ *pa-ni-šú-*[*nu x x x x*]
13e *i-s*[*a-ak-nu x x x x*]
14e *a-*⸢*x*⸣ [x x x x x]
15e *a-*[*x x x x x x x*]
s.1 [*x x x x x š*]*á* KUR.*ár-pad-da*
2 [*x x x* TA* L]Ú.KÚR *i-sa-as-nu-ma*
3 [LU]GAL *be-lí lu-u ú-di*

ABL 1422

1 To [the king, my lord]: yo[ur] servant [PN], the scribe [of ...], who [...] in [...]. Good health t[o the king, my lord]! [May] Nabû [and Marduk bless] the king, [my lord].

8 Arbayu [the ...], Qiltî [the ...], Ahu-šamši [the ...], Eriba-Issar [the ...]

12 *4* ...[...]

13 quickly [...]

14 what/of the king, [my] l[ord ...]

15 *did* [*n*]*ot* co[me ...]

(Break)

r.2 [PN], *cra*[*ftsman*] —

3 Ṣil-šarri the [...] has made common cause w[ith them]; they (plan to) destroy the [...] of the king, [*my lord*].

8 Two bodygu[ards ...]

9 because of him [...]

10 among the enemy [...]

11 The servants [of the king]

12 are ready to [......]

(Break)

s.1 [... o]f Arpad

2 [...] also serve [with the] enemy.

3 [The ki]ng, my lord, should know (it).

135 11 W 364. 12 The sign 4 could also be read *šá*, "who." 13 *kî arhiš* "quickly" is also attested in SAA 5 213:10. 15 Or: [*m*]*a-a il-l*[*a-ku-ni* "saying, '[they] will co[me].'" See coll. s.2 *i-sa-as-nu-ma* is G pf. pl. 3 m. of *lasāmu* "to run, serve" (< **iltasmūma*).

9. Letters Pertaining to Elam, Urarṭu, Media and Babylonia

FIG. 23. *Elamite deserters (reign of Assurbanipal).*
ANE 124801.

136. Deserters from the Governor of Der

K 518

1 *a-na* LUGAL *be-lí-ia*
2 ARAD.MEŠ-*ka* ^{md}PA—ÁG—UN.MEŠ$^{!}$-*šú*
3 *ù* ^{m}*sa-la-ma-nu*
4 *lu-u* DI-*mu a-na* LUGAL *be-lí-ni*
5 ^{d}PA *u* ^{d}AMAR.UTU *a-na* LUGAL *be-lí-ni*
6 *lik-ru-bu ina* UGU LÚ*.*ma-aq-tu-te*
7 *ša* LÚ*.EN.NAM *ša* URU.*de-ri*
8 *ú-še-bi-la-an-ni*
9 *ša* LUGAL *be-lí iš-pur-an-ni*
10 *ma-a šá-al ni-is-sa-al*
11 ^{m}*bur-si-la-a* LÚ*.3-*šú ša* DUMU—MAN
12 ^{m}*ku-dúr-ru* ARAD *ša* ^{m}*man-na-i-pi-te*
13 LÚ*.3-*šú ša* DUMU—MAN
14 PAB 2 LÚ*.NIM.MA-*a-a*
15 ^{m}*ra-me*—DINGIR
e.16 [URU].*arrap-ha-a-a*
r.1 LÚ*.A—SIG *ša* LÚ*.EN.NAM
2 ^{m}*ad-di-iq-ri-tú-šú*
3 ARAD.MEŠ *ša* ^{m}*ia-i-ru*
4 LÚ*.*gam-bu-la-a-a*
5 15 LÚ*.*ma-aq-tu-te*
6 *ša* LÚ*.EN.NAM *ša* URU.*de-ri*
7 *ú-še-bi-la-an-ni*
rest uninscribed

ABL 140

1 To the king, my lord: your servants Nabû-ra'im-nišešu and Salamanu. Good health to the king, our lord! May Nabû and Marduk bless the king, our lord.

6 As to the deserters whom the governor of Der sent to me (and) about whom the king, my lord, wrote to me: "Interrogate them!" — we have interrogated them.

11 Bur-Silâ, 'third man' of the crown prince; Kudurru, servant of Mannaipite, likewise a 'third man' of the crown prince. Total two Elamites. Rama-il, a man from Arrapha, chariot fighter of the governor, Addiqritušu, (and) servants of Iairu, the Gambulean:

r.5 Fifteen deserters whom the governor of Der sent to me.

137. The Kings have Made Peace with One Another

83-1-18,68

1 [*a-na* LUGAL EN-*ni*]
2 [ARAD.MEŠ-*ka* ^{md}PA—ÁG—UN.MEŠ-*šú*]
3 [^{m}*sa-la-ma-nu*] *lu-u* [DI-*mu*]
4 [*a-na* LUGAL E]N-*ni* ^{d}PA $^{⌈d⌉}$[AMAR.UTU]
5 [*a-na* LUGAL EN-*ni*] *lik-ru-bu*
6 *ina* [UGU DUMU—*šip-r*]*i ša* TA* EN.L[ÍL.KI]
7 *ša* LUGAL *iš-pu-ra-na-ši-an-ni*
8 *ma-a šá-ʾa-al-šú ni-is-sa-al-šú*
9 *ma-a* DUMU$^{!}$—*šip-ri ša* ^{m}*pa-ʾe-e*
10 LÚ*.*qe-e-pi ša* KUR.*a-ra-še*$^{!}$
11 *a-na* EN.LÍL.KI *it-tal-ka*
12 *ma-a* LUGAL.MEŠ *is-sa-he-iš is-sal-mu*

ABL 1115

1 [To the king, our lord: your servants Nabû-ra'im-nišešu (and) Salamanu]. Good [health to the king], our [lo]rd! May Nabû (and) [Marduk] bless [the king, our lord]!

6 Con[cerning the messeng]er from Nip[pur], about whom the king wrote to us: "Ask him!" — We asked him (and he replied): "The messenger of Pa'e, the legate of the land Araši, has come to Nippur (saying): 'The kings have made peace with one another, so

136 2 Y 76, W 62. r.2 For this person and the setting of this letter see the recent discussion by R. Rollinger and M. Korenjak, "Addikritušu: Ein namentlich genannter Grieche aus der Zeit Asarhaddons (680-669 v.Chr.). Überlegungen zu ABL 140," AoF 28 (2001) 325-337.
137 9f, 15 See coll.

13 *ma-a at-tu-nu a-ta-a*
14 *hu-ub-tú tah-bu-ta*
15 *ma-a* ⸢LÚ*!⸣.*mu*-⸢*šar*!-*kis*!-*a*!-*ni*! *iq*!⸣-*ṭí*!-*bu*!-*niš-šú*
16 *ma-a* [*x x x x x x x*]*x*.MEŠ-*ni*
17 [*x x x x x x x x x x*] *hur*
18 [*x x x x x x x x x x x*]*x*
e.19 [*x x x x x*] *ni* [*x x x*]
r.1 [*x x x x x x x x x*]
2 [*x x x x x x x*] *še x*[*x*]
3 [*x x x x x x x x*] *x*[*x*]
4 [*x x x x x x x x x x*]
5 [*x x x x x x x*] *be šú*
6 *la* [*x x x x x x x*]*x*
7 *ma-a* [*x x x x x x*]-*i*
8 *a-na* [*x x x x x x*]-*a*
9 *ma-a* [*x x x x x x*]-*u-ni*
10 *ina* URU.*x*[*x x x x x*] *e-tar-bu*
11 *ma-a x*[*x x x x x x*]-*ri*
12 *ša* [*x x x* LÚ*.ERIM].MEŠ—GIŠ.BAN
13 1 *x*[*x x x*] ANŠE.NITÁ.MEŠ
14 *x*[*x x x x*] *šúm-ma iš—ši-a-ri*
15 *š*[*úm-ma ina l*]*i-di-iš*
16 [*ina* URU.*arrap*]-*ha er-ra-bu-u-ni*
17 [*x x x x*] ⸢*x x*⸣ [*x x*] ⸢*x*⸣ [*x*]

why have you taken plunder/captives?' The recruitment officers told him: '[...]

(Break)

r.10 "They have entered the city [...]

11 "[......]

12 of [... ar]chers

13 1 [......] donkeys

14 They will enter [Arrap]ha either tomorrow, o[r the day] after tomorrow.

(Rest destroyed or too broken for translation)

138. Report on Araši and Elam

K 4690

1 [*a*]-*na* LUGAL [*be-lí-ia*]
2 ARAD.MEŠ-*ka* ^{m}[^{d}PA—ÁG—UN.MEŠ-*šú*]
3 ^{m}*sa-la-ma-n*[*u lu-u šul-mu*]
4 [*a-n*]*a* LUGAL *b*[*e-lí-ia*]
5 [^{d}P]A ^{d}AMAR.UTU *a-na* ⸢LUGAL⸣ [*be-lí-ia*]
6 [*lik-ru-bu is—su*]-*ri* LUGAL *be-lí i-qab*-[*bi*]
7 [*ma-a a-t*]*a-a ad-da-kan-ni* [*x x x*]
8 [*x x x x x*]-*ka-a-ni* ^{m}*pa-*ʾ*e*-⸢*e*⸣ [0]
9 [LÚ.*qe*]-⸢*e*⸣-*pu ša*! KUR.*a-ra-š*[*e x*]
10 [*iq-ṭi-b*]*a-na-a-ši ma-a x*[*x x x*]
11 [*x x x* KUR.NI]M.MA-*a-a x*[*x x x x x*]
12 [*x x x x x*]*x x*[*x x x x x x x x x*]
rest broken away
Rev. beginning broken away
1′ [*x x x x x*]*x*[*x x x x x*]
2′ [*x x x x*]*x x*[*x x x x x*]
3′ [*x x x x*] *an* [*x x x x x*]
4′ [*an-nu*]-⸢*rig*⸣ *a-n*[*a* LUGAL EN-*ia*]
5′ [*ni*]-*is-sap-r*[*a x x x*]
6′ [*a-d*]*u* LUGAL *be-lí* [*x x x x*]
7′ [*x x l*]*i it qi ab*? *x*[*x x x x*]
8′ [*x x*] DUMU ^{m}*um-ba-k*[*i-di-ni*]
9′ [*ina* IT]I *an-ni-e* [*x x*]
10′ [*x x x*]*x* URU.*de*-⸢*e*⸣-[*re x x*]
11′ [*x x x*]-*a ina* URU.[*x x x x*]
12′ [*x x x*] *a x*[*x x x x x*]

CT 53 70

1 T[o] the king, [my lord]: your servants [Nabû-ra'im-nišešu] (and) Salaman[u. Good health t]o the king [my lord]! [May Nabû and] Marduk [bless the king, my lord].

6 [Perh]aps the king, my lord, will sa[y]: "[W]hy [have you not ...] until now?"

8 Pa'e, [the deleg]ate of the land Araš[i, sai]d to us: "[...]

11 [... the Ela]mite(s) [...]

(Break)

r.4 [Now the]n [we] are writin[g] t[o the king, my lord].

6 [Un]til/[Whi]le the king, my lord, [...]

8 [...] the son of Umban-k[idinni]

9 [in] this [mont]h [...]

10 [...] the city of De[r ...]

11 [...] in the city [...]

(Last line destroyed)

139. Receiving Objects Sent by Umban-kidinni

Bu 91-5-9,105

1 *a-na* LUGAL EN-*ia*
2 ARAD-*ka* ^{md}PA—ÁG—UN.MEŠ-*šú*
3 *lu-u* DI-*mu a-na* LUGAL
4 [*be*]-*lí-ia* ^{d}PA ^{d}AMAR.UTU
5 [*a*]-*na* LUGAL *lik-ru-bu*
6 *a-nu-tú ša* ^{m}*um-ba-ki-di-ni*
7 *ša* ^{m}⸢*ri*$^{!}$⸣-*ši*—DINGIR
8 LÚ*.3.U_5
9 *ina* ŠÀ GIŠ.MÁ *ú-še-ri-du-u-ni*
10 *ina* ŠÀ URU.*su-da-ni-na*
11 *pi-it-ti* GIŠ.LI.U_5.UM
12 *e-taš-ru*
13 *it-tah-ru-šú*
14 *šul-mu a—dan-niš*
r.1 *me-me-e-ni*
2 *la ma-aṭ-ṭi*
rest uninscribed

ABL 425

1 To the king, my lord: your servant Nabû-ra'im-nišešu. Good health to the king, my [lo]rd! May Nabû (and) Marduk bless the king.

6 (As to) the objects of Umban-kidinni, which Riši-ilu the 'third man' brought down on a boat, they have checked them according to the writing-board and received them in the city of Sudanina. All is well. Nothing is missing.

140. Idri-aha'u has Brought the Shoes

Sm 268a

1 *a-na* LUGAL *be-lí-ia*
2 ARAD.MEŠ-*ka* ^{md}PA—ÁG—UN.MEŠ-*šú*
3 ^{m}*sa-la-ma-nu lu-u* DI-*mu*
4 *a-na* LUGAL *be-lí-ia*
5 ^{d}PA ^{d}AMAR.UTU *a-na* LUGAL *lik-ru-bu*
6 UD-16-KÁM *nu-bat-tu*
7 ^{m}*ad-ra—a-ha-ú it-tal-ka*
8 KUŠ.DA.E.SÍR *na-aṣ-ṣa*
9 UD-17-KÁM TA* [ŠÀ URU.*m*]*a*$^{!}$-*li-ki*
10 *nu-t*[*am-mì-iš ina* URU.*d*]*un-ni*—^{d}*šá-maš*
11 *š*[*a x x x x x x x x x x x*]*x*
12 [*x x x x x x x x x x x x*]
13 *bat* [*x x x x x x x x x x*]-*ni*
rest broken away
r.1 *ina* UGU KAS[KAL].⸢2$^{!}$⸣.MEŠ$^{!}$-*ni* [0]
2 *ša* LUGAL *be-lí iq-bu-u-ni*
3 *ma-a* TA* *an-na-ka*
4 TA* *an-na-kam-ma*
5 *ú-pa-su ma-a*ʾ*-da a-né-en-nu*
6 *ár-hiš ni-il-la-ka*
7 *i-*[*qa*]*b-ba-na-ši* ^{m}*um-ba-ki-di-ni*
8 [*ma*]-*a* KASKAL.2 ŠÀ-*bi ma-a-te*
9 *ni-il-lik la e-mu-qa-a-ni*
10 *ša la* LUGAL *ina* ŠÀ-*bi*

ABL 775

1 To the king, my lord: your servants Nabû-ra'im-nišešu (and) Salamanu. Good health to the king, my lord! May Nabû (and) Marduk bless the king.

6 Idri-aha'u came and brought the shoes in the evening of the 16th. On the 17th, we s[et out] from [M]alaku. [In D]unni-Šamaš [......]
(Break)

r.1 As to the cara[van]s of which the king, my lord, said: "They are ...ing much from here (and) there" — we will come quickly.

7 Umban-kidinni is [t]elling us: "We would like to go by the road inside the country (= Assyria)." We cannot bring him

139 Previous edition and translations: Fales and Lanfranchi Lettere (1992) 126f.; Oppenheim Letters (1967) 178, no. 126. 7 See coll.

140 9 See coll. 9f Coll. S. Parpola, 28.11.1966. r.1 See coll. r.3f Cf. *ša* TA* *na-ka* TA* *na-ka* "(captives) from here and there," SAA 5 166:4f; [TA* *an-na-ka*] TA* *an-na-kám-ma ú-*[*pa-har*]"I am [collecting] (tablets) from here and there," SAA 10 101:11 r.5 *ú-pa-su* is possibly a scribal error for *ú-pa-su-ku* "they are removing" (cf. SAA 5 229:11-19), hardly for *ú-pa-ṣu* (cf. *ú-pa-ṣi* "he robs/steals," no. 127:21).

11 *la nu-ub-bal-šú*
12 *mi-i-nu ša ši-ti-i-ni*
13 LUGAL *liš-pu-ra-na-ši*
14 DUMU—*šip-ri ina* ŠÀ URU.*de-e-re*
15 *ina pa-na-tu-un-ni*
16 *li-zi-zi*
17 UD-17-KÁM *ša ba-a-di*
18 ^{m}*ad-ra—a-ha-u*
s.1 *pa-an* LUGAL *be-lí-ia it-tal-ka*

there without the king('s permission).

[12] Let the king write us what to do, (and) let a messenger stay at our disposal in Der. Idri-aha'u left for the king, my lord, in the evening of the 17th.

141. Nobody has Gone Near His Equipment

K 1117

beginning broken away
1′ [*x*] ⌈*x x*⌉.MEŠ-⌈*šú a-nu-su*⌉
2′ *gab-bu i-si-šú*
3′ [in_6]—*ni-di a-nu-ti-šú*
4′ *me-me-e-ni la iq-ri-bi*
5′ *ú-ma-a šum-ma ina* IGI LUGAL
r.1 EN-*ia ma-hi-ir*
2 [*a-n*]*a* ^{m}*id-ri—a-ha-ú*
3 [*a-na* ^{m}]*qur-di*—^{d}15 *la-áš-al*
4 [*x x*] DUMU.MEŠ-*šú*
5 [*x x x*]*x an-na-ka*
6 [*x x x x*]*x šá ši* [[]]
7 [*x x x x x*]*x*[*x x*]
rest broken away

ABL 593

(Beginning destroyed)

[1] his [...] (and) his whole equipment (are) with him. Nobody has gone near his equipment.

[5] Now, if it is acceptable to the king, my lord, I will ask Idri-aha'u and Qurdi-Issar

[r.4] [...] his sons

[5] [...] here

(Rest destroyed)

FIG. 24. *Caravan on the move.*
ORIGINAL DRAWINGS I, 65.

142. Fragment Referring to Umban-kidinni

Bu 91-5-9,18

1 *a-na* LUGAL *be-lí-i*[*a*]
2 ARAD.MEŠ-*ka* ^{md}PA—ÁG—UN.MEŠ-*šú*
3 ^{m}*sa-la-ma-nu lu-u šul-mu*
4 *a-na* LUGAL *be-lí-ia*
5 ^{d}PA *ù* ^{d}AMAR.UTU
6 *a-na* LUGAL *lik-ru-bu*
7 ^{m}*um-ba-ki-di-ni*
8 [*x x x* URU.LUGAL—*i*]*q-bi*
9 [*x x x x x x x*]
Rev. beginning broken away
1′ *ú-ma-a an-nu-*[*rig*]
2′ *a-na* LUGAL *be-lí-ia*
3′ *ni-is-sap-ra*
4′ *mi-i-nu ša* LUGAL
5′ *i-qab-bu-u-ni*
rest uninscribed

ABL 777

1 To the king, m[y] lord: your servants Nabû-ra'im-nišešu (and) Salamanu. Good health to the king, my lord! May Nabû and Marduk bless the king.

7 Umban-kidinni

8 [.... the city Šarru]-iqbi

9 [......]

(Break)

r.1 Now then, we are sending (him) to the king, my lord. What are the king's orders?

143. Inscribing the Foundation Stone of the City Wall of Tarbiṣu

K 1247

1 [*a-na* LUGAL EN-*ia*]
2 [ARAD-*ka* ^{md}PA—ÁG]—UN.MEŠ-*šú*
3 [*lu-u* DI-*mu a-n*]*a* LUGAL EN-*ia*
4 [^{d}PA *ù*] ^{d}AMAR.UTU
5 [*a-na* LUG]AL *be-lí-ia lik-ru-bu*
6 NA$_4$.*pu-u-lu ša ina* ŠÀ *uš-še ša* BÀD
7 *ša* URU.*tar-bi-ṣi ni-ik-ru-ru-u-ni*
8 *šu-mu ša* LUGAL *be-lí-ia ina* UGU-*hi ni-iš-ṭur*
9 *ki-i ša ni-šaṭ-ṭa-ru-u-ni*
10 LUGAL *be-lí liš-pu-ra*
11 *i-na pi-it-te ni-iš-ṭur*
12 *ù ša* LUGAL *be-lí*
13 *i-na* ŠU.2 ^{m}*za-bi-ni iš-pur-an-ni*
14 *ma-a a-ta-a ti-ik-pi ša* NA$_4$.*pu-u-li*
15 1-*en id—da-at šá-ni-e*
16 *la il-lak*
17 *ma-a* ⌜*ša*⌝ *ra*!-*m*[*i*]-*ni-ka šu-u*
rest broken away
Rev. beginning broken away
1′ *m*[*a-a x x x x x x x*]
2′ *ma-*[*a x x x x x x x x*]
3′ *ma-a* [*x x x x x x x x*]
4′ *iš-kun-šú-nu ina* [ŠÀ UD-*me š*]*a*!
5′ DUMU—LUGAL *šu-*[*tu*]-*u-ni* ^{md}PA—MAN-*a-ni*
6′ *ina* É—*ku-tal-li ina pa-an* LUGAL
7′ *us-se-rib-šú-nu is-pi-lu-rat*
8′ *is-sak-nu-šu-nu*
9′ *ú-ma-a* ^{m}DI-*mu*—KUR *it-ta-lak*
10′ Á.2-*šú ina* UGU É *is-sa-kan*

ABL 628

1 [To the king, my lord: your servant Nabû-ra'im]-nišešu. [Good health t]o the king, my lord! May [Nabû and] Marduk bless [the ki]ng, my lord.

6 We shall write the name of the king, my lord, on the foundation stone which we laid in the foundations of the city wall of Tarbiṣu. Let the king, my lord, write me what we should write (on it) and we shall write accordingly.

12 And as to what the king, my lord, wrote to me via Zabinu: "Why do the limestone layers not go one after another? It is your own [......]"

(Break)

r.1 "[...... *Why*] has he put [*crosses*] on them?" —

4 At [the time when] he (= the king) was the crown prince, Nabû-šarrani brought them to the king into the Rear Palace, and the crosses were put on them (at that time).

9 Now Šulmu-mati has gone and started working on the palace. I am writing to the

143 r.4-8 This passage indicates that the letter dates from the early part of Assurbanipal's reign. Rev.9-10 probably refers to finishing work on the crown prince's palace in Tarbiṣu (cf. no. 34), which may have been only

11′ *a-na ša-ah-su-si šu-u*
12′ *a-na* LUGAL *be-lí-ia*
13′ *as-sap-ra*
14′ [LU]GAL *be-lí ki-i ša i-la-ú-ni*
15′ [*le*]-*pu-uš*

king, my lord, only as a reminder. [The k]ing, my lord, [may a]ct as he deems best.

144. Appeal for Royal Intervention

Rm 50

1 *a-na* LUGAL EN-*ia*
2 ARAD-*ka* ^{md}PA—ÁG—UN.MEŠ-*šú*
3 *lu-u šul-mu a-na* LUGAL EN-*ia*
4 ^{d}AG *u* ^{d}AMAR.UTU
5 *a-na* LUGAL EN-*ia lik-ru-bu*
6 ^{m}*šar-ú-ár-ri* [*x x x*]
7 URU.*lu-li-i*[*a*$^{?}$-*a-a*]
8 ARAD *ša* LUGAL [EN-*ia*]
9 *a-bat* LUGAL EN-*ia* [*iz-za-kar*]
10 *mi*$^{?}$-*i*$^{?}$-[*nu x x x x x*]
rest broken away
Rev. beginning broken away
1′ ⌈*x x*⌉ *x*[*x x x x x x x x*]
rest uninscribed

ABL 776

1 To the king, my lord: your servant Nabû-ra'im-nišešu. Good health to the king, my lord! May Nabû and Marduk bless the king, my lord.

6 Šar-uarri, a [... from] the town Luli[...], a servant of the king, [my lord, *has appealed for*] *the intervention* of the king, my lord.

(Rest destroyed or too broken for translation)

145. Fragment Referring to Locusts

K 13059

1 *a-na* LU[GAL EN-*ia*]
2 ARAD.MEŠ-*k*[*a* ^{md}PA—ÁG—UN.MEŠ-*šú*]
3 ^{m}*sa-la-m*[*a-nu lu-u šul-mu*]
4 *a-na* LUGAL [EN-*ia*]
5 ^{d}PA ^{d}AMA[R.UTU *a-na* LUGAL EN-*ia lik-ru-bu*]
6 4 UD.MEŠ-*te x*[*x x x*]
7 *ina* UGU *er-b*[*i-e x x*]
8 *x*[*x x x x x x x x*]
9 [*x x x x x x x x*]
Rev. beginning broken away
1′ *hi* [*x x x x x x x*]
2′ *x*[*x x x x x x x*]
3′ GIŠ.PA [*x x x x x x*]
4′ *ša tap* [*x x x x x x*]
5′ *ša tap* [*x x x x x x*]
6′ ŠE.*ta*[*b-ku*$^{?}$ *x x x x x x*]
7e UD-1[+*x*-KÁM *x x x x x x*]
8e *di-ni* [*x x x x x x*]
9e *ša* [*x x x x x x x*]
s.1 [*x x x x*] *e-te-tiq*
2 [*x x a-na* LUGAL] EN-*ia ni-is-sap-ra*

ABL 1351

1 To the ki[ng, my lord]: yo[ur] servants [Nabû-ra'im-nišešu] (and) Salam[anu. Good health] to the king, [my lord! May] Nabû (and) Ma[rduk bless the king, my lord].

6 4 days [...]
7 *Against* the locu[sts ...]
(Break)
r.3 staff/sceptre [......]
(Break)

6 *st*[*ored*] *grain* [...]
7 the 1[xth] day [...]
8 give [...]
(Break)
s.1 [...] has passed [...]
2 [*That is why*] we have written [to the king], my lord.

partially ready when Assurbanipal was appointed crown prince in 672. r.7f Cf. SAA 10 30 r.1.
144 7, 10, r.1 See coll.

146. Fragment Referring to Aid to Humbariš

K 7500

beginning broken away
1′ [*x x x* ^{m}*hu*]-*um-ba-ab-bi* ⸢LÚ*⸣.[SAG?]
2′ [*x x x x*] *uq-ṭar-ri-ib ma-a* [*x x*]
3′ [*x x x x*]-*bi ma-a ina* ŠU.2 ^{m}*hum-ba-r*[*i-iš*]
4′ [*x x x x*] *lu-ša-an-šil lid-di-na*
5′ [*x x bat-ti-b*]*at-ti-ia a-na* LUGAL KUR.[NIM.MA.KI]
6′ [*x x x x*]-*ba-bu e-ta-rab* [0]
7′ [*x x x x*] *iq-ṭi-bi ma-a a-ta-*⸢*a*⸣
8′ [*x x x x*]-*ti gab-bu i-rad-di*
9′ [*x x x x*] ⸢*a*⸣-*na* LÚ*.SAG *an-ni-i* [0]
10′ [*x x ina pa-n*]*i-šú lu la il-lak*
11′ [*x x x x-t*]*i-šú a-na* LUGAL *lid-din*
12′ [*x x x x*]*x ú-sa-an-šil a-na*
13′ [*x x x š*]*a* ^{m}*hum-ba-*⸢*ri-iš*⸣
14′ [*x x x x*] *x*[*x x x x x*]
rest broken away
Rev. beginning broken away
1′ [*x x x x x* KUR.NIM.MA.K]I-*a-a*
2′ [*x x x x x x x x*]-*u-ni*
rest broken away

CT 53 376

(Beginning destroyed)

1 [... Hu]mbappi th[e *eunuch*]

2 [...] presented [...], saying: "[...]

3 [...] "let *him* give me just as much [...] from the hands of Humbari[š]."

5 [... aro]und me (*belong*) to the king of [Elam].

6 [...] has entered [...]babu and said [to ...]: "Why does [...] lead all the [...]s?"

9 [...] to this eunuch [...]

10 He should not go [befo]re him

11 but give his [...]s to the king.

12 [...] equally much to

13 [... o]f Humbariš

(Break)

r.1 [...... the *Elamite*]*s*

(Rest destroyed)

147. Fragment Referring to Humbariš

K 15306

beginning broken away
1′ [*x x*] ⸢*ina* URU⸣.HAL.⸢ṢU⸣.M[EŠ *x x x*]
2′ [^{m}*hu*]*m-ba-re-e-še x*[*x x x*]
3′ [*a-n*]*a kit-ri ša* ^{m}*hu*[*m-ba-riš*]
4′ [(*x*) *x*]*x šúm-ma a-na kit-r*[*i x x*]
5′ [*x-l*]*i-im-ma ša* ^{m}*h*[*um?-ba-riš*]
6′ [*x* K]UR.NIM.MA.K[I *x x x x*]
rest broken away
Rev. completely broken away

CT 53 638

(Beginning destroyed)

1 [...] in the forts [...]

2 [Is Hu]mbariš [...]?

3 [... t]o the aid of Hum[bariš]

4 If [...] to the aid

5 [...] *of* H[umbariš]

6 [...] Elam [......]

(Rest destroyed)

148. Deserters from Mannea Sent to the Crown Prince

Bu 89-4-26,163

1 *a-na* LUGAL EN-*ia* ARAD-*ka*
2 ^{m}*aš-šur*—GI *lu-u* DI-*mu a-na* MAN EN-*iá*
3 *aš-šur* ^{d}UTU ^{d}EN ^{d}PA ^{d}U.GUR ^{d}*la-aṣ*
4 ^{d}*i-šum* ^{d}IM *ù* ^{d}*be-er*
5 DINGIR.MEŠ GAL.MEŠ *ša* AN-*e* KI.TIM
6 *a-du* 1-*lim-šú a-na* LUGAL EN-*ia*

ABL 434

1 To the king, my lord: your servant Aššur-ušallim. Good health to the king, my lord! May Aššur, Šamaš, Bel, Nabû, Nergal, Laṣ, Išum, Adad and Ber, (and) the great gods of heaven and earth bless the king, my lord, the

147 2 The lengthening of the vowel in Humbareše indicates a question.
148 Previous translation: Oppenheim Letters (1967) 171f, no. 119. Coll. SP 30.11.66. → no. 18. 2 In PNA 1/I p. 228, the name of the sender was rendered Aššur-ukin; however, the reading of the sign GI (without the complement NA) in NA names was not *ukīn* but *ušallim*, see e.g. PNA 1/II s.v. Bel-ušallim 3. 9 Or: "guards." 15 See coll. r.1

7 *a-na* DUMU—MAN KUR—*aš-šur*.KI *a-na* DUMU—MAN TIN.TIR.KI
8 *a—dan-niš a—dan-niš lik-ru-bu*
9 *ina* UGU EN.NUN.MEŠ *ša ina* UGU URU.HAL.ṢU
10 *ša* KUR.URI KUR.*man-na-a-a mad-a-a*
11 KUR.*hu-bu-us-ki pa-qa-da-a-ni*
12 *ša* LUGAL *be-lí iš-pur-an-ni*
13 *ma-a ṭè-e-mu šu-kun-šú-nu*
14 *ma-a bir-ti* IGI.2.MEŠ-*šú-nu ma-di-*[*id*]
15 *ma-a* : *a-na ma-ṣar-ti-ku*!*-nu*
16 *la ta-ši-ṭa ù ma-a uz-nu*
17 *a-na* LÚ.*ma-aq-tu-u-te*
18 *ša bat-bat-te-šu-nu lu šak-na-šu-nu*
19 *ma-a is—su-ur-ri*
e.20 LÚ.*ma-*[*aq*]*-tu*
21 TA KUR.*m*[*an-na-a-a mad-a*]*-a*
22 TA KUR.*hu-bu-*[*us-ki*]*-a*
r.1 *ina* UGU-*hi-šu-nu i*!!*-m*[*a-q*]*u-*[*t*]*a*!
2 *ma-a ár-hiš ina* ŠU.2 LÚ*.A—KIN-*ka*
3 *ta-šak-kan-šú a-na* DUMU—MAN
4 *tu-še-ba-la-áš-šu*
5 *ù ma-a šúm-ma i-ba-áš-ši*
6 *da-ba-bu ina pi-i-šu ma-a*
7 ⸢*a*!*-na*!⸣ A—LUGAL *ina ṭu-u-bi ta-qab-bi*
8 *ṭè-e-me* TA* *pa-ni-ka*
9 ⸢*da-mì*⸣*-iq ma-a* LÚ.A.BA 1!*-en*!
10 [*x x x*]*x a* ⸢*a ki*? *kit*? *nu x*⸣ *li*
11 [*x x x*]-⸢*ba*⸣*-ni*! *i-na-ṣa-*⸢*ru*!⸣*-u-ni*
12 TA* *pi-i-šu liš-ṭur*
13 *ina* ŠÀ NA_4.*is-pi-lu-ur-te*
14 *li-ik-nu-ku* ᵐPAB—BÀD—SIG
15 LÚ.GAL—*ki-ṣir ša* A—MAN
16 *ina* ŠÀ LÚ.*kal-li-i*
17 *ár-hiš a-na* UGU-*hi-ia*
18 *lu-bi-la ú-ma-a an-nu-rig*
19 2 LÚ.*ma-aq-tu-u-te*
20e TA* KUR.*man-na-a-a i-tuq-tu-u-ni*
21e 1 LÚ.SAG 1 LÚ.*šá*—EME
s.1 *e*!*-na* DUMU—MAN *us-se-bil-šú-nu da-ba-bu ina pi-šú-nu*
2 *i-ba-áš-ši*

crown prince of Assyria and the crown prince of Babylon a thousand times very greatly.

[9] As to the garrisons appointed to the fortresses of Urarṭu, Mannea, Media (and) Hubuškia, about whom the king, my lord, wrote to me:

[13] "Give them orders and make it very clear to them that they must not be negligent in their guard duty. Moreover, let them pay attention to the deserters from their surroundings. Should a deserter from M[annea, Medi]a or Hubu[ški]a fall in their hands, you are to put him immediately in the hands of your messenger and send him to the crown prince. And if he has something to say, you will tell it to the crown prince accurately. Make your report good!

[r.9] "Let one [...] scribe ... [who] guards [...]s write it down from his dictation, let it be sealed with the cross-shaped (stamp) seal, and let Ahu-dur-enši, the cohort commander of the crown prince, quickly bring it to me by express delivery."

[18] Now then two deserters from the land of the Manneans have arrived: one eunuch and one *informer*. I have sent them to the crown prince. They have things to say.

i!!-: tablet AD (scribal error). See coll. [r.7] See coll. [r.9-17] See LAS II p. 331f. [r.11] See coll. [s.2] Y 80.

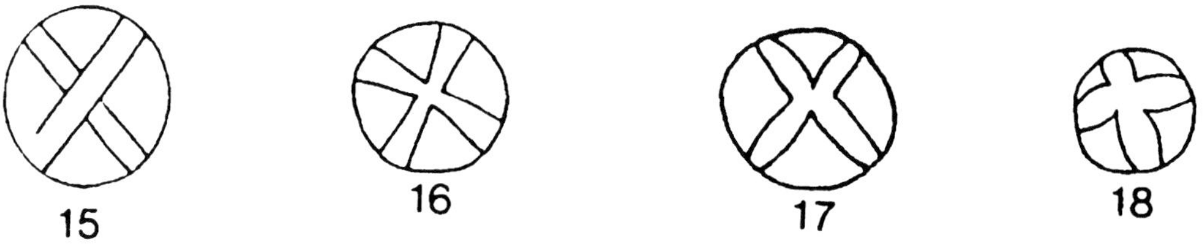

FIG. 25. *Impressions of the cross-formed stamp seal of the crown-prince.*
S. HERBORDT, *SAAS* 1, pl. 11.

149. Wounded in Bit-Hamban

K 1591

beginning broken away
1′ [*ina*]⸢É⸣.*ha*-⸢*b*⸣*a*[*n*]
2′ [*x x*] MU.AN.NA
3′ [*x x*] :. *it-ta-ha-su*
4′ [*ma*$^?$]-*ri-ṣi ir-ṭu-šu*
5′ [*it-t*]*a-bal* ^{md}PA—PAB—AŠ
6′ [LÚ.*qur-b*]*u-ti ša* DUMU—LUGAL
7′ [*ša ina* UGU]-*hi-šú-nu*
8′ [*x x x*] ⸢*e-ta*⸣-*mar-šú*
rest broken away
Rev. completely broken away

CT 53 190

(Beginning destroyed)

1 [in] Bit-Hamba[n]

2 [...] year [...] wounded him. He is [i]ll, but has *carried away* his ...

5 Nabû-ahu-iddina, [the bodyg]uard of the crown prince, [who is ... t]o them, has seen him.

(Rest destroyed)

150. Emissaries from Mazamua

82-5-22,159

beginning broken away
1′ [*x x x x*] *x*[*x x x*]
2′ [TA* LÚ.MA]H$^?$.MEŠ *šá* KUR.*ma*-⸢*za*⸣-[*mu-a*]
3′ [*ad-du*]-*bu-ub-ma*
4′ LUGAL *be-lí i-qab-bi*
5′ *ma-a ur-di is-si-ia-aṭ*
6′ *ma-a la ih-ru-up*
7′ *la iš-pu-ra*
8′ *ša a-de-e ú-di-na*
9′ TA* IGI LUGAL *be-lí-ia*
r.1 *la e-te-eq-q*[*u-u-ni*]
2 *la ug-da-ta-mu-*[*ru-u-ni*]
3 *ša e-gír-tu ina* I[GI *x x x*]
4 *a-du* ^{m}ARAD—^{d}15 *te-x*[*x x x*]
5 *e-mur-ú-*[*ni x x x*]
6 *it-tan-na-áš-*[*šu x x x*]
7 [*x x*]*x a-du* LUGAL EN [*x x x x*]
8 [^{m}*x x*]—SI.SÁ [*x x x x*]
9 [*x x x*]-*ub* ^{m}[*x x x x x*]
10 [*x x x*] *a*$^?$-*na*$^?$ [*x x x x*]
rest broken away

ABL 1235

(Beginning destroyed)

2 [*I* have] also [*sp*]*oken* [with the *emissa-ri*]*es* of Maz[amua].

3 (Perhaps) the king, my lord, will say: "My servant has been negligent; he did not send (a report) earlier."

8 Those who (came for) the treaty had not yet finished leaving the presence of the king, my lord, when the letter [...] before [...]. As soon as Urdu-Issar saw [...], he delivered it to hi[m].

r.7 [...] *while* the king, [my] lord [...]

8 [...]-lešir

(Rest destroyed or too broken for translation)

151. Fragment Referring to the King of Urarṭu

K 16056

beginning broken away
1′ [*x x x x x x* ^{d}PA] ⸢^{d}⸣AMAR.U[TU]
2′ [*x x x x x x a-na* LUGAL] EN-*ia*
3′ [*lik-ru-bu x x x x*]-*a-ri*
4′ [*x x x x x* LUGAL E]N-*ia*
5′ [*x x x x x x x*]*x-mu*

CT 53 731

(Beginning destroyed)

1 [May Nabû], Mard[uk],

2 [and DNN bless the king], my lord.

3 [May they ......]

4 [...... to the king], my [lo]rd,

149 4 *irṭu* is a *hapax legomenon.*
150 6f Or: "he didn't write me earlier."

6′ [*x x x x x x a-n*]*a*? NUMUN-*ka*
7′ [*x x x x x x x x x*]*x*
8′ [*x x x x x x x x x*]*x*
9′ [*x x x x x x x x x-n*]*i*
rest broken away
Rev. beginning broken away
1′ [*x x x x x x x x x*]*x*
2′ [*x x x x x x x* KUR.U]RI-*a-a*
3′ [*x x x x x x x b*]*é*?-*e-tú*
4′ [*x x x x x l*]*a i-*⸢*la*⸣*-pu-*[*t*]*ú*
5′ [*x x x x x a*]-*na* AD.MEŠ-*ka*
6′ [*x x x x x*]-*ia ina ti-ir-ṣi-ka*
7′ [*x x x x x x*] *ina* GÌR.2.MEŠ-*ka*
8′ [*x x x x x*] ⸢*i*⸣*-da-nu-ni-ka*
9′ [*x x x x x x*] *x*[*x x-ṭ*]*u*
rest broken away

5 [......]
6 [...... *t*]*o* your seed
(Break)

r.2 [...... the U]rarṭian
3 [......] ...
4 [...... do *n*]*ot* touch
5 [...... t]o your fathers
6 [...] in your time
7 [......] at your feet
8 [......] give to you
(Rest destroyed)

152. Fragment Referring to Babylonians

K 1198

1 *a-na* LUGAL *be-lí-iá*
2 [AR]AD-*ka* ^{m}*ṭu-di-i*
3 [*l*]*u* DI-*mu a-na* LUGAL *be-lí-iá*
4 [^{d}AG] ^{d}AMAR.UTU *a-na* LUGAL
5 [*be-lí-iá*] *lik-ru-bu*
6 [*ina* UGU-*hi* D]UMU.MEŠ KÁ.DINGIR.KI
7 [*ša* LUGAL *be-lí iš*]*-pur-an-ni*
rest broken away
Rev. beginning broken away
1′ [*x x x*] *iš-x*[*x x x*]
2′ [*x x ha-r*]*am-ma-ma a-ki*
3′ *ša* LUGAL *be-lí i-la-u-ni*
4′ *le-pu-uš*

ABL 986

1 To the king, my lord: your [ser]vant Ṭudî. [Go]od health to the king, my lord! May [Nabû] (and) Marduk bless the king, [my lord]!

6 [As to the] Babylonians [about whom the king, my lord, wr]ote to me: "[......]
(Break)

r.2 [... La]ter, the king, my lord, may do as he sees fit.

153. Letter from Borsippan Women

K 15124

1 [*a-na* LUGAL *be-lí-ni*]
2 [GEMÉ.M]EŠ-*ka* MÍ.*a-m*[*e-la-te*]
3 [MÍ.*bar-si*]*b-a-a-te lu* DI-[*mu*]
4 [*a—dan-niš a-n*]*a* LUGAL EN-*ni* [^{d}*x x*]
5 [^{d}EN] ⸢$^{d?}$⸣PA ^{d}U.G[UR *x x*]
6 [*x x x x*] ^{d}P[A.TÚG *x x x x*]
7 [*x x x x*] ⸢*x*⸣ [*x x x x x*]
rest broken away
Rev. completely broken away

CT 53 623

1 [To the king, our lord]: your [maid]s, the [Bors]ippan gen[tlewomen. The best of] hea[lth t]o the king, our lord! [May DN, Bel], Nabû, Nerg[al, ..., ...], N[usku, ...]
(Rest destroyed)

151 r.6 Taking *tirṣu* as a phonetic variant for *tarṣu*, cf., e.g., no. 96 r.8.
153 2 For the restoration cf. MÍ.LÚ-*te* URU.ŠÀ—URU-*te* "gentlewoman from Assur," StAT 2 313:4; the plural M]Í.*a-me-la-ti* is attested in K 1991 (unpub). [SP]

154. Assigning Houses to Sarrabaneans

K 1001

beginning broken away

1′ ⸢*x x x x*⸣ [*x x x x x x*]
2′ [*ik*]-*tar-b*[*u x x x x x*]
3′ *it-tal-ku-u-ni* UDU.SISKUR.[MEŠ]
4′ *e-tap-šú a-na* LUGAL EN-*iá i*[*k-tar*]-*bu*
5′ ^{d}EN *ù* ^{d}PA *ik-ri-ib-šú-nu*
6′ *a-na* LUGAL EN-*iá lu-ṭa-hi-u*
7′ LUGAL *be-lí ú-da ki-i*
8′ URU.*sa-rab-na-a-a ina* KÁ.DINGIR.RA.KI
9′ *ina* EN.LÍL.KI *ina* UNUG.KI
10′ *ù ina* ŠÀ-*bi* LÚ.*i-tú-ʾe*
11′ *ú-kal-lu-u-ni an-nu-rig*
12′ *e-ta-na-rab-u-ni* É.MEŠ
13′ *bat-ti-ba-ti ša* É—[*x x*]
14′ *uk-tal-lim-šú-nu*
e.15′ *ú-ṣa-lu-lu*
r.1 [*x x x*]-*u iq-ṭí-b*[*u-ni*]
2 [*x x x x*] *nu-uk*
3 [*x x x x*] UN.MEŠ *x*[*x x*]
4 [*x x x x*] *ù* LUGAL [*x x*]
5 [*x x x x i*]-*ba-áš-ši*
6 [*x x x x x*]*x ṭa-bu-te*
7 [*x x x x x*] *kam-mu-su*
8 [*x x x x x*] *uk-tal-lim-šú-nu*
9 [*x x x x x*]-*si a-na-ku*
10 [*x x x x x*] *a-na* URU.HAL.ṢU-*ú-te*
11 [*x x x x x*] LUGAL *i-ba-áš-ši*
12 [*x x x x x*] *ú-še-šib*
13 [*x x x x x*] LÚ*.*pu-qu-da-a-a*
14 [*x x x x x*] URU.*sa-rab-na-a-a*
15 [*x x x x x x x*] ⸢*x x*⸣
16 [*x x x x x x x x x*]

rest broken away

s.1 LUGAL *be-lí lu la i-šam-me a-du* [*x x x*]

ABL 572

(Beginning destroyed)

2 [have b]lessed [...].

3 The [...] have come, made sacrifice[s (and) bles]sed the king, my lord. May Bel and Nabû make their blessing reach the king, my lord.

7 The king, my lord, knows that the people of Sarrabanu hold (*houses*) in Babylon, Nippur and Uruk and in the Itu'u land. Recently, they have been entering my audience. I have showed them houses around Bit-[...] (and) they are roofing them.

r.1 [...] they tol[d me]:
2 "[...]." I said:
3 "[...] people [...]
4 [...] and the king [...]
5 there is [...]
6 good [...]s"
7 [...] are staying
8 I have showed them [...]
9 [......] I
10 [...] to the status of a fortress
11 there is [...] the king
12 [...] did [*not*] settle [...]
13 [...] the Puqudu
14 [...] the Sarrabaneans

(Rest destroyed)

s.1 May the king, my lord, not listen to [...] *until* [...].

155. Returning a Field to the Chaldeans

K 15175

beginning broken away

1′ [*ina* UGU A.ŠÀ? *ša* LUGAL *be-lí iš-p*]*ur-an*-⸢*ni*⸣
2′ [*ma-a x x x x x* LÚ].*kal-dà-a-a*
3′ [*x x x x x x t*]*a-áš-šú-u-ni*
4′ [*x x x x x x*]-*u-ni ma* A.ŠÀ
5′ [*x x x x x x*] *a-na* LÚ.*kal-dà-a-a*
6′ [*x x x x* ^{m}*k*]*u*?-*na-a-a aq-ṭí-bi*
7′ [*x x x x x x*]*x* TA* *pa-an*
8′ [*x x x x x*] ⸢*ú*⸣-*še-ṣa-an-ni*

CT 53 626

(Beginning destroyed)

1 [Concerning *the field* about which the king, my lord, wro]te to me: ["... of the] Chaldeans [... *which* y]ou took, [...; ...] the field [*and give it back*] to the Chaldeans" —

6 [...] I said [*to K*]*unaya*
7 [......] from
8 [......] *I* brought forth

154 This letter may also date from the reign of Sargon or Sennacherib.
155 8 Or: "he brought forth to me." r.4 Either a personal name or a word with interrogative intonation, e.g.

9′ [*x x x x x l*]*a im-ma-gúr-ru*
10′ [*x x x x x x x ap*$^{?}$-*t*]*a-làh*
rest broken away
Rev. beginning broken away
1′ [*x x x x x x*] ⌜*x*⌝ [*x x*]
2′ [*x x x x x* K]UG.UD *ia-ú*
3′ [*x x x x x aq-ṭí*]*-ba-áš-šú*
4′ [*x x x x x x-r*]*a-a-nu-u*
5′ [*x x x x x x x*] *it-ta-an-na*
6′ [*x x x x x x x*]*x ma-a a-lik*
7′ [*x x x x x x x*] A.ŠÀ KUG.UD
8′ [*x x x x x x i*]*š-ku-nu-u-ni*
9′ [*x x x x x x x*] 5 MA.NA TA* ŠÀ-*bi*
10′ [*x x x x x x x-t*]*a*$^{?}$*-lak ina* UGU-*hi-šú*
11′ [*x x x x x x x x x*]*x* ⌜DUMU—LUGAL⌝
rest broken away

9 [......] they refused to
10 [...... *I* became] scared
(Break)

r.2 [......] my [s]ilver
3 [...... *I* to]ld him
4 [......]...
5 [......] he gave
6 [......] saying: "Go
7 [......] field, silver
8 [...... p]laced
9 [......] 5 minas from it
10 [...... w]ent to him
11 [......] the crown prince
(Rest destroyed)

156. Fragment Referring to Akkad

Ki 1904-10-9,348 (BM 99316)

CT 53 972

beginning broken away
1′ [*x x x x x x*]*x x*[*x x x*]
2′ [*x x x x* KUR]—URI.KI *ma-*[*x x*]
3′ [*x x x x x-n*]*u*$^{?}$ *i-ba-áš-ši* [*x x*]
4′ [*x x x x x*] *al-la-*[*x x*]
5′ [*x x x x x*] *šud šuk-na* [*x x*]
6′ [*x x x x x x*]*x* [*x x x*]
rest broken away
Rev. completely broken away

(Beginning destroyed)

2 [...... the land of] Akkad [...]
3 [......] there is [...]
4 [......] ... [...]
5 [......] Place (pl.) [...]!
(Rest destroyed)

Miscellaneous Letters

10. Additions to SAA 10 and 13

FIG. 26. *Protective genie (apkallu) depicted as a scorpion-man.*
ORIGINAL DRAWINGS I, 17.

157. Fragment Referring to Scholars

K 14606

beginning broken away
1′ [*ša* LUGAL *be-lí*] *iš-*⸢*pur-an*⸣-[*ni*]
2′ [*x x x x x x*] UD-*mu* DÙG.GA
3′ [*x x x x x x*]*x qa-ni*
4′ [*x x x x* LÚ.*u*]*m-ma-ni gab-bu*
5′ [*x x x x x*]*-da-ni*
6′ [*x x x x x*] *ga-ri-na-te*
7′ [*x x x x x*]*x i-na-mir-a-ni*
8′ [*x x x x x*]*-mu*
9′ [*x x x x x*]*-ru*
10′ [*x x x x x x*]*x*
11′ [*x x x x x x*]*-ha*
12′ [*x x x x x x*]*-rab*
e.13′ [*x x x x x x*]
r.1 [*x x x x x x x*]*x*
2 [*x x x x x x*]-⸢*ri*?⸣-*šú*
3 [*x x x x x x*]*-e*
4 [*x x x x x x*]*-tú*
5 [*x x x x* LUGAL] *be-lí*
6 [*x x x x x ṭ*]*è-e-mu*
7 [*liš-kun ki-ma x x*] ⸢*e*⸣*-ta-at-qu*
8 [*x x x x lil-l*]*i-ku*
rest uninscribed

CT 53 541

(Beginning destroyed)
1 [As to what the king, my lord], wrote to m[e]:
2 [......] an auspicious day
3 [......] *outside*
4 [......] all the [s]cholars
5 [......]
6 [......] ...
7 [......] *at daybreak*
(Break)

r.5 [... The king], my lord, [should give o]rders [to ...]:
7 [After] the [...] have *passed*, they [should g]o [*to* ...]

158. Auspicious Days

DT 61

beginning broken away
1′ [*x*] *ina* IGI [*x x x x x x*]
2′ *a—mar* T[A? *x x x x x*]
3′ *an-nu-ri*[*g x x x x x x*]
4′ *ú-se-bi-l*[*a x x x x x*]
5′ UD-13-KAM UD-1⸢5?⸣-[KAM UD-*x*-KAM]
6′ UD-21-KAM UD-2[+*x*-KAM *x x x*]
7′ *an-na-te ši-na* [*x x x x*]
8′ [*x x x*] ⸢LUGAL⸣ [*x x x x x*]
rest broken away
Rev. completely broken away

CT 53 862

(Beginning destroyed)
1 [*which*] before [......]
2 all that [.......]
3 Now the[n ....]
4 I am sendin[g ....]
5 The 13th day, the 15th day, [the xth day],
6 the 21st day, the 2[xth day ...]:
7 these are the [days ....]
8 [...] the king [......]
(Rest destroyed)

157 6 Hardly "mothers."

159. Fragment Referring to Clothes

K 16504

beginning broken away
1′ [*x x x x x x x*]-*nu*
2′ [*x x x x x x*] *ni-iš-ši*
3′ [*x x x x x x*]*x ku-zip-pi-ma*
4′ [*x x x x x x*]*x* 3
e.5′ [*x x x x né-pu*]-*uš*
r.1 [*x x x x x x*]-*i*
2 [*x x x x x x-r*]*u-ni*
3 [*x x x x x x x*]*x-ti*
4 [*x x x x x x-a*]*k-ma*
5 [*x x x x x x x*]-*šá*
6 [*x x x x x x x*]*x*
rest broken away

CT 53 782

(Beginning destroyed)
2 [......] We will take
3 [......] garments
4 [......] three
5 [...... We will ma]ke
(Rest destroyed or too broken for translation)

160. Fragment Referring to a Ritual

K 16093

beginning broken away
1′ ⸢*lu*⸣ [DI-*mu a-na* LUGAL EN-*ia*]
2′ $^{d+}$EN ^{d}[PA *x x x x x x*]
3′ *a-na d*[*u-ur* UD-*me a-na* LUGAL EN-*ia*]
4′ *lu-ba*[*l-li-ṭu x x x x x*]
5′ *lu-pa*[*r-šim x x x x x x*]
6′ *lu-b*[*i*?-*x x x x x x x*]
7′ *e*[*l-x x x x x x x x*]
8′ *ni-*[*x x x x x x x x*]
rest broken away
Rev. beginning broken away
1′ ⸢*ina*⸣ [*x x x x x x x*]
2′ *ri* [*x x x x x x x*]
3′ *du*[*l-lu x x x x x x*]
4′ *né-*[*ta-pa-áš*? *x x x x*]
5′ *a-*[*x x x x x x x*]
6′ *a-na* ^{m}*b*[*i*?-*x x x x x x*]
7′ *ina* [*x x x x x x x*]
8′ *ir-t*[*a*?-*x x x x x x*]
9′ *a-na-k*[*u x x x x x x*]
10′ *me-me-ni* [*x x x x x x*]
11′ *me-m*[*e-ni x x x x x x*]
rest broken away

CT 53 751

(Beginning destroyed)
1 Good [health to the king, my lord]! May Bel, N[abû and ...] keep [the king, my lord], al[ive] forever. May he live lon[ger than ...]. May [......] *p*[*ure* ......]
8 We [......]
(Break)
r.1 in [......]
2 [......]
3 a ri[tual ......]
4 we p[erformed ......]
5 t[o ....]
6 for P[N ......]
7 in [......]
8 he [......]
9 I [......]
10 *somebody* [......]
11 *some*[*body* ......]
(Rest destroyed)

160 r.10 Or: "some/anything."

161. Ritual on the River

K 16096

beginning broken away
1′ [*x x x x*]*x* ⌜*x*⌝ [*x x x*]
2′ [*x x x*] *qab-si mar-*[*x x*]
3′ [*ina* Š]À-*bi* ÍD *ta-x*[*x x*]
4′ [*t*]*a-ri-ṣ*[*i* 0]
5′ [*l*]*il-li-ka* [0]
6′ [*ina* Í]D *lu-še-ṣ*[*i*]
rest broken away
Rev. completely broken away

CT 53 752

(Beginning destroyed)
2 [... in] the middle of [...]
3 *You* [... in the] river.
4 (If) it is all right,
5 he should come and [... to] the river
(Rest destroyed)

162. Ritual on the River Bank

K 13098

1 [*a-na* LUGAL EN-*ia*]
2 [ARAD-*ka* ^{m}*x x x x*]
3 [*lu* DI-*mu a-na* LUGAL EN-*ia*]
4 ^{d}[PA *u* ^{d}AMAR.UTU]
5 *a-na* L[UGAL EN-*ia lik-ru-bu*]
6 *ina* UGU-*hi š*[*a* LUGAL *be-lí*]
7 *iš-pur-an-*[*ni x x*]
8 *a-ta-mar x*[*x x x*]
9 *a—dan-niš ša* [*x x*]
10 *ṭè-e-mu a*[*s-sa-kan*]
11 *mu-uk lu* [*x x*]
12 *ina* ÍD *ur-r*[*ad x x*]
13 [*ina*] *ši-*[*a-r*]*i x*[*x x*]
14 [*x x x x x x*]
Rev. beginning broken away
1′ *an* [*x x x x*]
2′ *ša* U[GU *x x x*]
3′ *ú-šá-aṣ-*[*bat*]
4′ *a-na ši-a-*[*ri*]
5′ *ina nu-bat-t*[*i*]
6′ *ep-pa-áš*
rest uninscribed

ABL 1039

1 [To the king, my lord: your servant PN. Good health to the king, my lord! May] N[abû and Marduk bless] the k[ing, my lord].

6 Concerning wh[at the king, my lord], wrote to me, I have examined [...; ... is] very [...] that [...].

10 I have g[iven] orders that [...] be [...ed].
12 He will go dow[n] to the river [...].
13 [To]mo[rro]w [...]
(Break)

r.2 I will prepa[re the ritual] on [...].

4 He will perform it tomorrow evening.

163. Ritual on the River Bank

K 1094

beginning broken away
1′ [*x x*]*x x*[*x x x*]
2′ *šum-ma* LUGAL [*i-qab-bi*]
3′ *ina* UGU ÍD-*m*[*a*]
4′ *né-e-pu-u*[*š*]

ABL 583

(Beginning destroyed)
2 If the king [so orders], we will perfor[m] it t[oo] on the river bank.

162 13 See coll.

5′ *lu-bi-lu ina* UGU ÍD.*za-a*[*b-b*]*i ši-i*
6′ *li-ik-ru-ru*
7′ LUGAL *be-lí*
e.8′ *lip-ru-us*
r.1 *liš-pu-ra*
2 *ù* LÚ *man-nu*
3 *ša ub-bal-u-ni*
4 *i-kar-ra-ru-ru-ni*
5 *ṭè-e-mu liš-kun*
6 *ú-ma-a ṭup-pu* [*x*]
7 [*x*] *ʾa ši* [*x x*]
rest broken away

5 Let it be brought and thrown on the river Zab.

7 May the king, my lord, decide and write, and give orders to whoever man is to bring and throw it.

r.6 Now the tablet [...]
(Rest destroyed)

164. Explaining Asakku

83-1-18,825

1 [*a-na* LUGAL *be-lí-ia*]
2 A[RAD-*ka* ^{m}*x x x x*]
3 *lu* D[I-*mu a-na* LUGAL EN-*ia*]
4 ^{d}⸢PA⸣ [^{d}AMAR.UTU *a-na* LUGAL]
5 E[N-*ia lik-ru-bu*]
6 *ina* U[GU *x x ša* LUGAL *be-lí*]
7 *iš-*[*pur-an-ni*]
8 *ma-a* [*x x x x-a*]*b*$^{?}$*-bu*
9 *liš-ṭ*[*ur-u-ni*$^{?}$ *x x*]*x*
10 Á.S[ÌG *x x x x*]
11 Á GIŠ.⸢PA⸣ [*x x x*]
12 *a-sak-ku* [*x x x*]
rest uninscribed
Rev. uninscribed

CT 53 952

1 [To the king, my lord: your] se[rvant PN]. Good hea[lth to the king, my lord! May] Nabû [and Marduk bless the king, my] lo[rd].

6 Conce[rning the ... about *which* the king, my lord], wr[ote to me], saying, "May [*they*] wr[ite] ... [*for me*] —

10 Asakku [...]
11 power + sceptre [...]
12 Asakku [...]

165. A Lotion for the King

K 19986

Obv. broken away
e.1 *x x x*] ⸢*x x x*⸣ [*x x x*
r.1 *x x*] *u ni-iš-h*[*u*$^{?}$ *x x*
2 *x x*.M]EŠ *u* 15 LUGAL [*x x x*
3 *x x*]*-ni i—su-ur-r*[*i x x x*
4 *x x* LU]GAL EN-*ia x*[*x x x*
5 *x x mar*]*-hu-ṣu* LUG[AL *x x x*
6 *x x x*]*x la e-pa-á*[*š x x*
7 *x x* LUG]AL *be-lí* [*x x x*
rest broken away

K 19986

(Beginning destroyed)
r.1 [...] and *diarrh*[*oea* ...]
2 [the ...]s and the right hand of the king [...]
3 [...] Perhap[s ...]
4 [... *of*] the king, my lord [...]
5 [... lo]tion [...]
6 [...] will not do [...]
7 [...the kin]g, my lord [...]
(Rest destroyed)

163 3 See coll. r.4 Y 81.
164 10 Á.SÌG ("smiting power") was the logographic spelling for the demon/disease Asakku. 11 Reading the sign SIG as PA, the scholar "re-analyses" Á.SÌG as Á GIŠ.PA "side/power" + "staff/sceptre." 12 Asakku written syllabically.
165 Bottom fragment, sides are not extant. Previously unpublished; copy p. 218. The medical content and the distinctive spelling of the word *issurri* "perhaps" establish the writer of this letter as Urdu-Nanaya; cf. LAS II, Appendix M6.

166. Fragment of a Medical Report

K 15649

beginning broken away
1′ [*x* UD]-2-KÁM UD-*mu* [*x x x x x*]
2′ [*x x-g*]*a*?*-ni it-*[*x x x x*]
3′ [*š*]*u*[*l*]*-mu a—dan-niš* ⸢É⸣ [LUGAL *be-lí*]
4′ [*iš-p*]*ur-an-ni-ni* [*at-ta-lak*]
5′ [*x x x*] *a* [*x x x x x x*]
rest broken away
Rev. as far as preserved, uninscribed

CT 53 704

(Beginning destroyed)
1 [... *on*] the second day, the day [......]
2 [......]
3 He is very well [......]
4 [*I have gone where the king, my lord, se*]*nt me to.*
(Rest destroyed)

167. Fragment of a Medical Report

Sm 1851

beginning broken away
1′ [*a—dan-niš a-na*] ^{md}3[0—*x x x x*]
2′ [DI]*-mu* [*a—dan-niš*]
3′ [*a—dan-niš a*]*-na* ^{md}30—[*x x x*]
4′ [*x x mu*]*r-ṣi* [*x x x x*]
5′ [*x x-i*]*m-ma* [*x x x x*]
6′ [*x x x*] DI-*mu* [*a—dan-niš*]
7′ [*a—dan-niš a-na*] ⸢^{md}⸣[*x x x x*]
rest broken away
Rev. completely broken away

CT 53 855

(Beginning destroyed)
1 S[în-... is doing very, very well]. Sîn-[... is doing very, very we]ll.
4 [... sic]kness [...]
5 [......]
6 [... PN is doing very, very] well.
(Rest destroyed)

168. Advising the King

83-1-18,820

beginning broken away
1′ *ina gu-*⸢*mu*⸣*-ur-*⸢*ti*⸣ [ŠÀ-*bi a-na*]
2′ [LU]GAL EN-*ia* [*a-pal-làh*]
3′ [*ú*]*-ma-a a—ki-m*[*a x x x*]
4′ [*me-e*]*-te* LÚ.*pi-q*[*i-tu x x*]
5′ [*re*]*-e-šú ina pa-a*[*n x x x*]
6′ [*x*]*-šu-bu lib-b*[*u x x x*]
7′ [*ul*]*-lu-e-šú i-*[*x x x x*]
8′ [LUG]AL *dan-nu at-t*[*a x x x*]
9′ *ša i-šal-li-*[*mu-u-ni*]
10′ ŠÀ-*bu a-na* L[UGAL EN-*ia*]
11′ *ú-šá-áš-ka-*[*nu-ni x x*]
12′ [*x x x*] ⸢*x*⸣ [*x x x x*]
rest broken away
Rev. completely broken away

CT 53 950

(Beginning destroyed)
1 [I] whole[heartedly]
2 [fear the ki]ng, my lord.
3 [N]ow, as [...]
4 [is de]ad, a *war*[*d* ...]
5 [...] befo[re ...]
6 [...] *hear*[*t* ... to]
7 [*re*]*move him* [...]
8 Yo[u] are a strong [kin]g. [A *plan*]
9 which *will succe*[*ed and*]
10 encourag[e] the k[ing, my lord, ...]
(Rest destroyed)

167 1, 3 One, or even both of these royal patients, may be identified with the prince Sîn-perʾu-ukin, cf. SAA 10 222:7, 223:15. Fragment attributable to Adad-šumu-uṣur? *-im-ma* line 5 is often attested in his writings. 1-7 Cf. SAA 10 296:5-8 (Nabû-naṣir).
168 6 Possibly restore [*uš*]*-šu-bu* "they sit" or [*še*]*-šu-bu* "to seat, enthrone." 9 Or: "who will."

169. The King is like Adapa

Bu 91-5-9,78

1 [*a-na* LUG]AL EN-*ia* ARAD-*ka* [^{m}*x x x x*]
2 [*lu-u* DI]-*mu a-na* LUGAL EN-[*ia*]
3 [^{d}*x* ^{d}*x*] *a-na* LUGAL EN-*ia li*[*k-ru-bu*]
4 [*ša* LUGAL *be-l*]*í ina* UGU ARAD-*šú* ⸢*iš*⸣-[*pur-u-ni*]
5 [*x x x x d*]*i zi* [*x x x x*]
rest broken away
Rev. beginning broken away
1′ [*x x x x x*]*x-ta-te* [*x x x*]
2′ [*x x x x*]*x-me-ni* 2 GIŠ.ZU.[MEŠ]
3′ [*x x x x x-d*]*i*$^{?}$ LÚ*.KAŠ.LUL [*x x*]
4′ [*x x x x*] *aš-šur ni* [*x*]
5′ [*x x x* A]RAD-⸢*šú*⸣ *iš-pur-u-ni* [*x x x*]
6′ [*x x x*]-*ba-ti ša* UD *x*[*x x x*]
7e [*x x ma*]*n-nu ina* É—EN.M[EŠ-*šú x x*]
8e [*ki-i la ke*$^{?}$*-n*]*a-ku-ni la-a* [*x x x x*]
9e [LUGAL *b*]*e-lí a-ki a-da-p*[*i ga-mir*]
10e [*a-na-ku-ma*] ARAD *ša* TA* EN-*šú k*[*e-nu-u-ni*]

CT 53 963

1 [To the kin]g, my lord: your servant [PN. Good hea]lth to the king, [my] lord! May [*Nabû and Marduk* bless] the king, my lord.

4 [As to what the king], my [lord], w[rote] to his servant: "[...]"

(Break)

r.2 [...] ... 2 writing-board[s]

3 [... PN], cupbearer [...]

4 [...] Aššur [...]

5 [whom the king] sent [to] his [se]rvant [...]

6 [...] ... of *the day* [...]

7 [W]ho [would ...] in [his] lord's household

8 [that] I am [not loy]al (and) not [...]?

9 [The king], my [l]ord, [is as perfect] as Adap[a].

10 [As for me, I am] a servant who is l[oyal] to his lord.

170. ———

81-7-27,276

beginning broken away
1′ [*x x x x x*]*x* LÚ*.[*x x x*]
2′ [*x x x x m*]*u ša x*[*x x x*]
3′ [*x x x x x*]*x e-pa-*[*x x*]
4′ [*x x x ú-šam*$^{?}$]-*ra-aṣ-šú-nu*
5′ [*x x x x x*] *la i-zi-iz*
6′ [*x x x x*] ⸢*ú*⸣-*še-lu-ú-*[*ni*]
7′ [*x x x x* LÚ*].GAL—*da-ni-bat*
8′ [*x x x x x*] TA* *pa-ni-*⸢*i*⸣[*a*]
rest broken away
Rev. beginning broken away
1′ [*x x x x x x*]*x d*[*u-x*]
2′ [*x x x x* DI$^{?}$-*m*]*u a-*[*x x*]
3′ [*x x x x x* D]UMU.MÍ [*x x*]
rest broken away

CT 53 910

(Beginning destroyed)

3 [......] *do*[*es*]

4 [... is *hur*]*ting* them

5 [......] has not stood

6 [... whom ...] *promoted*

7 [...... the] chief victualler

8 [......] from m[e]

(Break)

3 [...... the d]aughter [......]

(Rest destroyed)

169 r.9 Cf. LAS II, discussion of letter 229.

171. Fragment Referring to Extispicies and a Treaty

K 5517

beginning broken away
1′ [*x x x x x x x*] LUGAL E[N-*iá x x x*]
2′ [*x x x x aq-ṭi-b*]*a-šú nu-uk* [*x x x*]
3′ [*x x x x x n*]*u-uk ba-a-si* [*x x x*]
4′ [*x x x x x*]*x-ṣi* TA* *a-he-iš ni-*[*x x x*]
5′ [*x x x a*]*-na* ^{md}PA—PAB.MEŠ—*šal-lim* ⸢LÚ*⸣.[*x x x*]
6′ [*x x x*]*-li ma-a* UDU.*pu-ha-du h*[*u*$^{?}$*-x x x*]
7′ [*x x x*] ARAD *ša* LUGAL *a-na-ku ma-a* [*šúm-ma ina pa-an*]
8′ [LUGAL *ma*]*-hi-ir* ^{md}PA—*tak-lak* LÚ*.HAL [*x x x*]
9′ [*x x* UD]U.*pu-ha-da-ni i-tak-s*[*u x x x*]
10′ [*x x x a-n*]*a-ku ar-tu-u*ʾ*-ba-šú* [*x x x*]
11′ [*ar-ta*]*-ka-as ù a-de-e i*[*s-se-e-šú x x*]
12′ [*x x x x x*]*x* ⸢*ni u*$^{?}$ *x*⸣ *du an* [*x x x*]
13′ [*x x x x x x x x x*] *x*[*x x x x*]
rest broken away
Rev. completely broken away

CT 53 266

(Beginning destroyed)

1 [......] the king, [my] lo[rd, ...]

2 [... I sai]d to him, "[...]

3 [...] I said, "*Soon* [...]

4 [...] we will [...] with each other."

5 [PN ... t]o Nabû-ahhe-šallim, th[e ...],

6 [...], saying: "[...] a lamb [...]

7 [...] "I am a servant of the king; [*if*]

8 [*it*] *is acceptable* [*to the king*, let] Nabu-taklak, the haruspex [...]."

9 [...] they sl[aughtered] lambs [......]

10 [...] I raged at h[im],

11 [bou]nd [...], and [made] a treaty w[ith him]

(Rest destroyed)

172. ———

K 16521

beginning broken away
1′ [*x x x x x x*]*x*
2′ [*x x x x x*]*x*
3′ [*x x x x-pu*]*r-an-ni*
rest broken away
Rev. beginning broken away
1′ [*x x x x x x*] ⸢*x x*⸣
2′ [*x x x x x*]*-ni* LÚ*.G[AL—*x x*]
3′ [*x x x x a-t*]*a-a*
4′ [*x x x x la*] ⸢*ú*⸣*-šah-kim* [0]
5′ [*x x x x x*]*x na-ṣu-u-ni*
rest uninscribed

K 16521

(Beginning destroyed)

3 [... wro]te to me

(Break)

2 [...] ... the ch[ief ...]

3 [wh]y did[n't] *he* explain [...]

5 [...] they have brought

171 This fragment can be certainly attributed to Mar-Issar on orthographical grounds (notice the spelling of the words *a-he-iš*, *ba-a-si*, *ma-hi-ir* and *nu-uk*, and the use of LÚ*, and see LAS II, Appendix M6). The tablet format also agrees with that of Mar-Issar.[SP]

172 Fragment from right-hand side. Previously unpublished; copy p. 217.

173. Enthroning [a Substitute King]

K 15626

beginning broken away
1′ [*x x x x*]*x me a* ⸢*šu-nu*⸣ *x*[*x x x x x x*]
2′ [*ma-a*] *me-me-ni la-a ú-še-šu-*[*bu x x x x*]
3′ [*an*]-*na-ka a—šá-šu-me* DINGIR.MEŠ *x*[*x x x x*]
4′ *a-sa-kan ma-a ša-ni-tú a-*[*bu-tú ma-a ki-i*]
5′ *ina pa-ni-ka at-ta-ni ma-*⸢*a*⸣ [*x x x x x*]
6′ [*x x x-r*]*uk-ka ma-a x*[*x x x x x*]
rest broken away
Rev. broken away

K 15626

(Beginning destroyed)
1 [...] they [......]
2 "[They] are not enthro[ning] anybody [......]
3 "[h]ere. The day before yesterday the gods [...]
4 "I placed. Another ma[tter: *When*]
5 "you were in *my* presence [......]
6 *your* [......]
(Rest destroyed)

174. ———

K 14580

1 *a-na* LUGAL *be-lí-ia*
2 ARAD-*k*[*a* ^{md}AG]—NUMUN$^{!}$—SUM-*na*
3 *lu-u* [DI-*mu a-na* L]UGAL
4 *b*[*e-lí-i*]⸢*a*⸣
5 [^{d}AG ^{d}AMAR.UT]U
6 [^{d}30 ^{d}NIN.GAL ^{d}]PA.TÚG
7 [*a-na* LUGAL *be-lí-i*]*a*
8 [*lik-ru-bu*]
rest broken away
Rev. completely broken away

CT 53 528

1 To the king, my lord: yo[ur] servant [Nabû]-zeru-iddina. Good [health to the k]ing, [m]y l[ord! May Nabû, Mardu]k, [Sîn, Nikkal and] Nusku bless the king, m]y [lord].
(Rest destroyed)

175. Fragment of a Horse Report

K 12949

1 [*a-na* LUGAL *be-lí*]-*ia*
2 [ARAD-*ka* ^{md}AG—MU]—SUM-*na*
3 [*lu* DI-*mu a-na* LUGAL EN-*ia*]
4 [*a—dan-niš a—dan*]-*niš* [0]
5 [^{d}PA ^{d}AMAR].UTU
6 [*a-na* LUGAL *be-lí*]-*ia*
7 [*lik-ru-bu x* K]UR.MEŠ
8 [*ša ni-i*]-*ri*
9 [*ša* LÚ.*tur*]-*tan-ni*
10 [*e-tar-bu-u-n*]*i*
11 [*x x x x x x*]*x*
12 [*x x x x x x*]
e.13 [*x x x x*]-*nu*

CT 53 437

1 [To the king], my [lord: your servant, Nabû-šumu]-iddina. [Very good health ind]eed [to the king, my lord]! [May Nabû and Mard]uk [bless the king], my [lord].

7 [x h]orses [trained to the yo]ke [have come i]n [from the comman]der-in-chief
(Break)

173 Previously unpublished; copy p. 217. [1] Readings after W. G. Lambert [4] *šanītu abutu*: cf. SAA 1 215:10 and SAA 10 74 r.4.
174 [5ff] For the restorations see SAA 10 343:5-8 (letter from Nabû-zeru-iddina's father, Urad-Ea); cf. also SAA

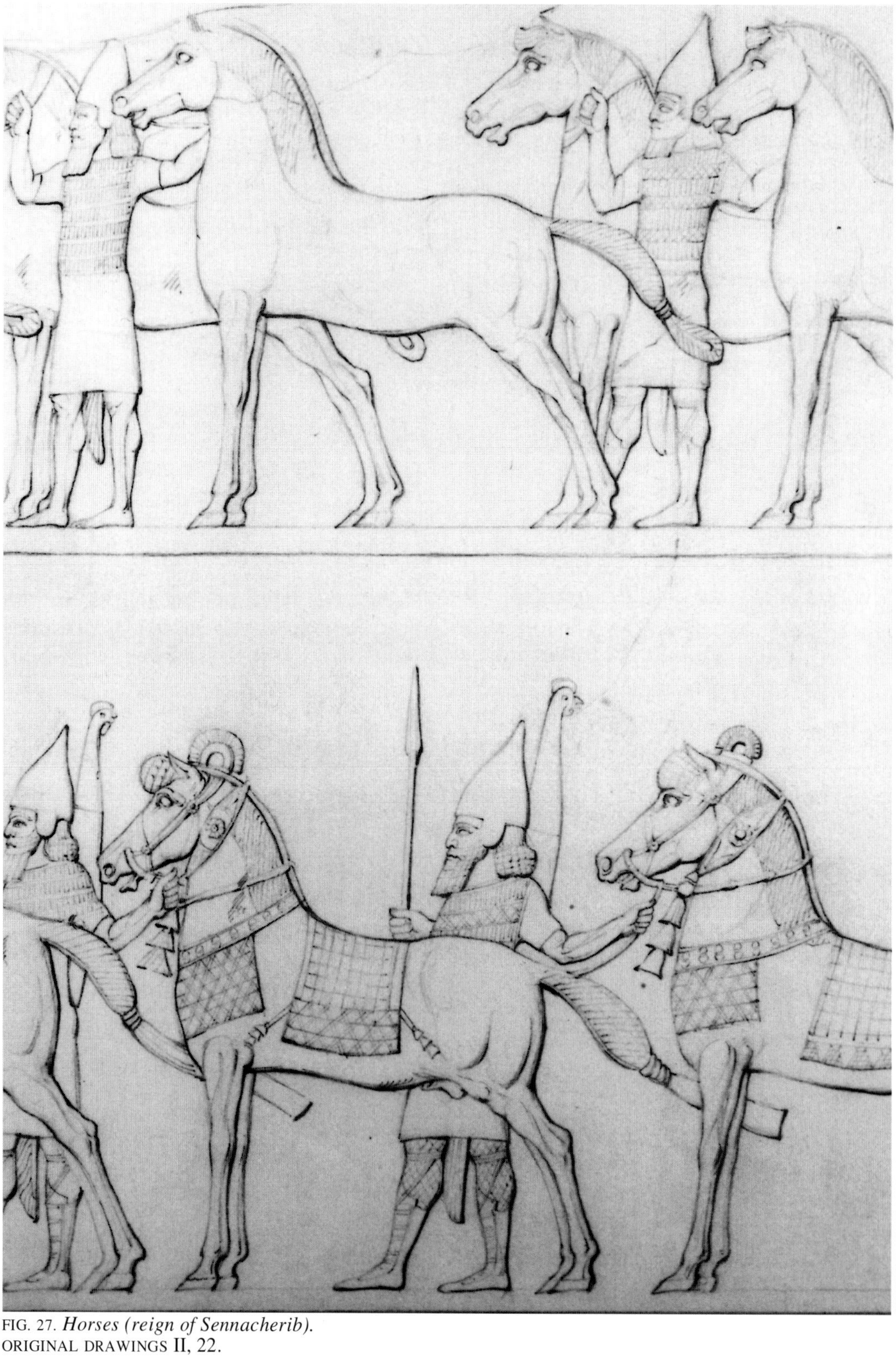

FIG. 27. *Horses (reign of Sennacherib).*
ORIGINAL DRAWINGS II, 22.

r.1 [*x x x x*]-⸢*i*⸣-*šú*
2 [*x x x x*]-*ri*
3 [*x x x x*]-*rab*
4 [*x x x*.M]EŠ
5 [*x x x x*]*x*
6 [*x x x x x*]
7 [*x x x x x*]
8 [*mi-nu ša* LUGAL] *be-lí*
9 [*i-šap-pa-r*]*a-an-ni*
rest uninscribed

r.8 [What are the written instru]ctions [of the king], my lord?

176. Fragment of a Horse Report

K 14625

beginning broken away
1′ ⸢*an-na-ka*⸣ *x*[*x x x x x*]
2′ *me-e-me-e-ni* [*x x x x*]
3′ *ša ni-i-ri x*[*x x x x x*]
4′ *ša*—BAD-HAL.ME[Š *x x x x*]
5′ LUGAL *be-lí* [*x x x x x*]
6′ *im—ma-te* [*x x x x x x*]
7′ ⸢*a-ni*⸣-*n*[*u x x x x x x x*]
rest broken away
Rev. beginning broken away
1′ *a*-[*x x x x x x x x x*]
2′ *a*-[*x x x x x x x x x*]
3′ ŠÀ-⸢*bu*⸣ [*x x x x x x x x*]
rest broken away

CT 53 551

(Beginning destroyed)
1 here [...]
2 any [...]
3 trained to the yoke [...]
4 riders [...]
5 the king, my lord, [...]
6 when [......]
7 we [......]
(Break)
3 [The king, my lord, can be] gla[d].
(Rest destroyed)

177. Fragment of a Horse Report

K 16501

beginning broken away
1′ [*x x x*]*x* 1 AN[ŠE.*x x x*]
2′ [PAB *x* K]UR.MEŠ 2 AN[ŠE.*ku-din*.MEŠ]
3′ [*x x x x*]*x-na-š*[*i x x x*]
rest broken away
Rev. completely broken away

CT 53 780

(Beginning destroyed)
1 [...], 1 [...] hor[se],
2 [total x ho]rses; 2 mu[les ...]
(Rest destroyed)

11. Varia and Unassigned

FIG. 28. *Inlaid couch (cf. no. 197).*
ORIGINAL DRAWINGS V, 42.

178. ———

K 1962

1 [*x x x x x* I]M ŠU.BA.T[I]
2 [*lu* DI-*mu a-na* LUGA]L EN-*i*[*a*]
3 [*x x x x a-na* L]UGAL EN-*ia*
4 [*x x x x x x*] *ta* [*x*]
5 [*x x x x x a-n*]*a* LUGAL EN-*i*[*a*]
6 [*x x x x x x x*]-*ut-ka*
7 [*x x x x x x la*]-*mur*
8 [*x x x x x x*] ⌈*x-u*⌉-*k*[*a*]
rest broken away
Rev. completely broken away

CT 53 218

1 [......] ...
2 [Good health to the kin]g, m[y] lord!
3 [*May DNN bless* the k]ing, my lord.
4 [*May they give* ...]
5 [... t]o the king, m[y] lord.
6 [*May I* s]ee your [...]
(Rest destroyed)

179. ———

83-1-18,264

1 *a-na* LUGAL EN-[*ia*]
2 ARAD-*ka* ^{md}MAŠ—*x*[*x x x*]
3 *lu šul-mu a-na* [LUGAL EN-*ia*]
4 ^{d}*aš-šur ù* ^{d}[15]
5 *a-na* LUGAL EN-*ia lik*-[*ru-bu*]
6 [*x x x x*]*x*[*x x x x x*]
rest broken away
Rev. broken away

ABL 1152

1 To the king, [my] lord: your servant Inurta-[...]. Good health to [the king, my lord]! May Aššur and [Ištar] bl[ess] the king, my lord.
(Rest destroyed)

180. ———

Ki 1904-10-9,256

1 *a-na* LUGAL *be-lí*-[*ia*]
2 ARAD-*ka* ^{md}AMAR.UTU—DÙ$^{?}$—[*x*]
3 *lu-u* DI-*mu a-na* LUGAL *be*-[*lí-ia*]
4 ^{d}PA ^{d}AMAR.UTU *a-na* LUGAL
5 [*be-lí-i*]*a lik-ru-bu*
6 [*x x x x x x*]*x x*[*x x*]
rest broken away
Rev. broken away

ABL 1399

1 To the king, [my] lord: your servant Marduk-*bani*-[...]. Good health to the king, [my] lo[rd]! May Nabû (and) Marduk bless the king m[y lord].
(Rest destroyed)

178 1 Obscure; possibly an otherwise unknown personal name. IM could be a logogram for "tablet" or "Adad," ŠU.BA.TI a logogram for *laqû* "to take." See coll.
180 2 See coll.

181. Nobody Knows What is in Balṭaya's Present

K 1589

1 *a-na* LUGAL EN-*ia*
2 ARAD-*ka* ^{md}PA—PAB.MEŠ—DI
3 *lu-u* DI-*mu a-na* LUGAL EN-*iá*
4 ^{d}PA ^{d}AMAR.UTU *a-*[*na* LUGAL EN-*iá*]
5 *lik-ru-bu ina* UGU [*ša* LUGAL *be-lí*]
6 *a-na* LÚ*.ARAD$^{!}$-*i-*[*šú iš-pur-an-ni*]
7 *ma-a šum-ma x*[*x x x x x*]
8 *ki-i a-n*[*a x x x x x x x*]
9 *šu-ú x*[*x x x x x x x x*]
10 *ma-a* TA* ⸢É⸣ [*x x x x*]
r.1 *šá-aṣ-*[*x x x x*]
2 *ma-a ú-l*[*a-a*]
3 *ši-i-ti-i-*[*ma*]
4 *lu ši-*[[]]*i* [0]
5 *ša ina* IGI ^{m}*bal-ṭa-a-*[*a*]
6 *man-nu ú-da me-me-ni*
7 *la ú-da ina* ŠÀ DINGIR.ME[Š]
8 *at-ta-ma šum-ma*
9 *a-na-ku-ma ú-du-ni*
10 *a-na man-ni ši-t*[*i-ni*]

ABL 695

1 To the king, my lord: your servant Nabû-ahhe-šallim. Good health to the king, my lord! May Nabû (and) Marduk bless the [king, my lord].

5 As to [what the king, my lord],
6 [wrote] to [his] servant:
7 "If [......],
8 "when t[o ......]
9 "he [......]
10 *"from the house of* [...]
r.1 *"pro*[*vide* ...].
2 "If n[ot],
3 *"she* may stay *as is*!"

5 Who knows what is in Balṭay[a]'s presence? Nobody knows! I swear by the gods that (at least) I do not know for whom *she* is.

182. ———

K 5506

1 [*a-na* LUGAL] EN-*ia*
2 [ARAD-*ka* ^{md}*x*]—MU—PAB
rest broken away
Rev. as far as preserved, uninscribed

CT 53 263

1 [To the king], my lord: [your servant DN]-šumu-uṣur.
(Rest destroyed)

183. Bread for the King's House

Bu 91-5-9,192

1 [*a*]*-n*[*a* LUGAL]
2 [EN-*i*]*a* ⸢ARAD⸣-*k*[*a* ^{m}*x x x x*]
3 [*lu*]*-u* DI-*mu a-na* L[UGAL EN-*ia*]
4 ⸢^{d}⸣AG [0] *ù* ^{d}[AMAR.UTU]
5 ⸢*a*⸣*-na* ⸢LUGAL EN⸣*-ia lik-*[*ru-bu*]
6 LUGAL *be-l*[*í ina* U]GU *sa-an-x*[*x x x*]
7 *ma-a a-ta-a* EN.NAM *ša ina* IG[I *x x*]
8 *dul-lu ša* É*-ia la e-pa-*[*áš*]
9 *ma-a ku-sa-pu a-na* É*-ia la* [*id-dan*]
10 *ma-a a-ta-a* Á.2.MEŠ*-šú is-sa-m*[*a*$^{?}$*-a*]
11 *ma-a ik-ku-u mi-i-nu du*[*l-la-ka*]
12 ⸢*ma-a*⸣ *la* LÚ.A.⸢BA *x*⸣ *x*[*x x x x*]
13 [*ma*]-⸢*a*⸣ *a-ta-a ina* ⸢UGU$^{?}$⸣ [*x x x x x*]

CT 53 970

1 [T]o [the king, m]y [lord]: yo[ur] servant [PN. Goo]d health to the k[ing, my lord]! May Nabû and [Marduk] bl[ess] the king, my lord.

6 The king, [my] lord, said concerning [...]: "Why does a governor in char[ge of ...] not d[o] the work of my (royal) house nor [give] bread to my house? Why are his arms *in*[*ept*]? What actually is your wo[rk]? [*You are*] not a scribe [...]. Why ... [...]?" —

14 [The words] from the k[ing my lord's]

181 6 See coll. 10 Hardly: "(ever) since." r.1 Maybe *šá-aṣ-*[*bi-it* or *ša-aṣ-*[*bu-su* or *ša-aṣ-*[*bu-tú*. r.3, 10 Or: "it." r.3f Cf. *šūtūma šû*, SAA 1 31:24, 97:14, and *šināma šina*, SAA 1 12 r.2.

14 [*da-ba-bu š*]*a* ⸢TA*⸣ *pi-i* L[UGAL EN-*ia x x*]
15 [*x x*] *ṭè*-⸢*e*⸣-[*m*]*u iš*-[*kun-x x x*]
16 [*x x x*]-*ni-šú ša* LUGAL *x*[*x x x*]
17 [*x x*] ⸢*a*⸣-*ta-a a*-[*x x x*]
18 [*x x x x x*]-*u-ni la* [*x x x*]
19 [*x x x x x x x*] *x*[*x x x x*]
rest broken away
Rev. beginning broken away
1′ [*x x x x x x*]*x ta a x*[*x x*]
2′ [*x x x x x*] LÚ.EN.NAM [*x x*]
3′ [*x x x*] *mi-i-nu dul-l*[*a-šú-nu*$^{?}$]
4′ [*x x*]-*šú-nu* GIŠ.MEŠ *a*-⸢*x x*⸣ *mi* [*x*]
5′ [*x-b*]*u*$^{?}$ *x*[*x x*]*x* [*x is*$^{?}$-*s*]*e-niš* URU [*x*]
6′ *a-na-ku i-di* ⸢*x*⸣ *šá-kín-tú taš-pu*-[*x*]
7′ GIŠ.IG.MEŠ *šá* LÚ*.*aš-šur-a-a ú-na*-[*x x*]
8′ *a*-⸢*x* LUGAL⸣ [*x*]*x* ⸢*x*⸣ *as-sa*-[*x x*]
9′ *a-na* LUGAL *be-lí-ia ú-šá*-⸢*áš*$^{?}$⸣-[*ma*]
10′ ⸢*ú*⸣-*ma-a* TA* IGI EN.NAM *ah*-[*x x x*]

11′ [*x x*] LUGAL EN-*ia i*-[*x x x*]
12′ *a-kil-tu ša* [*x x*] *a-he-i*[*š*$^{?}$ *x x*]
13′ ⸢*ag*$^{?}$⸣ EN UD *ma* [*x x x*] ⸢*šá*⸣ UR[U.*x x*]
14′ ⸢*x x*⸣ LUGAL *be-lí liš-al-šú-nu*
15′ ⸢*ma*⸣-*a* ⸢*a*⸣-[*ta*]-*a ku-sa-pu* [*x x x*]
16′ ⸢*dul-lu* LUGAL EN⸣-*ia* [*le-pu-šú*]
17′ ⸢*ú*⸣-*ma-a* [*x x x x x x*]
18′ *a-na* [*x x x x x x x x*]
s.1 [*x x x x x x x x*]*x-ku* ⸢*x*⸣ ŠU.2 LUGAL ⸢*be-lí-iá x*⸣ [*x x*]
2 [*x x x x x x x* L]UGAL EN-*ia ti*-[*x x x x*]

mouth [...]
15 [...] ga[ve] orders [...]
16 [...] him. (As to) what the king [...]
17 [...] Why [...]
18 [...] not [...]
(Break)
r.2 [...] the governor [...]
3 [...] what is [*their*] wor[k]?
4 Their [...] trees [...]
5 [... *like*]*wise* the town [...]
6 I ... the *harem manageress* [...]
7 The doors which the Assyrians [...]
8 ...... I have [*written down and*]
9 *I will* [...] to the king, my lord.
10 Now, I have [...] *from* the governor;
11 *he will* [... *to*] the king, my lord.
12 The consumption of [... ... each] oth[er].
13 ...... [...] of the cit[y ...]
14 Let the king, my lord, ask them w[h]y [...] bread, (and) [let them perform] the king's work!
17 Now [......]
18 to [......]
s.1 [......] the hands [of] the king, my lord, [...]
2 [...... the k]ing, my lord [...]

184. Fragment Referring to Building Activities

K 7305

1 [*a-na* LUGAL] *be*-[*lí-ia* (0)]
2 [ARAD-*k*]*a* $^{m⸢d⸣}$[*x x x x*]
3 [*lu* DI]-*mu a-n*[*a* LUGAL *be-lí-ia*]
4 [^{d}PA] ⸢*ù*⸣ ^{d}A[MAR.UTU *a-na* LUGAL *be-lí-ia*]
5 [*lik-r*]*u-bu a-n*⸢*a*⸣ [*x x x x*]
6 [*ša*$^{?}$ LUGA]L *be-lí-i*[*á x x x x*]
7 [*x x*] ⸢*il*$^{?}$⸣ *x*[*x x x x x*]
rest broken away
Rev. beginning broken away
1′ [*x x x*] *ú*-⸢*ma*$^{?}$⸣-[*x x x x*]
2′ [*x x x*]*x ina* ŠÀ-*bi x*[*x x x x*]
3′ [*x x a*]*n-nu-rig a*-[*x x x x*]
4′ [*x x*]-*a ra-ṣi-i*[*b x x x x*]
5′ [*x x x*] *pa-hi-ú ni*-[*x x x x x*]
6′ [*x x x*]-*ri-e* ⸢*ku*$^{?}$⸣ [*x x x x*]
7′ [*x x x*]-*ni*$^{?}$ *ù x*[*x x x x x*]
8′ [*x x x x*]*x* ⸢*x*⸣ [*x x x x x*]
rest broken away

CT 53 309

1 [To the king, my] lo[rd: yo]ur [servant PN. Good heal]th t[o the king, my lord! May Nabû] and M[arduk ble]ss [the king, my lord].
5 The [... of the kin]g, m[y] lord, [is well].
(Break)

r.1 [...] *no*[*w* ...]
2 [...] *there* [...]
3 [Now t]hen [...]
4 [...] *has been* buil[t ...]
5 *We* [...] *closed* [...]
(Rest destroyed)

183 r.10 Or: "because of." *ah*-[*x x x*] possibly to be restored *uh*-[*tar-rid* "I have ca[utioned]." r.12 Or, for example, *a-hi-i*[*a* "m[y] arms."

185. ———-

K 7320

lines 1-2 destroyed
3 ⌜*lu*⌝ [DI-*mu a-na x x x*]
4 ⌜^{d}⌝[*x x x x x x x*]
5 *l*[*ik-ru-bu x x x x*]
6 *ina* [UGU *x x x x x*]
line 7 obliterated
8 *nu*-[*x x x x x x x*]
9 LÚ*.[*x x x x x x x*]
10 *a-x*[*x x x x x x x*]
11 LÚ*.*i*-[*x x x x x x x*]
12 LÚ*.*x*[*x x x x x x x*]
13 *i*-[*x x x x x x x*]
14 *i*-[*x x x x x x x*]
15 LÚ*.[*x x x x x x x*]
16 *qu*-[*x x x x x x x*]
Rev. uninscribed

CT 53 317

(Beginning destroyed)

3 Good [health to the king, my lord! May DNN] b[less the king, my lord].

6 [Conc]erning [the ......]

(Rest destroyed)

186. ———-

K 1088

1 *a-na* LUGA[L EN-*ia*]
2 ARAD-*ka* ^{m}[*x x x x*]
3 *lu* DI-*mu* [*a-na* LUGAL EN-*ia*]
4 ^{d}PA ^{d}ME[S *x x x*]
5 [*x x*]*x x*[*x x x x x*]
rest broken away
Rev. beginning broken away
1′ *x*[*x x x x x x x*]
2′ ⌜LÚ*⌝.[*x x x x x x x*]
3′ *me-m*[*e-ni x x x x x*]
4e *la-a* [*x x x x x x*]
5e *hal-q*[*u x x x x x x*]

CT 53 162

1 To the kin[g, my lord]: your servant [PN]. Good health [to the king, my lord]! [May] Nabû (and) Mard[uk bless the king, my lord].

(Break)

r.3 nob[ody ......] is [...]

5 They have fle[d ......]

187. ———-

K 14660

1 *a*-[*na* LUGAL *be-lí-ia*]
2 ARAD-[*ka* ^{m}*x x x x*]
3 LU D[I-*mu a-na* LUGAL *be-lí-ia*]
4 ^{d}PA *u* [^{d}AMAR.UTU *a-na* LUGAL *lik-ru-bu*]
5 *ina* UGU [*x x x x x x x*]
6 LÚ.GA[L$^{?}$—*x x x x x*]
7 *a-sa*-[*ʾa-al x x x*]
8 *an*-[*x x x x x x*]
rest broken away
Rev. as far as preserved, uninscribed

CT 53 570

1 T[o the king, my lord: your] servant [PN]. Good he[alth to the king, my lord]! [May] Nabû and [Marduk bless the king].

5 As to the [......]

6 *the chi*[*ef* ......]

7 I *as*[*ked* ......]

(Rest destroyed)

188. ———

K 19979

1 ⸢*a*⸣-*na* LUG[AL *be-lí-ia*]
2 ARAD-*ka* [^{m}*x x x x x*]
3 *lu* DI-*mu* ⸢*a*⸣-[*na* LUGAL EN-*ia*]
4 ^{d}PA ^{d}AMAR.[UTU *a-na* LUGAL EN-*ia*]
5 *lik*-[*ru-bu*]
6 *x*[*x x x x x x*]
rest broken away
Rev. beginning broken away
1′ ⸢*nu*?⸣-[*x x x x x x x x*]
2′ *lib*-⸢*bu*? *ša*⸣ [LUGAL EN-*ia lu x x*]
3′ *mì-i-nu š*[*a x x x x x x*]
4′ *la pa-ṭu-ru-u-n*[*i x x x x*]
5′ *lu-še-b*[*il-u-ni*]

K 19979

1 To the kin[g, my lord]: your servant [PN]. Good health t[o the king, my lord]! May Nabû (and) Mar[duk] bl[ess the king, my lord].
(Break)

r.2 [*The king, my lord, can be*] *glad.*
3 Let [them] sen[d me] whatev[er] was not *detached* [*from* ...].

189. ———

K 15379

1 *a-na* [LUGAL EN-*ia*]
2 ARAD-*ka* ^{m}[*x x x x*]
3 *lu-u šul-m*[*u a-na* LUGAL EN-*ia*]
4 ^{d}AG *u* ^{d}[AMAR.UTU *a-na* LUGAL]
5 EN-*ia* [*lik-ru-bu*]
6 [*ina t*]*i-ma-l*[*i x x x x*]
7 [*mu-uk*] *la-l*[*i*?-*ka x x x x*]
8 [*x x*] ⸢*x*⸣ [*x x x x x*]
rest broken away
Rev. as far as preserved, uninscribed

CT 53 650

1 To [the king, my lord]: your servant [PN]. Good healt[h to the king, my lord]! [May] Nabû and [Marduk bless the king], my lord.
6 [Ye]sterda[y I said ...]: "Let me co[me ...]"
(Rest destroyed)

190. ———

K 16482

1 ⸢*a*⸣-*na* L[UGAL *be-lí-ia*]
2 ARAD-*ka* ^{m}[*x x x x*]
3 *lu* DI-*m*[*u a-na* LUGAL EN-*ia*]
4 ^{d}PA ^{d}[AMAR.UTU *a-na* LUGAL EN-*ia*]
5 ⸢*lik*⸣-[*ru-bu*]
rest broken away
Rev. as far as preserved, uninscribed

CT 53 769

1 To the k[ing, my lord]: your servant [PN]. Good healt[h to the king, my lord]! May Nabû (and) [Marduk] bl[ess the king, my lord].
(Rest destroyed)

188 Near top left-hand part of tablet. Previously unpublished; copy p. 218.

191. ———

83-1-18,147

1 [_a-n_]_a_ ⸢LUGAL⸣ [EN-_ia_]
2 [AR]AD-_ka_ ^{m}⸢_x_⸣ [_x x x_]
3 [_l_]_u-u_ DI-_mu a-_[_na_ LUGAL EN-_ia_]
4 ^{d}EN _u_ ^{d}⸢AG⸣ [_a-na_ LUGAL EN-_ia_]
5 [_l_]_ik-ru-_[_bu_]
6 [_x x_] ⸢_e_? _x_⸣ [_x x_]
7 [_x x_] ⸢_x x x_⸣ [_x x_]
8 ⸢_ma_⸣-_a_ʾ-_du_ ⸢_x_⸣ [_x x_]
9 ⸢LUGAL⸣ _a-_[_x_] ⸢_x x_⸣ [_x x_]
10 _a-na_ LÚ*.[_x x x x_]
11 [_m_]_a-a_ GEŠTIN.MEŠ TA* [_x x_]
12 [_x x x_]_x-a-ni ma-a_ [_x x_]
13 [_x x x_]-_te tu-x_[_x x_]
14 [_x x x_]_x ina ma-_[_x x_]
one line and edge broken away
Rev. two lines broken away
3 [_x x x x x_] _x_[_x x_]
4 [_x x x_]_x bi ni_ [_x x_]
5 [_š_]_a_ LUGAL TA* KUR.[_x x_]
6 _ú-ba-_⸢_ru_⸣ ⸢_ù_⸣ [_x x x x_]
7 TA* ⸢_x x x_⸣ [_x x x_]
8 _i-_⸢_x x_⸣-_u-ni_ [_x x x_]
9 [_x x_]-_a_ ⸢_x_⸣ [_x x x_]
10 [_x x x_] ⸢_x x x_⸣ [_x x x_]
11 [_x x n_]_i_ ⸢_x x_⸣ [_x x x_]
12 [_x x x_]_x_ DINGIR.MEŠ [_x x x_]
13 [_x x x_]_x x_ [_x x x x_]
rest broken away

83-1-18,147

1 [T]o the king, [my lord]: your [ser]vant [PN. G]ood health t[o the king, my lord]! [M]ay Bel and Nabû bles[s the king, my lord].
(Break)

8 much [...]
9 The king [said] to [the ...]
10 (and) to the [...] (officials):
11 "[...] _me_ wine from [...]
(Break)

r.5 They will catch [the _enemies_ o]f the king from the land of [...]
6 and [...]
7 from/with [...]
(Break)

12 [...] the gods [...]
(Rest destroyed)

192. ———

83-1-18,707

1 _a-na_ LUG[AL _be-lí-ia_]
2 ARAD-_ka_ ^{m}[_x x x x_]
3 _lu_ DI-_m_[_u a-na_ LUGAL EN-_ia_]
4 _aš-šur_ ^{d}[UTU ^{d}PA ^{d}AMAR.UTU]
5 _a-na_ [LUGAL _be-lí-ia_]
6 _li-_[_ik-ru-bu x x x_]
7 _ma-_⸢_a_?⸣ [_x x x x x x_]
8 _ša_ [_x x x x x x_]
9 _ša_ [_x x x x x x_]
10 _š_[_a x x x x x x_]
11 _š_[_a x x x x x x_]
12 _š_[_a x x x x x x_]
13 _x_[_x x x x x x x_]
14 _x_[_x x x x x x x_]
15 ⸢_pa_?⸣-[_x x x x x x_]
Edge uninscribed

CT 53 940

1 To the kin[g, my lord], your servant: [PN]. Good healt[h to the king, my lord]! May Aššur, [Šamaš, Nabû and Marduk bless the king, my lord].
(Break)

191 Previously unpublished. Almost every single sign on this tablet is damaged or broken. Transliterated by S. Parpola, 27.3.68.

Rev. beginning (one or two lines) broken away

1′ *x*[*x x x x x x x*]

2′ *ša* [*x x x x x x*]

3′ *ina* [*x x x x x x*]

4′ *is*-[*x x x x x x*]

5′ *ša* [*x x x x x x*]

6′ *ša* [*x x x x x x*]

7′ *a-na* [*x x x x x x*]

8′ *da*-[*x x x x x x*]

9′ *la i*[*l-x x x x x*]

10′ *la is*-[*x x x x x x*]

11′ *ú-ma*-⸢*a*⸣ [*x x x x x*]

12′ *šak-na* ⸢LUGAL⸣ [*be-lí x x*]

13′ *liš-pur ina* ⸢É⸣ [*x x x*]

14′ *lu-še-r*[*i-bu-ši-na*]

one line uninscribed

r.11 Now [...] are in place. Let the king, [my lord], send [...] to bri[ng them] into the *house* of [...].

193. ———

K 19787

1 *a-na* [LUGAL EN-*i*]*a*

2 ARAD-*k*[*a* ^{m}*x x x x x*]

3 *lu-u* [DI-*mu a-na* LUGA]L EN-*ia*

4 *aš-šur* [^{d}*x x*]*x* ^{d}MES

5 ^{d}⸢15⸣ [*x x x x l*]*i*$^{?}$

remainder and reverse uninscribed

K 19787

1 To [the king, m]y [lord]: yo[ur] servant [PN]. Good [health to the kin]g, my lord! [May] Aššur, [DN], Marduk, Ištar [......]

(Rest destroyed)

194. ———

K 15381

1 [*a-na* LUGAL *be-lí*]-*ia*

2 [ARAD-*ka* ^{m}*x x x* DINGIR.MEŠ *a*] AN-*e*

3 [*a-na* LUGAL *be-lí-ia*] *lik-ru-bu*

4 [*x x x x x x*]-*hi pa-an*

5 [*x x x x x x x*] [LU]GAL *be-lí-ia*

rest broken away

Rev. beginning broken away

1′ [*x x x x x x x*]*x-ia*

2′ [*x x x*] *mu*$^{?}$ [*x x* LUG]AL EN-*iá*

3′ [*x x*] ⸢*a*⸣ *x*[*x x x*]-⸢*ú*⸣-*ni*

rest uninscribed

CT 53 652

1 [To the king], my [lord: your servant PN]. May [the gods of] heaven bless [the king, my lord].

5 [...... the k]ing, my lord

(Break)

r.1 [...] my [...]

2 [...... the ki]ng, my lord [......]

192 r.13 Or: "temple of."

193 Previously unpublished. Copy p. 218.

195. ———

K 15390

beginning broken away
1′ [*x x x* UD.MEŠ *ar-ku-t*]*i* ⌜MU.AN⌝.[NA.MEŠ *da-ra-ti*]
2′ [*ṭu-ub* ŠÀ-*bi ṭu-ub* U]ZU.MEŠ *a-na* LUGA[L EN-*ni liš-ru-ku*]
3′ [*x x x x x*] NUMUN.MEŠ *ù lu*-[*ub-bur* BALA-*e*]
4′ [*x x x ša* LUGA]L EN-*ni iš-pur-a*-[*na-ši-ni*]
5′ [*x x x x x x*]*x qa*$^{?}$ [*x x x x x x x x x*]
rest broken away
Rev. completely broken away

CT 53 657

(Beginning destroyed)

1 [May DNN grant lon]g [days, everlasting] yea[rs, happiness and phy]sical [well-being] to the kin[g, our lord. May they give him ...] descendants and a l[ong reign]!

4 [Concerning what the kin]g, our lord, wrote t[o us ...]

(Rest destroyed)

196. Asking for Further Instructions

K 670

1 *a-na* L[UGAL EN-*ia*]
2 ARAD-*k*[*a* ^{m}*x x x*]
3 *lu-u* [DI-*mu a-na* LUGAL EN-*ia*]
4 *ina* UGU [*ṭè-e-me ša* LUGAL EN-*ia*]
5 *iš-kun*-[*an-ni*]-*ni*
6 DI-*mu a-na* LUGAL EN-*ia*
7 *as-sap-ra*
8 DI-*mu ša* LUGAL EN-*ia*
9 *la-áš-me*
10 *ù mi-i-nu*
11 *ša šu-tu-ú-ni*
e.12 LUGAL *liš-pu-ra*
13 *lib-bu*
r.1 *a-na* LÚ.ARAD-*šu*
2 *liš-kun*
rest broken away

ABL 554

1 To the k[ing, my lord]: yo[ur] servant [PN]. Good [health to the king, my lord]!

4 As to the [orders which the king, my lord], gave me, (hereby) I am sending greetings to the king, my lord. May I hear about the health of the king, my lord, and may the king write me what the matter is, and encourage his servant.

197. Golden Plate for a Couch

K 1116

beginning broken away
1′ [*x x*] *pa x*[*x x x x x*]
2′ [ZU] *ša* LÚ*.BU[R.GUL *x x x*]
3′ *ša e-piš-u-ni* [*x x x x x*]
4′ *ši-in pu-us-ki a-x*[*x x x*]
5′ UD-*mu* UD-3-KAM *ša* ITI.BA[RAG 0]
6′ *le-ʾu-u* KUG.GI *ša* BUR.G[UL]
7′ *ina* UGU *e-ṣi ni-ik-ta-r*[*a-ar*]
r.1 ZU *ša né-me-di* [*x x*]
2 6 *ina* 1 KÙŠ *i-ta-lak* [*x x*]
3 *an*-⌜*x x x x x*⌝ LUGAL
rest broken away

ABL 592

(Beginning destroyed)

2 [the plate] of the scu[lptor ...]

3 which was made [......]

4 a (piece of) *ivory* a palm (wide) [...]

5 On the 3rd of Ni[san] (I) we fit[ted] the gold plate of the scul[ptor] on the wood. The plating of the couch measured 6 cubits [...]

r.3 [......] the king

(Rest destroyed or too broken for translation)

195 1-3 Cf. SAA 13 193:4-8.
196 4-r.2 Oppenheim, JAOS 61 (1941) 264.
197 5-r.2 → LAS II 315:6.

198. Making Cursers Talk

K 1150

obverse completely broken away
r.1 *me-me-ni* [*x x x*]
2 *il-lak ú-š*[*e-rab*?]
3 *a-na-ku al-*[*la-ka*]
4 *ki-i* ŠÀ-*b*[*i x*]
5 *a-ra-r*[*i*? *x*]
6 *ú-šá-ad-ba-ab* [0]
rest (about 6 lines) uninscribed

ABL 613

(Beginning destroyed)

r.1 Somebody will go (and) br[ing *in* ...].

2 I shall go too (and) make the *curs*[*ers*] talk according to the wis[h of ...].

199. Report on Work

Sm 562

beginning broken away
1′ [*x*]*x x*[*x x x x x x*]
2′ *i-na-ṣu-r*[*u x x x*]
3′ *ša* LUGAL *be-lí iš-*[*pur-an-ni ma-a*]
4′ *a-di* UD-20-KÁM *dul-*[*lu x x x*]
5′ *le-pu-šú ma-a x*[*x x x x*]
6′ *dul-la-šú-nu x*[*x x x x x*]
7′ UD-3-KÁM *ša* IT[I.*x x x x*]
8′ *it-tal-ku-u-ni* [*x x x x x*]
9′ LÚ*.*qur-bu-ti* [*x x x x x*]
10′ [*x*]*x x*[*x x x x x x x x*]
Rev. beginning broken away
1′ *a-*[*x x x x x x*]
2′ UZ[U.Á].⌈2⌉-*šú-n*[*u*! *ina* UGU-*hi*]
3′ *ú-mu-du* [*ep-pu-šu*]
rest uninscribed

ABL 1055

(Beginning destroyed)

2 they are guard[ing ...]

3 As to what the king, my lord wr[ote to me]: "Let them do [...] wor[k] until the 20th. [...] their work [...]."

7 On the 3rd day of the mon[th ...]

8 they came [......]

9 a bodyguard [...]

(Break)

r.2 They will set to [work and do it].

200. All the Lands Belong to The King

83-1-18,148

obverse broken away
Rev. beginning broken away
1′ [*x x x x x*] 2 *e kal x*[*x x x x*]
2′ [*x x x x x*]-*i-ni ni-il-x*[*x x x*]
3′ [*x x x x*]*x-ʾa-ka is-si-*[*x x*]
4′ [*x x x*] TA* É ^{d}UTU *i-nap-pa-ha*!-[*an-ni*]
5′ [*a-di* É] ⌈*i*⌉-*rab-bu-u-ni šá* LUGAL *š*[*u-nu*]
6′ [UN.MEŠ] KUR.KUR *gab-bu* ARAD-*a-nu-tú šá* [LUGAL *e-pu-šú*]
7′ LÚ.SAG.MEŠ LÚ.*šá—ziq-*[*ni*.MEŠ *ina* GIŠ.MI]
8′ [LUGAL] NINDA.HI.A *e-ku-lu* [*x x x x*]

ABL 1139

(Beginning destroyed)

r.2 [......] we will c[ome ...]

3 [......] *with* [...]

4 [*All the lands*] from where the sun rise[s to where] it sets be[long] to the king.

6 [The people] of all the lands [are] obedient to [the king].

7 The eunuchs (and) the bearded court[iers] eat bread [*under the king's protec-*

198 r.1f See coll. r.4f See coll.
199 r.2 See coll.
200 r.4f Cf. no. 127:10ff // no. 128:10-13. This phrase was particularly popular in the reign of Esarhaddon, cf. SAA 9 3 i 30-34 and (in almost identical form) ibid. ii 4-5 (680 BC), SAA 2 6:6, SAA 10 185 r.17-8 (both 672 BC). The present text could accordingly be associated either with the coronation or (more likely) with the succession treaty

9′ [*x x*]*x-mu ù ina* É.MEŠ [*x x x*]
10′ [*x x x*]*x ár-hiš šá ma x*[*x x x x*]
11′ [*x x x x*] *hi*? *x*[*x x x x x x*]
rest broken away

tion ...]

9 [...] and in the houses [...]

10 [...] quickly ... [...]

(Rest destroyed)

201. Revering the King

83-1-18,160

beginning broken away
1′ *ma-a ina* É.GAL *a-x*[*x x x x*]
2′ 1-*en ina* ŠÀ-*bi-ku-nu at-*[*x x x*]
3′ *ina* ŠÀ AD-*ka* AD—AD-*ni*
4′ *i-te-te-li*
r.1 LUGAL *ip-ta-al-hu*
2 *ina šad-daq-diš i-ti-te-iq*
3 LUGAL *be-lí ip-ta-al-hu*
4 *ú-ma-a la im-*[*ma-gúr*]
5 LUGAL *la i-p*[*al-lu-hu*]
6 [*x x*]*x*[*x x x x x x*]
Rest broken away

ABL 1144

(Beginning destroyed)

1 saying: "I [will ...] in the palace. One of you [...]."

3 In the reign of your father, (when) our grandfather went up (there), they revered the king.

r.2 Last year, (when) he passed by, they revered the king, my lord. But now they ref[use] to rev[ere] the king.

(Rest destroyed)

202. Go and Ask!

83-1-18,280

beginning broken away
1′ *ta-x*[*x x x x x x*]
2′ LUGAL *be-l*[*i*] *i*[*q-ṭi-bi-a*]
3′ *ma-a* UD-28?-KÁM *tal-l*[*a-ka*]
4′ *ta-šá-ʾa-a-l*[*a*]
5′ *ú-ma-a mi-i-nu*
6′ *ša* LUGAL *be-li* [0]
7′ [*i-qab-bu-u-ni*]
Rev. broken away

ABL 1158

(Beginning destroyed)

2 The king, my lord, t[old me]: "On the 28th you will g[o] (and) ask!" Now, what is it that the king, my lord, [commands]?

(Rest destroyed)

203. ———

Sm 540

obverse broken away
Rev. beginning broken away
1′ [*x x x*]*x ina* UGU [*x x x*]
2′ [*x x x*]*x-i lil-*[*x x x x*]
3′ [*x x*]*x-a la-a pu*?-[*x x x*]
4′ [*x x*]-*at-tú ina pi-i* [*x x x*]
5′ [*x x* Š]U.2.MEŠ-*šú-nu lil-*[*x x x*]
6′ [*x x x x x x x x x x*]

ABL 1268

(Too broken for translation)

of Esarhaddon (SAA 2 6). r.5 See coll.
202 2 See coll.

204. Glazing Bricks

K 4799

beginning broken away

1′ [*x x x x x x x x x x x x*]*x*
2′ [*x x x x x x x x* LÚ].*tur-tan*
3′ [*x x x x x x x i*]-*qab-bi-ú*
4′ [*x x x x x x x*] *kal*? *e ru x*
5′ [*x x x x x x x*] ⸢*ep*⸣-*pu-šu*
6′ [*x x x x x x x a*]*q-ṭi-bi*
7′ [*x x x x x x x*]*x* TA* LUGAL
8′ [*x x x x x x x*]*x ana-ku* LÚ.*ú-ra-si*
9′ [*x x x x x x x*] LÚ.GAL—LAM
10′ [*x x x x x is-s*]*a-ah-ṭu*
11′ [*x x x x x x*]-*te i-ba-áš-ši*

e.12′ [*x x x x x*]*x-ia* LUGAL *ih-tar-ṣa*
13′ [*x x x x x*] *is-sa-al*
14′ [*x x x x x*]-*du-u-ni*

r.1 [*x x x x x*]-*ú-ni ni-sa-al*
2 [*x x x x x*]-*u-ni ma-a* 2 3
3 [*x x x x x*]*x i-ba-áš-ši*
4 [*x x x x x*] *ina* ŠÀ-*bi* 2 3
5 [*x x x x x*] *ni-il-lik pa-ni*
6 [*x x x x x x*]*x iq-bu-u-ni*
7 [*x x x x x x*]*x ina maš-kan-i-šú*
8 [*x x x x x x*] EN—MUN *ni-ih-ru-uṣ-ṣa*

9 [*x x x x x x*] LUGAL *ni-qab-bi*
10 [*x x x x x x x-k*]*a mu-šam-hi-iṣ-ṣu-u*
11 [*x x x x x x*]-*hu*?-*u a-na-ku-u-ni*
12 [*x x x x x x x*]*x* LÚ.*x*[*x x*] *tan*

rest broken away

ABL 1310

(Beginning destroyed)

2 [...... the] commander-in-chief
3 [......] they say
4 [......] ...
5 [......] they do
6 [...... I] said
7 [......] with the king
8 [......] I (*and*) the brick masons
9 [......] the chief ...
10 [... have *gla*]*zed* [bricks]
11 [...] there are
12 [...] the king *made clear*
13 [...] asked
14 [...] ...
r.1 [...] we asked
2 [...] they said: "2 or 3
3 [...] there are
4 [...] with(in) 2 or 3
5 [...] we will go and [...] *the face*
6 [...] said
7 [...] *in its place*
8 [...] We shall clear up (who is) a friend
9 [... and] tell [it to] the king.
10 [*Perhaps the king will say*: "Is yo]ur [...] an instigator?"
11 [... that] I am [...]
12 [......] the c[*ommander-in-c*]*hief*

(Rest destroyed)

205. Appointing Guards

K 10911 + K 14628

Obv. completely broken away

r.1 ⸢2 LÚ*.*šá*—EN⸣.NUN.MEŠ 2 LÚ*.[*x x x*]
2 *ina pa-ni-šú-nu ap-ti-*[*qid*]
3 *ina* UGU NINDA.MEŠ-*šú-nu bir-*[*ti*]
4 IGI.2 *um-ta-di-i*[*d*]
5 *nu-uk bé-et ṣi-la-*⸢*a*⸣-[*te*]
6 [*i-ba-šu*]-⸢*ni x*⸣-*ru še-ri-d*[*a*]
7 [*ú-ma-a* m]⸢d⸣AMAR.UTU—*rém-a-ni*
8 [*x x m*]*a-a* LÚ*.ARAD.MEŠ URU.[*x x*]
9 [*x x du*]*l-li-i-ni* [*x x x*]

CT 53 109

(Beginning destroyed)

r.1 I ap[point]ed two guards and two [...s] in their service. Concerning their bread I made it very clear that they are to bring the [...] down where [there are] shelters.

7 [Now] Marduk-remanni [..., say]ing: "The servants of the city [GN ...] our [wo]rk."

204 10 For another interpretation of *šahāṭu*, see Radner, AfO 44/45 (1997/98) 159ff and Saggs, CTN 5 (2001) 122. r.5 Or: "we did[n't] go." r.7 Or: "from his tents."
205 r.5 Besides this letter, the form *ṣillāte* is attested only in no. 117:15.

10 *[it-t]a-at-lak* [*x x x*]
rest broken away

[10] [*He* we]nt off [...]
(Rest destroyed)

206. ———

K 1584

beginning broken away
1′ ⸢*ša*⸣ É.GAL *ša a-x*⸣-[*x*]
2′ *ú-qar-ra-bu-u-*⸢*ni*⸣
3′ *an-nu-rig*
4′ *né-e-ta-mar*
5′ ⸢*i-ba*⸣*-áš-ši*
rest broken away
Rev. beginning broken away
1′ [*x x x x x*]*x*
2′ [*x x x x*]-*a-te*
3′ LUGAL [*be-lí ina*] UGU-*hi*
4′ *la*$^{?}$ [*x x x x x x*]
5′ *ni-*[*x x x x x x*]
rest broken away

CT 53 189

(Beginning destroyed)

1 Now then, we have seen [the ...] of the palace who produce the [...]. There is [...]

(Break)

r.3 The king, [my lord], should not [*be concerned*] about it.

5 We [......]

(Rest destroyed)

207. Promoting Chariot Drivers and 'Third Men'

K 5478

beginning broken away
1′ [*x x x x x x*]*x-*⸢*ia*⸣ *x*[*x x x x x x*]
2′ [*x x x x x x*] ⸢*a*⸣*-na* DUMU—LUG[AL *x x x x*]
3′ [*k*]*i-ma* DINGIR.MEŠ-*ka pa-*⸢*ni*⸣ *ša* LUGAL EN-⸢*ia i*⸣-[*x x x x*]
4′ [*p*]*i-*⸢*i-šú*⸣ LUGAL *be-lí em-*⸢*mar* LÚ*⸣.ARAD *ša* [TA* EN-*šú*]
5′ [*k*]*e-nu-ú-ni* LÚ*.ARAD *ša* ⸢*x*⸣ *ša* EN-*š*[*ú x x x*]
6′ ⸢LÚ*⸣.ARAD *ša* UGU É—⸢EN.MEŠ⸣*-š*[*ú i-ma-qa-tu-ni*]
7′ [*i*]*-mu-tú-u-ni ú-ma-a* ⸢*šúm-ma ina*⸣ [U]GU *x*[*x x x x*]
8′ [LÚ*.D]IB—PA.MEŠ LÚ*.3-*šú*.MEŠ *ina* IGI LUGAL E[N-*ia x x x*]
9′ [*il-lak*]*-u-ni lu-u-sa-te-li ina* UGU GIŠ.[*x x x x x*]
10′ [2 LÚ*.D]IB—PA.MEŠ 2 LÚ*.3-*šú*.MEŠ *ina* U[GU *x x x x*]
11′ [MU.MEŠ-*šú*]*-nu liš-ṭu-ru ba-si l*[*u-x x x x x x*]
12′ [*x x x* ^{m}]⸢^{d}⸣PA—*mu-še-zib* [*x x x x x x x*]
rest broken away
Rev. completely broken away

CT 53 249

(Beginning destroyed)

1 [...] *my* [......]

2 [......] to the cro[wn] prince [...]

3 As soon as your gods [have ...ed] the face of the king, my lord, the king, my lord, will see his statement: a servant who is loyal [*to his lord*], a servant who [...]s the [...] of h[is lord], a servant who [falls] and die[s] on behalf the house of h[is] lords.

7 Now, if on [... the ch]ariot-driver(s) and the 'third men' [com]e before the king, [my] lo[rd], let him be promoted. As to [...], let the overseer of the [...] write [the names of two ch]ariot-drivers and two 'third men' on [...], so that [...]

12 [...] Nabû-mušezib [......]

(Rest destroyed)

207 4 See coll. 4-7 → Fales, HANEM 4 (2000) 238b. 7-12 → Parpola *apud* Nissinen, SAAS 7 (1998) 130.

208. ———

K 5497

beginning broken away
1′ [*x x x x x x*]*x* ⸢*ri*⸣ [*x x x x x x*]
2′ [*x x x x x*]*x-ka lu* [*x x x x x x*]
3′ [*x x x x x* L]UGAL EN-*i*[*a x x x x x x*]
4′ [*x x x x x x*] ⸢*a*⸣-*ki bir*-[*x x x x x x x*]
5′ [*x x x x x x*] *la hu-ul*-[*x x x x x x x*]
6′ [*x x x x x*]-*u*?-*tú ina te*-[*x x x x x x x*]
7′ [*x x x x x* U]D *bi i-x*[*x x x x x x x*]
8′ [*x x x x x x*]*x si*? [*x x x x x x x*]
rest broken away
Rev. completely broken away

CT 53 259

(Too broken for translation)

209. ———

K 5527

Obv. completely broken away
e.1′ [*x x x x*] ⸢*an*?⸣ *x*[*x x x x*]
2′ [*x x x* L]Ú.GAL—*ki-ṣir* [*x x*]
r.1 [*x x x*]*x ha-an-ni*-[*šá*]
2 [*x x x g*]*a*? GIŠ.GEŠTIN.MEŠ [(*x*)]
3 [*x x x* K]UG.UD *ba-áš-lu* [(*x*)]
4 [*x x x x*] ⸢*x x x te*?⸣ [*x*]
rest broken away

CT 53 270

(Beginning destroyed)
2 [... t]he cohort commander [...]
r.1 [...] hith[er]
2 [...] wine
3 [...] refined [s]ilver
(Rest destroyed)

210. ———

K 5545

beginning (one line only?) broken away
1′ [*x x x x x x x*] *x*[*x x x*]
2′ [*x x x x x*] *ù ad-ru x*[*x x x*]
3′ [*x x x x i*]*l*?-*lak la-a a*-[*x x x*]
4′ [*x x x x*] ⸢d?⸣MAŠ d⸢UTU? SAG?⸣ *x*[*x x x*]
5′ [*x x x x x*]-*iá lu-ub*-[*x x x x x*]
6′ [*x x x x x x*] *an x*[*x x x x x x*]
rest broken away
Rev. completely broken away

CT 53 278

(Too broken for translation)

211. Should I Come to Calah?

K 5598

Obv. completely broken away
Rev. beginning broken away
1′ [*l*]*a*-⸢*li*⸣-*k*[*a-a*]
2′ *a-na* URU.*kal*-[*ha*]
3′ *mi-i-nu ša* LUGAL ⸢*be*⸣-[*lí*]
4′ *i-qab-bu-u-ni*
rest uninscribed

CT 53 292

(Obverse destroyed)
r.1 Should I come to Cal[ah]?
3 What is it that the king, [my l]ord, commands?

212. Good Advice

K 5597

beginning broken away
1′ *ú-ma-*⸢*a*⸣ [*x x x x x*]
2′ *nu-uk* [*x x x x x*]
3′ *ša ra-m*[*i-ni-x x x*]
4′ *nu-uk* [*x x x x x*]
5′ *q*[*a-x*] *x*[*x x x x x*]
6′ ⸢*nu-uk*⸣ *a-t*[*a-a x x x*]
7′ ⸢LUGAL$^{?}$⸣ *x*[*x x x x*]
Edge broken away
r.1 ⸢*x x*⸣ [*x x x x x*]
2 [*m*]*a-a a-ta-*[*a x x x*]
3 [*ma*]*-a a-ṣu-du* [*x x x*]
4 ⸢*la*⸣ *tu-šá-kal š*[*a x x x*]
5 *ša* LÚ.2-⸢*e*⸣ [*x x x x*]
6 *a-ta-a* [*x x x x x*]
7 *e-*[*x x x x x x x*]
rest broken away
s.1 [*x x x*].MEŠ *ša* LUGAL *i*[*t-x x x*]
2 [*m*]*ì-il-ku šú-u* SIG$_5$ *a—*[*dan-niš*]

CT 53 294

(Beginning destroyed)
1 Now [......]
2 I said: "[......]
3 of [*your*]se[lf ...]
4 I said: "[......]
5 [......]
6 I said: "Wh[y ...]
7 *the king* [......]
r.1 [......]
2 [He sa]id: "Wh[y *don't you agree*]
3 "to feed an *aṣūdu*-bowl [to ...]? *O*[*f* ...]
5 *of* the deputy [...]
6 Why [......]
(Break)
s.1 [The ...]s *of* the king [...].
2 That is a ve[ry] good advice.

213. ———

K 7418

beginning broken away
1′ [*x x x*]*x an za* [*x x x x*]
2′ [*x x*]*-ni*$^{?}$ *a-na x*[*x x x x*]
3′ [*x x x*]*x* MU.AN.NA [*x x x x*]
4′ [*x x x*] *a-na na lu* [*x x x x*]
5′ [*x x x*].MEŠ *la-ak-*[*x x x x*]
6′ [*x x x*].MEŠ *lu-qar-*[*ri-ib x x x*]
7′ [*x x x-i*]*a la-a*[*n-tu-uh*$^{?}$ *x x*]
8′ [*x x x x*]*x-ia* [*x x x x x*]
rest broken away
Rev. completely broken away

CT 53 354

(Too broken for translation)

214. ———

K 7502

Obv. completely broken away
e.1′ [*x x*] LUG[AL *x x x x*]
2′ [*i*]*t-ta-la*[*k x*]
r.1 [*x*] *lu* [*x x*]*x* LÚ*.A—K[IN]
2 [*x i*]*š-p*[*ur*]*-ra-an-ni* [0]
3 [*x x x x*]*x* [*i*]*m—ma-te*
4 [*x x x x*] ⸢É⸣.S⸢IG$_4$$^{?}$⸣
5 [*x x x x-a*]*l*

CT 53 377

(Beginning destroyed)
1 [...] the kin[g ...]
2 [w]ent [...]
r.1 [......] the messe[nger]
2 [...] wrote me
3 [... w]hen
4 [......] *the* [*w*]*al*[*l*]

212 3 Or: "[my/him]self."

6 [*x x x x x*].MEŠ *am-ma-te*
7 [*x x x x*]-*ni*
8 [*x x x x-n*]*i*
rest broken away

6 [...] those [...]s
(Rest destroyed)

215. ———

K 7539

1 [*a-na* LUGAL *be-lí-ia*]
2 ARAD-[*ka* ^{m}*x x x x x*]
3 LÚ*.A.[BA *x x x x x*]
4 *lu* [DI-*mu a-na* LUGAL EN-*ia*]
5 ^{d}[*x x x x x x*]
6 ⸢*a*⸣-[*na x x x x x x*]
rest broken away
Rev. beginning broken away
1′ *an*-[*x x x x x x*]
2′ ^{m}NU—MAN—[E$^{?}$ *x x x x*]
3′ LÚ*.GAL—[*x x x x x*]
4′ *i-tu*-[*bi-la*$^{?}$ 0$^{?}$]

CT 53 381

1 [To the king, my lord: your] servant [PN], the sc[ribe of ...]. Good [health to the king, my lord]!
(Break)
r.2 Ṣalam-šarri-[*iqbi* ...]
3 the chief [......]
4 *bro*[*ught me* (...)]

216. ———

K 12998

beginning broken away
1′ [*i—ti-ma-li i*]*—šá*-[*šu-me x x x*]
2′ [*x x x x*]*x a*[*s x x x x*]
3′ ⸢LÚ*⸣.[*x x x š*]*a* LÚ*.[*x x x x x*]
4′ *m*[*a-a x x-a*]*n-ni* [*x x x x x*]
5′ *ma-a* [*x x x l*]*a x*[*x x x x x*]
6′ *ú-ma-a il-t*[*i-bi x x x x*]
7′ *ú-ta-me-i*[*š x x x x x x*]
8′ *i-du-nu* [*x x x x x x x*]
9′ *i—šá-šu-me* [*x x x x x x x*]
10′ *i-ka-ṣur* [*x x x x x x x*]
11′ SÍG.ZA.GÌN.MI [*x x x x x x*]
e.12′ *si-ih-pu* [*x x x x x x*]
vitrified
Rev. vitrified
2 *an* [*x x x x x x x x x*]
3 *ú*-[*x x x x x x x x x*]
4 *a-na* ⸢*x*⸣[*x x x x x x x*]
5 ⸢*i*⸣-*x*[*x x x x x x x x*]
6 LÚ*.⸢*za*⸣-[*x x x x x x x*]
7 *it-t*[*i-ši*$^{?}$ *x x x x x x x*]
8 *li-i*[*r-x x x x x x x x*]
9 *ba*-[*x x x x x x x x*]
10 *dul-la*-[*x x x x x x x x*]
11 *i*-[*x x x x x x x x x*]
rest broken away

CT 53 456

(Beginning destroyed)
1 [*Previ*]*o*[*usly*]......]
3 the [... o]f the [...] official
4 said: "[...] ... [......]"
6 Now he has go[ne around ......]
7 set ou[t ......]
8 they *sell* [......]
9 Previously [......]
10 they used to knit [......]
11 dark-blue wool [......]
12 bast [......]
(Break)

r.4 to [......]
5 [......]
6 the *ex*[*empts* ...]
7 has *ta*[*ken* ......]
8 let [......]
9 [......]
10 [their] work [......]
(Rest destroyed)

216 6 The verb is probably *labû*, which usually does not display the Neo-Assyrian assimilation *lt* > *ss* in the perfect (the assimilated form *issibi* is attested only in PKTA 19:13 and CT 53 326:1). 8 Or: "give." 9 Or: "the day before yesterday." 10 For *i-ka-ṣur* as pl., cf. SAA 1 77:17, r.3. See also Hämeen-Anttila, SAAS 13 (2000) 111f for the aspectual use of the present.

217. ———

K 13069

beginning broken away
1′ *[x x x x x x* T]A ⌜LUGAL *be-lí-ia*⌝
2′ *[x x x x x x x]-ba ina* UGU
3′ *[x x x x x x x s]a-mi-ik-te*
4′ *[x x x x x x x x]* ⌜LÚ⌝.A.BA
5′ *[x x x x x x x x x x x]x*
6′ *[x x x x x x x x x x]-ni*
rest broken away
Rev. beginning broken away
1′ *[x x]-nu-šú ina* IGI *[x x x x x x x]*
2′ *[x x] a-šá-ad-da-*⌜*du*⌝*-u-n[i x x x x]*
3′ *[x x]x-šu-u-ni ki-i x[x x x x]*
4′ [*x* LUG]AL *be-lí-ia l[i-x x x x x]*
5′ *[x x]-ni mu-šá-[x x x x x x x]*
6′ *[iq]-ṭi-bi [x x x x x x x x]*
7′ *[x x]x aš-šu[r x x* É$^{?}$—*k]u*$^{?}$*-tal-li*
8′ *[x x x]* EN-⌜*ú*$^{?}$⌝-*[tú x x x x]-u-ni*
9′ *[x x x x x x x x x x]-ti*
10′ *[x x x x x x x x x x]x-ti*
11′ *[x x x x x x x x x x]x gab-bi*
12′ *[x x x x x x x x x x]-u-ni*
rest broken away

CT 53 475

(Beginning destroyed)
1 [...... wi]th the king, my lord
2 [......] *upon*
3 [......] *terrible*
4 [......] scribe
(Break)

r.1 *his* [...] *before* [......]
2 [which] I am hauling [...]
3 [...] ... [...]
4 [.. the kin]g, my lord [...]
5 [...] ... [...]
6 [s]aid [......]
7 [...] Aššu[r ... *the R*]*ear* [*Palace*]
8 [...] lord*s*[*hip* ...]
(Rest destroyed or too broken for translation)

218. Who is This Goldsmith?

K 13123

1 *[a-na* LUGAL EN-*ia]*
2 [ARAD-*ka* ^{m}*x x x x*]
3 *[lu* DI]*-mu a-na* MAN [EN-*ia*]
4 ⌜^{d}⌝PA *ù* ^{d}AMA[R.UTU]
5 *a-na* LUGAL EN-*i[a]*
6 *lik-ru-bu* [0]
7 *ina* UGU LÚ*.SIMUG.KUG.[GI]
8 *ša* LUGAL *iq-bu-[u-ni]*
9 *ma-a man-nu šu-[ú]*
10 ⌜*i x x x*⌝ *[x x x]*
rest broken away
Rev. completely broken away

CT 53 488

1 [To the king, my lord: your servant PN. Good hea]lth to the king, [my lord]! May Nabû and Mar[duk] bless the king, m[y] lord.

7 As to the go[ld]smith about whom the king sai[d]: "Who is he?"

(Rest destroyed)

219. ———

K 14604

Obv. completely broken away
r.1 *[x x a]-na-ku am-[x x]*
2 *[x x x x]* LUGAL *be-[lí]*
3 *[x x x-i]a it-tu-b[il]*
4 *[ma-a x x-k]a is-si-k[a]*
5 *[x x x]-it li-te-[x]*
6 *[x x x x]-li is-sa-ka[n]*

CT 53 539

(Beginning destroyed)
r.1 [...] I [...]
2 [...] the king, [my] lo[rd], broug[ht] (me) my [..., saying: "*Let* yo]ur [...] with you!"
6 [*The king*], *my* [*lor*]*d* pla[c]ed

7 [*x x x*] *ša šu-u*[*n-x*]
8 [*x x x x x*] *e-mur-u-*[*ni*]
9 [*x x x* LUGAL *be-l*]*í lu* [*ú-di*?]
10 [*x x x x x-l*]*i-k*[*u* 0?]
11 [*x x x x x x x*]*x* [*x*]
rest broken away

7 [...] of ...
8 [... *which* I] saw
9 [... The king], my [lor]d, should [*know it*].
(Rest destroyed)

220. ———

K 15328

beginning broken away
1′ [*x x x x x x x*]*x* ⸢*x-a*⸣*-šu*
2′ [*x x*] ⸢*an-ni-ú*⸣ *šu-u*
Edge uninscribed
r.1 [*x x x x x x x x*]*x a—dan-niš*
2′ [*x x x x x x x x*].MEŠ
rest broken away

CT 53 643

(Too broken for translation)

221. ———

K 15386

beginning broken away
1′ *lu-b*[*i-la*? *x x x x x*]
2′ *an-na-ka* [*x x x x x*]
3′ *liš-ši-a x*[*x x x x x*]
4′ *ša* LUGA[L *x x x x x*]
e.5′ ⸢*a-na*⸣ [*x x x x x x*]
Rev. completely broken away

CT 53 654

(Beginning destroyed)
1 Let *him br*[*ing* ......]
2 here [......]
3 let him *take* [......]
4 of/which the kin[g ......]
5 to [......]
(Rest destroyed)

222. ———

K 15387

beginning broken away
1′ [*x x x x ina* UG]U LUGAL ⸢EN⸣-[*ia*]
2′ [*x x x x a-n*]*a šul-me*
3′ [*x x x* LUGAL EN-*i*]⸢*a*⸣ *a-ta-mar*
4′ [*x x x x x* LUGA]L EN-*ia*
5′ [*x x x x x x x*]*x*
rest broken away
Rev. beginning broken away
1′ [*x x x x x x*] ⸢TA⸣ IGI ⸢LÚ*?⸣.[*x x*]
2′ [*x x x x x x x*]*x-tú*
3′ [*x x x x x x a-n*]*a* LUGAL
rest broken away

CT 53 655

(Beginning destroyed)
1 [...... to] the king, [my] lord
2 [...... *t*]*o greet* [...]
3 I saw the [... of the king, m]y [lord]
4 [...... the kin]g, my lord
(Break)
r.1 [......] *because of* [......]
3 [...... t]o the king
(Rest destroyed)

223. It is a Royal Order

K 15414

beginning broken away
1′ [*x x x x*] ⸢*x x*⸣ [*x x x x*]
2′ [*x x x x*]*x* IGI.2.ME ^{m}*x*[*x x x*]
3′ [*x x m*]*a-a a-bat* LUGAL *ši*-[*ti*]
4′ [*x x x*]-*an-ni ša an*$^{?}$-[*x x x*]
5′ [*x x x x x*] ⸢*x*⸣ [*x x x x*]
rest broken away
Rev. completely broken away

CT 53 669

(Beginning destroyed)
2 [...] eyes [...]
3 [...] He said: “It is a royal order
4 [...] *me* ... [...]
(Rest destroyed)

224. ———

K 15621

beginning broken away
1′ 1 [*x x x x x x x x*]
2′ *a*-[*x x x x x x x x*]
3′ ⸢*x*⸣ [*x x x x x x x x*]
4′ ⸢*x*⸣ [*x x x x x x x x*]
e.5′ ⸢*x*⸣ *x*[*x x x x x x x x*]
r.1 *mu-x*[*x x x x x x x x*]
2 [*a*]-*na* ⸢LÚ*⸣.[*x x x x x x x*]
3 [*x*] *qa x*[*x x x x x x x*]
4 [LU]GAL *x*[*x x x x x x x*]
5 [*r*]*a*$^{?}$-*mì-ni* [*x x x x x x x*]
6 ⸢*i*⸣-*si*-[*x x x x x x x x*]
7 [*x*]*x x*[*x x x x x x x x*]
rest broken away

CT 53 688

(Too broken for translation)

225. Sold for Money

K 15632

beginning broken away
1′ [*x x x*]*x-šú-ni ma-a a-ta-a x*[*x x x x*]
2′ [*x x*] *ša* É—EN.MEŠ-*ia ina kas-pi x*[*x x x*]
3′ [*x x*] ⸢*i*⸣-*sa-par i-sa-kan it-t*[*al-ka x x x*]
4′ [*x x x x*] ⸢*x x*⸣ *ma-a* [*x x x x x*]
rest broken away
Rev. completely broken away

CT 53 690

(Beginning destroyed)
1 [...] saying, “Why [*has* ... *sold* the ...] *of* my lord’s household for money[...?]”
3 [...] sent, placed, and ca[me ...]
4 [......] saying, “[......]”
(Rest destroyed)

226. ———

K 15639

1 [*x x x x x x x x* LUG]AL
2 [*x x x x x x x x* ^{d}]PA
3 [*x x x x x x x x-n*]*u-ú*
4 [*x x x x x x x x*]-*u-ni*
5 [*x x x x x x x x*]-*nu-šú-u-ni*

CT 53 696

1 [...... the ki]ng
2 [......] Nabû
(Rest destroyed or too broken for translation)

6 [*x x x x x x x*]-*a*? *a*[*k*?-*x*]
7 [*x x x x x x x*] *x*[*x*]
8 [*x x x x x x x*]-*u*?-*n*[*i*]
9 [*x x x x x x x x*]*x* [*x*]
rest broken away
Rev. as far as preserved, uninscribed

227. ———

K 15641

beginning broken away
1′ 5 *x*[*x x x x x x*]
2′ PAB *an-ni*-[*x x x x x*]
3′ *ša i-x*[*x x x x x x*]
4′ ⸢*ta*? *x*⸣ *x*[*x x x x x*]
rest broken away
Rev. as far as preserved, uninscribed

CT 53 698

(Beginning destroyed)
1 5 [......]
2 all this [......]
3 *that* [......]
(Rest destroyed)

228. ———

K 15654

1 [*a-na* LUGAL *be-lí-ia*]
2 ⸢ARAD-*ka*⸣ [^{m}*x x x x*]
3 *lu* DI-*mu* ⸢*a*⸣-[*na* LUGAL *be-lí-ia*]
4 ^{m}*kab-ti-i* [*x x x x x*]
5 *iq-ṭí-bi* [*ma-a x x x x*]
6 *ma-a ša da*-[*x x x x x*]
rest broken away
Rev. completely broken away

CT 53 705

1 [To the king, my lord]: your servant [PN]. Good health t[o the king, my lord]!

4 Kabtî [...] has said: "[......]
(Rest destroyed)

229. We Shall Stay Awake

K 15681

beginning broken away
1′ [*x x x x x x x*]*x-li*
2′ [*x x x x x x*] *ni-da-lip*
3′ [*x x x x x x*]-*te*-⸢*x*⸣-*li*
one line obliterated
Edge uninscribed
r.1 [*x x x x x x*]*x an x*[*x*]
2 [*x x x x x x x*] ITI
3 [*x x x x x x x*]-*sa-su*
4 [*x x x x x x x*] ⸢*x*⸣
5 [*x x x x x x x x*]-*is*?
6 [*x x x x x x x x*] ⸢*a*?⸣
rest broken away

CT 53 713

(Beginning destroyed)

2 [......] we shall stay awake
(Break)

r.2 [......] month
3 [......] him
(Rest destroyed)

230. ———

K 15683

Obv. completely broken away
e.1′ [*ša ina p*]*a-ni-it-t*[*i*]
r.1 [0 LUGA]L *be-lí*
2 [*iš-pu*]*r-an-ni*
3 [*x x x*]*x x*[*x x*]
rest broken away

CT 53 714

(Beginning destroyed)
1 [Concerning what the kin]g, my lord, [pr]eviousl[y wrot]e to me [......]
(Rest destroyed)

231. Fragment of a Military Report

K 16060

beginning broken away
1′ [*x x x x x x* LÚ*.*ka*]*l-lab*.MEŠ
2′ [*x x x x x x x x x*]-*u*$^{?}$-*ni*
3′ [*x x x x x x x x* K]ASKAL.MEŠ
4′ [*x x x x x x x x x*] *qa-a-lu* [0]
5′ [*x x x x x x x x š*]*a-an-hu-ṣ*[*u*]
6′ [*x x x x x x x x x*]-*i-te* [0]
7′ [*x x x x x x x x x x*] *ma* [(*x*)]
rest broken away
Rev. beginning broken away
1′ [*x x x x x*] *i-x*[*x x x*]
2′ [*x x x x*]-*šá-ba e-tab-ku-šú-nu*
3′ [*x x x x x*]*x ma-zi-i*
4′ [*x x x x x*]*x-da*
5′ [*x x x x x*]*x-ši*
rest broken away

CT 53 735

(Beginning destroyed)
1 [...... *out*]*riders*
2 [......]
3 [...... *r*]*oads*
4 [......] they are silent
5 [......] the[y] are [*pr*]*ovoked to fight*
(Break)

r.2 [......] *they led them in*
3 [......] *tureen*(*s*) [......]
(Rest destroyed)

232. ———

K 16084

beginning broken away
1′ [*x x x x*]-*ia qar-b*[*a-x x*]
2′ [*x x x x*] ZÍD$^{?}$.DA PAB 3 [*x x x*]
3′ [*x x x x*] ⌈*x x*⌉ *qa-ti x*[*x x x*]
4′ [*x x x x x i*]*na* URU.BÀ[D—*x x*]
5′ [*x x x x x x*]*x ina* URU.[*x x x*]
6′ [*x x x x x x*]-⌈*u-ni*⌉ [*x x x*]
rest broken away
Rev. completely broken away

CT 53 744

(Beginning destroyed)
1 [...] *my* [...]
2 [...] *flour*, in all three [...]
3 [...] *hand* [...]
4 [... i]n Du[r-...]
5 [...] in the city [...]
(Rest destroyed)

231 4 Or: “passive/inactive.” r.2 Or: “they drove/kept them away.”

233. Let them Learn!

K 16092

beginning broken away
1′ [*x x x x x x*]-*šú-nu*
2′ [*x x x x x x*]*x-ni*
3′ [*x x x x x x*]*x-nu*
e.4′ [*x x x x x x*]*x*—DÙ
a blank space of two lines
r.1 [*x x x x x x*]*x-te-šú-nu x*[*x*]-*u-nu*
2 [*x x x x x x*]*x lil-mu-du*
3 [*x x x x x x*] *a-na-ku* 1
4 [*x x x x x x*].MEŠ
5 [*x x x x x* K]Á.GAL
6 [*x x x x x x*] ⸢*x x*⸣.MEŠ
rest broken away

CT 53 749

(Beginning destroyed)
1 [......] *them*
(Break)

r.1 [...] their [...]s [...]
2 [......] *let them learn*
3 [......] I one
4 [......]s
5 [...... city g]ate
6 [......]s
(Rest destroyed)

234. ———

K 16099

beginning broken away
1′ *ša* L[UGAL *be-lí*]
2′ *iš-p*[*ur-an-ni*]
3′ *ma-a* [*x x x x*]
4′ *i*-[*x x x x*]
5′ *ia*-[*x x x x*]
Edge uninscribed
r.1 *dul-l*[*u x x x*]
2 *e*-[*pa-áš x x*]
3 LUGAL [*x x x x*]
4 *lu*-⸢*ú*⸣ [*x x x*]
rest uninscribed

CT 53 755

(Beginning destroyed)
1 [...] about which the k[ing, my lord] wro[te me]: "[......]."

r.1 [I am] d[oing] the wor[k]. The king, [*my lord*], can [*be at ease*].

235. ———

K 16100

beginning broken away
1′ ⸢*li*⸣-[*x x x x x x x*]
2′ UD.MEŠ [*x x x x x x x*]
3′ *a-na* [*x x x x x x*]
4′ *ib*-[*x x x x x x x*]
5′ *ú*-[*x x x x x x x*]
6′ *ki*-[*x x x x x x x*]
7′ *ú-x*[*x x x x x x x*]
8′ ⸢*ú*⸣-[*x x x x x x x*]
rest broken away
Rev. beginning broken away
1′ ^{m}DINGIR—⸢*ú*$^{?}$⸣-[*x x x x*]
2′ *ina* É *x*[*x x x x x x x*]
rest uninscribed

CT 53 758

(Beginning destroyed)
2 days [......]
(Break)
r.1 Ilu-[......]

236. A Haruspex and Sheep

K 16476

beginning broken away
1′ [*x x x x x x*] ˹LUGAL˺ *be*-˹*lí*˺
2′ [*x x x x ina* UG]U LÚ.HAL
3′ [*ša* LUGAL *be-lí i*]*š-pur-an-ni*
4′ [*x x x x* UDU.*k*]*ab*$^{?}$*-su*
5′ [*x x x x x*]*-me* UDU.MEŠ
6′ [*x x x x x*] *a-ta-na-áš-šú*
7′ [*x x x x x*] ˹*lu* 50$^{?!}$˺*-šú*
rest broken away
Rev. as far as preserved, uninscribed

CT 53 764

(Beginning destroyed)
1 [......] the king, my lord.
2 [*Concerning the*] haruspex
3 [about whom the king, my lord, w]rote to me,
4 [... x] old male sheep
5 [... x] hundred sheep
6 [...] I gave him
(Rest destroyed)

237. ———

K 16485

beginning broken away
1′ [*x x x x x*] ˹*x-pat*˺
2′ [*x x x x-p*]*u-uš*
3′ [*x x x x x*]*x pu-ut*
4′ [*x x x x x*] *šu-ú*
5′ [*x x x x x*]*-lak*
e.6′ [*x x x x x*]*-za*
r.1 [*is—s*]*u-ri*
2 [LUGAL *be-l*]*í i-qab-bi*
3 [*ma-a x*] ˹*a*˺*-a-im-ma*
4 [*x x x ep*]*-pu-šú*
5 [*x x x x x x*]*x*
6 [*x x x x x x*]*x*
7 [*x x x x x x*]*x*
rest broken away

CT 53 772

(Beginning destroyed)

3 [...] *opposite*
4 [...] he (is)
5 [... *we*]*nt*
5 [.......]
r.1 [Per]haps [the king], my [lord], will say: "[*With*] *whom* are they [d]oing [the work]?"
(Rest destroyed)

238. ———

K 16492

beginning broken away
1′ [*x x x x x x*] ˹*x*˺ [*x x x x*]
2′ [*x x x x x x x*]*x-li*[*k x x x x*]
3′ [*x x x x x a-n*]*a* LUGA[L *x x x x*]
e.4′ [*x x x x x x*]*x li-in-*[*x x x x x*]
rest broken away
Rev. completely broken away

CT 53 776

(Beginning destroyed)

3 [... t]o the kin[g, my lord ......]
(Rest destroyed)

239. Fragment Mentioning a Bed

K 16527

beginning broken away
1′ ˹*ina* UGU˺ *x*[*x x x x x*]
2′ *ú-la-b*[*a*$^{?}$*-x x x x*]

CT 53 792

(Beginning destroyed)
1 Concerning [......]

3′ *lu la* ⌜*i*⌝-[*x x x x*]
4′ *qa-di-t*⌜*u*?⌝ [*x x x x*]
5′ *ša šu-r*[*u-x x x x*]
Edge broken away
r.1 *ši-i* [*x x x x x*]
2 GIŠ.NÁ [*x x x x x*]
3 *x*[*x x x x x x*]
rest broken away

2 he *dres*[*ses* ......]
3 may *he* not [......]
4 ... [......]
5 *which* [......]
r.1 *she* [......]
2 the bed [......]
(Rest broken away)

240. ———

Sm 354

beginning broken away
1′ [*x x x x*]*x-ra-a-a* [*x x x*]
2′ [*x x x x*]*-hi-mu x*[*x x x x*]
3′ [*x x x* L]Ú.*ma*-[*x x x x*]
4′ [*x x x x*]*-lak-ti* [*x x x x*]
5′ [*x x x* KAS]KAL *lit-bal x*[*x x x x*]
6′ [*x x x x*]*x ú ma* [*x x x x*]
7′ [*x x x x x*] *ti* [*x x x x*]
rest broken away
Rev. completely broken away

CT 53 815

(Too broken for translation)

241. ———

Sm 2190

beginning broken away
1′ [*x x x x x x x*] *a*-⌜*ta*?⌝-[*a*?]
2′ [*x x x x x x x x-k*]*a*
3′ [*x x x x x x x*]*x* GUD
4′ [*x x x x x x x*] *ú-ma-a*
5′ [*x x x x x x x*]*-ga-ma*
6′ [*x x x x x x x x*]*x x*[*x*]
rest broken away
Rev. completely broken away

CT 53 860

(Beginning destroyed)
1 [......] *why*
3 [......] an ox
4 [......] now
(Rest destroyed)

242. Reporting the Deficit of Silver

82-5-22,155

Obv. completely broken away
Rev. beginning broken away
1′ LU⌜GAL?⌝ *b*[*e-lí x x is—su-ri*]
2′ LUGAL EN *i*-[*qa-bi ma-a a-ta-a*]
3′ LAL-*e ša* ⌜KUG.UD⌝ [*x x x x*]
4′ *la taš-pu-ra* [*x x x x*]
5′ *i-na* ŠÀ-*bi* ⌜*i*⌝-[*x x x x*]
6′ *i-na* ŠÀ-*bi e-p*[*u-šu x x x*]
7′ *ki-ma an-te-se ú-ṣa-*[*ri-pi* 0]

CT 53 922

(Beginning destroyed)

r.1 the king, [my] l[ord, ... Perhaps] the king, my lord, wi[ll say: "Why] have you not written about the deficit of silver [...]?"

5 [......] *there*

6 [They are] work[ing] *there* [...].

7 After I have washed (and) purif[ied] (the

240 4 Either *tallaktu* or *alaktu*.
242 r.7ff → Deller and Mayer, Or. 53 (1984) 85; Radner in Dercksen (ed.), *Trade and Finance in Ancient*

8′ LAL-*e ša* KUG.UD *a-na* LUG[AL EN-*ia*]
9′ *ú-ša-áš-ma*
rest uninscribed

silver), I will notify the kin[g, my lord], about the deficit of silver.

243. A Battle and a Treaty

83-1-18,268

beginning broken away
1′ *x*[*x x x x x x x x x x*]
2′ *mu*-⸢*uk*⸣ [*x x x x x x x x x*]
3′ *ni-du-uk-šú-nu* ⸢*x*⸣[*x x x x x*]
4′ *is-su-uh-ra u an*-[*x x x x x*]
5′ *a-na* LUGAL EN-*ia* [*x x x x*]
6′ LÚ.ERIM.MEŠ-*e ša* LUGA[L EN-*ia x x*]
7′ *ke-e-tu a-na-ku* [*x x x x x*]
8′ *as-sap*-[*ra x x x x x x x x*]
rest broken away
Rev. beginning broken away
1′ 1-*en* [*x x x x x x x x x x*]
2′ *qa-ra-b*[*u x x x x x x x x x*]
3′ LÚ*.*e-mu-qi ša* [*x x x x x*]
4′ *ina* UGU *an-ni-e* LUGA[L *x x x x x*]
5′ 30 *a-ni-nu* [*x x x x x*]
6′ *a-de-e is-sa-he-iš* [*is-sak-nu*]
7′ *ma a-du* LUGAL KUR—*aš-šur*.[KI *x x x x*]
8′ [*x x x x*]-⸢*nu mi*⸣-[*x x x x x*]
rest broken away

CT 53 935

(Beginning destroyed)
2 I said: "[......]
3 We shall kill them [......]
4 has returned, *but* [......]
5 to the king, my lord, [...]
6 [*Are they*] men of the kin[g, my lord]?
7 In truth, I have sen[t ......]
(Break)
r.1 one [......]
2 battl[e ......]
3 the troops of [the ......]
4 On account on this the kin[g ...]
5 We are 30 [......]
6 [They have made a] treaty with one another,
7 saying: "*As long* as the king of Assyria [...]
(Rest destroyed)

244. ———

Ki 1904-10-9,216 (BM 99184)

beginning broken away
1′ [*x*] *x*[*x x x x x x x*]
2′ ⸢*ú*?⸣-*ka*-[*x x x x x*]
3′ [*x*]-*na a-x*[*x x x x x*]
4′ [*a*]*n-ni-u* ⸢*ú*?⸣-[*x x x x*]
Rev. completely broken away

CT 53 978

(Too broken for translation)

245. ———

K 16550

beginning broken away
1′ [*x x šá*?]-*ni*-⸢*ú*⸣-*t*[*e x x x*]
2′ [*x x l*]*a nu-da* ⸢*ú*⸣-[*ma-a*]
3′ [*an-nu-r*]*ig* LUGAL *x*[*x x x*]
4′ [*x x ṣ*]*a-lam x*[*x x x x*]
rest broken away
Rev. broken away

K 16550

(Beginning destroyed)
1 [... the *o*]*ther* ones [...]
2 [...] we do [n]ot know. N[ow the]n, the king
4 [... i]mage [......]
(Rest destroyed)

Mesopotamia (1999), 133.
245 Small fragment from centre. Previously unpublished; copy p. 217. [1] Or *pa*]-*ni-u-te*, "the previous ones."

246. ———

K 20565

1 *a-na* LUG[AL *be-lí-ia*]
2 *dan-niš* [*dan-niš lu-u šul-mu*]
3 ⸢d⸣P[A *x x x x x x x x x*]
rest broken away
Rev. broken away

K 20565

1 The very [best of health] to the kin[g, my lord!]

2 [May] Na[bû ......]

(Rest destroyed)

246 Small fragment from top left-hand corner. Previously unpublished; copy p. 217. 1f For the restorations cf. SAA 1 133:1-3 and SAA 10 249.6.

GLOSSARY AND INDICES

Logograms and Their Readings

A → *mar'u;* A—LUGAL, A—MAN → *mār šarri;* A.ŠÀ → *eqlu;* AD → *abu;* AD—AD → *ab abi;* AMA → *ummu;* AMA—LUGAL → *ummi šarri;* AN → *šamê;* AN.BAR → *parzillu;* ANŠE.KUR.RA → *sissû;* ANŠE.NITÁ → *imāru;* ARAD → *urdu;* Á, Á.2 → *ahu B;* Á.SÌG → *asakku;*

BÀD → *dūru;* BALA → *palû;* BARAG → *parakku;* BÁR.SIPA.KI → *Barsip;* BE → *bēlu;* BUR.GUL → *parkullu;* BURU$_5$ → *erbiu;*

^{d}AG, ${}^{d+}$AG → *Nabû;* ^{d}AMAR.UTU → *Marduk;* ^{d}BE → *Illil;* ^{d}DI.KUD → *Madānu;* ^{d}EN, ${}^{d+}$EN → *Bēl;* ^{d}É.A → *Ēa;* ^{d}GAŠAN → *Bēlet,* ^{d}IM → *Adad;* ^{d}MAŠ → *Inūrta;* ^{d}MES → *Marduk;* ^{d}NIN.GAL → *Nikkal;* ^{d}NIN.LÍL → *Mullissu;* ^{d}NIN.URTA → *Inūrta;* ^{d}PA → *Nabû;* ^{d}PA.TÚG → *Nušku;* ^{d}ŠÚ → *Marduk;* ^{d}U.GUR → *Nergal;* ^{d}UTU → *Šamaš, šamšu;* ^{d}ZA.BA$_4$.BA$_4$ → *Zabāba;* ^{d}15 → *Issār;* ^{d}30 → *Sîn;* ^{d}60 → *Nabû;*

DAG.GAZ → *takkassu;* DI → *šulmu;* DINGIR → *ilu;* DU → *alāku;* DUB → *ṭuppu;* DÙG, DÙG.GA → *ṭiābu;* DUG$_4$.DUG$_4$ → *dabābu;* DUMU → *mar'u;* DUMU—DUMU → *mār mar'i;* DUMU—É.GAL → *mār ekalli;* DUMU—KÁ.DINGIR.KI → *Bābili;* DUMU—LUGAL, DUMU—MAN → *mār šarri;* DUMU.MÍ → *mar'utu;* DUMU.MÍ—LUGAL → *mar'at šarri;* DUMU.ŠU.SI → *mār banê;* DÙ → *kalu;*

EDIN → *ṣēru;* EME → *lišānu;* EN → *adi, bēl, bēlu, Bēl;;* EN—É → *bēl bēti;* EN.LÍL.KI → *Nippur;* EN—MUN → *bēl ṭābti;* EN.NAM → *pāhutu;* EN.NUN → *maṣṣartu;* ERIM → *ṣābu;* ERIM—É.GAL → *ṣāb ekalli;* ÉŠ.QAR → *iškāru;* É → *bēt, bētu;* É—AD → *bēt abi;* É—DINGIR → *bēt ili;* É—EN → *bēt bēli;* É.GAL → *ekallu;* É—GIBIL → *bētu eššu;* É.SIG$_4$ → *igāru;* É.ŠÁR.RA → *Ešarra;* É—ŠU.2 → *bēt qāti;* É—UŠ → *bēt rēdūti;* É—1-*te* → *bēt issēte;*

GADA → *kitû;* GAG → *sikkutu;* GAL → *rabû;* GAL—MÁŠ → *rab ṣibti;* GAL—NÍG.ŠID → *rab nikkassi;* GAŠAN—É → *bēlat bēti;* GEMÉ → *amtu;* GEŠTIN → *karānu;* GIBIL → *eššu;* GÍD, GÍD.DA → *arāku;* GIN → *kuānu;* GÍN → *šiqlu;* GÍR, GÍR.AN.BAR → *patru;* GÍR.TUR → *uṣultu;* GÌR.2 → *šēpu;* GIŠ → *iṣu;* GIŠ.BANŠUR → *paššūru;* GIŠ.DA → *lē'u;* GIŠ.ERIN.BAD → *supuhru;* GIŠ.GEŠTIN → *karānu;* GIŠ.GIGIR → *mugirru;* GIŠ.GU.ZA → *kussiu;* GIŠ.IG → *dassu;* GIŠ.KIN.GEŠTIN → *ishunnutu;* GIŠ.LI.U$_5$.UM → *lē'u;* GIŠ.MÁ → *eleppu;* GIŠ.MI → *ṣillu;* GIŠ.NÁ → *eršu;* GIŠ.PA → *haṭṭu;* GIŠ.SAR → *kiriu;* GIŠ.ŠÚ → *šibšutu;* GIŠ.ZU → *lē'u;* GU.ZA → *kussiu;* GUD → *alpu;* GÚ → *kišādu, libānu;* GÚ.UN → *biltu;*

HAR → *sabirru;*

ÍD → *nāru;* IGI → *pānu;* IGI.2 → *ēnu;* IM → *ṭuppu;* IM.GÍD, IM.GÍD.DA → *liginnu;* ITI → *urhu;* ITI.AB → *kanūnu;* ITI.APIN → *arahsamnu;* ITI.BARAG → *nisannu;* ITI.DU$_6$ → *tašrītu;* ITI.GUD → *aiāru;* ITI.KIN → *elūlu;* ITI.SIG$_4$ → *simānu;* ITI.ŠE → *addāru;* ITI.ŠU → *tamūzu;* ITI.ZÍZ → *šabāṭu;*

KALAG → *danānu;* KAR → *kāru;* KASKAL, KASKAL.2 → *harrānu, hūlu;* KÁ.DINGIR.KI, KÁ.DINGIR.RA.KI → *Bābili;* KÁ.GAL → *abullu;* KI.LAL → *šuqultu;* KI.LAM → *mahīru;* KI.MIN → *šanīš;* KI.TA → *šapal;* KI.TIM → *kaqquru;* KUG.GI → *hurāṣu;* KUG.UD → *ṣarpu;* KUR, KUR.KUR → *mātu;* KUR.NIM.KI, KUR.NIM.MA, KUR.NIM.MA.KI → *Elamtu;* KUR—URI → *Urarṭu;* KUR—URI.KI → *Māt Akkadî;* KUŠ.DA.E.SÍR → *maš'ennu?;* KÙŠ → *ammutu;* KÚ → *akālu;*

LAL → *muṭê;* LUGAL → *šarru, šarrūtu;* LÚ → *amēlu;* LÚ.A.BA → *ṭupšarru;* LÚ.A.BA—É.GAL, LÚ.A.BA—KUR → *ṭupšar ekalli;* LÚ.A.BA.URU → *ṭupšar āli;* LÚ.A—KIN → *mār šipri;* LÚ.A—SIG → *mār damqi;* LÚ.A—SIG$_5$ → *mār damqi;* LÚ.A.ZU → *asû;* LÚ.AB.BA → *paršumu;* LÚ.ARAD → *urdu;* LÚ.BUR.GUL → *parkullu;* LÚ.DAM.QAR → *tamkāru;* LÚ.DIB—PA → *mukīl appāti;* LÚ.DUB.SAR → *ṭupšarru;* LÚ.EN—DÙG.GA → *bēl ṭābtūtu;* LÚ.EN—GIŠ.GIGIR → *bēl mugirri;* LÚ.EN.NAM → *pāhutu;* LÚ.EN—URU → *bēl āli;* LÚ.ENGAR → *ikkāru;* LÚ.ERIM → *ṣābu;* LÚ.ERIM—GIŠ.BAN → *ṣāb qassi;* LÚ.GAL → *rabiu;* LÚ.GAL—A.BA → *rab ṭupšarri;* LÚ.GAL—É → *rab bēti;* LÚ.GAL—É.GAL → *rab ekalli;* LÚ.GAL—KA.KÉŠ → *rab kāṣiri;* LÚ.GAL—KAR → *rab kāri;* LÚ.GAL—KUR → *rab ekalli;* LÚ.GAL—MU → *rab nuhatimmi;* LÚ.GAL—NÍG.ŠID → *rab nikkassi;* LÚ.GAL—NINDA → *rab āpie;* LÚ.GAL—SAG → *rab ša-rēši;* LÚ.GAL—TIN → *rab etinnāti;* LÚ.GAL—URU → *rab ālāni;* LÚ.GAR, LÚ.GAR.KUR

→ *šaknu;* LÚ.GIŠ.GIGIR → *sūsānu;* LÚ.GUB.BA → *mazzāz pāni;* LÚ.HAL → *bārû;* LÚ.IGI → *ša-pān;* LÚ.IGI.DUB → *masennu;* LÚ.Ì.DU$_8$ → *atû;* LÚ.KAŠ.LUL → *šāqiu;* LÚ.KÚR → *nakru;* LÚ.LUL → *parrisu;* LÚ.MAH → *ṣīru;* LÚ.MUŠEN.DÙ → *ušandû;* LÚ.NAM → *pāhutu;* LÚ.NAR → *nuāru;* LÚ.NAR.GAL → *nargallu;* LÚ.NIM.MA → *Elamtu;* LÚ.NINDA → *āpiu;* LÚ.NU.GIŠ.SAR → *nukaribbu;* LÚ.PA → *ša-huṭāri;* LÚ.SAG → *ša-rēši;* LÚ.SAG.DU → *kaqqudu;* LÚ.SANGA → *sangû;* LÚ.SIMUG—AN.BAR → *nappāh parzilli;* LÚ.SIMUG.KUG.GI → *ṣarrāpu;* LÚ.SIPA → *rā'iu;* LÚ.SUKKAL → *sukkallu;* LÚ.TUR → *ṣehru;* LÚ.URU → *ālāiu;* LÚ.UŠ.BAR → *ušpār ṣiprāti, ušpāru;* LÚ.ÚŠ → *pagru;* LÚ.3, LÚ.3.U$_5$ → *tašlīšu, tašlīšūtu;*

MA.NA → *manû;* MAN → *šarru;* MÍ → *issu B;* MÍ.AMA—MAN → *ummi šarri;* MÍ.ANŠE → *atānu;* MÍ—É.GAL → *sēgallu* MÍ.É.GI$_4$.A → *kallutu;* MÍ—KUR → *sēgallu;* MÍ.TUR → *ṣahurtu;* MU → *šumu;* MU.AN.NA → *šattu;* MU.IM.MA → *šaddaqdiš;* MUL → *kakkubu;* MUL.GAG.SI.SÁ → *Šukūdu;* MUL.SAG.ME.GAR → *Sagmegar;* MUN → *ṭābtu;* MURUB$_4$ → *qablu;*

NAM.MUŠEN → *erbiu;* NA$_4$ → *abnu;* NA$_4$.BABBAR.DIL → *pappardaliu;* NA$_4$.IGI.ZAG.GA → *igizaggû;* NA$_4$.ŠU.GUR → *unqu;* NÍG.ŠID → *nikkassu;* NIM → *elītu;* NIN → *ahātu;* NINA.KI → *Nīnuwa;* NINDA, NINDA.HI.A → *kusāpu;* NUMUN → *zar'u;*

PAB → *ahu, gimru;* PI.2 → *uznu;*

QÀL → *qallu;*

SAG → *rēšu;* SAG.DU → *kaqqad Pazūzi;* SÍG → *šāptu;* SÍG.MI → *šāptu ṣalimtu;* SÍG.SA$_5$ → *šāptu sāntu;* SÍG.ZA.GÌN.MI → *ṣalittu;* SIG$_4$ → *libittu;* SIG$_5$ → *damāqu;* SIPA → *rā'iu;* SUHUŠ → *išdu;* SUM → *tadānu;*

ŠÀ → *libbu;* ŠE → *še'u;* ŠE.GIG → *kibtu;* ŠE.GIŠ.Ì → *šamaššammi;* ŠE.NUMUN → *zar'u;* ŠE.PAD → *kurummutu;* ŠE.ZÍZ → *kunāšu;* ŠEŠ → *ahu;* ŠEŠ—AD → *ah abi;* ŠU → *qātu;* ŠU.BA.TI → *laqû;* ŠU.SI → *ubānu;* ŠU.2 → *qātu;* ŠÚ → *kiššatu;*

TA → *issi/u;* TI, TI.LA, TIN → *balāṭu;* TIN.TIR.KI → *Bābili;* TU → *erābu;* TÚG.BAR.DIB → *kusītu;* TÚG.GÚ.È → *nahlaptu;* TUR → *ṣahāru;* TÙR → *tarbāṣu;*

U → *bēlu;* UD → *ūmu;* UD.KIB.NUN.KI → *Sippar;* UDU → *immeru;* UDU.MÍ.ÁŠ.GÀR → *unīqu;* UDU.NITÁ → *iābilu;* UDU.SISKUR → *niqiu;* UGU → *muhhu;* UMBIN → *magarru;* UN → *nīšī;* UNUG.KI → *Uruk;* UR.KU → *kalbu;* URU → *ālu;* URU.HAL.ṢU → *bīrtu;* URU.KASKAL, URU.KASKAL.KI, URU.KASKAL.2 → *Harrānu;* URU.NINA, URU.NINA.KI → *Nīnuwa;* URU.ŠÀ—URU → *Libbi āli;* URU.ŠE → *kapru;* ÙR → *ūru;* ÚŠ → *dāmu, muātu;* UZU → *šīru;* UZU.Á.2 → *ahu B;* UZU.GÚ → *kišādu, libānu;*

ZI → *napšutu;* ZÍD.DA → *qēmu;* ZU → *lē'u;*

1 → *issēn, issēt;* 2 → *šaniu B, šinīšu;* 3 → *šalšu, šallussu;*

10 → *ešer;*

15 → *imittu;*

20 → *ešrā;*

30 → *šalāšā;*

40 → *erbā;*

50 → *hanšā;*

80 → *samānā;*

150 → *šumēlu;*

Glossary

abāku "to drive away, to lead in; (vent.) to fetch": *a-ba-ak-ka* 121:11, *e-tab-ku-šú-nu* 231 r. 2, *a-bu-uk* 11 r. 4, *li-b]u-ku-u-niš-šú-nu* 90 r. 13,

abat šarri "king's word, royal intervention": *a-bat—šar-ra-a-te* 64:1, see also *amatu,*

abbūtu "intercession": *ab-bu-ti* 52 r. 8,

abnu "stone": NA$_4$.MEŠ 60 s. 1,

abu "father": [A]D 96:9, AD-*ia* 34:10, 18, r. 12, 35:6, 53:12, 60 r. 7, AD-*ka* 30:5, 32 r. 8, 34:5, r. 14, 35 r. 7, 45:5, 60:5, 61:5, 201:3, AD-*k*]*a* 33 r. 2, AD-[*ka* 59:4, AD]-*ka* 59:4, A]D-*k*[*a* 60:5, [AD]-*ka* 96:8, AD.MEŠ-*ka* 77 r. 6, 151 r. 5, AD-*šú* 63:12, A]D-*šú* 71 r. 3, AD-*u-a* 12:4, 34 r. 13, 45:3, 56:3, r. 10, AD-*u-ka* 59:10, AD-*ú-a* 34:8, 105:14, e. 22,

abullu "(city) gate": KÁ.GAL 54 r. 3, 59 r. 6, 95 r. 5, 100 r. 10, 11, K]Á.GAL 233 r. 5, KÁ.GAL.MEŠ 133:8,

abutu "word, matter": *a-bat* 2:1, 3:1, 21 r. 15, 28:1, 31:9, 59 r. 4, 105:12, 144:9, 223:3, [*a-bat* 5:1, [*a-bat*] 4:1, *a-bat-su* 52 e. 10, *a-ba-tu-ni* 127 r. 1, *a-bi-it* 62:5, *a-bi-te* 63:6, 78 r. 15, *a-bi-ti* 62:1, *a-bu-tu-u* 62:4, *a-bu-tu-u-ni* 105 r. 6, *a-bu-tú* 47 r. 6, 63 r. 29, 64:4, 78:11, r. 6, 115 r. 10, *a-b*[*u*]-*tú* 63 r. 12, *a-*[*bu-tú* 173:4, *iá-bu-tú* 60 r. 7, see also *amatu,*

ab abi "grandfather": AD—AD-*ia* 34 r. 6, 13, AD—AD-*ka* 34 r. 8, A[D—AD-*ka*] 96:8, 9, AD—AD-*ni* 201:3, AD—AD-*šú* 34 r. 11,

adakanni see *akanni,*

adanniš "very": *a—dan-niš* 2 r. 2, 14:8, 15:10, 19, 26:6, 10, 37:2, 38:2, 44:7, 48:4, r. 3, 52:8, 60 r. 7, 71 e. 10, 78 r. 3, 105:6, 106:4, 108:8, 111:5, 6, 113:5, 114:5, 119 r. 1, 126:8, 134:4, 139:14, 148:8, 162:9, 166:3, 220 r. 1, *a—dan-*[*niš* 114:5, 118:7, *a—dan*]-*niš* 118:10, 175:4, *a—d*]*an-niš* 101 s. 1, *a—*[*dan-niš*] 212 s. 2, *a—*[*dan*]-*niš* 118:10, *a*]*—dan-niš* 27:5, [*a—dan-niš* 27:5, 38:2, 153:4, 167:1, 3, 7, 175:4, [*a—dan-niš*] 96:7, 113:5, 167:2, 6, see also *danniš,*

addāru (Adar, name of the 12th month): ITI.ŠE 62:7,

adê "treaty": *a-de-e* 21:9, r. 5, 59:4, 60:5, 61:5, 71 r. 3, 126:19, 25, 150:8, 171:11, 243 r. 6, *a-de-e-ka* 59:5, *a-de-e-ka*] 61:5, *a-de-ka* 60:5,

adi "until, plus": *a-di* 27 r. 3, 29:15, 34 r. 21, 52 r. 5, 53:8, 199:4, [*a-di* 200 r. 5, *a-du* 36:11, r. 1, 59 s. 4, 60 r. 18, 21, 122 r. 8, 148:6, 150 r. 4, 7, 154 s. 1, 243 r. 7, *a-*[*du*] 93:4, [*a-d*]*u* 138 r. 6, EN 101:5,

adru "threshing floor": *ad-ri* 5:18, *ad-ru* 210:2,

adû "until, as long as": *a-du-u* 49 r. 6, *a-du-ú* 126:14, 127:11, [*a-du*]-*ú* 128:11,

adunakanni see *akanni,*

aganni see *akanni,*

agarinnu "crucible; mother": *ga-ri-na-te* 157:6,

agê see *akê,*

ahāiš "each other": *a-*[*ha-iš*] 63 r. 2, *a-he-iš* 15:27, 60:3, 171:4, *a-he-i*[*š* 183 r. 12, *is-sa-he-iš* 137:12, 243 r. 6,

ahātu "sister": NIN 8:2, NIN-*sa* 28:6, NIN-*šu* 123:10,

ahāzu "to take": *ta-ta-ha-za* 53:3,

ahhūr "still": *ah-ru* 65 s. 2,

ahu A "brother": PAB-*iá* 57:4, ŠEŠ-*ia* 1:6, 57:3, ŠEŠ-*i*[*a* 103 r. 1, Š[EŠ-*ia*] 1:2, ŠEŠ.MEŠ-*ka* 9 r. 1, ŠEŠ.MEŠ-*ni* 95:13, ŠEŠ-*u-a* 29:4, 30:6, ŠEŠ-*u-ni* 40:9, ŠEŠ-*ú-ni* 21 r. 14,

ahu B "arm, strength": *a-hi-ia* 34 r. 4, Á 164:11, Á.2-*e-*[*a*] 121:10, Á.2.MEŠ-*ia* 36:7, Á.2.MEŠ-*šú* 183:10, Á.2-*ni* 97 r. 17, Á.2-*šú* 63:23, 91 r. 3, 143 r. 10, Á.2-*š*[*ú*] 63 r. 6, UZ[U.Á].2-*šú-n*[*u* 199 r. 2,

ah abi "uncle": ŠEŠ—AD.MEŠ-*ka* 59 s. 2,

aiāka "where": *a-a-ka* 84:10, 117 r. 7,

aiāru (Iyyar, name of the 2nd month): ITI.GUD 125 r. 14,

aiāši "me": *a-a-ši* 2:3, 5:2, *a-a-š*[*i*] 118:6, *a-a-*[*ši*] 1:3, *a-*[*a-ši* 129:13, *ia-a-ši* 3:3, 4:2, 45:4, r. 11, 99 r. 5,

aiēša "whither?": *a-a-e-šá* 63:28, *a-a-e-*[*šá* 63 e. 33,

aiu "what, who?": *a-a-i* 126 r. 21, *a-a-im-ma* 237 r. 3,

akālu "to eat, consume, utilize; (Š) to feed": *a-kal-li-ia* 53 r. 9, *a-kul-u-ni* 114 r. 10, *ek-ka-la* 112:10, *e-ku-lu* 200 r. 8, *e-ta-kal* 15:16, KÚ 43:13, KÚ] 43 r. 2, *le-kul-šú*] 126:21, *le-ku-la-šú*] 126:20, *né-ta-kal* 63 r. 4, *ta-kal* 26:10, *tu-šá-kal* 212 r. 4,

akanni "now": *ad-da-kan-ni* 138:7, *a-da-ka-an-ni* 62:3, *a-du-na-k*[*a-ni* 7:2, *a-ga-ni* 126 r. 9, *a-kan-ni* 74:5, *a-ka-ni* 45 r. 12,

akāšu "(D) to be detained, tarry": *ú-kaš* 64 e. 12, *ú-ku-uš* 64:2,

akê "how?": *a-ge-e* 127:14, *a-ke-e* 6:4, 36:13, 54:7, 60 r. 6, 62 r. 8, 65 r. 16, *a-ke-*(*e*) 78:6, [*a-k*]*e-e* 6 e. 9,

akī "as; as if; thus": *ak* 112 r. 15, *a*]*k* 122 r. 3, *a-ki* 15:7, 8, 20 r. 3, 36 r. 7, 43:7, 60:15, 78:13, 14, 18, e. 22, r. 4, 82 r. 3, 101 r. 3, 7, 126:13, 152 r. 2, 169 r. 9, 208:4, [*a-ki* 110:6, *a-ki-i* 86 r. 18, 87 r. 7, 126:10, 19, 25,

akiltu "consumption": *a-kil-tu* 183 r. 12,

ālāiu "townsman": LÚ.URU.MEŠ-*n*[*i*] 76 r. 2,

alāku "to go, come": *al-ka* 54 r. 4, *al-ka-ni* 5 r. 25, *al-*[*la-ka*] 85 r. 3, 198 r. 3, [*al-la-k*]*a* 5 r. 19, *al-la-kan-ni* 25:7, *at-ta-lak* 27:7, [*at-ta-lak*] 166:4, *a-lik* 21:17, 155 r. 6, *a-ta-lak* 15:9, DU-*ka* 48 r. 1, *il-lak* 127 e. 26, 143:16, 146:10, 198 r. 2, *i*]*l-lak*

210:3, *il-lak-u-ni* 36:12, [*il-lak*]-*u-ni* 207:9, *il-la-ak* 2 r. 6, *il-la-ka* 34:21, 120 r. 8, 127 e. 27, r. 2, *il-l*[*a-ka*] 5:4, *il-la-kan-ni* 127:18, *il-la-ku-u-ni* 84 r. 10, *il-la-ku-ú* 27 r. 4, *il-la-k*[*u-ú-ni* 126:20, *il-la-*[*ku-ú-ni* 126:21, *il-lik-an-ni* 21 r. 11, *il-lik-u-ni* 90 r. 10, 124 r. 1, *i*]*l-li-ku-ni* 104:4, *il-li-ku-u-ni* 59 r. 13, *il-l*[*i-x* 135:15, *il-lu-*[*ku*] 52 r. 3, *it-tal-ka* 21 r. 12, 103 e. 6, 137:11, 140:7, s. 1, *it-t*[*al-ka* 225:3, *it-tal-*[*ku* 95:16, *it-tal-ku-nu* 49 r. 4, *it-tal-ku-u-ni* 154:3, 199:8, [*it-tal-ku-u-ni* 55:4, *it-tal-ku-ú-ni* 105:18, [*it-t*]*a-at-lak* 205 r. 10, *it-ta-lak* 78:19, 95 r. 17, 143 r. 9, *it-*[*ta-lak* 15:21, *i*[*t-ta-lak* 15:25, [*it-t*]*a-lak* 16:2, [*i*]*t-ta-la*[*k* 214 e. 2, [*i*]*-lak* 64 r. 1, *i-la-ku-u-ni* 64 r. 4, *i-tal-ku* 40 r. 16, *i-ta-al-ka* 124 r. 5, *i-ta-lak* 197 r. 2, *i-ta-la*[*k* 103 r. 2, [*la-a*]*l-li-ka* 37:9, *la-l*[*i-ka* 189:7, [*l*]*a-li-k*[*a-a*] 211 r. 1, *lil-li-ka* 26 r. 1, 88:15, 111 r. 5, *lil-li-k*[*a* 48 r. 13, *lil-l*[*i-ka* 96 r. 20, 100 r. 18, [*l*]*il-li-ka* 161:5, [*li*]*l-li-ki* 70 e. 7, *lil-li-ku* 90 r. 12, *lil-l*]*i-ku* 157 r. 8, [*lil-li-k*]*u* 132:6, *li-il-li-ku-u-n*[*i* 90 r. 2, *li-li-ku-u-ni* 64:3, *ni-il-la-ka* 140 r. 6, *ni-il-lik* 140 r. 9, 204 r. 5, *ni-lak* 88:18, *ni-t*[*a-lak* 95 r. 4, *tal-lak* 125 r. 15, *tal-l*[*a-ka*] 202:3, *tal-la-kan-ni* 27 r. 3, *tal-lik-a-ni* 105 r. 2, *tal-lik-a-ni*] 7:3, *tal-li-ka* 12:3, *ta-tal-ka*] 6:6,

ali "where?": *a-le-e* 40 r. 14, *a-li-ma* 52:9, r. 6, 105 r. 21,

alpu "ox": GUD 241:3,

ālu "city, town": URU 43:12, 63:31, 76 r. 1, 100:8, 10, 14, r. 14, 183 r. 5, [UR]U-*ku-nu* 63 r. 9, URU.MEŠ 15 r. 1, 68:19, see also *ālāiu,*

amāru "to see, behold": *a-mar* 6 r. 1, *a-mur* 5:19, r. 13, 15:7, 48:10, 89:8, 91:2, *a-mur-u-ni* 60:13, 78:11, *a-ta-mar* 15:9, 162:8, 222:3, *a-ta-mar-ku-nu* 88:13, *em-mar* 207:4, *e-mar* 5 r. 12, 63 r. 34, *e-mur-ru* 21:19, *e-mur-u-*[*ni*] 219 r. 8, *e-mur-ú-*[*ni* 150 r. 5, *e-ta-mar* 34:5, 37 r. 7, 65:11, [*e*]*-ta-mar* 74:1, *e-ta-mar-šú* 149:8, *in-na-mar-u-ni* 73 r. 3, *la-a-mur* 63 s. 2, *la-mur* 29:11, 37:6, *la*]*-mur* 178:7, *l*]*e-e-mu-ru* 11 r. 11, *le-mur* 125 r. 10, *le-mur-ši* 26 r. 2, *le-mu-ru* 17 r. 14, [*l*]*e-mu-ru* 116 r. 5, *l*]*e-mu-ur* 100 r. 18, *né-e-ta-mar* 206:4, *né-mur* 63:23, 97 r. 16, *né-ta-mar* 95 r. 10, *ta-mar-u-*[*ni*] 66:5, *ta-m*[*u-ru-ni* 59 r. 17, *ta-na-mar* 64 r. 5, *ta-ta-ma-a-ra* 5 r. 22,

amatu "word, matter": *a-mat* 17 r. 4, see also *abutu, abat šarri,*

amēltu "gentlewoman": MÍ.*a-m*[*e-la-te*] 153:2,

amēlu "man": LÚ 5 r. 6, 34:21, 36 r. 16, 48 r. 10, 60 s. 1, 65 r. 6, 115 r. 7, 121 r. 2, 163 r. 2, L]Ú 33 r. 9,

amēlūtu "mankind": *a-me-lu-ti* 126 r. 13, LÚ-*ti* 126:10, 12,

ammar see *mar,*

ammiu "that": *am-ma-te* 5 r. 20, 78:13, 214 r. 6, *am-mì-i* 70:2, [*am*]*-mì-ú* 70 r. 2, *am-mu-te* 15:8, 79:13, *am-mu-t*[*i* 126 r. 2, *am-mu-ú-ti* 27 r. 4, [*a*]*m-mu-ú-*[*ti*] 94:2,

ammutu "forearm, cubit": KÙŠ 100:12, 197 r. 2,

amtu "maid, slave-girl": GEMÉ 26:8, 59 r. 2, 7, GEMÉ-*ka* 49:2, GEMÉ.MEŠ 78 e. 22, [GEMÉ.M]EŠ-*ka* 153:2,

ana "to": *ana* 19:1, 3, 4, 188:4, *a-na* 1:2, 4, 5, 6, 7, 8, 13, 2:1, 4, r. 4, 3:2, 4:1, 5:1, 14, r. 5, 6 r. 2, 10:11, 12, 14:3, 5, 15:2, 24, 17:1, 3, 4, 9, 18:3, 20:1, 2, r. 2, 11, 21:1, 3, 4, 12, r. 3, 4, 8, 9, 10, 22:1, 3, 4, 23:3, 7, 24:1, 3, 25:3, 5, 26:1, 3, 5, 27:3, 4, 28:1, 29:3, 4, 6, 13, 16, 30:1, 5, 31:1, 4, 5, 32:1, 4, 13, 33:4, r. 9, 34:2, 3, 8, 19, 21, e. 25, r. 1, 5, 9, 35:1, 3, 4, r. 1, 36:5, 6, 12, 14, r. 3, 6, 7, 15, 39:3, 4, 14, 40 r. 12, 41:6, 7, 10, 42:1, 6, 7, 13, r. 1, 43 r. 5, 44:1, 4, 5, 45:1, 8, 9, 14, e. 17, 47 r. 1, 48:1, 3, 5, 7, r. 8, 49:1, 5, 7, r. 2, 50:2, 14, 52:3, 7, r. 1, 6, 53 r. 1, 54 r. 2, 55:6, 56:1, 8, 57:3, 4, 58:1, 59:1, 6, r. 4, 10, 11, 16, 60:1, 2, 14, r. 8, 9, 11, s. 2, 61 r. 5, 62:2, 5, 8, 9, 10, r. 4, 12, 63:1, 9, 29, e. 33, 35, r. 1, 21, 22, 64 r. 1, 8, 10, 65:1, 7, 14, r. 11, 13, 67 r. 9, 68 r. 8, 69:1, e. 8, 70:1, 6, 71:5, 6, 72:5, 75:9, 78:1, 2, 3, 5, 8, 9, 12, 17, r. 1, 8, 14, 17, 79:1, 3, 5, 16, r. 1, 6, 81:1, 5, r. 4, 7, 82:1, 3, 5, 16, 83:1, 3, 4, 84:1, 3, 5, 7, 9, 12, r. 3, 5, 85:1, 3, 5, 86:3, 4, 87:1, 3, 4, 9, 10, 16, 88:1, 4, 5, 89:3, 90 r. 4, 7, 91:4, 6, 92:3, 93:8, r. 7, 95:6, 15, r. 7, 11, 12, 96:1, 4, r. 5, 97:6, 8, r. 4, 10, 11, 15, 17, 98:1, 5, 7, 9, r. 3, 11, 99:6, 7, e. 11, r. 2, 5, 100:1, 3, 4, 101 r. 1, 5, 102:4, 103:5, r. 1, 104:1, 5, 105:1, 3, 6, 8, 9, r. 7, 15, 106:1, 3, 11, r. 3, 5, 107:1, 4, 6, 108:1, 3, 109:1, 3, 4, 110:4, 6, r. 5, 111:1, 3, 5, 12, r. 3, 112:1, 3, 8, 14, 113:1, 3, 4, 114:1, 3, r. 4, 6, 115:1, 3, 9, r. 11, 117:5, 9, 118:3, 4, 5, 6, r. 2, 119:3, 120:1, 3, 5, r. 3, 121:1, 3, 4, 9, 12, 16, r. 5, 11, 17, 122:1, 2, 124:1, 3, 5, 125:14, r. 5, 126:1, 3, 9, 15, 16, 20, 21, r. 8, 17, 20, 127:3, 9, 17, 18, 20, e. 26, r. 8, 11, 12, 13, 128:1, 3, 9, r. 4, 5, 9, 11, 12, s. 3, 129:3, 5, 9, 10, 13, 131:3, 4, r. 3, 132:4, 133:5, 134:1, 2, 3, 135:1, 7, 136:1, 4, 5, 137:11, r. 8, 138:5, 139:1, 3, 140:1, 4, 5, 142:1, 4, 6, r. 2, 143 r. 11, 12, 144:1, 3, 5, 145:1, 4, 5, s. 2, 146:5, 9, 11, 12, 147:4, 148:1, 2, 6, 7, 15, 17, r. 3, 7, 17, 150 r. 10, 151:2, 152:1, 3, 4, 154:4, 6, r. 10, 155:5, 160:1, 3, r. 6, 162:3, 5, r. 4, 164:3, 4, 168:10, 169:2, 3, 174:1, 3, 175:3, 178:2, 3, 179:1, 3, 5, 180:1, 3, 4, 181:1, 3, 6, r. 10, 183:3, 5, 9, r. 9, 18, 184:4, 5, 185:3, 186:1, 187:3, 4, 188:1, 189:1, 3, 4, 190:1, 3, 4, 191:10, 192:1, 3, 5, r. 7, 193:1, 3, 195:2, 196:1, 3, 6, r. 1, 207:2, 211 r. 2, 213:2, 4, 215:4, 216 r. 4, 218:3, 5, 221 e. 5, 235:3, 242 r. 8, 243:5, 246:1, *a-na*] 77 r. 3, 95 s. 1, 99 r. 10, 129 r. 5, 167:1, 7, 168:1, *a-n*[*a* 18:4, 20:3, 43:5, 60 s. 1, 61 r. 3, 63 s. 1, 79 r. 5, 91:5, 102:6, 138 r. 4, 181:8, 184:3, *a-n*]*a* 46:3, 66 r. 3, 132:2, 143:3, 151:6, 153:4, 178:5, 222:2, r. 3, 238:3, *a-*[*na* 23:4, 39:1, 67:6, 122:3, 129:12, 135:5, 181:4, 187:1, 188:3, 191:3, 215:6, 228:3, *a-*[*na*] 79:11, 90 r. 7, *a*]*-na* 110:3, 151 r. 5, 167:3, 171:5, [*a-na* 15:1, 18:1, 24:5, 25:1, 27:1, 29:1, 33:1, 8, 10, 38:1, 43:1, 57:2, 60:4, 61:1, 4, 67 r. 2, 72 r. 5, 77 r. 5, 78:20, 81:7, 89:1, 92:1, 4, 97:1, 102:1, 110:1, 114:4, 116:1, 5, r. 4, 118:7, 8, 119:1, r. 4, 127:1, r. 22, 132:1, 137:1, 4, 5, 141 r. 3, 143:1, 5, 153:1, 162:1, 164:1, 169:1, 174:7, 175:1, 6, 182:1, 184:1, 186:3, 191:4, 194:1, 3, 215:1, 218:1, 228:1, [*a-na*] 15:3, 34:1, 64 r. 5, 86:8, 96:6, 117:1, [*a-n*]*a* 23:1, 66:1, 68 r. 10, 118:1, 138:4, 141 r. 2, 147:3, 191:1, [*a*]*-na* 14:1, 41:1, 66:3, 86:1, 131:1, 138:1, 139:5, 224 r. 2, [*a*]*-n*[*a* 183:1, *e-na* 148 s. 1,

anāhu "to be weary, exhausted": *a-na-hu* 19 e. 9,

anāku "I": *ana-ku* 6:4, 121:11, 204:8, *ana-k*[*u* 99 r. 8, [*ana-k*]*u* 63:27, *an-na-ku* 56 r. 13, *a-na-ku* 2:10, 5 r. 2, 16, 10:5, 17 r. 10, 29:4, 11, 15, 30 r. 3, 32 r. 11, 34:17, e. 26, r. 4, 18, 35:6, 36:4, 6, 13,

r. 5, 7, 53 r. 9, 63 r. 8, 67 r. 15, 70:6, 71 r. 2, 78:6, 9, 82:8, 105 e. 21, 112 r. 2, 122:12, 127 r. 11, 15, 128 r. 9, 15, 129 r. 4, 154 r. 9, 171:7, 183 r. 6, 198 r. 3, 233 r. 3, 243:7, *a-na-ku*] 60:11, 61:11, 63 r. 33, *a-na-k*[*u* 160 r. 9, *a-na*]-*ku* 132:10, *a-n*]*a-ku* 90:3, 171:10, *a*-[*na-ku* 63 s. 2, *a*]-*na-ku* 219 r. 1, [*a-na-ku* 33 r. 5, [*a-na-ku*] 34 r. 20, *a-na-ku-ma* 181 r. 9, [*a-na-ku-ma*] 169 r. 10, [*a-na-ku-ni*] 45:11, *a-na-ku-u-ni* 204 r. 11, *a*]-*na-ku-u-ni* 62 r. 16,

anāšu "to be weak": *an-šu* 5 r. 8,

anīna "hear me!": *a-ni-na* 32 r. 7, 70:5, 59:8, 12, 60 r. 18, s. 1,

anīnu "we": *a-né-en-nu* 140 r. 5, *a-né-e-nu* 63 r. 5, *a-ni-nu* 42 r. 7, 79:9, 95 r. 6, 13, 243 r. 5, *a-ni-n*[*u* 176:7, *a-ni*-[*nu* 60 r. 22, see also *anīna,*

annāka "here": *an-na-ka* 9 r. 2, 49 r. 3, 67:3, 86 r. 14, 95 r. 3, 128 r. 8, 140 r. 3, 141 r. 5, 176:1, 221:2, [*an*]-*na-ka* 173:3, *an-na-kam-ma* 140 r. 4, *an-na-kan-ni* 36:11, 73:2, *an-na*-[*kan-ni* 36 r. 1,

annēša "hither": *ha-an-ni*-[*šá*] 209 r. 1,

anniu "this": *an-na-te* 63 r. 15, 158:7, *an-ni-e* 36 r. 7, 40:11, 64 r. 7, 65:13, 66:3, 86 r. 19, 128 r. 4, 138 r. 9, 243 r. 4, *an-ni-e*] 59:12, *a*[*n-ni-e* 64 r. 9, *an-ni-i* 15:6, 17:11, 43 r. 7, 60:16, r. 5, 127 r. 8, 146:9, *a*[*n-ni-i*] 15:11, [*an-ni-i*] 8:5, *an-ni-im-ma* 35 r. 8, (*an*)-*ni-im-ma* 112 r. 15, *an-ni-te* 62:5, 78:8, r. 5, 15, 100 r. 8, *an-ni-ti* 17 r. 12, 128:14, *an-ni-tu-u* 28:6, *an-ni-tú* 60 r. 16, 62:9, 63:17, r. 12, 78 r. 6, 104:5, *an-ni*-[*tú* 6:4, 59 r. 14, *an-ni-u* 73:5, [*a*]*n-ni-u* 244:4, *an-ni-ú* 35 r. 5, 60:8, 63 r. 18, 115:7, 220:2, [*an-ni-ú*] 61:8, *an-ni*-[*x* 129 e. 15, 227:2, *an-nu-te* 16:3, 52:3, 7, 63:6, 91 r. 9, 115 r. 4, *an-nu-te-am-ma* 62 r. 7, *an-nu-ti* 60:4, 99 r. 6, *an-nu-t*]*i* 60 r. 14, *ha-an-ni-i* 99:6, *ha*-[*an-ni-u* 59 r. 12, *ha-an-nu-ti* 4:3, *ha-nim-ma* 37 r. 8, 126:13,

annurig "right now, at the moment": *an-nu-ri* 16:5, 48:11, *an-nu-rig* 1:9, 39:13, 49 r. 3, 9, 52 r. 1, 55 r. 1, 62:7, 82:13, r. 2, 105 r. 3, 114 r. 6, 120:8, 124 r. 3, 125:8, 131 r. 2, 148 r. 18, 154:11, 206:3, *an-nu-ri*[*g* 158:3, *an-nu-ri*[*g*] 62 r. 4, *an-nu-ri*]*g* 5:3, *an-nu*-(*rig*) 32 r. 10, *an-nu*-[*rig*] 142 r. 1, *an*]-*nu-rig* 1:14, *a*]*n-nu-rig* 184 r. 3, [*an-nu-r*]*ig* 245:3, [*an-nu*]-*rig* 138 r. 4,

anšu see *anāšu,*

anūtu "equipment": *a-nu-su* 141:1, *a-nu-ti-šú* 141:3, *a-nu-tu* 89 r. 2, *a-nu-tú* 139:6, *a-nu*-[*ut* 56:11,

apālu "to answer": *e-tap-lu-u-ni* 63 r. 2, *e-ta-pal* 63 e. 34,

āpiu "baker": LÚ.NINDA 40:9,

appāru "reed": GI.*ap-p*[*a-ri* 79:12,

appu "nose, tip": *ap-pi* 1:13,

aptu "window": *ap-te* 100:19,

arahsamnu (Marchesvan, name of the 8th month): ITI.APIN 61:10, I[TI.APIN 60:10,

arāku "to be long; (D) to lengthen": *ar-ku-te* 117:8, *ar-ku-t*]*i* 195:1, *ar-ku-ú-te* 72:2, GÍD.[MEŠ 59:3, GÍD.DA.MEŠ 29:13, 49:6, 98:8, 126:6, 127:6, GÍ[D.D]A.MEŠ 128:6, *lu-ur-rik* 60 s. 2,

arāru "to curse": *a-ra-r*[*i* 198 r. 5,

arhiš "quickly": *ár-hiš* 59:7, 60 r. 15, 135:13, 140 r. 6, 148 r. 2, 17, 200 r. 10, *ár-hi*]*š* 60 r. 17, *ár*-[*hiš* 60 r. 10, [*ár-hiš* 5:5, [*ár-h*]*iš* 132:7,

arku see *arāku,*

asakku (a demon and disease): *a-sak-ku* 164:12, Á.S[ÌG 164:10,

askupputu "threshold": *as-ku-pe-te* 34 r. 18,

asû "physician": LÚ.A.ZU 26:13,

aṣūdu (a bowl for fruit and dough): *a-ṣu-di* 92:8, *a-ṣu-du* 41 r. 14, 212 r. 3,

ašarēdūtu "foremost, first-class": *a-šá-re-du-te* 131 r. 3,

ašāru "to check, review, take care of": *a-še-er* 48 r. 10, *a-šur* 5:16, *e-taš-ru* 139:12,

āšipūtu "magic, exorcism": LÚ.*a-ši-pu-te* 65:7,

ašlu "tow, string, rope": *áš-li* 95 r. 4, 17,

atâ "why?": *a-ta-a* 10:8, 15:11, 28:3, 33 r. 1, 43:15, 45:3, 62:3, 64 r. 8, 70 r. 2, 95 r. 13, 105 r. 1, 114 r. 8, 127 r. 4, 137:13, 143:14, 146:7, 183:7, 10, 13, 17, 212 r. 6, 225:1, *a-ta-a*] 242 r. 2, *a-ta*-[*a* 212 r. 2, *a-ta*-[*a*] 241:1, *a-t*[*a-a* 212:6, *a-t*]*a-a* 138:7, 172 r. 3, *a*-[*ta*]-*a* 59 r. 17, 183 r. 15, [*a-ta-a* 63 s. 3, [*a-ta-a*] 97 r. 4,

atānu "(donkey) mare": MÍ.ANŠE.ME 88:7,

atta "you": *at-ta* 5 r. 4, 9, 9 r. 4, 10:6, 32 r. 17, 36 r. 9, 96:11, r. 1, 3, *at-ta*] 59 s. 3, *at-t*[*a* 8 r. 2, 168:8, [*at-ta* 60 s. 2, [*at-t*]*a* 77 r. 7, *at-ta-ni* 173:5,

atti "you": *at-ti* 28 r. 5,

attunu "you": *at-tu-nu* 12:2, 137:13, *at-t*[*u-nu* 63 r. 7,

atû "gate-guard": LÚ.Ì.DU$_8$ 81 r. 5,

baʾāru "to catch, hunt": *ú-ba-ru* 191 r. 6,

baʾʾû "to seek": *lu-ba-ʾi-a* 5 r. 3, *ú-ba-ʾa* 86:12,

baddudu "to squander": *ba-du-du-ni* 42 r. 3, *ub-ta-di-du* 42:9,

bādu "evening": *ba-a-di* 140 r. 17,

bakû "to weep": *ba-ke-e* 95 r. 7, *i-ba-ki-ú* 95:4, *ni-bak-ki* 95 r. 13,

balāt "without": *ba-la-at* 7 e. 6, 45 r. 7, 15,

balāṭu "to live, (D) to keep alive, to heal; life": *bal-lu-ṭi* 36:4, 63 r. 25, *ba*]*l-u-ṭi* 86 r. 6, *bal-ṭu* 16:4, *ba-la-ṭi* 52:6, 72:1, *ba-l*[*i-iṭ* 60 r. 19, *lu-ba*[*l-li-ṭu* 160:4, *lu-bal-li-ṭu-u-ka* 61:4, *lu-bal-li-ṭ*]*u-u-ka* 60:4, *lu-bal-l*[*iṭ*] 52 r. 4, *lu-ú-bal-liṭ* 27:12, TIN 106:10, TI-*ku-ni* 20 s. 1, TI.LA 86:5, T[I.LA] 87:6, *ub-tal-liṭ* 126 r. 19, *ub-tal*-[*liṭ-a*]-*ni* 127 r. 16, *ú-bal-liṭ-ú-ni* 31:3, *ú-ba-l*[*a-ṭu-u-ni*] 118:5,

baqāru "to claim": *i-ba-qu*-[*ru-ni*] 116 r. 1,

bārtu "rebellion": *bar-tu* 60:8,

bārû "haruspex, diviner": LÚ.HAL 21:22, 171:8, 236:2,

bārûtu "extispicy": LÚ.*ba-ru-u-te* 65:9,

basi "in order to, duly, soon": *ba-a-si* 171:3, *ba-si* 207:11,

bašālu "to cook, boil": *ba-áš-lu* 209 r. 3,

bašû "to exist": *i-ba-áš-ši* 10:8, 11 r. 6, 62:12, 63:6, 65:8, 11, r. 5, 67 r. 13, 72 r. 4, 86:14, 148 r. 5, s. 2, 154 r. 11, 156:3, 204:11, r. 3, 206:5, *i-ba-áš*-[*ši* 59 r. 1, *i*]-*ba-áš-ši* 86 r. 5, 154 r. 5, *i-ba-áš-ši-i* 62:13, 75:2, *i-ba-áš-ši-ma* 11 r. 10, *i-b*]*a-áš-šú-u-ni* 41 r. 15, [*i-ba-šu*]-*ni* 205 r. 6, *i-ba-šú-ni* 41 r. 6,

batāqu "to cut off, parcel out; to repair": *ba-di-qu-nu* 126 r. 22, *i-ba-ta-q*[*u-ni* 67:11, *la-ab-tu-qu* 63:24, *ub-ta-ti-qu* 63:19, *ú-ba-at-ti-qu* 63:20,

bātiqūtu "information": [*b*]*a-te-qu-tú* 124 r. 6,

batqu "repair": *bat-qu* 89:14,

battatāia "systematically": *bat-ta-ta-a-a* 127 r. 10, 128 r. 7,

battibatti "around": *bat-bat-te-šu-nu* 148:18, *bat-ti-bat-ti* 105:19, *bat-ti-b*]*at-ti-ia* 146:5, *bat-ti-*

ba-ti 154:13, *ba-tu-ba-ti-ni* 97:12,
battu "side": *i–ba-ti* 15:12,
baṭālu "to quit, stop": *ib-ta-aṭ-l[u]* 84 s. 1,
bēlat bēti "lady of the house": GAŠAN–É 28 r. 5,
bēlu "lord": *be-li* 32 r. 7, 15, 33 r. 11, 34 r. 25, 43:7, r. 6, 8, 46:2, 59:8, 12, 60:15, r. 18, 61:9, 77 r. 9, 80:2, 202:6, *be-li*] 77 r. 2, *be-l[i]* 202:2, [*be-li*] 60 s. 1, *be-li-ia* 32:1, 33:1, 43:6, 98:1, *be-li-ia*] 43:1, *be-li-[ia]* 23:1, *be-li-ni* 79:1, 3, *be-l[i-ni]* 79:4, *be-lí* 20 r. 3, 26:11, 29:10, 16, r. 15, 31:7, 34:22, r. 3, 6, 10, 19, 20, 35 r. 2, 36:5, 10, 15, r. 9, 12, 13, 44 r. 7, 45 r. 14, 48 r. 6, 9, 11, 49 r. 8, 51:3, 54:2, 5, 6, 62:3, 5, 6, 13, r. 7, 12, 63:8, r. 19, 22, 25, 27, 33, s. 1, 3, 64:2, e. 12, r. 2, 9, 11, 65:14, r. 7, 11, s. 1, 2, 66:12, 67:6, 11, r. 1, 3, 10, 68 r. 13, s. 1, 69 r. 3, 74:3, 77 r. 4, 78:5, 8, 14, 15, 21, r. 5, 16, 79 r. 7, 82:8, 9, 13, r. 1, 3, 11, 83:6, 84:6, 86:7, r. 7, 18, 87 r. 2, 89:6, 90:1, 98:3, r. 7, 101 r. 7, 105 r. 5, 16, 108:6, 111:9, r. 2, 112 s. 1, 115:6, 10, 13, r. 13, 120 r. 10, 123 r. 7, 126:10, r. 8, 10, 21, 23, 127:13, r. 3, 14, 129:6, r. 4, 132:11, 134 r. 4, 135 s. 3, 136:9, 138:6, r. 6, 140 r. 2, 143:10, 12, r. 14, 148:12, 150:4, 152:7, r. 3, 154:7, s. 1, 155:1, 157 r. 5, 163:7, 165 r. 7, 175 r. 8, 176:5, 183 r. 14, 199:3, 201 r. 3, 207:4, 230 r. 1, 236:1, 3, *be-lí*] 60:9, 66:2, 67:2, r. 8, 87 r. 6, 157:1, 162:6, 164:6, 166:3, 181:5, 234:1, *be-l[í* 64:6, 183:6, *be-l[í]* 70:5, *be-l]í* 39:9, 169:4, 219 r. 9, 237 r. 2, *be-[lí* 66:8, *be-[lí]* 92:6, 211 r. 3, 219 r. 2, *be]-lí* 68 r. 15, *b[e-lí* 129 r. 2, 135:14, 242 r. 1, *b]e-lí* 34:14, 62 r. 3, 169 r. 9, [*be-lí* 192 r. 12, 206 r. 3, [*be-lí*] 55 r. 4, 64 r. 7, 85:6, [*be*]-*lí* 44 r. 4, *be-lí-ia* 14:1, 4, 6, 7, 15:1, 2, 3, 4, 17:1, 3, 21:3, 22:1, 5, 25:12, 30:1, 39:14, 49:8, 81:1, 82:1, 3, 5, 86:1, 3, 92:5, 12, 98:5, 100:1, 3, 105:1, 106:4, 11, 111:1, 112:1, 115:1, r. 11, 119:1, 126:3, 9, 15, 17, 136:1, 140:1, 4, s. 1, 142:4, r. 2, 143:5, 8, r. 12, 150:9, 174:1, 183 r. 9, 194:5, 217:1, r. 4, *be-lí-ia*] 18:1, 3, 4, 23:4, 39:1, 3, 89:1, 3, 92:1, 3, 126 r. 2, 135:1, 5, 164:1, 184:3, 4, 187:1, 3, 188:1, 190:1, 192:1, 5, 194:3, 215:1, 228:1, 3, *be-lí-i[a]* 21:1, 142:1, *be-lí-i]a* 38:1, 39:4, 174:7, *be-lí-[ia]* 180:1, *be-lí-[[ia]]* 119:5, *be-lí]-ia* 175:1, 6, 194:1, *be-l]í-ia* 88:1, *be-[lí-ia* 184:1, *be-[lí-ia]* 180:3, *b[e-lí-ia]* 23:3, 138:4, *b[e-lí-i]a* 174:4, *b]e-lí-ia* 24:1, [*be-lí-ia* 135:7, [*be-lí-ia*] 138:1, 5, [*be-lí-i*]*a* 38 r. 3, 98:10, 180:5, [*be*]-*lí-ia* 139:4, *be-lí-iá* 21:4, 25:4, 29:1, 3, 13, 34:16, 81 r. 7, 86:4, 6, 100:4, 119 r. 1, 152:1, 3, 183 s. 1, *be-lí-i[á* 184:6, *be*]-*lí-iá* 29:6, [*be-lí-iá*] 152:5, [*be-lí*]-*iá* 81:6, *be-lí-ni* 79:11, r. 5, 97:1, 6, 8, 136:4, 5, *be-lí-ni*] 102:1, 153:1, *be-li*$_{8}$ 52 r. 4, *be-li*$_{8}$*-ia* 52 r. 1, 7, *be-li*$_{8}$*-iá* 52 r. 8, *bé-li-ni* 42:1, 13, r. 1, BE 115 r. 3, BE-*i-ni* 21:20, BE-*ni* 41:1, 6, 8, 9, r. 5, EN 17:7, 45 r. 14, 53 r. 10, 11, 81 r. 10, 112:6, r. 4, 114:7, r. 7, 121:6, r. 4, 13, 127:3, 14, r. 6, 16, 128 r. 13, 150 r. 7, 183 r. 13, 242 r. 2, EN-*ia* 17:4, 20:1, 22:3, 26:1, 3, 27:3, 29:9, 31:1, 4, 6, r. 2, 32 r. 14, 33:4, r. 8, 34:1, 3, e. 25, r. 5, 35:1, 3, 4, r. 2, 36:6, 8, 9, r. 3, 7, 11, 15, 37 r. 3, 5, 44:1, 4, 5, 45:11, r. 13, 49:1, 5, 7, 53 r. 7, 59 r. 10, 60:1, 11, 61:11, 63:9, 69:1, 78:1, 2, 3, 7, 9, 12, 17, r. 1, 8, 14, 81:7, 83:1, 3, 4, 84:1, 5, 85:1, 3, 5, 87:1, 7, 88:4, 98:7, r. 3, 9, 11, 99 e. 11, r. 2, 10, 101 s. 1, 105:3, 6, 8, 10, r. 4, 7, 15, 19, 106:1, r. 3, 7, 107:5, 6, 111:5, 112:3, 113:1, 3, 4, 114 r. 7, 119:3, 120:1, 3, 5, 121 r. 5, 124:1, 3, 126:1, 11, 13, 16, r. 20, 127:1, 3, 9, 12, 16, r. 6, 7, 11, 13, 19, 20, 22, 128:1, 9, r. 10, 129 r. 6, 131:1, 3, 4, r. 3, 7, 132:1, 2, 4, 6, 7, 134:1, 139:1, 141 r. 1, 143:3, 144:1, 3, 5, 9, 145:5, s. 2, 148:1, 6, 151:2, 162:5, 165 r. 4, 168:2, 169:1, 3, 178:3, 179:5, 181:1, 182:1, 183:5, 14, r. 11, 16, s. 2, 189:5, 193:3, 196:6, 8, 207:3, 222:4, 243:5, 6, EN-*ia*] 20:2, 3, 27:1, 61:1, 114:3, 4, 116:1, 121 r. 11, 138 r. 4, 143:1, 145:1, 160:1, 3, 162:1, 3, 164:3, 168:10, 175:3, 179:3, 183:3, 186:1, 3, 188:3, 4, 189:1, 3, 190:3, 4, 191:3, 4, 192:3, 196:1, 3, 4, 215:4, 218:1, 242 r. 8, EN-*i[a* 208:3, EN-*i[a]* 34:2, 87:3, 110:4, 178:2, 5, 218:5, EN-*i]a* 63 s. 2, 193:1, 222:3, EN-[*ia* 45:15, 124:5, 126:18, 132:9, EN-[*ia*] 34:6, 37:1, 84:3, 87:4, 90 r. 4, 107:1, 118:1, 134:2, 3, 169:2, 179:1, 222:1, EN]-*ia* 110:1, E[N-*ia* 164:5, 207:8, E[N-*ia*] 87:10, 134:6, E[N-*i*]*a* 35 r. 9, E[N]-*i[a* 82:17, 132:8, E]N-*ia* 33:8, 55 r. 3, 116:5, 151:4, [EN-*ia*] 114:1, 144:8, 145:4, 191:1, 218:3, [EN-*i*]*a* 59:1, 183:2, [EN]-*ia* 36:14, [E]N-*ia* 47 r. 2, EN-*iá* 19:1, 24:3, 5, 25:1, 5, 26:5, 27:4, 29:16, 32:4, 48:1, 3, 5, r. 1, 5, 56:1, r. 8, 62:2, r. 4, 63:13, r. 10, 28, 33, s. 2, 64:5, r. 7, 65:2, 12, r. 14, 66:1, r. 6, 67 r. 2, 16, 68:15, 70:1, 72:5, 75:8, 88:5, 90 r. 10, 108:1, 3, 4, 109:1, 3, 110:3, 111:3, 115:3, 118:5, 7, 121:1, 3, 4, 12, 128:3, 12, r. 2, 12, 17, s. 1, 129:1, 3, 4, 5, 9, 12, s. 1, 148:2, 154:4, 6, 181:3, 194 r. 2, EN-*iá*] 90:12, 181:4, EN-[*iá* 129:2, E[N-*iá* 171:1, E[N-*iá*] 110 r. 5, E[N]-*iá* 64 r. 6, 128 s. 3, E]N-*iá* 72 r. 5, [EN-*iá* 63:1, 118:10, [EN-*iá*] 64 r. 4, EN-*i-ni* 58:1, 117:6, 10, 11, r. 3, [EN-*i-ni*] 117:1, EN-*ka* 32 r. 19, EN-*ku-nu* 21:12, EN.MEŠ-*šú* 36 r. 5, 6, 52 e. 10, 82:7, 91 s. 2, E]N.MEŠ-*šú* 126 r. 13, EN-*ni* 42:6, 7, r. 4, 97 r. 10, 15, 153:4, 195:2, 4, EN-*ni*] 96:4, r. 11, 19, 102:4, 6, 137:1, 5, EN-[*ni*] 96:1, 6, E]N-*ni* 137:4, EN-*šú* 33 r. 9, 64:9, 169 r. 10, EN-*šú*] 207:4, EN-*š[ú* 207:5, U-*iá* 19:3, 4,
bēlūtu "lordship": EN-*ú-[tú* 217 r. 8,
bēl adê "treaty partner": EN–*a-de-e* 60:11, 61:11, EN–*a-[de-e* 63 r. 4,
bēl āli "city lord": LÚ.EN–[URU.MEŠ 15:26,
bēl bēti "master of the house": EN–É 34 r. 26,
bēl dāmē "avenger, mortal enemy": EN–*da-me* 78:18, EN–*da-me-šú* 78 r. 4,
bēl dēni "adversary in court": EN–*de-ni-šu* 42 r. 5,
bēl dulli "worker": EN–*dul-li* 34 r. 15, 16,
bēl hiṭṭi "criminal, offender": EN–*hi-iṭ-ṭi* 99 r. 1, E]N–*hi-i[ṭ-ṭi* 9 r. 7,
bēl mugirri "chariot owner/fighter": LÚ.EN–GIŠ.GI[GIR 63 e. 34,
bēl piqitti "official": LÚ.EN–*pi-qit-ta-a-te*.MEŠ 86:13, LÚ.EN–*pi-qit-tú-ia* 5 r. 2, LÚ.EN–*pi-qi-te-ma* 67 r. 6,
bēl sīhi "insurgent": EN–*si*]-*i-hi* 130:6,
bēl ṭābti "friend": EN–MUN 204 r. 8, EN–*ṭa-ab-ti-ia* 48 r. 2,
bēl ṭābtūtu "friendship": L[Ú.EN–D]ÙG.GA-*ti-ni* 1:13,
bēl ṭēmi "reporter": EN–*ṭe-e-[mì-ia* 6:6,
bēl [...]: LÚ.EN–[*x*] 46:3,
bēt unqi see *Unqi*,
bētānu "interior, inside": É-*an-ni* 112 r. 2,
bēt "house; (in st. constr.) where, what, when": *bé-et* 25:6, 98 r. 7, 125 r. 4, 127:10, 13, 128:10, 205 r. 5, *bé-et*] 59 r. 12, *b*]*é-e-tú* 151 r. 3, É 5 r. 23,

34:13, s. 1, 40:9, 42 r. 7, 15, s. 1, 45 r. 8, 49 r. 6, 52 r. 5, 59 r. 6, 7, s. 4, 60:15, 63 r. 13, 20, 21, 65:3, 5, 66:9, 78 e. 24, 79:15, 81:4, 8, 82:13, 89:4, 5, 9, 12, r. 1, 91 r. 2, 96:13, r. 16, 98:4, 99:5, 100 r. 6, 8, 111:7, 10, 11, 112 r. 4, 116:9, 117 r. 1, 125 r. 8, 127 r. 8, 128 r. 4, 129:6, 143 r. 10, 166:3, 181:10, 192 r. 13, 200 r. 4, 235 r. 2, É] 200 r. 5, É-*ia* 5 r. 19, 56 r. 12, 82:15, 183:8, 9, É-*ka* 34 r. 12, 14, 18, É-*ma* 51:2, É.MEŠ 96 r. 11, 117 r. 4, 154:12, 200 r. 9, [É-*šú*] 78:16, É—[*x* 154:13,

bētu eššu "New Palace": É—GIBIL 107:3,

bēt abi "father's house, paternal estate": É—AD-*ia* 32 r. 11, É—AD-*i*[*a* 53:2, É—A]D-*ia* 33 r. 5, É—AD-*k*[*u-nu* 63 r. 8, É—AD-*šú* 29:10,

bēt bēli "government department": É—EN.MEŠ-*ia* 36:3, 112 r. 4, 6, 11, 113:7, 115:5, 225:2, É]—EN.MEŠ-*ia* 86:14, É—EN.MEŠ-*iá* 86 r. 15, 17, É—EN.MEŠ-*ka* 86:11, É—EN.MEŠ-*ni* 42:8, r. 3, É—EN.[MEŠ-*ni* 79:8, É—EN.MEŠ-*š*[*ú* 114 r. 8, 207:6, É—EN.M[EŠ-*šú* 169 r. 7, É—EN.MEŠ-*šú-nu* 86 r. 3, É—EN.ME-*šú-nu* 41:15,

bēt ili "temple": É—DINGIR 100:15, 20,

bēt issēte (a building): É—[I-*te*] 100 r. 13, É—I-*te* 100 r. 6, 15,

bēt kutalli "Rear House/Palace": É—*ku-tal-li* 143 r. 6, É—*k*]*u-tal-li* 217 r. 7,

bēt maiāli "bedroom": É—*ma-a-a-*[*li-i*]*a* 89 r. 5,

bēt maṣṣarti "garrison": É—*ma-ṣar-te* 100 r. 14,

bēt qāti "storehouse": É—ŠU.2.MEŠ-[*i*]*a* 89 r. 4,

bēt ramāki "bathroom": É—*ra-ma-ki* 116:10,

bēt rēdūti "Succession Palace": É—*re-du-ti* 95 r. 16, É—UŠ.MEŠ-*te* 28 r. 2, 6,

bēt ṭuppi "school": É—*ṭup-pi* 52 r. 3,

biādu "to stay overnight": *t*]*a-bi-da* 61:11,

biltu "talent": GÚ.UN 82 r. 5, 6, 7, 8, 9, 10, 97:17, [GÚ.U]N 83 r. 2,

birmu "multi-coloured textile": *bir-me* 84 r. 12,

birti "between, through, in the midst of": *bir-te* 43:12, 64:9, r. 2, 125 r. 2, *bir-ti* 45 r. 3, 48 r. 7, 55:1, 64:7, 148:14, *bir-*[*ti*] 205 r. 3, *b*]*ir-ti* 119 r. 2, [*b*]*ir-ti* 86:9, *bir-tú-*[*x* 95:14,

bīrtu "fort": URU.HAL.ṢU 148:9, URU.HAL.ṢU.M[EŠ 147:1,

bīrtūtu "status as fortress": URU.HAL.ṢU-*ú-te* 154 r. 10,

bis "at once, duly": *bi-is* 62:6, r. 9, 64 r. 3, 87 r. 5,

bubūtu "hunger": *bu-bu-ti* 29:5, 31 r. 4,

bulê "firewood": *bu-le-e* 40:12,

bunbullu "cone": *bu-un-bu-ul-li* 63:22,

daʾānu "to be strong, hard; (D) to strengthen; force": *da-a-ni* 65 r. 9, *i-da-nu* 40 r. 9, see also *dannu,*

dabābu A "to talk, plot, contest; (Š) to incite, provoke": *ad-da-bu-ub* 78:7, *ad-da-bu-*[*ub*] 112:12, *ad-du-bu-bu* 112 r. 9, *ad-du-bu-ub-ma* 150:3, *a-da-bu-bu* 62 r. 10, *a-da-bu-u-ni* 78 r. 11, *da-ba-ab-šú* 63 s. 1, 2, *da-ba-bi* 59:12, 63 r. 30, 64 r. 5, 9, 65:13, *da-ba-bu* 32 r. 5, 59:8, r. 3, 60:8, 61:8, 62 r. 3, 148 r. 6, s. 1, [*da-ba-bu* 183:14, [*da-ba*]-*bu* 72 r. 3, *id-bu-bu* 59 r. 17, *id-bu-bu-ni* 10:4, 51:4, *id-du-ub-bu* 10:2, *i-*[*da-ba-bu-ni*] 61:6, *i-*[*da-ba-bu-u*]-*ni* 60:6, *i-da-bu-bu* 43 s. 1, *i-da-bu-bu-u-ni* 42 r. 6, *i-da-bu-ub* 64 e. 11, 112 r. 10, *i-da-bu-u*[*b* 60 r. 21, [*i-da-bu-ub*] 78:18, *lid-bu-bu* 59 r. 11, 63:8, *lid-bu-ub* 48 r. 12, *ni-da-bu-bu-ni* 42 r. 7, *ta-dáb-*[*b*]*u-ba* 63 r. 7, *ta-da-bu-bu* 59 r. 4, *ta-da-bu-bu-u-ni* 78 r. 10, *ú-šá-ad-ba-ab* 198 r. 6, *ú-šá-da-b*[*a-bu-u-ni* 68 s. 2,

dabābu B "lawsuit, dispute": DUG_4.DUG_4 43 r. 7, DUG_4.DUG_4.ME 30:4,

dagālu "to look, regard, see (a vision)": *a-da-gal* 61:10, 78:11, *a-*[*d*]*a-gal* 60:10, *id-da-gal-an-ni* 78 r. 4, *it-ta-gal* 20 r. 4, *i-da-gal* 32 r. 6, *i-da-gal-an-ni* 78:18, *i-da-gal-an-ni-ni* 78:14, *i-da-gul* 21 r. 2,

dāgil iṣṣūri "augur": LÚ.*da-gíl*—MUŠEN.[MEŠ 8:7, LÚ.*da-gíl*—M[UŠEN.MEŠ 8:1,

daiālu "courier, scout": [LÚ].*da-a-a-lu* 97 r. 7,

dalālu "to glorify": *la-ad-lul* 31 r. 3,

dalāpu "to stay awake": *ni-da-lip* 229:2,

dalīlu "praise": *dà-lí-lí* 31 r. 2,

damāqu "to be good, beautiful; (D) to do well, to feign": *dam-mì-iq* 59:7, *dam-qa* 129:3, 12, *dam-qu-ti* 126 r. 3, *da-an-qa-a-te* 72:8, *da-mì-iq* 148 r. 9, *da-mu-qi* 126 r. 24, *de-e-iq* 34:7, *de-e-qe* 3 r. 2, SIG_5 2 r. 2, 23:7, 55 r. 2, 59 r. 3, 89:13, 91:9, 212 s. 2, [SIG_5].MEŠ 37:6, *ú-da-mì-qa* 126 r. 18,

dāmu "blood": ÚŠ.MEŠ-*ka* 20 r. 8,

dannatānu "powerful man": *da-an-na-ta-a-nu* 63 r. 19,

danniš "greatly": *dan-niš* 246:2, see also *adanniš,*

dannu "strong, big": *dan-na-*[*te* 91 r. 2, *dan-nu* 28 r. 4, 29:3, 36:3, 128 r. 5, 168:8, *dan-nu-ti* 126:13, KALAG 116:10, see also *daʾānu, dannutu,*

dannutu "legal document": *dan-na-a-te* 96 r. 15,

dappastu "rug, blanket": TÚG.*dáp-pa-sat* 53:9,

darû "everlasting": *da-ra* 34 r. 3, *da-ra-a-ta* 29:13, *da-r*[*a*]-*a-ta* 128:7, *da-ra-a-te* 117:9, 127:7, *da-ra-a-ti* 126:7, *da-ra-ti*] 195:1, *da-r*]*a-ti* 59:3, *dà-ri* 36 r. 12,

dassu "door": GIŠ.IG 95 r. 18, GIŠ.IG.MEŠ 183 r. 7,

daššu (an implement): *da-áš-šú* 53 r. 3,

dātu "after": *da-te-ka* 5 r. 9, *id—da-at* 143:15, *id—da-a-te* 85 r. 4, *id—da-te* 34 r. 8, *i*]*d—da-tú* 20:7, *i—da-at* 25:7, [*i—da*]-*a-te* 78 e. 22, *i—da-te* 56 r. 7, [*i—d*]*a-te* 62 r. 4, *i—da-tu-uk-ka* 120 r. 7, *i—da-tu-uš-šú* 34 s. 1,

dēku see *duāku,*

dēnu "judgment, lawsuit, case": *de-en-ku-nu* 41:12, *de-en-šú-nu* 55 r. 4, *de-e-ni* 32 r. 4, *de*]-*e-ni* 39:12, *de-e-n*[*i-šú-nu* 64:3, *de-e-nu* 32 r. 7, 41:15, [*de-e-nu* 33 r. 3, *de-na-ni* 42 s. 1, *de-ni-ni* 41 r. 12, *di-in-šú* 39 r. 4,

dibbī "words": *di-ib-bi* 60:12, *di-ib-*[*bi* 61:12, *di*]-*ib-bi* 99 r. 6,

diglu "vision": *di-ig-lu* 61:10, *di-ig-lu*] 60:10,

duāku "to kill": *de-e-ke* 30:7, *du-a-ki* 30 r. 3, 36:4, *d*[*u-a*]-*k*[*i-ia*] 112 r. 9, *du-a-ki-i-ka* 10:4, *i-du-ak* 95 s. 1, 127:21, *i-du-kan-ni* 112 r. 14, *i-du-ku-uš* 105 r. 9, *i-du-ku-u-ni* 44 r. 3, *id-*[*du-kan-ni*] 114 r. 11, *ni-du-uk-šú-nu* 243:3,

duālu "to run about, serve": *ad-du-al* 30 r. 4, [*a-du-a*]*l* 34 r. 19, *i-du-lu-u-ni* 63 r. 16, [*i-d*]*u-lu-u-ni* 33 r. 10,

duhšiu "tanned leather": *duh-ši-e* 97:20,

dullu "work, ritual, treatment": *dul-la-a-ni* 62:8, *du*[*l-la-ka*] 183:11, *dul-l*]*a-ku-nu* 5 r. 16, *dul-la-ni* 34:24, 40 r. 8, 79:4, *dul-la-ni-šú* 62:6, *dul-la-šú-nu* 199:6, *dul-l*[*a-šú-nu*] 183 r. 3, *dul-la-*[*x* 216 r. 10, *dul-li* 34:8, 10, 14, 45:2, 86 r. 15, *dul-[li* 126 r. 16, *dul-li-ia* 37:8, *du]l-li-ia* 32:16, *du]l-li-i-ni* 205 r. 9, *du]l-li-šú-nu* 119 r. 4, *dul-lu* 25 r. 2, 34:4, 12, 17, 40:10, 45:8, 53 r. 7, 59 r. 7, 79:6, 86:11, r. 20, 126 r. 21, 183:8, r. 16, *dul-l[u* 234 r. 1, *dul-[lu* 86 r. 3, 87 r. 5, 199:4, *du[l-lu* 160 r. 3, *dul-lu-ni* 79:8, *dul-lu-nu* 126 r. 22,

dumāqu "jewellery, decor": *du-ma-qi* 127 r. 17,

dūru A "city wall": BÀD 30 r. 1, 32 r. 15, 100:10, 101 r. 3, 121 r. 2, 143:6,

dūru B "continuity, duration": *d[u-ur* 160:3,

egirtu "letter, document": *e-gír-a-te-ia* 63 r. 28, *e-gír-a-ti* 95 r. 1, 97 r. 14, *e-gír-ti* 73:3, *e-gír-t[i-šú* 60:16, *e-gír-tu* 59:14, 81 r. 6, 150 r. 3, *e-gír-tú* 5:15, 6:5, e. 9, 17 r. 13, 21:8, r. 9, 60 r. 16, 80:1, 99:10, *e-gír-tú]* 6:1, e. 10, *e-gí[r-tú* 6 e. 7,

ekallu "palace": É.GAL 45:12, 47:1, 60:5, r. 8, 62 r. 14, 63 e. 32, 66 r. 1, 82:15, 84 r. 2, 88:8, 12, 95:2, 4, r. 16, 98 r. 4, 99 r. 4, 120 r. 1, 127:22, r. 19, 20, 128 r. 16, 201:1, 206:1, É.[GAL 60:14, É.[GAL] 90:10, É.[G]AL 128 s. 1, É].GAL 63:22, É.GAL-*ka* 59:6, s. 3, 61 r. 2, É.GA]L-*ka* 61:8, É.[GAL-*ka* 60:8, É.GAL.MEŠ 40 r. 8, 16,

ekal māšarti "Review Palace": KUR—*ma-šar-ti* 21 r. 15,

ekeltu "darkness": *e-kel-ti* 29:5,

ekit (mng. obscure): *e-ki-it* 64 e. 11,

eleppu "boat, ship": GIŠ.MÁ 139:9, GIŠ.MÁ.MEŠ 127:15, GIŠ.MÁ-*šú* 127:21,

elītu "upper part": NIM.[MEŠ] 92:7,

elû "to go up; (D) to remove, set aside; (Š) to promote, raise, set aside, donate": *e-la-a-ni* 127:16, *e-te-li-ú* 118:13, *il-la-ni* 127:20, *i-te-te-li* 201:4, *lu-u-sa-te-li* 207:9, *né-e-l[i]* 93 r. 4, *né-e-[li]* 93:5, *tu-še-li]* 59:11, *ul-li* 20 r. 7, *[ul]-lu-e-šú* 168:7, *us-se-la-an-ni* 31:8, *ú-se-li* 68 r. 14, *[ú-se]-li-ia-a* 76 r. 2, *ú-še-lu-u-ni* 115:10, 13, r. 3, *ú-še-lu-ú-[ni]* 170:6,

elūlu (Elul, name of the 6th month): ITI.KIN 100:6,

emādu "to impose, lean": *e-mì-du-ni-ni* 83 r. 4, *le-mì-du-šú* 73 r. 5, *ú-mu-du* 199 r. 3,

emūqu "strength, (armed) forces, army": *e-mu-qa-a-ni* 140 r. 9, *e-mu-qa-a-a* 88 r. 7, *e-mu-qi-ia* 62 r. 11, *la-mu-qa-ni* 40:7, LÚ.*e-mu-qi* 243 r. 3, *mu-qa-a-a* 60:12, 61:12, 63:25,

enna "now": *en-n[a* 4:4,

ēnu "eye": *e-ni* 32 r. 6, IGI.2 64:7, 119 r. 2, 205 r. 4, IGI.2.ME 223:2, IGI.2.MEŠ 64 r. 2, 65 s. 2, 86:9, IGI.2.MEŠ-*ia* 36:9, IGI.2.MEŠ-*šú* 48 r. 7, 78:11, IGI.2.MEŠ-*šú-nu* 148:14, IGI.2-*šú* 64:9, IGI.2-*[š]ú-nu* 64 r. 12,

epāšu "to do, make, perform; (D) to do, practice, exercise; (N) to be done": *ep-pa-áš* 34:24, 123:4, 162 r. 6, *ep-pa-áš]* 79:9, *ep-pa-su-nu* 126 r. 23, *ep-pa-šu-u-ni* 36 r. 9, *ep-pu-šu* 204:5, *[ep-pu-šu]* 199 r. 3, *ep-pu-šú* 41:13, 84 r. 4, 11, 126:16, *ep]-pu-šú* 237 r. 4, *e[p]-sa-tu-ni* 127:14, *ep-šat* 62:11, *ep-šá* 5 r. 16, *ep-šu-u-n[i* 61 r. 2, *ep-šú* 29 r. 4, *e-pa-as* 97 r. 3, *e-pa-áš* 32 r. 4, 41 r. 18, 86 r. 16, *e-pa-á[š* 165 r. 6, *e-pa-[áš]* 183:8, *e-[pa-áš* 234 r. 2, *e-pa-áš-u-ni* 53 r. 11, 77 r. 6, 86 r. 13, *e-pa-še* 104:5, *e-pa-ši* 62:8, *e-piš-u-ni* 197:3, *e-pu-su-nu* 126 r. 18, *e-pu-su-su-nu* 126 r. 21, *e-pu-[šu* 60:8, *e-p[u-šu* 242 r. 6, *e-pu-šu]-ni* 126:26, *e-pu-šu-[u-ni]* 34:4, *e-pu-šú* 41 e. 16, *e-pu-šú]* 200 r. 6, *e-pu-šú-u-ni* 32 r. 8, 78:8, *e-pu-uš* 5 r. 6, 21:15, 34 e. 26, *e-pu-uš]* 6:4, 45:2, *e-pu-[uš* 114 r. 6, *[e-p]u-uš* 70:5, *e-pu-uš-u-ni* 75:7, *e-pu-u]š-u-ni* 33 r. 3, *e-tap-šu* 76 e. 3, *e-tap-šú* 60:13, 154:4, *e-ta-pa-áš* 34:6, *e-t[a-pa-áš]* 121 r. 8, *e-[ta-pa-áš]* 45:8, *i-né-pa-áš-u-ni* 86 r. 20, *le-e-pu-šú* 34 r. 3, *le-e-pu-uš* 11 r. 12, 34:19, e. 27, 35 r. 4, 36:13, *le-pu-šu* 39 r. 4, 83 r. 6, *le-[pu-šu]* 83 r. 3, *le-pu-šú* 25 r. 3, 59:8, r. 8, 125 r. 13, 129 r. 5, 131 r. 5, 199:5, *[le-pu-šú]* 183 r. 16, *le-pu-uš* 32 r. 3, 16, 39:13, 42 s. 1, 53 r. 12, 55 r. 4, 62:7, 82 r. 4, 115 s. 1, 134 r. 5, 152 r. 4, *le-pu-u[š* 101 r. 8, *le-pu-[uš]* 87 r. 8, *[le-p]u-uš* 33 r. 13, *[le]-pu-uš* 143 r. 15, *lu-pi-šu]* 77 r. 8, *lu-pi-šú* 82:10, *lu-up-pi-šu* 5 e. 25, *né-ep-pa-áš* 27 r. 1, *né-e-pu-u[š]* 163:4, *né-pa-áš* 40:8, *né-pu-uš* 79:9, *né-pu]-uš* 159 e. 5, *né-ta-pa-áš* 40:5, *né-[ta-pa-áš* 160 r. 4, *ta-né-pi-šu-u-ni* 63:18, *te-ep-pa-šá* 79:6, *tu-pa-áš* 96 r. 8, *ú-tu-pi-eš* 124 r. 6,

epēšu "to do, make, perform": *e-pi-še* 82:16, *e-pu-uš-ma* 127:23,

epšetu "deed": *ep-še-te-ka* 72:7,

eqlu "field": A.ŠÀ 29 r. 3, 43:11, 155:1, 4, r. 7, A.ŠÀ-*in-ni* 40 r. 5, A.ŠÀ-*šú* 40 r. 4,

equ "to anoint, daub": *e-ti-qi-ši* 65 r. 8,

erābu "to enter; (Š) to bring in": *er-ra-bu-u-ni* 137 r. 16, *e-rab* 89:11, 99 r. 4, *e-r[a]b-u-ni* 51 r. 2, *e-rab-ú-ni* 90 r. 6, *e-ra-bu-u]-ni* 63 s. 1, *e-ru-ub* 11 r. 5, 48:8, *e-tar-ba* 25:8, *e-tar-bu* 137 r. 10, *e-tar-bu-u-ni* 62:7, *[e-tar-bu-u-n]i* 175:10, *e-ta-na-rab-u-ni* 154:12, *e-ta-rab* 45 r. 6, 64 r. 7, 146:6, *i-tar-bu* 40 r. 17, *le-ru-ub* 15:4, 64:4, *le-r]u-ub* 62 r. 15, *lu-še-r[i-bu-ši-na]* 192 r. 14, *us-se-rib-šú-nu* 143 r. 7, *us-se-ri-ba* 80:4, *[ú-s]e-ri-ba-an-ni* 71 r. 4, *ú-se-ri-ib-ši* 95:2, *ú-š[e-rab]* 198 r. 2, *ú-še-ra-ba-na-ši-na* 49 r. 7,

erāšu "to cultivate ": *e-ra-šu-u-ni* 86 r. 12,

erbâ "forty": 40 57:5,

erbiu "locust": $BURU_5$ 121 r. 6, *er-b[i-e* 145:7,

ēribu "enterer": LÚ.*e-rib-u-te* 50 r. 1, TU.MEŠ 51 r. 3,

eršu "bed": GIŠ.NÁ 53:8, 239 r. 2,

ešer "ten": 10 63 r. 15, 82 r. 9,

ešrā "twenty": 20 5:10, 83 r. 2, 25 40:3,

eššu "new": GIBIL-*tu* 52 r. 5,

etāku "to be alert": *e-ta-ka-ni* 93:4,

etāqu "to pass (through), to move on; (Š) to transfer, avert": *e-ta-at-qu* 157 r. 7, *e-te-eq-q[u-u-ni]* 150 r. 1, *e-te-tiq* 145 s. 1, *e-ti-qu-u-ni* 35 r. 7, *i-ti-te-iq* 201 r. 2, *le]-e-ti-qu* 35 r. 10, *šu-te-tu-qe-e* 62:10, *te-te-qe* 78:10,

eṭāru "to save": *i-te-ṭi-ra* 100:11,

eṭûtu "darkness": *e-ṭu-ti* 29:15,

ezābu "(Š) to rescue, escape": *lu-še-zib-an-ni* 30 r. 6, *še-zib* 59 s. 4, 60 r. 10, s. 3, *še-zib]* 60 r. 16, *[še-zib* 59:9, 60 s. 3, *[še]-zib-an-ni* 127 r. 18, *us-se-zib* 29:5, *ú-še-zib* 105 r. 11,

Enūma Anu Illil (astrological omen series): UD-*mu*—AN—EN.LÍL 21 r. 1, UD—*a-na*—^{d}EN.LÍL 65:10,

gabbu "all, whole, entire": *gab-bi* 217 r. 11, 29:14, 40:11, 112 r. 11, 127:17, 129:8, r. 3, *gab-bi-šu* 100:8, *gab-bi-šu-nu* 16 e. 7, *gab-bi-šú* 126 r. 20, 24, *[gab]-bi-šú* 89 r. 8, *gab-bu* 32 r. 11, 33 r. 5, 35 r. 6, 36 r. 8, 40 r. 2, 60:5, 63 r. 28, 86 r. 20, 100:10, 15, 18, 106 r. 6, 141:2, 146:8, 157:4, 200 r. 6,

gabrû "reply": *gab-ru-ú* 97 r. 16,

gabû "alum": NA$_4$.*ga-bu-u* 82 r. 8,
gamāru "to come to an end, finish; (D) to complete; to abolish": *ga-mir*] 169 r. 9, *ga-mur-ak-ka* 60 s. 4, *ga-mur-u-ni* 36 r. 6, *ug-dam-me-ru* 125:4, [*ug-da*]*m-mì-ru* 41 r. 4, *ug-da-ta-mu-*[*ru-u-ni*] 150 r. 2, *ú-gam-mu-ru* 126:16, 129:5, *ú-ga-mar* 64 e. 12,
gammalu "camel": ANŠE.*gam-mal*.MEŠ 5:9,
gammurtu "totality": *gu-mu-ur-ti* 168:1,
garāru A "to become scared; (Š) to frighten, scare": *ig-ru-r*[*u*] 94:7, *ú-sa-ag-ri-r*[*i* 15:22,
garāru B "(Ntn) to writhe, grovel": *it-at-na-ag-ra-ra* 20 r. 5,
garinnu see *agarinnu,*
gaṣṣānu "calcareous": *ga-ṣa-a-nu* 125:7,
gimru "total": PAB 50 r. 1, 53:7, r. 4, 82 r. 10, 91 r. 9, 136:14, 227:2, 232:2, [PAB 177:2, [P]AB 51 r. 3,
gulgullu "skull": *gul-gu-lat-ku-nu* 88:13,
habālu "to borrow, be indebted": *ih-bil-šú-ni* 29:8,
habāru "to be noisy": *ih-tu-bur* 121 r. 7,
habātu "to plunder": *tah-bu-ta* 137:14,
hadû "to be glad": *ha-di-u* 15:19,
hadūtu "joy": *ha-du-te-e* 63:20,
hakāmu "to understand; (Š) to explain, clarify": *li-ih-kim* 65 s. 1, *tah-ti-ik-im* 10:3, *ú-šah-kim* 172 r. 4,
halālu "to sound": *uh-tal-lil* 9 r. 5,
halāpu "to clothe, dress": *hal-lu-pu* 95 r. 9,
halāqu "to disappear, flee, run away; (D) to cause to be lost, destroy": *ah-tal-qa* 29:6, *hal-li-qí* 59:6, *hal-lu-qi* 61 r. 5, *hal-qa-ku* 30 r. 4, *hal-q*[*u* 186 r. 5, *ih-tal-q*[*u*] 34:13, *i-hal-liq* 34 r. 13, s. 1, *li-ih-li-iq* 59 r. 10, *tu-hal-la-qa* 59:11, 61:8, *tu-hal-la-qa*] 43 r. 1, 60:8, *uh-ta-li-qi* 43:12, *uh-ta-li-qu-u-ni* 82:12, *ú-hal-la-qa* 59 r. 5, *ú-hal-l*[*u-qu* 135 r. 7,
hallupu "covered": ANŠE.*ha-lup*.MEŠ 88:9,
hannēša see *annēša,*
hanniu see *anniu,*
hanšā "fifty": 50 1 r. 2, 3, 105:15, 50] 1 r. 2, 50-*šú* 236:7,
hanṭiš "quickly": *ha-an-ṭiš* 52:8,
hapû "to break, destroy": *ih-ti-pi* 97:10, *t*[*a-hi-bi*] 126:23,
harādu "to watch, attend, prompt; (N) to be vigilant": *at-ta-ah-*[*rid*] 34:5, *i-har-ri-di* 62 r. 10, *la-ah-ri-id* 32 r. 13, 33 r. 7, *li-ih-hi-ri-id* 105 r. 17,
harammāma "later, afterwards": *ha-r*]*am-ma-ma* 152 r. 2, *ha-ra-me-ma* 92:9,
harāpu "to be early, first": *ih-ru-up* 150:6, *i-ha-ru-pu-ni* 59 s. 4, *i-ha-ru-*[*pu-u-ni*] 60 r. 18, *i-h*]*a-ru-pu-u-ni* 60 r. 21,
harāṣu "to clear up, delve into": *har-ṣa* 63 s. 1, *hu-ur-*[*ṣa*] 92:8, *ih-tar-ṣa* 204 e. 12, *i-har-ra-ṣi* 127 r. 2, *ni-ih-ru-uṣ-ṣa* 204 r. 8,
harpūtu "spring": *i—har-pu-u-te* 86 r. 19,
harrānu "caravan": KASKAL.MEŠ 131 r. 3, KASKAL.MEŠ-*tú* 131 r. 2, KAS[KAL].2.MEŠ-*ni* 140 r. 1, see also *hūlu,*
hasā'u "to mistreat, molest": [*ih*]*-ta-sa-'u-šu* 76 r. 3, *i-ha-si-šú* 48 r. 9, *i-ha-as-su-na-ši* 42 r. 8,
hasāsu "to remember; (Š) to remind": *li-ih-su-su* 23:8, *ša-ah-su-si* 143 r. 11,
haṣānu "to take care of, protect": *ni-ha-*[*ṣi-in* 40:15,
haṭṭu "sceptre": GIŠ.PA 145 r. 3, 164:11, GIŠ.PA] 63 r. 5,
haṭû "to make a mistake, sin": *ah-ti-ṭi* 36:3, *ih-ṭi* 75:5, *i*]*h-ṭu-ni* 74:4, *ih-ṭu-u-ni* 59:5, *i-ha-aṭ-ṭi* 75:6, *i-ha-ṭu-u-n*[*i* 60:6, [*i-ha-ṭu-u-ni*] 61:6,
hazannu "mayor; (police) inspector": LÚ.*ha-*[*za-na-te*] 96:2, LÚ.*ha-za-na-ti* 97:2, r. 11, LÚ.*ha-za-ni* 95:9, LÚ.*ha-za-nu* 69 r. 1, 97:9,
hazannūtu "mayor's office": LÚ.*ha-za-nu-ti* 95:6, 97 r. 4,
hiāṭu "to weigh": [*ih-ti*]*-ṭu* 67:6,
hibiltu "debt": *ha-ba-la-ta-ia* 29:16, *hi-bil-a-te-šú* 29:17, *hi-bil-a-te-šú-nu* 43 r. 9, *hi-bi-la-te*]*-šú* 29:8,
hiddu (mng. uncertain): *hi-id-du* 65 r. 8, 10,
hirṣu "cut, slice": *hi-ir-ṣu* 63 r. 3,
hissutu "reminder, memorandum": *hi-is-su-tú* 23:6, r. 1,
hiṭṭu "fault, crime, sin": *hi-iṭ-ṭa-a-a* 34 r. 17, *hi-iṭ-ṭa-šú-nu* 63:10, *hi-iṭ-ṭu* 75:5, *hi-ṭa-a-te* 62:11, *hi-ṭa-ni-šú-nu* 63:8, *hi-ṭa-šú-nu* 63:12, *hi-ṭu* 36:3, 122:10, 129:7,
hubtu "booty, captives": *hu-ub-tú* 137:14, LÚ.*hu-ub-tú* 45:9,
hudû "joy": *hu-du-ú* 126:8, 127:8, 128:8,
hullānu "cloak, wrap": TÚG.*hu-la-nu* 17 r. 7,
hūlu "road, way; expedition, caravan": KASKAL 48 r. 14, KAS]KAL 240:5, KA]SKAL 5:5, K]ASKAL.MEŠ 231:3, KASKAL.2 31:6, 127:19, 140 r. 8, see also *harrānu,*
hurāṣu "gold": KUG.GI 60 s. 1, 63:30, r. 17, 64 r. 5, 67:7, 12, 69:5, 95:8, 97:18, 197:6,
huṭāru "staff": *hu-ṭa-ru* 125 r. 11,
iabutu see *abutu,*
iābilu "ram": UDU.NITÁ.MEŠ 5:16,
iāu see *ijû,*
ibissu "bundle(?)": *ib-bi-is-si* 123 r. 4,
iddāti see *dātu,*
idu "side": [*in*$_6$]*—ni-di* 141:3,
idû "to know": *i-di* 183 r. 6, *ud-da-áš-šú* 42 r. 2,
igāru "wall": É.SIG$_4$ 214 r. 4,
igizaggû (a semi-precious stone): NA$_4$.IGI.ZAG.GA 81 r. 3,
ijû "mine": *ia-u* 34 r. 16, *ia-ú* 155 r. 2,
ikīsu "brother-in-law": LÚ.*i-ki-i-su* 63 r. 26,
ikkāru "farmer": LÚ.ENGAR 79:10, LÚ.ENGAR.MEŠ 5:22, L]Ú.ENGAR.[M]EŠ 5 r. 13,
ikkillu "scream, wail": *ki-il-lu* 36:14,
ikkû "yours": *ik-ku-u* 183:11,
ikribu "blessing": *ik-ri-ib-šú-nu* 154:5,
ilku "state service, duty": *il-ki* 40 r. 15, *il-ki-ia* 44 r. 6,
ilu "god": DINGIR 126:10, 12, DINGIR-*a-a* 127 r. 17, DINGIR.MEŠ 16:3, 23:5, 52:3, 7, 72:9, 97:7, 98:6, 99:5, 110 r. 2, 118:4, 122:7, 11, 126:13, 129:4, 8, 11, s. 1, 148:5, 173:3, 191 r. 12, 194:2, DINGIR.ME[Š] 128 s. 2, 181 r. 7, DINGIR.[MEŠ 122:10, DINGIR.[ME]Š 126:24, [DINGIR.MEŠ 96:5, 127 r. 21, 132:4, DINGIR.MEŠ-*ia* 5 r. 19, DINGIR.MEŠ-*ka* 61:3, 207:3, DINGIR.MEŠ-*k*[*a* 36 r. 2, DINGIR.MEŠ]-*ka* 60:3, DINGIR.MEŠ-*ni* 100:17, DINGIR.MEŠ-*šú* 126:2,
imāru "donkey": ANŠE.ME 88:18, [AN]ŠE.NITÁ-*ma* 89:10, ANŠE.NITÁ.MEŠ 137 r. 13,
imittu "right side, south": 15 126:20,

immati "when?": *a-na—ma-ti* 126 r. 17, *im—ma-te* 176:6, [*i*]*m—ma-te* 214 r. 3,

immeru "sheep": UDU 56:10, UDU.MEŠ 48 r. 5, 236:5,

ina "in; by means of; from": *ina* 2:6, 10, 3:5, 5:5, 19, 20, e. 26, r. 2, 9, 12, 20, 23, 6:2, 6, e. 10, 8:6, r. 4, 9:5, 10:2, 4, 14:7, 15:3, 7, 10, 13, 21, 25, 16:3, 4, 17:6, r. 4, 8, 18:7, 20 r. 4, 7, 21:9, 17, 20, r. 6, 13, 15, 25:6, 8, 9, 29:5, 9, 14, 15, 30:6, 8, r. 5, 31:9, r. 4, 32 r. 20, 22, 34:6, 10, 18, 21, 23, r. 4, 8, 14, 16, 18, 35:6, 8, r. 8, 36:3, 8, 15, r. 4, 13, 39:6, 7, 11, 40:9, 14, r. 5, 9, 11, 41 r. 2, 10, 13, 42 r. 9, 12, 15, 43:3, r. 7, 11, s. 1, 44 r. 4, 45:6, 7, 10, 11, r. 1, 6, 12, 13, 15, 16, 47 r. 5, 48:10, r. 1, 5, 14, 49 r. 4, 5, 51:3, 52 e. 10, r. 2, 3, 7, 8, 53 r. 7, 9, 54:1, 12, 55:1, 56 r. 8, 59:4, 5, 6, 7, 15, r. 2, 3, 6, 7, 8, 11, 15, s. 3, 60:5, 6, 7, 9, 10, 11, 13, 16, r. 5, 6, 17, 61:4, 5, 6, 7, 9, 11, r. 2, 62:2, 14, r. 6, 9, 63:6, 11, 13, 14, 16, 20, 22, 24, r. 5, 16, 27, 28, 29, 30, s. 1, 2, 64:1, 3, 5, 6, 7, 8, 10, e. 11, r. 1, 3, 5, 7, 9, 12, 65:5, 7, 13, r. 4, 15, s. 1, 66:4, 67 r. 5, 13, 68:20, r. 12, 69:7, 71:8, r. 3, 5, 73:3, r. 2, 4, 76 r. 1, 77 r. 2, 7, 78:4, 6, 8, 9, 10, 13, 15, 16, r. 2, 5, 7, 9, 10, 15, 79:4, 10, 15, r. 6, 80:6, 82:17, 84:6, 8, r. 11, 12, 85:6, 86:12, 87:8, 18, r. 3, 88:8, 11, 12, 19, 89:10, 15, r. 2, 4, 5, 90:6, 12, r. 3, 4, 9, 10, 91:3, r. 3, 92:6, 10, 11, 93:2, r. 1, 3, 94:4, 95:2, 9, 11, 14, r. 4, 6, 15, 16, 17, 19, 96:15, r. 7, 8, 11, 16, 22, 97:13, 98:4, 99 r. 1, 4, 100:14, 102 r. 1, 105:13, 14, 17, 19, r. 4, 10, 16, 108:5, 110 r. 4, 111:7, 8, 112:4, 9, r. 4, 6, 9, 17, 113:7, 114 r. 9, 10, 11, 120:9, r. 5, 121:6, 7, 10, 14, r. 14, 15, 17, 122:6, 9, r. 11, 12, 14, 123:4, r. 6, 124 r. 4, 125:10, 13, r. 1, 2, 7, 8, 126:22, r. 16, 127:12, 16, r. 7, 128 r. 2, 7, 13, 16, 129:7, 14, r. 1, 5, 10, 131 r. 4, 7, 132:6, 8, r. 2, 134:5, 6, r. 3, 135:4, r. 10, 136:6, 137:6, r. 10, 15, 138 r. 11, 139:9, 10, 140:10, r. 1, 10, 14, 15, 141:5, 143:6, 8, r. 4, 6, 10, 145:7, 146:3, 10, 147:1, 148:9, r. 1, 2, 6, 7, 13, 16, s. 1, 149:7, 150 r. 3, 151 r. 6, 7, 154:8, 9, 10, 155 r. 10, 158:1, 160 r. 1, 7, 162:6, 12, r. 5, 163:3, 5, 164:6, 168:1, 5, 169:4, r. 7, 171:7, 173:5, 181:5, r. 5, 7, 183:6, 7, 13, 184 r. 2, 185:6, 187:5, 191:14, 192 r. 3, 13, 196:4, 197:7, r. 2, 199 r. 2, 200 r. 7, 9, 201:1, 2, 3, r. 2, 203 r. 1, 4, 204 r. 4, 7, 205 r. 2, 3, 207:7, 8, 9, 10, 208:6, 217:2, r. 1, 218:7, 222:1, 225:2, 230 e. 1, 232:5, 235 r. 2, 236:2, 239:1, 243 r. 4, *ina*] 8 r. 9, 19:7, 64:4, 78:17, 104:2, 116 r. 3, 127 r. 19, 206 r. 3, *in*[*a* 122 r. 7, *i*[*na* 63 r. 6, *i*]*na* 232:4, [*ina* 4:3, 5:4, 10:8, 15:5, 27:6, 33 r. 7, 35 r. 7, 36 r. 15, 37:8, 55 r. 3, 59:12, 60:5, r. 9, 61:10, 62:1, 63:1, 66:8, 68 r. 9, 70:2, 78 e. 24, 79:17, 86:7, 89:4, 5, 97:14, 119 r. 3, 125 r. 12, 128:12, 137 r. 16, 138 r. 9, 149:1, 152:6, 155:1, 161:3, 6, 189:6, [*ina*] 8:3, 25 r. 3, 41:14, 44 r. 3, 63 e. 32, 72:9, 83:7, 88:15, 91:2, 162:13, [*in*]*a* 64:5, [*i*]*na* 40 r. 16, *i-na* 27:11, 29:11, 47 r. 6, 65:12, 123 r. 11, 126:12, 18, 19, 127:19, r. 5, 10, 16, 143:11, 13, 242 r. 5, 6, *i-n*[*a* 126:25, *i-n*[*a*] 126:11, [*i-n*]*a* 16 r. 1,

irkalla "netherworld": (*i*)*-ri-kal-la* 31:8,

irtu "breast": *ir-te* 84 r. 12, *ir-ti* 63:11, 95 r. 6,

irṭu (mng. unknown): *ir-ṭu-šu* 149:4,

ishunnutu "grape": GIŠ.KIN.GEŠTIN.MEŠ 5:13,

isītu "tower": URU.*i-si-ti* 29:6,

ispillurtu "cross": *is-pi-lu-rat* 143 r. 7, NA$_4$.*is-pi-lu-ur-te* 148 r. 13,

issēn "one": 1-*en* 9:3, 22:6, 8, 26:13, 42 r. 9, 63:10, s. 1, 90:4, 105 r. 10, 143:15, 148 r. 9, 201:2, 243 r. 1, 1-*e*[*n*] 100 r. 7,

issēniš "likewise, at the same time, in addition": *is-se-niš* 25:10, 81 r. 6, *is-s*]*e-niš* 183 r. 5, *is-se-niš-ma* 125 r. 9,

issēt "one": 1-*et* 17 r. 7, 100 r. 13, 15, 1-*te* 53 r. 2, 3, 63 r. 29,

issi "with": *is-se-e-ni* 21:10, *i*[*s-se-e-šú* 171:11, *is-si-ia* 29:7, 16, 36 r. 10, *is-si-i*[*a* 32 r. 2, *is-si-ka* 59 r. 16, 60 s. 4, *is-si-k*[*a* 52:6, *is-si-k*[*a*] 219 r. 4, [*is-si-ka*] 60 r. 15, *is-si-ni* 60 r. 20, *is-si-šá* 78 r. 11, *is-si-šu-nu* 44 r. 5, 49 r. 9, *is-si-šú* 5 e. 24, 39 r. 2, *is-s*[*i-šú* 60 r. 12, *is-si-šú-nu* 21:18, r. 5, 59 r. 9, s. 1, 60 r. 13, *i*[*s-si-šú-nu*] 135 r. 4, *is-si-*[*x* 200 r. 3, *i-se-e-šú* 43 r. 8, *i-si-ia* 43:10, *i-si-ni* 62 r. 6, *i-si-šú* 64:10, 141:2, *i-si-šú-nu* 63:7,

issi/u "with/from": TA 5 r. 3, 15:27, r. 3, 16 r. 3, 17 r. 9, 11, 20:5, 32 r. 11, 19, 33 r. 5, 34:9, r. 6, 12, 22, 35:7, 36:9, 40 r. 1, 15, 42 r. 5, 45:13, 48:6, r. 4, 11, 51:4, 52 r. 2, 53 r. 5, 56 r. 5, 59:6, 7, 8, 9, 10, 11, r. 3, 8, 11, 13, 16, s. 1, 60:3, 5, 8, 14, r. 13, 61:7, 62 r. 5, 10, 11, 63:19, 27, r. 6, 14, 27, 66:6, 67:10, 78:7, 13, 15, 81:8, 82:10, 11, 13, 15, r. 13, 84:10, r. 2, 87:7, 91 s. 2, 95:4, 10, 13, r. 3, 8, 14, 98 r. 7, 100:12, r. 8, 15, 103:4, 107:8, 112:6, 10, r. 2, 4, 8, 115:11, r. 2, 8, 119:4, 120 r. 1, 121 r. 19, 122:8, 124 r. 1, 125 r. 4, 126:10, 14, r. 11, 127:10, 22, r. 9, 128:10, r. 3, 129 r. 7, 11, 135 r. 9, s. 2, 137:6, 140:9, r. 3, 4, 148 e. 21, 22, r. 8, 12, 20, 150:9, 155:7, r. 9, 169 r. 10, 170:8, 171:4, 181:10, 183:14, r. 10, 191:11, r. 5, 7, 200 r. 4, 204:7, 222 r. 1, T[A 158:2, T]A 11 r. 9, 217:1, [TA 5:11, 29:4, 6, 31:8, 60:7, 61:8, 67:1, 5, 86:6, 207:4, [TA] 63:28, [T]A 10:9, 44 r. 6, 55:3,

issi-ekalli see *sēgallu,*

issurri "perhaps": *is—su-ri* 54:6, 59 r. 1, 67 r. 8, *is—su-ri*] 242 r. 1, *is—su*]*-ri* 138:6, [*is—s*]*u-ri* 237 r. 1, *is—su-ru* 127 r. 3, *is—su-ur-ri* 148:19, *i—*[*su-ri*] 64 e. 12, *i—su-ur-r*[*i* 165 r. 3,

issu B "woman, wife": MÍ 27 r. 3, 63:1, MÍ.MEŠ 5 r. 20, MÍ.MEŠ-*šú-nu* 63 r. 26, MÍ.ME-*šú-nu* 54:9, MÍ-*šú* 27:8, 10, 50:7, 9, 63:5, r. 23, 24, 78 r. 10, 95:5, [MÍ]-*šú* 95:1,

iṣu "tree, wood": *e-ṣi* 197:7, GIŠ.MEŠ 125 r. 1, 183 r. 4,

išdu "foundation, base": [SUHUŠ 33:9,

iškāru "assigned quota, impost": ÉŠ-*iš*-QAR.MEŠ 43:13, ÉŠ.QAR 63:13, ÉŠ.QAR.MEŠ 43 r. 2,

kabāsu "to tread upon, trample": *ni-ka-ba-su-u-ni* 125 r. 3, *ú-ka-ba-as* 63:22,

kabsu "old male sheep":

ka'i see *kullu, kab-su* 5 r. 6, UDU.*kab-su* 22:8, UDU.*k*]*ab-su* 236:4,

kaiamānīu "constant, permanent": *ka-a.*(*a*)*-ma-nu-te* 115:12,

kaiamānu "constant(ly)": *ka-a-a-man* 29:9, *ka-a-a-ma-nu* 36:9, 10, 59:6, *ka-a-a-ma-*[*nu* 119 r. 4, *ka-a-a-*[*m*]*a-nu* 60 s. 1,

kakkubu "star": MUL.MEŠ 21:19,

kalāma "all, everything": [*ka*]*-la-me* 72 r. 1,

kalbu "dog": *kal-ba-a-*[*ni* 132:10, *kal-bi* 31 r. 3, 32 r. 12, 33 r. 6, 127 r. 15, 128 r. 15, *kal-bi-šú* 36:5, r. 4, *kal-bu* 132:10, UR.KU 34 r. 17, UR.KU-*šú* 29:11,

kallāpu "outrider(?)": LÚ.*ka*]*l-lab*.MEŠ 231:1, LÚ.*kal-lap* 90:7, 8, 9, 10, LÚ.*kal-*[*lap*.MEŠ] 90 r. 5,

kallāp šipirti "dispatch rider(?)": LÚ.*kal-lap—[ši-pir-ti* 6 r. 4,

kalliu "mule express": LÚ.*kal-li-i* 148 r. 16,

kallumu "to show, display": *lu-kal-lim-an-ni* 31 r. 1, *lu-[kal-li-mu]* 36 r. 3, *lu-kal-li-mu-na-ši* 117 r. 4, *uk-tal-lim-šú-nu* 154:14, r. 8, *uk-tal-li-mu-šú* 65:9, *ú-kal-lam-ka* 65 r. 13,

kallutu "bride, daughter-in-law": *kal-lat* 28 r. 5, MÍ.É.GI$_4$.A-*su* 50:11,

kalu "all": [DÙ]-*šú-nu* 41 r. 2, *ka-li-šú-nu* 132:5,

kal ūmi "daytime": *kal-la*—UD-*mu* 21 r. 2,

kammusu "to sit, live, stay": *kam-mu-su* 105 e. 20, 154 r. 7, *kam-mu-su-u-ni* 121:8, *k[a-mu]-sa* 120:10,

kanāku "to seal": *ik-nu-ku-u-ni* 49 r. 8, *ik-ta-an-ku* 63:17, *li-ik-nu-ku* 148 r. 14,

kanāšu "to submit": *lu-š]a[k-ni-šú]* 132:8, *ú-sak-niš* 127:12, *[ú-šak-ni]-iš* 128:13, *ú-šak-nu]-šú* 126:18,

kanūnu (Kanun, name of the 10th month; a festival): ITI.AB 45:10, 117:13,

kappu "list(?)": *kap-pu* 50:1,

kapru "village": URU.ŠE.MEŠ-*ti* 5 r. 12,

kaqqad Pazūzi "Pazuzu head": SAG.DU—*pa-zu-za-a-ni* 65 r. 4,

kaqqudu "head, principal (person)": LÚ.SAG.DU.MEŠ 97:3,

kaqquru "earth, ground, region": *kaq-qar* 126:22, KI.TIM 127 r. 21, 128 s. 2, 148:5,

karābu "to bless": *ik-ra-bu-[šú-nu* 126 r. 5, *i[k-tar]-bu* 154:4, *[ik]-tar-b[u* 154:2, *ik-tar-bu-ka* 96 r. 6, *i-kar-ru-bu* 126 r. 20, *lik-ru-bu* 14:6, 15:3, 17:5, 20:4, 21:5, 22:5, 23:5, 25:5, 26:7, 27:5, 29:3, 31:6, 35:5, 41:8, 42:8, 43:6, 48:5, 49:6, 69:2, 70:1, 78:3, 81:7, 82:5, 83:5, 84:5, 86:4, 87:5, 88:6, 92:5, 97:8, 98 r. 11, 99:7, 100:5, 105:7, 107:7, 111:6, 112:4, 113:5, 115:4, 120:5, 121:5, 127 r. 22, 128 s. 3, 131:4, 132:4, 134:4, 136:6, 137:5, 139:5, 140:5, 142:6, 143:5, 144:5, 148:8, 152:5, 180:5, 181:5, 194:3, 218:6, *lik-ru-bu]* 114:5, 135:7, 145:5, 162:5, 164:5, 187:4, *lik-ru-b]u* 38:2, 125:1, *lik-ru-[bu]* 18:5, *lik-r[u-bu]* 34:3, *lik-r]u-bu* 124:5, *lik-[ru-bu]* 39:5, 85:5, 96:7, 179:5, 183:5, 188:5, 190:5, *lik]-ru-bu* 24:5, *li[k-ru-bu]* 169:3, *li[k-ru-b]u* 19:5, *l[ik-ru-bu* 185:5, *[lik-ru-bu* 138:6, 151:3, 175:7, *[lik-ru-bu]* 37:3, 44:6, 174:8, 189:5, *[lik-ru-b]u* 57:5, 116:6, *[lik-ru]-bu* 119:4, *[lik-r]u-bu* 184:5, *[lik]-ru-bu* 110:5, *[l]ik-ru-[bu]* 191:5, *lik-ru-bu-ka* 52:4, *lik-ru-bu-šú]* 36 r. 2, *lik-ru-ub* 65:2, 98:7, *li-ik-ru-bu* 33:8, *li-[ik-ru-bu* 192:6,

karāku "to collect, wrap (up)": *ik-ri-ka-a* 9:6, *ik-te-rik* 112 r. 12, *ik-ti-ri-ik* 89 r. 3,

karāmu "to stock up": *kar-mat* 111 r. 1, *kar-ma-tu-ú-ni* 117:14,

karānu "wine": GEŠTIN 5:8, GEŠTIN.MEŠ 191:11, GIŠ.GEŠTIN 117 r. 6, GIŠ.GEŠTIN.MEŠ 209 r. 2, [GIŠ].GEŠTIN.MEŠ 117 r. 1,

karāru "to lay, throw, cast; to place, put, set; to deposit, pile up": *ak-ta-ra-ar* 60:14, *ik-tar-ru* 95:14, *ik-ta-ra-ra* 63 r. 6, *[i]k-ta-[ra-ra]* 89 r. 6, *ik-ter-ru* 63:19, *ik-te-r[u* 8 r. 1, *i-kar-ra-ru-ru-ni* 163 r. 4, *i-kar-ru-ru* 119 r. 5, *kar-rak* 29:15, *kar-ru* 56 s. 1, 95 r. 10, 14, *ka-ra-ri* 111:12, 125:5, *kur-ru* 5:17, 21:17, *li-ik-ru-ra* 111 r. 6, *li-ik-ru-ru* 163:6, *ni-ik-ru-ru-u-ni* 143:7, *ni-ik-ru-ur* 125 r. 12, *ni-ik-ta-r[a-ar]* 197:7, *tak-ru-ur* 59:7, *ta-kar-ra-ár* 17 r. 8,

karṣī "slander, calumny": *kar-ṣi-ia* 47 r. 2,

kāru "quay, port, harbour; trade": *ka-a-ru* 127:16, 17, 20, KAR 83 r. 1,

kasāpu "to break": *i[t-t]ak-sap* 25:11,

kaspu "money": *kas-pi* 41 r. 2, 10, 225:2, *kas-p]i* 123 r. 6, *kas-pi-šú-nu* 54:3,

kaṣāpu "to reckon, figure out": *tak-ṣip* 54:7,

kaṣāru "to knot, knit": *i-ka-ṣur* 216:10,

kašādu "to reach, conquer; (Š) to fulfil": *lu-šak-š]i-d[u]* 132:9,

kāšunu "you (pl.)": *ka-šá-nu-u-ma* 63 r. 1,

kēnu "righteous, just, truthful": *ke-e-nu* 126:1, *ke-nu-ti* 8 r. 3, *ki-i-nu* 29:3, see also *kuānu,*

kēttu "truth; truly": *ket-te* 78:6, *ket-tu* 78:7, *ket-tú* 16 r. 2, 130:9, *ke-e-tu* 243:7, *ke-ti-ia* 10:2,

kî "as; if, whether": *ki* 2:8, r. 3, 65 s. 2, *k[i* 8 r. 5, *ki-i* 5:13, 7:3, 8:5, r. 3, 29:12, 31 r. 3, 32 r. 12, 16, 34 r. 8, 39:10, 42 r. 2, 4, 60:13, 16, r. 5, 63:18, r. 2, 14, 15, 65:4, 66:3, 68 r. 9, 70:3, 71:6, 73:5, 105 r. 6, 115 r. 14, 117:12, 121:6, r. 6, 124:6, 129 r. 4, 131 r. 4, 134 r. 4, 135:13, 143:9, r. 14, 154:7, 181:8, 198 r. 4, 217 r. 3, *ki-i]* 173:4, *ki]-i* 37 r. 8, *k[i-i]* 17:11, *k[i]-i* 15:11, *[ki-i* 33 r. 6, 12, 77 r. 6, 169 r. 8, *[ki-i]* 45:10, *[ki]-i* 15:6, 35 r. 5, 8,

kibtu "wheat": ŠE.GIG.MEŠ 5:12,

kidinnu "protection; protégé": *ki-din-nu* 105 r. 12,

killu see *ikkillu,*

kīma "when; after; if; as soon as; like": *a—ki-ma* 78 r. 15, *a—ki-m[a* 168:3, *ki-ma* 6:5, 29:14, 34 e. 26, 65 r. 8, 79:9, 115 r. 6, 157 r. 7, 242 r. 7, *[k]i-ma* 207:3,

kinaltu "congregation, assembly": LÚ.*ki-na-al-ti* 20:5,

kinātu "colleague": *ki-na-ta-te-ia* 36 r. 8,

kīnu see *kēnu,*

kīpu (mng. uncert.): *ki-pa-ni* 40:3,

kiriu "orchard, garden": GIŠ.SAR.MEŠ 29 r. 3,

kispu "funerary offering": *ki-is-pi* 52 r. 3,

kissutu "fodder": *ki-[su-tú* 112:13,

kiṣru "cohort": *ki-ṣir* 43:4,

kišādu "neck(-stone), neck seal, amulet": NA$_4$.*ki-šá-du* 65 r. 3, see also *libānu,*

kiššatu "world, universe": ŠÚ 28 r. 4,

kitru "aid, auxiliary troops": *kit-ri* 147:3, *kit-r[i* 147:4,

kitû "flax, linen; tunic": GADA 82 r. 5,

kuānu "to be firm, loyal, true; (D) to confirm, establish, determine, settle": GIN 96 r. 1, *i-ku-u-nu* 99:4, *ke-na-a-ka* 9 e. 9, *ke-n]a-ku-ni* 169 r. 8, *[ke-nu-ni* 91 s. 2, *k[e-nu-u-ni]* 169 r. 10, *ke-nu-u-nu* 126:10, *[k]e-nu-ú-ni* 207:5, *ki-na-a-te* 121:1, *lu-ki]n-nu* 59 r. 10, *lu-ki-ii-ni* 44 r. 5, *lu-ki-in-ma* 78 r. 5, *lu-ki-in-nu* 33:11, *lu-ki-na-an-ni-ni* 78 r. 12, *lu-ki-na-a-ni* 43 r. 9, *uk-ti-i-nu* 1:12, see also *kēnu,*

kūdunu "mule": AN[ŠE.*ku-din*.MEŠ] 177:2, [ANŠE.*ku-d]in*.MEŠ 5:9,

kullu "to hold, deploy, wield": *lu-ka-i* 128 r. 17, *ú-kal-lu-u-ni* 154:11, *ú-ka-la* 63 r. 18,

kūmu "instead; lest": *i—ku-me* 36:6, *ku-me* 78:9, *ku-um* 63 r. 31, 90 r. 3, *ku-um-mu-šu* 45:4,

kunāšu "emmer": ŠE.ZÍZ.MEŠ 5:12,

kurummutu "barley (ration)": ŠE.PAD.MEŠ 5:12, e. 26, 35:5, 7, 8, 52 r. 5,

kusāpu "bread": *ku-sa-pi* 26:10, *ku-sa-pu*

183:9, r. 15, NINDA.HI.A 31 r. 5, 200 r. 8, NINDA.MEŠ 53 r. 9, NINDA.MEŠ-*šú-nu* 205 r. 3,

kusītu "robe": *ku-si-a-ti* 95:8, TÚG.BAR.DIB.MEŠ 84:8,

kussiu "throne, seat, chair": GIŠ].GU.ZA 11 r. 2, GIŠ.GU.ZA 29:10, 34 r. 8, GIŠ.GU].ZA 33:9, G]IŠ.GU.ZA 11 r. 6, GIŠ.GU.ZA.MEŠ 53:11, GU.ZA 11 r. 9,

kuzippu "garment, cloth": *ku-zip-pi* 5:6, 83 r. 3, *ku-zip-pi-ia* 5:6, *ku-zip-pi-ma* 159:3,

lā "not": *la* 82:16, 5 r. 10, 11, 12, 6:3, 4, r. 1, 7 r. 2, 9:6, 7, r. 2, 10:12, 11:6, 12:3, 20 r. 10, 21:21, r. 12, 26:10, 28:3, 4, 29 r. 1, 3, 6, 31 r. 5, 32 r. 5, 19, 34:15, 21, r. 10, 11, 13, 19, 35 r. 3, 40:8, 13, 15, r. 2, 7, 41:14, 42:10, r. 6, 45 r. 4, 5, 8, 15, 48 r. 10, 49 r. 7, 52 r. 3, 54:3, 59:3, 11, 13, 60:9, 12, r. 14, 18, 21, 61:12, r. 3, 4, 7, 62:4, 6, 11, r. 7, 63:12, 17, 20, 25, e. 32, r. 25, 34, s. 1, 3, 64:2, 5, e. 11, 65 r. 10, 14, 66:2, 6, r. 5, 67 r. 9, 68:15, r. 16, 73:2, 74 r. 2, 77 r. 5, 78:7, 16, 17, r. 8, 11, 79:9, r. 3, 81 r. 9, 82:17, r. 2, 14, 88:10, r. 7, 89:11, 90 r. 6, 91 s. 2, 94:7, 97 r. 8, 16, 19, 105 r. 11, 112 r. 7, 114 r. 10, 115 r. 9, 121:11, r. 8, 9, 20, 127:15, 16, r. 4, 5, 6, 12, 18, 128 r. 12, 137 r. 6, 139 r. 2, 140 r. 9, 10, 11, 141:4, 143:16, 146:10, 148:16, 150:6, 7, r. 1, 2, 154 s. 1, 165 r. 6, 169 r. 8, 170:5, 181 r. 7, 183:8, 9, 12, 18, 188 r. 4, 192 r. 9, 10, 201 r. 4, 5, 206 r. 4, 208:5, 212 r. 4, 239:3, 242 r. 4, *la*] 88 r. 8, 172 r. 4, *l*[*a* 32 e. 23, 45:16, 61:9, 63 e. 32, *l*]*a* 3:7, 11 r. 4, 151 r. 4, 155:9, 216:5, 245:2, [*la* 33 r. 11, 45:2, 59 s. 4, 61:12, 126:26, [*la*] 41 e. 16, [*l*]*a* 62:4, 70 r. 1, 88:18, 91:2, *la-a* 29:15, 32 r. 4, 34:20, e. 26, r. 7, s. 1, 36:4, 12, 14, r. 7, 64 e. 12, 98 r. 6, 128 r. 14, 169 r. 8, 173:2, 186 r. 4, 203 r. 3, 210:3, *la*]-*a* 132 r. 4, [*l*]*a-a* 135:15,

la'û "to be able": *i-la-'u-nu*] 129 r. 4, *i-la-'u-u-ni* 33 r. 12, *i-la-u-ni* 32 r. 16, 82 r. 3, 115 r. 14, 134 r. 5, 152 r. 3, [*i-la-u-ni*] 87 r. 7, *i-la-ú-ni* 143 r. 14,

labāru "to grow old": *lu-*[*ub-bur* 195:3,

labāšu "to dress": *la-bu-šú* 95:8, *ú-lab-bi-i*[*š*]*-ú-*[*ka-ni*] 63:29, *ú-la-b*[*a-x* 239:2,

labīru "old": *la-bi-ru* 125:12,

labû "to go around, surround": *al-ti-*[*bi* 122 r. 15, *il-t*[*i-bi* 216:6,

lamādu "to learn": *lil-mu-du* 233 r. 2, [*li*]*l-mu-du* 8:8,

lamānu "to be bad, evil": *la-ma-a-nu* 65 r. 12,

lapātu "to touch, affect": *i-la-pu-*[*t*]*ú* 151 r. 4,

laplaptu "parching thirst": *lap-lap-tú*] 126:22,

laqānu (mng. obscure): *la-qa-ni* 121 r. 19,

laqû "to take, buy": *i-si-qi* 65:5, ŠU.BA.T[I] 178:1,

lasāmu "to run, to serve": *i-sa-as-nu-ma* 135 s. 2,

laššu "is not": *la-aš-šú* 88:17, *la-áš-šú* 34:20, 53 r. 10, 54:4, 63:7, 117 r. 1, [*l*]*a-áš-šú* 128 r. 9, *la-áš-šú-ni* 40 r. 6, *la-a-šú* 40 r. 5,

latāku "to check, test": *lu-ut-ka* 92:9,

la pān "from": *la—pa-ni* 29:5,

lē'u "board, writing-board, plate, plating": *le-'u-u* 197:6, GIŠ.DA 53:8, GIŠ.*le-'i* 43 r. 11, GIŠ.*l*[*e-'u* 43 r. 12, GIŠ.LI.U$_5$.UM 5:19, 139:11, GIŠ.ZU.[MEŠ] 169 r. 2, ZU 197 r. 1, [ZU] 197:2,

lēpu "generation": *le-bu* 96 r. 4, *le-e-bi* 96 r. 5,

libānu "neck, neck seal": GÚ-*šá* 17 r. 8, UZU.GÚ 63:14, UZU.GÚ-*šú-nu* 63:16, 19, see also *kišādu*,

libbu "heart": *lib-bu* 106 r. 6, 196 e. 13, *lib-b*[*u* 168:6, *lib*^{ib}*-bi* 52:5, ŠÀ 5 r. 9, 16:3, 29:6, 15, 32 r. 11, 33 r. 5, 34 r. 4, 52 r. 2, 59:4, 5, 6, r. 3, 60:5, 8, 14, 16, 61:5, 8, 78:8, r. 15, 84 r. 2, 88:12, 95:4, 13, 98:11, 99 r. 4, 103:3, 120 r. 1, 125 r. 7, 135:4, r. 10, 139:9, 10, 140 r. 14, 143:6, 148 r. 13, 16, 181 r. 7, 201:3, ŠÀ] 61:4, 125 r. 12, 127 r. 20, Š[À 60:13, Š]À 31:8, 59:12, 60:5, 128 s. 1, [ŠÀ 140:9, 143 r. 4, ŠÀ-*ba-ka* 3:4, ŠÀ-*ba-k*[*a* 60 s. 4, ŠÀ-*ba-*[*ka* 4:2, ŠÀ-*ba-šú-nu* 60 s. 4, ŠÀ-*bi* 5:19, 15:22, 23 r. 2, 4, 30 r. 5, 35:7, 36:7, 40:14, r. 11, 49:6, 60:9, 61:9, 11, 63:13, 14, 16, r. 28, 29, s. 2, 64:10, 65:5, 7, 66:4, 67 r. 5, 71 r. 3, 76 r. 1, 78 r. 7, 82 r. 13, 87 r. 3, 89:15, 100:12, r. 8, 15, 105:7, 106:8, 108:4, 122 r. 14, 126:7, 8, 14, 19, 25, r. 19, 127:8, 22, r. 19, 23, 128:7, 8, r. 2, 16, 129:14, 131:5, 140 r. 8, 10, 154:10, 155 r. 9, 184 r. 2, 195:2, 204 r. 4, 242 r. 5, 6, ŠÀ-*b*[*i* 40 r. 1, 60:11, 129:7, 198 r. 4, ŠÀ-[*b*]*i* 64 e. 11, ŠÀ]-*bi* 123:4, Š[À-*bi* 123 r. 11, Š]À-*bi* 62 r. 14, s. 1, 161:3, [ŠÀ-*bi* 168:1, [ŠÀ-*bi*] 89 r. 2, ŠÀ-*bi-ka* 48:6, ŠÀ-*bi-ku-nu* 201:2, ŠÀ-*bi-ni* 116:8, ŠÀ-*bi-šá-ni* 53 r. 5, ŠÀ-*bi-šu-nu* 105 r. 10, ŠÀ-*bi-šú* 89:10, [ŠÀ]-*bi-šú-nu* 134 r. 3, ŠÀ-*bu* 5 r. 15, 36:11, 168:10, 176 r. 3, [ŠÀ-*bu* 38 r. 2, 101 s. 1, 119 r. 1, ŠÀ-*bu-šú* 36 r. 6, Š]À-*ka* 5:2,

libittu "brick": SIG$_4$ 79:12, SIG$_4$.MEŠ 25:9, 111 r. 1,

līdiš "the day after toworrow": *l*]*i-di-iš* 137 r. 15,

liginnu "one-column tablet, lesson, homework": IM.GÍD-*ki* 28:4, IM.GÍD.DA 65:6,

līmu "thousand": *li-mu* 127 r. 16, 1-*lim* 35:5, r. 9, 1-*lim-šú* 148:6,

liqtu "excerpt": *li-iq-te* 65:10,

lišānu "tongue": EME.MEŠ-*šú-nu* 122 r. 9,

littūtu "extreme old age": *lit-tu-tu* 98:9,

lū "let, may, be it": *lu* 1:6, 7, 8, 2:4, 3:4, 4:2, 5 r. 10, 11, 12, 9 e. 9, 14:3, 17:3, 19:3, 20 r. 10, 24:3, 25:3, 31 r. 5, 34 r. 11, 13, 19, 35 r. 3, 38 r. 3, 39:3, 42 r. 2, 44:4, r. 7, 47 r. 3, 48:3, 59:10, 60:9, 17, r. 16, 61:9, r. 4, 62:6, r. 11, 64:2, r. 12, 65:11, 66:2, 77 r. 2, 5, 78:2, 79:3, 82:3, 97:5, r. 19, 98:5, 101 s. 1, 102:4, 105 e. 23, 106 r. 8, 108:4, 109:3, 111:3, 112 s. 1, 114:3, 118:7, 121:3, r. 20, 126:23, 127 r. 6, 18, 19, 146:10, 148:18, 153:3, 154 s. 1, 160:1, 162:11, 164:3, 179:3, 181 r. 4, 185:3, 186:3, 188:3, 190:3, 192:3, 208:2, 213:4, 214 r. 1, 215:4, 219 r. 9, 228:3, 236:7, 239:3, *lu*] 29 r. 15, 59:6, *l*[*u* 135 r. 9, *l*[*u*] 118:10, [*lu* 5:3, 15:2, 18:3, 57:3, 110:3, 131:3, 132:2, 162:3, 175:3, 178:2, 184:3, 218:3, [*lu*] 23:3, 64 e. 11, 119 r. 1, [*l*]*u* 64 e. 12, 152:3, *lu-u* 6 r. 3, 20:2, 21:3, 22:3, 26:3, 31:4, 32:4, 34:7, r. 3, 35:3, 36 r. 12, 41:6, 42:6, 79:7, 81:5, 83:3, 84:3, 85:3, 87:3, 88:4, 100:3, 105:3, 106:3, 107:4, 108:3, 113:3, 117:5, 120:3, 124:3, 126:3, r. 7, 134:2, 135 s. 3, 136:4, 137:3, 138:3, 139:3, 140:3, 142:3, 144:3, 145:3, 148:2, 174:3, 180:3, 181:3, 189:3, 193:3, 196:3, [*lu-u* 27:3, 33:4, 92:3, 127:3, 143:3, 169:2, [*lu-u*] 34:2, 86:3, 89:3, 96:4, [*lu*]*-u* 183:3, [*l*]*u-u* 191:3, *lu-ú* 6 r. 3, 4, 127 r. 14, 128:3, 234 r. 4, [*lu-ú* 6 e. 9, 126:24,

luādu "to be embarrassed(?)": *al-tu-u-da* 63 r. 30,

lumnu "bad luck, ill fate, misfortune": *lum-*[*n*]*a-a-ni* 62:10,

luppu "bag": *lub-bi* 65 r. 15,

mā "thus": *ma* 5 r. 18, 8 r. 5, 15:11, 17 r. 10,

21:9, 17, 27 s. 1, 59 r. 16, 66:2, 67 r. 17, 105 e. 21, 121:15, 155:4, 183 r. 13, 200 r. 10, 231:7, 240:6, 243 r. 7, *ma-a* 5 r. 24, 6:1, 11:2, 15:4, 6, 7, 9, 10, 11, 12, 13, 14, 15, 17, 19, 21, 24, 25, 26, 17:8, 10, r. 5, 6, 7, 9, 13, 18:9, 21:11, 13, 22, r. 11, 12, 13, 27:8, 28:6, 29:17, r. 1, 34:12, 39:9, 11, 40 r. 14, 41:10, 12, 43 r. 3, 4, 45:3, 49 r. 5, 6, 53:13, 54:3, 4, 7, 56:7, r. 4, 11, 59:2, 7, r. 2, 3, 4, 5, 11, 12, 14, 15, 17, 60:3, 4, 5, 6, 8, 9, 10, 11, 12, 13, 16, 17, r. 2, 3, 5, 6, 7, 8, 12, 21, 22, 61:10, 62 r. 8, 63:10, 17, 18, 23, 28, 29, 30, 31, e. 33, 34, r. 1, 2, 3, 4, 5, 7, 8, s. 3, 64 e. 11, r. 1, 65 r. 12, 66:4, 5, 67 r. 11, 68:16, 69:4, r. 3, 70:3, r. 2, 71:5, 73 r. 2, 74:2, 4, 78:6, 79:5, 84:8, r. 1, 3, 6, 8, 85 r. 2, 3, 4, 86:11, 87:15, 88:11, 12, 14, 89:8, 90 r. 5, 91:6, 92:7, 95:3, 12, r. 18, 96 r. 13, 99 r. 1, 4, 6, 8, 9, 10, 105:14, 15, e. 22, 112 r. 2, 114 r. 5, 120 r. 3, 5, 121:10, 125:12, 126:20, 21, 22, 127:22, 23, r. 4, 134:7, 136:10, 137:8, 9, 12, 13, 15, 16, r. 7, 9, 11, 138:10, 140 r. 3, 143:14, 17, r. 3, 146:2, 3, 7, 148:13, 14, 15, 16, 19, r. 2, 5, 6, 9, 150:5, 6, 155 r. 6, 164:8, 171:6, 7, 173:4, 5, 6, 181:7, 10, r. 2, 183:7, 9, 10, 11, 12, r. 15, 191:12, 192:7, 199:5, 201:1, 202:3, 204 r. 2, 216:5, 218:9, 225:1, 4, 228:6, 234:3, 242 r. 2, *ma-a*] 17:12, 63 r. 6, 199:3, *ma-*[*a* 6:3, 59:7, 60 r. 9, 143 r. 2, *ma*]*-a* 9:3, 29 r. 3, *m*[*a-a* 15:16, 17 r. 2, 74:3, 143 r. 1, 216:4, *m*[*a-a*] 20 r. 9, *m*]*a-a* 9:7, 55:4, 60:1, 205 r. 8, 223:3, [*ma-a* 29:8, 39:12, 61:11, 63:24, e. 35, 71 r. 3, 5, 90:2, 138:7, 155:2, 219 r. 4, 228:5, 237 r. 3, [*ma-a*] 16:1, 67:7, 71 e. 10, 173:2, [*ma*]*-a* 60:14, 63 r. 1, 64:10, 71:8, 99 r. 12, 120 r. 1, 140 r. 8, 183:13, 212 r. 3, [*m*]*a-a* 15:7, 10, 63 r. 8, 64:10, 71 r. 2, 88:17, 94:6, 7, 191:11, 212 r. 2,

maʾādu "to be much, many, numerous": *ma-aʾ-da* 89:14, 117 r. 7, 140 r. 5, *ma-aʾ-d*[*a*] 90:8, *ma-aʾ-di* 64 r. 5, *ma-aʾ-du* 65 r. 12, 191:8, *ma*]*-aʾ-du* 67:13, *ma-aʾ-du-te* 62 r. 11, 64 r. 4, *ma-aʾ-du-*[*te*] 98:8, *ma-du-ti* 127 r. 7, *ma-du-ti*] 128 r. 1,

madādu "to measure": *lu-ma-di-du* 64:9, r. 3, *lu-*[*ma-di-d*]*u* 64:8, *ma-di-di* 48 r. 8, *ma-di-*[*id*] 148:14, *um-ta-di-i*[*d*] 205 r. 4, *un-ta-ad-*[*di-di*] 119 r. 3, *ú-ma-di-du-u-ni* 86:10,

magarru "wheel": [UMBI]N 25:10,

magāru "to agree, (with neg.) to refuse": *a-ma-gúr-u-ni* 78 r. 11, *im-*[*ma-gúr*] 201 r. 4, *im-ma-gúr-ru* 155:9, *i-ma-ga-ru-u-ni* 63:12, *i-ma-gúr* 29 r. 1, 41:14, *i-ma-gu-ru* 88:10, *le-ma-gúr* 65 r. 13,

mahāru "to accept, receive; to turn to, appeal to, implore, petition": *ah-hur-u-ni* 29:16, *at-ta-har* 35 r. 2, 52 r. 6, 114 r. 7, *a-hur-u-ni* 30:4, *a-hu-ru-ú-*[*ni*] 87:11, *a-mah-har* 5 r. 17, *a-ta-har* 82:8, *it-tah-raš-ši* 95:1, *it-tah-ru-šú* 139:13, *it-tah-ru-u-*[*ni*] 94:6, [*i-hu-ru-u-ni*] 39:8, *i-mah-har* 82:7, *mah-hur-u-ni* 53 r. 8, *mah-ra-tu-*[*u-ni*] 64:4, *mah-r*[*a-tu-u-ni*] 64:5, *mah-ri* 78:16, *ma-hir* 36 r. 14, *ma-hir-u-ni* 125:14, *ma-hi-ir* 34:16, 90:12, 92:11, 131 r. 6, 141 r. 1, *ma*]*-hi-ir* 171:8, [*ma-h*]*i-ru-u-ni* 131 r. 5, *mu-hur* 29 r. 1, *t*[*a-hur-u-ni*] 52:7,

mahāṣu "to strike, fight; to wound, hit": [*it-t*]*a-ha-aṣ* 25:11, *it-ta-ha-su* 149:3, *mah-ṣi-ni* 63:23, *ma-hu-uṣ* 15:14, *mì-h*[*iṣ*] 20 r. 8, *š*]*a-an-hu-ṣ*[*u*] 231:5,

mahīru "market price": KI.LAM 5:13,

makû "to be weak, feeble": *ma-ki-i* 32 r. 15, [*ma*]*-ki-i* 30 r. 1, *ma-ki-u* 5 r. 8, *ma-ki-*[*u-te*] 131 r. 2,

māla "once": *ma-a-la* 86:8,

malāhu "to tear out": *i-ta-am-la-ah* 100:13,

malāku "to advise, counsel": *im-mal-ku* 45 r. 8, *i-ta-ma-lik* 63:28,

malû "to be full; (D) to fill": *i-ma-la* 104:3, *ú-ma-lu-šú-*[*nu* 126 r. 6,

mannu "who?": *man-ni* 63:26, 65 r. 10, 181 r. 10, *man-nu* 32 r. 17, 63 r. 24, 65 r. 12, 68:16, 73 r. 2, 122:7, 11, 163 r. 2, 181 r. 6, 218:9, *ma*]*n-nu* 169 r. 7, *man-nu-ma* 5 r. 10, [*man-nu-ma* 79:9, *man-nu-um-ma* 34 e. 27,

manû A "mina": MA.NA 5:10, 32:14, 54:5, 10, 67:1, 69:4, 82 r. 12, 97:19, 155 r. 9, MA.N[A 56:7, MA.NA-*a-a* 54:8, 9,

manû B "to count, recite, deliver to": *ma-né-e* 34:8, *mu-nu* 5:14, *ú-man-na* 62:10,

maqaltānu (mng. obscure): *ma-qa-al-ta-a-nu* 63 r. 10,

maqātu "to fall, collapse; to defect": *i-ma-qa-tu-ni*] 207:6, *i-m*[*a-q*]*u-*[*t*]*a* 148 r. 1, *i-tuq-tu-u-ni* 148 r. 20, *i-tu-qu-tu* 100 r. 12, *i-tu-qu-ut* 100:14, r. 9, *i-tu-uq-tu* 100 r. 7, LÚ.*ma-*[*aq*]*-tu* 148 e. 20, LÚ.*ma-aq-tu-te* 136:6, r. 5, LÚ.*ma-aq-tu-u-te* 148:17, r. 19, *ma-qa-t*[*e* 101 r. 5, *ta-ma-qu-ta-an-*[*ni*] 52 r. 5, *ta-tu-qu-ut* 100 r. 16,

mār "as much/many as; all (those) who/which": *am—mar* 52:7, 79:8, 89 r. 2, 99:3, 121 r. 15, *a*[*m—mar* 60 r. 13, *a—mar* 158:2, *a—ma*[*r* 67 r. 15, *mar* 66:5, 78:15, *ma-ri* 126:17, r. 22,

marādu "to damage(?)": *i-me-ri-du-n*[*i* 101 r. 4, see also *marāṭu,*

mār ahi "nephew": DUMU ŠEŠ-*šú* 76 r. 5,

marāqu "to crush, destroy": *mu-ru-uq* 5:16, *ú-mar-ra-qa* 88:14,

marāṣu "to be ill, in trouble; (Š) to hurt": *mar-ṣa* 82:8, *mar-ṣa-at* 26:10, *mar-ṣa-šu-un-ni* 82:6, [*ma*]*-ri-ṣi* 149:4, *ú-šam*]*-ra-aṣ-šú-nu* 170:4,

marāṭu "to rub, scratch, damage": *i-ta-am-ri-ṭi* 100:9, *i-ta-*[*am-r*]*iṭ* 100:15, see also *marādu,*

marʾat šarri "princess": DUMU.MÍ—LUGAL 28:1,

marʾu "son": DUMU 15:20, 21:6, 7, 31:2, 34 r. 15, 16, 50:8, 63 r. 16, 67:4, 69:6, 99:9, 105:11, 115:8, 138 r. 8, DU]MU 9 r. 3, DUMU-*a-a* 30:8, 63:10, DUMU-*ka* 96 r. 3, DUMU.MEŠ 95 s. 1, 122 r. 13, D]UMU.MEŠ 152:6, DUMU.MEŠ-*ia* 1:7, 5:7, DUMU.MEŠ-*iá* 66 r. 6, DUMU.MEŠ-*ka* 1:4, DUMU].MEŠ-*ka* 59 s. 2, DUMU.MEŠ-*ni* 63 r. 1, 3, DUMU.MEŠ-*šá* 53:4, 63 r. 25, DUMU.MEŠ-*šú* 141 r. 4, DU]MU.MEŠ-*šú* 58:3, 5, DUMU-*šu* 99 r. 4, DUMU-*šú* 63 r. 13, 14, 65:7,

marʾutu "daughter": DUMU.MÍ 28 r. 2, 50:10, 60:6, D]UMU.MÍ 170 r. 3, DUMU.MÍ.MEŠ-*ia* 1:7, DUMU.MÍ.MEŠ-*ka* 1:4, DUMU.MÍ.MEŠ-*ni* 63 r. 3, DUMU.MÍ.MEŠ-*šú* 95:10, DUMU.MÍ-*sa* 53:6, 13, *ma-rat* 28 r. 5,

marʾūtu "sonship": DUMU-*ut-te* 53 r. 1,

mār banê "nobleman": DUMU—ŠU.SI.MEŠ 89:13,

mār damqi "nobleman; chariot fighter": LÚ.A—SIG 11:10, 68:18, 136 r. 1, LÚ.A—SIG$_5$ 34:10,

mār ekalli "courtier": DUMU—É.GAL 50:5, 6, 14,

marhuṣu "lotion": *mar*]*-hu-ṣu* 165 r. 5,

mār marʾi "grandson": DUMU—DUMU-*ka* 96 r. 4,

mār šarri "crown prince": A—LUGAL 148 r. 7, A—MAN 20 r. 11, 148 r. 15, DUMU.M[EŠ—LU]GAL 63 r. 14, DUMU—LUGAL 21:21, r. 8, 29:6, 7, 10, 16,

34:1, 2, 3, 15, 16, 19, 21, 22, 24, e. 25, r. 1, 3, 5, 6, 10, 17, 19, 20, 22, s. 1, 35:1, 3, 4, r. 1, 2, 36:10, 11, r. 1, 38:1, 41 r. 1, 65:4, 70:5, 106:1, r. 3, 7, 107:1, 4, 6, 116:1, 5, 124:1, 3, 133:1, 143 r. 5, 149:6, 155 r. 11, DUMU—LUGAL] 29:5, DUMU—LUG[AL 207:2, DUMU—LU[GAL 60:2, DUMU—L[UGAL 60:1, DUMU—[LUGAL] 70:6, DUMU]—LUGAL 70:1, DUM]U—LUGAL 116 r. 4, [DUMU—LUGAL] 34 r. 25, DUMU—MAN 28 r. 6, 35 r. 8, 37 r. 5, 63 e. 32, r. 20, 69:1, r. 1, 106:3, 11, 107:9, 124:5, 136:11, 13, 148:7, r. 3, s. 1, DUMU—MAN] 37 r. 3, DUMU—MA]N 37:1, DUMU—M[AN] 38 r. 2, DUMU]—MAN 118:6,

mār šipri "messenger": DUMU—*šip-ri* 137:9, 140 r. 14, DUMU—*šip-r]i* 137:6, DUMU—*šip-ri*.MEŠ 63 r. 22, LÚ].A—KIN 29:7, LÚ.A—KIN 6 r. 2, 87:12, LÚ.A—K[IN] 214 r. 1, LÚ.A—KIN-*ka* 148 r. 2, LÚ.A—*šip-ri* 56:4, LÚ.A—*šip-[ri* 96 r. 19,

masennu "treasurer": LÚ.IGI.DUB 21 r. 11, 63:15, 112:9,

masû "to wash": *an-te-se* 242 r. 7,

maṣātānu "influental man": *ma-ṣa-ta-a-nu* 63 r. 19,

maṣi "(as) much (as); (how) many, (how) long?": *ma-ṣi* 65 s. 2,

maṣṣartu "watch, guard": EN.NUN 25:9, 105 r. 1, 108:5, [EN.NUN 33 r. 8, EN.NUN-*ka* 59 s. 2, EN.NUN.MEŠ 105:9, 106 r. 5, 148:9, *ma-ṣar-ti-ku-nu* 148:15, *ma-ṣar-tu* 32 r. 14, 86 r. 16, 93 r. 5, 98 r. 9, *ma-ṣar-[tu]* 93:6,

maṣṣuru "guard": *ma-ṣar* 52:6, 86:5, 87:6,

mašālu "to be like, resemble": *lu-ša-an-šil* 146:4, *maš-la-ku* 66:2, *ú-sa-an-šil* 146:12,

maš'ennu? KUŠ.DA.E.SÍR 140:8,

maškunu "place, tent": *maš-kan-i-šú* 204 r. 7,

matāhu "to lift, pick up": *[in-ta]-at-ha* 97 r. 1, *la-a[n-tu-uh* 213:7, *li-im-tu-[hu* 59:10,

mātu "land, country": KUR 45 r. 10, 48 e. 13, 82 r. 6, 7, 105:14, 127:13, 128:14, KUR-*ia* 1:5, KUR-*ka* 1:8, KUR.KUR 29:14, 35 r. 6, 127:1, 128:1, 200 r. 6, *ma-a-te* 140 r. 8, *ma-a-ti* 126 r. 20,

māt nakiri "enemy land": KUR—*na-ki-ri* 105:14, 122:9,

maṭû "to be defective, lacking, missing": *ma-aṭ-ṭi* 139 r. 2,

maziu (a dish for serving soup, "tureen"): *ma-zi-i* 231 r. 3,

mazzassu "stand, post, position": *ma-za-as-su* 34 r. 12,

mazzāz pāni "courtier; entourage": LÚ.GUB.BA—*pa-ni-šu* 42 r. 10, LÚ.*man-za-za—pa-ni* 127 r. 7, 128 r. 2,

mazzāz pānūtu "position of a courtier": *ma]-za-az—pa-nu-te* 91:5,

meat "hundred": 1-*me* 1 r. 3, 40:2, 129 r. 10, 1-*m[e* 1 r. 2, 1-[*me* 1 r. 1, 1-*me*-58 82 r. 10, 2-*me* 40:1, 4, 74 r. 4, 2-*me-ma* 40:6, 4-*me* 35:7, 6-*me* 35:8,

memmēni "anybody, anything": *me-e-me-e-ni* 176:2, *me-me-e-ni* 34:20, 35 r. 4, 127 r. 12, 139 r. 1, 141:4, *me-me-ni* 29:15, 40:12, r. 4, 7, 60:6, 64:10, 82 r. 13, 98 r. 6, 112 r. 6, 160 r. 10, 173:2, 181 r. 6, 198 r. 1, *me-m[e-ni* 160 r. 11, 186 r. 3, *mi-i-mi-ni* 39 r. 2, *mi-mi-[i-ni* 87:17, *mì-mì-i-ni* 128 r. 11,

mētūtu "death": *mi-tu-ti* 97 r. 17,

mihru "equal, counterpart; colleague, comrade": *me-eh-ri-šu* 64 r. 1, *mì-hi-ri-šu* 115 r. 8,

mihṣu "blow; raid": *mi-ih-iṣ* 129 r. 7, *mi-ih-zi-a-ni* 129 r. 12,

milku "advice, counsel": [*m*]*ì-il-ku* 212 s. 2,

mīnu "what?": *mi-i-ni* 21:11, 62:9, 63 e. 35, 105 r. 21, 127 e. 27, r. 1, 129 e. 17, *mi-[i-ni* 10:11, *mi-i-nu* 34 r. 16, 36:6, r. 9, 52:9, r. 6, 66 r. 5, 78:9, 140 r. 12, 142 r. 4, 183:11, r. 3, 196:10, 202:5, 211 r. 3, *mi]-i-nu* 63 r. 7, *m]i-i-nu* 75:11, *mi-nim-ma* 5 r. 5, *mi-nu* 53 r. 11, 125:13, [*mi-nu* 175 r. 8, [*mi-nu*] 63:26, *mì-i-ni* 2 r. 4, 45 r. 12, 48 r. 8, *mì-i-nu* 10:5, 37:3, 59 r. 15, 17, 69 r. 3, 98 r. 3, 120 r. 9, 188 r. 3, *mì-i-[nu* 96 r. 13, 144:10, *mì*]*-i-nu* 71 r. 5, [*mì-nu* 31:9,

mišlu "half": *meš-lu* 93:12, r. 2, 1:2 54:8, 9, 10, 82 r. 12, 100:12, 127 r. 12, 128 r. 11,

mithuru "corresponding": *mit-hu[r-r]u* 5:8,

muātu "to die": *a-mu-at* 34:22, 39:12, *a-mu-[a]t* 127 r. 18, *a-mu-'a-at* 31 r. 5, *i-mu-at* 40:10, *i-mu-a]t* 33 r. 11, *i-mu-tú* 63:18, [*i*]*-mu-tú-u-ni* 207:7, *i-mu-u-at* 70 r. 1, *li-mu-tu* 59:7, 9, *li-mu-tú* 60 r. 14, 16, 17, *li-mu]-tú* 59 s. 4, [*li-mu-tú*] 59 s. 1, *me-e-te* 31:2, 34 r. 26, [*me-e*]*-te* 168:4, *me-e-ti* 105:15, e. 23, 127 r. 15, 128 r. 15, *me-tu* 126 r. 7, *mé-e-ti* 95:3, *uš-mat-tan-ni* 29:4, ÚŠ 97 r. 13,

mugirru "chariot": GIŠ.GIGIR 25:10, GIŠ.*mu-gir* 36:8,

muhhu "top, on": UGU 2:6, 3:5, 6:6, 10:4, 15:3, 7, 10, 21, 25, 17:6, 18:7, 20 r. 4, 21:20, r. 15, 25 r. 3, 27:6, 29:9, 34:18, r. 16, 36:15, r. 4, 13, 39:6, 41 r. 13, 42 r. 15, 43:14, r. 7, s. 1, 45 r. 12, 13, 48 r. 5, 54:1, 59:6, 60:6, 9, 61:6, 62:1, 14, 63:6, 22, r. 5, 27, 28, 30, 64:1, 7, r. 5, 9, 65:13, r. 15, 77 r. 7, 78:4, 17, r. 5, 9, 79:4, 10, r. 6, 83:7, 84:6, 8, 85:6, 87:8, 90:6, 91:2, 92:6, 10, 93:2, r. 1, 95:11, r. 17, 19, 96:15, r. 11, 97:13, 99 r. 1, 104:2, 105 r. 16, 112:9, r. 6, 9, 114 r. 10, 119:4, 125 r. 1, 127 r. 11, 129 r. 1, 5, 134:5, 136:6, 140 r. 1, 143 r. 10, 145:7, 148:9, 155:1, 163:3, 5, 169:4, 181:5, 183:13, 187:5, 196:4, 197:7, 203 r. 1, 205 r. 3, 207:6, 9, 217:2, 218:7, 239:1, 243 r. 4, UGU] 89:4, 5, UG]U 4:3, 63:1, 68 r. 9, 78 e. 24, 86:7, 95 r. 4, 222:1, 236:2, U[GU 59 r. 2, 162 r. 2, 164:6, 207:10, U[GU] 128 r. 5, U]GU 14:7, 37:8, 66:8, 70:2, 183:6, [UGU 137:6, 185:6, [UGU] 64:6, [U]GU 207:7, UGU-*hi* 5 r. 20, 15:13, 21 r. 13, 30:6, 51:3, 59 r. 3, 15, 64 r. 3, 68:20, 72:9, 77 r. 2, 95 r. 4, 108:5, 111:7, 114 r. 11, 116 r. 3, 121:7, r. 14, 125:10, 126:11, 12, 128 r. 9, 143:8, 152:6, 162:6, 206 r. 3, UGU-*hi*] 199 r. 2, UG]U-*hi* 79:17, UGU-*hi-ia* 8 r. 4, 34:23, 49 r. 4, 60 r. 6, 71:8, 78:10, r. 10, 148 r. 17, UGU-*hi-ia-a-ni* 78:15, UGU-*hi-ia-m[a* 6 e. 10, UGU-*hi-ka* 6:2, 9:5, 21:9, 60 r. 17, UGU-*hi-k]a* 5:4, UGU-*hi-ni* 40 r. 9, 88:15, 96 r. 7, UGU-*hi-šá* 59 r. 8, UGU-*hi-šu-nu* 148 r. 1, UGU-*hi-šú* 64 r. 12, 155 r. 10, UGU-*h[i-š]ú* 64:8, UGU]-*hi-šú-nu* 119 r. 3, 149:7, UG[U-*hi-š*]*ú-nu* 90 r. 9, UGU-*šá*] 39:7, UGU-*š*]*ú* 97:14, UGU-*šú-nu* 17 r. 4,

muk "thus": *mu-ku* 36 r. 8, 9, *mu-uk* 5 r. 6, 34:6, 78 r. 12, 81 r. 7, 112:13, 121:13, r. 6, 13, 162:11, 243:2, [*mu-uk*] 189:7, [*m*]*u-uk* 29:10,

mukīl appān/ti "chariot driver": LÚ.D]IB—PA.MEŠ 207:10, [LÚ.D]IB—PA.MEŠ 207:8, LÚ.*mu-kil*—KUŠ.*a-pa-a-ni* 63:21, LÚ.*m[u-kil*—KUŠ.*a-pa-a-ni*] 63:3, LÚ.*mu-kil*—KUŠ.PA.MEŠ 69:7, 78:4,

mukīl appātūtu "position of a chariot driver":

LÚ.*mu-kil*—K[UŠ.PA.MEŠ-*u-tú*] 68 r. 10,
mūlû "height, hill": *mu-le-e* 77 r. 7,
mūqu see *emūqu*
murabbānūtu "tutorship": *mu-rab-[ba-nu-te* 91:4,
murṣu "disease, sickness": *mu*]*r-ṣi* 167:4,
muṣappıtu "female dyer": MÍ.*mu-ṣap-pi-tú* 54:10,
mušamhiṣu "instigator of rebellion": *mu-šam-hi-iṣ-ṣu-u* 204 r. 10,
mušarkisu "recruitment officer": LÚ.*mu-šar-kis* 105:12, LÚ.*mu-šar-kis-a-ni* 137:15,
muššuru "to let go, abandon": *um-taš-šir* 123 r. 2,
mūšu "night": *mu-šu* 21 r. 2,
mūtānu "plague, pestilence": *mu-ta-ni* 127 r. 16,
muṭê "deficit, (with numbers) less": LAL-*e* 242 r. 3, 8,
nabalkutu "(Š) to turn upside down": *ú-sa-bal-ki-tú* 32 r. 10, *ú-sa-ba*]*l-ki-tú* 33 r. 4,
nādu "waterskin": *na-da-te-ku-ni* 126:23,
nagaru see *nakru,*
nahlaptu "armour; wrap, covering": TÚG.GÚ.È.MEŠ 95 r. 9,
nakāpu "to butt, push, thrust": *a-ti-kip* 63 r. 32,
nakāsu "to cut, dissect, slaughter": *i-nak-ki-su* 21:20, *i-tak-s[u* 171:9,
nakīru see *māt nakiri,*
nakkamtu "treasure, treasury": *na-kam-te* 63:21,
nakru "enemy": LÚ.KÚR 15:12, 129:2, 135 r. 10, L]Ú.KÚR 135 s. 2, LÚ.KÚR.MEŠ-*te* 132:7, *na-ga-ru-ti-ni* 126:17,
namāru "to be bright; (Š) to let shine": *i-na-mir-a-ni* 157:7, *nam-ru* 29:14, *na-ma-a-ru* 132:11, *na-mir* 67 r. 14,
nammušu "to set out": *nu-t[am-mì-iš* 140:10, *ú-ta-me-i[š* 216:7,
nāmurtu "audience gift": *na-mur-tú* 117:13,
nāmuru "tower": *na-mi-ri* 100 r. 10,
napāhu "to blow, ignite, light up; to rise": *i-nap-pa-ha-[an-ni*] 200 r. 4, *i-nap-pa-ha-an-nu* 127:10, 128:10,
nappāh parzilli "ironsmith": LÚ.SIMUG—AN.BAR 40 r. 3,
napšutu "life; person": *nap-šá-te* 129 e. 18, ZI.MEŠ 49 r. 1, 53:7, 56:9, 59:9, ZI.ME[Š 60 r. 8, Z[I.MEŠ 60 r. 7, [ZI.MEŠ 60 s. 3, ZI.MEŠ-*ia* 43 s. 1, ZI.MEŠ-*ka* 59:9, 11, s. 4, 60 r. 10, 19, s. 3, 61:6, ZI.MEŠ-*k[a* 60 r. 16, ZI.MEŠ-*k*]*a* 60:6, ZI].MEŠ-*ka* 60 s. 2,
nargallu "chief singer": LÚ.NAR.GAL 123:5,
narû "stele": *na-ru-u* 125 r. 7,
nāru "river": ÍD 161:3, 162:12, Í]D 161:6, ÍD-*m[a*] 163:3,
nâru see *nuāru,*
nasāhu "to pull out, uproot; to exact, extract, quote": *a-ta-as-ha* 45:14, *it-ta-as-ha* 112 r. 18, *i-na-su-[hu*] 96:17, *i-[na-su-hu*] 96 r. 9,
naṣāru "to watch, guard": *a-na-ṣar* 86 r. 17, 98 r. 10, *i-na-ṣa-ru-u-ni* 148 r. 11, *i-na-ṣu-r[u* 199:2, *la-aṣ-ṣur* 33 r. 8, *la-ṣur* 32 r. 14, *li-ṣur-ú-ka* 52:4, *li-ṣu-ru* 59 s. 2, *ni-iṣ-[ṣ]ur* 93 r. 5, *ni-n[a-ṣ]a-a[r*] 93:7, *ta-ta-aṣ-[ra*] 60 r. 7, *ú-ṣur* 60 s. 2,
naṣû "to strive(?)": *iṣ-ṣi-a* 60:17,
našû "to lift, carry; to take, bring": *at-ta-ṣa* 47:2, *at-ta-ṣa-áš-šú* 8:5, [*a-na-áš*]-*ši* 5 r. 20, *iṣ-ṣa* 5:15, *iš-šu-ú* 49 r. 1, *it-ta-ṣa* 16 e. 7, *it-ta-ṣu* 34:12, *it-ti-ši* 31:7, *it-t[i-ši* 216 r. 7, *i-na-áš-ši* 67 r. 7, *i-na-šu-ni* 56 s. 1, *i-ti-ši* 67:2, *liš-ši-a* 221:3, *li-ši* 56 s. 2, *li-ši-ú* 56 r. 10, *na-aṣ-ṣa* 140:8, *na-ṣa* 134 r. 3, *na-ṣ[a* 47 r. 7, *na-ṣa-ni-ni* 120:7, *na*]-*ṣu-niš-šú* 31:10, *na-ṣu-u-ni* 55 r. 2, 172 r. 5, *ni-iš-ši* 117 r. 5, 159:2, *t*]*a-áš-šú-u-ni* 155:3, *ta-ši* 15:11,
nazāru "to curse; (Š) to make accursed, hateful": *li-iz-zi-ru-u-ni* 36 r. 8, *us-sa-an-zi-ir-an-ni* 78 r. 3,
nēmudu "couch": *né-me-di* 197 r. 1,
nēmulu "profit, gain": *né-mal-šu* 36 r. 3,
nērubu "entrance, pass": *né-ri-bi* 88:8,
niālu "to lie, rest": *at-[te*]-ʾ*i-la* 30 r. 5, *i-ti-i-la* 64:10,
nību "name, amount, number": *ni-bu* 63:16,
nibzu "tablet, document": *ni-ib-zi* 63:13, 14,
nikkassu "accounts": NÍG.ŠID 92:10, NÍG.ŠID-*ia* 34:16, 82:10, NÍG.ŠID.MEŠ-*šú-nu* 5 e. 25,
niqittu "revenge(?)": *ni-qi-it-te* 62 r. 1,
niqiu "offering, sacrifice": UDU.SISKUR.[MEŠ] 154:3,
nīru "yoke": *ni-i-ri* 176:3, *ni-i*]-*ri* 175:8,
nisannu (Nisan, name of the first month): ITI.BA[RAG 197:5,
nišhu "diarrhea": *ni-iš-h[u* 165 r. 1,
nišī "people": UN.MEŠ 21 r. 3, 49 r. 3, 56 r. 11, 59:7, r. 9, s. 1, 4, 60 r. 13, 15, 17, 64 r. 3, 154 r. 3, UN.[MEŠ 60 r. 14, [UN.MEŠ] 200 r. 6, UN.MEŠ-*a* 45 r. 9, UN.MEŠ-*ia* 5 r. 3, UN.MEŠ-*šú* 36:15, UN.M]EŠ-*šú-nu* 59:5,
nitiru "natron": NA_4.*ni-ti-ru* 82 r. 9,
nuāru "singer, musician": LÚ.NAR 95:10,
nubattu "evening": *nu-bat-ti* 59 r. 11, *nu-bat-t[i*] 162 r. 5, *nu-bat-tu* 140:6,
nuk "thus": *nu-uk* 20 r. 6, 43:15, 64 r. 6, 7, 65 r. 16, 95 r. 13, 154 r. 2, 171:2, 205 r. 5, 212:2, 4, 6, *n*]*u-uk* 171:3, [*nu*]-*uk* 8:7,
nukaribbu "gardener": LÚ.NU.GIŠ.SAR.MEŠ 5:18, 23,
nūru "light": *nu-ú-ru* 29:11, 31 r. 1,
nusāhu "corn tax": ŠE.*nu-sa-hi* 96:17, ŠE.*nu-sa-hi-ni* 96 r. 9,
paʾāṣu "to remove, take away, steal": *up-te-ii-ṣi* 63 r. 21, *ú-pa-ṣi* 127:21,
pagru "corpse, body": LÚ.ÚŠ 95 r. 6,
pahāru "to assemble, gather": *ip-hur-[u-ni* 15:28, *lu-pa-ah-hi-ir* 59 s. 3, *pa-hi-ra-a-ni* 63 e. 32, *up-ta-hir-šú-nu* 21 r. 5,
pāhizu (an occupation or profession): LÚ.*pa-hi-zu* 30:3,
pahû "to close up, caulk": *pa-hi-ú* 184 r. 5,
pāhutu "governor": EN.NAM 48 r. 11, 107:9, 183:7, r. 10, LÚ.EN.NAM 29:8, r. 1, 42:11, 49:9, 63:5, 27, 29, 31, r. 5, 68:17, 71:3, 79:16, 88:11, 136:7, r. 1, 6, 183 r. 2, LÚ.E]N.NAM 63:25, LÚ.NAM 68:19, LÚ.NAM.MEŠ 32 r. 6, 42:9, LÚ.NAM-*šú* 64:7,
pakku (an implement or weapon): *pa-ki* 40:4, 6, [[*pa-ki* 40:7,
palāhu "to fear, respect, revere; (D) to frighten, scare": *ap-ta-làh* 71 e. 10, *ap-t*]*a-làh* 155:10, *a-pal-làh* 5 r. 19, [*a-pal-làh*] 168:2, *a-pa-làh* 82:15, *ip-ta-al-hu* 201 r. 1, 3, *i-p[al-lu-hu*] 201 r. 5, *la-ap-làh* 34 r. 5, *ni-ip-ta-làh* 41 r. 7, 95 r. 11, *pal-ha-ak* 127 r. 5, *pa-lih-šú* 29:11, *pa-lìh* 15:10, 48 r. 4,

ta-pa-làh 60 r. 14, *ú-pal-làh-u-ni* 127 r. 10, *ú-p[a-l]a-hu-nu* 128 r. 7,

palû "reign": BALA-*e* 29:13, BALA-*e*] 195:3,

pānāt "fore": *pa-na-at* 132:6, *pa-(na)-at* 56:5, *pa-na-tu-un-ni* 140 r. 15, *pa-na-tu-u-a* 45 r. 1, 112 r. 17,

pāniu "previous, former": *p]a-ni-it-t[i]* 230 e. 1, *pa-ni-iu-u[m-ma* 62 r. 2, *pa-ni-ti*] 62:2, *pa*]*-ni-tú* 112:13, *pa-ni-u* 125:6, *pa-ni-u-*[*te*] 88:18, *pa-ni-ú* 31:6,

pānu "face, presence": IGI 5 r. 3, 7 r. 1, 8:6, r. 9, 32 r. 19, 20, 22, 36 r. 15, 18, 42 r. 12, 43:3, 44 r. 4, 45:13, 52 e. 10, r. 7, 8, 53 r. 7, 55 r. 3, 56 r. 8, 59:7, 62 r. 6, 63 e. 32, s. 1, 64:4, 5, r. 1, 7, 67:1, 10, 73 r. 4, 79 r. 1, 82:17, 84 r. 12, 88:8, 11, 90:12, r. 10, 91 r. 2, 92:11, 121:10, 14, r. 17, 123:9, 125:13, 131 r. 4, 7, 134:6, 141:5, 150:9, 158:1, 181 r. 5, 183 r. 10, 207:8, 217 r. 1, 222 r. 1, IGI] 5:11, IG[I 102 r. 1, 183:7, I[GI 150 r. 3, I]GI 60 r. 9, IGI-*ia* 105:13, 124 r. 4, IGI-*i*[*a* 10:9, I]GI-*ia* 10:8, 62 r. 10, IGI-*ia-ni* 12:1, IGI-*iá* 19:7, IGI-*šú* 59:4, 78:13, 16, r. 2, 135 r. 9, *pa-an* 29:15, 34:6, 15, 21, 35:6, r. 8, 40 r. 15, 42 r. 9, 45:11, r. 6, 13, 48 r. 1, 4, 54 r. 3, 95:9, 105 r. 4, 115 r. 8, 121 r. 19, 122 r. 12, 140 s. 1, 143 r. 6, 155:7, 194:4, *pa-an*] 171:7, *pa-a*[*n* 168:5, *pa*]*-an* 35 r. 7, *p*]*a-an* 47 r. 2, *pa-ni* 15:7, 48:8, 9, 49 r. 5, 63 s. 2, 65:12, 67 r. 13, 126 r. 2, 12, 129 r. 7, 204 r. 5, 207:3, *pa-ni-ia* 35:8, 120 r. 5, *pa-ni-i*[*a*] 170:8, [*pa*]*-ni-ia* 6 e. 10, *pa-ni-iá* 66:6, *pa-ni-ka* 37:5, 148 r. 8, 173:5, *pa-n*]*i-ka* 15:5, [*pa-n*]*i-ku-nu* 63 e. 34, *pa-ni-ni* 63 r. 5, 129 r. 10, *pa-ni-šú* 15:9, 34:23, r. 15, 73 r. 2, 78:15, 127:17, 18, r. 5, *pa-ni-*[*šú* 121 r. 15, *pa-ni-*[*šú*] 130:4, *pa-n*]*i-šú* 146:10, *pa-ni-šú-nu* 41:14, 73:3, 88:19, 95:11, 205 r. 2, *pa-ni-šú-*[*nu* 135 r. 12,

pappardaliu (a precious stone, perhaps "agate"): [N]A_4.BABBAR.DIL 81 r. 2,

paqādu "to appoint, entrust, assign": *ap-ti-*[*qid*] 205 r. 2, *ip-qid-an-ni-ni* 78:16, *ip-qid-da-ni-ni* 112 r. 5, *ip-qi-da-an-ni-ni* 98 r. 8, *ip-qi-da-ni* 98:4, *ip-qi-da-ni-ni* 82:14, 108:7, 111:9, *ip-qí-du-u-ni* 34:9, *ip-taq-da-an-ni* 52 r. 7, *ip-taq-da-na-a-ši* 43:8, *ip-*[*taq-du-ni*] 45:4, *ip-ta-aq-du* 96:16, *i-ba-qi-du-šú-nu-*[*ni* 91:10, *i-pa-qid* 129 r. 1, *i-pa-qi-du-ni-ši* 97 r. 12, *lip-qid* 34:17, 42 r. 16, *lip-*[*qid* 96 r. 21, *lip-qi-dan-ni* 82:9, *lip-qi-du*] 52:6, *lip-qi-d*[*u*] 87:7, [*li*]*p-qi-id* 32 r. 2, *lip-qí-dan-ni* 44 r. 4, *lip-qí-du* 86:6, *li-ip-qid-du* 39 r. 3, *li-ip-qi-da-na-ši* 42 r. 11, [*li*]*-ip-qi-du-ni-šú* 97 r. 5, *pa-qa-da-a-ni* 148:11, *pa-qa-di-ia* 78:17, *pa-*[*qid-u-ni*] 18:8, *pa-qí-id* 34:12, *pa-qu-du-u-ni* 34:11,

parāhu "to obstruct(?)": *ip-par-ri-hi* 5 r. 11,

parakku "dais, sanctuary": BARAG.MEŠ 21:17,

parāsu "to separate; to decide, determine": *a-pa-ra-as-ka* 112 r. 3, *lip-ru-us* 163 e. 8, *li*]*p-ru-us* 19:8, *pu-ru-us* 5 r. 1, *ú-par-ri-su-u-ni* 115:7, see also *parsu,*

parkullu "stonecutter, sculptor": BUR.G[UL] 197:6, LÚ.BU[R.GUL 197:2,

parriṣu "criminal, traitor": LÚ.LUL.ME 68 s. 2, [*par-r*]*i-ṣu* 97 r. 6, *pa-ri-ṣu* 43:10,

parsu "definite": *pa-ri-is-tu* 27 r. 5, see also *parāsu,*

paršumu "old man, elder; to grow old": *lu-pa*[*r-šim* 160:5, LÚ.AB.BA.MEŠ 63:31, [LÚ.*pa*]*r-šú-mu-te* 96:3,

parzillu "iron": AN.BAR 40:2, 3, 4, 6, 63:24, 95 r. 14, 115 r. 7, AN.BAR]] 40:7,

paṣādu "(D) to break, crack, shatter": *up-ta-ta-ṣi-*[*d*]*i* 100:16,

paṣāṣu "to withdraw": *ni-ip-ta-ṣa* 40 r. 11,

pašāhu "to relax": *ni-ip-šah* 105 r. 18,

pašāqu "to be narrow, difficult; (D) to explain": *up-ta-ši-iq* 121:12,

paššūru "table": GIŠ.BANŠUR 53:11,

patāhu "to pierce": *pát-hat-ú-ni* 5 r. 14,

patû "to open; (D) to dismiss": *a-pa-ti* 6 r. 1, *ip-te-ti* 95 r. 5, *i-pa-ti*] 6 e. 7, *ni-ip-tu-ni* 97:14, *pa-te* 111:11, *pi-ta-a-ni* 95 r. 18, *tap-ti*] 6:3, *up-ta-*[*ti-iu-u*] 45 r. 7,

paṭāru "to dissolve, release; (D) to loosen, demolish": *ap-ṭu-ra* 132 r. 4, *i-pa-ṭa-ra* 74:2, *nu-pa-ṭi-ru-ni* 125:6, *pa-aṭ-ru-u-ni* 99:3, *pa-ṭu-ru* 98 r. 5, *pa-ṭu-ru-u-n*[i] 188 r. 4, *up-ta-ṭi-ir* 111:10,

pazû (mng. obscure): *pa-zu-u* 129:7,

pazzuru "to conceal, hide": *tu-pa-zar* 32 r. 19, [*tu-pa-za*]*r* 66:6, *up-ta-z*[*i-x* 66:7, *ú-pa-az-z*]*a-ar* 61:12, *ú-*[*pa-az-za-ar* 60:12,

piqittu "charge, ward; official": LÚ.*pi-qi-ta-*[*te*] 87:9, LÚ.*pi-q*[*i-tu* 168:4,

pitti "according to": *pi-it-te* 53 r. 5, 143:11, *pi-it-ti* 139:11, *pi-te-ma* 2:10, see also *pūtu,*

pû "mouth, utterance, command": *pi-i* 21:18, 132 r. 2, 183:14, 203 r. 4, *pi-i-ia* 21 r. 13, *pi-i-šu* 148 r. 6, 12, *pi-i-šú* 30:8, 135 r. 4, *pi-i-*[*šú*] 110 r. 4, [*p*]*i-i-šú* 207:4, *pi-i-šú-nu* 59:5, *pi-ni* 97:13, *pi-šú-nu* 148 s. 1,

puāgu "to take away": *ip-tu-ag-ga* 42 e. 15,

puhādu "lamb": UDU.*pu-ha-da-a-ni* 21:19, UD]U.*pu-ha-da-ni* 171:9, UDU.*pu-ha-du* 171:6,

pūhu "exchange, loan": *pu-u-hi* 5 e. 26,

pūlu "limestone, foundation stone": NA_4.*pu-u-li* 143:14, NA_4.*pu-u-lu* 125:8, 143:6, *pu-u-li* 125 r. 2, *pu-u-lu* 65 r. 15, 125:6,

purkullu see *parkullu,*

purṭû (a weapon): *pur-ṭí-e* 40:2,

pusku "palm": *pu-us-ki* 197:4,

pussu? *ú-pa-su* 140 r. 5,

pūtu "front, opposite; according to": *pu-ut* 237:3, *pu-u-ti* 80:6, see also *pitti,*

qabassīu "middle, central": *qab-si-te* 100 r. 10,

qabassu "middle, center": *qab-si* 25:8, 78 r. 9, 100:14, 161:2,

qablu "middle part, waist": $MURUB_4$ 20 r. 7, 132:5,

qabû "to say, tell, command": *aq-bi* 36 r. 7, *aq-bu-u-ni* 30:5, 78 r. 8, 99 r. 3, 134:7, *aq-ṭi-ba-áš-šú* 20 r. 6, *aq-ṭi-ba-šú* 15:10, *aq-ṭi-b*]*a-šú* 171:2, *aq-ṭi-ba-šú-nu* 105 e. 21, *aq-ṭi-bi* 2 r. 1, 20 r. 2, 121:13, r. 5, *aq-ṭi-*[*bi* 121 r. 12, *a*]*q-ṭi-bi* 204:6, [*aq*]*-ṭi-bi* 10:3, *aq-ṭí*]*-ba-áš-šú* 155 r. 3, *aq-ṭí-bi* 155:6, *a-qa-bi* 62 r. 4, 63 s. 2, 67 r. 14, *a-qa-bu-u-ni* 43:14, 63 r. 31, *iq-ab-bu-ni* 90 r. 5, *iq-ban-ni* 20 r. 3, *iq-ba-áš-šá-nu-u-ni* 63:10, *iq-bi-ia* 45 r. 5, *iq-bi-ú* 66 r. 5, *iq-bu-ni* 15:4, *iq-bu-u-ni* 1:11, 17:7, 63:26, 68:16, 92:7, 140 r. 2, 204 r. 6, *iq-bu-u-n*[*i* 68 r. 15, *iq-bu-u-n*[*i*] 54:2, *iq-bu-*[*u-ni*] 218:8, [*iq-ṭi-b*]*a-na-a-ši* 138:10, [*i*]*q-ṭi-ba-na-ši* 88:12, *iq-ṭi-bi* 15:6, 12, 16:1, 20 r. 9, 53:12, 146:7, *i*]*q-ṭi-bi* 3:8, [*iq-ṭi-bi*] 56 r. 10, [*iq*]*-ṭi-bi* 217 r. 6, *iq-ṭi-bi-a* 70:3, *i*[*q-ṭi-bi-a*] 202:2, [*iq-ṭi-bi-a*] 120:12, *iq-ṭi-bi-ia* 69:4, *iq-ṭi-bi-u* 17 r. 5, *iq-ṭi-bu-u-ni* 60:8, 120 r. 2,

121 r. 3, *iq-ṭí-bi* 64:7, 65:8, 68 r. 11, 228:5, *iq-ṭí-bi-ú* 73 r. 1, *iq-ṭí-bi-[ú* 66 r. 4, *iq-ṭí-b[u-ni]* 154 r. 1, *iq-ṭí-bu-niš-šú* 137:15, *iq-ṭí-bu-u-ni* 63 r. 12, *i-[qa]b-ba-na-ši* 140 r. 7, *i-qab-ba-šú* 127 r. 2, *i-qab-bi* 11:7, 21:21, 60:4, 71 r. 2, 96 r. 18, 111 r. 2, 123 r. 7, 125:9, 12, 127 r. 3, 150:4, 237 r. 2, *i-qab-[bi]* 138:6, *i-qab-[b]i* 27 r. 6, *i-qa[b-bi]* 46:2, *[i-qab-bi]* 163:2, *i-qab-bi-a* 112 r. 1, *i-qab-bi-ʾa-a* 99 e. 13, r. 5, *i-qab-bi-ú* 28:5, *i]-qab-bi-ú* 204:3, *i-qab-bu-ni]* 101 r. 7, *i-qab-bu-niš-š[u]* 127 e. 24, *i-qab-bu-ni-ka* 11 r. 8, *i-qab-bu-u-ni* 120 r. 11, 142 r. 5, 211 r. 4, *[i-qab-bu-u-ni]* 202:7, *i-qab-bu-ú-ni* 42 r. 13, 69 r. 4, *i-qa-bi* 54:6, 63 s. 3, 64 r. 1, *i-[qa-bi* 242 r. 2, *[i-qa-b]i* 67:3, *i-qa-bu-ni-ni* 63 e. 33, *la-aq-ba]-ak-ka* 99 r. 8, *la-aq-bi* 78:12, *[la-aq-bi]* 98 r. 3, *[la-aq]-bi* 72 r. 6, *la-qa-bi* 63:9, 25, 64 r. 2, *liq-bi* 105 r. 7, 125 r. 4, *liq-bi-ú* 32 r. 22, *[li]q-bu-ni-šú* 89 r. 7, *li-iq-bi* 90 r. 8, 117 r. 3, *li-iq-bi-u* 73 r. 4, *li-iq-bi-ú* 64:3, *[l]i-iq-bu-nik-ka* 60 r. 14, *ni-iq-bu-ni* 95:11, *ni-iq-te-bi* 97 r. 10, *ni-iq-ṭi-bi* 21 r. 8, *ni-iq-ṭí-bi* 95 r. 12, *ni-qab-bi* 204 r. 9, *q[a-b]i* 60 r. 5, *qa-bu-u-ni]* 126:25, *[qa-bu-u-ni]* 126:19, *qi-ba-a-ni* 63 r. 2, *q]i-ba-na-ši* 63 e. 35, *qi-bi* 32 r. 20, *qi-bi-a* 78:6, *qi-bi-iʾ* 49 r. 5, *qí-ba-áš-šú* 15:8, *qí-bi-a* 15:5, *taq-bi-ni* 2 r. 3, *taq-bu-u-ni* 2:9, *ta-qab-bi* 148 r. 7, *ta-qab-bi-a* 21:12, *ta-qab-bi-i* 28:4,

qadītu (mng. obscure): *qa-di-tu* 239:4,

qalālu "to be small; (D) to slight": *qa-li-la-šu* 21 r. 13,

qallilu "small, insignificant": *qàl-li-su* 62:4,

qallu "small; slave": QÀL.MEŠ-*šú-nu* 52 r. 2,

qallulu "tiny, vile": *qa-lál* 89:9,

qalû "to burn": *taq-ṭu-lu* 95:5,

qanni "outside": *qa-an-ni* 34:11, *qa-an-ni-ma* 62 r. 5, *qa-ni* 11:11, 100 r. 11, 13, 132:10, 157:3, *qa-[ni* 120:9, *q[a-n]i* 59 r. 2,

qarābu A "to approach, arrive; (stat.) to be present; (D) to present, offer": *aq-ri-i[b]* 121:11, *iq-ri-bi* 141:4, *i-qar-ri-ib* 77 r. 5, *lu-qar-[ri-ib* 213:6, *ni-iq-ri-ib* 121 r. 18, *ni-qar-rib-u-ni* 121 r. 16, *ni-qar-ri-ib* 121 r. 20, *qí-ri-ib* 121:10, *qu-ru-ub* 125:9, *qur-ba-ku* 78 r. 16, *qur-ba-ku-u-ni* 78 r. 7, *qur-bu* 90:7, *uq-ṭar-ri-ib* 146:2, *ú-qar-rab-an-ni* 29:15, *ú-qar-ra-bu-u-ni* 206:2,

qarābu B "battle, fight": *q]a-ra-bi* 77 r. 5, *qa-ra-b[u* 243 r. 2, *qa-r[a-bu* 15:27, 77 r. 8,

qarādu "to be brave, (D) to encourage": *uq-ṭa-ri-da-áš-šú* 63:26,

qarbāti "personally(?)": *[qa]r-bat-te-šú* 6 e. 7, *qar-ba-ti-ia* 7:4, *[q]ar-ba-ti-ia* 8:6, *qar-b[a-x* 232:1,

qarrāru "bedspread": TÚG.*qar-ra-ru* 53:10,

qātu "hand; responsibility (of)": *qa-ti* 232:3, ŠU 67 r. 7, ŠU.2 5:20, r. 2, 34:9, 69:7, 82:11, 143:13, 146:3, 148 r. 2, 183 s. 1, ŠU.2-*ia* 112 r. 8, ŠU.2-*iá* 62 r. 9, ŠU.2-*i-ka* 86:12, ŠU.2-*k[a* 59:11, ŠU.2-*k]a* 61:7, ŠU.2-*[ka* 60:7, Š]U.2.MEŠ-*šú-nu* 203 r. 5, ŠU.2-*šú* 63 r. 6, 64:5, 105:16, ŠU.2-*šú-nu* 105:17, 128 r. 13,

qēmu "flour": ZÍD.DA 232:2,

qēpu "(royal) delegate": LÚ.*qe-ba-a-ni* 96:14, LÚ.*qe-e-pi* 137:10, LÚ.*qe-[e-pu]* 92:14, [LÚ.*qe]-e-pu* 138:9,

qiāpu "to believe": *i-qi-[ap* 67 r. 9,

qinnu "nest, family": *qin-ni-ka* 59:9, 60 s. 3,

qinnutu "anus": *qi-in-ni-te* 63:24,

quālu "to be silent": *qa-a-lu* 231:4, *qa-la-ka* 5 r. 4,

qulālē "belittlement, slight, insult": *qu-la-a-li* 63 r. 23, *qu-la-le-e-a* 112:15,

qurbu see *qarābu,*

raʾābu "to get angry, rage": *ar-tu-uʾ-ba-šú* 171:10, *ir-tu-ʾa-ba* 76 r. 3, *ir-tu-[a-ba]* 121:9, *[ir-t]u-ú-bu* 71:9,

raʾāmu "love; to love": *i-ra-am* 34 r. 15, *i-ra-ma-ka-a-ni* 105 r. 14, *ra-a-mu* 126:2, *ra-ʾi-mu* 36 r. 5,

rāʾiu "shepherd": LÚ.SIPA 79:10, 124 r. 3, LÚ.SIPA.ME 88:7, LÚ.SIPA.MEŠ 5:22, 63:13, 114:6, LÚ.SIP]A.MEŠ 5 r. 15, SIPA 27 r. 8,

rab ālāni "village manager": LÚ.GAL—URU.MEŠ 68 r. 7, 134:5, LÚ.[GAL—URU.MEŠ] 68:20, LÚ.GAL—URU.MEŠ-*te* 63:15, L]Ú.GAL—URU.MEŠ-*te* 86 r. 10,

rab āpie "chief baker": LÚ.GAL—NINDA 93:8,

rab bēti "major-domo": LÚ.GAL—É 42:3, LÚ.[GA]L—É 112:11,

rab danibāti "chief victualler": LÚ].GAL—*da-ni-bat* 170:7, LÚ.GAL—*da-[ni-bat]* 46:4,

rab ekalli "palace manager": LÚ.GAL—É.GAL 50:2, LÚ.GAL—KUR 50:7,

rab etinnāti "chief master builder": LÚ.GAL—TIN.MEŠ 111 r. 3,

rab kāri "chief of trade": LÚ.GAL—KAR 20:6,

rab kāṣiri "chief tailor": GAL—*ka-ṣir* 63 r. 16, LÚ.GAL—KA.KÉŠ 76 r. 4,

rab kiṣri "cohort commander": LÚ.GAL—*ki-ṣir* 148 r. 15, LÚ.G[AL—*ki-ṣir* 67:9, L]Ú.GAL—*ki-ṣir* 209 e. 2, LÚ.GAL—*ki-ṣir-a-ni* 40 r. 12, LÚ.(GAL)—*ki-ṣir*.MEŠ 43 r. 5,

rab kiṣrūtu "rank of cohort commander": LÚ.GAL—*ki-ṣir-u-tú* 115:9,

rab mūgi (a high military official): GAL—*mu-gi* 51:4, LÚ.GAL—*mu-gi* 59 r. 18, 123:9, LÚ.GAL—*mu-gi-ka* 59 r. 5,

rab nikkassi "chief of accounts": GAL—NÍG.ŠID.MEŠ 48 r. 12, LÚ.GAL—NÍG.ŠID.MEŠ 63:4, r. 15,

rab nuhatimmi "chief cook": LÚ].GAL—MU 120:11,

rab pilkāni "chief of public works": GAL—*pil-ka-ni* 50:4,

rab ṣibti "sheep-tax master": GAL—MÁŠ 48 e. 12,

rab ša-rēši "chief eunuch": LÚ.GAL—SAG 60 r. 9,

rab ṭupšarri "chief scribe": LÚ.GAL—A.BA 89:5, 9, 125 r. 5,

rabiu "magnate": LÚ.GAL.MEŠ 41:10, 47 r. 4, 59:10, 62 r. 6, 63 r. 20, 64 r. 2, 83:8, L]Ú.GAL.MEŠ 133:3, LÚ.GAL.MEŠ-*ia* 1:5, LÚ.GAL.MEŠ-*ka* 1:8, 77 r. 3, [LÚ.G]AL.MEŠ-*ka* 77 r. 8, LÚ.GAL].MEŠ-*te* 118:8,

rabû A "to be great, grow; (D) to rear, bring up": GAL 28 r. 4, 6, 97:5, 134 r. 2, GAL.MEŠ 52:3, 118:4, 148:5, GAL-*tú* 28 r. 2, *ir-bu-uʾ* 29 r. 5, *ú-ra-bu-ú-ni* 126:15,

rabû B "to go down, set": *i-rab-bu-un-nu* 128:11, *i-rab-bu-u-ni* 200 r. 5, *i-rab-bu-ú-nu* 127:11,

râbu "to tremble": *ir-tu-bu* 100:7,

radādu "to persecute": *i]r-tu-du-u-ni* 62 r. 13,

raddiu "follower": *rad-di-u* 5 r. 7,

radû "to lead, rule; (D) to add to": *i-rad-di* 146:8, *ta-ra-di* 64 e. 11,
rahāṣu "to be confident; to trust, rely on": *ir-ti-hi-i*[*ṣ* 60:9, *li-ir-hi-ṣa-áš-šú* 48 r. 6, *ra-hi-*[*iṣ*] 77 r. 2,
rakābu "to ride, mount": *i-ra-ak-ku-b*[*u* 119 r. 6,
rakāsu "to bind, attach": [*ar-ta*]*-ka-as* 171:11, [*ir*]*-ta-kas* 66 r. 4,
raksu "recruit, mercenary(?); bound, scheduled": LÚ.*rak-su*.MEŠ 68:18, *ra-a*[*k-su-t*]*e*.MEŠ 132:5,
ramanu see *ramunu,*
rammû "to leave, release, reject, forsake": *lu-ra*]*-am-mi* 64:6, *lu-ra-ma-an-na-*[*ši*] 93:11, *ra-am-mu-u* 98 r. 5, *ra-mu-u-a-ku-nu* 62 r. 8, *tu-ra-am-me-a* 105 r. 2, *ur-tam-mi-ú* 21:15, *ur-ta-am-me* 45:2, 60:11, *ur-ta-am-m*[*e* 20:7, *ur-ta-am-me-u* 34:13, *ú-r*[*am-man-ni*] 34 s. 1, *ú-ra-am-mu* 127:15, *ú-ra-ma* 97 r. 19, *ú-ra-man-ni* 34 r. 11, 19, 35 r. 3, *ú-ra-ma-an-ni* 128 r. 14, *ú-ra-mu-šá-nu-u-ni* 62 r. 6,
ramunu "self": *ra-*[*man*]*-ka* 60 s. 2, *ra-ma-ni-šú-nu* 21:15, *ra-mi-ni-šú* 65:5, *ra-m*[*i-ni-x* 212:3, [*r*]*a-mì-ni* 224 r. 5, [*r*]*a-mì-ni-ka* 15:9, *ra-m*[*ì*]*-ni-ka* 143:17, *ra-mì-ni-šú* 60:11, *ra-mì-ni-ia* 32 r. 13, *ra-mì-ni*]*-ia* 33 r. 7,
rapāšu "to be wide, extensive": *ra-pa-áš-tu* 78 r. 13,
raṣāpu "to build, brick up": *ni-ir-ṣi-ip* 125:11, *ra-ṣi-i*[*b* 184 r. 4, *ri-iṣ-pa* 125:13,
rēhtu "rest, remainder; (pl.) leftovers": *re-eh-te* 34:14, [*re-e*]*h-te* 86 r. 15, *re-eh-tú* 79:14, *re-e*[*h*]*-tú* 54:11, *re-ha-a-te* 106 r. 1,
rēmu "compassion, mercy": *re-e-mu* 29:6, 36:5, 15, r. 4, *re-e*]*-mu* 36 r. 13, *r*[*e-e-mu*] 121 r. 13, [*re e*] *mu* 46:1,
rēšu "head, top, beginning": *re-eš* 5 r. 19, *re-e-ši* 31:7, *re-e-š*]*i* 29:4, *re-e-šu* 117 r. 5, [*re*]*-e-šú* 168:5, *re-ši* 56 r. 9, *re-šú-un-ni* 95 r. 15, SAG 8:3, 63 r. 18, SAG-*šú* 65 r. 4,
riāhu "to be left": *re-e-ha-at* 35:8, *re-hu-u-te* 62 r. 10, 79 r. 6,
riāqu "to be empty, free": *i*]*r-ti-aq* 97:11,
rību "earthquake": *ri-i-bu* 100:7,
rihṣu "devastation": *rih-ṣi* 13:1,
rikalla see *irkalla,*
riksu "bond, agreement, obligation, ordinance": *ri-ik-sa-a-ni* 98 r. 4, *ri-i*[*k-s*]*a-t*[*i*] 99:2,
ruāqu "to be distant": *ru-qi* 128 r. 6,
rūbu "maturity, adulthood": *ru-ú-bu* 126:14,
rupšu "width": *ru-up-šá-šá* 81 r. 2,
sabāʾu "to rock, bound": *a-sa-ab-bu-uʾ* 32 r. 12, *a-sa-a*]*b-bu-uʾ* 33 r. 6,
sabirru "ring, torc, bracelet": HAR 53 r. 2, 63 r. 17, H]AR 63:30, HAR.MEŠ 63 e. 32, 95:8,
sadāru "to array, line up, itemize, list": *a-sa-*[*dir*] 85 r. 4, [*a*]*-sa-*[*dir*] 54:11, [*a-si-di*]*r* 43 r. 11, *i-sa-dir* 120 r. 6,
sāgu "sash": *sa-gu* 20 r. 7,
sahāru "to turn, go around, return": *is-su-*[*hur* 103 r. 3, *is-su-hu-ru-nu* 129 r. 9, *is-su-uh-ra* 243:4, *i-sa-hu-ru* 99:4, *i-su-hu-ra* 45 r. 2, [*la*]*-as-hu-ra* 37:7, *lu-sah-hi-ri* 65 r. 16, *l*]*u-sa-hi-ru* 75:10, *sa-ha-ra* 29:17, *ta-sa-hu-r*[*a* 61 r. 4, *tu-sa-har* 29:8, r. 3, *us-sah-hir* 127:17, *us-sa-hi-ir* 80:4, *us-sa-hi-ra* 34:23, *ú-sa-ah-*(*ha*)*-ra* 115 r. 9, *ú-sa-hi-ir* 78:9, *ú-sa-hi-x*[*x* 60:13,
salāmu A "to make peace": *is-sal-mu* 137:12, *ni-sa-al-lam* 17 r. 11,
salāmu B "alliance": *sa-la-mu* 128 r. 5,
salû "to lie": *is-sa-na-al-lu-ka* 11 r. 7,
samāhu "to unite; (D) to mix": *ú-sa-ma-*[*hu-ni* 60:3,
samāku "to be terrible, bad": *s*]*a-mi-ik-te* 217:3,
samānā "eighty": 80 82 r. 6,
samû "to hesitate, to slacken(?)": *a-sa-me* 63:27, *is-sa-m*[*a-a*] 183:10, *i-sa-ma-*[*x*]*-a* 5 r. 10,
sanāqu "to approach; (D) to question": *lu-sa-ni-qi* 65 r. 6,
sangû "priest": LÚ.SANGA 62 r. 5, 63:3, 26, r. 25,
sapāqu "to suffice": *i-sa-ap-*[*pi*]*-qa* 5 r. 4,
sarāhu "to be enraptured(?)": *sa-ar-ha-at* 59 r. 3, [[*su*]]*-ur-ha* 5:11,
sarruru "to pray": *sa-ri-ir* 60 s. 2,
sartennu "chief judge": LÚ.*sar-ten-ni* 133:2, LÚ.*sar-tin-n*[*i* 64 r. 10,
sāru "(palm frond) broom": *sa-a-ri* 128 r. 16, [*sa-a-ri* 127 r. 19,
sasû "to read": *as-si*] 6 e. 9, *a-s*[*a-as-si*] 6 r. 1, *is-si-si-ú* 73:4, *i-s*]*a-si* 95 r. 3, *ta-sa-su-u-ni* 32 r. 18,
sēgallu "queen": MÍ—É.GAL 63 r. 20, 65:3, 81:4, 111:7,
sihpu "bast": *si-ih-pu* 216 e. 12,
sikkutu "peg, nail": GAG 40:3,
simānu (Sivan, name of the 3rd month): ITI.SIG$_4$ 52 r. 4, 59 r. 3,
simunu "time, moment": *si-mu-nu* 59 r. 12, *ši-mu-nu* 129:11,
sinqu "distress": *si-in-qi* 31 r. 4,
sippu "doorjamb": *si-ip-pa-ni* 125 r. 8,
siqqurrutu "ziggurat": É.*si-qur-ra-*[*te*] 100 r. 5, *ziq-qur-r*[*a-te*] 93 r. 1,
sissiktu "hem": TÚG.*zi-zi-ik-tú* 36 r. 16,
sissû "horse": ANŠE.KUR.RA 22:6, 70:2, ANŠE.KUR.RA] 70 e. 7, [ANŠE.K]UR.RA 119 r. 6, ANŠE.KUR.RA.MEŠ 63:11, 21, 105:16, 112:5, 14, [ANŠE.K]UR.RA.MEŠ 70 r. 3, K]UR.MEŠ 175:7, 177:2,
sukkallu "vizier": LÚ.SUKKAL 92:12, 95 r. 11,
supuhru (a cedar resin): GIŠ.ERIN.BAD.MEŠ 5:17,
sūsānu "horse trainer, chariot-man": LÚ.GIŠ.GIGIR 68:19,
ṣabātu "to seize, capture; (D) to fasten; (Š) to prepare": *a-ṣab-bat-si* 127 r. 6, *a-ṣa-bat* 29:5, *iṣ-bat-ú-ni* 21 r. 4, *iṣ-ṣa-bat* 29:6, *i-ṣab-tu-u-ni* 105:17, *i-ṣa-bat* 52 r. 8, *li-iṣ-bat* 29:10, 36 r. 2, *li-ṣi-bat* 64:5, *ni-ṣa-bat* 95 r. 19, *ni-ṣi-bat* 63:28, *nu-ṣa-bi-it* 105 r. 11, *nu-šá-aṣ-bat-ka* 11:9, *nu-šá-aṣ-bat-u-ni* 78 e. 23, *ṣa-ab-t*]*a* 60 s. 4, *ṣa-bit* 21 r. 16, *ta-aṣ-bat-si* 127 r. 4, *tu-šá-aṣ-bat-šá-nu-ni* 11:6, *ú-šá-aṣ-*[*bat*] 162 r. 3,
ṣābu "men, troops": ERIM.MEŠ 4:3, 51 r. 3, 59 r. 18, 60:7, r. 19, 115 r. 4, ER]IM.MEŠ-*ia* 60 r. 9, E[RI]M.MEŠ-*šú* 64 e. 12, LÚ.ERIM.MEŠ 40 r. 14, 15, 63:1, 64:1, 66:4, 105:15, LÚ.ERIM.M[EŠ 68 r. 5, 19, LÚ.[ERIM.MEŠ] 64:2, LÚ.ERIM.MEŠ-*e* 243:6, LÚ.ERIM.MEŠ-*šú* 95 r. 8, 14,
ṣāb ekalli "palace personnel, troops of the palace": ERIM—É.GAL 47 r. 1,
ṣāb qassi "archer": LÚ.ERIM].MEŠ—GIŠ.BAN 137 r. 12,

ṣad (mng. obscure): *ṣa-ad* 5 r. 9,
ṣahāru "to be small, young": TUR 97:5,
ṣahittu "wish, desire": *ṣa-hi-it-tú* 64 r. 4,
ṣahurtu "girl servant": MÍ.TUR-*a* 45 r. 9,
ṣalittu "dark-blue wool": SÍG.ZA.GÌN.MI 216:11,
ṣallulu "to cover, roof": *ú-ṣa-lu-lu* 154 e. 15,
ṣallumu "black wood": GIŠ.*ṣal-lu-ma-a-ni* 65 r. 3,
ṣalmāt qaqqadi "black-headed people, human beings": *ṣal-mat*—SAG.DU 126:12,
ṣalmu "image, likeness": *ṣ*]*a-lam* 245:4,
ṣarāpu "to burn, refine (silver)": *ú-ṣa-*[*ri-pi* 242 r. 7,
ṣarpu "silver": KUG.UD 5:10, 34:13, 43 r. 13, 45:13, 53 r. 3, 54:4, 5, 63:13, 16, 65:5, 81 r. 1, 97:17, 19, 127 r. 8, 128 r. 3, 155 r. 7, 242 r. 3, 8, KUG.U[D] 53 r. 2, KU[G].UD 53 r. 4, K]UG.UD 155 r. 2, 209 r. 3,
ṣarrāpu "goldsmith": LÚ.SIMUG.KUG.GI 65:3, 81:3, LÚ.SIMUG.KUG.[GI] 218:7,
ṣehru "apprentice, manservant": LÚ.TUR.MEŠ-*te* 118:8, LÚ.TUR-*šú* 5:14,
ṣehēru "childhood": *ṣe-he-ru* 126:14,
ṣēru "open country, plain, steppe": EDIN 100:8, 10,
ṣētu "shine, light": *ṣe-e-ta* 29:14, *ṣe-e-ti-ka* 29:14,
ṣillu "shadow, shelter, sheltered place, protection, aegis": GIŠ.MI] 200 r. 7, GIŠ.MI-*šú* 29:11, *ṣi-il-la-a-te* 117:15, *ṣi-la-a-*[*te*] 205 r. 5,
ṣīru "emissary": LÚ.MA]H.MEŠ 150:2, [LÚ].MAH.MEŠ-*ni* 35 r. 6,
ṣītu "exit; (pl.) distant times": *ṣa-a-ti* 33:10, *ṣa-at* 59 r. 10,
ṣīt pî "command": *ṣi-it*—*pi-i* 126:11,
ṣullû "to pray; prayer": *ṣu-le-e-ka* 29:12, *ú-ṣal-li* 29:9,
ṣumāmītu "thirst": *ṣ*[*u-ma-mit* 126:22,
ṣummurāti "wish, objective": *ṣu-um-mu-rat* 132:9,
ša "that; what; of": *ša* 1:9, 10, 14, 2:6, 7, 8, r. 3, 3 r. 3, 5:18, e. 26, r. 14, 6:1, 2, 7 r. 1, 8:4, 9:5, 10:4, 11 r. 9, 15:6, 23, 28, r. 3, 16:4, 17 r. 9, 18:7, 8, 20:6, r. 3, s. 1, 21:11, 14, 15, 16, r. 11, 22:7, 9, 23:6, 7, 25:10, 26:8, 27:10, r. 2, 6, 28 r. 1, 2, 3, 5, 6, 7, 29:8, 16, 30:4, r. 3, 31:3, r. 2, 5, 32 r. 5, 6, 8, 14, 16, 18, 33 r. 2, 3, 9, 34:4, 8, 10, 14, 18, 24, r. 11, 12, 17, 18, 35:5, r. 5, 6, 36:4, 8, r. 5, 6, 11, 40:3, 10, r. 4, 5, 8, 41:9, 15, r. 1, 42:11, 12, r. 12, s. 1, 43:3, 4, 10, 11, 12, 13, 14, r. 1, 10, 12, 13, 44:3, 45:12, 15, r. 4, 10, 13, 15, 46 r. 7, 48:8, 9, e. 13, r. 3, 49:4, 5, 8, 9, 50:7, 9, 12, 52:7, 9, r. 3, 4, 53 r. 7, 11, 54:2, 56:6, r. 12, 59:7, 61:3, r. 2, 63:1, 5, 6, 9, 10, 12, 13, 15, 16, 26, 29, e. 32, r. 3, 4, 11, 13, 14, 15, 20, 22, 24, 25, 26, 28, 30, 33, s. 1, 2, 3, 64:1, 5, 6, 8, 9, r. 2, 4, 5, 6, 65:3, 9, 10, 12, r. 10, 11, 67:1, 7, 9, r. 10, 14, 68:15, 17, 19, r. 15, 69 r. 3, 70 r. 3, 71:3, 6, r. 2, 5, 73 r. 2, 74 r. 3, 75:7, 8, 76 r. 5, 78:4, 5, 8, 10, 11, 20, e. 24, r. 3, 9, 10, 79:4, 8, 12, 15, 80:1, 2, 3, 82:6, r. 3, 83:6, r. 4, 84:6, r. 9, s. 1, 85:6, r. 1, 86:7, 9, 11, r. 11, 15, 17, 87:9, 10, 12, r. 7, 88:3, 89:16, 90:1, 10, r. 9, 91:4, 6, 8, r. 2, s. 2, 92:6, 8, 95:1, 2, 96:9, 13, r. 2, 19, 97:4, 7, 13, 98:3, r. 4, 9, 99:3, 5, 9, 10, r. 2, 10, 100:6, 10, 17, 19, 20, r. 5, 6, 10, 11, 13, 14, 17, 101 r. 7, s. 1, 102 r. 2, 105:4, 5, 10, 16, 19, r. 1, 6, 12, 13, 14, 106:7, r. 2, 7, 107:3, 9, 108:6, 111:8, 9, 112:5, 7, 11, r. 8, 17, 114:6, 7, r. 10, 115:5, 6, 9, 11, r. 2, 10, 14, 117:13, r. 2, 6, 118:7, 9, 119:5, r. 2, 120:7, r. 10, 121:14, 16, 122:4, 8, 10, 12, 123:2, r. 5, 125:5, 126:2, 5, 6, 10, 11, 13, 14, 18, 19, 20, 21, 24, 25, r. 2, 11, 19, 21, 23, 127:6, 12, 14, 16, 18, 20, 23, r. 1, 5, 7, 8, 19, 20, 21, 128:5, 12, r. 2, 3, 17, s. 1, 129:2, 4, 8, 11, r. 5, 7, 11, 13, s. 1, 131 r. 4, 132:4, 7, 8, 9, 133:2, 6, 134:5, 6, 7, r. 2, 135:4, 14, r. 6, 136:7, 9, 11, 12, 13, r. 1, 3, 6, 137:6, 7, 9, 10, r. 12, 138:9, 139:6, 7, 140 r. 2, 10, 12, 17, 142 r. 4, 143:6, 7, 8, 9, 12, 14, 17, r. 14, 144:8, 145 r. 4, 5, 9, 147:3, 5, 148:5, 9, 10, 12, 18, r. 15, 149:6, 150:8, r. 3, 152 r. 3, 154:13, 155:1, 162:9, r. 2, 163 r. 3, 164:6, 168:9, 169 r. 6, 10, 170:2, 171:7, 175 r. 8, 176:3, 181 r. 5, 183:7, 8, 16, r. 12, 192:8, 9, r. 2, 5, 6, 195:4, 196:4, 8, 11, 197:2, 3, 5, 6, r. 1, 199:3, 7, 202:6, 206:1, 207:3, 4, 5, 6, 211 r. 3, 212:3, r. 5, s. 1, 218:8, 219 r. 7, 221:4, 223:4, 225:2, 227:3, 228:6, 234:1, 239:5, 242 r. 3, 8, 243:6, r. 3, *ša*] 27:6, 33 r. 8, 12, 63 s. 1, 86 r. 3, 96:5, 119 r. 1, 127 r. 21, *š*[*a* 6:5, 59:10, 64:4, 74:1, 79:6, 96:3, 129:11, r. 4, 140:11, 162:6, 188 r. 3, 192:10, 11, 12, 212 r. 4, *š*[*a*] 51 r. 1, *š*]*a* 12:4, 19:6, 33:6, 7, 38 r. 2, 51:2, 59 s. 1, 60 r. 19, 61:10, 66:8, 77 r. 6, 10, 81:10, 110 r. 4, 127:5, 130:8, 133:1, 143 r. 4, 146:13, 183:14, 216:3, (*ša*) 49 r. 8, ((*ša*)) 126:11, [*ša* 3:6, 4:4, 5:7, r. 21, 37:4, 43 r. 2, 63:23, 25, 30, r. 11, 86:14, 96 r. 11, 118:5, 123 r. 6, 125:3, 135 r. 11, 149:7, 152:7, 157:1, 169:4, 175:8, 9, 181:5, 184:6, 230 e. 1, 236:3, [*ša*] 15:4, 27:9, 69 r. 1, 70:4, 84 r. 13, 89:6, 126:17, [*š*]*a* 8:1, 51:3, 64 r. 11, 83:8, 88:19, 94:4, 134 r. 5, 191 r. 5, *šá* 15:7, 23, r. 2, 17:7, r. 12, 13, 21 r. 3, 12, 29:8, 10, 13, 36:4, 39:7, 59:3, 4, 8, 9, r. 2, 5, 6, 9, 10, 17, 60:3, 5, 6, 9, 10, 11, 12, 13, r. 4, 7, 8, s. 1, 61:3, 4, 5, 6, 11, 12, 62:10, 11, 12, 13, r. 1, 5, 63:15, 65:15, r. 9, 66 r. 2, 6, 67 r. 3, 74 r. 5, 81:4, r. 3, 95:11, 122 r. 5, 8, 123:11, 125:6, 10, 13, r. 2, 7, 8, 11, 127 r. 1, 141 r. 6, 150:2, 183 r. 7, 13, 200 r. 5, 6, 10, *šá*] 60 s. 3, 62:1, *š*[*á* 61:5, *š*]*á* 135 s. 1, (*šá*) 60:3, [*šá* 61:9, 62:2, 11, 116 r. 3, [*šá*] 6 r. 2, 59 r. 6, 116 r. 1,
šaʾālu "to ask, inquire, interrogate": *as-sa-ʾa-al* 84:13, r. 6, *as-sa-ʾa-al-šú* 27:7, *a-sa-a*[*l-ku-nu*] 63 r. 1, *a-sa-al-šú* 15:5, *a-sa-*[*ʾa-al* 187:7, *a-*[*sa-ʾa-al*] 87:13, *is-sa-al* 204 e. 13, *is-sa-al-šú-nu* 121 r. 4, *iš-al* 62:4, *iš-a*[*l* 45 r. 4, *i*]*š-al-u-ni* 81:9, *i-sa-al-šú-nu* 63 e. 33, *la-áš-al* 141 r. 3, *la-áš-a*[*l*] 93:2, *liš-al* 30 r. 2, 34 r. 6, 45 r. 14, 59 r. 6, 71:6, 81 r. 10, 82 r. 11, 101 r. 2, *liš-al-šu* 105 r. 5, *liš-al-šú* 29 r. 7, 74:3, *liš-al-*[*šú*] 16:2, *liš-al-šú-nu* 43 r. 6, 183 r. 14, *liš-ʾa-al* 40 r. 10, 13, 78:21, *liš-u-lu* 17:8, *liš-ú-lu* 59 r. 2, *li-šá-al* 62 r. 3, 8, 67 r. 11, *li-šá-al*] 67:6, *ni-is-sa-al* 136:10, *ni-is-sa-al-šú* 137:8, *ni-sa-al* 204 r. 1, *ni-*[*sa-ʾa-al*] 96 r. 14, *šá-al* 136:10, *šá-al-šu* 15:5, *šá-ʾa-al* 84:10, *šá-ʾa-al-šú* 137:8, *šá-ʾa-al-šú-nu* 60 r. 13, *šá-ʾa-la* 63 r. 1, *ta-šá-al-an-na-*[*ši*] 63 e. 35, *ta-šá-ʾa-a-l*[*a*] 202:4,
šaʾūdu "to inform; (Štn) to spread tales": *us-sa-ta-ʾi-da-ni* 78:19,
šabāšu "to collect": *i-šab-bu-šú* 96:18, *i-*[*šab-bu-šú*] 96 r. 10,
šabāṭu (Shebat, name of the 11th month): ITI.ZÍZ 62:7,
šadādu "to drag, haul": *a-šá-ad-da-du-u-n*[*i* 217

r. 2,

šadattūnu (mng. uncert.): *šá-ad-da-tu-u-nu* 121:7,

šaddaqdiš "last year": MU.IM.MA 45:10, 90 r. 9, *šad-daq-diš* 201 r. 2, *šá-daq-diš* 112:4,

šaddû "mountain": KUR.MEŠ-*ni* 55:1,

šahāṭu "to glaze": *is-s]a-ah-ṭu* 204:10,

šakānu "to place, set": *as-sa-kan* 41:11, *a[s-sa-kan]* 162:10, *áš-kun* 36:14, *a-sa-kan* 60:10, 65 r. 15, 173:4, [*is-sak-nu*] 243 r. 6, *is-sak-nu-šu-nu* 143 r. 8, *is-sa-kan* 21:10, 18, r. 6, 36:5, 112:16, r. 13, 143 r. 10, *is-sa-ka[n]* 219 r. 6, [*is-sa-kan*] 87:14, *is-sa-kan-an-n[a-ši]* 121 r. 10, *iš-ka-nu-šá-nu-u-ni* 21:14, *iš-kun* 60 r. 6, *iš-kun-[an-ni]-ni* 196:5, *iš-kun-ni-ni* 89:7, *iš-kun-šu-u* 34 r. 10, *iš-kun-šú-nu* 143 r. 4, *iš-kun-u-nu* 129:13, *iš-[kun-x* 183:15, *iš]-ku-na-an-ni* 119:6, *iš-ku-ni-ni* 127:13, *iš-ku-n[u]* 130:5, *iš-ku-nu-u-ni* 32 r. 9, *iš-ku-nu-u-[ni]* 33 r. 2, *i]š-ku-nu-u-ni* 155 r. 8, *i-s[a-ak-nu* 135 r. 13, *i-sa-kan* 63:23, 135 r. 5, 225:3, *i-sa-ka[n* 63 r. 6, *i-sa-ka-[nu* 96 r. 17, *i-šak-kan* 127:19, *i-šak-ku-nu*] 129:3, *i-šá-kan-an-ni* 36:11, *i-šá-kan-u-ni* 125 r. 9, *i-šá-ka-an-šú-nu*] 60:7, *i-šá-ka-nu-šu-nu* 61:7, *i-šá-ka-nu-u-ni* 63 r. 24, *la-áš-kun* 63:25, *liš-ka-nu-[šú-nu]* 46:1, *liš-kun* 26:12, 48 s. 1, 65 r. 7, 79 r. 7, 125 r. 6, 163 r. 5, 196 r. 2, *liš-kun*] 121 r. 14, [*liš-kun* 157 r. 7, [*l*]*iš-kun* 25 r. 2, *liš-kun-an-ni* 78 r. 17, *liš-kun-šú-nu* 90:5, [*liš-k*]*un-šú-nu* 90 r. 12, *liš-ku-nu* 34:16, 111 r. 4, *liš-ku-[nu]* 93:10, *li-i[š-kun]* 36 e. 16, r. 4, [*li-iš-kun* 36 r. 14, *ni-iš-kun* 117 r. 8, *ni-šak-kan-u-ni* 117 r. 2, *šak-na* 25:9, 36:10, 192 r. 12, *šak-na-ka-ni* 70:4, *šak-na-šu-nu* 148:18, *š[a]k-n[u* 63 r. 5, *ša-áš-kin* 5 r. 15, [*š*]*a-ka-na-ku-u-ni* 94:3, *šá-ak-nu* 95:9, *šá-ka-an* 1:14, *šá-kín* 36:8, *šá-ki-in* 59:5, *šuk-na* 156:5, *šu-kun* 77 r. 3, 120 r. 4, [*šu-kun*] 5:6, *šu-kun-šú-nu* 148:13, *tas-sa-[ka]n* 5 r. 9, *t[a-sa-kan]* 96:12, *t]a-sa-kan* 60 r. 8, *ta-šak-kan-šú* 148 r. 3, *ú-šá-áš-ka-[nu-ni* 168:11,

šakāru "to be drunk": *i-šak-ki-ru* 115 r. 6,

šakintu "(harem) manageress": *šá-kín-tú* 183 r. 6,

šaknu "governor; prefect": LÚ.GAR-*nu*.MEŠ 43 r. 5, LÚ.GAR.KUR 95:1, 4, 13, r. 8, 14, 19, 96 r. 16, LÚ.GAR].KUR 95:16, LÚ.[GAR.KUR] 96:13, LÚ.*šak-ni* 59 r. 13, LÚ.*šak-ni-šu* 64:7, 8,

šakrānu "drunkard": *šá-ak-ra-nu-tú* 115 r. 5,

šakru "drunk": LÚ.*šak-ru-te* 34:9, r. 2,

šalāmu "to be sound, whole, safe, to succeed; (D) to complete, repay": *i-šal-li-[mu-u-ni]* 168:9, *liš-li-mu* 62 r. 9, *lu-šal-lim* 80:6, *l[u-šal-li-mu-ka]* 52:4, *ú-[sa-l]i-mu* 1:12, *ú-šal-lam* 126 r. 14, *ú-šal-lim* 36:7, *ú-šal-lim-u-ni* 80:2, see also *šalmu*,

šalāšā "thirty": 30 23 r. 3, 82 r. 8, 100:12, 129 r. 10, 243 r. 5, 31 82 r. 5, 32 53 r. 4,

šalāṭu "to have authority, rule": *šal-ṭa-ak* 112 r. 7,

šallussu "one third": 3-*su* 66:10,

šalmu "integer, sincere": *šá-al-mu* 126:1, see also *šalāmu*,

šalšu "third": 3-*šú* 78 e. 24,

šalšūmi "the day before yesterday": *a—šá-šu-me* 173:3, *i—šá-šu-me* 216:9, *i*]—*šá-[šu-me* 216:1,

šamaššammi "sesame": ŠE.GIŠ.Ì.MEŠ 5:8,

šamê "heaven(s), sky": AN-*e* 21 r. 2, 63 r. 27, 127 r. 21, 128 s. 2, 148:5, 194:2, AN]-*e* 44:7, A]N-*e* 132:4,

šamšu "sun": dUTU-*ši* 29:14, *šá-an-ši* 53 r. 4,

šamû "to hear, heed; (Gtn) to listen; (Š) to inform, notify": *as-sa-nam-me* 90:3, *as-se-me* 54:4, [*as*]-*se-me* 11:2, *áš-mu-u-ni* 78:12, r. 7, 9, *a-se-me* 99:2, [*a-šam*]-*mu-ú-ni* 71 r. 6, *iš-me* 32 r. 5, 61 r. 3, *iš-mu-u-ni* 34:11, *iš-mu-ú-ni* 29:12, *i-šam-man-ni* 98 r. 6, *i-šam-me* 41 r. 8, 63 r. 24, 154 s. 1, *i-šam-[me]* 114 r. 9, *i-šam-me-ú* 64 r. 3, *i-šá-am-mu-[u-ni* 122:5, *i-šá-man-ni* 34:20, *la-áš-me* 105 r. 20, 196:9, *ni-is-se-me* 21 r. 7, *ni-iš-mu-ni* 95:2, *šá-me-e* 29 r. 4, *taš-mu-u-ni* 63 s. 3, *ta-š[am-me]* 71 r. 6, *ta-šá-ma-a-ni* 21:11, *ú-ša-áš-ma* 242 r. 9, *ú-šá-áš-[ma]* 183 r. 9, [*ú-šá-áš-man-ni*] 6 e. 8, [*ú-šá-áš-mu*]-*ú-ni* 62:3, 1?šanīš *ḫ*alternatively; ditto*ḫ*: KI.MIN 60 s. 2, 3, [K]I.MIN 60 s. 3,

šaniu A "deputy": LÚ.2-*e* 11 r. 9, 212 r. 5, LÚ.[2]-*u* 63:4, LÚ.2-*ú* 78 r. 2,

šaniu B "second, other, different": *ša-ni-tú* 173:4, *šá-ni-e* 68 s. 3, 143:15, *šá-ni-iu-um-ma* 62 r. 2, *šá-ni-iu-um-[ma]* 62 r. 3, *šá-ni-iu-u-te* 63:8, *šá-ni-u* 125:8, *šá-ni-ú* 63:12, *šá*]-*ni-ú-t[e* 245:1, 2-*e* 59 r. 16, 2-*tú* 15 r. 2,

šanuttu "second time": *ša-nu-te-šú* 121 r. 11,

šapal "under": KI.TA 36:8, 132:8, KI.[TA 112:6, *sa-pal* 126:18, 127:12, *sa*]-*pal* 128:12, *šap-a-lu-[a]* 70 r. 3, *šap-la* 59 r. 6, *šap-lu-uš* 112 r. 12, *šá-pa-lu-[uš-šú]* 68 r. 12,

šapāru "to send; to write to": *as-pur-an-[ni* 129 e. 16, *as-sap-ra* 39:15, 129 r. 2, 143 r. 13, 196:7, *as-sap-[ra* 243:8, [*as-sap-ra*] 52 r. 1, *as-sa-pa-ra* 115 r. 12, *áš-par* 65 r. 14, *áš-pur-an-ni* 63 r. 29, 64 r. 6, 78 r. 1, *áš-pur-an-ni*] 63:1, [*áš-pur-u-ni*] 6:2, [*á*]*š-pu-rak-kan-ni-ni* 5 r. 21, *áš-pu-r[a-x* 13:2, *a-sap-ra* 7:5, *a-sa-[pa-ra]* 56 r. 8, *is-sap-ra* 29:7, *is-sap-[ra* 17:12, *is-sa-ap-ra* 21 r. 10, *is-sa-ap-ru-u-ni* 21:8, *is-sa-nap-[pu-r]u* 11:3, *is-sa-par-u-ni* 127:22, [*i*]*š-pur-an-na-ši-i-ni* 71:7, *iš-pur-an-na-ši-ni* 41:9, *iš-pur-an-[na-ši-ni]* 96 r. 12, *iš-pur-an-ni* 27:6, 65 r. 11, 79:5, 84:7, 136:9, 143:13, 148:12, *iš-pur-an-ni*] 181:6, *iš-pur-an-[ni* 162:7, *iš-pur-an-[ni]* 157:1, *iš-pu*]*r-an-ni* 90:1, *iš-p[ur-an-ni]* 234:2, *iš-p*]*ur-an-ni* 155:1, *iš-[pur-an-ni* 199:3, *iš-[pur-an-ni]* 164:7, *iš*]-*pur-an-ni* 152:7, *i*]*š-pur-an-ni* 236:3, [*iš-pur-an-ni*] 129:6, [*iš-pu*]*r-an-ni* 230 r. 2, [*iš-p*]*ur-an-ni-ni* 166:4, *iš-pur-a-[na-ši-ni]* 195:4, *iš-pur-ni-ni* 15:6, *i*]*š-p[ur*]-*ra-an-ni* 214 r. 2, *iš-pur-šu-u-ni* 21:16, *iš-pur-u-ni* 29:16, 83:8, 169 r. 5, *iš-[pur-u-ni]* 169:4, *iš-pu-ra* 62 r. 12, 150:7, *iš-pu-ra-an-ni* 78:5, *iš-pu-ra-na-ši-an-ni* 137:7, *i-s[a-ap-ra]* 66:3, *i-sa-par* 225:3, *i-ša[p-par-u-ni]* 77 r. 1, [*i-šap-pa-r*]*a-an-ni* 175 r. 9, *i-šá-par-an-ni* 63 r. 23, *la-áš-pu-rak-ka* 10:5, *liš-pur* 192 r. 13, *liš-pu-ra* 27 r. 5, 64 r. 8, 125:15, 143:10, 163 r. 1, 196 e. 12, *liš-pu-[r]a* 65:14, *liš-pu-ra-na-ši* 140 r. 13, *liš-pu-ru* 93 r. 12, 116 r. 4, *liš-[pu]-ru* 39:16, *ni-is-pur-an-ni* 129 r. 6, *ni-is-sap-ra* 142 r. 3, 145 s. 2, [*ni*]-*is-sap-r[a* 138 r. 5, *ni-sap-ra* 97 r. 15, *ni-sa-par* 129:11, *šap-r[u]-ni* 89:16, *šup-ra* 5 r. 2, 84:11, *šup-ru* 65 r. 17, *šu-pur* 17:8, *taš-pur-an-ni* 3 r. 3, *taš*]-*pur-an-ni* 3:6, *t*]*a[š-pur*]-*an-ni* 94:5, [*taš-pur-an-ni* 6:1, *ta*]*š-pur-a-ni* 4:4, *taš-pur-in-ni* 2:7, *taš-pu-ra* 242 r. 4, *taš-p*]*u-ra* 63 s. 3, *taš-pu-[x]* 183 r. 6, *ta-sa-nap-par-u-ni* 9 r. 3, *ta-šap-par-an-ni*] 6:5,

šāptu "wool": SÍG.MEŠ 5:7,

šāptu sāntu "red wool": SÍG.SA$_5$ 63:29, 82 r. 6, 84 r. 1, 6, SÍG.SA$_5$] 83 r. 1, SÍ[G.SA$_5$] 83 r. 5,

šāptu ṣalimtu "black wool": (SÍG).MI 82 r. 7,

šāqiu "cupbearer": LÚ.KAŠ.LUL 169 r. 3,

šarāku "to present, grant, bestow": *liš-ru-ku*] 195:2, *liš-*[*ru-ku-ka*] 52:8, *li-iš-ru-ku* 72:6,

šarru "king": LUGAL 1:2, 6, 2:1, 3:1, 4:1, 5:1, 14:1, 3, 5, 7, 15:3, 4, 17:1, 3, r. 4, 18:1, 3, 4, 20 r. 3, 21:1, 3, 4, 9, 14, 16, 20, r. 12, 15, 22:1, 3, 4, 23:1, 3, 4, 24:5, 25:3, 5, 7, 9, 12, 26:1, 3, 5, 8, 11, 27:1, 3, 4, 6, r. 5, 6, 29:6, 9, 13, 15, 16, r. 1, 7, 15, 30:1, r. 1, 2, 5, 6, 31:1, 3, 4, 5, 7, 9, r. 1, 2, 32:1, 4, r. 5, 7, 14, 15, 19, 20, 22, 33:4, 8, r. 8, 9, 11, 34:5, r. 14, 35:5, 36:5, 6, 8, 9, 15, r. 3, 4, 7, 9, 11, 12, 15, 39:1, 3, 4, 8, 12, 14, 40 r. 10, 13, 41:1, 6, 7, 9, r. 8, 42:1, 6, 7, 10, 12, r. 1, 4, 9, 12, 43:1, 7, 11, 13, r. 1, 2, 6, 8, 13, 44:1, 4, 5, r. 4, 7, 45:2, 8, 9, 11, 14, 15, r. 4, 6, 7, 8, 10, 13, 14, 47 r. 2, 3, 5, 48:9, 59:1, 7, 8, 12, r. 7, 10, 60:9, 11, 15, r. 18, s. 1, 61:1, 9, 62:2, 3, 5, 6, 13, r. 4, 7, 63:1, 8, 9, 11, r. 10, 19, 22, 25, 27, 28, 33, s. 1, 2, 3, 64:2, 4, 5, 6, 10, e. 12, r. 2, 4, 6, 7, 9, 11, 65:1, 4, 12, 14, r. 7, 11, s. 1, 2, 66:1, 8, r. 6, 67:2, 6, r. 1, 3, 7, 8, 10, 16, 68:15, r. 8, 13, 15, s. 1, 69 r. 3, 71:5, 6, 8, r. 2, 72:5, r. 5, 73 r. 4, 75:9, 76 r. 3, 77 r. 4, 78:1, 2, 3, 5, 7, 8, 12, 14, 15, 17, e. 24, r. 1, 5, 8, 12, 14, 16, 79:1, 3, 4, 11, 15, r. 7, 80:2, 81:1, 5, r. 7, 10, 82:1, 3, 5, 8, 9, 11, 13, 17, r. 1, 3, 11, 83:1, 3, 4, 6, 84:1, 3, 5, 6, s. 1, 85:1, 5, 6, 86:1, 3, 4, 7, r. 18, 87:1, 3, 4, 7, 10, r. 2, 88:4, 5, 89:1, 6, 90:1, r. 4, 8, 11, 91 s. 1, 92:1, 3, 6, 95:1, 3, 96:1, 6, r. 11, 19, 97:6, 8, r. 10, 15, 18, 98:1, 3, 5, 6, 7, 9, r. 3, 7, 9, 11, 99:6, e. 11, r. 2, 10, 100:1, 3, 4, 17, 101 r. 2, s. 1, 102:1, 4, 6, 105:1, 10, 12, r. 1, 4, 5, 16, 19, 108:1, 3, 4, 6, 109:1, 3, 4, 110:1, 3, 4, r. 2, 5, 111:1, 3, 5, 9, r. 2, 112:1, 3, 6, r. 4, s. 1, 113:1, 3, 4, 114:1, 4, 7, r. 3, 7, 9, 11, 115:1, 6, 10, 13, r. 3, 11, 13, 117:1, 9, 11, r. 2, 3, 6, 118:1, 7, 9, 119:3, 5, r. 1, 120:1, 3, 5, r. 10, 121:1, 3, 4, 6, 9, 12, 14, 16, r. 4, 5, 13, 124:6, 125:13, 126:1, 3, 9, 10, 11, 13, 15, 16, 17, 18, 24, r. 2, 10, 20, 21, 23, 127:9, 12, 13, 14, 16, r. 3, 5, 6, 7, 11, 13, 14, 16, 17, 19, 20, 128:1, 3, 9, 12, r. 10, 12, 13, 17, s. 1, 129:2, 4, 6, 9, r. 2, 4, 6, 11, s. 1, 131:1, 3, 4, r. 3, 4, 132:1, 2, 4, 6, 7, 8, 9, 11, 134:1, 2, 6, 135:5, 7, 14, r. 6, 136:1, 4, 5, 9, 137:1, 4, 5, 7, 138:1, 4, 5, 6, r. 4, 6, 139:1, 3, 5, 140:1, 4, 5, r. 2, 10, 13, s. 1, 141:5, 142:1, 4, 6, r. 2, 4, 143:1, 3, 8, 10, 12, r. 6, 12, 144:1, 3, 5, 8, 9, 145:4, 5, 146:5, 11, 148:1, 6, 12, 150:4, 9, r. 7, 151:4, 152:1, 3, 4, 7, r. 3, 153:1, 4, 154:4, 6, 7, r. 4, 11, s. 1, 155:1, 157:1, 158:8, 160:1, 3, 162:1, 3, 6, 163:2, 7, 164:1, 3, 6, 165 r. 2, 169:2, 3, 4, 171:1, 7, 174:1, 7, 175:1, 3, 6, 176:5, 178:5, 179:1, 5, 180:1, 3, 4, 181:1, 3, 4, 5, 183:5, 6, 16, r. 8, 9, 11, 14, 16, s. 1, 184:3, 4, 186:3, 187:1, 3, 4, 188:3, 4, 189:3, 190:3, 4, 191:1, 3, 4, 9, r. 5, 192:3, r. 12, 194:1, 3, 196:3, 4, 6, 8, e. 12, 197 r. 3, 199:3, 200 r. 5, 201 r. 1, 3, 5, 202:2, 6, 204:7, e. 12, r. 9, 206 r. 3, 207:3, 4, 8, 211 r. 3, 212:7, s. 1, 215:1, 4, 217:1, 218:1, 5, 8, 219 r. 2, 9, 222:1, 3, r. 3, 223:3, 228:1, 3, 234 r. 3, 236:1, 3, 242 r. 1, 2, 243:5, r. 7, 245:3, LUGAL] 15:1, 24:3, 29:1, 33:1, 43:5, 62 r. 12, 63 r. 4, 64:3, 66:12, 67 r. 2, 79 r. 5, 92:4, 97:1, 114 r. 6, 118:5, 119:1, 127:1, r. 22, 129:11, 135 r. 11, 145 s. 2, 151:2, 157 r. 5, 164:4, 175 r. 8, 182:1, 183:1, 184:1, 189:4, LUGA[L 67:12, 186:1, 195:2, 221:4, 238:3, 243:6, r. 4, LUGA]L 25:1, 123 r. 7, 178:2, 184:6, 193:3, 195:4, 222:4, 230 r. 1, LUG[AL 64 r. 8, 87 r. 6, 89:3, 101 r. 7, 165 r. 5, 188:1, 192:1, 214 e. 1, 242 r. 8, 246:1, LUG[AL] 60:1, 134:3, LUG]AL 29:3, 143:5, 169:1, 194 r. 2, 217 r. 4, 226:1, LU[GAL 61:11, 63 r. 33, 87:12, 88:1, 102 r. 2, 121 r. 11, 129:5, 145:1, LU[GAL] 121 r. 17, LU]GAL 81:7, 86 r. 7, 165 r. 4, L[UGAL 85 r. 1, 129:3, 8, 162:5, 168:10, 183:3, 14, 190:1, 196:1, 234:1, L[UGAL] 90 r. 10, 100 r. 17, 117:5, L]UGAL 5 r. 17, 46:2, 86:6, 174:3, 178:3, 183 s. 2, 208:3, [LUGAL 24:1, 34:14, 36 r. 13, 39:9, 45 r. 15, 62 r. 3, 66:2, 77 r. 2, 90:12, 96:4, 114:3, 135:1, 166:3, 169 r. 9, 171:8, 179:3, 189:1, 192:5, 193:1, 200 r. 6, 237 r. 2, [LUGAL] 41 r. 5, 63 s. 2, 77 r. 9, 78:21, 92:11, 200 r. 8, [LUGA]L 67:11, [LUG]AL 74:3, 168:8, [LU]GAL 135 s. 3, 143 r. 14, 168:2, 194:5, 224 r. 4, [L]UGAL 134 r. 4, LUGAL-*ma* 64 r. 1, LUGAL.MEŠ 45 r. 3, 127:3, 137:12, LUGAL.MEŠ-*ni* 45 r. 14, 77 r. 6, LUG]AL-*ni* 66:11, MAN 1:1, 15:2, 6, 16:2, 4, r. 3, 17:4, 7, r. 9, 19:1, 3, 4, 20:1, 3, 28 r. 4, 7, 36:14, 63:12, 65 r. 13, 75:8, 85:3, 105:3, 6, 8, r. 7, 15, 115:3, 123 r. 5, 125:9, 10, 12, r. 4, 6, 7, 11, 128 r. 2, s. 3, 131 r. 7, 148:2, 218:3, [MAN 20:2,

šarrūtu "kingship, kingdom": LUGAL-*te* 8:3, LUGAL-*ti* 29:13, 60:4, LUGAL]-*ti* 61:4, LUGAL-*ti-ka* 33:9, LUGAL-*t*[*u*] 20 r. 10, LUGAL-*u-tu* 59:11, r. 4, LUGAL-*u-tú* 96 r. 7, LUGAL-*ú-tú* 29:10,

šatiši (mng. obscure): *šá-ti-ši* 65 r. 14,

šattu "year": MU.AN.NA 8:4, 15:23, 63:17, 149:2, 213:3, MU.A[N.NA 15:23, MU].AN.NA 81:8, MU.AN.NA.MEŠ 35 r. 9, 59:3, 98:8, 117:8, 126:7, 128:6, MU.AN.[NA.MEŠ 195:1, M]U.AN.NA.MEŠ 20 s. 1, [M]U.AN.NA.MEŠ 127:7,

šatû "to drink": NAG 47 r. 5, *ši-t*[*i-a*] 92:10, *ta-as-si* 6:3,

šaṭāru "to write": *a-s*[*a-ṭar*] 56 r. 7, *i-sa-ṭa-ru* 63:14, *i-šá-ṭar* 95 r. 3, *liš-ṭur* 125 r. 7, 148 r. 12, *liš-ṭ*[*ur-u-ni* 164:9, *liš-ṭu-ru* 125:10, 207:11, *ni-iš-ṭur* 143:8, 11, *ni-šaṭ-ṭa-ru-u-ni* 143:9, *šá-ṭi-ir* 60:16, *šu-ṭur* 5:20, *ta-šaṭ-ṭi-ri* 28:3,

ša-huṭāri "staff-bearer": LÚ.PA.MEŠ 51 r. 4, LÚ.*šá—hu-ṭa-ri* 69:3,

ša-lišāni "informer": LÚ.*šá*—EME 148 r. 21,

ša-maṣṣarti "guard": LÚ.*šá*—EN.NUN 6 r. 3, LÚ.*šá*—EN.NUN.MEŠ 205 r. 1,

ša-muhhi-āli "city overseer": LÚ.*šá*—UGU—URU 59 r. 12,

ša-muhhi-huluhhi "overseer of frit": LÚ.[*šá*—UGU—*hu-luh-hi*] 32:3, [LÚ.*šá*—UG]U—*hu-luh-hi* 33:3,

ša-pān-bēt-qāti "storehouse supervisor": LÚ.*ša*—IGI—É—ŠU.2 91:8,

ša-pān-ekalli "palace supervisor, palace superintendent": LÚ.*ša*—IGI—É.GAL 98:4, LÚ.*šá*—IGI—É.GAL 88:3,

ša-pān-manê "accountant": LÚ.IGI—*ma-né-e* 34 r. 2,

ša-pān-nērebi "entrance supervisor": LÚ.*ša*—IGI—*né-re-bi* 91:7,

ša-pēthalli "cavalryman": *ša*—BAD.HAL.ME[Š 176:4,

ša-qurbūti "bodyguard": LÚ.*qur-b*[*u-te* 135 r. 8, LÚ.*qur-*[*bu-te*] 93 r. 6, LÚ.*qur-bu-ti* 199:9, [LÚ.*qur-b*]*u-ti* 149:6, LÚ.*qur-bu-tú* 42 r. 14, LÚ.*qur*-ZAG

83:6, 88:14, LÚ.*qur*-ZAG.MEŠ 115 r. 2, L[Ú.*qu*]*r*-ZAG.MEŠ 90 r. 8,

ša-rēši "eunuch": LÚ.SAG 34 r. 7, 49 r. 8, 63 r. 10, 89:16, 100 r. 17, 146:9, 148 r. 21, LÚ.[SAG] 146:1, LÚ].SAG.MEŠ 60 s. 3, LÚ.SAG.MEŠ 87:8, 90:4, 112:7, 200 r. 7, LÚ.SAG.MEŠ-*šú* 95:7, LÚ.SAG-*šú* 95:6,

ša-ṣilli "parasol": TÚG.*ša*—GIŠ.MI 123:3, TÚG.*šá—ṣi-il-li* 63 r. 17,

ša-šēpi "(king's) personal guard": LÚ.*ša*—GÌR.2 27:9, LÚ.*še-e-pi* 59 r. 6,

ša-šērāti "morning": *šá—še-r*]*a-a-t*[*i* 122 r. 7, *šá—še-ra-ti* 122 r. 11,

ša-ziqni "bearded (courtier)": LÚ.*šá—ziq*-[*ni*.MEŠ 200 r. 7,

šeʾu "corn": ŠE 93:2,

šebû "to get sated, enjoy; satisfaction": *šeb-e* 106:10, *še-bé-e* 98:9,

šēpu "foot": GÌR.2 15:21, 25, 20 r. 4, 126:18, 127:12, [GÌR.2 29:5, [GÌR.2] 128:12, GÌR.2-*ia* 34 r. 4, GÌR.2.MEŠ 132:8, GÌR.2.MEŠ-*ia* 36:7, GÌR.2.MEŠ-*ka* 151 r. 7, GÌR.2.MEŠ-*šú* 5:5, GÌR.2.M[EŠ-*šú*] 48 r. 14, GÌR.2-*šú* 127:19,

šî "she, it": *ši-i* 59 r. 4, 60 r. 11, 62:5, 63 r. 29, 163:5, 239 r. 1, *ši*-[[]]*i* 181 r. 4,

šiāru "tomorrow": *iš—ši-a-ri* 137 r. 14, *ši-a-*[*ri*] 162 r. 4, *ši-*[*a-r*]*i* 162:13, *ši-ia-a-ri* 114 r. 9,

šiāṭu "to be negligent, disregard": *is-si-ia-aṭ* 150:5, *i-ši-aṭ*] 61:9, *i-*[*ši-aṭ*] 60:9, *i-ši-ia-ṭa* 62:6, *ta-ši-*[*aṭ* 59:13, *ta-ši-ṭa* 148:16,

šibšu "straw tax": ŠE.*ši-ib-še* 96:18, ŠE.*ši-ib-še-ni* 96 r. 10,

šibšutu "door-beam, architrave": GIŠ.ŠÚ.MEŠ 101 r. 6, *ši-ib-šú-tú* 100:19,

šimunu see *simunu,*

šina "they": *ši-na* 158:7,

šinīšu "twice": *ši né-e-šu* 86:8, 2-*šú* 78 e. 24,

šinnu "tooth": *ši-in* 197:4,

šipirtu "message": *ši-pir-ti* 129:6,

šipru "art, accomplishment": *ši-pir* 72:7,

šiptu "incantation, spell": *ši-ip-tú* 60 r. 16,

šipṭu "judgment, punishment": [*šip*]-*ṭa* 73 r. 5, *ši-ip-ṭi* 78 r. 17,

šiqlu "shekel": GÍN 53 r. 4, 127 r. 12, 128 r. 11,

šīru "flesh": UZU 126:8, 127:8, 128:8, UZU.MEŠ 49:7, 52:5, 65:8, 105:8, 106:9, U]ZU.MEŠ 195:2,

šīti "she, it": *ši-i-ti-i-*[*ma*] 181 r. 3, *ši-*[*ti*] 223:3, *ši-ti-i-ni* 140 r. 12, *ši-ti*]-*ni* 37:4, *ši-t*[*i-ni*] 181 r. 10,

šû "he": *šu-u* 15:13, 48 r. 3, 63:20, r. 15, 17, 19, 26, s. 2, 64:6, 68 r. 11, 13, 75 r. 10, 79:5, 105 r. 8, 120 r. 5, 121 r. 9, 125:7, 143:17, r. 11, 220:2, *šu-*[*u*] 62 r. 1, [*šu-u* 60:9, *šu-ú* 5 r. 7, 43:10, 60:9, 61:9, 79:17, 97 r. 6, 127 e. 25, 26, r. 5, 181:9, 237:4, *šu-*[*ú*] 218:9, [*šu-ú* 72 r. 4, *šú-u* 9:7, 104:3, 212 s. 2, *šú-ú* 130:6,

šubalkutu see *nabalkutu,*

šubtu "seat, settlement; ambush": *šu-ub-tú* 60 r. 20,

šulmānu "gift, present, bribe": *šul-ma-na-te* 44 r. 3, 112 r. 13, 15, *šul-ma-*[*nu* 99 r. 12,

šulmu "health, well-being": DI 17:3, DI-*me* 36:12, 48:10, DI-*mu* 2:3, 4, 3:3, 14:3, 18:3, 19:3, 20:2, 21:3, 22:3, 23:3, 25:3, 26:3, 31:4, 32:4, 41:6, 45 r. 4, 48:3, 78:2, 79:3, 81:5, 82:3, 83:3, 84:3, 85:3, 86:3, 5, 87:3, 6, 88:4, 89:3, 92:3, 96:4, 100:3, 18, 105:3, 9, r. 19, 106:3, r. 5, 107:4, 108:3, 8, 109:3, 110:3, 111:3, 113:3, 114:3, 116:9, 117:5, 118:6, 10, 121:3, 124:3, 128:3, 132:2, 135:5, 136:4, 139:3, 140:3, 143:3, 148:2, 152:3, 162:3, 167:6, 175:3, 178:2, 180:3, 181:3, 183:3, 186:3, 188:3, 191:3, 196:6, 8, 228:3, DI-*mu*] 15:2, 118:7, DI-*m*[*u* 15:18, 190:3, 192:3, DI-*m*]*u* 33:4, 170 r. 2, DI-[*mu* 24:3, DI-[*mu*] 153:3, DI]-*mu* 27:3, 131:3, 169:2, 184:3, 218:3, D[I-*mu* 39:3, 164:3, 187:3, D]I-*mu* 57:3, [DI-*mu* 5:2, 102:4, 118:6, 160:1, 174:3, 185:3, 193:3, 196:3, 215:4, [DI-*mu*] 118:3, 137:3, [DI-*m*]*u* 118:4, [DI]-*mu* 4:2, 167:2, *šul-me* 52:6, 222:2, *šul-mu* 1:3, 4, 5, 6, 7, 8, 34:2, 35:3, 42:6, 44:4, 97:5, 98:5, 120:3, 122:3, 126:3, 134:2, 139:14, 142:3, 144:3, 179:3, *šul-mu*] 138:3, 145:3, *šul-m*[*u* 122:2, 4, 189:3, *š*[*ul-mu* 122:1, *š*]*ul-mu* 127:3, [*š*]*u*[*l*]-*mu* 166:3, *šu-lam-šú* 122:6,

šumēlu "left, north": 150 126:21,

šumma "if": *šum-ma* 27 r. 6, 34:15, 22, 63:17, 64 r. 6, 81 r. 8, 9, 85 r. 2, 88:17, 90:12, 111 r. 2, 125:9, 126:26, 141:5, 163:2, 181:7, r. 8, *šum-m*[*a* 99 r. 6, [*šum-ma* 46:2, 123 r. 7, [*šum-ma*] 126:25, *šum-mu* 97 r. 11, *šúm-ma* 63:6, 7, s. 3, 64:8, 66 r. 4, 67 r. 15, 99:1, 131 r. 6, 137 r. 14, 147:4, 148 r. 5, 207:7, *š*[*úm-ma* 137 r. 15, *š*]*úm-ma* 9:4, 36 r. 14, [*šúm-ma* 67:2, 171:7, [*šúm-m*]*a* 66 r. 5, [*šúm*]-*ma* 64 r. 9, [*šú*]*m-ma* 78 r. 6, [*š*]*úm-ma* 64:6, *šúm-mu* 92:11,

šumu "name": MU 15 r. 2, 59 r. 5, 9, 10, MU-*ka* 60:4, MU-*ka*] 61:3, [MU.MEŠ-*šú*]-*nu* 207:11, MU-*šú* 15 r. 2, MU-*šú-nu* 59:6, 60:7, MU-[*šú-nu* 61:7, *šu-me* 1:14, *šu-mì* 34:6, *šu-mu* 34 r. 11, 125:10, r. 7, 129:3, 12, 143:8,

šunu "they": *šu-nu* 49 r. 1, 3, 56 r. 12, 59:10, 60:4, 7, r. 12, 62:8, 63:29, r. 25, 76 e. 2, 124 r. 2, 127 r. 9, 173:1, *šu-n*[*u* 61:4, 68:16, *šu*]-*nu* 73:1, *š*[*u-nu*] 200 r. 5, [*šu-nu* 61:7, [*šu*]-*nu* 68 r. 8, *šu-nu-ma* 63:7, 126:16, *šú-nu* 15:26, 21 r. 1, 51:2, 61 r. 7, 84 r. 3, 115 r. 5, 126 r. 15,

šupuhru see *supuhru,*

šuqultu "weight": KI.LAL 53 r. 4,

šūtu "he": *šu-tu-u-ni* 63 r. 14, 67 r. 8, 143 r. 5, *šu-tu-ú-ni* 196:11, *šu-tú* 15:13, 17:10, *šu-tú-u-ni* 96 r. 14, *šu-tú-ú* 45 r. 10, *šu-u-tu* 53 r. 8,

tabāku "to pour, shed": *lit-bu-ku* 27 r. 7,

tabālu "to carry away, remove": [*it-t*]*a-bal* 149:5, *lit-bal* 240:5,

tabku "stored grain": ŠE.*tab-ki-šú-nu* 55:3, ŠE.*ta*[*b-ku* 145 r. 6, *tab-ku* 52 r. 4,

tabû "to rise, get up; (Š) to remove": *šat-bu-a-ku-u* 44 r. 6,

tadānu "to give, sell": *ad-dan* 34 e. 25, 127 r. 12, 13, *ad-dan-nu* 128 r. 13, *ad-din-u-ni* 99 e. 12, *at-ta-na-šú* 80:4, *at-ti-din* 35:7, *a-dan-nu* 128 r. 12, *a-di-ni* 31:9, *a-ta-na-áš-šú* 236:6, *a-ti-din* 81 r. 5, [*a-ti-din* 45:14, [*a-ti-din*] 45:9, *di-in* 112:14, *di-na* 29:17, [*di-na-áš-šú*] 5:10, *di-ni* 5:15, 145 r. 8, [*d*]*i-ni* 81 r. 8, *id-dan* 29 r. 1, [*id-dan*] 183:9, *id-da-nu-na-ši* 84 r. 7, *id-da-nu-ni* 84:11, *id-da-nu-u-ni* 86:15, 16, 133:7, *id-din* 81 r. 9, *id-din-ak-kan-ni* 29 r. 14, *id-din-an-ni* 99:10, *id-din-*[*u-ni* 99 r. 11, *id-di-na* 34:15, *id-di-nu-u-ni* 21 r. 4, 42 e. 14, *id-di-nu-u-nu* 127 r. 8, *id-du-nu* 126:16, *id-du-nu*] 129:5, *it-tan-nu* 29:13, *it-ta-an-na* 155 r. 5, [*it-t*]*a-an-nu* 41 r. 3, *it-ta-nu* 78 r. 14, *it-ti-din* 81 r. 8, 112:8, [*it-t*]*i-din* 55 e. 7, *it-ti-din-šu-nu* 49 r. 2, *i-da-nu-ni* 125 r. 4, *i-da-nu-ni-ka* 151 r. 8, *i-da-nu-u-ni* 65 r. 10, *i-di-na* 29 r. 6, 82 r. 14, *i-di-nak-kan-ni* 63:30, *i-di-na-na-še* 40 r. 7, *i-di-na-na-*[*še*] 40:13, *i-di-nu* 63:17, *i-di-nu-u-nu* 128 r. 4, *i-du-nu* 216:8, *i-tan-na* 71:2, *i-ta-an-na-ka-a* 67 r. 12, [*i*]-*ta-nu-ni-ka-nu-u* 67:8, *i-ti-din* 63 r. 13, 21, 112 r. 16, *it-tan-na-áš-*[*šu* 150 r. 6, *la-ad-din* 34:19, 83 r. 6, *lid-din* 146:11, *lid-din-nu* 106:12, *lid-di-na* 146:4, *lid-di-nu* 49:7, 105:9, 117:10, 126:9, 127:9, *lid-di-n*[*u*] 128:9, [*lid*]-*di-nu* 23 r. 5, *lid-di-nu-ni* 80:5, [*lid-di-nu-ni-ka*] 52:5, *li-di-nu-ni* 83 r. 5, *li-di-nu-nik-ka* 59:4, *li-di-nu-ni-šú* 39 r. 1, *li-di-nu-u-ni* 65 r. 9, 83 r. 2, *li-id-din* 34 r. 1, *li-id-*[*din*] 98:10, *ni-dan* 84 r. 2, *ni-din* 56 r. 6, *ni-ti-din* 40:5, 97 r. 18, SUM-*u-ni* 88:9, *ta-ad-nu-u-ni* 123 r. 6, *ta-dan-áš-šú* 29:8, r. 3, *ta-da-ni* 91:6, *ta-di-na-ni* 5 r. 1, *ta-ti-din* 53 r. 6,

tahūmu "border": *ta-h*[*u-me*] 18:7,

takālu "(D) to trust, have faith": *ta-ku-la* 60 r. 11, *ta-ku-la-ak* 128 r. 10, *tak-ku-lak* 127 r. 11,

takkassu "(unfinished) piece": DAG.GAZ 81 r. 3,

takmīsu (mng. uncert.): *tak-mis* 43:7,

takrimāti "autumn(?)": *tak-ri-ma-a-*[*ti*] 90 r. 3,

tamkāru "merchant": LÚ.DAM.QAR 105 r. 8, LÚ.DAM.QAR.MEŠ 54:8, 128 r. 3, LÚ.DAM.QAR.[MEŠ] 54:1, LÚ.D[AM.QAR.MEŠ] 45:13, LÚ.DAM.QAR.MEŠ-*ni* 45 r. 11, LÚ.DAM.QAR.MEŠ 127 r. 9,

tamû "to swear, (D) to adjure": *at-ta-a-ma* 10:3, *at-ta-ma* 181 r. 8, *ut-ta-me-šú-nu* 21 r. 7,

tamūzu (Tammuz, name of the 4th month): ITI.ŠU 50:12,

taqānu "to be safe, keep in safety": *tu-qu-nu* 59 s. 3, *tu*]-*qu-nu* 60 s. 2,

tarammu "corn heap": *ta-ra-am* 43 r. 3, 4,

tarāṣu "to be proper, in order, all right": *ta-ri-iṣ* 121:13, [*t*]*a-ri-ṣ*[*i* 161:4,

tarbāṣu "courtyard, pen, stall": TÙR.MEŠ 5 r. 7,

tašlimtu "reimbursement, compensation": *taš-li-ma-a-ti* 80:1, 6,

tašlīšu "third man (in a chariot team)": LÚ.3-*šú* 78 r. 10, 136:11, 13, LÚ.3-*šú*.MEŠ 207:8, 10, LÚ.3.U_5 78:4, 139:8, LÚ.3.U_5.MEŠ 115:11, LÚ.3.U_5.ME[Š 68:17,

tašlīšūtu "rank of third man": LÚ.3.U_5-*u-tú* 68 r. 10,

tašrītu (Tishri, name of the 7th month): ITI.DU_6 90 r. 4,

tidintu "gift": *ti-din-tu* 42:12,

tikpu "layer": *ti-ik-pi* 143:14,

timāli "yesterday": *it—ti-ma-li* 25:6, [*i—ti-ma-li* 216:1, *ti-ma-a-l*[*i*] 94:4, *t*]*i-ma-l*[*i* 189:6,

tirṣu "reign": *ti-ir-ṣi-ka* 151 r. 6, *ti-ir-ṣ*[*i-ka*] 96 r. 8,

tuāru "to turn (into), become": *a-tu-ar* 34:22, *a-tu-ur*] 82:17,

tumuṣu (mng. obscure): *tu-mu-ṣu* 123 r. 3,

tūra "again": *tu-ur-a* 11:4,

turtānu "commander-in-chief": LÚ].*tur-tan* 204:2, LÚ.*tur*]-*tan-ni* 175:9,

ṭaʾtu "gift, bribe": *ṭa-aʾ-tú* 63:18,

ṭabāhu "to slaughter": *ṭa-bi-ih* 30:9,

ṭābtānu "benefactor": *ṭa-*[*ab-t*]*a-ni-ma* 128 r. 8,

ṭābtu "goodness, favour, patronage": MUN 78:8, MUN-*ú* 78:10, *ṭa-ab-ta-ka* 32 r. 21, *ṭa-ab-ti* 32 r. 20, 59:4, [*ṭa-ab-ti* 60:5, [*ṭa-ab-ti*] 61:5, *ṭa-ab-tu* 121 r. 8, *ṭa-a*[*b-tú* 126 r. 15, *ṭa-ba-te* 62:11,

ṭābu see *ṭiābu*,

ṭahû "to approach, advance": *lu-ṭa-hi-u* 154:6,

ṭēmu "mind, order, report, news": [*ṭe*]-*en-šú* 6 e. 8, [*ṭè*]-*en-šú-*[*nu*] 17:10, *ṭè-e-me* 148 r. 8, [*ṭè-e-me* 196:4, *ṭè-e-mu* 21:14, 25 r. 1, 32 r. 9, 41:11, 60 r. 6, 64 r. 6, 65 r. 7, 70:4, 79 r. 7, 87:14, 89:7, 90:5, r. 11, 111 r. 4, 120 r. 4, 125 r. 6, 148:13, 162:10, 163 r. 5, *ṭè-e-*[*mu*] 93:9, *ṭè-e-*[*m*]*u* 183:15, *ṭè-*[*e-mu* 46 r. 3, *ṭ*]*è-e-mu* 157 r. 6, [*ṭè-e-mu* 33 r. 2, *ṭè-ma-ni* 62 r. 9, *ṭè-*[*me*] 17 r. 13, *ṭè-mi* 26:12, *ṭè-mì-ni* 42 r. 12, *ṭè-mì-šú-nu* 84 r. 3, *ṭè-mu* 45:12, [*ṭè-mu* 77 r. 3, 119:6, *ṭè-mu-ni* 127 r. 1,

ṭiābu "to be good, pleasing": DÙG-*ka* 5:3, DÙG.GA 38 r. 3, 48:6, 101 s. 1, 108:4, 125 r. 10, 157:2, [DÙG.GA 119 r. 2, DÙG.GA-*ka* 3:4, DÙG.GA.MEŠ 62:8, DÙG.GA-*šú* 106 r. 8, *li-ṭi-ba-a*[*n-ni*] 62 s. 1, [*lu-ṭ*]*i-ib-bu* 72 r. 2, *ṭa-a-ba* 62:9, *ṭa-ab-ka*] 4:2, *ṭa-ba-kan-ni* 127:23, *ṭa-bu-te* 154 r. 6, *ṭa-bu-u-ni* 3:7, 126:12,

ṭību "twine, thread": *ṭi-bu* 82 r. 5,

ṭībūtu "goodness(?)": *ṭi-bu-te* 16:4,

ṭūbu "goodness": *ṭu-bi* 121 r. 17, *ṭu-ub* 49:6, 7, 52:5, 105:7, 8, 106:8, 9, 126:7, 8, 127:8, 128:7, 8, 195:2, [*ṭu-ub* 195:2, *ṭu-u-bi* 148 r. 7,

ṭuppu "tablet, letter, document": DUB-*pi* 1:1, I]M 178:1, [IM 57:1, *ṭup-pi-ki* 28:3, *ṭup-pu* 163 r. 6, [*ṭ*]*u*[*p*]-*pu* 128 r. 1,

ṭupšarru "scribe, secretary": LÚ.A.BA 21 r. 1, 32 r. 17, 34:7, 12, 42:5, 43:3, 44:2, 45:1, r. 1, 56:6, 59 r. 12, 14, 63:2, 15, r. 13, 68 r. 6, 88:3, 99:8, 100:2, 107:3, 112:11, r. 8, 16, 135:3, 148 r. 9, 183:12, 217:4, LÚ.A.B[A 59 r. 19, LÚ.A.B]A 123:8, LÚ.A.[BA 215:3, LÚ.A.BA.MEŠ 82:10, 11, LÚ.DUB.SAR 98:2, LÚ.DUB.[SAR].MEŠ 43 r. 10,

ṭupšarrūtu "scribal art; position/post of scribe": LÚ.A.BA-[*ú*]-*te* 34 r. 9, *ṭup-šar-ru-tú* 62:9,

ṭupšar āli "city scribe": LÚ.A.BA—URU 97:3,

ṭupšar ekalli "palace scribe": LÚ.A.BA—É.GAL 49:1, r. 5, 78:10, LÚ.A.BA—KUR 48:1, 78:4, 20, 87:13,

u "and": *u* 19:4, 20:3, 23:4, 25:4, 29:3, 9, 11, 12, 31:5, 32:5, 34:3, r. 21, 23, 35:4, 44:6, 48:4, 60:5, 61:5, 70:1, 72:4, 78 r. 13, 81:6, 86 r. 1, 88:5, 94 r. 2, 98 r. 10, 99:5, 100:4, 110:4, 112 r. 4, 118:8, 119:3, 121:4, 124:4, 126:10, 12, 127:16, 128 s. 2, 134:3, 136:5, 144:4, 162:4, 165 r. 1, 2, 171:12, 187:4, 189:4, 191:4, 243:4, [*u* 135:6, *ú* 240:6, *ù* 1:8, 3 r. 2, 5 r. 18, 6 r. 2, 8 r. 2, 9 r. 6, 10:7, 21:4, r. 3, 26:4, 27:4, 28 r. 5, 29:14, 15, 32 r. 11, 34:10, 17, 36:10, 42 r. 7, 14, 46 r. 6, 48 r. 4, 7, 52:1, 2, 54 r. 1, 57:4, 59:5, 60:5, 7, 61 r. 6, 63 r. 22, 78:15, 20, 82:4, 84 r. 5, 12, 85:4, 87:5, 6, 90:6, 91:6, r. 1, 92:13, 93 r. 6, 111:4, 112 r. 1, 8, 114:4, 117:15, 120:4, 121:14, r. 9, 125 r. 8, 126:2, 11, 17, r. 4, 12, 16, 19, 22, 127 r. 17, 18, 21, 23, 128 r. 5, 136:3, 142:5, 143:12, 148:4, 16, r. 5, 154:5, 10, r. 4, 163 r. 2, 171:11, 179:4, 183:4, 184:4, r. 7, 191 r. 6, 195:3, 196:10, 200 r. 9, 210:2, 218:4, *ù*] 143:4, [*ù* 63 s. 1, 78:17,

ubālu "to bring, (Š) to send": *bi-la-a-ni* 63:11, 24, *it-tu-b*[*il*] 219 r. 3, *i-tu-*[*bi-la* 215 r. 4, *lu-bíl* 63:11, *lu-bi-la* 148 r. 18, *lu-b*[*i-la* 221:1, *lu-bi-la-ni* 5 e. 24, *lu-bi-lu* 60 s. 2, 163:5, *lu-bi-lu-ni* 59 r. 8, *lu-bi-lu-ni-ši* 59 r. 7, *lu-še-b*[*il-u-ni*] 188 r. 5, *lu-še-bi-la* 54:5, [*lu-še-bi-l*]*a-šú-nu* 123 r. 8, [*l*]*u-u-bi-la-na-ši* 88:16, *lu-ú-bi-lu* 6 r. 5, *nu-bil* 125 r.

11, *nu-ub-bal-šú* 140 r. 11, *še-bi-la* 5:21, *še-[bi-la* 8 r. 4, [*še*]*-bi-la* 3 r. 1, *tu-še-ba-la-áš-šu* 148 r. 4, [*u*]*b-bal-áš-ša-nu-[u-ni* 86 r. 2, *ub-bal-u-ni* 163 r. 3, *us-se-bil-šú-nu* 148 s. 1, *us-se-bi-la* 105 r. 15, [*us-se-b*]*i-la* 110 r. 6, *us-se-bi-la-áš-šú* 105 r. 4, *ú-ba-la* 59:3, *ú-ba-lu-ni-ni* 95 r. 2, *ú-bi-lu-ni* 59 r. 7, *ú-bi-lu-ú-ni* 71 r. 2, *ú-se-bi-la* 106 r. 4, *ú-se-bi-l[a* 158:4, [*ú*]*-se-bi-la* 131 r. 4, *ú-še-bi-la* 69 r. 2, *ú-š[e]-(bi)-la* 54:3, *ú-še-bi-la-an-ni* 136:8, r. 7,

ubānu "finger": ŠU.SI 81 r. 2,

udē- "alone": *in-nu-di-šu* 91:9, *ú-de-[e-ka]* 36 r. 10, *ú-de-e-šú* 21:22, *ú-de-šu* 79:6,

udīna "yet": *ud-di-ni* 16 r. 2, *ú-di-na* 45:16, 150:8, *ú-[di-ni* 73:1,

udû "to know": *nu-da* 245:2, *tu-ud-da* 10:6, *ú-da* 17:11, 29 r. 15, 34 r. 20, 25, 42:10, r. 4, 53 r. 10, 60:15, 61 r. 3, 78:14, 86 r. 18, 91 s. 1, 112 s. 1, 117:12, 127 r. 19, 154:7, 181 r. 6, 7, *ú-d[a* 39:10, *ú-[da* 59:8, *ú-di* 44 r. 7, 129 r. 3, 135 s. 3, *ú-[di* 82 r. 1, [*ú-di*] 219 r. 9, *ú-du* 127:14, r. 6, 14, *ú-du-ni* 78 r. 6, 181 r. 9, *ú-du-u* 9 r. 2, 63:7, 68 r. 8, *ú-du-u*] 126:24, *ú-du-u-ni* 59 s. 1, 123 r. 9, *ú-du-u-[ni* 59:7, *ú-du-[u-ni*] 59 r. 9, 60 r. 13, *ú-du-ú-ni* 115 r. 10,

ula "no, not": *ú-la* 64 r. 2,

ulâ "if not; otherwise, alternatively": *ú-la-a* 27 r. 4, 28:5, 125:11, *ú-l[a-a]* 181 r. 2,

ūmâ "now": *ú-ma-a* 9 r. 4, 16:5, 21:13, r. 7, 26:8, 11, 27 r. 2, 29 r. 1, 32 r. 3, 10, 34:7, 15, r. 10, 35:6, 36 r. 14, 43:9, 45 r. 5, 51 r. 1, 67:2, r. 8, 70:2, 78 e. 22, 87 r. 6, 88:10, 96:13, 97:16, 105 r. 3, 120 r. 9, 131 r. 6, 141:5, 142 r. 1, 143 r. 9, 148 r. 18, 163 r. 6, 183 r. 10, 17, 192 r. 11, 201 r. 4, 202:5, 207:7, 212:1, 216:6, 241:4, *ú-[ma-a* 1:14, *ú-[ma-a]* 245:2, *ú*]*-ma-a* 72 r. 4, [*ú-ma-a* 33 r. 4, 120:11, 205 r. 7, [*ú-ma-a*] 55 r. 1, [*ú*]*-ma-a* 25:12, 131 r. 2, 168:3,

umma "thus": *um-ma* 4:4,

ummânu "scholar, expert": LÚ.*u*]*m-ma-ni* 157:4,

ummi šarri "queen mother": [AM]A—LU[GAL 94:5, MÍ.AMA—MAN 2:2, 5, 8,

ummu "mother": AMA-*ka* 59:10, AMA.MEŠ 105 r. 14,

ūmu "day": UD 169 r. 6, U[D 65 s. 1, UD-*me* 75 r. 5, 143 r. 4, 160:3, UD-*me*] 33:10, UD-*mu* 35 r. 5, 95:2, 115:6, 125 r. 10, 126:6, 127:6, 128:6, 157:2, 166:1, 197:5, [UD-*mu* 63 s. 1, UD.ME 59 r. 16, [UD.ME 59 r. 10, UD.MEŠ 49:6, 59:3, 63 r. 15, 78:13, 87:18, 98:8, 117:7, 195:1, 235:2, UD.ME[Š] 72:1, UD.MEŠ-*te* 145:6, UD-*x*]*x*-KÁM 125 r. 13, UD-*x*-KAM] 158:5, UD-*x*-KÁM 61:10, UD-[*x*-KÁM] 121 r. 16, UD.1.KÁM-*ma* 52 r. 2, UD].2.KÁM 166:1, UD.3.KAM 197:5, UD.3.KÁM 199:7, UD.4.KAM 65 s. 1, UD.6.KÁM 60:10, UD.8.KÁM 50:12, UD.1[*x*-KÁM 145 r. 7, UD.13.KAM 158:5, UD.15.[KAM 158:5, UD.16.KÁM 140:6, UD.17.KÁM 140:9, r. 17, UD.2[*x*-KAM 158:6, UD.20.KÁM 199:4, UD.21.KAM 158:6, UD.21.KÁM 100:6, UD.27.KÁM 59 r. 11, UD.28.KÁM 59 r. 15, 202:3, UD.29.KAM 27 r. 6,

unīqu "young she-goat": UDU.MÍ.ÁŠ.GÀR 95:5,

unqu "signet ring, sealed order": [N]A_4.ŠU.GUR.MEŠ 116 r. 2, [*un-q*]*a-a-te* 63:19, *un-qi* 63:16, *un-qu* 39:15, *un-q[u* 7:3,

urādu "to descend, (Š) to bring down": *še-ri-d[a]* 205 r. 6, *ur-r[ad* 162:12, *ú-še-ra-da-a-ni* 63 r. 27, *ú-še-ri-du-u-ni* 139:9,

urāsu "brick mason(?)": LÚ.*ú-ra-si* 90:6, 204:8,

urdānūtu "servitude": ARAD-*a-nu-tú* 200 r. 6,

urdu "servant, subject": ARAD 2:6, 63 r. 33, 64:6, 91 s. 2, 99:9, 136:12, 144:8, 169 r. 10, 171:7, ARAD-*i-šu* 86:9, ARAD-*ka* 15:1, 17:2, 19:2, 21:2, 22:2, 25:2, 26:2, 29:1, 30:2, 31:1, 32:2, 34:1, 35:2, 44:2, 48:2, 59:2, 60:2, 65 r. 17, 78:1, 81:2, 82:2, 83:2, 84:2, 85:2, 87:2, 88:2, 98:2, 100:2, 105:2, 106:2, 107:2, 108:2, 109:2, 111:2, 112:2, 113:2, 114:2, 115:2, 120:2, 121:2, 124:2, 126:2, 128:2, 134:1, 139:2, 144:2, 148:1, 169:1, 179:2, 180:2, 181:2, 186:2, 188:2, 189:2, 190:2, 192:2, 228:2, ARAD-*k[a* 24:2, 135:2, 174:2, 183:2, 193:2, 196:2, ARAD-[*ka* 187:2, 215:2, ARAD-[*ka*] 127:2, ARAD]-*ka* 132:1, A[RAD-*ka* 39:2, 164:2, [ARAD-*ka* 18:2, 20:1, 27:2, 33:2, 61:2, 89:2, 92:2, 110:2, 116:2, 119:2, 143:2, 162:2, 175:2, 182:2, 194:2, 218:2, [ARAD-*k*]*a* 118:2, 184:2, [ARAD]-*ka* 23:2, 43:2, 86:2, 131:2, [ARA]D-*ka* 14:2, 70:6, [AR]AD-*ka* 152:2, 191:2, ARAD-*ki* 56:2, ARAD.MEŠ 17 r. 9, 43:11, 56 r. 11, 63:5, r. 20, 115:5, 123 r. 5, 136 r. 3, ARAD.M[EŠ 43 r. 1, ARA[D.MEŠ 43 r. 13, [ARAD.ME]Š 41 r. 1, ARAD.MEŠ-*ia* 67:10, ARAD.MEŠ-*ka* 42:2, 79:2, 136:2, 138:2, 140:2, 142:2, ARAD.MEŠ-*k[a* 145:2, A[RAD.MEŠ-*ka* 102:2, [ARAD.MEŠ-*ka* 137:2, [ARA]D.MEŠ-(*ka*) 96:2, [AR]AD.MEŠ-*ka* 97:2, ARAD.MEŠ-*ni* 49:8, 79:15, ARAD.MEŠ-*ni-ka* 41:2, [ARAD.MEŠ]-*ni-ka* 117:2, [AR]AD.MEŠ-*šu* 63 r. 7, ARAD.MEŠ-*šú* 52 r. 4, 79:5, 105 r. 9, ARAD-*su* 29:11, ARAD-*šú* 36 r. 13, 42 r. 15, 62 r. 12, 64 r. 8, 65:14, r. 11, 66:3, 67 r. 9, 75:9, 78:5, 8, 84:7, 86:8, 112:8, 125:14, 169:4, ARAD-[*šú* 77 r. 10, A]RAD-*šú* 169 r. 5, LÚ.ARAD 36 r. 5, 6, 71 r. 2, 82:6, 207:4, 5, 6, LÚ.[ARA]D 121:14, LÚ.ARAD-*i-[šú* 181:6, LÚ.ARAD.MEŠ 135 r. 11, 205 r. 8, LÚ.ARAD.MEŠ-*ka* 97 r. 13, LÚ.ARAD.MEŠ-*šú* 78:20, 97 r. 18, LÚ.ARAD.M[EŠ-*šú* 121 r. 14, [LÚ.ARAD].MEŠ-*šú* 119:5, LÚ.ARAD-*šu* 196 r. 1, LÚ.ARAD-*šú* 29:4, 121:9, *ur-di* 150:5, *ur-du* 64:8,

urhu "month": ITI 76 e. 3, 229 r. 2, IT]I 138 r. 9, ITI.MEŠ 62:8, 75:3,

urû "team (of horses)": *ú-rat* 112:5,

ūru "roof": ÙR 93 r. 3,

uṣṣuṣu "to investigate": *lu-ṣi-ṣi* 40 r. 10, *ú-ṣi-ṣi* 62:4,

uṣû "to go out, (vent.) to come out, emerge; (Š) to bring/send out, banish": *lu-ṣi* 62 r. 15, *lu-ṣi-a* 90:4, *lu-še-ṣ[i]* 161:6, *lu-še-ṣi-a* 65 r. 6, *l*]*u-še-ṣu-ni* 89 r. 10, *lu-še-ṣu-u-ni* 80:5, *ni-tu-ṣi* 95 r. 7, *ṣi-a* 63:31, *u-ṣu-u-ni* 86 r. 11, *ú-se-ṣi* 95 r. 5, *ú-se-ṣi-a* 95:5, *ú-se-ṣi-u* 1:13, *ú-ṣa* 99 r. 4, *ú-še-ṣa-an-ni* 80:3, 155:8,

uṣultu "knife, dagger": GÍ]R.TUR 63:24,

ušābu "to sit, dwell; (Š) to enthrone, settle": *a-šib* 98:6, *a-ši-b[u-ti* 118:4, *ši-bi* 59 s. 3, *ú-se-še-eb* 95:7, *ú-[se-ši-bu* 60 r. 20, *ú-se-ši-ib-šú* 65:6, *ú-si-ib-u-ni* 34 r. 9, *ú-šab* 34 r. 22, *ú-še-šib* 154 r. 12, *ú-še-šu-[bu* 173:2, *ú-ši-ib* 75:4,

ušandû "fowler": LÚ.MUŠEN.DÙ 47 r. 3, 4,

ušpāru "weaver": LÚ.UŠ.BAR.MEŠ 83:7, 84 r. 8,

ušpār ṣiprāti "scarf weaver": LÚ.UŠ.BAR—*ṣip-rat* 55:2,

uššē "foundation": *uš-še* 111:11, 12, r. 5, 125:5, 143:6,

utāru "to exceed, be in surplus": *ú-tú-ru-te* 96:12,

uznu "ear, understanding": PI.2-*ka* 61 r. 4,

PI.2.MEŠ-*šú-nu* 122 r. 10, *uz-ni-ia* 63 s. 2, *uz-nu* 78 r. 13, 148:16,

uzuzzu "to stand, to be present; (Š) to station": *a-ti-it-zi* 45:5, *a-za-za* 88 r. 8, *a-za-zu-ni* 78:13, *it-ti-it-zi* 10:7, *it-ti-ti-is-su* 34 r. 14, *iz-za-zu* 16 r. 2, 59:4, 60 r. 15, *iz-zi-zi* 34 r. 7, *i-t*[*i-iz*] 77 r. 7, *i-ti-*[*ti-zi*] 45 r. 3, *i-za-zu* 55 r. 3, 88:10, 95:9, r. 15, *i-za-zu-u-ni* 88:9, *i-zi-iz* 170:5, *i-zi-su-u-ni* 62 r. 7, *li-iz-zi-iz* 27 r. 3, *li-zi-zi* 140 r. 16, *l*]*i-zi-zu* 60 s. 4, [*l*]*u-šá-zi-zu* 90 r. 11, *ni-ti-it-zi* 41:13, *šá-zi-iz* 77 r. 4, *ta-za-az* 17 r. 10, *ta-za-za* 88 r. 6,

zaʾānu "to decorate": *lu-za-in* 127 r. 20, [*lu-za-i*]*n* 128 s. 2,

zakāru "to pronounce, call": *iz-kur-u-ni* 60:4, 61:4, *iz-za-kar* 17 r. 5, [*iz-za-kar*] 144:9, [*i-zak-ka-ru-u-ni*] 64:1, *i-za-kar* 105:13,

zakkû "exempt": LÚ.*zak-ku-ú* 120:6, LÚ.*za-ku-ú* 63 r. 21,

zakû "to be clean, exempt; (D) to exempt": *ú-*[*za-ki-ú*] 96:10,

zamāru "to sing": *i-za-mu-ru* 95:11,

zaqāpu "to plant; (Š) to implant": *ú-šar-qu-up* 65 r. 5,

zarʾu "seed, offspring": NUMUN 59 r. 5, 9, 10, 68 r. 2, 99:7, NUMUN-*ka* 151:6, NUMUN.MEŠ 96 r. 1, 195:3, NUMUN-*šú-nu* 59:6, ŠE.NUMUN.MEŠ 40 r. 6, NUMUN-*šú* 99:6, 7,

zēru see *zarʾu,*

ziāru "to hate": *i-zi-ir-ra-an-ni* 71:4, *i-zi-ru-u-ni* 29 r. 2,

zuāzu "to divide, distribute": *ú-za-zi* 112 r. 14,

zūku "exempt, professional soldier": LÚ.*zu-k*[*u* 90:11,

Index of Names

Personal Names

Paramu[...] (Phraortes?): ^{m}*pa-ra-m[u* 15:24,
Parruṭu (goldsmith of the queen's household): ^{m}*pa-ru-ṭi* 81:3, ^{m}*pa-ru-ṭu* 65:2,
Puṭi-Širi: ^{m}*pu]-ṭi-ši-ri* 57:2,
Qīltî: ^{m}*qi-il-ti-[i* 135:9,
Qīsāia (singer): ^{m}*qi-sa-a-a* 95:10,
Qurdî (chariot driver): [^{m}*qur-d]i-i* 63:21, ^{m}*qur-di-i* 63:3,
Qurdi-Issār: ^{m}]*qur-di*—^{d}15 141 r. 3,
Rāhiṣ-Dādi: ^{m}*ra-hi-iṣ*—U.U 15:3,
Rāma-il: ^{m}*ra-me*—DINGIR 136:15,
Rāši-ili ('third man'): ^{m}*ri-ši*—DINGIR 139:7,
Rūkibtu: ^{m}*ru]-ki-ib-t[ú]* 130:7,
Salāmānu: [^{m}*sa-la-ma-nu]* 137:3, ^{m}*sa-la-ma-nu* 136:3, 140:3, 142:3, ^{m}*sa-la-ma-n[u* 138:3, ^{m}*sa-la-m[a-nu* 145:3,
Salmānu-ašarēd (Shalmaneser III, king of Assyria): ^{m}DI-*ma-nu*—MAŠ 99:9,
Samsi-nātan: [^{m}]*sam-si*—*na-tan* 51:7,
Sangil-rāmat: MÍ.*sa-an-gíl*—*ra-mat* 27:8,
Sārai: MÍ.*sa-ra-a-a* 49:2,
Sasî (city overseer 54, mayor 64): [^{m}*sa]-si-i* 59 r. 11, ^{m}*sa-si-i* 17:9, 59:7, r. 4, 7, 9, 15, 16, s. 1, 60 r. 10, 11, 19, 62 r. 5, 65 r. 2, 71:5, ^{m}*sa-s[i-i* 59:6, ^{m}*sa-s[i]-i* 69 e. 8, ^{m}*s[a-si-i* 60 r. 13,
Sē'-abī: ^{m}*si-i*—AD 5:11,
Sē'-rahî: ^{m}*se-e'*—*ra-hi-i* 55:4,
Sē'-rapâ (province; governor 29): ^{m}*se-e'*—*ra-pa-a'* 29 r. 1,
Sîn-ahhē-rība (Sennacherib, king of Assyria): ^{md}30—PAB.MEŠ—SU 59 r. 5, 96 r. 2,
Sîn-balāssu-iqbi (son of Nikkal-iddin): ^{md}30—TI-*su*—*iq-bi* 69:5,
Sîn-[...]: ^{md}3[0—*x* 167:1, ^{md}30—[*x* 167:3,
Sukki-Aia: ^{m}]TE-*a-a* 67:5,
Sulāia: ^{m}*su-la-a-a* 21 r. 14,
Sumutî (scribe): ^{m}*su-mu-ti-i* 68 r. 6,
Ṣalam-šarri-iqbi: ^{m}NU—MAN—[E 215 r. 2,
Ṣallāia (major-domo 40): ^{m}*ṣal-la-a-a* 42:3, ^{m}*ṣil*—LUGAL 135 r. 3,
Šamaš-ēmuranni (governor): ^{md}UTU—IGI.LAL-*ni* 63:27,
Šamaš-ibni: ^{md}UTU—*ib-ni* 31:2,
Šamaš-mētu-uballiṭ (son of Esarhaddon): ^{md}GIŠ.NU$_{11}$—UG$_{5}$.GA—TI.LA 25:2, 26:2, ^{md}GIŠ.NU$_{11}$—UG$_{5}$.GA—TI.LA] 27:2,
Šamaš-šumu-ukīn (crown prince of Babylon, brother of Assurbanipal): ^{md}GIŠ.NU—MU—GI.NA 22:2, ^{md}GIŠ.NU—MU—[GI.NA] 23:2, ^{md}GIŠ.NU$_{11}$—MU—GI.N[A] 21:2, ^{md}GIŠ].NU$_{11}$—MU—GI.NA 24:2,
Šamaš-zēru-iqīša: ^{md}UTU—NUMUN—BA-*šá* 21:13, 23, r. 10,
Šar-uarri: ^{m}*šar-ú-ár-ri* 144:6,
Šarīdu: ^{m}*šá-ri-du* 21:5,
Ša-[...]-anēnu: ^{m}*ša*—^{d}[*x*]*x*—*a-né-nu* 79 r. 4,
Šērū'a-ēṭerat (daughter of Esarhaddon): MÍ.^{d}EDIN—*e-ṭè-rat* 28 r. 1,
Šulmu-māti: ^{m}DI-*mu*—KUR 143 r. 9,
Šumāia: ^{m}*šu-ma-a-a* 35:2, ^{m}*šu-ma-a-[a]* 34:1,
Šumma-ilu (son of Aramiš-šar-ilani): ^{m}*šúm-mu*—DINGIR 105:10,
Šumma-šarru (chariot fighter): ^{m}*š]um-ma*—MAN 11:10,
Tabālāiu (cohort commander): ^{m}*tab*-URU-*a-a* 115:8,
Tabnî: ^{m}*tab-ni-i* 48:2,
Tarība-Issār: ^{m}SU—^{d}15 135:11,
Tarṣî (scribe of Guzana): ^{m}LAL-*i* 63 r. 24, ^{m}*tar-ṣi-i* 63:5, r. 14, 16, 18, 26, ^{m}*ta-ra-ṣi-i* 63 r. 12, 23,
Tattî (son of PN 62): [^{m}*ta]-at-ti-i* 67:4,
Tutî (scribe): ^{m}*tu-ti-i* 63:2, 9,
Ṭudî: ^{m}*ṭu-di-i* 152:2,
Uaksatar: ^{m}*ú-ak-sa-t[a-ar* 15:20,
Ubru-Nabû (scribe of New Palace 94): ^{m}]SUHUŠ—^{d}PA 110:2, ^{m}SUHUŠ—^{d}PA 59:9, 105:2, 106:2, 107:2, 108:2, 109:2,
Umba-kidinni: ^{m}*um-ba-ki-di-ni* 139:6, 140 r. 7, 142:7, ^{m}*um-ba-k[i-di-ni]* 138 r. 8,
Umītê: ^{m}*ú-mi-te-e* 129:10,
Urdu-Issār: [^{m}ARAD]—^{d}15 70:3, ^{m}ARAD—^{d}15 150 r. 4, ^{m}ARAD—15 60 r. 12,
Urdu-Nabû: ^{m}ARAD—^{d}PA 21 r. 9,
Urtaku (king of Elam): ^{m}*ur-ta-ku* 1:2, 6,
Zabīnu: ^{m}*za-bi-ni* 143:13,
Zār-Issār (chief of public works): ^{m}NUMUN—15 50:4,
Zāzâ (wife of Tarṣî): MÍ.*za-za-a* 63:5, r. 24,
Zazakku: ^{m}*za-za-ki* 95 s. 1,
Zēru-kēn: ^{m}NUMUN—GIN 68 r. 9,
broken: [MÍ.*x* 27:10, ^{md}[*x* 43:2, 56 r. 1, 2, 119 r. 2, 167:7, 184:2, ^{md}*x*]—MAN—PAB 66 r. 7, ^{md}*x*]—MU—PAB 182:2, ^{m}DINGIR—*ú-*[*x* 235 r. 1, ^{m}*iz-*[*x* 46 r. 4, ^{m}*ur-x*[*x* 8 s. 1, [^{m}*x* 67:4, 76 r. 5, 91:6, 129 r. 8, 134:1, 135 r. 2, 150 r. 8, 169:1, 188:2, 228:2, ^{m}*x* 17 r. 2, 39:2, 89:2, 92:2, 102:2, 135:2, 162:2, 164:2, 183:2, 187:2, 191:2, 193:2, 194:2, 196:2, 215:2, 218:2, ^{m}[*x* 39:7, 56:6, 74:2, 102:3, 117:2, 150 r. 9, 186:2, 189:2, 190:2, 192:2, ^{m}*x*[*x* 223:2, [^{m}*x*]-*i-pi-di* 58:2, ^{m}*x-l]i-i* 5:1,

Place Names

Adia (town in central Assyria, Mosul?): URU].*a-di-a* 125:3,
Arāši (region in the Zagros, near mod. Ilam): KUR.*a-ra-še* 137:10, KUR.*a-ra-š[e* 138:9,
Arbail (Arbela, Erbil): *arba-ìl*.KI 126:6, 127:6, DUMU—URU.*arba-ìl* 123:7, D]UMU—URU.*arba-ìl* 123:6, URU.*arba-ìl* 1:10, 33:7, 49:5, 59:3, 60:3, 84 r. 9, 93 r. 9, 106:7, 121:6, 128:5, URU.*ar]ba-ìl* 120:9, ((URU.*arba-ìl*)) 93 r. 10, [URU.*arba-ìl* 61:3,
Arbāiu ("Arab"): *ar-b[a-a-a* 129 r. 5,
Armāiu ("Aramean"): *ar-me-tú* 99:10, *ár-ma-a-a* 63:14, LÚ.*ar-ma-a-ú* 123:8, MÍ.[*ár]-me-ti* 17 r. 6,
Arpadda (city N of Aleppo, Tell Rifat): KUR.*ár-pad-da* 135 s. 1, URU.*ar-pad-dà* 48 e. 13,
Arrapha (city in Assyria, now Kerkuk): URU.*arrap-ha* 42:11, URU.*arrap]-ha* 137 r. 16, [URU].*arrap-ha-a-a* 136 e. 16,
Aššūrāiu "Assyrian": *aš-šur-a-a* 63:13, 64:9, 67

148:10, KUR.U]RI-*a-a* 151 r. 2,
Uruk (city in Babylonia, Bibl. Erech, now Warka): UNUG.KI 154:9,
Zāba (river Zab): ÍD.*za-a*[*b-b*]*i* 163:5,
broken: KUR.[*x* 191 r. 5, URU.BÀ[D—*x* 232:4, URU.*ub*-[*x*] 90:9, URU.[*x* 138 r. 11, 205 r. 8, 232:5, UR[U.*x* 45:6, 110:6, 183 r. 13, U[RU.*x* 60:10, 122 r. 13, URU.*x*[*x* 103:4, 137 r. 10,

God, Star and Temple Names

Adad (storm god): ^{d}IM 72:4, 84 r. 13, 100 r. 1, 148:4,
Aššūr (supreme god of Assyria): *aš-šur* 14:5, 15:2, 17:4, 18:4, 32:5, 11, 41:7, 65:1, 96 r. 6, 148:3, 169 r. 4, 192:4, 193:4, *aš-šu*[*r* 217 r. 7, [*aš-šur* 33:5, 127:4, 131:4, ^{d}*aš-šur* 1:9, 31:5, 72:3, 98:6, 117:6, 126:4, 128:4, 179:4, ^{d}*aš-š*[*ur* 102:5, [^{d}*aš-šur*] 132:3,
Baʾal-rakkābu (city god of Sam'al): ^{d}]*bi-iʾ-li—ra-kab-bi* 63 r. 11,
Bēl ("Lord," an appellative of Marduk): $^{d+}$EN 31:5, 32:5, 44:6, 160:2, ^{d}EN 1:9, 9:7, 14:5, 15:2, 17:4, 18:4, 29:12, 33:5, 49:3, 59:2, r. 10, 60:2, 10, r. 15, s. 1, 61:2, 65:1, 78:3, r. 13, 87:5, 92:4, 105:4, 106:5, 117:7, 126:4, 127:4, 128:4, 148:3, 154:5, 191:4, [^{d}]EN 52:1, [^{d}EN 60 s. 2, [^{d}EN] 86:5, 153:5, [^{d}E]N 29:9,
Bēlet ("Lady," an appellative of Ištar): ^{d}]GAŠAN 60:2, ^{d}GAŠAN 61:2, ^{d}GA[ŠAN 59:2,
Bēlet Bābili ("Lady of Babylon," Zarpanitu): ^{d}*be-let*—KÁ.DINGIR.RA.KI 49:3,
Bēlet Kidmūri ("Lady of Kidmuri," Ištar of Calah): ^{d}GAŠAN—*ki-di-mu-ri* 105 r. 13, 106:6,
Bēltīa ("My Lady," an appellative of Zarpanitu): ^{d}GAŠAN-*ia* 52:1, ^{d}GAŠAN-*ti*-[*ia*] 49:3,
Bēr: ^{d}*be-er* 148:4,
Ēa (god of wisdom): ^{d}É.A 62:12, 13,
Ešarra (temple of Aššur in Assur): É.ŠÁR.RA 97:7, É.ŠÁR.[RA] 96:5, 98:6,
Gula (goddess of healing): ^{d}*gu-la* 52:2,
Illil (Enlil, head of the Sumerian pantheon): ^{d}BE 116:3,
Inūrta (Ninurta, son of Enlil, god of victory): ^{d}MAŠ 210:4, [^{d}]MAŠ 52:2, [^{d}NIN.URTA] 29:2,
Issār (Ištar, goddess of love): ^{d}[15] 179:4, ^{d}15 1:10, 49:4, 5, 59:3, 60:3, 10, 12, 61:3, 84 r. 9, 105:4, 5, 106:7, 122 r. 8, 126:5, 6, 127:5, 128:5, 193:5, ^{d}15] 63:23, [^{d}15 33:6, 7, 61:3, 127:5, [^{d}15] 127:6,
Išum (god of war and fire): ^{d}*i-šum* 148:4,
Kidmūri: É—*kad-mu-ru* 126:5, É—*kid-mur-ra* 127:5, É—*ki-di-mu-ri* 105:5,
Lāṣ (consort of Nergal): ^{d}*la-aṣ* 52:2, 148:3,
Madānu (divine judge): ^{d}DI.KUD 29:2,
Manziniri (Elamite god): ^{d}[*m*]*a*-[*a*]*n-zi-ni-ri* 1:11,
Marduk (supreme god of Babylon): ^{d}AMAR.UTU 20:3, 21:4, 22:4, 23:4, 25:4, 26:4, 27:4, 34:3, 35:4, 42:7, 43:5, 69:1, 70:1, 72:4, 81:6, 82:4, 83:4, 84:4, 85:4, 86:4, 87:4, 98 r. 10, 100:4, 107:5, 109:4, 111:4, 112:3, 113:4, 114:4, 115:3, 119:3, 120:4, 124:4, 131 r. 1, 134:3, 136:5, 138:5, 139:4, 140:5, 142:5, 143:4, 144:4, 152:4, 180:4, 181:4, ^{d}AMAR.UTU] 135:6, 162:4, 192:4, ^{d}AMAR.UT]U 110:4, 174:5, ^{d}AMAR.U[TU] 151:1, ^{d}AMAR.[UTU 188:4, ^{d}AMAR].UTU 24:4, 175:5, ^{d}AMA[R.UTU 145:5, ^{d}AMA[R.UTU] 218:4, ^{d}A[MAR.UTU 184:4, ^{d}[AMAR.UTU 189:4, 190:4, ^{d}[AMAR.UTU] 137:4, 183:4, ^{d}[AMAR.U]TU 19:4, [^{d}AMAR.UTU 39:4, 164:4, 187:4, ^{d}MES 48:4, 57:4, 86 r. 1, 121:4, 193:4, ^{d}ME[S 186:4, ^{d}ŠÚ 88:5,
Mullissu (consort of Aššur, Queen of Heaven): ^{d}NIN.LÍL 60:9, r. 15, 105 r. 12, 106:6, ^{d}NIN.LÍ]L 61:9,
Nabû (Nebo, son of Marduk): ^{d}60 88:5, $^{d+}$AG 44:6, ^{d}AG 1:9, 21:4, 23:4, 32 r. 21, 33:5, 35:4, 48:4, 8, 49:4, 52:1, r. 6, 8, 78 r. 13, 81:6, 82:4, 83:4, 84:4, 85:4, 86:5, 92:4, 98 r. 10, 107:5, 111:4, 112:3, 114:4, 117:7, 120:4, 124:4, 135:6, 144:4, 183:4, 189:4, 191:4, [^{d}]AG 113:4, [^{d}AG 29:3, 174:5, [^{d}AG] 86:4, 152:4, ^{d}]PA 226:2, ^{d}PA 14:5, 15:2, 17:4, 18:4, 19:4, 20:3, 22:4, 25:4, 26:4, 29:9, 12, 31:5, 32:5, 39:4, 42:7, 43:5, 59:2, r. 6, 10, 60:2, 10, r. 15, 61:2, 65:1, 69:1, 78:3, 87:4, 5, 99:5, 100:4, r. 1, 105:4, 106:5, r. 2, 109:4, 115:3, 121:4, 126:4, 127:4, 128:4, 134:3, 136:5, 137:4, 139:4, 140:5, 142:5, 145:5, 148:3, 153:5, 154:5, 164:4, 180:4, 181:4, 186:4, 187:4, 188:4, 190:4, 192:4, 218:4, ^{d}PA] 151:1, ^{d}P[A 247:3, ^{d}[PA 160:2, 162:4, [^{d}]PA 27:4, 34:3, [^{d}PA 24:4, 70:1, 110:4, 143:4, 175:5, [^{d}PA] 57:4, 119:3, 184:4, [^{d}P]A 138:5,
Nergal (god of power, lord of the underworld): ^{d}U.GUR 29:2, 52:2, 86:5, 126:4, 127:4, 128:4, 148:3, ^{d}U.G[UR 153:5, ^{d}[U.GUR] 87:5,
Nikkal (consort of Sin): ^{d}NIN.GAL 59:5, 8, 132:3, 174:6, ^{d}NIN.[GAL 59:12,
Nušku (son of Sin): ^{d}]PA.TÚG 174:6, ^{d}PA.TÚG 59 r. 4, 8, ^{d}P[A.TÚG 153:6,
Sagmegar (Jupiter, reading uncert.): MUL.SAG.ME.GAR 21 r. 6,
Sîn (moon, god of understanding): ^{d}30 1:9, 33:5, 36 r. 18, 63 r. 27, 72:3, 132:3, ^{d}30] 127:4, [^{d}30 174:6,
Šamaš (sun, god of justice): ^{d}]*šá-maš* 33:5, ^{d}*šá-maš* 41:7, 132:3, ^{d}UTU 1:9, 29:9, 12, 31:5, 63 r. 33, 65:1, 72:3, 96 r. 6, 126:4, 127:4, 10, 128:4, 10, 148:3, 200 r. 4, 210:4, ^{d}UTU] 131:4, ^{d}[UTU 192:4, ^{d}[UTU] 32:5, 117:6,
Šukūdu (Sirius): MUL.GAG.SI.SÁ 21 r. 6,
Taškāti ("Triplets," α Herculis): M[UL].*taš-k*[*a-ti* 60:14,
Tašmētu (consort of Nabû): ^{d}*taš-me-tum* 49:4, 52:1, 60:2, 99:5, ^{d}*taš-me-tum*] 61:2, ^{d}*taš-me*]-*tum* 59:2,
Zabāba (city god of Kiš): ^{d}ZA.BA$_4$.BA$_4$ 29:2,
broken: ^{d}*x*] 169:3, ^{d}[*x* 93:8, 185:4, 215:5, [^{d}*x* 153:4, 169:3, 193:4,

Subject Index

kings 45 66 127 137
kingship 20 29 59 60 61 96
knit 216
Kushite 78
lady 28 56 67
lambs 21 171
lands 127 128 200
lawsuit 30 41 42 44
league 60
learn 8 78 233
leather 97
leftovers 106
legal 96
legate 137
letter 1 6 17 21 32 59 60 73 81 99 150
letters 9 63 95 97
life 43 59 60 61 72 86 87 106 129
light 29 31 59 78
limestone 143
linen 82
list 50
literature 65
litigate 42 64 78
loan 5
locusts 15 121 145
lordship 217
lore 62
lotion 165
love 34 36 105
loyal 8 9 60 91 169 207
magnates 1 41 47 59 62 63 64 77 83 118 133
maid 49 153
major domo 42 112
manager 63
manageress 183
mankind 126
manservant 5 118
mares 88
masons 90 204
masters 82
maturity 126
mayor 69 95 96 97
mayorship 97
Media 148
men/troops 59
merchants 45 54 105 127 128
mercy 36 46 121
message 129
messenger 6 29 56 63 87 96 136 137 140 148 214
mina 5 32 54 56 67 69 82 97 155
mistreat 42 45 48
molest 76
money 41 54 123 225
moon 63
mortal 78
mother 2 59 105
mules 5 177
multi-coloured 84
nails 40
natron 82
neck-seals 63
neck-stone 65
neglectful 60 61
negligent 148 150
netherworld 31
news 13 127
nobleman 89
nobles 34
offender 9 99
offering 52 113
omens 65
orchards 29
ordinances 98 99
outriders 90 231
overseer 32 33
palace 4 40 47 49 59 60 61 62 63 65 66 78 82 84 87 88 90 95 98 107 111 127 128 143 201 206
Palace 45 63 95 99 120 143 217
palace manager 50
palace supervisor 88
parasol 63 123
pay 63 80 148
Pazuzu-heads 65
peace 17 48 137
perfect 169
persecuted 62
pestilence 127
petition 82
Phraortes 15
physician 26
plate 197
plot 60 61 78
plunder/captives 137
port 83 127
pray 29 52 60
prefect 43 64
price 5
priest 62 63
prince 28 29 34 63
principals 97
privileges 96
promote 68 115 170
property 53
protection 29 64 105 200
punish 73 78
purified 242
purple 63
queen 63 65 81 111
queen mother 94
question 43 59 105 121 136
quota 43 63
raid 129
ram 5 22
rank 115
read 6 17 32 60 73 95
Rear Palace 143 217
rebellion 60
recite 28
recruitment officer 105 137
recruits 68
red wool 82 83 84
refined 209
regular offering 113
reign 8 29 30 63 96 195 201
reimbursements 80
reminder 143
report 5 15 17 21 45 59 62 64 148 150
reporter 6
revere 34 48 82 201
Review Palace 5 21
revive 13 31 126 127
riders 176

List of Text Headings

1. Letter to Urtaku, King of Elam
2. King's Word to the Queen Mother
3. King's Word to Issar-na'di
4. King's Word to Ištar-[...]
5. Settling Accounts and Preparing for Royal Visit to Harran
6. Reading Letters to the King
7. Sealed Order
8. Augurs from Hamath
9. Fragment Referring to Bel and Offenders
10. They are Plotting to Kill You
11. Fragment Referring to Chairs
12. ———-
13. ———-
14. ———-
15. Report on the Cimmerians of Iyazê
16. Cimmerians in Mindâ
17. Report on Kunaya and Kudurru
18. Report on the Border of Urarṭu
19. ———-
20. Milki-nuri Curses the Crown Prince
21. Treacherous Astrologers
22. Audience Gifts for the King
23. ———-
24. ———-
25. A Broken Chariot Weel
26. Doctor for a Sick Maid
27. Report on Two Women
28. Dressing Down the Wife of the Crown Prince
29. Debts of the Governor of Barhalza
30. May the King Save Me
31. May the King Let me See Light
32. Justice Turned Upside Down
33. Partial Duplicate of No. 32
34. Let me Finish my Father's Work in Calah
35. Paying back Father's Debts
36. May the King Have Mercy on his Dog
37. ———-
38. Fragment of a Letter to the Crown Prince
39. Appeal on Behalf of a Woman
40. Complaints by Blacksmiths
41. Magnates Obstructing Justice
42. Governor Appropriates a Royal Gift
43. My Associate is a Criminal
44. May my Lord Appoint me
45. Complaints from Nasibina
46. Asking for Mercy
47. Slander
48. Petition on Behalf of a Tax Master
49. Petition on Behalf of Servants not Allowed to Enter the Palace
50. List of People Entering the Palace
51. List of Staff-bearers Coming in
52. Food for Schoolboys
53. Adopting a Daughter
54. Silver for the Merchants
55. Petition on Behalf of Weavers
56. Petition Concerning a Will
57. ———-
58. ———-
59. The Conspiracy of Sasî
60. More on the Conspiracy of Sasî
61. Partial Duplicate of No. 60
62. The Case of Nabû-kabti-ahhešu and Sasî
63. Crimes in Guzana
64. How to Deal with Appeals for Royal Intervention
65. Divination Taught to a Goldsmith's Son
66. Fragment Mentioning Kar-Mullissi
67. Stolen Gold
68. Disloyal Officials
69. Sin-balassu-iqbi Sends Gold to Sasî
70. May the Horse not Die!
71. Fragment Mentioning Sasî
72. I have Something to Tell the King
73. May They Inform the King
74. Fragment Referring to Trespassing
75. A Crimc Committed
76. Fragment mentioning a Nephew of Hanbî
77. Instructions for a Battle
78. The Matter of the 'Third Man' of the Palace Scribe
79. Work on the Inner City, Nineveh and Dur-Šarrukin
80. Reimbursements
81. Jewellery for the King
82. Marduk-šarru-uṣur in Trouble
83. Wool for Weavers
84. Providing Weavers with Red Wool
85. Itemising Textiles
86. Working for the Royal Household
87. Eunuchs for Officials
88. Donkey Trade at Nineveh
89. The House of the Chief Scribe
90. Outriders for Brick Masons
91. Candidates for Courtiers
92. Drink on the Accounts!
93. May the Chief Baker Release Us
94. An Appeal to the Queen Mother
95. The Governor Acts after the King's Death
96. Privileges in Assur at Stake
97. The Mayor is a Criminal
98. Dissolved Ordinances
99. Information on Accomplices of Aššur-da''in-aplu
100. An Earthquake Hits Assur

Index of Texts

By Publication Number

By Museum Number

Sm 540	203	82-5-22,150	33	83-1-18,268	243	(Bu 91-5-9,137+)	5
Sm 562	199	82-5-22,158	44	83-1-18,272	134	(Bu 91-5-9,149+)	47
Sm 1034	111	82-5-22,159	150	83-1-18,280	202	Bu 91-5-9,157	42
Sm 1072	39	82-5-22,174	26	83-1-18,283	16	Bu 91-5-9,192	183
Sm 1851	167	83-1-18,20	97	83-1-18,508	61	Bu 91-5-9,46	110
Sm 1942	3	83-1-18,22	19	83-1-18,707	192	Bu 91-5-9,78	169
Sm 2077	55	83-1-18,55+	126	83-1-18,742+	47	Ki 1904-10-9,8	45
Sm 2190	241	83-1-18,62	88	83-1-18,820	168	Ki 1904-10-9,84+	66
DT 61	158	83-1-18,64	90	83-1-18,825	164	Ki 1904-10-	
Rm 50	144	83-1-18,68	137	83-1-18,838	75	9,121+	10
80-7-19,43	27	83-1-18,90	87	83-1-18,861	77	Ki 1904-10-	
81-2-4,52	82	83-1-18,111	35	Bu 89-4-26,4	32	9,216+	244
81-2-4,65	95	83-1-18,115	81	Bu 89-4-26,16	99	Ki 1904-10-9,256	180
81-2-4,75	86	83-1-18,118	85	Bu 89-4-26,31	92	9,348+	156
81-2-4,113	98	83-1-18,121	65	Bu 89-4-26,71	91	Th 1932-12-	
81-2-4,388	133	83-1-18,147	191	Bu 89-4-26,163	148	10,301	100
81-2-4,425	58	83-1-18,148	200	Bu 91-5-9,3	17	BM 99055	66
81-2-4,492	135	83-1-18,153	76	Bu 91-5-9,12	84	BM 99092	10
81-7-27,276	170	83-1-18,155	124	Bu 91-5-9,18	142	BM 99184	244
82-5-22,155	242	83-1-18,157	113	(Bu 91-5-9,86+)	126	BM 99309	245
82-5-22,100	41	83-1-18,160	201	Bu 91-5-9,105	139	BM 99316	156
82-5-22,108+	59	83-1-18,257+	5	Bu 91-5-9,110	31	BM 123358	100
82-5-22,146	132	83-1-18,264	179	Bu 91-5-9,111	104	BM 135586	21

List of Joins

K 1034 (CT 53 17) + K 7395 (ABL 1031) + K 9204 + K 10541 + K 11021 (+) K 9821 (CT 53 107)	60
K 1366 (ABL 633) + K 11448 (= CT 53 46)	63
K 4279 (CT 53 226) (+) K 5425 (ABL 1026)	15
K 5432a (CT 53 78) + K 11465 (CT 53 426)	64
K 10911 + K 14628 (= CT 53 109)	205
K 13737 (+) 82-5-22,108 (CT 53 118)	59
83-1-18,257 (CT 53 930) + Bu 91-5-9,137 (CT 53 967)	5
83-1-18,55 (ABL 1110) + Bu 91-5-9,86 (= CT 53 148)	126
83-1-18,742 + Bu 91-5-9,149	47

List of Illustrations

COPIES

K 1273 (= no. 52)

Obv.

Rev.

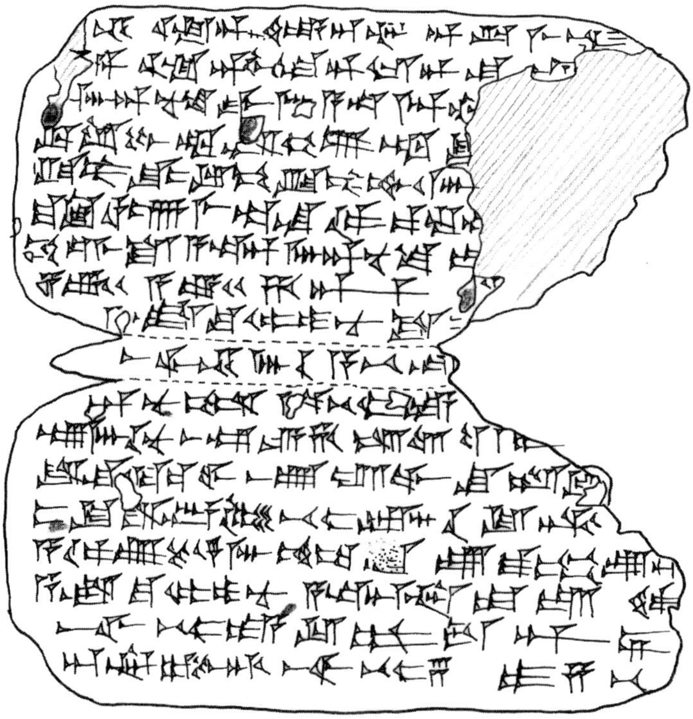

K 15626 (= no. 173)

K 16521 (= no. 172)

K 16550 (= no. 246)

Obv.

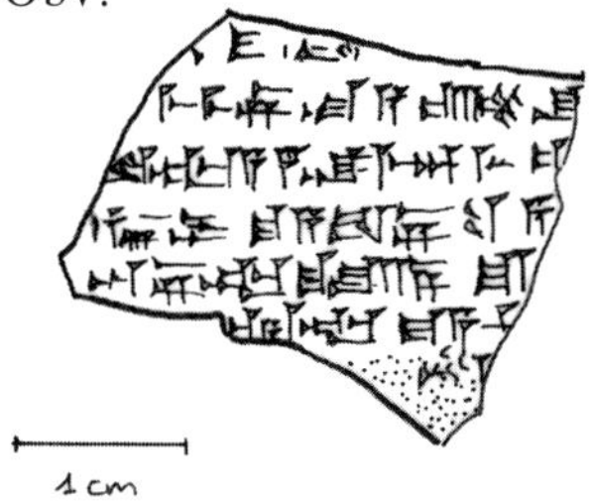

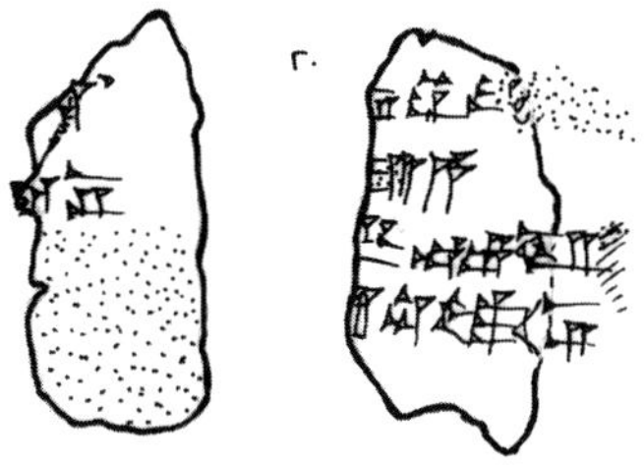

Obv.

K 19787 (= no. 193)

Obv.

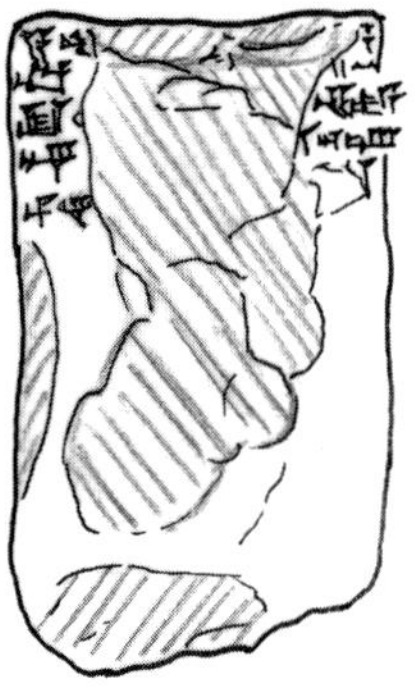

K 19979 (= no. 188)

Obv.

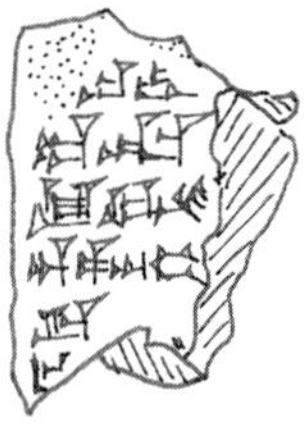

Rev.

K 20565 (= no. 247)

Obv.

K 19986 (= no. 165)

Rev.

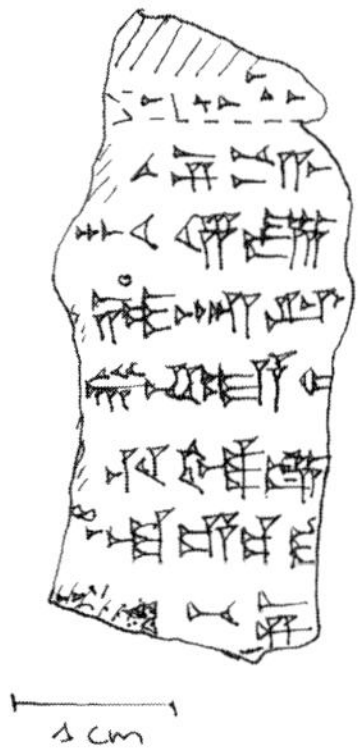

83-1-18,153 (= no. 76)

Edge

Rev.

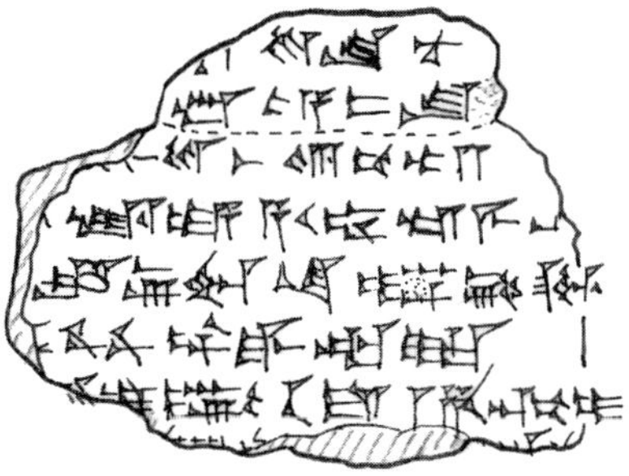

83-1-18,742+ Bu 91-5-9,149 (= no. 47)

Obv.

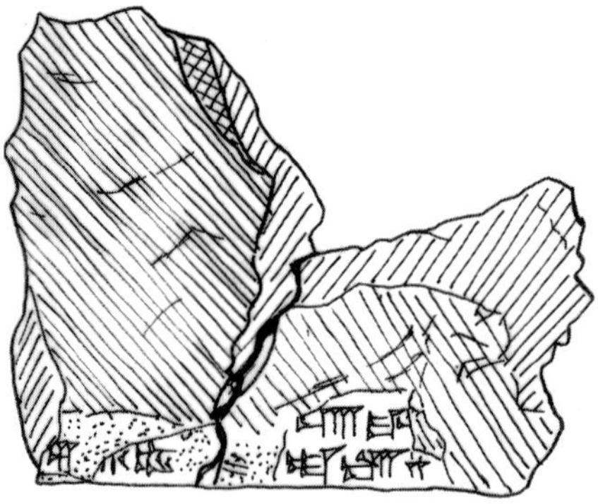

Rev.

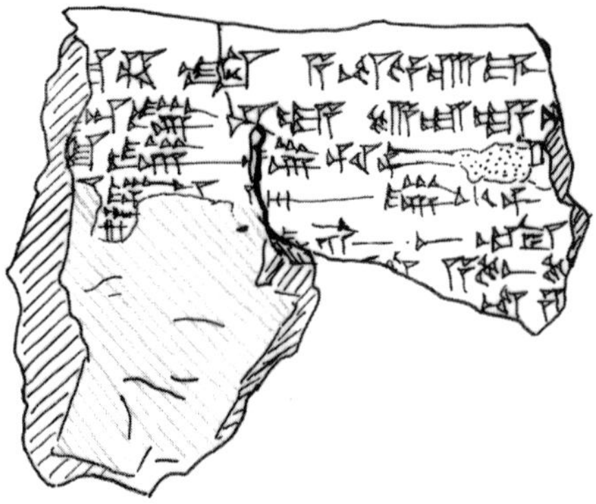

COLLATIONS

1: 11 -*zi-ni-ri*

13 .[EN]– -*ti-ni a-na ap-* *ú-se-* -*u*

5: 17

r.8 *an-*

8: 8

9

11: 2

10 LÚ*.A-

15: 7 -*a* *pa-ni šá* m*ia-ze-e*

10 LÚ*. -[*m*]*i*[*r-a-a*]

11 *ta-*

16: 2 [*it*]- -*lak* MAN -[*šú*]

3

4 MAN-*ṭu*

r.3

23 r.5 -*di-nu* [

24: 3

25: 10

29: 15

17 *sa-* -*ra*

r.1 *mu-*

3 .ŠÀ

30 r.1 -*ki-i*

4 *ad-* -*al*

31 r.1 *lu-* -*an-ni*

32: 2

16 -*li-ia*

r.3 -*pu-uš*

33: 3 [LÚ.*šá*]- -*hu-* -*hi*

r.4 *ú-šá*]- -*ki-tú*

7 -*ah-ri-id*

11 *i-mu*]-

34: 1 m*šu-* -*a-*[*a*]

13 *ih-tal-*

15

r.1 -*id-*

2 LÚ*. -*te*

4 .2-*ia*

8

18 *a-na-*

25

35 r.9

36: 2

r.3 *a-*

41: 12 *de-en-* -*nu*

13 *ni-ti-it-*

14

r.1

2 *ina*

15 *i*]- -*áš-šú-u-ni*

42: 9 LÚ.NAM. -*ta-di-*

43 r.5

44: 8	[cuneiform]		**84**: 2	ᵐᵈPA–MAN– [cuneiform]
r.2	[cuneiform]		r.12	ù [cuneiform] -me ina IGI [cuneiform] -te
3	[cuneiform] -na-te		13	nu [cuneiform]
6	[cuneiform] il-ki- [cuneiform]		**85** r.4	id-da-a- [cuneiform] -[dir]
45: 7	[cuneiform]		**86** r.15	[re]- [cuneiform] -te
r.10	[cuneiform] -ú		**89**: 16	šap- [cuneiform]
14	liš- [cuneiform]		**92**: 4	[cuneiform]
54: 11	[cuneiform] -[dir]		**95**: 8	ku- [cuneiform] -ti
56: 5	[cuneiform] –NUMUN–AŠ		r.1	e- [cuneiform] -a-ti
62: 6	[cuneiform]		6	LÚ*. [cuneiform] –
9	ṭa-a- [cuneiform]		**96**: 9	[A]D ša [cuneiform]
r.7	la i- [cuneiform] -su-u-ni		12	[cuneiform] -[sa-kan]
13	[cuneiform] -tu-du-u-ni		18	i-šab-bu- [cuneiform]
16	a]- [cuneiform] -ku-u-ni		**97**: 4	URU.ŠÀ– [cuneiform] -a-a
63: 35	[cuneiform] -ba-na-ši		12	ba-tu-ba- [cuneiform]
r.6	Á.2- [cuneiform]		r.2	[cuneiform] -na- [cuneiform]
65: 2	ᵐpa- [cuneiform]		4	LÚ.ha-za-nu- [cuneiform]
3	ša [cuneiform]		19	lu la [cuneiform] -ra-ma
10	li-iq-te [cuneiform]		**98** r.9	ma-ṣar- [cuneiform]
r.16	lu [cuneiform]		**99** r.8	ana- [cuneiform]
67 r.16	ú- [cuneiform]		9	8 [cuneiform]
68: 19	LÚ*.GIŠ. [cuneiform]		**112**: 4	ina URU. [cuneiform]
r.9	[cuneiform]		11	LÚ*.A.BA [cuneiform]
69 r.1	[cuneiform]		**116**: 10	[cuneiform]
71: 2	[cuneiform] -kan- [cuneiform]		**117** r.3	li- [cuneiform] -bi
r.3	[cuneiform]		**119**: 7	[cuneiform] -nu
72 r.1	[ka]- [cuneiform] -me		**120** r.7	i– [cuneiform] -tu-uk-ka
80: 3	1. [cuneiform].AB-a-a-u		**121** r.17	[cuneiform] -bi
81: 3	1. [cuneiform] -ṭi		**122** r.7	šá–še]- [cuneiform]
9	[cuneiform] -u-ni		13	(U[RU?]) [cuneiform]
10	š]a [cuneiform]		**123**: 2	x]- [cuneiform]
r.8	[cuneiform] -ni		3	[cuneiform] .ša–GIŠ.MI
82: 8	a- [cuneiform] -har		**124**: 6	[cuneiform]
9	lip- [cuneiform] -dan-ni		r.6	[cuneiform] -te-qu-tú
16	[cuneiform]		**132**: 4	[cuneiform] -e

5 -[*su-t*]*e*.MEŠ

135: 15

137: 9 *ma-a* -*ri*

10 KUR.*a-ra-*

15 *ma-a* -*šú*

139: 7 1. -*ši*–DINGIR

140: 9 URU.] -*li-ki*

r.1 *ina* UGU

144: 7 URU.*lu-li-*

10 -[*nu*

r.1

148: 15 *ma-ṣar-ti-* -*nu*

r.1 -[*q*]*u-*

7 (*a-na*)

11 *ba-* -*i na-ṣa-* -*u-ni*

162: 13 [*ina*] -[*a*]-

163: 3 ÍD-

178: 1

180: 2 mdAMAR.UTU–

181: 6 LÚ*. -*i*-[*šú*

198 r.1 *me-me-*

2 *ú-* -[*rab*?]

4 ŠÀ.

5 *a-ra-*

199 r.2 UZ[U.Á].2-*šú-*

200 r.5 -[*nu*]

202: 2 -[*ṭi-bi-a*]

207: 4 *pi-*

STATE ARCHIVES OF ASSYRIA

VOLUME I
THE CORRESPONDENCE OF SARGON II, PART I
Letters from Assyria and the West
Edited by Simo Parpola
1987

VOLUME II
NEO-ASSYRIAN TREATIES AND LOYALTY OATHS
Edited by Simo Parpola and Kazuko Watanabe
1988

VOLUME III
COURT POETRY AND LITERARY MISCELLANEA
Edited by Alasdair Livingstone
1989

VOLUME IV
QUERIES TO THE SUNGOD
Divination and Politics in Sargonid Assyria
Edited by Ivan Starr
1990

VOLUME V
THE CORRESPONDENCE OF SARGON II, PART II
Letters from the Northern and Northeastern Provinces
Edited by Giovanni B. Lanfranchi and Simo Parpola
1990

VOLUME VI
LEGAL TRANSACTIONS OF THE ROYAL COURT OF NINEVEH, PART I
Tiglath-Pileser III through Esarhaddon
Edited by Theodore Kwasman and Simo Parpola
1991

VOLUME VII

IMPERIAL ADMINISTRATIVE RECORDS, PART I

Palace and Temple Administration

Edited by F. M. Fales and J. N. Postgate

1992

VOLUME VIII

ASTROLOGICAL REPORTS TO ASSYRIAN KINGS

Edited by Hermann Hunger

1992

VOLUME IX

ASSYRIAN PROPHECIES

Edited by Simo Parpola

1997

VOLUME X

LETTERS FROM ASSYRIAN AND BABYLONIAN SCHOLARS

Edited by Simo Parpola

1993

VOLUME XI

IMPERIAL ADMINISTRATIVE RECORDS, PART II

Provincial and Military Administration

Edited by F. M. Fales and J. N. Postgate

1995

VOLUME XII

GRANTS, DECREES AND GIFTS OF THE NEO-ASSYRIAN PERIOD

Edited by L. Kataja and R. Whiting

1995

VOLUME XIII

LETTERS FROM PRIESTS TO THE
KINGS ESARHADDON AND ASSURBANIPAL

Edited by Steven W. Cole and Peter Machinist

1998

VOLUME XIV

LEGAL TRANSACTIONS OF THE ROYAL COURT OF NINEVEH, PART II

Assurbanipal through Sin-šarru-iškun

Edited by Raija Mattila

2002

VOLUME XV

THE CORRESPONDENCE OF SARGON II, PART III

Letters from Babylonia and the Eastern Provinces

Edited by Andreas Fuchs and Simo Parpola

2001

VOLUME XVI

THE POLITICAL CORRESPONDENCE OF ESARHADDON

Edited by Mikko Luukko and Greta Van Buylaere

2002